BUSINESS MATH USING

Calculators

with 10-Key Computer-Assisted Instruction

Jo Burton
David Burton

PEARSON

Prentice
Hall

Upper Saddle River, New Jersey
Columbus, Ohio

To Amanda

Library of Congress Cataloging-in-Publication Data

Burton, Jo
  Business math using calculators/Jo Burton, David Burton.—1st ed.
    p. cm.
  Includes index.
  ISBN 0-13-099140-6
  1. Business mathematics. 2. Calculators. I. Burton, David, II.
  Title.
  HF5691.B48 2006
  650'.01'513—dc22

                                     2005007367

Senior Acquisitions Editor: Gary Bauer
Editorial Assistant: Jacqueline Knapke
Production Editor: Louise N. Sette
Production Coordination: Kelly Crooks, Techbooks/GTS, York, PA
Design Coordinator: Diane Ernsberger
Cover Designer: Linda Sorrells-Smith
Production Manager: Pat Tonneman
Marketing Coordinator: Leigh Ann Sims

This book was set in Sabon by Techbooks/GTS, York, PA. It was printed and
bound by Banta Book Group. The cover was printed by Coral Graphic Services, Inc.

Pearson Education Ltd.
Pearson Education Singapore Pte. Ltd.
Pearson Education Canada, Ltd.
Pearson Education—Japan

Pearson Education Australia Pty. Limited
Pearson Education North Asia Ltd.
Pearson Educación de Mexico, S.A. de C.V.
Pearson Education Malaysia Pte. Ltd.

10 9 8 7 6 5 4 3 2 1
ISBN: 0-13-099140-6

preface

ABOUT THIS BOOK

In today's world, knowledge of current business practices is important to anyone dealing with business situations or personal finance matters. Business students will also find a working knowledge of business math and 10-key skills invaluable. In the words of one office manager, "Everyone working in a business office today needs to know business math and how to operate a 10-key calculator by touch." This book provides the means necessary for the business student to acquire the business math and 10-key skills necessary to be successful in the workplace.

FEATURES

- **Clear explanations** are used to take the mystery out of solving business math problems. For ease of understanding, many visual aids are used to outline solutions to business math problems in a clear, concise, and easy-to-remember format.
- **Procedures for solving business math problems are given for both the desktop calculator and the pocket calculator.** The Windows® calculator is discussed for situations when only a computer is available.
- **Desktop calculator key sequences** and illustrations of resulting paper tapes are provided to help each students learn new techniques.
- **Pocket calculator key sequences** are provided for many business math problems to help students learn how to use this tool properly.
- **Terminology and exercise reviews** are provided at the end of each chapter. Answers to odd-numbered problems are provided in an appendix.
- The **Be a Math Star** feature promotes critical thinking and reasoning skills.
- **Use of the Internet** for banking applications, finding insurance quotes, and so on is incorporated into the text.
- **Reference tables** are conveniently located in the chapters in which they are introduced.

Touch Key 10-key software, included with the book, takes the student through lessons, drills, and tests leading to speed and accuracy on the 10-key using the computer numeric keypad.

INTEGRATED 10-KEY SOFTWARE FEATURES

- **Ten-key keystroking technique** is developed using the desktop calculator.
- **One-, 3-, or 5-minute timing drill exercises** are provided in every chapter using the desktop calculator.
- **Software and text are fully integrated.** The text clearly indicates when certain software lessons, tutorials, drills, and tests are appropriate.
- A complete **Touch Key user's manual** is included in an appendix.
- Icons are used within each chapter to help identify which activities require Touch Key software, the desktop calculator, and/or the pocket calculator.

Business Math FUNdamentals, an optional Windows-based CD-ROM product, offers tutorials and drills correlated with Part 3 of every chapter. It can be ordered online at www.prenhall.com (ISBN: 0-13-086204-5).

ORGANIZATION OF THE BOOK

The 33 chapters in this text are organized into four units:

Unit I: Arithmetic Operations

Unit II: Business Applications

Unit III: Business Mathematics for Accounting

Unit IV: Financial Mathematics for Business

Each chapter is divided into four parts as follows, to allow instructors flexibility in course coverage:

 **PART 1** *Speed and Accuracy Building Using Touch Key Software*

Beginning with Chapter 2, part 1 of each chapter covers 10-key by touch using the computer numeric keypad and Touch Key software included with the book. This part provides a quick, fun, and efficient way to master 10-key by touch on the computer numeric keypad. Correct keystroking techniques are discussed, suggested speed and accuracy goals are provided, suggestions for assignment of Touch Key lessons, drills, and tests are given, and space for the student to record his or her scores is provided.

 **PART 2** *Business Math Skills*

This part of each chapter explains business math theory. Key terms are highlighted in bold in the text. Many illustrations simulating problem solving on a chalkboard are given in each chapter. Explanations are clear and easy to understand and attempt to answer the "why" questions students often have. Step-by-step procedures are shown for example problems. Business math exercises are included at the end of each Part 2. Answers to selected problems are included in Appendix B.

 **PART 3** *Pocket and Windows Calculators*

In Part 3 of the chapter, students are taught how to solve business math problems using either a pocket (personal) calculator or the pop-up Windows calculator as appropriate. Procedures listing exact pocket calculator keystrokes are given for business math problems presented in this part. Exercises are included at the end of the part as appropriate. The problems and exercises in Part 3 reinforce the business math theory presented in Part 2 of each chapter. Answers to selected problems are given in Appendix B.

Part 3 also includes suggestions for using the optional software **Business Math FUNdamentals** for review and practice. Space is given to record scores for assigned computerized drills to help the student be aware of his or her progress. This software can be purchased online at **www.prenhall.com.**

 # PART 4 *Desktop Calculator*

Part 4 of the chapter has two purposes: (1) solving business math problems similar to those presented in Part 2 of the chapter using the desktop calculator as appropriate, and (2) building 10-key speed and accuracy on the desktop calculator. Correct keystroking techniques as well as the use of special-purpose keys are presented. Procedures listing exact keystrokes and illustrations of the resulting paper calculator tapes are included for each business math problem presented in the section. Additional attention is given to the types of calculations required to complete various business forms. Exercises covering business math problems are included at the end of Part 4 as appropriate. Every chapter includes a speed and accuracy drill sufficient in length for 1-, 3-, or 5-minute 10-key timings on the desktop calculator. Only keys previously presented are included in the drills. Answers to selected questions are included in Appendix B.

END-OF-CHAPTER EXERCISES

End-of-chapter exercises include a terminology review, with questions about key terms discussed in the chapter, and chapter review exercises, which may be solved using the method and machine chosen by the instructor or student (pen and paper, pocket calculator, or desktop calculator). Answers to selected problems are included in Appendix B.

SUPPLEMENTS

An instructor's manual with test item file (ISBN: 0-13-099152-X) is available.

Business Math FUNdamentals, an optional Windows-based CD-ROM product, offers tutorials and drills correlated with Part 3 of every chapter. It can be ordered at **www.prenhall.com** (ISBN: 0-13-086204-5).

ACKNOWLEDGMENTS

We thank all who provided help, suggestions, and support for this project. We appreciate Janis Rollins, Caroline Garrett, and Mark Henry of Victoria College for their help in testing the software and for their invaluable input, Amanda Burton for many of the images in the book, and Joan Schramek for her unfailing help and encouragement. We appreciate very much the hard work of our editor, Gary Bauer, and media editor, Michelle Churma. In particular, we thank the following reviewers for their valuable time, insights, and recommendations: Emily Martin, Faulkner State; Christy Bryant, Lamar State; Annetta Jones, Chemeketa Community College; and Billie Miller-Cooper, Consumnes River College. This book would not have been possible without you.

contents

UNIT I

Arithmetic Operations

CHAPTER 1

Numbers and Calculators

Before beginning, you will need to install Touch Key software. Turn to Appendix A for Touch Key installation instructions. You will need a blank formatted disk labeled Touch Key. Be sure to include your name and your instructor's name on the labels. If you have purchased the supplemental software Business Math FUNdamentals, install it. The same data disk may be used for both software packages.

 **PART 1** *Business Math Skills*

NUMBERS IN BUSINESS

Numbers are the universal language of business. If we think of the value of a number as an idea, then a number is a symbol that represents that idea. Our system of numbers is based on 10 and uses the **Arabic numerals** 0, 1, 2, 3, 4, 5, 6, 7, 8, and 9, which may be written alone or in combinations. This set of numerals, also referred to as digits, represents all the symbols we need to write **whole numbers**, which are numbers that may be used for counting. Contrast the Arabic symbols with the Roman numerals for 1 through 10—I, II, III, IV, V, VI, VII, VIII, IX, and X. In the Roman numeral system, additional symbols are used to represent 50 (L), 100 (C), and others. Roman numerals are sometimes used for special applications such as outlines, publication volume numbers, and dates. Which set of characters would you rather use for everyday business problems?

THE PLACE VALUE OF NUMBERS

Numbers must be **read** correctly in many situations. During a club meeting, the treasurer will report orally on the club's finances. During telephone conversations, numbers must be read and spoken accurately. Numbers must be **spelled** correctly on legal documents such as contracts and checks, where both numerals and the complete spelling are used for important numbers and amounts.

In the Arabic system, digits have **place value**. A digit's value is determined by its name and its position in the number. Each position has a specific name. Beginning at the right, the first place in a whole number is the ones place. In Figure 1.1, the numeral in the ones place is 6.

The place immediately left of the ones place is the tens place. The number 56 is spelled and read as *fifty-six*. Notice the hyphen. Beginning with the number 21, the written forms of all two-place numbers without zeros up to and including 99 are hyphenated if they stand alone or if they are part of a number greater than 100; for example, forty-three, sixty-nine, one hundred ninety-eight.

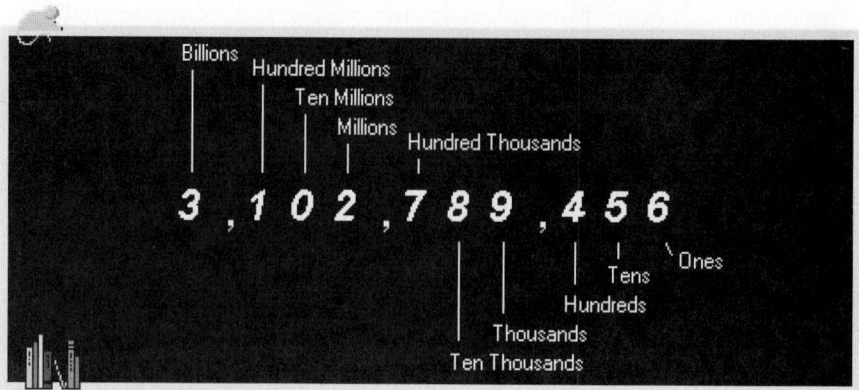

FIGURE 1.1   Numbers have place values.

The third place from the right is the hundreds place (Figure 1.1). The number 456 is spelled and read as *four hundred fifty-six*.

Let's look at this in another way. The number 456 may be represented as follows:

$$4 \times 100 = 400$$
$$5 \times 10 = 50$$
$$6 \times 1 = \underline{6}$$
$$= 456$$

Large whole numbers are written in groups of three numerals beginning at the right. Commas separate the groups of three. The first right-hand comma represents the separation of the thousands place from the hundreds, tens, and ones places. Read this comma as "thousand."

Still referring to Figure 1.1, let's look at more examples of reading and writing larger numbers:

    9,456   nine <u>thousand</u> four hundred fifty-six

   89,456   eighty-nine <u>thousand</u> four hundred fifty-six

  789,456   seven hundred eighty-nine <u>thousand</u> four hundred fifty-six

You will notice a certain amount of repetition for each successive category. The categories following thousands are millions, then billions, then trillions. Each category contains a ones, a tens, and a hundreds place. The second comma from the right always represents millions, the third comma from the right always represents billions, and so on. Notice in the second example below that the 0 in the ten millions place is not read or written.

Examples:

2,789,456   two <u>million</u> seven hundred eighty-nine <u>thousand</u> four hundred fifty-six

102,789,456   one hundred two <u>million</u> seven hundred eighty-nine <u>thousand</u> four hundred fifty-six

3,102,789,456   three <u>billion</u> one hundred two <u>million</u> seven hundred eighty-nine <u>thousand</u> four hundred fifty-six

DIFFERENT BUSINESSES USE DIFFERENT LINGOES

You've probably heard 1,200 read as twelve hundred. This form is easier to understand than one thousand two hundred. However 1,245 should be expressed as one thousand two hundred forty-five, NOT twelve hundred forty-five. You may have heard a real estate agent refer to a $98,500 price of a house as ninety-eight five instead of ninety-eight thousand five hundred dollars. However, in formal correspondence, reports, and legal documents, it is imperative that numbers be referenced accurately rather than casually to avoid misunderstandings.

Handling Huge Numbers with Lots of Zeros

For ease in understanding large numbers such as 3,000,000 and 45,000,000,000, use the words million and billion instead of all those zeros.

Write	3,000,000	as	3 million.
Write	45,000,000,000	as	45 billion.

EXAMPLE: As of 2001, the United States had a $10 trillion economy (the total of all spending).

Name _____

Class/Section _____

Score (Correct Answers ÷ No. of Assigned Problems) _____

PART 1 *Business Math Skills*

Exercise 1

Write the following numbers in words.

1. 35 _____

2. 1,351 _____

3. 622 _____

4. 3,802 _____

5. 144 _____

6. 96 _____

7. 115 _____

8. 4,339 _____

9. 10,004 _____

10. 53,782 _____

Exercise 2

Write the following numbers using Arabic numerals.

11. One hundred twenty-three _____

12. Eleven _____

13. Fifty-six _____

14. Eighteen_____

15. One hundred twenty-three thousand one hundred _____

16. Thirty-one thousand one_____

17. Three hundred sixty-five thousand _____

18. Ninety-six million three hundred five thousand one hundred sixty-five_____

19. One million thirty-five thousand _____

20. Twelve thousand six hundred fifty-five_____

 **PART 2**   *Review and Practice Using Business Math FUNdamentals*

Instructions: *If you have purchased the supplemental software Business Math FUNdamentals, complete Tutorial 1 Numbers, Numbers, Numbers; Tutorial 2 Place Value of Numbers; and Drill 1 Place Values of Numbers. If you are not satisfied with your score, repeat Drill 1. Write your scores below.*

Business Math FUNdamentals Drill 1

Today's Date	Score

 PART 3   *Tools for Calculations Commonly Used by Businesses*

Before exploring business math further, we consider some of the tools commonly used by businesses to work with numbers. Calculators and computers are found in most offices and are used to complete math problems quickly and accurately.

Computers may be used to make repetitive calculations using programs written for specific business applications such as calculating payments for a home loan, calculating insurance premiums, and so on. The computer is, after all, a calculating machine. How are these calculations made? Who determines whether the calculations have been made correctly? People! Just like you!

You will learn to make these and many other types of business calculations using a desktop calculator and a pocket calculator. Conveniently, Windows comes with a calculator accessory that looks and works much like a pocket calculator. The Windows calculator is accessed by selecting, respectively, Start, Programs, Accessories, and Calculator.

Calculations to be learned include the **arithmetic operations**—addition, subtraction, multiplication, and division. The term **order of entry** refers to the sequence for entering numbers and the arithmetic operation keys necessary for solving a math problem. (The appropriate order of entry will be shown for each machine for the various types of problems.)

THE DESKTOP CALCULATOR

A typical desktop calculator keyboard is shown in Figure 1.2. The keys labeled 1 through 28 are identified and described in Table 1.1. Most newer desktop calculators include a percent-of-change key, a tax key, and a gross-profit-margin key. If your desktop calculator does not feature these keys, you will still be able to work these types of problems. Methods will be given in appropriate chapters.

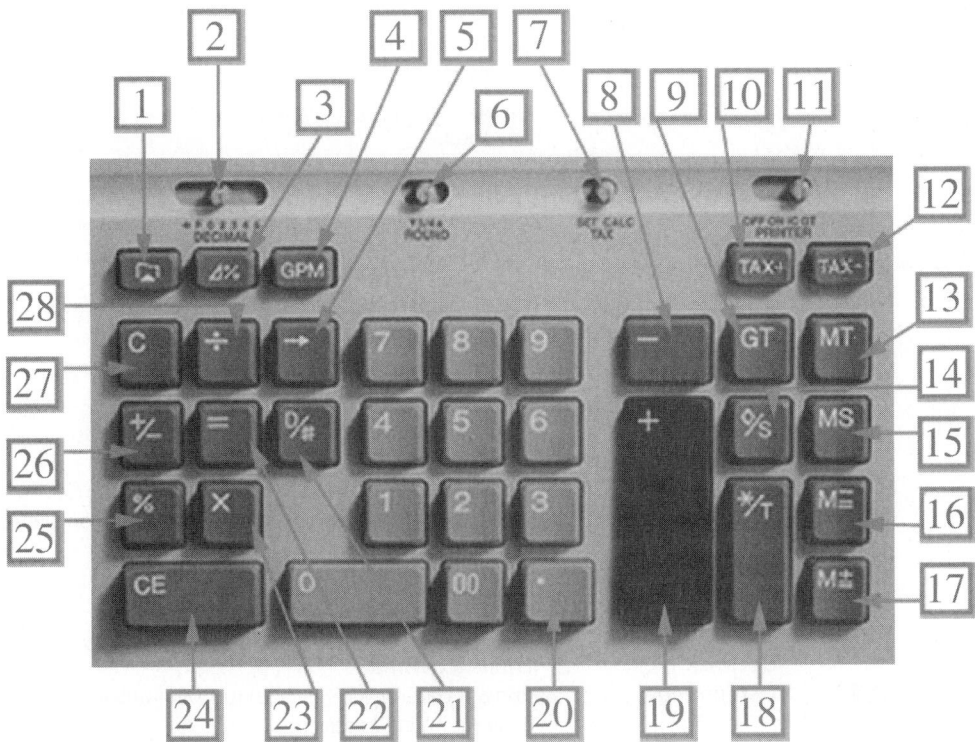

FIGURE 1.2 Keyboard of the TI 5660 desktop calculator.

THE COMPUTER NUMBERPAD

The numberpad on a computer has two kinds of keys: number keys and arithmetic operation keys (see Figure 1.3). To use the keys on the numberpad, **Num Lock** must be on. On some computers, Num Lock is on by default. Most keyboards have a Num Lock indicator light above the numberpad. If Num Lock is not on, press the top left key on the numberpad

TABLE 1.1 Identification and Description of Desktop Calculator Keys

	Symbol	Name	Description
1	↑	Paper feed	Advances the paper tape
2	DECIMAL	Decimal selector	a. +, allows addition and subtraction of numbers without entering the decimal point (the decimal point is automatically placed at two places in any number entered) b. F, the number of decimal places varies based on the result c. 0 2 3 4 6, sets the number of decimal places at 1, 2, 3, 4, or 6
3	Δ%	Percent change	Computes percent of increase/decrease
4	GPM	Gross profit margin	Calculates selling price and profit or loss on an item
5	→	Correction	Removes the last digit entered in the display
6	ROUND	Rounding switch	Sets the type of rounding: down, 5/4, or up
7	TAX	Tax switch	a. SET, sets the tax rate to perform tax calculations b. CALC, stores the tax rate
8	−	Subtraction	Subtracts the number from the value in the display
9	GT	Grand total	Displays and prints the grand total of all totals
10	TAX+	Tax plus	Adds the stored tax rate to value in display
11	PRINTER	Printer switch	a. OFF, calculations are displayed but not printed b. ON, calculations are displayed and printed c. IC, both printer and item counter are active; press */T or MT key to clear item counter d. GT, accumulates a running grand total of all calculations; press GT key to print a grand total; press GT key again to clear the grand total
12	TAX−	Tax minus	Subtracts stored tax rate from value in display
13	MT	Memory total	Displays and prints value in memory, clears the memory, and resets the item counter to zero
14	◇/S	Subtotal	Displays and prints total, but does not clear the total
15	MS	Memory subtotal	Displays and prints total in memory, but does not clear memory
16	M−=	Memory minus	Subtracts displayed value from memory; if a multiplication or division operation is pending, M−= completes it and subtracts the result from memory
17	M+=	Memory plus	Adds displayed value to memory; if a multiplication or division operation is pending, M+= completes it and adds the result to memory
18	*/T	Total	Displays and prints the total, clears the total, and resets the item counter to zero
19	+	Addition	Adds the number to the value in the display
20	.	Decimal	Enters a decimal
21	D/#	Date/number	Prints a date or a reference number without affecting calculations
22	=	Equals key	Displays products and quotients
23	×	Multiplication	Sets the machine up to multiply the value in the display by the next number entered
24	CE	Clear entry	Clears an entry, error, or overflow
25	%	Percent	Interprets the number in display as a percentage
26	+/−	Reverse	Reverses the sign (+ or −) of the displayed number
27	C	Clear	Clears entire pending operation except memory or grand total
28	÷	Division	Prepares the machine to divide the value in the display by the next number entered

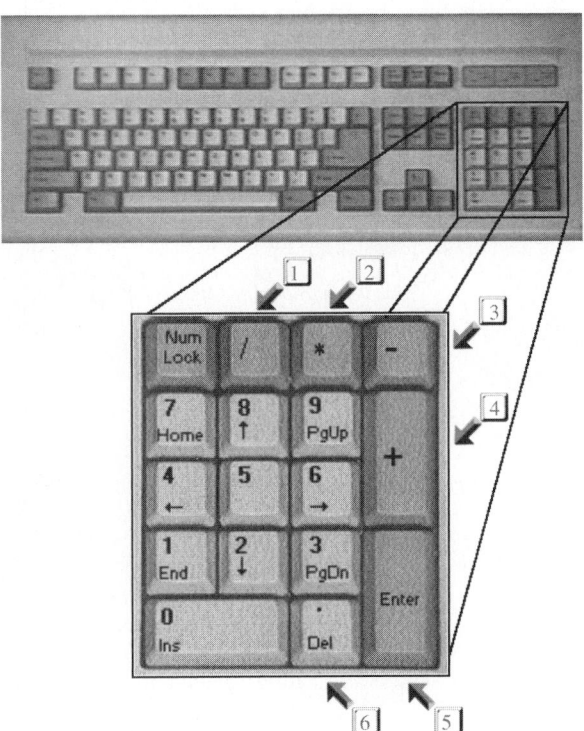

FIGURE 1.3 The computer numberpad.

marked Num Lock. Table 1.2 identifies the arithmetic operation keys, describes what each does, and lists the symbols used to identify the keys.

TABLE 1.2 The Computer Numberpad Arithmetic Operation Keys

	Operation	Symbol	Description
1	Division	/	Division function
2	Multiplication	*	Multiplication function
3	Subtraction	−	Subtraction function
4	Addition	+	Addition function
5	Total or equals	**Enter**	Completes the previously entered arithmetic operation
6	Decimal	**. Del**	Enters a decimal into the number

THE POCKET CALCULATOR

The pocket calculator used for problem solving in this book contains the standard arithmetic operation, percent, and memory keys. Notice the difference in symbols used on the two types of calculators for multiplication, division, clear entry, and square root as you refer to Figures 1.4 through 1.6.

The Windows operating system is packaged with a calculator accessory that emulates a pocket calculator. This program may be left running simultaneously with other programs. Just click Calculator on the task bar at the bottom of the Windows screen to display the calculator on top of any other program you are using.

There are two calculator views: standard and scientific. For most applications in this book, the standard view is used. You will be instructed when to use the scientific view. To change views, first select View on the calculator menu bar, then select either Standard or Scientific.

FIGURE 1.4   Pocket calculator.

FIGURE 1.5   Pocket calculator.

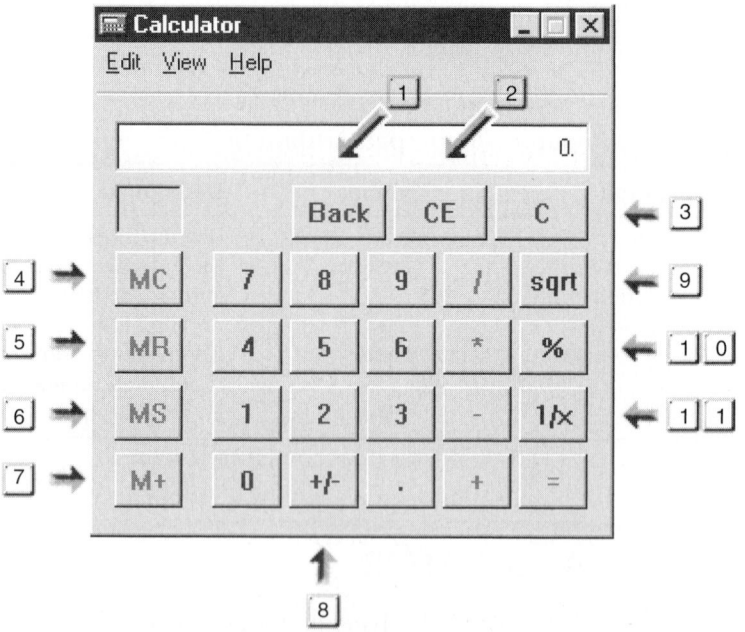

FIGURE 1.6   The Windows calculator, standard view.

Listed in Table 1.3 are some of the functions of the pocket and Windows calculators. The functions of the Windows calculator may be accessed by clicking the appropriate key on the screen or by pressing the equivalent key on the computer keyboard. For example, instead of clicking the CE button to clear an entry, you can use the delete key on the keyboard to delete it. Keyboard equivalent keys are listed in column two of Table 1.3.

TABLE 1.3   The Windows and Pocket Calculator Function Keys

Name/Function	Keyboard Equivalent (Windows Calculator Only)	Description
1 Back (backspace) (Windows calculator only)	← **Backspace**	Removes the last digit of the displayed number
2 CE or ON/CE or ON/C (clear entry)	**Delete**	Clears incorrect numbers to allow correct reentry
3 C (clear all)	**Esc**	Clears the current calculation
4 MC (memory clear)	**Ctrl + L**	Clears any number stored in memory
5 MR (memory recall)	**Ctrl + R**	Recalls the number stored in memory; the number remains in memory
6 MS (memory store)	**Ctrl + M**	Stores the displayed number in memory
7 M+ (memory plus)	**Ctrl + P**	Adds the displayed number to any number already in memory
8 +/− (reverse)	**F9**	Changes the sign of the displayed number
9 Sqrt or √ (square root)	**Shift + @**	Calculates the square root of the displayed number
10 % (percent)	**Shift + %**	Displays the result of multiplication as a percentage; enter the first number, click *, enter the second number, click %. Example: 100* 5% will display 5; 100 + 5% = will display 105
11 1/× (reciprocal)	**R**	Calculates the reciprocal of the displayed number

Note: If you choose to use a scientific or business analyst calculator, refer to your calculator manual for differences in keying problems.

 **PART 4**   *Learning the 10-Key Numberpad by Touch*

Numbers are entered on calculators and computers with the 10-key numberpad. The arrangement of numbers is the same on both machines. The size of the keys on the computer numberpad and on the desktop calculator such as the one shown in Figure 1.7

FIGURE 1.7   The TI 5660 desktop calculator.

allows for keying by touch. Just as typing by touch is more efficient, keying numbers by touch is much faster. Most pocket calculators, however, do not have numberpads suitable for touch keying. Use the computer numberpad or desktop calculator numberpad for practicing touch keying of numbers.

PREPARING TO 10-KEY BY TOUCH

Organization of the Workspace

If you are using a desktop calculator, position the calculator slightly to the right of your body (Figure 1.8). Adjust your chair and calculator. If you are using a computer, position the keyboard so that the J key is centered in front of your body (Figure 1.11).

Sit with your feet flat on the floor. Lean forward slightly. Your arm should hang comfortably at your side from shoulder to elbow. Raise your right hand, curve your fingers, and position them over the number keys.

When keying from paper copy, place the paper copy so that you can keep your place using the left hand (Figure 1.9).

FIGURE 1.8   Posture.

FIGURE 1.9   Keeping your place.

Keystroking Technique: The 4, 5, and 6 Keys

Home Row.   The 4, 5, and 6 keys are the home row keys on a numberpad. Curl the fingers of the right hand. Place the index finger on the 4 key, the middle finger on the 5 key, and the ring finger on the 6 key (Figure 1.10). The 5 key usually has a small raised dot or bar on its surface to help you identify it by touch.

If you are using a computer keyboard, the edge of the keyboard should be at the edge of the table or desk. Refer to Figure 1.11 for correct hand position on the home row of a computer numberpad.

Notice with both types of keyboards the fingers are in position to strike the home row keys with a straight downward motion. The wrist is straight. To correctly key the home row keys, visualize a small hammer striking a tack. Your fingers should deliver the same sharp rap on the home row keys as a hammer on a tack (Figure 1.12).

FIGURE 1.10   The 4, 5, and 6 keys.

FIGURE 1.11   Correct hand position.

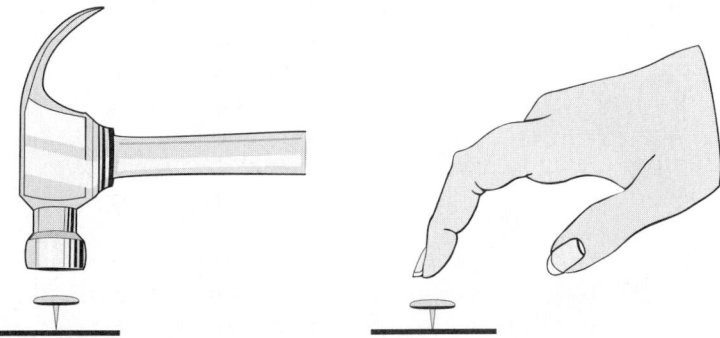

FIGURE 1.12   Similar to a small hammer striking a tack, strike the key with a sharp rap.

Remember, bend your fingers, not your wrists!

ADDITION ON DESKTOP CALCULATORS

The order of entry for a typical addition problem on the desktop calculator involves keying each of the addends followed by the plus key. Press the total key to print the sum on the paper tape, reset the item counter, end the problem, and clear the machine for the next problem. (The sum will still be shown in the display, but the machine's register is ready for the next problem.)

KEYSTROKING TECHNIQUE: ADDITION

With the index, middle, and ring fingers in position over the 4, 5, and 6 keys (the home row), respectively, use the little finger to press the addition key (Figure 1.13) and the total key (Figure 1.14). Attempt to press the keys without moving the home row fingers from their positions over the home row keys.

FIGURE 1.13   Addition key.

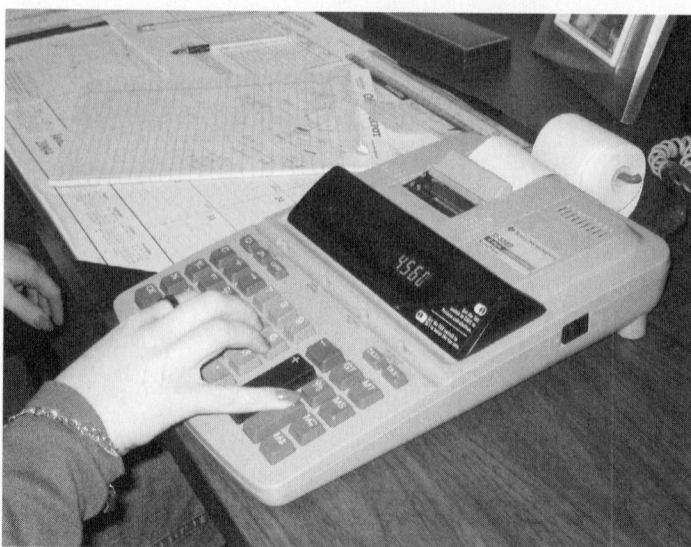

FIGURE 1.14   Total key.

CORRECTING KEYING ERRORS

To clear an incorrect number that has been keyed, press the clear entry (CE) key before pressing an operation key. To clear the last digit from the display, press the backspace (→) key before pressing an arithmetic operation key or the equals key. To cancel an addition or subtraction operation, press the opposite operation key. To cancel an addition-to-memory or subtraction-from-memory operation, press the opposite memory operation key.

MACHINE SETUP

Set the decimal selector on F or 0. Set the rounding switch on 5/4. (More will be given on the decimal selector and rounding switch in later chapters.) Set the tax switch on CALC.

Set the printer switch on IC (item counter). With the printer switch set on IC, the number of items entered for each problem will be **counted and printed on the left side of the paper tape** when the total key is pressed.

Note: In future, the total key will be indicated by T.

Problem	Procedure	Check
47	47+	54+
46	46+	46+
+54	54+ */T	47+ */T
	147	147

ADDITION PRACTICE PROBLEMS: KEYS 4 THROUGH 6

Key the following addition problems, using the plus (+) key after each addend and the total key (*/T) to find the sum.

Note: Remember that it is not necessary to clear the display after pressing the total key. Compare your answers with the ones given.

	1.	2.	3.	4.	5.	6.	7.	8.
	44	45	54	56	44	65	66	64
	54	55	56	65	46	55	65	65
	46	56	64	64	45	54	46	55
	46	54	65	66	45	54	64	54
	44	55	55	64	44	56	66	44
	45	54	64	65	44	55	65	46
	46	54	66	66	46	66	66	46
	54	54	64	46	65	64	64	66
	45	56	65	44	66	46	65	55
	64	66	66	45	64	56	56	55
	488	549	619	581	509	571	623	550

PRINT A DATE

If your instructor wishes for you to print the date on the paper tapes you key in class, print the numerals for the date and then press the D/# key. For example, for the date April 4, 2004, key **4042004**. A pound sign (#) and the numerals will print to the left side of the tape without commas or decimals. This number will not be included in any calculations.

PART 5   *Speed and Accuracy Building Using Touch Key Computer Software*

COMPLETING AND PRINTING TOUCH KEY LESSONS

Each of the 11 lessons consists of fifty 3- to 6-digit numbers (problems) to be keyed. In each lesson, the number to be keyed appears in a white box. The numbers are keyed in a yellow box. The enter key must be pressed after each number (Figure 1.15). A progress bar is displayed so that you will have an indication of the number of problems remaining in the lesson. The number box will turn red when you reach the last problem to be keyed in the lesson.

FIGURE 1.15   Enter key.

Numbers (problems) in lessons to be keyed are selected randomly so that no two lessons are alike. Therefore, lessons may be repeated as many times as desired in an attempt to improve keystrokes.

You may correct errors with the backspace key BEFORE the enter key is pressed. However, the time clock will be running, so each correction will cost time. It is recommended that you do NOT correct while keying Touch Key Lessons because correcting is detrimental to creating an even keystroking technique.

After the last problem has been entered, the Lesson Results are displayed. At this point, you may either print or return to the main menu. If print is selected, the problems and your actual keystrokes will be printed on a report called Lesson Results. An asterisk beside a problem in the student keystrokes column indicates one or more errors. This is an important diagnostic tool. By comparing the two columns containing the problems and your keystrokes, you can identify troublesome keys. Strokes per Hour, Total Errors, and Percent Accuracy are also printed on the Lesson Results report.

It is important that students wait until the print job has finished and that they check for a successful print job before returning to the main menu. *Once the main menu has been selected, the actual keystrokes can no longer be printed.* However, Strokes per Hour, Errors, and Percent Accuracy are stored permanently in the Lesson Log and may be printed at any time. This feature conserves disk space. Select the print menu, Lesson Log.

Note: It is strongly recommended that you print logs on a regular basis and either submit the printed logs to the instructor or retain them in a folder in case of disk failure. All logs will be personalized with your name, course, the current date, and current time for each lesson, drill, application, or test taken.

GOALS: Your speed goal is 6,000 strokes per hour.
Your accuracy target goal range is 95% to 100%.

With each repetition of the lesson, try to improve your speed without lowering your accuracy score. If your percent-of-accuracy score falls below 95%, review your finger position and technique. Then try again.

Instructions: *Turn to the Touch Key User Guide in Appendix A and follow the instructions for starting and using Touch Key. Complete Lesson 1, Parts A through E. Write your scores for strokes per hour and percent of accuracy below.*
    Note: Ask your instructor how often you should print logs of your scores.

Touch Key Lesson 1—The 4, 5, and 6 Keys

Today's Date	Strokes per Hour	Percent of Accuracy
A.		
B.		
C.		
D.		
E.		

CHAPTER 1 *Terminology Review*

    Arabic numerals
    Arithmetic operations
    Order of entry
    Place value
    Whole numbers

Insert the missing words to complete the following statements.

1. _____ are commonly used to write numbers in the business world.
2. The value of a digit in a number is partially determined by its _____.
3. _____ is the sequence that should be used when keying the numbers and functions to solve a problem on a calculator.
4. Addition and subtraction are examples of _____.
5. Write an example of a whole number with two digits. _____.

Chapter 1 Review Exercises

Identify the place value of the digit printed in blue. The first one has been completed for you.

1. 5,632 *thousand* _____

2. 6,009 _____

3. 10,251 _____

4. 12,662 _____

5. 12 _____

6. 103,239 _____

7. 4,692,104 _____

8. 21,426,920 _____

9. 1,456,220,000 _____

10. 1,105,233,000 _____

Write out the following numbers.

11. 16 _____

12. 21 _____

13. 44 _____

14. 99 _____

15. 182 _____

16. 10,004 _____

17. 1,000,000 _____

18. 132,550,000 _____

19. 4,159,000,000 _____

20. 326,456 _____

Write the following numbers using Arabic numerals.

21. One hundred sixty-nine _____

22. Fifty-seven _____

23. Two million _____

24. Four hundred thousand _____

25. Twelve thousand one hundred two _____

26. Sixty-nine billion _____

27. One hundred thirty-two thousand fourteen _____

28. Eight thousand nine hundred thirty-two _____

29. Twenty-three million one hundred ninety-one thousand _____

30. Eight billion _____

Write the number in parentheses as you might see it reported in a news caption.

31. It is (93,000,000) _____ miles from the Earth to the Sun.

32. When the World Trade Center collapsed in September 2001, (231,000,000) _____ dollars worth of silver and gold was buried beneath it. Gold accounted for over (110,000,000) _____ dollars worth of this amount.

CHAPTER 2

Addition, Grand Total

 **PART 1** *Speed and Accuracy Building Using Touch Key*

KEYSTROKING TECHNIQUE

Top Row

Strike the upper row keys with the pad or fleshy part of the finger (see Figure 2.1). After striking a key on the top row, return your finger to the appropriate key on the home row. The 4 (or index) finger reaches upward to strike the 7 key, the 5 (or middle) finger strikes the 8 key, and the 6 (or ring) finger strikes the 9 key.

FIGURE 2.1

GOALS: Your speed goal is 6,000 strokes per hour.
Your accuracy target goal range is 95% to 100%.

With each repetition of the lesson, try to improve your speed without lowering your accuracy score. If your percent-of-accuracy score falls below 95%, review your finger position and technique, then try again.

Instructions: *Start Touch Key. Complete Lesson 2, Parts A through E. Record your scores for strokes per hour and percent of accuracy.*

Touch Key Lesson 2—The 7, 8, and 9 Keys

	Today's Date	Strokes per Hour	Percent of Accuracy
A.			
B.			
C.			
D.			
E.			

 **PART 2** *Business Math Skills*

ADDITION

Addition is the combining of like items to find a total. It is one of the arithmetic operations.

Example: At a pet shop, 12 kittens were sold July 24 and 36 kittens were sold July 25. How many kittens were sold on these two days?

COMPONENTS OF ADDITION

Amounts or numbers to be added are called **addends** (Figure 2.2). The answer or total is called the **sum**. The plus sign (+) is used to indicate addition. In vertical addition the addends are aligned vertically beginning at the ones place of whole numbers. A horizontal line is drawn under the problem to indicate that a sum follows.

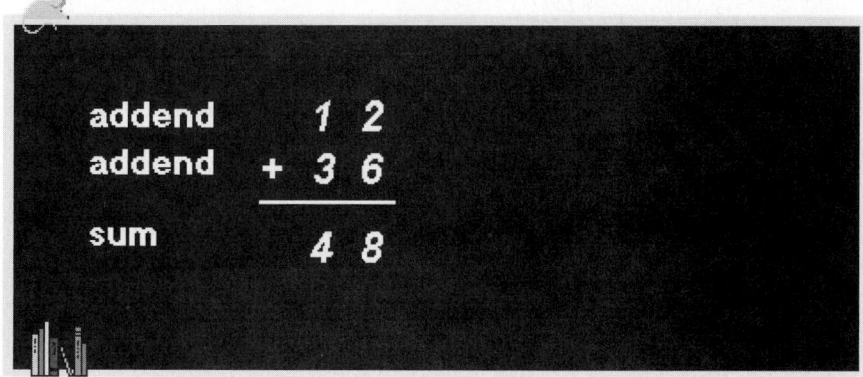

FIGURE 2.2

CHECKING ADDITION

Addition problems are checked by reversing the addends and adding a second time (Figure 2.3). A problem may also be checked without rewriting by beginning at the bottom of a column and adding from bottom to top.

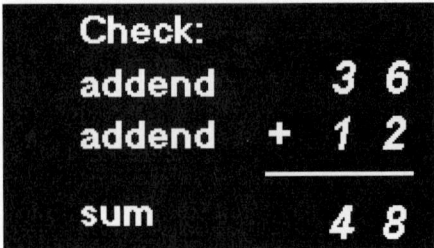

FIGURE 2.3

ADDITION PROPERTIES

The **order property of addition** (commutative property of addition) allows us to add together two numbers in any order without changing the result. The **grouping property of addition** (associative property of addition) allows us to group three or more addends in any order before adding without changing the sum.

TABLE OF ADDITION

To use the table of addition (Table 2.1), note that the addends are at the top of each column and at the beginning of each row. The sums are in the intersecting cells of the columns and rows. To find the sum of 8 + 7, look down the column containing 8 and across the row containing 7. The point where the column and row intersects is the cell containing the answer, 15. If you are not comfortable with the addition facts in this table, now is the time to memorize the ones that give you trouble.

Note: Any number plus zero equals that number.

TABLE 2.1 Table of Addition

+	1	2	3	4	5	6	7	8	9	10
1	2	3	4	5	6	7	8	9	10	11
2	3	4	5	6	7	8	9	10	11	12
3	4	5	6	7	8	9	10	11	12	13
4	5	6	7	8	9	10	11	12	13	14
5	6	7	8	9	10	11	12	13	14	15
6	7	8	9	10	11	12	13	14	15	16
7	8	9	10	11	12	13	14	15	16	17
8	9	10	11	12	13	14	15	16	17	18
9	10	11	12	13	14	15	16	17	18	19
10	11	12	13	14	15	16	17	18	19	20

WHY BOTHER WHEN WE HAVE CALCULATORS?

Although it is true that businesses and individuals rely heavily on the calculator, it is not always convenient to do so. Perhaps you are making a presentation using a chart tablet or whiteboard and someone has a question. You would not want to stop and fumble with a calculator.

You may not have a calculator with you. Perhaps you are picking up office supplies and need to mentally check the cashier's total. In this case a quick estimate would suffice.

Short calculations can be done more quickly mentally than with a calculator. Perhaps you call someone on the phone to increase your boss' cell phone minutes. She needs about 2,000 minutes. The company representative tells you that your boss currently has a plan with 1,000 minutes and you may add 1,250 minutes for an additional $9.95. You quickly add the 1,000 to 1,250 mentally, and decide that 2,250 minutes will be just right.

MATH STAR 2.1

BE A Math★!

Do you panic when faced with a column of numbers? Try the grouping method. With this method, you will look for familiar number combinations. One of the most popular combinations is two numbers that equal 10. Another combination is the number 9 and another number. (To add nine to any number that ends in a number other than zero, decrease the ones place by 1 and increase the tens place by 1; for example, $4 + 9 = 13$, $25 + 9 = 34$, $66 + 9 = 75$.) Let's see how this works. Notice in the following column of numbers we have a 3 and 7 in the ones column. We envision 10, the sum of 7 and 3. Then we notice the next two numbers are 9 and 4, and we envision the sum, 13. We can handle adding 10 and 13 together mentally for a sum of 23.

```
  3       ┌─────────────┐
  7       │ 3 + 7 = 10  ├──────────────────┐
  9       ├─────────────┤  10 + 13 = 23    │
 +4       │ 9 + 4 = 13  │                  │
          └─────────────┴──────────────────┘
```

Another grouping to watch for is repeated numbers such as $8 + 8$. (Most of us are quick to recognize doubles and to remember their sums.) Below we have two 8s in the ones column, followed by a 6, a 4, and a 9. Follow the steps below to find the sum mentally.

```
  8       ┌─────────────┐
  8       │ 8 + 8 = 16  ├──────────────────┐
  6       ├─────────────┤  16 + 10 = 26    │
  4       │ 6 + 4 = 10  │                  │
 +9       └─────────────┴───────┬──────────┘
                                 │  26 + 9 = 35   │
                                 └────────────────┘
```

CARRYING IN ADDITION

In the last step of Be a Math Star 2.1, you were required to add 1 to the tens place. This is known as carrying. Study the following example:

```
  1       Step 1: Add the numbers in the ones column: 6 + 9 = 15. Write 5 in the ones
 26       column below the total line. Carry the 1 and write it at the top of the tens column.
 +9
 ──
  5
```

```
  1       Step 2: Add the numbers in the tens column, including the carried number:
 26       2 + 1 = 3. Write 3 in the tens column below the total line.
 +9
 ──
 35
```

FIGURE 2.4

In Figure 2.4, two large numbers are added together. In step 1, the numbers in the ones column are added, $8 + 2 = 10$. Write 0 in the ones place below the total line and carry the 1 above the tens column. In step 2, the numbers in the tens column are added, including the number that was carried in step 1, for $1 + 7 + 9 = 17$. Write 7 in the tens column below the total line and carry the 1 to the hundreds column. In step 3, the numbers in the hundreds column are added, including the number that was carried in step 2, for $1 + 5 + 5 = 11$. Because there are no numbers in the thousands column to be added in this problem, write 1 in the hundreds place and, instead of carrying 1 to the thousands column, simply write 1 in the thousands place—followed by a comma—below the total line.

MATH STAR 2.2

BE A *Math* ★ !

How do you handle double-digit columns of numbers like those below? No, you don't have to run for a calculator. First add down the tens column, then add up the ones column. Working with the resulting smaller numbers is easy!

	Add down the tens column:	*Continue adding up the ones column:*
56	50 + ↓	260 + 6 = 266—final answer!
92	90 = 140 + ↓	258 + 2 = 260 ↑
12	10 = 150 + ↓	256 + 2 = 258 ↑
84	80 = 230 + ↓	252 + 4 = 256 ↑
+22	20 = 250 →	250 + 2 = 252 ↑

HORIZONTAL ADDITION

Often you will see numbers to be added listed across the page in business documents. It takes more concentration to add these numbers, but it can be done. Add the ones-place numbers, then the tens-place numbers and so on. Study the following example.

1 55 + 65 + 123 = __3 ↑ ↑ ↑	**Step 1:** Add the numbers in the ones place: $5 + 5 + 3 = 13$. Write 3 in the ones place of the answer and carry the 1 to the tens place of one of the addends.
1 1 55 + 65 + 123 = _43 ↑ ↑ ↑	**Step 2:** Add the numbers in the tens place, including the carried number: $1 + 5 + 6 + 2 = 14$. Write 4 in the tens place of the answer and carry the 1 to the hundreds place of one of the addends.
1 1 55 + 65 + 123 = 243 ↑	**Step 3:** Add the numbers in the hundreds place, including the carried number: $1 + 1 = 2$. Write 2 in the hundreds place of the answer.

MATH STAR 2.3

BE A *Math*★ !

Here's another method for handling mental arithmetic when faced with more than two numbers. Begin by looking at the first number, then count by tens to add the tens in the next number, then add the ones in the second number, and so on.

56 + 43 + 28 = _____

Step 1: To add 56 + 43, think 56, 66, 76, 86, 96 + 3 = 99.
(Count by tens to add the 40 in 43.)

Step 2: To add 28 to the sum in step 1, continue counting by tens for the 20 in 28, then add 8 and you're done: 99, 109, 119 + 8 = 127.

This method also works with vertical addition.

```
  62
  33
 +54
 ────
```

Step 1: Think 62, 72, 82, 92 + 3 = 95.
(Count by tens to add the 30 in 33.)

Step 2: Think 95, 105, 115, 125, 135, 145 + 4 = 149.
(Count by tens to add the 50 in 54.)

VERTICAL AND HORIZONTAL ADDITION

Many business problems require that column or row totals be calculated. These totals are then added to find a **grand total**. In the example that follows, we must find totals for the rows and columns. In tables, columns are vertical (up and down) and rows are horizontal (across the page). The grand totals for the rows and columns should match. This is the most efficient way to check the addition for this type of problem.

PROBLEM

Calculate daily and weekly hours worked. Check by finding grand totals of daily and weekly hours worked.

Dusty Rag Housekeeping Service
Hours Worked Week of July 2, 2001

	Monday	Tuesday	Wednesday	Thursday	Friday	Saturday	Sunday	Totals
Jerri Chandler	8	8	0	6	6	4	0	1. ____
Carlee Daggett	8	8	0	6	6	4	0	2. ____
Kathy Ley	6	6	0	8	8	4	0	3. ____
Mary Tinsley	6	6	0	8	8	4	0	4. ____
Totals	6. ____	7. ____	8. ____	9. ____	10. ____	11. ____	12. ____	5. ____

Grand Total 13. _____

1.	*32*
2.	*32*
3.	*32*
4.	*32*
5.	*128*

Procedure

1. Add across each employee row and write the sums in the totals column.
2. Add all totals in cells 1 through 4 and write the first grand total in cell 5.
3. Add down the columns (Monday through Sunday), and write the sums in the totals area beneath each column.

Totals	6. *28*	7. *28*	8. *0*	9. *28*	10. *28*	11. *16*	12. *0*

Grand Total 13. *128*

4. Add across the totals row and write the second grand total in answer blank number 13. Make sure that the two grand totals (in answer blanks 5 and 13) match.

Name _____

Class/Section _____

Score (Correct Answers ÷ No. of Assigned Problems) _____

PART 2 *Business Math Skills*

Exercise 1

Add and check. Two blanks are provided, one for the first answer and one for the check answer. Use the grouping method as appropriate.

4	8	3	6	12	2	9
5	6	6	7	4	9	10
2	9	1	51	7	5	3
+11	+7	+4	+9	+1	+2	+6

1. _____ 2. _____ 3. _____ 4. _____ 5. _____ 6. _____ 7. _____

Add and check. Remember to use commas in answers when necessary.

289	831	69	70	22	321	443
11	34	56	24	56	38	99
45	68	170	45	77	17	29
+87	+57	+33	+21	+651	+29	+100

8. _____ 9. _____ 10. _____ 11. _____ 12. _____ 13. _____ 14. _____

Add and check.

99 + 122 + 11 = _____   12 + 55 + 290 = _____   77 + 8 + 140 = _____
15. _____   16. _____   17. _____

24 + 144 + 65 = _____   43 + 85 + 572 = _____   33 + 1 + 762 = _____
18. _____   19. _____   20. _____

Exercise 2

21. Adopt-a-Pet-or-2 has 31 cats, 4 kittens, 9 dogs, and 1 ferret. How many animals are in the shelter?_____
22. Action Shippers has a customer who needs to ship 9 cases of bottled water, 5 cases of juice, and 20 cases of sports drink. The shipper needs to reserve space for how many cases on his truck for this shipment?_____
23. At a recent employee appreciation dinner, all employees were asked to list their years of work experience. What is the total work experience represented in the room?_____

Employee	Years of Experience
Jim Grant	15
Elaine Robinson	12
Jayne Ramirez	14
Tim Summers	2
Gladys Treadway	16
John Tims	9
Total	23. _____

Exercise 3

Complete the following report of hours worked. Add vertically and horizontally. Check sums by finding grand totals.

Adopt-a-Pet-or-2
Hours Worked Week of July 2, 2001

	Monday	Tuesday	Wednesday	Thursday	Friday	Saturday	Sunday	Totals
Janis Carter	8	0	8	8	4	4	0	24. ___
Heidi Chanfield	8	6	0	8	8	0	0	25. ___
Joanne Jones	7	8	0	9	7	0	0	26. ___
Johnny Chanfield	8	8	0	0	5	8	8	27. ___
Totals	29. ___	30. ___	31. ___	32. ___	33. ___	34. ___	35. ___	28. ___

Grand Total 36. _____

 PART 3 *The Pocket and Windows Calculators*

The order of entry for a typical addition problem on the pocket and Windows calculators is usually the same. Key all the addends followed by a plus key, except the last addend. Key the last addend of the problem followed by the equals key. Pressing the equals key readies the calculator's register for the next problem. **It is not necessary to clear the display before beginning the next problem.** To check the addition, reverse the addends and add again.

Problem	Procedure	Check
47	47+	29+
16	16+	16+
+29	29 =	47 =
	[92]	[92]

CORRECTING ERRORS

Pocket Calculator

Most pocket calculators have an on/correct key. It may be labeled [on/c] or [on/ce]. This button will clear the last keyed number if pressed once before the equals key has been pressed. The on/correct key will completely clear the problem and allow you to start over when pressed twice.

> **Example:** You are in the process of keying the problem 24 + 22 on a pocket calculator. You key 24 + 24 and notice that the second number you keyed is incorrect. To correct, press the on/c key once. Then key the correct number. Finish the problem by pressing the equals key. Your display should show the correct answer, 46.

Procedure: 24 + 24 . . . oops!

$$\boxed{\text{on/c}} \quad 22 = \boxed{46}$$

Windows Calculator

When using the Windows calculator, the backspace key may be used before an operation key has been pressed to remove the last digit in the display. Then key the correct digit and continue the problem. The CE key works like the on/c key on a pocket calculator. The C key clears the problem completely and allows you to start over.

THE MEMORY FEATURE, HORIZONTAL AND VERTICAL ADDITION, AND FINDING A GRAND TOTAL

Pocket calculators have a memory register. With this feature the number in the display may be added to the memory register using the **memory plus key** (M+) or subtracted from the memory register using the **memory minus key** (M−). The amount in the memory register may be recalled to the display using the memory recall (MR) key. The memory clear (MC) key may be used to clear the memory register.

PROBLEM

In the following problem involving both horizontal and vertical addition, the memory register is used to find the grand totals and thus check the horizontal and vertical addition.

Newberry Ice Crème Shops
Weekend Sales Report for August 4, 2001 ($)

		Saturday		Sunday		Totals
Northeast store		8,190		7,960	1.	16,150
Glendale store		6,900		4,500	2.	11,400
Mountain View store		12,115		15,300	3.	27,415
Totals	5.	27,205	6.	27,760	4.	54,965

Grand Total 7. $ 54,965

Procedure

1. Add across the rows for each store. Place each total in memory. Use memory recall to display the first grand total. Clear memory if necessary before beginning the problem.

   $\boxed{\text{MC}}$ 8,190 + 7,960 = $\boxed{16,150}$ $\boxed{\text{M+}}$

            6,900 + 4,500 = $\boxed{11,400}$ $\boxed{\text{M+}}$

          12,115 + 15,300 = $\boxed{27,415}$ $\boxed{\text{M+}}$ $\boxed{\text{MR}}$ $\boxed{54,965}$ These two grand totals should match, proving that both the vertical and horizontal sums are correct.

2. Add down the Saturday and Sunday columns. Place each total in memory. Use memory recall to display the second grand total.

   $\boxed{\text{MC}}$ 8,190 +   7,960 +

          6,900 +   4,500 +

      12,115 = $\boxed{27,205}$ $\boxed{\text{M+}}$ 15,300 = $\boxed{27,760}$ $\boxed{\text{M+}}$ $\boxed{\text{MR}}$ $\boxed{54,965}$

PART 3 *Pocket or Windows Calculator*

Exercise 1

Add and check. Two blanks are provided; one for the first answer and one for the check answer.

14	28	37	16	38	3	32
5	6	26	27	24	19	1
6	9	15	56	15	22	5
+55	+17	+24	+29	+16	+6	+2

1. _____ 2. _____ 3. _____ 4. _____ 5. _____ 6. _____ 7. _____

Add and check. Remember to use commas in answers when necessary.

512	58	369	71	14	691	471
27	17	156	52	26	18	100
25	28	74	45	77	42	60
+175	+17	+6	+70	+639	+63	+505

8. _____ 9. _____ 10. _____ 11. _____ 12. _____ 13. _____ 14. _____

Add and check.

99 + 691 + 51 = _____   17 + 25 + 226 = _____   37 + 8 + 736 = _____
15. _____   16. _____   17. _____

77 + 788 + 64 = _____   45 + 89 + 178 = _____   61 + 9 + 169 = _____
18. _____   19. _____   20. _____

Exercise 2

Complete the following weekly sales report. Add horizontally and vertically. Check sums by finding grand totals.

Abacus Sales Co. Region 10 Weekly Sales
Week of June 25, 2001 ($)

	Monday	Tuesday	Wednesday	Thursday	Friday	Totals
Rodriguez, Joe	15,696	19,699	14,774	28,896	25,654	21. _____
James, John	19,687	18,578	24,597	19,664	25,885	22. _____
Carter, Patrick	36,647	35,779	34,987	27,587	24,687	23. _____
Koslo, Mark	29,684	28,495	34,965	34,876	29,648	24. _____
Totals	26. _____	27. _____	28. _____	29. _____	30. _____	25. _____

Grand Total 31. _____

PART 3 *Review and Practice Using Business Math FUNdamentals*

GOAL: Complete 9 of the 10 problems correctly.

Instructions: *Start Business Math FUNdamentals. Complete Tutorial 3 Addition, Tutorial 4 Carrying in Addition, and Drill 2 Addition. If you are not satisfied with your score, repeat Drill 2. Write your scores below.*

Business Math FUNdamentals Drill 2

Today's Date	Score

 **PART 4** *The Desktop Calculator*

KEYSTROKING TECHNIQUE: THE 7, 8, AND 9 KEYS

Strike the upper row keys with the pad or fleshy part of the finger (Figure 2.5). Use the index finger to key number 7, the middle finger to key the number 8, and the ring finger to key the number 9 on the upper row of a desktop calculator. After keying a number on the upper row, return the finger to its correct position on the home row.

Machine Setup

Set the decimal selector on F or 0.

Set the rounding switch on 5/4.

Set the tax switch on CALC.

Set the printer switch on IC (item counter).

FIGURE 2.5

ADDITION PRACTICE PROBLEMS: KEYS 4 THROUGH 9

Key the following addition problems, using the plus (+) key after each addend and the total key (*/T) to find the sum.

Note: Remember that it is not necessary to clear the display after pressing the total key. Compare your answers with the ones given.

1.	64	2.	55	3.	84	4.	96	5.	54	6.	95	7.	46	8.	74
	54		55		67		65		46		58		99		79
	47		56		74		64		45		57		56		85
	46		88		75		86		58		44		67		87
	48		57		57		67		47		86		68		74
	69		59		78		68		44		55		65		79
	84		94		89		69		99		96		66		76
	94		84		97		76		95		67		74		96
	45		87		79		74		96		46		69		48
	64		86		76		75		97		56		97		85
	615		721		776		740		681		660		707		783

THE MEMORY FEATURE

Desktop calculators also have a memory register. With this feature the number in the display may be added to the memory register using the memory plus (M+=) key or subtracted from the memory register using the memory minus (M−=) key. An M in the display indicates that the memory register contains a value.

The amount in the memory register may be recalled to the display using the memory subtotal (MS) key. Using the memory subtotal key does not clear the memory, and thus additional numbers may continue to be added to or subtracted from the current total in memory.

The memory total (MT) key is used to display the value in memory and to clear the memory register. The MT key clears M from the display and resets the memory item counter to zero.

FINDING A GRAND TOTAL

For the grand total feature to be active, the printer switch must be set on GT. The item counter is also active when the printer switch is set to GT. The GT key may be used to display and print the grand total of all totals. Press the GT key *twice* to clear the grand total.

HORIZONTAL AND VERTICAL ADDITION ON FORMS

Forms containing several columns of numbers may be checked by adding across the rows and finding a grand total, then adding down the columns and finding a second grand total. The two grand totals should match.

In the following problem, the grand total feature is used to find the grand totals and thus to check the vertical and horizontal additions.

Newberry Ice Crème Shops
Weekend Sales Report for February 3, 2001 ($)

		Saturday		Sunday		Totals
Northeast store		4,779		4,556	1.	*9,335*
Glendale store		4,589		4,455	2.	*9,044*
Mountain View store		7,664		8,469	3.	*16,133*
Totals	5.	*17,032*	6.	*17,480*	4.	*34,512*

Grand Total 7.   *$ 34,512*

MACHINE SETUP   Decimal Selector—F
Rounding Switch—5/4
Tax Switch—CALC
Printer Switch—GT

PROCEDURE

1. Add across the rows and find a grand total.

C MT   4,779+
4,556+   */T   9,335

4,589+
4,455+   */T   9,044

7,664+
8,469+   */T   16,133   GT   34,512   GT   GT

2. Add down the columns and find a grand total.

4,779+
4,589+
7,664+   */T   17,032

4,556+
4,455+
8,469+   */T   17,480   GT   34,512   GT   GT

> These two grand totals should match, proving that both the vertical and horizontal sums are correct.

TAPE 2.1:

```
                        0   C
000

                        0   M*

                4,779    +
                4 556    +
002
                9 335   G+

                4 589    +
                4,455    +
002
                9 044   G+

                7 664    +
                8 469•   +
002
                6,133   G+

                34,5 2  G◇
                34 512  G*

                        0   G*

                4,779    +
                4 589    +
                7,664    +
003
                7 032   G+

                4 556    +
                4,455    +
                8 469    +
003
                7 480   G+

                34 5 2  G◇
                34 5 2  G*

                        0   G*
```

 **PART 4** *Desktop Calculator*

Exercise 1

Add and check. Two blanks are provided, one for the first answer and one for the check answer.

4	8	7	6	88	4	9
5	6	6	7	4	9	77
6	9	5	56	5	5	5
+55	+7	+4	+9	+6	+6	+6

1. _____ 2. _____ 3. _____ 4. _____ 5. _____ 6. _____ 7. _____

Add and check. Remember to use commas in answers when necessary.

589	858	69	74	44	696	474
47	47	56	54	56	58	99
45	68	474	45	77	47	69
+875	+57	+66	+69	+659	+69	+565

8. _____ 9. _____ 10. _____ 11. _____ 12. _____ 13. _____ 14. _____

Add and check.

99 + 696 + 55 = _____   47 + 55 + 796 = _____   77 + 8 + 746 = _____
       15. _____   16. _____   17. _____

74 + 744 + 65 = _____   48 + 85 + 578 = _____   66 + 9 + 769 = _____
       18. _____   19. _____   20. _____

Exercise 2

Complete the following weekly sales report. Add horizontally and vertically. Use the grand total feature to check addition.

Amadeus Equipment Company
Region 4 Weekly Sales Week of June 25, 2001 ($)

	Monday	Tuesday	Wednesday	Thursday	Friday	Totals
Rodriguez, Joe	45,696	39,699	44,774	58,896	65,654	21. _____
James, John	59,687	58,578	54,597	49,664	55,885	22. _____
Carter, Patrick	46,647	45,779	44,987	47,587	44,687	23. _____
Koslo, Mark	69,684	48,495	64,965	64,876	59,648	24. _____
Totals	26. _____	27. _____	28. _____	29. _____	30. _____	25. _____

Grand Total 31. _____

Exercise 3

Accuracy Score (Correct Strokes ÷ Total Strokes) _____

One-Minute Addition Timing (Keys 4 through 9)

(Optional: Your instructor may wish you to use Touch Key on the computer for all your timings. Check with your instructor before completing this exercise.)

Complete as many of the problems as possible in 1 minute by adding. Work quickly and accurately. The number preceding each closing parenthesis indicates the cumulative number of strokes for problems attempted. For example, if you complete Problems 1 through 5 in 1 minute, your strokes-per-minute score is 155. Optional: 3-to 5-minute timings. (See instructions for longer timings below.)

1.	44	2.	45	3.	54	4.	56	5.	44	6.	65	7.	66	8.	64
	54		55		57		65		46		58		69		69
	47		56		74		64		45		57		46		85
	46		58		75		66		48		54		67		87
	48		57		87		67		47		56		68		74
	49		59		78		68		44		55		65		79
	84		54		89		69		49		66		66		76
	94		84		97		76		95		67		64		96
	45		87		79		74		96		46		69		88
	64		86		76		75		97		56		96		85
31)		62)		93)		124)		155)		186)		217)		248)	

9.	74	10.	47	11.	45	12.	65	13.	66	14.	77	15.	76	16.	84
	49		84		75		46		86		74		79		58
	84		94		58		58		76		75		67		86
	85		47		95		59		96		76		47		48
	47		46		98		57		56		78		75		78
	48		48		96		45		46		79		78		89
	45		49		65		58		69		97		79		85
	44		45		55		59		67		67		87		87
	46		44		57		57		68		57		74		84
	94		64		75		56		66		47		77		86
279)		310)		341)		372)		403)		434)		465)		496)	

17.	94	18.	85	19.	74	20.	76	21.	84	22.	65	23.	99	24.	86
	96		88		84		78		87		86		49		88
	95		84		94		47		95		69		65		58
	68		86		57		49		94		76		79		85
	89		87		57		95		99		46		58		78
	84		89		58		69		85		54		98		48
	57		95		59		96		76		58		57		85
	59		96		55		76		64		68		97		86
	69		76		56		77		95		76		75		89
	67		74		64		87		55		86		76		87
527)		558)		589)		620)		651)		682)		713)		744)	

25.	44	26.	58	27.	67	28.	96	29.	95	30.	89	31.	76	32.	64
	84		56		46		99		97		59		85		69
	96		89		56		59		67		58		76		68
	95		86		87		89		98		68		74		67
	85		57		89		69		69		67		79		46
	76		48		88		67		76		57		98		65
	74		89		84		69		48		94		97		86
	57		68		85		68		87		68		96		85
	59		58		59		64		89		86		59		89
	56		57		65		69		86		69		64		96
775)		806)		837)		868)		899)		930)		961)		992)	

Note: If you wish to take longer timings, divide your total strokes by the number of minutes in the timing. For example, if you take a 3-minute timing, divide your total strokes by 3 to get your strokes-per-minute score.

To calculate your percent-of-accuracy score, use the following method.

Using the calculator tape, check each key stroke. For incomplete problems, count each number and each operation key as one stroke and add to the total strokes indicated beside the previous problem. Subtract incorrect strokes from total strokes to find total correct strokes. Divide correct strokes by total strokes. Convert to a percent. This is your percent-of-accuracy score.

Example

190 total strokes, 178 correct strokes.

178 correct strokes divided by 190 total strokes = .94 (rounded).

Convert to a decimal number. Then 94% is your percent-of-accuracy score.

Some instructors may prefer to use total problem accuracy when calculating a grade. To use this method, check *answers only* for all completed problems. Divide the number of correct problems by the number of problems attempted. This will give you the percent of problem accuracy.

Example

6 problems were attempted, 5 were correct.

5 divided by 6 = .8333, or 83% problem accuracy.

Or, you may add together keystrokes for problems with correct answers only. (In this exercise, there are 31 strokes in each problem.) Divide the number of correct problem keystrokes by the total keystrokes for all problems attempted.

Example

6 problems were attempted, 5 were correct.

$5 \times 31 = 155$.

155 keystrokes divided by 186 keystrokes = .8333, or 83%.

CHAPTER 2 *Terminology Review*

Addends

Grand total

Grouping property of addition (associative property of addition)

Memory minus key

Memory plus key

Order property of addition (commutative property of addition)

Sum

Insert the missing words to complete the following statements.

1. To check vertical and horizontal addition on one form, find the _____.
2. The _____ allows numbers to be placed in any order without affecting the result of addition.
3. Numbers that are to be added together are called _____.
4. The _____ allows more than two numbers to be grouped in different ways without affecting the result of addition.
5. The result of adding numbers together is called the _____.

Chapter 2 Review Exercises

Exercise 1

Add and check. Two blanks are provided, one for the first answer and one for the check answer.

64	58	97	46	88	44	69
45	76	96	77	54	49	77
46	49	75	56	75	75	65
+55	+47	+54	+99	+86	+76	+56

1. _____ 2. _____ 3. _____ 4. _____ 5. _____ 6. _____ 7. _____

Add and check. Remember to use commas in answers when necessary.

4,589	9,858	8,769	8,774	5,944	4,696	6,474
8,747	7,647	6,556	7,654	6,856	8,758	8,899
5,645	5,568	9,474	6,645	6,577	5,447	7,869
+7,875	+9,457	+4,566	+7,569	+9,659	+5,769	+6,565

8. _____ 9. _____ 10. _____ 11. _____ 12. _____ 13. _____ 14. _____

Add and check.

49 + 596 + 45 = _____   87 + 85 + 896 = _____   97 + 6 + 946 = _____
        15. _____   16. _____   17. _____

64 + 844 + 75 = _____   49 + 95 + 644 = _____   57 + 5 + 889 = _____
        18. _____   19. _____   20. _____

Exercise 2

21. On Monday, a wholesaler ordered 500 pounds of apples, 900 pounds of bananas, and 600 pounds of oranges to be delivered Tuesday. He has 100 pounds of apples, 200 pounds of bananas, and 150 pounds of oranges on hand. A customer needs 550 pounds of apples delivered Wednesday. Will the wholesaler have enough apples on hand to fill this order?
22. Bill's business mileage was 65 miles on Monday, 56 miles on Tuesday, 44 miles on Wednesday, 76 miles on Thursday, and 58 miles on Friday. What was his total mileage for the week?

Exercise 3

Complete the following weekly production report. Add horizontally and vertically. Check sums by finding grand totals.

School Furniture Company
Weekly Production Report Week of June 25, 2001

	Monday	Tuesday	Wednesday	Thursday	Friday	Totals
Model A desks	5,696	3,699	4,774	5,896	5,654	23. _____
A-line chairs	5,685	5,578	4,595	9,664	5,985	24. _____
Library tables	645	775	957	587	657	25. _____
All-in-1 desks	9,684	8,495	5,965	4,875	4,649	26. _____
Totals	28. _____	29. _____	30. _____	31. _____	32. _____	27. _____

Grand Total 33. _____

CHAPTER 3

Subtraction,
Subtotals

 PART 1   *Speed and Accuracy Building Using Touch Key*

KEYSTROKING TECHNIQUE
Bottom Row

Strike the keys on the bottom row with the fingernail portion of the fingertips and then re-turn the finger to the home row. Strike the 1 key with the 4 (index) finger, strike the 2 key with the 5 (middle) finger, and strike the 3 key with the 6 (ring) finger (Figure 3.1).

FIGURE 3.1

GOALS: Your speed goal is 6,000 strokes per hour.
Your accuracy target goal range is 95% to 100%.

With each repetition of the lesson, try to improve your speed without lowering your accuracy score. If your percent-of-accuracy score falls below 95%, review your finger position and technique. Then try again.

37

Touch Key Lesson 3—The 1, 2, and 3 Keys

	Today's Date	Strokes per Hour	Percent of Accuracy
A.			
B.			
C.			
D.			
E.			

PART 2 *Business Math Skills*

SUBTRACTION

Subtraction is the opposite of addition. It is one of the arithmetic operations. **Subtraction** is used to decrease a number by a specified amount.

Example: A pet shop had 384 pets for sale. On Monday, 21 pets were sold. How many pets were left?

COMPONENTS OF SUBTRACTION

The number to be decreased in a subtraction problem is the **minuend.** The number to be subtracted is the **subtrahend.** The remainder, or answer, is the **difference** (see Figure 3.2).

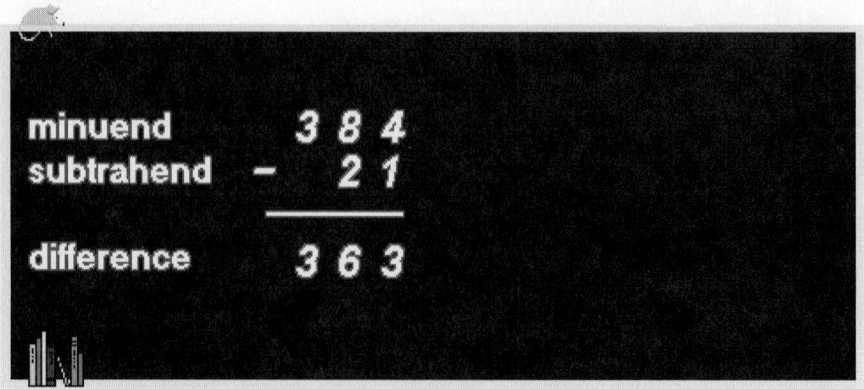

FIGURE 3.2

In vertical subtraction numbers should be aligned according to place value beginning with the ones place. A horizontal line is drawn under the problem to indicate a total follows. The minus sign indicates subtraction.

CHECKING SUBTRACTION

Because subtraction is the opposite of addition, subtraction may be checked by adding the subtrahend and the difference. If the sum equals the minuend of the subtraction problem, the answer is correct (see Figure 3.3).

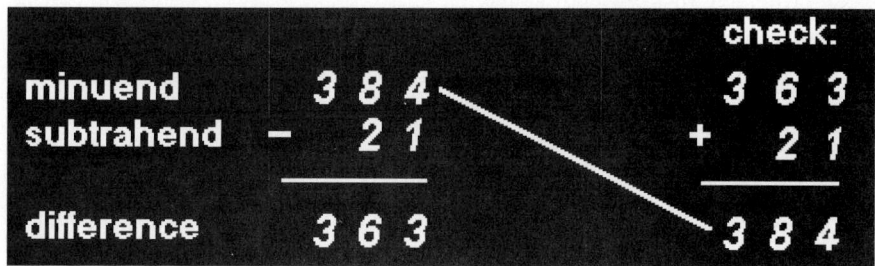

FIGURE 3.3

SUBTRACTION PROPERTIES

The order of the numbers in a subtraction problem is extremely important and cannot be changed without affecting the difference.

Example: $9 - 4 = 5$, but
$4 - 9 = -5$

The same is true for grouping three or more numbers to be subtracted. Only two numbers are subtracted at a time. The grouping of these numbers may not be changed without affecting the difference.

Example: $9 - 6 - 2 = 1$, but
$6 - 2 - 9 = -5$, and
$2 - 9 - 6 = -13$

TABLE OF ADDITION USED FOR SUBTRACTION

Because subtraction is the opposite of addition, the table of addition may be used to find a difference (Table 3.1). Use the table to find the difference of $11 - 10 = $ ___. Find the subtrahend (10) in the first column. Find the minuend (11) in the same row as the subtrahend, but **within the body** of the table. The difference is the number at the top of the column containing the minuend (1).

Note: Any number minus zero is equal to that number.

TABLE 3.1   Table of Addition/Subtraction

+/−	1	2	3	4	5	6	7	8	9	10
1	2	3	4	5	6	7	8	9	10	11
2	3	4	5	6	7	8	9	10	11	12
3	4	5	6	7	8	9	10	11	12	13
4	5	6	7	8	9	10	11	12	13	14
5	6	7	8	9	10	11	12	13	14	15
6	7	8	9	10	11	12	13	14	15	16
7	8	9	10	11	12	13	14	15	16	17
8	9	10	11	12	13	14	15	16	17	18
9	10	11	12	13	14	15	16	17	18	19
10	11	12	13	14	15	16	17	18	19	20

MATH STAR 3.1

BE A *Math*★ !

It is easier to subtract numbers like 30, 70, and 90, that end in zero. If the same number is added (or subtracted) to both the minuend and the subtrahend, the result will not be affected, but working the problem is easier.

128 +3 131	Example 1: Mentally, add 3 to both the minuend and the subtrahend.
−67 +3 −70	Subtract mentally: 131 − 70 = 61. Note: In this shortcut we are
‾‾‾‾‾‾‾‾ 61	increasing the subtrahend, 67, by 3. We are NOT adding a negative number to a positive number.
134 −3 131	Example 2: Subtract 3 from the minuend and subtrahend.
−63 −3 −60	Subtract: 131 − 60 = 71.
‾‾‾‾‾‾‾‾ 71	

BORROWING IN SUBTRACTION

Sometimes one or more of the digits in the subtrahend will be larger than the corresponding number in the minuend. We must then borrow from the digit in the next higher place in the minuend. In the problem shown in Figure 3.4, the ones place contains a 9 to be subtracted from a 1. This cannot be done without borrowing.

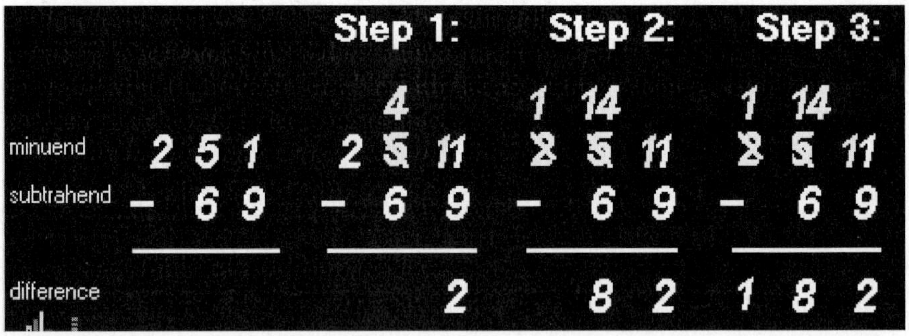

FIGURE 3.4

Step 1: Borrow 10 from the tens place in the minuend. Cross out 5 and replace it with 4. In effect, this reduces 50 to 40 and allows 10 to be added to the ones place. Change the 1 in the ones place in the minuend to 11. Subtract 9 from 11 and place 2 in the ones place of the answer.

Step 2: Look at the numbers in the tens place. Six cannot be subtracted from 4 without borrowing. Borrow 100 by crossing out the 2 in the hundreds place in the minuend and replace it with 1. Write the 1 beside the 4 in the tens place, making it 14. Subtract 6 from 14 and write 8 in the tens place of the answer.

Step 3: There is no digit in the hundreds place of the subtrahend to subtract. Bring down the 1 in the hundreds place in the minuend by writing it in the hundreds place of the answer.

Because of borrowing, subtracting columns of numbers is considered too complex when subtracting mentally or with pencil and paper. Subtract only two numbers at a time.

NEGATIVE NUMBERS

If the subtrahend is larger than the minuend, the difference will be a **negative number.** Visualize the answer to the problem $4 - 6$ by drawing a number line. Begin with 4 and move to the left 6 digits. The answer is -2.

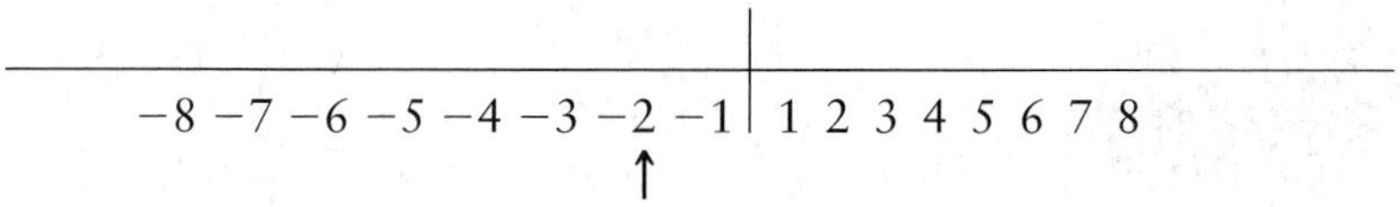

FIGURE 3.5

What does a negative number mean? It could mean a shortage as in a checking account. Assume Bill has $999 in his checking account. He then writes a check for $1,054. If the bank honors the check, Bill's checking account will have a negative balance, or a **credit balance.** In this case Bill will owe the bank money.

Problem		Rewrite the Problem
Minuend	999	$-1,054$
Subtrahend	$-1,054$	$+999$
Difference		-55

To solve this type of problem, subtract the smaller number (the minuend) from the larger number (the subtrahend) and place a minus sign before the answer (the difference) to indicate a negative number. Sometimes negative numbers are shown on business forms in parentheses; for example, (55) signifies -55.

ADDING NEGATIVE NUMBERS

If another check clears the bank before money is deposited in the account, the negative balance increases. Therefore, two negative numbers are added and a negative sign is placed before the sum:

$$
\begin{array}{rl}
-55 & \text{negative balance} \\
-24 & \text{additional check} \\
\hline
-79 & \text{negative new balance}
\end{array}
$$

ADDING A NEGATIVE NUMBER AND A POSITIVE NUMBER

If $500 is deposited in the foregoing account, the deposit is greater than the shortage (negative balance). The result is a positive balance:

$$
\begin{array}{rl}
-79 & \text{negative balance} \\
+500 & \text{deposit} \\
\hline
421 & \text{positive new balance}
\end{array}
$$

Note: A number with no sign in front of it is assumed to be a positive number.

However, if only $50 is deposited into the account with a negative balance of −$79, the amount of the shortage will decrease, but the balance will still be negative:

$$
\begin{array}{rl}
-79 & \text{negative balance} \\
+50 & \text{deposit} \\
\hline
-29 & \text{negative new balance}
\end{array}
$$

MATH STAR 3.2

BE A *Math★* !

Is there a way to easily subtract numbers that normally require borrowing? Yes, there is! You are already familiar with the first method.

Method 1: Adjust Minuend, Adjust Subtrahend, Subtract

$$
\begin{array}{ll}
231 & +1\ 232 \\
-19 & +1\ -20 \\
\hline
& 212
\end{array}
$$

Example 1: The subtrahend has a 9 in the ones place and the minuend has a 1 in the ones place. To avoid having to borrow, convert the subtrahend to a number that does not require borrowing. In this example, add 1 to it. Add 1 to the minuend also. Then mentally subtract: $232 - 20 = 212$.

Method 2: Adjust Subtrahend, Subtract, Adjust Difference

In the second method, the subtrahend is adjusted by adding or subtracting a small number. After finding the difference, it is then adjusted by the same amount used to adjust the subtrahend.

$$
\begin{array}{ll}
167 & 167 \\
-29 & -2\ -27 \\
\hline
& 140 - 2 = 138
\end{array}
$$

Example 2: Rather than borrowing to subtract numbers in the ones place, alter the subtrahend, 29, by subtracting 2. It is then easy to find the difference: $167 - 27 = 140$. Adjust the answer by subtracting 2. The answer is 138.

HORIZONTAL SUBTRACTION

Business forms frequently list numbers to be subtracted across the form in rows. In the following example, each item has a selling price and a cost. Subtract cost from selling price to find the amount of markup for each item.

7/24 Shops

Item Number	Selling Price ($)	Cost ($)	Amount of Markup ($)
724AAA1	5	3	1. _____
724AAA13	8	2	2. _____
724AAA29	9	4	3. _____
724AAA35	12	7	4. _____
Totals	6. _____	7. _____	5. _____

The amounts of markup are as shown:

Amount of Markup ($)	
1.	2
2.	6
3.	5
4.	5

To check this type of problem, use the following procedure:

Step 1: Total the markup column.

Amount of Markup ($)	
1.	*2*
2.	*6*
3.	*5*
4.	*5*
5.	*18*

Step 2: Total the selling price and cost columns:

Totals   6. *$34*   7. *$16*

Step 3: Subtract the total cost from the total selling price. The total should match the total from step 1: $34 − $16 = $18.

Name _____

Class/Section _____

Score (Correct Answers ÷ No. of Assigned Problems) _____

PART 2   *Business Math Skills*

Exercise 1

Subtract. Check by adding. The first problem has been completed for you.

	148	883	60	112	277	902	522
	−62	−58	−47	−94	−269	−10	−288
1.	86	2. _____	3. _____	4. _____	5. _____	6. _____	7. _____
	+62						
	148	_____	_____	_____	_____	_____	_____

Add and check. Remember to use commas in answers when necessary.

	1,289	8,031	69	70	222	8,321	4,430
	−11	−1,934	−56	−24	−156	−7,938	−2,999
8. _____	9. _____	10. _____	11. _____	12. _____	13. _____	14. _____	
_____	_____	_____	_____	_____	_____	_____	

Subtract and check.

15. 135 − 59 = __76__ + 59 = __135__   16. 290 − 55 = _____ _____
17. 1,112 − 290 = _____ _____   18. 8,140 − 6,036 = _____ _____
19. 324 − 144 = _____ _____   20. 143 − 85 = _____ _____
21. 762 − 339 = _____ _____   22. 1,003 − 798 = _____ _____

23. John bought a car with 20,460 miles on it. The odometer now shows 86,951 miles. How many miles has John driven the car? _____

24. What is the difference of one hundred twenty-two thousand four hundred sixty-three and one hundred twenty thousand sixty-one? _____

25. Jan's weekly gross (total) pay was $600. Her paycheck was written for $486. How much were Jan's withholdings (items deducted from total pay)? _____

26. Janice's new printer can print 12 color pages per minute. Her old printer produced 4 color pages per minute. How many more color pages can the new printer produce per minute? _____

27. A pair of name-brand sports shoes regularly costs $85. The shoes were advertised for sale at $59. How much would the purchaser save by buying the shoes during the sale? _____

28. A pet shop had 34 kittens, 15 puppies, and 24 freshwater hermit crabs for sale. During the day, it sold 19 freshwater hermit crabs. How many crabs were left? _____

Exercise 2

Complete the following travel expense report. Each week Joe is given an advance. His weekly expenses are deducted from this advance. Joe usually has surplus advanced money, which is used for next month's expenses. Check your answers.

Travel Expense Report for Joe Smith ($)
Month of August 2001

Week of	Advance	Hotel	Meals	Bus, Taxi, Miscellaneous	Totals
August 4	160	92	32	25	29. ____
August 13	160	79	29	15	30. ____
August 20	160	109	27	20	31. ____
August 27	160	56	22	18	32. ____
Totals	34. ____	35. ____	36. ____	37. ____	33. ____

Exercise 3

38. The Johnson Buildings Company had $6,592 in its checking account on July 1. During the month of July, the following checks were written. Deduct the checks to find the current balance. Check your answer using one of the methods in this chapter.

Checking account balance ($)	$6,592
Rent	$525
Utilities	$269
Truck loan	$562
Insurance	$560
Lumber	$2,699
Hardware	$1,042
Gasoline	$126
Balance	$_____

 PART 3 *The Pocket and Windows Calculators*

SUBTRACTION

The order of entry for a typical subtraction problem on the pocket and Windows calculators involves keying the minuend followed by the minus key, then the subtrahend followed by the equals key.

Check the subtraction problem by adding the subtrahend to the difference. With the difference showing in the display, press the plus key. This sets the number in the display as an addend. Key the subtrahend followed by the equals key. The total should match the minuend in the original problem.

Problem	Procedure	Check
57 −16	57− 16= 41	41 + 16 = 57

Pocket calculators make it easy to subtract columns of numbers, even when borrowing is involved. To check, add the difference and all the subtrahends. The result should equal the minuend of the original problem.

Problem	Procedure	Check
899 −57 −30 −27	899− 57− 30− 27= 785	785 + 57 + 30 + 27 = 899

COMPLETING AND CHECKING A FORM WITH HORIZONTAL SUBTRACTION

Along with the memory plus key, the pocket calculator also has a **memory minus key**. Pressing the memory minus key subtracts the number in the display from the memory register.

PROBLEM

Subtract cost from selling price to find markup. Add the difference to memory.

Newberry Ice Crème Shops

Item	Selling Price ($)	Cost ($)	Markup ($)
Small cone	2	1	1. _____
Double cone	3	2	2. _____
Sundae	4	3	3. _____
Totals	5. _____	6. _____	4. _____

Procedure

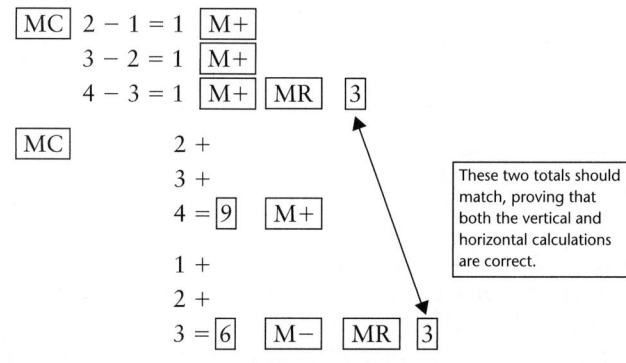

These two totals should match, proving that both the vertical and horizontal calculations are correct.

 PART 3 *Pocket or Windows Calculator*

Exercise 1

Subtract. Check by adding. The first problem has been completed for you.

	953	83	760	912	277	1,902	529
	−162	−58	−647	−594	−69	−710	−28
1.	791	2. ____	3. ____	4. ____	5. ____	6. ____	7. ____
	+162						
	953	____	____	____	____	____	____

Add and check. Remember to use commas in answers when necessary.

	289	6,039	469	270	9,222	8,355	4,430
	−11	−1,934	−54	−124	−956	−7,938	−3,002
8. ____	9. ____	10. ____	11. ____	12. ____	13. ____	14. ____

____   ____   ____   ____   ____   ____   ____

Subtract and check.

15. 14,135 − 559 = <u>13,576</u> + 559 = <u>14,135</u>   16. 2,290 − 1,155 = ____ ____

17. 10,112 − 2,090 = ____ ____   18. 8,944 − 6,836 = ____ ____

19. 813 − 514 = ____ ____   20. 963 − 585 = ____ ____

21. 462 − 339 = ____ ____   22. 1,221 − 998 = ____ ____

Exercise 2

Complete the following sales/returns report. Returns should be deducted from sales each week. Check answers using the memory feature.

Week of	Sales ($)	Returns ($)	Totals ($)
August 5	15,696	699	23. ____
August 12	19,687	578	24. ____
August 19	36,647	779	25. ____
August 25	29,684	495	26. ____
Totals	28. ____	29. ____	27. ____

Exercise 3

30. Angela's account at her family physician's office had a balance on May 1 of $569. She has since made the following payments: June $200, July $150, and August $200. What is her current balance? _____

PART 3 *Review and Practice Using Business Math FUNdamentals*

GOAL: Complete 9 of the 10 problems correctly.

Instructions: *Start Business Math FUNdamentals. Complete Tutorial 5 Subtraction, Tutorial 6 Borrowing in Subtraction, Tutorial 7 Negative Numbers in Subtraction, and Drill 3 Subtraction. If you are not satisfied with your score, repeat Drill 3. Write your scores below.*

Business Math FUNdamentals Drill 3

Today's Date	Score

PART 4 *The Desktop Calculator*

SUBTRACTION

The order of entry for a typical subtraction problem on the desktop calculator involves first keying the minuend followed by the plus key, then keying the subtrahend followed by the minus and total keys. On a desktop calculator with a two-color ribbon, the items subtracted and any negative differences will print in red.

For example, 30 + 10 − T $\boxed{20}$.

Checking the Problem

With the difference still displayed, press the plus key, and then add the subtrahend. The difference should equal the minuend of the original problem. Assume the difference is still shown in the display: $\boxed{20}$ + 10 + T $\boxed{30}$.

KEYSTROKING TECHNIQUE: SUBTRACTION

With the index, middle, and ring fingers in position over the 4, 5, and 6 keys, respectively, use the little finger to press the subtraction key (Figure 3.6). Attempt to press the key without moving the home row fingers from the correct position over the home row keys.

Machine Setup

Set the decimal selector on F or 0.

Set the rounding switch on 5/4.

Set the printer switch on IC (item counter).

FIGURE 3.6

Problem	Procedure	Check
47	47+	31 +
−16	16− */T	16 + */T
	31	47

SUBTRACTION PRACTICE PROBLEMS USING KEYS 1 THROUGH 9

Key the following subtraction problems, using the plus key after each positive number, the subtraction key after each negative number, and the total key to find the answer. Compare your answer with the one given.

1. 1,164	2. 2,155	3. 8,184	4. 3,496	5. 8,154	6. 2,395	7. 7,146	8. 9,674
−24	−52	−64	−35	−246	−58	−399	−279
−17	−53	−71	−164	−345	−57	−56	−385
−16	−82	−72	−226	−158	−144	−61	−187
−18	−51	−51	−37	−247	−86	−62	−171
−39	−53	−72	−268	−544	−255	−65	−373
−24	−91	−83	−36	−199	−96	−63	−173
−34	−81	−91	−116	−195	−367	−174	−393
−15	−82	−73	−224	−296	−46	−69	−142
−64	−83	−−73	−135	−397	−256	−37	−282
913	1,527	7,534	2,255	5,527	1,030	6,160	7,289

SUBTOTAL FEATURE

Columns of numbers may be subtracted as well as added using the desktop calculator. It may be necessary to display and print the current amount contained in the calculator register without clearing the register. This procedure is called obtaining a **subtotal** and may be accomplished using the subtotal key. Subsequent numbers may continue to be added and subtracted after the subtotal key is pressed.

To check columns of numbers with both addends and subtrahends: With the total in the display, press the plus key, and then add any numbers that were previously subtracted and subtract any numbers that were previously added. The total should equal the original beginning addend.

Alternatively, you may simply begin a new problem and add or subtract from the bottom to the top of the problem. The second total should equal the first. Study the following example.

MACHINE SETUP	Decimal Selector—F
	Rounding Switch—5/4
	Printer—IC

Problem		Procedure		Check 1		Check 2	
188		188 +		82 +		23 −	
−51		51 −		51 +		32 −	
−32		32 −	◇/S	32 +		51 −	
———	Subtotal	105		23 +	*/T	188 +	*/T
−23		23 −	*/T	188		82	
		82					

SUBTOTAL PRACTICE PROBLEMS

Find subtotals and totals as indicated below. Remember to key the addition key **after** each positive number and the subtraction key **after** each negative number. Use the subtotal key and total keys as necessary. Compare your answers with the ones given.

	688		4,567		417		1,425
	−24		+159		−5,223		−35
1. Subtotal	664		+652		421	7. Subtotal	1,390
	+125	3. Subtotal	5,378	5. Subtotal	−4,385		−248
	+211		−1,211		6,333	8. Subtotal	1,142
2. Total	1,000	4. Total	4,167	6. Total	1,948		−369
						9. Total	773

MEMORY MINUS FEATURE, HORIZONTAL SUBTRACTION, AND CHECKING PROCEDURE

Find the Difference in Total Markup between the First and Second Quarters

To complete the following problem, it will be necessary to compute markup for several items during the first and second quarters and the total markup for each of the quarters, and then to find the difference in total markup between the two quarters. To efficiently solve this problem, use the grand total feature to find total markup, store the first-quarter total markup in memory using the memory plus (M+=) key, and then find and subtract the second-quarter total markup from memory using the memory minus (M−=) key. The difference can then be displayed using the memory subtotal (MS) or memory total (MT) key.

PROBLEM

Subtract cost price from selling price to find markup for each item. Find total markup for each quarter. Find the difference in total markup between the first and second quarters. 9.$ _____

TAPE 3.1:

```
              0 · C

000

              0 · M*

          675 · +
          449 · −
002

          226 · G+

          833 · +
          624 · −
002

          209 · G+

          537 · +
          385 · −
002

          152 · G+

          587 · G◇
          587 · M+
          587 · G◇
          587 · G*

          673 · +
          452 · −
002

          221 · G+

          845 · +
          634 · −
002

          211 · G+

          535 · +
          386 · −
002

          149 · G+

          581 · G◇
          581 · M−
002

            6 · M*

          581 · G◇
          581 · G*
```

First Quarter ($)

Item	Selling Price	Cost Price	Markup
Awx	675	449	1. _____
Bwx	833	624	2. _____
Cwx	537	385	3. _____
Total markup			4. _____

Second Quarter ($)

Item	Selling Price	Cost Price	Markup
Awx	673	452	5. _____
Bwx	845	634	6. _____
Cwx	535	386	7. _____
Total markup			8. _____

MACHINE SETUP Decimal Selector—F or 0
Rounding Switch—5/4
Printer Switch—GT

PROCEDURE

C MT 675 + 449 − */T 226
         833 + 624 − */T 209
         537 + 385 − */T 152 GT 587 M+=

GT GT
         673 + 452 − */T 221
         845 + 634 − */T 211
         535 + 386 − */T 149 GT 581 M−= MT 6

GT GT

Note: It is not necessary to press the clear and memory total keys at the beginning of each problem. Do this only if you are not certain that the last problem was ended with the total key and memory total key (if memory was used).

 # PART 4 *Desktop Calculator*

Exercise 1

Subtract. Check by adding. The first problem has been completed for you.

95	38	76	91	27	922
−16	−25	−64	−59	−19	−71
1. __79__	2. _____	3. _____	4. _____	5. _____	6. _____
+16					
95	_____		_____	_____	_____

Subtract and check. Remember to use commas in answers when necessary.

28	331	46	627	5,228
−11	−34	−24	−124	−156
7. _____	8. _____	9. _____	10. _____	11. _____
_____	_____	_____	_____	_____

Subtract and check.

12. 4,132 − 551 = _____   _____   13. 2,291 − 1,144 = _____   _____

Find subtotals and totals as indicated below.

	451		922		723		2,583
	−124		−51		−432		−1,535
14. Subtotal	_____		−412		+169	20. Subtotal	_____
	−123	16. Subtotal	_____	18. Subtotal	_____		+243
	−28		+365		−523	21. Subtotal	_____
15. Total	_____	17. Total	_____	19. Total	_____		−1,263
						22. Total	_____

Exercise 2

Complete the following sales/returns report. Returns should be deducted from sales each week. Use the grand total feature to check answers. Use the memory feature to store and subtract totals to find the difference in total returns between August and September. 37. $_____

ABC School Supplies
Sales and Returns August 2001 ($)

Week of	Sales	Returns	Totals
August 5	145,696	9,699	23. _____
August 12	159,687	8,578	24. _____
August 19	146,647	5,779	25. _____
August 26	169,684	8,495	26. _____
Totals	28. _____	29. _____	27. _____

ABC School Supplies
Sales and Returns September 2001 ($)

Week of	Sales	Returns	Totals
September 2	122,696	4,699	30. _____
September 9	178,687	18,323	31. _____
September 16	192,647	25,379	32. _____
September 23	153,684	8,325	33. _____
Totals	35. _____	36. _____	34. _____

Exercise 3

38. On August 1, Roman borrowed $1,500 to pay part of his college tuition. He made the following payments: September $365, October $445, November $260. If he wishes to pay off the loan in December, how much should he pay? _____

Exercise 4

Strokes per Minute Score _____

Accuracy Score (Correct Strokes ÷ Total Strokes) _____

One-Minute Addition Timing (Keys 1 through 9)

(Optional: Your instructor may wish you to use Touch Key on the computer for all your timings. Check with your instructor before completing this exercise.)

Complete as many of the problems as possible in 1 minute by adding. Work quickly and accurately. The number preceding each closing parenthesis indicates the cumulative number of strokes for problems attempted. For example, if you complete Problems 1 through 5 in 1 minute, your strokes-per-minute score is 155. Optional: 3- to 5-minute timings.

1.	34	2.	41	3.	24	4.	26	5.	14	6.	62	7.	36	8.	61
	52		55		27		62		16		28		39		63
	47		53		74		61		15		27		16		82
	16		58		78		63		18		24		37		81
	28		57		57		64		17		26		38		44
	25		59		75		65		14		25		35		43
	41		51		59		63		19		33		33		16
	21		81		91		79		35		37		34		36
	52		87		73		71		36		16		31		82
	58		83		73		72		37		26		32		25
31)		62)		93)		124)		155)		186)		217)		248)	

9.	74	10.	47	11.	45	12.	65	13.	66	14.	77	15.	76	16.	84
	49		84		75		46		86		74		79		58
	84		94		58		58		76		75		67		86
	85		47		95		59		96		76		47		48
	47		46		98		57		56		78		75		78
	48		48		96		45		46		79		78		89
	45		49		65		58		69		97		79		85
	44		45		55		59		67		67		87		87
	46		44		57		57		68		57		74		84
	94		64		75		56		66		47		77		86
279)		310)		341)		372)		403)		434)		465)		496)	

17.		18.		19.		20.		21.		22.		23.		24.	
	64		82		71		76		24		32		79		86
	66		88		84		78		27		36		49		82
	65		84		94		47		35		13		65		52
	38		86		57		49		34		32		79		85
	29		87		57		95		39		13		52		72
	24		89		58		69		25		31		92		42
	87		95		59		96		16		58		57		85
	89		96		55		76		34		38		97		83
	39		76		56		77		25		16		75		89
	37		74		64		87		21		56		73		81
527)		558)		589)		620)		651)		682)		713)		744)

25.		26.		27.		28.		29.		30.		31.		32.	
	11		88		61		96		25		29		16		34
	81		86		45		93		91		59		25		39
	96		83		53		53		61		58		16		62
	95		86		27		83		92		68		14		61
	85		51		29		63		69		61		19		43
	16		18		82		61		76		51		38		65
	14		89		81		63		42		24		37		83
	51		68		22		38		27		68		36		85
	53		28		53		64		29		86		29		86
	56		51		68		39		26		69		34		36
775)		806)		837)		868)		899)		930)		961)		992)

CHAPTER 3 *Terminology Review*

Credit balance
Difference
Memory minus key
Minuend
Negative number
Subtotal
Subtraction
Subtrahend

Insert the missing words to complete the following statements.

1. When an account has a negative balance, it may be referred to as a(n) _____
   _____.

2. The number to be decreased in a subtraction problem is called the _____
   _____.

3. The _____ key displays the amount currently contained in the calculator register without clearing the register.

4. When the minuend is smaller than the subtrahend, the difference will be a(n)
   _____.

5. The result of subtracting two numbers is called the _____.

6. The number to be subtracted from another is called the _____.

7. The opposite of addition is _____.

Chapter 3 Review Exercises

Exercise 1

Subtract and check. Indicate negative answers with a minus sign. Two blanks are provided, one for the first answer and one for the check answer.

	64		58		97		246		88		544		69
	−45		−76		−16		−77		−54		−49		−77
1. _____		2. _____		3. _____		4. _____		5. _____		6. _____		7. _____

_____ _____ _____ _____ _____ _____ _____

Subtract and check. Remember to use minus signs and commas in answers when necessary.

	4,589		9,858		8,769		8,774		5,944		4,696		6,474
	−747		−7,647		−6,556		−7,654		−5,856		−3,758		−3,899
8. _____		9. _____		10. _____		11. _____		12. _____		13. _____		14. _____

_____ _____ _____ _____ _____ _____ _____

Subtract and check.

15. $596 - 45 =$ _____   16. $875 - 685 =$ _____   17. $97 - 76 =$ _____

_____   _____   _____

18. $844 - 75 =$ _____   19. $49 - 28 =$ _____   20. $57 - 49 =$ _____

_____   _____   _____

Find subtotals and totals as indicated:

	2,355		3,652		5,641		1,635
	−1,263		−83		−3,522		−1,187
21. Subtotal _____			−1,547		+1,523	26. Subtotal _____	
	−35	23. Subtotal _____			−217		+2,754
	−31		+1,351		−325	27. Subtotal _____	
22. Total _____		24. Total _____		25. Total _____		−2,631
						28. Total _____	

Exercise 2

Complete the following inventory report. Subtract items going out of inventory from items coming in. Check your answers.

	In ($)	Out ($)	Totals ($)
Model A desks	15,696	13,699	29. _____
A-line chairs	25,685	25,578	30. _____
Library tables	33,645	21,775	31. _____
All-in-1 desks	59,684	48,495	32. _____
Totals	34. _____	35. _____	33. _____

Exercise 3

36. On Monday, a wholesaler had 950 pounds of oranges on hand. He received an order for 150 pounds of oranges, 200 pounds of bananas, and 100 pounds of apples Monday morning and another order for 600 pounds of oranges Monday afternoon. Does the wholesaler have enough oranges to fill the orders? If so, how many will he have left after the orders are filled? _____

37. Bill filled his truck with 100 gallons of fuel. During the next 3 days, he used 31 gallons, 14 gallons, and 22 gallons of fuel, respectively. How many gallons of fuel does he have left? _____

38. Janet budgeted $300 for college texts this semester. The prices of her books were as follows: math $45, English $56, economics $94, word processing $39, dictionary $15, and sociology $49. How much, if any, did she have left after paying for the books? _____

Rounding Whole Numbers

 **PART 1** *Speed and Accuracy Building Using Touch Key*

KEYSTROKING TECHNIQUE

A pencil can be held in the crease of the thumb and the right hand when it is necessary to record results of calculations on a paper copy (Figure 4.1).

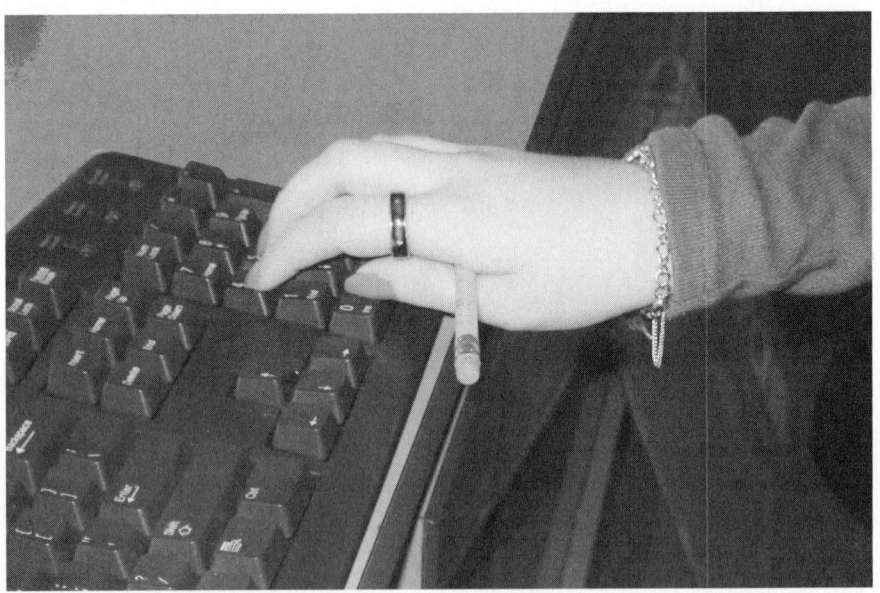

FIGURE 4.1

GOALS: Your speed goal is 6,500 strokes per hour.
Your accuracy target goal range is 95% to 100%.

With each repetition of the lesson, try to improve your speed without lowering your accuracy score. If your percent-of-accuracy score falls below 95%, review your finger position and technique. Then try again.

Instructions: *Start Touch Key. Complete Lesson 4, Parts A through E. Record your scores of strokes per hour and percent of accuracy.*

Touch Key Lesson 4—The 4, 5, 6, 7, 8, and 9 Keys, Three-Digit Numbers

	Today's Date	Strokes per Hour	Percent of Accuracy
A.			
B.			
C.			
D.			
E.			

 # PART 2 *Business Math Skills*

ROUNDING WHOLE NUMBERS

Numbers may be rounded for convenience, ease of understanding, or quick estimations. An estimate is an approximate value. If a department processed 31,255 envelopes in June, it might be reported in the company newsletter that the department processed "over 30,000 envelopes in June." Although the 30,000 figure is not as accurate, it is easier for the reader to grasp the idea of how many envelopes were processed by the department in June. **Rounding** is used to **estimate** or find an approximate number.

Unofficial reports may be prepared with all numbers rounded to thousands. Presentation materials such as handouts and slides may contain rounded numbers.

PROBLEM 1

A speaker at a meeting informed the group, "The number of units sold last quarter was just under 125,000." The actual number of units sold, however, was 124,897. What are the steps for rounding 124,897 to 125,000 (Figure 4.2)?

First, decide to which place the number will be rounded.

Round 124,897 to the **thousands place**. The digit in the thousands place is 4.

Second, examine the digit to the right of the place to be rounded.

1 2 4 ,8 9 7 round up to **1 2 5 ,0 0 0**

FIGURE 4.2

Because the number 124,<u>8</u>97 is being rounded to the thousands place, the digit in the hundreds place should be examined.

Third, if the digit in the place being examined is **5 or greater**, round up by increasing the number in the place being rounded by 1. If the digit in the place being examined is less than 5, do not change the digit in the place being rounded.

In the number 124,<u>8</u>97 the digit in the **hundreds place** is 8. Since this number is greater than 5, the number in the thousands place is increased by 1.

Fourth, change the digit(s) in the place(s) to the right of the place being rounded to zero(s).

Because the number is being rounded at the thousands place, the hundreds place, the **tens place**, and the **ones place** should be changed to zeros. The result of rounding 124,897 to the thousands place is 125,000.

Following are more examples.

PROBLEM 2

Round 456 to the hundreds place (Figure 4.3).

Examine the digit in the tens place. It is 5; therefore, the number in the hundreds place will be increased by 1 and the digits in the tens and ones places will be changed to 0s.

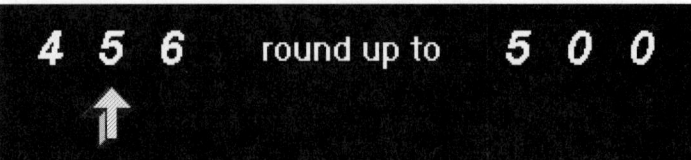

FIGURE 4.3

PROBLEM 3

Round 214,585 to the ten thousands place (Figure 4.4).

Examine the digit in the thousands place. It is less than 5, so do not change the digit in the ten thousands place. Change the digits to the right of the ten thousands place to 0s.

2 1 4 ,5 8 5   rounded to   2 1 0 ,0 0 0

FIGURE 4.4

MATH STAR 4.1

BE A *Math ★* !

Use rounding to speed up addition or subtraction problems. To add quickly, round up one of the addends. Add, then subtract the amount used to round up from the answer. If you have been studying the math star tips carefully, you will note that this one is quite similar to a previous math star tip.

Problem: Add 57 + 27

57 + 27 + 3	**Step 1:** Round 27 up to the nearest 10.
	Note: Make a mental note that in rounding to 30, we increased 27 by 3.
57 + 30 = 87	**Step 2:** Add: 57 + 30 = 87.
87 − 3 = 84	**Step 3:** Subtract the 3 that was used for rounding 27 to 30 from the result obtained in step 2: 87 − 3 = 84. The answer is 84.

Problem: Subtract 87 − 18

87 − 18 + 2	**Step 1:** Round 18 up.
87 − 20 = 67	**Step 2:** Subtract.
67 + 2 = 69	**Step 3:** To the result of 67 (obtained in step 2), add the 2 that was used in rounding 18 up to 20 in step 1. The answer is 69.

ROUNDING USED FOR ESTIMATION

"Give me a rough estimate."

"Give me a ballpark figure."

"Are we in the ballpark?"

"What is your best guesstimate?"

"Off the top of your head . . ."

You may have heard some of the foregoing expressions used in conversations regarding numbers in business. All of them are an attempt to obtain an unofficial estimated number. In other words, all are attempts to get an idea of the cost, size, or amount of something.

"Does the answer make sense?"

After calculating the answer to a problem, take a moment to look at the answer to check for its reasonableness. For example:

When two numbers each less than 50 are added together, the answer should be less than 100.

When two numbers each between 501 and 999 are added together, the answer should be greater than 1,000.

Name _____

Class/Section _____

Score (Correct Answers ÷ No. of Assigned Problems) _____

PART 2   *Business Math Skills*

Exercise 1

Round to the tens place.

1. 39 _____   2. 35 _____   3. 62 _____   4. 87 _____   5. 33 _____   6. 45 _____   7. 51 _____

Round to the hundreds place.

8. 310 _____   9. 859 _____   10. 725 _____   11. 692 _____   12. 225 _____   13. 356 _____   14. 341 _____

Round to the thousands place.

15. 1,359 _____   16. 2,905 _____   17. 1,290 _____   18. 6,140 _____   19. 3,459 _____

20. 8,501 _____   21. 3,592 _____   22. 1,009 _____   23. 61,668 _____   24. 49,500 _____

25. A loan application asked for Paul's yearly salary. Round his salary of $42,769 to the hundreds place. _____

26. Round twenty-five thousand four hundred fifty-nine to the thousands place. _____

Exercise 2

John needs to budget for an office computer. He has obtained prices for the equipment. Round the prices at the first digit (the leftmost digit), then add. How much should he budget for the computer?

CPU	$799	27. _____
Monitor	$459	28. _____
Wireless keyboard and mouse	$99	29. _____
Operating system	$95	30. _____
		31. _____

Exercise 3

You have been asked to estimate costs for a planned business trip. Two travel companies provided the following flight costs. Round the prices to the hundreds place and add. Which company should be used?

	Company A ($)		Company B ($)	
Los Angeles to London	799	32. _____	795	37. _____
London to China	1,589	33. _____	1,490	38. _____
China to Taiwan	189	34. _____	145	39. _____
Taiwan to Los Angeles	2,229	35. _____	2,460	40. _____
		36. _____		41. _____

The company with the lowest total price for this trip is 42. _____

 **PART 3** *The Pocket and Windows Calculators*

ROUNDING

There is no special feature for rounding on a pocket or Windows calculator. Round mentally, then key the numbers, or work the problem and then round the answer mentally, according to instructions given with the problem.

PROBLEM 4

Consider the following list of monthly postage expenses in dollars. Add to find total postage expense. Check your answer, then round to the hundreds place.

Problem	Procedure	Check
January 56	56+	120+
February 49	49+	92+
March 74	74+	48+
April 89	89+	52+
May 75	75+	55+
June 64	64+	47+
July 47	47+	64+
August 55	55+	75+
September 52	52+	89+
October 48	48+	74+
November 92	92+	49+
December 120	120+ =	56+ =
	821	821

Answer rounded to the hundreds place: 800.

 PART 3   *Pocket or Windows Calculator*

Exercise 1

Add, then round answers to the hundreds place. The second blank is for the rounded answer.

953	83	760	912	277	1,902	529
+162	+58	+647	+594	+169	+1,710	+428

1. _____   2. _____   3. _____   4. _____   5. _____   6. _____   7. _____

Add, then round answers to the thousands place. The second blank is for the rounded answer.

9,289	6,039	7,469	5,270	9,222	8,355	4,430
+11	+1,934	+54	+124	+956	+7,638	+3,982

8. _____   9. _____   10. _____   11. _____   12. _____   13. _____   14. _____

Subtract, then round answers to the hundreds place.

15. $4,135 - 559 =$ _____ _____ 16. $2,490 - 1,155 =$ _____ _____
17. $19,112 - 2,090 =$ _____ _____ 18. $8,944 - 7,836 =$ _____ _____
19. $1,813 - 814 =$ _____ _____ 20. $3,963 - 582 =$ _____ _____
21. $5,462 - 2,339 =$ _____ _____ 22. $11,221 - 798 =$ _____ _____

Exercise 2

Complete the following estimated sales report. Round each sales figure to thousands, then add.

Week of	Actual Sales ($)	Rounded Sales ($)
August 5	15,496	23. _____
August 12	19,587	24. _____
August 19	36,747	25. _____
August 26	29,384	26. _____
Total		27. _____

Exercise 3

28. Mary's office supply purchases for the first quarter were as follows: January $169, February $362, and March $113. What was her office expense for the first quarter? Round your answer to hundreds. _____

 PART 3   *Review and Practice Using Business Math FUNdamentals*

GOAL: Complete 9 of the 10 problems correctly.

Instructions: Start Business Math FUNdamentals. Complete Tutorial 8 Rounding and Drill 4 Rounding. If you are not satisfied with your score, repeat Drill 4. Write your scores on the following table.

Business Math FUNdamentals Drill 4

Today's Date	Score

 PART 4 *The Desktop Calculator*

KEYSTROKING TECHNIQUE: WHILE HOLDING A PENCIL

Refer to Figure 4.5 for the correct method of holding a pencil while keying numbers. The pencil is held between the thumb and the first joint of the index finger. The point of the pencil should extend slightly past the first joint of the little finger. The pencil may be switched to a position for writing simply by moving the thumb to the left. This shifts the pencil to an upright position and allows the fingers and the thumb to move to the normal position used in writing. The reverse of these movements will place the pencil back in the position that allows for the keying of numbers.

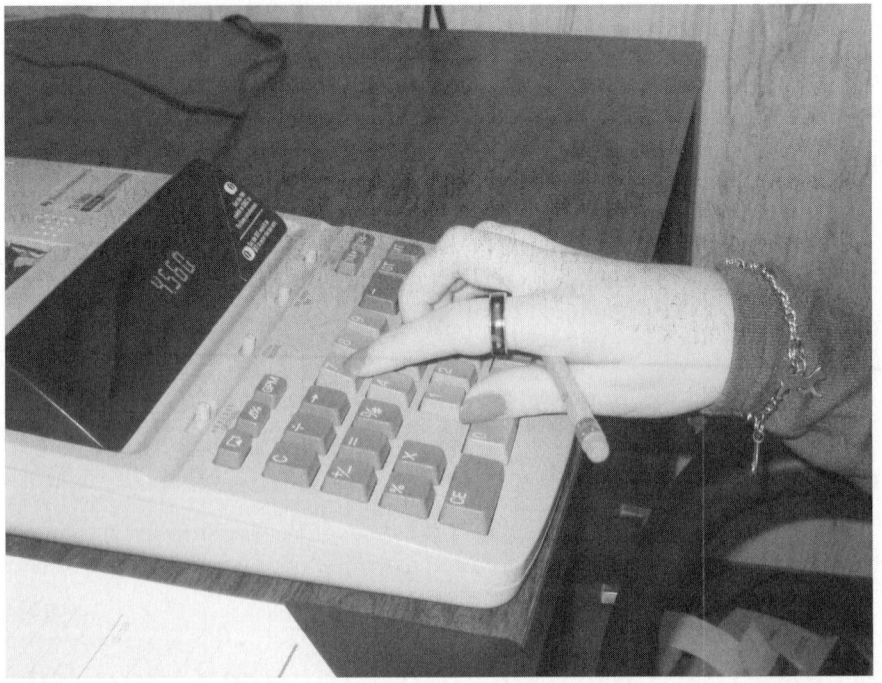

FIGURE 4.5

Note: If you write with your left hand, there is no need for you to hold a pencil in your right hand while keying. Simply record answers as you normally would while keying numbers with your right hand.

Add the following problems while holding a pencil. As you complete each problem, write your answer below the problem. After you have completed all the problems, check your answers with those given.

1.	2.	3.	4.	5.	6.	7.	8.
64	55	84	96	54	95	46	74
24	52	64	35	46	58	99	79
17	53	71	64	45	57	56	85
16	82	72	26	58	44	61	87
18	51	51	37	47	86	62	71
39	53	72	68	44	55	65	73
24	91	83	36	99	96	63	73
34	81	91	16	95	67	74	93
15	82	73	24	96	46	69	42
64	83	73	35	97	56	37	82
315	683	734	437	681	660	632	759

ROUNDING

The desktop calculator does not have a feature for rounding whole numbers. Whole numbers must be rounded mentally. The rounding and decimal switches may be used to round decimal numbers only. This feature will be discussed in Chapter 7.

Name _____

Class/Section _____

Score (Correct Answers ÷ No. of Assigned Problems) _____

 PART 4 *Desktop Calculator*

Exercise 1

Add. Round answers to the tens place. The second blank is for your rounded answer.

95	238	476	791	827	922	852
+216	+125	+364	+259	+ 619	+471	+328

1. _____ 2. _____ 3. _____ 4. _____ 5. _____ 6. _____ 7. _____

Add. Round answers to the hundreds place. The second blank is for your rounded answer.

7,528	4,331	7,846	4,627	5,228	8,352	7,436
+211	+634	+324	+7,124	+9,156	+3,936	+3,652

8. _____ 9. _____ 10. _____ 11. _____ 12. _____ 13. _____ 14. _____

Subtract. Round answers to the thousands place.

15. 64,132 − 1,551 = _____ _____   16. 34,291 − 1,147 = _____ _____
17. 64,225 − 8,363 = _____ _____   18. 53,916 − 8,136 = _____ _____
19. 32,413 − 9,514 = _____ _____   20. 23,463 − 4,385 = _____ _____
21. 39,462 − 6,139 = _____ _____   22. 52,221 − 10,558 = _____ _____

Exercise 2

Complete the following estimated sales report. Round the total to the thousands place.

Week of	Sales ($)
August 5	145,696
August 12	159,687
August 19	146,647
August 26	169,684
Total	23. _____
	24. _____

Exercise 3

25. Roland's grandmother has agreed to help pay for his physical therapy for a sports injury. The costs for the 5 months of therapy are as follows: January $465, February $450, March $469, April $490, and May $510. How much does he need rounded to thousands? _____

Exercise 4

Strokes per Minute Score _____

Accuracy Score (Correct Strokes ÷ Total Strokes) _____

One-Minute Addition Timing (Keys 4 through 9)

(Optional: Your instructor may wish you to use Touch Key on the computer for all your timings. Check with your instructor before completing this exercise.)

Complete as many addition problems as possible in 1 minute. Work quickly and accurately. The number preceding each closing parenthesis indicates the cumulative number of strokes for problems attempted. For example, if you complete Problems 1 through 5 in 1 minute, your strokes-per-minute score is 155. Optional: 3- to 5-minute timings.

1.		2.		3.		4.		5.		6.		7.		8.	
	64		48		74		86		84		67		76		65
	58		55		97		65		86		78		69		69
	47		56		76		67		75		87		46		85
	56		58		78		69		98		54		67		84
	98		57		57		64		97		96		98		44
	85		59		75		65		94		95		75		46
	46		59		59		69		49		68		97		46
	95		87		98		79		45		87		94		96
	57		89		75		75		46		76		59		87
	58		86		76		76		47		96		98		85
31)		62)		93)		124)		155)		186)		217)		248)	

9.		10.		11.		12.		13.		14.		15.		16.	
	74		47		45		65		66		77		76		84
	49		84		75		46		86		74		79		58
	84		94		58		58		76		75		67		86
	85		47		95		59		96		76		47		48
	47		46		98		57		56		78		75		78
	48		48		96		45		46		79		78		89
	45		49		65		58		69		97		79		85
	44		45		55		59		67		67		87		87
	46		44		57		57		68		57		74		84
	94		64		75		56		66		47		77		86
279)		310)		341)		372)		403)		434)		465)		496)	

17.		18.		19.		20.		21.		22.		23.		24.	
	64		86		79		76		64		84		79		86
	66		88		84		78		67		86		49		85
	65		84		94		47		95		76		65		54
	98		86		57		49		94		77		79		85
	89		87		57		95		69		47		58		74
	84		89		58		69		85		74		96		46
	87		95		59		96		56		58		57		89
	89		96		55		76		74		98		97		87
	49		76		56		77		75		96		75		89
	47		74		64		87		48		56		79		84
527)		558)		589)		620)		651)		682)		713)		744)	

25.		26.		27.		28.		29.		30.		31.		32.	
	54		88		69		96		75		59		76		94
	85		86		45		99		98		59		75		99
	96		89		58		56		65		58		76		68
	95		86		77		86		95		68		74		67
	85		54		89		66		69		67		79		46
	56		78		85		64		76		55		98		65
	54		89		84		69		45		74		97		89
	57		68		77		78		67		68		96		85
	59		98		59		64		89		86		89		86
	56		57		68		79		76		69		94		76
775)		806)		837)		868)		899)		930)		961)		992)	

CHAPTER 4 *Terminology Review*

Estimate
5 or greater
Hundreds place
Ones place
Rounding
Tens place
Thousands place

Insert the missing words to complete the following statements.

1. When rounding to the thousands place, the digit in the hundreds place is used to determine whether the digit in the _____ should be changed.

2. When rounding to the _____, the digits in the tens and ones places should be changed to zeros.

3. A(n) _____ is an approximate value.

4. _____ may be used for convenience, ease of understanding, and quick estimates.

5. When rounding, the digit in the ten thousands place will be increased by one if the digit in the thousands place is _____.

Chapter 4 Review Exercises

Exercise 1

Mental addition. Add using the rounding method presented in Math Star 4.1. Check your answers.

64	9	92	49	88	44	69
9	27	19	18	94	58	27

1. _____ 2. _____ 3. _____ 4. _____ 5. _____ 6. _____ 7. _____

Mental subtraction. Subtract using the rounding method presented in Math Star 4.1. Check your answers.

89	58	169	74	94	96	47
−77	−66	−58	−69	−86	−29	−38

8. _____ 9. _____ 10. _____ 11. _____ 12. _____ 13. _____ 14. _____

Subtract. Round answers to the tens place. The second answer blank is for your rounded answers.

15. $6,596 - 445 =$ _____   17. $1,578 - 586 =$ _____   19. $2,397 - 677 =$ _____
   16. _____   18. _____   20. _____

21. $8,844 - 7,775 =$ _____   23. $2,349 - 2,896 =$ _____   25. $3,257 - 1,549 =$ _____
   22. _____   24. _____   26. _____

Find the subtotals and totals as indicated below. Round the totals to the hundreds place.

1,623	329	712	1,324
469	465	368	692
133	578	119	813
27. Subtotal _____	30. Subtotal _____	33. Subtotal _____	36. Subtotal _____
−262	−984	−275	−1,621
28. Total _____	31. Total _____	34. Total _____	37. Total _____
29. (Rounded) _____	32. (Rounded) _____	35. (Rounded) _____	38. (Rounded) _____

Exercise 2

Round the following numbers to the thousands place. Add the rounded numbers.

Model AB	$15,496	39. _____
Model AX	$25,985	40. _____
Model CF	$33,545	41. _____
Model AC	$59,684	42. _____
Total		43. _____

Exercise 3

The following chart indicates some representative charter costs versus full coach-fare round-trip air travel. Round each amount to the tens place.

	Charter Fare ($)		Coach Fare ($)	
Atlanta to Nashville	2,755	44. _____	948	45. _____
Denver to Albuquerque	3,296	46. _____	1,010	47. _____
New York City to Pittsburgh	4,528	48. _____	423	49. _____

CHAPTER 5

Multiplication, Multiplication of Constants, Accumulation of Products, Sales Reports

 **PART 1** *Speed and Accuracy Building Using Touch Key*

GOALS: Your speed goal is 6,500 strokes per hour.
Your accuracy target goal range is 95% to 100%.

With each repetition of the lesson, try to improve your speed without lowering your accuracy score. If your percent-of-accuracy score falls below 95%, review your finger position and technique. Then try again.

Instructions: Start Touch Key. Complete Lesson 5, Parts A through E. Record your scores for strokes per hour and percent of accuracy.

Touch Key Lesson 5—The 1, 2, 3, 4, 5, and 6 Keys, Three-Digit Numbers

	Today's Date	Strokes per Hour	Percent of Accuracy
A.			
B.			
C.			
D.			
E.			

 **PART 2** *Business Math Skills*

MULTIPLICATION

Just as subtraction is the opposite of addition, multiplication can be viewed as an extension of addition. Multiplication is a quicker way of combining many like items.

PROBLEM 1

A wholesaler wrote a contract to provide three 1-carat diamonds per month to a retailer for 5 months. How many diamonds will the wholesaler need to supply (Figure 5.1)?

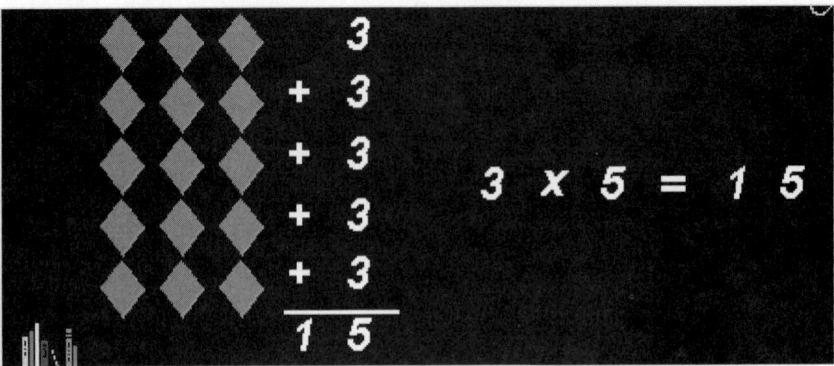

FIGURE 5.1

The 3 diamonds could be added together 5 times to achieve a result of 15. However, it would be quicker to multiply the 3-diamonds by 5 to find the same result.

COMMUTATIVE PROPERTY OF MULTIPLICATION

Chapter 1 discussed the commutative property of addition; that is, the order of the addends may be changed without affecting the sum. Similarly, the order of the numbers in a multiplication problem may be changed without affecting the result. This is known as the **commutative property of multiplication**.

    Example: $500 \times 2 = 1,000$ and $2 \times 500 = 1,000$.

COMPONENTS OF MULTIPLICATION

The number to be multiplied in a subtraction problem is the **multiplicand**. The number we are multiplying by is the **multiplier**. The result, or answer, is the **product** (see Figure 5.2).

$$
\begin{array}{lr}
\text{multiplicand} & 3\ 0 \\
\text{multiplier} & \times\quad 2 \\
\hline
\text{product} & 6\ 0
\end{array}
$$

FIGURE 5.2

In vertical multiplication, numbers should be aligned according to place value beginning with the ones place. A horizontal line is drawn under the problem to indicate a result follows. The symbol $\times$ is used to indicate the arithmetic operation of multiplication.

The multiplicand and multiplier may be referred to as **factors**. **Multifactor multiplication** refers to problems containing more than two factors.

CHECKING MULTIPLICATION

To check a multiplication problem, rewrite the problem reversing the multiplicand and multiplier, and solve. The result should match the first product. Note that this is possible because of the commutative property of multiplication.

LONGER MULTIPLICATION PROBLEMS

When a multiplication problem contains a multiplier with more than one digit, working the problem with pencil and paper will result in a **partial product** for each digit in the multiplier.

multiplicand		3	0
multiplier	X	1	2
partial product		6	0	result of 1st step
partial product	3	0		result of 2nd step
product	3	6	0	result of 3rd step

FIGURE 5.3

The multiplier in Figure 5.3 contains two digits; therefore, the problem will have two partial products. To solve the problem:

Step 1: Beginning at the ones place in the multiplicand, multiply each digit by the 2 in the ones place of the multiplier.

Because any number times zero is zero, write 0 in the ones place in the first partial product. Then multiply the 3 in the tens place of the multiplicand by 2 in the ones place of the multiplier. Write the resulting 6 in the tens place of the first partial product.

Step 2: Multiply each digit in the multiplicand, beginning at the ones place, by the 1 in the tens place of the multiplier. This results in the second partial product.

One times zero equals zero. Write 0 in the tens place of the second partial product. One times three equals three. Write 3 in the hundreds place of the second partial product.

Note: *The ones place in the second partial product is left blank. It is very important that numbers in the partial products be aligned correctly.*

Step 3: Being careful not to change the alignment of the numbers, add the two partial products together to find the product of this problem (360).

MULTIPLICATION WITH ZEROS

When a multiplier contains multiple zeros beginning in the ones place, a shortcut may be used to find a product. However, we should first look at the longer traditional method shown in Figure 5.4.

The first partial product is the result of multiplying the 0 in the ones place of the multiplier by each digit in the multiplicand.

Long method:	3 3 3		Short method:	3 3 3
X 3 0 0			X 3 0 0	
0 0 0	step 1		9 9 ,9 0 0	
+ 0 0 0	step 2			
+ 9 9 9	step 3			
9 9 ,9 0 0	step 4			

FIGURE 5.4

The second partial product is the result of multiplying the 0 in the tens place of the multiplier by each digit in the multiplicand.

The third partial product is the result of multiplying the 3 in the hundreds place of the multiplier by each digit in the multiplicand. The three partial products are then added to find the product (99,900).

Contrast this with the short method. Zeros are contained in the ones and tens places in the multiplier. Write zeros in the ones and tens places in the product. Multiply the three digits in the multiplicand by the 3 in the hundreds place of the multiplier, aligning the result carefully. The resulting product is the same as when using the longer method (99,900).

TABLE OF MULTIPLICATION

To use Table 5.1, find the desired multiplicand and multiplier in the column and row headers, respectively. The intersecting cell in the table will contain the product.

Example: $5 \times 9 = 45$.

Note: Any number times zero equals zero.

TABLE 5.1   Table of Multiplication

×	1	2	3	4	5	6	7	8	9	10
1	1	2	3	4	5	6	7	8	9	10
2	2	4	6	8	10	12	14	16	18	20
3	3	6	9	12	15	18	21	24	27	30
4	4	8	12	16	20	24	28	32	36	40
5	5	10	15	20	25	30	35	40	45	50
6	6	12	18	24	30	36	42	48	54	60
7	7	14	21	28	35	42	49	56	63	70
8	8	16	24	32	40	48	56	64	72	80
9	9	18	27	36	45	54	63	72	81	90
10	10	20	30	40	50	60	70	80	90	100

MATH STAR 5.1

BE A *Math*★ !

Multiplying with Zeros

The quickest way to multiply numbers containing zeros beginning in the ones place is to disregard the zeros, solve the problem, then replace the appropriate number of zeros in the product.

Example: 130×20

$13 \times 2 = 26$ **Step 1:** Mentally, disregard the zeros and multiply.

2,600   **Step 2:** Place two zeros in the product beginning in the ones place. The answer is 2,600.

CARRYING IN MULTIPLICATION

The method for carrying in multiplication is the same as the method for carrying in addition. The problem in Figure 5.5 requires the use of carrying as demonstrated in the following:

Step 1: Multiply the 2 in the multiplier by the 9 in the ones place of the multiplicand: $2 \times 9 = 18$. Write 8 in the ones place of the product and carry the 1 above the tens place in the multiplicand.

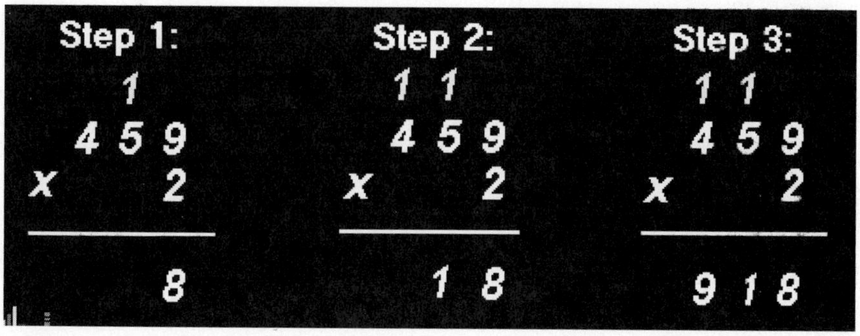

FIGURE 5.5

Step 2: Multiply the 2 in the multiplier by the 5 in the tens place of the multiplicand: $2 \times 5 = 10$. Add the 1 that was carried to the tens place: $10 + 1 = 11$. Write 1 in the tens place of the product and carry 1 above the hundreds place in the multiplicand.

Step 3: Multiply the 2 in the multiplier by the 4 in the hundreds place of the multiplicand: $2 \times 4 = 8$. Add the 1 that was carried to the hundreds place: $8 + 1 = 9$.

MULTIPLYING BY 10, 100, 1,000, AND SO ON

When multiplying by 10, 100, 1,000, and so on, simply write the multiplicand and then add the appropriate number of zeros. This is your new product.

$$32 \times 10 = 320 \qquad 32 \times 100 = 3,200$$
$$32 \times 1,000 = 32,000 \qquad 32 \times 10,000 = 320,000$$

MATH STAR 5.2

BE A *Math★*!

Multiplying by 4

You are presiding at a meeting at which the topic is fundraising. A local businesswoman stands to announce that if the club can raise $3,600, she will quadruple the amount. Quick! Multiply by 4 to find out the total amount of money this will mean for the club.

To quickly multiply by 4, mentally double the number twice.

$36 \times 2 = 72$ **Step 1:** Using the shortcut learned earlier, disregard the two zeros and double 36.

$72 \times 2 = 144$ **Step 2:** Double the resulting number, 72, from step 1.

14,400   **Step 3:** Replace the two zeros that were disregarded in step 1. The answer is $14,400.

Try it for yourself.

1. 34×4
2. 23×4
3. 48×4

Answers: 1. 136   **2.** 92   **3.** 192

Multiplying by 101

The easiest shortcut of all is available when multiplying a number by 101.

One-digit multiplicand

5×101 Write the digit in the multiplicand twice, inserting a zero between: 5—0—5.
505

(continued)

MATH STAR 5.2 *(continued)*

Two-digit multiplicand

25 × 101   Write the two digits of the multiplicand twice: 25—25.
2,525

Multiplying by 1,001

One-digit multiplicand

5 × 1,001   Write the digit in the multiplicand twice, inserting two zeros between:
5,005   5—00—5.

Two-digit multiplicand

25 × 1,001   Write the two digits of the multiplicand twice, inserting a zero between:
25,025   25—0—25.

Three-digit multiplicand

225 × 1,001   Write the three digits of the multiplicand twice: 225—225.
225,225

Try it!

1. 3 × 101
2. 32 × 101
3. 8 × 1,001
4. 28 × 1,001
5. 228 × 1,001

Answers: 1. 303 **2.** 3,232 **3.** 8,008 **4.** 28,028 **5.** 228,228

Multiplying by 11

While we are working with the magical one digits, let us learn to multiply by 11. How would we multiply a two-digit number by 11? Begin by writing the two digits of the multiplicand leaving space between them. Then add (yes, ADD) the two digits and write the sum in the space you reserved.

Problem: 26 × 11

2__6   Step 1: Write the two digits of the multiplicand leaving space between them.
2 + 6 = 8   Step 2: Add the two digits of the multiplicand.
2<u>8</u>6   Step 3: Write the sum in the reserved space. You're finished!

If the sum of the two digits is greater than 9, it will be necessary to carry.

Problem: 85 × 11

8__5   Step 1: Write the two digits of the multiplicand, leaving space between them.
8 + 5 = 13   Step 2: Add the two digits.
1
8<u>3</u>5   Step 3: Write the 3 between the two digits, and carry the 1 to the hundreds place.
935   Step 4: Add the 8 in the hundreds place to the 1 carried in step 3. The answer is 935.

Try it for yourself.

4. 21 × 11
5. 16 × 11
6. 34 × 11

Answers: 4. 231 **5.** 176 **6.** 374

PART 2 *Business Math Skills*

Exercise 1

Multiply and check. When applicable, use shortcuts presented in Math Star 5.1 and 5.2.

148	882	60	121	277	902	522
×2	×5	×4	×11	×30	×10	×28
1. _____	2. _____	3. _____	4. _____	5. _____	6. _____	7. _____

Multiply and check. When applicable, use shortcuts presented in Math Star 5.1 and 5.2. Remember to use commas in answers when necessary.

1,290	8,032	69	70	222	325	4,430
×4	×40	×11	×240	×5	×25	×9
8. _____	9. _____	10. _____	11. _____	12. _____	13. _____	14. _____

Multiply and check. When applicable, use shortcuts presented in Math Star 5.1 and 5.2.

15. 35 × 11 = _____   16. 280 × 4 = _____
17. 112 × 250 = _____   18. 140 × 60 = _____
19. 324 × 40 = _____   20. 143 × 85 = _____
21. 7,620 × 330 = _____   22. 1,300 × 980 = _____
23. What is one thousand two hundred sixty-six times four thousand forty-three? _____
24. The Children's Products Company can produce 700 baby strollers in one day. How many can be produced by this company in one work week (5 days)? _____
25. Janice's new printer can print 12 color pages per minute. How many color pages can the new printer produce in 1 hour (60 minutes)? _____
26. A pair of name-brand sports shoes regularly costs $85. The shoes were advertised for sale at $59. Janey has three children and wishes to buy each of them a pair of the shoes while they are on sale. How much will the shoes cost? _____
27. A pet shop can purchase a 20-pound bag of puppy food for $15. How much will five bags (100 pounds) of puppy food cost? _____
28. David wishes to purchase three emergency flashlights for his business at $29 each. How much money will he need? _____

Exercise 2

Complete the following sales slip. Multiply units by unit price to find total price. Find a grand total.

Fabrics R Us
September 22, 2001

Units	Item Number	Unit Price ($)	Total Price ($)
6 yards	35689	5	29. _____
1 yards	25878	3	30. _____
5 yards	54123	10	31. _____
2 yards	89888	8	32. _____
9 yards	45187	15	33. _____
		Total	34. _____

Exercise 3

Multifactor multiplication. When applicable, use shortcuts presented in Math Star 5.1 and 5.2.

35. $12 \times 50 \times 5 = $ _____   36. $12 \times 10 \times 4 = $ _____

37. $11 \times 25 \times 2 = $ _____   38. $25 \times 9 \times 3 = $ _____

 PART 3   *The Pocket and Windows Calculators*

MULTIPLICATION

The order of entry for a typical multiplication problem on the pocket and Windows calculators involves keying the multiplicand followed by the multiplication key, then the multiplier followed by the equals key.

Check the multiplication problem by reversing the multiplicand and multiplier and solving again. The second product should match the product in the original problem.

Problem	Procedure	Check
55 ×16	55 × 16 = 880	16 × 55 = 880

A multifactor multiplication problem may be worked using the same procedure as above.

Example: 3 ⊠ 12 ⊠ 55 ⊠ 450 ⊟ 891,000

COMPLETING AND CHECKING A FORM WITH HORIZONTAL MULTIPLICATION

PROBLEM 2

Complete the following sales report.

Multiply the selling price for each item by the units sold for each item. Use the memory plus key to add each product to memory. Use the memory recall key to display the accumulated total.

Newberry Ice Crème Shops
Sales Report for July 4, 2001

Item	Selling Price ($)	Units Sold	Daily Totals ($)
Small cone	2	10,000	1. _____
Double cone	3	8,905	2. _____
Sundae	4	3,675	3. _____
		Total	4. _____

Procedure: MC $2 \times 10,000 = 20,000$ M+

$3 \times 8,905 = 26,715$ M+

$4 \times 3,675 = 14,700$ M+   MR   61,415

Checking: Clear the memory register and work the problem a second time, working from the bottom of the columns to the top. The result should match the first product.

PART 3 *Pocket or Windows Calculator*

Exercise 1

Multiply and check.

953	83	760	912	277	1,902	529
×16	×58	×47	×94	×69	×71	×28
1. _____	2. _____	3. _____	4. _____	5. _____	6. _____	7. _____

Multiply and check. Remember to use commas in answers when necessary.

289	6,039	469	270	9,222	8,355	4,430
×11	×934	×545	×124	×956	×7,938	×3,002
8. _____	9. _____	10. _____	11. _____	12. _____	13. _____	14. _____

Multiply and check.

15. $14,135 \times 559 =$ _____   16. $2,290 \times 1,155 =$ _____
17. $10,112 \times 2,090 =$ _____   18. $8,944 \times 6,836 =$ _____
19. $813 \times 514 =$ _____   20. $963 \times 585 =$ _____
21. $462 \times 339 =$ _____   22. $1,221 \times 998 =$ _____

Exercise 2

Complete the following sales report. Selling price for each model should be multiplied by the number of units sold. Use memory features to accumulate products and to display an accumulated total. Check your answers.

ABC Mobile Homes
Yearly Sales Report

Model Number	Selling Price ($)	Units Sold	Totals ($)
A335	$15,696	99	23. _____
A336	$19,687	78	24. _____
A339	$36,647	79	25. _____
A340	$29,684	95	26. _____
		Total	27. _____

Exercise 3

28. Ann makes monthly payments on her business building and land of $890. How much does she pay for the building and land each year? _____

Multifactor multiplication:

29. $44 \times 10 \times 12 =$ _____   30. $68 \times 5 \times 16 =$ _____
31. $100 \times 34 \times 5 =$ _____   32. $50 \times 34 \times 2,067 =$ _____

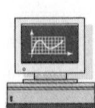

PART 3   *Review and Practice Using Business Math FUNdamentals*

GOAL: Complete 9 of the 10 problems correctly.

Instructions: *Start Business Math FUNdamentals. Complete Tutorial 9 Multiplication, Tutorial 10 Multiplication with Zeros, Tutorial 11 Carrying in Multiplication, and Drill 5 Multiplication. If you are not satisfied with your score, repeat Drill 5. Write your scores below.*

Business Math FUNdamentals Drill 5

Today's Date	Score

PART 4   *The Desktop Calculator*

KEYSTROKING TECHNIQUE

On the desktop calculator, the equals key (=) is used to find the product of a multiplication problem, not the total key. The equals key and the multiplication key (×) (if located on the left side of the keyboard) are both pressed with the index finger. If you are reaching to the left for the equals or multiplication key, try to leave the ring finger anchored on the 6 key. After keying the equals or multiplication key, bring the index finger back to the 4 key.* Feel for the raised bar or dot on the five key to make sure your fingers are in the correct position on the home row before continuing to key numbers. Although it is not necessary to use the multiplication and equals keys strictly by touch, it is important to use correct fingering, which will help you to become more efficient. Productive employees are valuable employees!

*Note: Check with your instructor for fingering instructions if the desktop calculator you are using has the multiplication and other keys located to the right of the numberpad.

MULTIPLICATION

The order of entry for a typical multiplication problem on the desktop calculator involves first keying the multiplicand followed by the multiplication key, then keying the multiplier followed by the equals key. To check the problem, reverse the multiplicand and multiplier. Solve again. The two products should match.

Problem	Procedure	Check
42	42 ×	12 ×
×12	12 =	42 =
	$\boxed{504}$	$\boxed{504}$

MULTIFACTOR MULTIPLICATION

Problems containing more than two factors may be easily solved. Key the factors and signs as follows for a problem containing four factors:

$$55 \; \boxed{\times} \; 42 \; \boxed{\times} \; 3 \; \boxed{\times} \; 11 \; \boxed{=} \; \boxed{76,230}$$

MULTIPLICATION OF CONSTANTS

A **constant** is a value that will be used more than once as a multiplicand. Fortunately, most modern desktop calculators automatically recognize the first number entered in a multiplication problem as the constant. Therefore, it is not necessary to enter the value of the constant more than once.

Note: Desktop calculator models vary. Check with your instructor for the correct procedure for your model.

PROBLEM 3

Island Boutique wishes to order one dozen pairs of four types of shoes for resale. Type A cost $36 per pair, type B cost $39 per pair, type C cost $45 per pair, and type D cost $42 per pair. What is the total for each type of shoe ordered?

Note: Twelve is the constant because 12 pairs of each type of shoe will be ordered.

MACHINE SETUP   Decimal Selector—F or 0
Rounding Switch—5/4
Tax Switch—CALC
Printer Switch—ON

$\boxed{C}$	Problem:	Procedure:	
	12×36	$12 \times 36 =$	$\boxed{432}$
	12×39	$39 =$	$\boxed{468}$
	12×45	$45 =$	$\boxed{540}$
	12×42	$42 =$	$\boxed{504}$

TAPE 5.1:

0 •	C
12 •	x
36 •	=
432 •	*
39 •	=
468 •	*
45 •	=
540 •	*
42 •	=
504 •	*

CALCULATOR FUN

Using the constant feature, perform the following calculations to complete the chart. Set the decimal selector on F.

$987,654,321$	$\times$	9	$=$
$987,654,321$	$\times$	18	$=$
$987,654,321$	$\times$	27	$=$
$987,654,321$	$\times$	36	$=$
$987,654,321$	$\times$	45	$=$
$987,654,321$	$\times$	54	$=$
$987,654,321$	$\times$	63	$=$
$987,654,321$	$\times$	72	$=$
$987,654,321$	$\times$	81	$=$

1. Underline the last digit of each multiplier and the last digit of each product. Do they match?

2. Beginning with the second divisor, underline the first digit of each divisor. Beginning with the second product, underline the first digit of each product. Do they match?

USING MEMORY KEYS TO ACCUMULATE PRODUCTS

Many business problems require the calculation of several products, which are then added together. This totaling of products is commonly referred to as the **accumulation of products**. In the following example, the products are accumulated using the memory plus (M+=) feature. The M+= key is used to find the product of a multiplication problem and add the product to memory.

TAPE 5.2:

```
       0 • C

       0 • M*

       6 •  x
      42 •  =
     252 • M+

      12 •  x
      65 •  =
     780 • M+

      10 •  x
      26 •  =
     260 • M+

   1,292 • M*
```

EXAMPLE

Island Boutique wishes to order the following merchandise for resale. What is the total of the order?

6	Dresses #10442	$42 each
12	Swimsuits #22314	$65 each
10	Shirts #84421	$26 each

MACHINE SETUP   Decimal Selector—F or 0
Rounding Switch—5/4
Tax Switch—CALC
Printer Switch—ON

[C] [MT]   *Problem:*   *Procedure:*

6 × 42	6 × 42 [252] [M+=]
12 × 65	12 × 65 [780] [M+=]
<u>10 × 26</u>	<u>10 × 26</u> [260] [M+=]
	[MT] [1,292]

Name _____

Class/Section _____

Score (Correct Answers ÷ No. of Assigned Problems) _____

PART 4 *Desktop Calculator*

Exercise 1

Multiply and check.

95	38	76	91	27	922	52
×16	×25	×64	×59	×19	×71	×28

1. _____   2. _____   3. _____   4. _____   5. _____   6. _____   7. _____

Multiply and check.

28	331	46	627	5,228	8,352	7,436
×11	×34	×24	×124	×156	×936	×952
8. _____	9. _____	10. _____	11. _____	12. _____	13. _____	14. _____

Multiply and check.

15. 4,132 × 551 = _____   16. 2,291 × 144 = _____

17. 4,225 × 363 = _____   18. 3,916 × 136 = _____

19. 413 × 514 = _____   20. 3,463 × 1,385 = _____

21. 53,462 × 139 = _____   22. 72,221 × 258 = _____

Exercise 2

Complete the following sale of grain contracts report. Use the memory feature to accumulate products.

Grain Contracts for August 2001

Units	Contract Type	Unit Amount ($)	Total Amount ($)
9	B015	145,696	23. _____
4	B225	159,687	24. _____
1	R554	146,647	25. _____
2	D711	169,684	26. _____
Total			27. _____

Complete the following book order. Use the memory feature to accumulate products.

Order #0078943

Units	Order #	Cost per Unit ($)	Total ($)
35	001245	28	28. _____
56	046923	32	29. _____
Order total			30. _____

Exercise 3

31. The ADC Testing Co. wishes to purchase three of each of the following models for consumer testing. Calculate the total cost. Use the constant and memory features.

Model AK8 fire extinguisher	$198
Model AL3 fire extinguisher	$254
Model 903C smoke detector	$39
Model 89B gas detector	$62
Total	31. $ _____

Multifactor multiplication:

32. 13 × 112 × 12 = _____   33. 2,455 × 12 × 9 = _____

34. 312 × 98 × 120 = _____   35. 2,557 × 36 × 22 = _____

Exercise 4

Accuracy Score (Correct Strokes ÷ Total Strokes) _____

One-Minute Addition Timing (Keys 1 through 6)

(Optional: Your instructor may wish for you to use Touch Key on the computer for all your timings. Check with your instructor before completing this exercise.)

Complete as many of the addition problems as possible in 1 minute. Work quickly and accurately. The number preceding each closing parenthesis indicates the cumulative number of strokes for problems attempted. For example, if you complete Problems 1 through 5 in 1 minute, your strokes-per-minute score is 155. Optional: 3- to 5-minute timings.

1.	2.	3.	4.	5.	6.	7.	8.
64	11	54	26	14	32	36	41
52	65	51	32	16	25	63	33
14	23	14	61	15	21	16	52
16	26	16	33	12	24	31	61
55	25	24	34	13	26	32	64
25	12	15	45	14	25	25	13
41	41	23	43	16	33	33	16
51	51	31	13	35	34	54	36
52	54	43	21	36	16	61	52
25	53	23	12	31	26	52	55
31)	62)	93)	124)	155)	186)	217)	248)

9.	10.	11.	12.	13.	14.	15.	16.
14	23	15	35	36	22	16	54
43	24	45	16	56	34	13	26
64	34	52	24	36	65	64	46
45	42	15	54	26	36	14	42
16	16	32	21	56	35	45	62
13	43	36	45	46	31	23	63
15	46	65	36	32	41	13	65
14	15	25	53	13	62	53	67
16	44	51	21	52	54	24	64
64	34	45	16	16	14	11	46
279)	310)	341)	372)	403)	434)	465)	496)

17.	18.	19.	20.	21.	22.	23.	24.
34	52	61	36	34	12	13	16
66	22	64	45	21	26	23	22
65	54	34	41	15	33	35	32
32	26	21	53	64	42	63	45
26	27	51	65	53	53	52	52
24	46	31	16	45	61	32	62
51	65	51	26	46	56	55	15
23	63	55	36	54	22	21	23
36	56	35	44	25	36	15	33
34	34	64	21	21	56	43	11
527)	558)	589)	620)	651)	682)	713)	744)

25.	26.	27.	28.	29.	30.	31.	32.
44	22	61	36	25	23	16	34
41	16	45	63	31	26	25	66
56	63	53	23	43	32	16	32
65	46	14	53	12	55	14	61
55	51	26	63	51	41	13	43
56	62	32	61	26	11	32	65
64	13	61	63	32	54	31	53
51	25	62	35	13	56	36	25
43	22	53	34	56	53	26	56
66	31	62	31	46	66	34	36
775)	806)	837)	868)	899)	930)	961)	992)

CHAPTER 5 *Terminology Review*

Accumulation of products
Commutative property of multiplication
Constant
Factors
Multifactor multiplication
Multiplicand
Multiplier
Partial product
Product

Fill in the blanks with the best answer.

1. A number to be repeated in more than one multiplication problem. _____
2. The number to be multiplied. _____
3. Allows the interchange of numbers in a multiplication problem without affecting the result. _____
4. The totaling of several products. _____
5. The number used to multiply by. _____
6. The result of a multiplication problem. _____
7. A problem containing several numbers to be multiplied. _____
8. Another name for multiplier and multiplicand. _____
9. An intermediate result of a multiplication problem. _____

Name _____

Class/Section _____

Score (Correct Answers ÷ No. of Assigned Problems) _____

Chapter 5 Review Exercises
Exercise 1

Multiply and check.

	64	58	97	246	88	544	69
	×45	×76	×16	×77	×54	×49	×77
	1. _____	2. _____	3. _____	4. _____	5. _____	6. _____	7. _____

Multiply and check. Remember to use commas in answers when necessary.

	4,589	9,858	8,769	8,774	5,944	4,696	6,474
	×47	×647	×556	×54	×856	×58	×99
	8. _____	9. _____	10. _____	11. _____	12. _____	13. _____	14. _____

Multiply and check.

15. $3,596 \times 45 =$ _____   16. $1,875 \times 685 =$ _____
17. $2,697 \times 476 =$ _____   18. $9,844 \times 375 =$ _____
19. $5,149 \times 9,128 =$ _____   20. $2,357 \times 649 =$ _____

Exercise 2

Complete the following order. Unit × unit cost = Total. Accumulate products.

Order #001345778

Units	Model	Unit Cost ($)	Total ($)
35	Model A desks	56	21. _____
35	A-line chairs	25	22. _____
6	Library tables	33	23. _____
15	All-in-1 desks	59	24. _____
Order total			25. _____

Exercise 3

26. In 2000, the college bookstore sold 3,000 copies of book #032956, which sells for $45. In 2001, the bookstore sold 3,056 copies of the same book for $45. What is the amount of the increased sales in dollars? _____

27. At an average speed of 65 miles per hour, how many miles will a trucker cover in 8 hours? _____

28. Pencils are bulk packaged at 144 per box. How many pencils are there in 12 boxes? _____

29. Staples are packaged 100 per box. There are 10 boxes per case. How many staples are there in 9 cases? _____

30. James can paint an average of 800 square feet in a day. How many square feet should he contract to paint in 4 weeks if he normally works 5 days per week? _____

CHAPTER 6

Division, Constants in Division, Accumulation of Quotients

 ## PART 1   *Speed and Accuracy Building Using Touch Key*

GOALS: Your speed goal is 6,500 strokes per hour.
Your accuracy target goal range is 95% to 100%.

As you complete each succeeding part of the lesson, try to improve your speed without lowering your accuracy score. If your percent-of-accuracy score falls below 95%, review your finger position and technique. Then try again.

Instructions: *Start Touch Key. Complete Lesson 6, Parts A through E. Record your scores for strokes per hour and percent of accuracy.*

Touch Key Lesson 6—The 1 through 9 Keys, Three-Digit Numbers

Today's Date	Strokes per Hour	Percent of Accuracy
A.		
B.		
C.		
D.		
E.		

 ## PART 2   *Business Math Skills*

DIVISION

The arithmetic operation of **division** is used to calculate the number of times one number is contained in another. Division is the opposite of multiplication. Division may be used to split an amount into equal portions. For example, if we would like to give eight children an equal number of cookies and we have 24 cookies, we would divide to see how many cookies each child may receive (Figure 6.1).

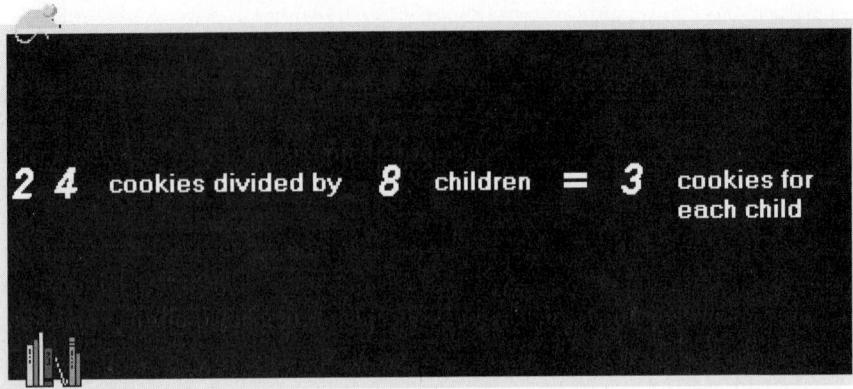

FIGURE 6.1

COMPONENTS OF DIVISION

The number to be split in a division problem is the **dividend**. The number we are dividing by (the number of portions desired) is the **divisor**. The result, or answer, is the **quotient**.

Several symbols may be used to indicate the arithmetic operation of division, including the symbol shown in Figure 6.2, which is usually used when working division problems with pencil and paper. The alignment of numbers is extremely important when working division problems without a calculator to avoid confusion and mistakes. You will also see the symbols / and ÷ used to indicate division.

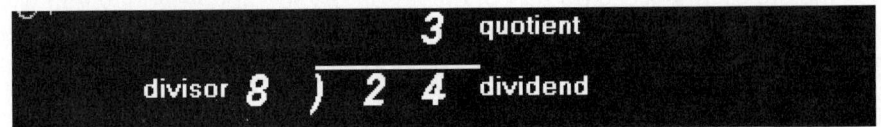

FIGURE 6.2

PROPERTIES OF DIVISION

The divisor and the dividend are not interchangeable in a division problem. Numbers in a division problem may not be changed without affecting the result.

SOLVING AND CHECKING DIVISION

To solve the problem in Figure 6.3, ask yourself, "What number times 8 equals 24?" We know that 3 times 8 equals 24. Write 3 in the ones place of the quotient. Write the product of 3 × 8 (24) beneath the dividend and subtract. The difference is 0, which means there is no remainder; in other words, 24 is **evenly divisible** by 8. To check a division problem, multiply the quotient by the divisor. The result should equal the dividend.

$$
\begin{array}{r}
3 \text{ quotient} \\
\text{divisor } 8\,)\overline{\,2\ 4\,}\ \text{dividend} \\
-\ 2\ 4 \\
\hline
0
\end{array}
$$

check: 3 × 8 = 2 4

FIGURE 6.3

DIVISION PROBLEMS WITH REMAINDERS

If a dividend is not **evenly divisible** by the divisor, the quotient will contain a **remainder**.

EXAMPLE

Twenty-one dozen cookies are needed for a fundraiser. Five volunteers are available to bake cookies. How many dozen cookies should each volunteer bake? Divide 21 by 5. Since no number times 5 equals 21, ask yourself, "What number times 5 equals a number which is slightly smaller than 21?" Since $5 \times 4 = 20$, write 4 in the ones place of the quotient. Multiply 4×5 and write the product (20) below the dividend. Subtract. The difference is 1. Write r (for remainder) and a 1 to the right of the quotient (see Figure 6.4). What have we learned? Each of the five volunteers will need to bake four dozen cookies, and one volunteer will need to bake one dozen additional cookies.

$$
\begin{array}{r}
4\ r\,1 \quad \text{quotient} \\
\text{divisor}\ 5\ \overline{)\ 2\ 1}\ \ \text{dividend} \\
-\ 2\ 0 \\
\hline
1 \\
\end{array}
$$

check: $4 \times 5 = 20$

$+\ 1 = 21$

FIGURE 6.4

To check a quotient containing a remainder, multiply the divisor by the quotient and add the remainder to the product. The answer should match the dividend in the problem being checked. In Figure 6.4, $4 \times 5 = 20$, and $20 + 1 = 21$. This answer matches the dividend of 21 in the problem; therefore, 4 remainder 1 is the correct answer.

LONGER NUMBERS IN DIVISION

There are six steps required in a division problem containing a large dividend: (1) identify a partial dividend, (2) divide, (3) multiply, (4) subtract, (5) compare, and (6) bring down the next digit of the dividend. These steps are repeated until all the digits of the dividend have been divided. Each of the steps is illustrated below.

Step 1: Identify a partial dividend. In Figure 6.5, the 2 in the hundreds place of the dividend is too small to divide by 6. Use 29 as the first **partial dividend**.

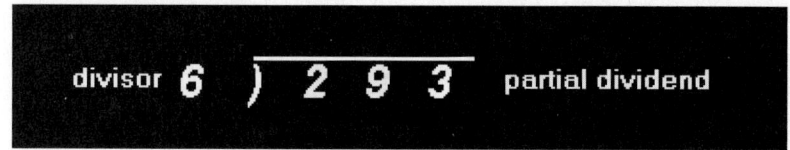

divisor $6\ \overline{)\ 2\ 9\ 3}$ partial dividend

FIGURE 6.5

Step 2: The partial dividend (29) is not evenly divisible by 6. However, $4 \times 6 = 24$, a number slightly smaller than 29. Write 4 in the quotient area above the 9 in the partial dividend (Figure 6.6). The 4 is a **partial quotient**.

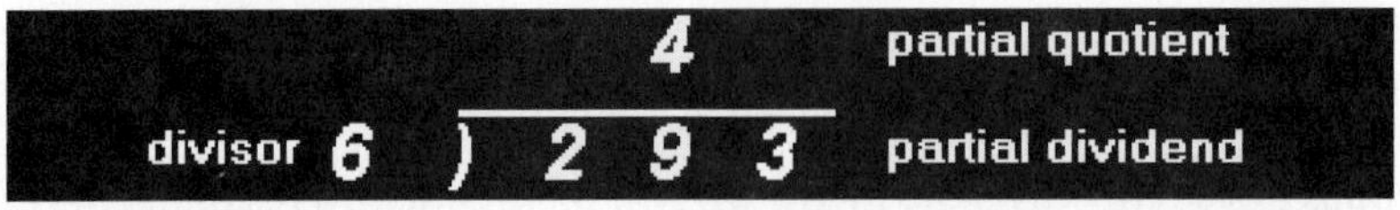

FIGURE 6.6

Step 3: Multiply the partial quotient (4) by the divisor (6) and write the result (24) below the partial dividend. Be careful to align place values (Figure 6.7).

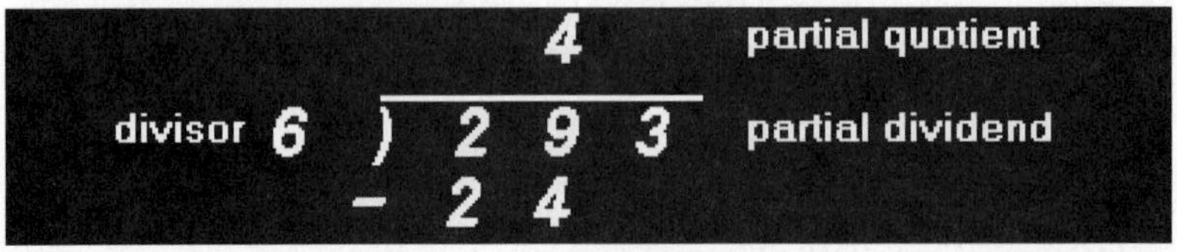

FIGURE 6.7

Step 4: Subtract. Draw a line below the amount to be subtracted (24). Subtract. Write the difference (5) below the line, being careful to align place values (Figure 6.8).

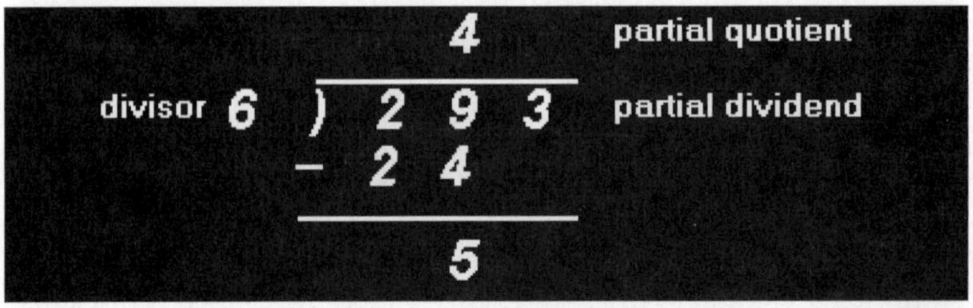

FIGURE 6.8

Step 5: Compare the difference of 5 with the divisor of 6 (Figure 6.9). The difference should be smaller than the divisor. If the difference is not smaller than the divisor, repeat steps 2 through 5 using a larger number as the partial quotient. If the difference is smaller than the divisor, continue to step 6.

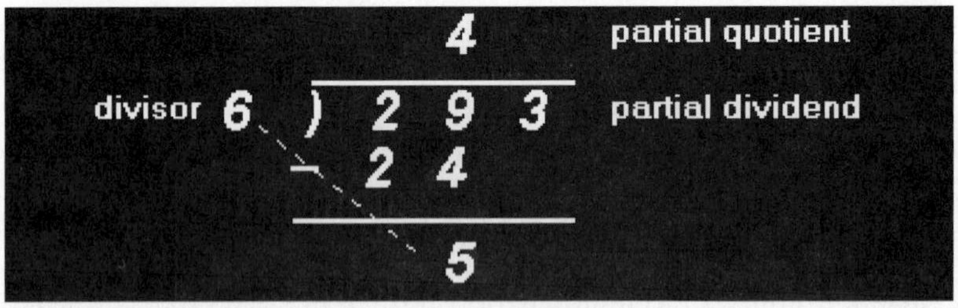

FIGURE 6.9

Step 6: Bring down the next digit of the dividend. Write the next digit (3) at the right of the difference calculated in step 5. Again, make sure to keep the digits aligned correctly (Figure 6.10).

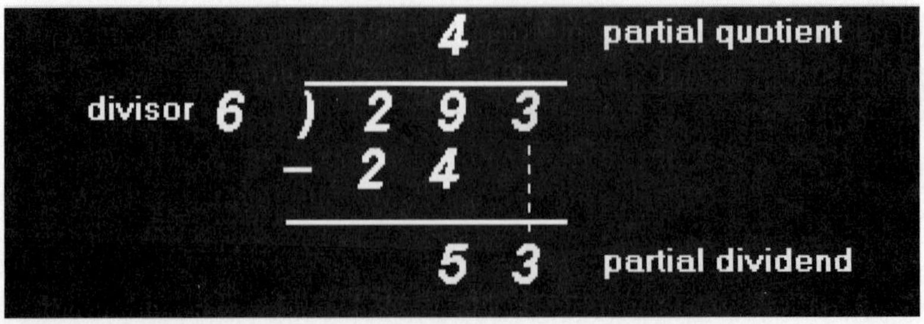

FIGURE 6.10

Repeat steps 2 through 6 until all digits in the dividend have been divided.

Step 2 repeated: Divide the partial dividend (53) by the divisor (6). Since $8 \times 6 = 48$, which is slightly smaller than 53, write 8 in the quotient area above the 3 in the dividend (Figure 6.11).

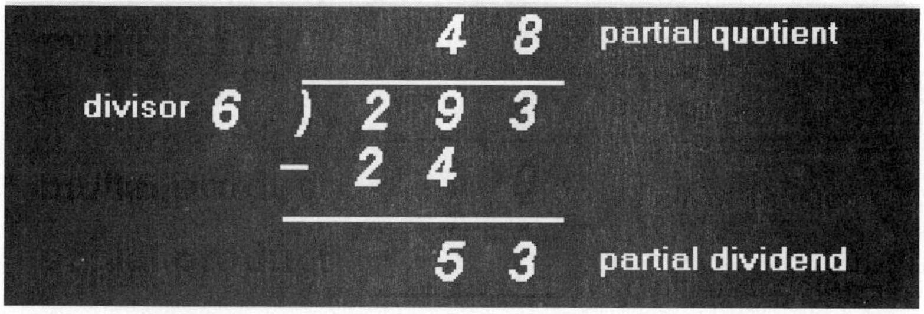

FIGURE 6.11

Step 3 repeated: Multiply 8 times $6 = 48$. Write 48 below the partial dividend of 53 (Figure 6.12).

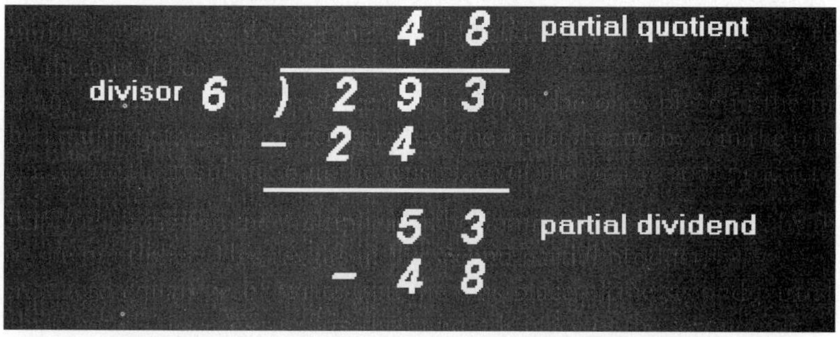

FIGURE 6.12

Step 4 repeated: Subtract 53 minus 48 $= 5$. Draw a line and write 5 below it (Figure 6.13).

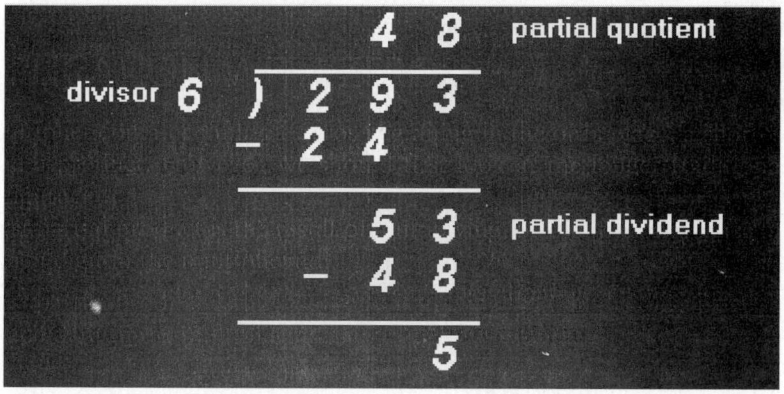

FIGURE 6.13

Step 5 repeated: Compare the difference (5) and the divisor of 6 (Figure 6.14). The difference is smaller, so continue to step 6.

Step 6 repeated: There are no more digits in the dividend to bring down, which means 5 is the remainder. Write r5 in the quotient area. The problem shows that 293 may be divided by six 48 times with 5 left over.

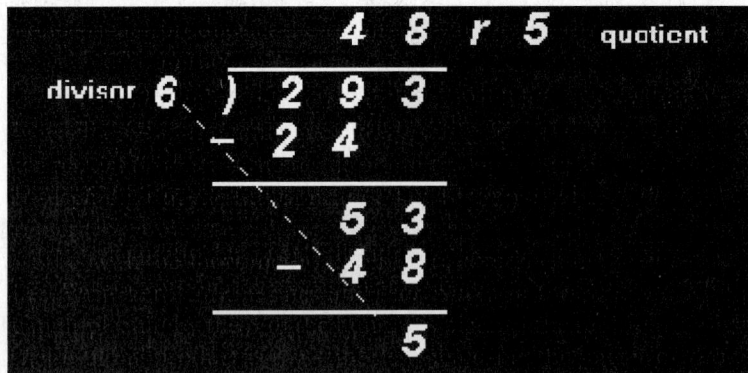

FIGURE 6.14

MORE ABOUT REMAINDERS

Remainders may be simply noted in the quotient, as in Figure 6.14; that is, 48 remainder 5. Remainders may also be converted to fractions by placing the remainder over the divisor. The quotient would then be 48 and 5/6 (more on fractions in Chapter 9). Lastly, remainders may be converted to decimal numbers by dividing the remainder by the divisor (more on decimal numbers in Chapter 8).

Using the answer in Figure 6.14 as an example, listed below are three ways to write uneven quotients (quotients with remainders) and how to read them:

48 r5	forty-eight remainder five
48 5/6	forty-eight and five sixths
48.83	forty-eight and eighty-three hundredths

USING THE TABLE OF MULTIPLICATION FOR DIVISION

To use the multiplication table for division (Table 6.1), find the desired divisor in the top row of the table. Locate the dividend in the column beneath it. The quotient will be the first item in that row.

Example: $45 \div 9 = 5$.

Note: The result of dividing a number by zero is considered to be an undefined number. A calculator will return an error message if this is attempted.

TABLE 6.1   Table of Multiplication/Division

×/)	1	2	3	4	5	6	7	8	9	10
1	1	2	3	4	5	6	7	8	9	10
2	2	4	6	8	10	12	14	16	18	20
3	3	6	9	12	15	18	21	24	27	30
4	4	8	12	16	20	24	28	32	36	40
5	5	10	15	20	25	30	35	40	45	50
6	6	12	18	24	30	36	42	48	54	60
7	7	14	21	28	35	42	49	56	63	70
8	8	16	24	32	40	48	56	64	72	80
9	9	18	27	36	45	54	63	72	81	90
10	10	20	30	40	50	60	70	80	90	100

MATH STAR 6.1

BE A *Math* ★ !

Dividing Numbers with Trailing Zeros

Quick! At a meeting, you need to divide 3,600 by 900. When dividing, you may cancel an equal number of trailing zeros from the dividend and divisor without affecting the result.

Problem 1: 3,600 ÷ 900.

$36 ÷ 9 = 4$ Mentally, cancel the two trailing zeros in both the dividend and the divisor. Divide. The answer is 4.

Too easy? Ok, next you need to divide 5,400 by 90. Cancel one zero from both the dividend and the divisor. Disregard the remaining zero in the dividend. Divide. Replace the disregarded zero in the quotient. You're finished!

Problem 2: 5,400 ÷ 90.

$540 ÷ 9$ **Step 1:** Mentally, cancel one zero in both the dividend and the divisor.

$54 ÷ 9 = 6$ **Step 2:** Disregard the remaining zero in the dividend.
60   Divide: $54 ÷ 9 = 6$. Replace the disregarded zero in the answer. The answer is 60.

Dividing by 4

To quickly divide by four, simply halve the number once, then halve the result.

Problem 3: 368 ÷ 4.

$368 ÷ 2 = 184$ **Step 1:** Halve the number. Working left to right, half of 36 is 18; half of 8 is 4. The result is 184.

$184 ÷ 2 = 92$ **Step 2:** Halve the result. Half of 18 is 9; half of 4 is 2. The answer is 92.

In the next problem, cancel the zeros, then halve the dividend and the result.

Problem 4: 4,800 ÷ 400.

$48 ÷ 2 = 24$ **Step 1:** Cancel the two trailing zeros in both the dividend and the divisor. Halve the dividend.

$24 ÷ 2 = 12$ **Step 2:** Halve the result. The answer is 12.

In the next problem, cancel two zeros from each number, disregard the remaining trailing zero, halve the number, halve the result, and then replace the disregarded zero in the quotient. Sound complicated? It isn't.

Problem 5: 52,000 ÷ 400.

$520 ÷ 4$ **Step 1:** Cancel the two trailing zeros in the dividend and in the divisor.

$52 ÷ 2 = 26$ **Step 2:** Disregard the remaining trailing zero. Halve the dividend.

$26 ÷ 2 = 13$ **Step 3:** Halve the result. Replace the disregarded zero in the result. The
130   answer is 130.

Try it yourself!

1. 52 ÷ 4
2. 120 ÷ 4
3. 60 ÷ 4
4. 9,200 ÷ 40
5. 76,000 ÷ 4,000
6. 12,800 ÷ 400

Answers: 1. 13 **2.** 30 **3.** 15 **4.** 230 **5.** 19 **6.** 32

(continued)

MATH STAR 6.1   *(continued)*

Multiplying by 5

Multiply by dividing? Yes, it's true in the case of 5 and 25. When you need to quickly multiply by 5, think 2 and 10. Why? Because to multiply by 5, you can divide by 2 and multiply by 10 instead. If you remember that to multiply by 10, you simply add a zero, the problem is greatly simplified. Try these examples:

Problem: 58×5.

$58 \div 2 = 29$	**Step 1:** Divide by 2.
$29 \times 10 = 290$	**Step 2:** Multiply by 10 (or, place a 0 in the ones place).

Problem: 60×5.

$6 \div 2 = 3$	**Step 1:** Disregard the 0. Divide by 2.
$3 \times 10 = 30$	**Step 2:** Multiply by 10.
300	**Step 3:** Replace the 0 that was disregarded in step 1.

Try it for yourself.

1. 34×5
2. 26×5
3. 48×5
4. 62×5
5. 120×5
6. 72×5

Answers: 1. 170 **2.** 130 **3.** 240 **4.** 310 **5.** 600 **6.** 360

Multiplying by 25

Instead of multiplying by 25, try dividing by 4, then adding one zero for each number in the multiplier (in this case two zeros).

Problem: 36×25.

$36 \div 4 = 9$	**Step 1:** Divide by 4, or using the shortcut learned earlier, halve 36, then halve again: $36 \div 2 = 18$, and $18 \div 2 = 9$.
900	**Step 2:** Place two trailing zeros in the answer because there are two places in the multiplier.

Dividing by 25

Conversely, instead of dividing by 25, it is possible to multiply by 4, then mark off two places in the answer.

$5,200 \div 25$ $5,200 \times 4 =$ $20,800$	**Step 1:** Multiply by 4 (or, double, then double again): $5,200 \times 2 = 10,400$, and $10,400 \times 2 = 20,800$.
20,8~~00~~ 208	**Step 2:** Remove two trailing zeros because there are two places in the divisor.

Try it!

1. 8×25
2. $1,200 \times 25$
3. 40×25
4. $225 \div 25$
5. $3,000 \div 25$
6. $100 \div 25$

Answers: 1. 200 **2.** 30,000 **3.** 1,000 **4.** 9 **5.** 120 **6.** 4

 **PART 2**   *Business Math Skills*

Exercise 1

Divide and check.

1. $2\overline{)162}$	2. $5\overline{)880}$	3. $10\overline{)950}$	4. $6\overline{)42}$
5. $2\overline{)74}$	6. $12\overline{)720}$	7. $3\overline{)429}$	8. $9\overline{)666}$
9. $8\overline{)288}$	10. $15\overline{)3,195}$	11. $7\overline{)8,841}$	12. $4\overline{)5,652}$
13. $26\overline{)286}$	14. $22\overline{)462}$	15. $13\overline{)559}$	16. $78\overline{)936}$
17. $32\overline{)4,352}$	18. $29\overline{)5,655}$	19. $34\overline{)6,426}$	20. $56\overline{)9,296}$

Exercise 2

21. The Farmer's Wife Co-op has an order for 114 sets of quilted placemats. Nineteen members make quilted products. How many placemat sets should each produce? _____
22. A local nursery has agreed to enroll 60 babies for child care. State law requires no more than 5 babies per teacher or worker. How many child care teachers or workers should be hired? _____
23. A rough draft of a report consists of 48 pages. If the printer can produce 12 pages per minute, how much time will be required to print 3 copies of the report? _____
24. Joe worked 40 hours last week. His gross pay was $520. How much does he earn per hour? _____
25. Janie wants to package 890 pounds of pet food into bags that hold 24 pounds each. How many bags will she be able to fill with 24 pounds of pet food in each? How many pounds will be left over? _____

 **PART 3**   *The Pocket and Windows Calculators*

DIVISION

The order of entry for a typical division problem on the pocket and Windows calculators involves keying the dividend followed by the division key, then the divisor followed by the equals key.

Check the division problem by multiplying the quotient by the divisor. The product should match the dividend of the original problem.

Problem	Procedure	Check
188 ÷ 4 =	188 ÷ 4 = $\boxed{47}$	4 × 47 = $\boxed{188}$

NUMBERS THAT ARE NOT EVENLY DIVISIBLE

Calculators do not have the capability of displaying remainders. Instead, a calculator will convert a quotient with a remainder into a decimal number. The quotient will be the number to the left of the decimal. The calculator will automatically divide the remainder by the divisor and the result will be placed to the right of the decimal. Decimal numbers will be explained in Chapter 7.

Name _____

Class/Section _____

Score (Correct Answers ÷ No. of Assigned Problems) _____

 ## PART 3   *Pocket or Windows Calculator*

Exercise 1

Divide and check.

1. 104 ÷ 13 = _____
2. 112 ÷ 8 = _____
3. 216 ÷ 9 = _____
4. 96 ÷ 6 = _____
5. 136 ÷ 8 = _____
6. 78 ÷ 6 = _____
7. 352 ÷ 22 = _____
8. 480 ÷ 24 = _____
9. 836 ÷ 44 = _____
10. 1,192 ÷ 4 = _____
11. 676 ÷ 26 = _____
12. 2,916 ÷ 9 = _____
13. 3,840 ÷ 15 = _____
14. 4,776 ÷ 4 = _____
15. 6,588 ÷ 27 = _____
16. 2,114 ÷ 302 = _____
17. 4,554 ÷ 33 = _____
18. 9,880 ÷ 152 = _____
19. 5,850 ÷ 78 = _____
20. 8,364 ÷ 123 = _____
21. 2,550 ÷ 34 = _____
22. 8,640 ÷ 540 = _____
23. 9,108 ÷ 138 = _____
24. 5,882 ÷ 346 = _____
25. 2,520 ÷ 840 = _____
26. 10,980 ÷ 180 = _____
27. 9,538 ÷ 19 = _____

Exercise 2

28. Mary Ann has been given a raise of $1,800 per year. How much more will she earn each month? _____
29. A local nonprofit group wishes to sell 4,000 boxes of candy. The group has 160 members. How many boxes of candy must each member sell to meet the group's goal? _____
30. The amount of money available for company manager bonuses is as follows: Department A $50,000, Department B $35,000, and Department C $11,000. How much of the bonus money will each of the eight company managers receive if the bonus money is divided equally? _____

 ## PART 3   *Review and Practice Using Business Math FUNdamentals*

GOAL: Complete 9 of the 10 problems correctly.

Instructions: *Start Business Math FUNdamentals. Complete Tutorial 12 Division, Tutorial 13 Division with Remainders, Tutorial 14 Longer Numbers in Division, and Drill 6 Division with Remainders. If you are not satisfied with your score, repeat Drill 6. Write your scores below.*

Business Math FUNdamentals Drill 6

Today's Date	Score

 **PART 4** *The Desktop Calculator*

KEYSTROKING TECHNIQUE

If the division key is located to the left of the numberpad on your calculator, use your index finger to key the division key. As you reach for the division key, try to keep the ring finger anchored to the 6 key so that you can easily return your fingers to the home row after pressing the division key. It is not necessary to use the division key by touch only; however, correct fingering is still important.

DIVISION

The order of entry for a typical division problem on the desktop calculator involves first keying the dividend followed by the division key, then keying the divisor followed by the equals key. To check the problem, multiply the quotient by the divisor. The result should match the dividend in the original problem.

Problem	Procedure	Check
5,500 ÷ 11	5,500 ÷	500 ×
	11 =	11 =
	500	5,500

MULTIFACTOR DIVISION

Problems containing more than one divisor—**multifactor division**—are easily solved on a calculator. Key the dividend followed by the division key, the first divisor followed by the division key, the second divisor followed by the division key, then the equals key. It is important that the order of the dividend and the divisors not be changed.

PROBLEM 1

Headquarters for a chain discount store confirmed that their order for 9,000 brand A televisions would be shipped in 2 weeks. Management decided to divide them equally among 500 retail territories. Three outlet stores are located within territory WTX. How many brand A televisions will each store in territory WTX receive?

$$9,000 \div 500 \div 3 = \boxed{6}$$

DIVISION PROBLEMS WITH CONSTANTS

A **division constant** is a value that will be used more than once as a divisor. Fortunately, most modern desktop calculators automatically recognize the second number entered in a division problem as the constant. Therefore, it is not necessary to enter the value of the constant more than once.

PROBLEM 2

City Toy Wholesalers wishes to equally distribute three very popular toys to its 43 retail chain customers. The wholesaler has 34,830 units of toy A, 67,000 units of toy B, and 135,000 units of toy C. How many units of each toy should each retail chain customer receive?

TAPE 6.1:

```
      0 · C

 34,830 · ÷
     43 · =
    810 · *

 66,994 · =
  1,558 · *

135,020 · =
  3,140 · *
```

MACHINE SETUP

Decimal Selector—F or 0
Rounding Switch—5/4
Tax Switch—CALC
Printer Switch—ON

C	*Problem:*	*Procedure:*
	34,830 ÷ 43	34,830 ÷ 43 = [810]
	66,994 ÷ 43	66,994 = [1,558]
	135,020 ÷ 43	135,020 = [3,140]

ACCUMULATION OF QUOTIENTS FOR DIVISION PROBLEMS WITH CONSTANTS

Many business problems require the calculation of several quotients, which are then added together. This totaling of quotients is commonly referred to as the **accumulation of quotients**. In the following example, the products are accumulated using the memory feature.

TAPE 6.2:

```
        0 · C

  8,000 · ÷
      5 · =
  1,600 · *

  1,600 · M+
335,000 · =
 67,000 · *

 67,000 · M+
280,000 · =
 56,000 · *

 56,000 · M+
 80,000 · =
 16,000 · *

 16,000 · M+

140,600 · M*
```

PROBLEM 3

On his death, Mr. Brown wishes his assets to be distributed equally among his five grandchildren. His assets consist of the following: $8,000 cash, certificates of deposit and government bonds worth $335,000, real estate valued at $280,000, and stocks and bonds valued at $80,000. At today's values, calculate the amount of each asset each grandchild will receive, as well as the total value of assets each grandchild will receive.

MACHINE SETUP

Decimal Selector—F or 0
Rounding Switch—5/4
Tax Switch—CALC
Printer Switch—IC

C	MT	*Problem:*	*Procedure:*		
		8,000 ÷ 5	8,000 ÷ 5 =	[1,600]	M+=
		335,000 ÷ 5	335,000 =	[67,000]	M+=
		280,000 ÷ 5	280,000 =	[56,000]	M+=
		80,000 ÷ 5	80,000 =	[16,000]	M+=
			MT	[140,600]	

ACCUMULATION OF QUOTIENTS USING THE MEMORY PLUS EQUALS KEY

The M+= key can be used to complete both multiplication and division problems and accumulate the products or quotients in memory. The total of the products or quotients can then be displayed by pressing the MT key.

MACHINE SETUP   Decimal Selector—F or 0
Rounding Switch—5/4
Tax Switch—CALC
Printer Switch—IC

$\boxed{\text{C}}$	$\boxed{\text{MT}}$	*Problem*	*Procedure*	
		6,900 ÷ 3	6,900 ÷ 3 M+=	$\boxed{2,300}$
		7,500 ÷ 5	7,500 ÷ 5 M+=	$\boxed{1,500}$
		28,000 ÷ 7	28,000 ÷ 7 M+=	$\boxed{4,000}$
			$\boxed{\text{MT}}$	$\boxed{7,800}$

TAPE 6.3:

```
              0 . C
              0 . M*
        6,900.  ÷
            3.  =
        2,300. M+

        7,500.  ÷
            5.  =
        1,500. M+

       28,000.  ÷
            7.  =
        4,000. M+

        7,800. M*
```

Name _____

Class/Section _____

Score (Correct Answers ÷ No. of Assigned Problems) _____

 # PART 4 *Desktop Calculator*

Exercise 1

Divide and check.

1. 91 ÷ 13 = _____
2. 816 ÷ 8 = _____
3. 273 ÷ 3 = _____
4. 266 ÷ 7 = _____
5. 522 ÷ 18 = _____
6. 267 ÷ 3 = _____
7. 364 ÷ 7 = _____
8. 705 ÷ 15 = _____
9. 440 ÷ 8 = _____
10. 975 ÷ 25 = _____
11. 2,288 ÷ 26 = _____
12. 1,216 ÷ 8 = _____
13. 2,925 ÷ 45 = _____
14. 2,232 ÷ 62 = _____
15. 1,593 ÷ 27 = _____
16. 2,646 ÷ 98 = _____
17. 1,254 ÷ 33 = _____
18. 1,845 ÷ 15 = _____

Multifactor division:

19. 5,600 ÷ 700 ÷ 2 = _____
20. 10,800 ÷ 120 ÷ 9 = _____
21. 8,976 ÷ 34 ÷ 33 = _____
22. 5,040 ÷ 4 ÷ 84 = _____

Exercise 2

Mike Jackson owned MJACK Oil wells 14, 15, 16, and 17. His four children inherited the oil wells equally. How much of the proceeds from each oil well will each child receive? Check the problem. Total distributions should equal total income produced.

Production Figures for September 2001, Oil Field #890

Oil Well	Total Income Produced ($)	Distribution of Income ($)			
		Adam Jackson	Bob Jackson	Patricia Maine	Harold Jackson
14	8,000	23. _____	24. _____	25. _____	26. _____
15	16,000	27. _____	28. _____	29. _____	30. _____
16	24,000	31. _____	32. _____	33. _____	34. _____
17	4,000	35. _____	36. _____	37. _____	38. _____
Totals	44. _____	39. _____	40. _____	41. _____	42. _____

Total distributions   43. _____

Exercise 3

45. ABC Co. received fuel shipments of 150 gallons on September 3, 150 gallons on September 15, and 150 gallons on September 21. If divided equally among the company's six tractors, how much fuel did each tractor use in September? _____

Exercise 4

Strokes per Minute Score _____

Accuracy Score (Correct Strokes ÷ Total Strokes) _____

One-Minute Addition Timing (Keys 1 through 9)

(Optional: Your instructor may wish you to use Touch Key on the computer for all your timings. Check with your instructor before completing this exercise.)

Complete as many of the problems as possible in 1 minute by adding. Work quickly and accurately. The number preceding each closing parenthesis indicates the cumulative number of strokes for problems attempted. For example, if you complete Problems 1 through 5 in 1 minute, your strokes-per-minute score is 155. Optional: 3- to 5-minute timings.

1.	55	2.	15	3.	58	4.	28	5.	36	6.	32	7.	36	8.	71
	47		65		52		27		56		38		63		83
	69		25		59		21		53		53		37		92
	58		26		96		55		52		24		38		41
	54		35		57		52		33		26		32		54
	56		12		51		23		13		25		25		63
	51		41		54		29		15		33		33		16
	51		67		53		51		35		34		34		26
	52		64		25		21		36		39		61		32
	53		53		23		12		37		37		57		55
31)		62)		93)		124)		155)		186)		217)		248)	

9.	84	10.	83	11.	75	12.	95	13.	96	14.	82	15.	76	16.	74
	43		24		45		16		56		34		13		26
	44		94		42		84		66		95		94		76
	45		42		85		54		26		36		14		42
	76		76		92		81		86		95		75		92
	83		43		36		45		46		31		23		63
	95		16		35		96		92		71		73		95
	14		15		25		53		13		62		53		67
	26		74		81		81		78		84		84		94
	54		34		45		16		16		14		11		46
279)		310)		341)		372)		403)		434)		465)		496)	

17.	94	18.	82	19.	91	20.	96	21.	37	22.	18	23.	19	24.	19
	66		22		64		45		21		26		23		22
	95		84		94		11		18		39		38		38
	32		26		21		53		64		42		63		45
	86		87		81		95		59		59		58		58
	24		46		31		16		45		61		32		62
	81		95		71		86		49		59		58		18
	23		63		55		36		54		22		21		23
	96		86		65		74		28		39		85		33
	34		34		64		21		21		56		43		17
527)		558)		589)		620)		651)		682)		713)		744)	

25.	26.	27.	28.	29.	30.	31.	32.
47	28	67	39	28	29	19	37
41	16	45	63	31	26	25	66
59	69	59	29	49	38	19	38
65	46	14	53	12	55	14	61
58	57	29	69	57	47	19	49
56	62	32	61	26	11	32	65
67	19	67	69	38	57	39	59
51	25	62	35	13	56	36	25
49	28	59	37	59	59	29	59
66	31	62	31	46	66	34	36
775)	806)	837)	868)	899)	930)	961)	992)

CHAPTER 6 *Terminology Review*

Accumulation of quotients
Dividend
Division
Division constant
Divisor
Evenly divisible
Multifactor division
Partial dividend
Partial quotient
Quotient
Remainder

Insert the missing words to complete the following statements.

1. _____ is used to determine how many times one number is contained in another number.

2. The number being divided is called the _____.

3. To check a quotient containing a remainder, multiply the _____ by the quotient and add the _____.

4. A division problem is _____ by the divisor if its answer contains no remainder.

5. In a longer division problem, a(n) _____ may be divided in the first step instead of the entire dividend.

6. A division problem containing more than one divisor is called _____ _____.

7. The result obtained after dividing a partial dividend is called a(n) _____.

Questions 8 and 9 pertain to the desktop calculator.

8. Desktop calculators recognize the second number entered in a division problem as the _____.

9. _____ is the adding together of quotients and may be done easily using the memory feature.

Chapter 6 Review Exercises

Exercise 1

Complete the following division problems mentally. Use the shortcuts mentioned in Math Star 6.1.

1. $4\overline{)2,800}$ 2. $40\overline{)480}$ 3. $5\overline{)1,250}$ 4. $70\overline{)770}$

5. $80\overline{)2,800}$ 6. $22\overline{)264}$ 7. $3\overline{)990}$ 8. $5\overline{)430}$

Complete the following division problems.

9. $1,296 \div 48 =$ _____   10. $208 \div 4 =$ _____   11. $180 \div 12 =$ _____

12. $244 \div 4 =$ _____   13. $574 \div 82 =$ _____   14. $1,088 \div 17 =$ _____

15. $650 \div 50 =$ _____   16. $460 \div 5 =$ _____   17. $810 \div 45 =$ _____

18. $216 \div 3 =$ _____   19. $248 \div 4 =$ _____   20. $1,640 \div 40 =$ _____

Exercise 2

Sails Aloft has received an order for 85 biminis. A checklist has been prepared that lists the materials required. Compare the materials required with the amounts in inventory. Complete the following checklist. If there are sufficient materials on hand for each part needed to manufacture the 85 biminis, write "yes" in the column. If sufficient materials for each part needed to manufacture the biminis are not in inventory, write "no" in the order materials column for that part. If sufficient quantities of all needed materials are available for fabrication of the biminis, authorize the production department to begin manufacture. If any materials need to be ordered, do not authorize the production department to begin manufacture.

Sails Aloft
Materials Check List
Current Orders: Order #86233, 85 Pacific Blue Biminis, Model S292

Inventory (Materials on Hand)	Materials Required for Order #86233	Sufficient Materials on Hand? Yes/No	Order Materials? Yes/No
3,500 square yards of Pacific blue Sunbrella® fabric	16 square yards of Pacific blue Sunbrella® each	21. _____	25. _____
350 six-foot YYK® zippers	4 six-foot zippers each	22. _____	26. _____
600 bobbins of white marine-grade thread	6 bobbins of white marine-grade thread each	23. _____	27. _____
1,200 yards of 1-inch Pacific blue webbing	12 yards of 1-inch Pacific blue webbing each	24. _____	28. _____
Begin manufacture? Yes/No			29. _____
Warehouse supervisor Signature:		Date:	

Exercise 3

30. The Smooth Sailing Club advertises a 36-hour sailing class that usually extends over 1 week. The club has decided to offer the class over two 3-day weekends. How many hours of instruction should be planned for each day if the time is divided equally? _____

31. A grocer purchased 75 pounds of sirloin steak for $150. How much did she pay for each pound of steak (cost per pound)? _____

Reading, Rounding, Adding, and Subtracting Decimal Numbers

PART 1   *Speed and Accuracy Building Using Touch Key*

GOALS: Your speed goal is 7,000 strokes per hour.
Your accuracy target goal range is 95% to 100%.

With each part of the lesson, try to improve your speed without lowering your accuracy score. If your percent-of-accuracy score falls below 95%, review your finger position and technique. Then try again.

Instructions: *Start Touch Key. Complete Lesson 7, Parts A through E. Record your scores for strokes per hour and percent of accuracy.*

Touch Key Lesson 7—The 0 through 9 Keys, Three-Digit Numbers

	Today's Date	Strokes per Hour	Percent of Accuracy
A.			
B.			
C.			
D.			
E.			

PART 2   *Business Math Skills*

DECIMAL NUMBERS

A **decimal number** contains a period or dot, referred to as a **decimal point,** which separates the two parts of the number: (1) the part of the number that is a whole number and (2) the part of the number that is less than one. You are probably already familiar with the most common use of decimal numbers. Money amounts are expressed as decimal numbers preceded by the dollar ($) sign. The dollar amounts are placed to the left of the decimal point. The portion of the amount less than 1 dollar is placed to the right of the decimal point. For example, ten dollars and fifty cents can be expressed as $10.50. Because 205 pennies equals two dollars and five cents, the decimal number is $2.05. In general, numbers that are smaller than one or contain a part smaller than one can be written as a decimal number. For example, two and five tenths is written as 2.5. Read the decimal point as the word "and."

DECIMAL NUMBERS HAVE PLACE VALUES

You have already learned the place values of whole numbers. Beginning at the decimal, the decimal places are **tenths, hundredths, thousandths, ten thousandths, hundred thousandths,** and **millionths** (see Figure 7.1).

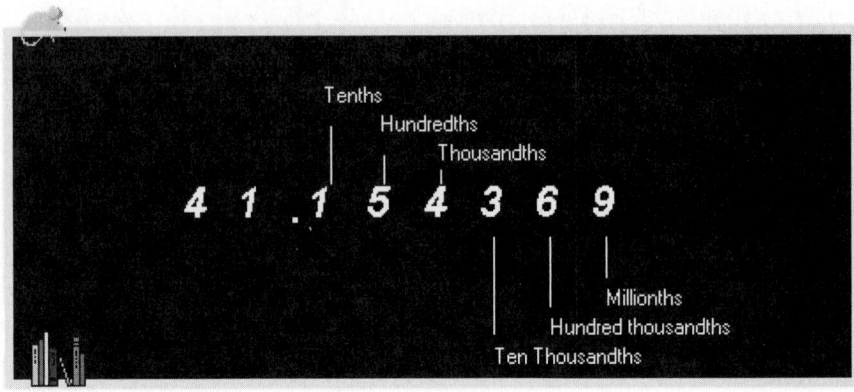

FIGURE 7.1

The number 41.1 is read as forty-one and one tenth.

The number 41.15 is read as forty-one and fifteen hundredths.

The number 41.154 is read as forty-one and one hundred fifty-four thousandths.

The number 41.1543 is read as forty-one and one thousand five hundred forty-three ten thousandths.

The number 41.15436 is read as forty-one and fifteen thousand four hundred thirty-six hundred thousandths.

The number 41.154369 is read as forty-one and one hundred fifty-four thousand three hundred sixty-nine millionths.

ROUNDING DECIMAL NUMBERS

Dollars and cents are written as decimal numbers with two decimal places, the tenths and the hundredths. Why? There are 100 cents in 1 dollar ($1.00). Any number of cents less than 100, that is, 1 to 99 cents, represents the decimal portion of dollars and cents when written as a decimal number.

Examples: 100 cents = $1.00   50 cents = $.50

199 cents = $1.99   5 cents = $.05

105 cents = $1.05   1 cent = $.01

If a calculation involving dollars and cents results in more than two decimal places, round to the hundredths place. To round to the hundredths place, look at the digit in the thousandths place. If it is 5 or greater, add 1 to the digit in the hundredths place and delete any digits to the right of the hundredths place. On the other hand, if the digit in the thousandths place is less than 5, do not change the digit in the hundredths place. Delete any digits to the right of the hundredths place.

In Figure 7.2, the first example contains a 6 in the thousandths place. Six is greater than 5, so round the 8 in the hundredths place up to 9 and delete any digits to the right of the hundredths place. The result is $56.59.

Examples:	Results after rounding:
5 6 . 5 8 6	$ 5 6 . 5 9
5 6 . 5 9 6	$ 5 6 . 6 0
5 6 . 5 9 4	$ 5 6 . 5 9

FIGURE 7.2

In the second example, the 6 in the thousandths place is greater than 5. Therefore, add 1 to 59 hundredths to round it to 60 hundredths and delete any digits to the right of the hundredths place. The result is $56.60.

In the third example, the 4 in the thousandths place is less than 5, so do not change the number in the hundredths place. Delete any digits to the right of the hundredths place. The result is $56.59.

Round decimal numbers to other places using the same procedure. To round 1.68971 to the thousandths place, look at the number to the right (the ten thousandths place). If it is 5 or greater, add 1 to the digit in the thousandths place. In this case the number in the ten thousandths place is 7, so add 1 to the 9 in the thousandths place. Delete all digits to the right of the thousandths place. The rounded number is 1.690.

A CASE OF FOLLOWING DIRECTIONS

Decimal Numbers Less Than One. When writing decimal numbers using digits, it is customary to place a zero before the decimal point when there are no whole numbers in the decimal number. For example, write nine tenths as 0.9, and write one thousandth as 0.001.

Trailing Zeros. When solving problems involving decimal numbers there are often questions involving unnecessary zeros. The zero in the number 1.690 is merely a place-holder. The zero is unnecessary because it has no value and may be referred to as a trailing zero. However, if we have been instructed to round to thousandths, we need the zero to show that we have indeed carried the answer out to three decimal places.

Rounding. However, you may sometimes be instructed to round to a certain decimal place, but not to use any unnecessary zeros. In this case the zero in the answer 1.690 would be omitted.

Rounding Dollars and Cents. In answers involving dollars and cents, two decimal places are used, even if the hundredths place contains a zero. However, watch for instructions that require you to round to dollars, when no decimal places would be written.

Rounding to the First Digit. Sometimes instructions will specify that you round at the first digit. This means round to whatever place the leftmost number of the digit occupies. For example, "round 398 to the first digit" means round to the hundredths place because the leftmost digit is in the hundredths place. Three hundred ninety-eight rounded to the first digit is four hundred.

Rounding the Final Answer. Another instruction you will sometimes see in a problem that requires multiple calculations is one that asks you to avoid rounding until the final answer. In this case, you would make all necessary calculations. Then round the final answer to the specified decimal place.

To summarize, look for any instructions that will help you when recording answers in order to avoid penalty points.

WRITING DECIMAL NUMBERS AS FRACTIONS

At the beginning of this chapter we learned that a portion of a dollar can be written as a decimal number. For example, 10 cents can be written as $0.10. Ten cents represents one tenth of a dollar because there are 10 dimes in 1 dollar ($10 \times 10 = 100$). A **fraction** also represents a portion. We can write any decimal number as a fraction by placing it over the appropriate number to represent tenths, hundredths, and so on. In Figure 7.3 we see that 0.1 equals one tenth, 0.21 equals twenty-one hundredths, and 0.303 equals three hundred three thousandths, and that each of these can be expressed as a fraction.

$$.1 = \frac{1}{10}$$

$$.21 = \frac{21}{100}$$

$$.303 = \frac{303}{1000}$$

FIGURE 7.3

ADDING AND SUBTRACTING DECIMAL NUMBERS

Before adding or subtracting decimal numbers, write the numbers so that the decimals in each number align vertically—a procedure called **decimal alignment**. The decimal should remain aligned when it is written in the answer as shown in Figure 7.4.

```
Add:        1.121        Subtract:
        2 0 2.3                  2 0 9.7 2
            5.9 7 8                  5.1
    1,0 0 2.1                  2 0 4.6 2
    1,2 1 1.4 9 9
```

FIGURE 7.4

MATH STAR 7.1

BE A *Math*★ !

Quick! You have gone to the supermarket for an elderly friend. She has given you $40 and a list. You are standing in the checkout line after selecting the items on her list when you notice her favorite magazine. Will the $40 cover the items on her list and the magazine? You live in a state with no sales tax.

(continued)

MATH STAR 7.1 (continued)

Mentally, round the cost of each item in the market basket to the nearest dollar. Round and add as you move down the column. Will the $40 cover all the items and the magazine?

Item Cost($)	Step 1 Round		Step 2 Add
2.79	3		
2.79	3	→	6
2.21	2	→	8
.59	1	→	9
1.09	1	→	10
5.07	5	→	15
2.89	3	→	18
3.09	3	→	21
8.82	9	→	30
1.79	2	→	32
1.99	2	→	34
2.39	2	→	36
Magazine $2.39	$2	→	$38

Name _____

Class/Section _____

Score (Correct Answers ÷ No. of Assigned Problems) _____

PART 2 *Business Math Skills*

Exercise 1

Write the following numbers in words.

1. 35.4 _____

2. 51.25 _____

3. 22.355 _____

4. 32.4667 _____

5. 14.45598 _____

Exercise 2

Write the following numbers using Arabic numerals.

6. One and twenty-three hundredths _____

7. Fourteen and three tenths _____

8. Fifty and one hundred twenty-six thousandths _____

9. One hundred eighteen and five ten thousandths _____

10. One hundred twenty-three thousandths _____

Exercise 3

Round to dollars and cents. Be sure to put a dollar sign and a decimal point in your answer.

11. 39.688 _____   12. 35.1003 _____   13. 62.999 _____
14. 87.9674 _____   15. 33.561 _____

Round to the thousandths place. Be sure to use a decimal point in your answer.

16. 0.3101 _____   17. 0.2859 _____   18. 1.4725 _____
19. 66.2692 _____   20. 4.2215 _____

Round to the ten thousandths place.

21. 13.5967459 _____   22. 29.0563324 _____   23. 92.5439995 _____
24. 140.5432576 _____   25. 3.4596611 _____

Add the following numbers. Round the answers to the tenths place unless the answer is for dollars and cents.

26. 16.45 + 25.4 _____   27. 26.55 + 100.44 _____
28. 39.65 + 9.98 _____   29. $55.003 + $69.356 _____
30. $108.673 + $1,000.34 _____

Subtract the following numbers. Round all answers except dollars and cents to the thousandths place.

31. 69.793467 − 6.4902 _____   32. 59.6711345 − 49.998329 _____
33. $2.32008 − $0.688 _____   34. $1.034 − $0.322 _____

Write the following decimal numbers as fractions.

35. 0.1 _____   36. 0.25 _____   37. 0.98 _____
38. 0.45 _____   39. 0.5 _____   40. 0.298 _____

 ## PART 3   *The Pocket and Windows Calculators*

LIMITATIONS

Most pocket calculators do not have a facility for rounding. When rounding is required, use mental rounding. To solve a problem containing decimals, enter the amounts including decimal points as well as any required arithmetic operation keys. Round the final answer mentally.

Problem	Procedure	Round
$55.135 +16.556	55.135 + 16.556 = 71.691	Since the answer contains dollars and cents, mentally round the answer to two places. The answer is $71.69.

The number of characters in a decimal number that will display on a pocket or Windows calculator is limited (usually to eight characters). You can determine the number of characters that will display on your model by keying the characters 1.23456789 . . . until the display is full. The last character displayed is the limit for your calculator.

PART 3 *Pocket or Windows Calculator*

Exercise 1

Add the following numbers. Round the answers to the thousandths place unless the answer is for dollars and cents.

1. 316.455 + 25.4 _____
2. 66.5579 + 100.443 _____
3. 139.6533 + 29.987 _____
4. $35.077 + $39.359 _____
5. $8.679321 + $1.345299 _____
6. $0.25 + $0.799 + $0.89321 + $1.675 _____

Subtract the following numbers. Round all answers except dollars and cents to the tenths place.

7. 1,069.4346 − 646.4902 _____
8. 559.671 − 292.998 _____
9. $22.3289 − $11.6892 _____
10. $21.634 − $9.329 _____

Exercise 2

Johnnelle opened a checking account on January 14 with a deposit of $600. During the week she wrote checks and made deposits as shown below in her check register. Subtract each check and add each deposit to find the balance of Johnnelle's checking account.

Date	Check Number	Amount of Check (−)	Amount of Deposit (+)	Balance ($)
1/14			600.00	600.00
1/16	100	255.65		11. _____
1/17	101	65.99		12. _____
1/19			55.50	13. _____
1/19	102	275.75		14. _____
1/19			120.55	15. _____

Exercise 3

Round the following prices to whole numbers, then add.

7.49	16. _____
109.99	17. _____
22.49	18. _____
24.99	19. _____
79.99	20. _____
21.49	21. _____
198.88	22. _____
199.28	23. _____
399.99	24. _____
Total	25. _____

PART 3   *Review and Practice Using Business Math FUNdamentals*

GOAL: Complete 9 of the 10 problems correctly.

Instructions: *Start Business Math FUNdamentals. Complete Tutorials 15 through 18 and Drills 7 through 10. If you are not satisfied with your scores, repeat the drills. Write your scores below.*

Business Math FUNdamentals Drill 7

Today's Date	Score

Business Math FUNdamentals Drill 8

Today's Date	Score

Business Math FUNdamentals Drill 9

Today's Date	Score

Business Math FUNdamentals Drill 10

Today's Date	Score

PART 4   *The Desktop Calculator*

KEYSTROKING TECHNIQUE

Decimal Key

Use the 6 (ring) finger to press the decimal key. Try to leave the index finger hovering above the 4 key. The index finger should work as an anchor in order for you to bring the ring finger back to the 6 key on the home row after pressing the decimal key. If your fingers do leave the home row, feel for the small dot or other mark on the 5 key to make sure your fingers are on the home row before continuing to key. Although awkward at first, this motion will become automatic with practice.

In numbers such as 0.3410 the 0 preceding the decimal is referred to as a **leading zero**. The ending zero is referred to as a **trailing zero**. It is not necessary to key preceding zeros or trailing zeros because both are merely placeholders. Simply key .341 and continue the problem.

Exception: See Setting the Add Mode below. However, when recording answers such as 0.56, the zero is always written in front of the decimal.

USING THE FLOATING DECIMAL SETTING

To add numbers with varying decimal places without rounding the answer, set the decimal selector on the **floating decimal setting**.

MACHINE SETUP Decimal Selector—F (the decimal will be entered by the operator)

Rounding Switch—5/4 (the rounding function is inoperative when the decimal selector is set at F; therefore, the rounding switch setting is not important)

Tax Switch—CALC

Add. Key decimals as indicated. Check your answers.

1.	2.	3.	4.	5.
1,164.45	62,155.10	184.2	96.777	15.4
16.24	6.152	6.964	33.5	2.46
0.6717	0.353	2.71	1.64	34.5
9.16	4.9982	9.72	2.226	0.158
3.318	145.1	0.151	0.37	12.47
1,193.8397	62,311.7032	203.745	134.513	64.988

SETTING THE ADD MODE

The **add mode** setting allows you to key numbers that all have two decimal places without pressing the decimal key. When using add mode, it will be necessary to key trailing zeros, as in the number 11.50.

MACHINE SETUP Decimal Selector—+ (add mode)

Rounding Switch—5/4 (the rounding function is inoperative when the decimal selector is set at +; therefore, the rounding switch setting is not important)

Tax Switch—CALC

Add, using the add mode. DO NOT key the decimal point. Check your answers.

6.	7.	8.	9.	10.
.39	4.53	22.72	2.68	575.44
1.20	6.91	45.83	56.36	381.99
.34	7.81	24.91	161.58	921.95
.15	9.82	67.73	224.68	652.96
.64	1.83	81.53	13.21	673.97
2.72	30.90	242.72	458.51	3,206.31

SETTING THE ROUNDING SWITCH

The **rounding switch** works in conjunction with the decimal selector to round answers automatically at the decimal place selected by the 10-key operator. There are usually three settings for the rounding switch: rounding down, the 5/4 position, and rounding up. We will first look at the 5/4 position.

The 5/4 position is usually the middle position. When the calcultor is set at the 5/4 rounding position and the decimal selector has been set at the desired number of decimal places, results are rounded in the same manner as discussed at the beginning of this chapter under Business Math Skills; that is, results are rounded depending on value and decimal setting.

Example: If the decimal selector is set at 2, the number 2.33<u>8</u> will be rounded to 2.34. The number 2.33<u>4</u> will be rounded to 2.33.

EXAMPLE

Add the following numbers, rounding the answer to two decimal places. Add the numbers again without rounding. Compare the two results. Did the calculator round the first answer correctly?

Calculation 1

TAPE 7.1:

```
47,678·339  +
 9,165·332  −
38,513·01   *
```

MACHINE SETUP   Decimal Selector—2
Rounding Switch—5/4

Problem:	Procedure:
47,678.339	47,678.339 +
−9,165.332	9,165.332 − */T
	38,513.01

Notice that the rounding does not take place until the total key is pressed.

Calculation 2

TAPE 7.2:

```
47,678·339  +
 9,165·332  −
38,513·007  *
```

MACHINE SETUP   Decimal Selector—F (no decimals will be cut off or rounded)
Rounding Switch—5/4 (the setting of the rounding switch does not matter when the decimal selector is set at F; no rounding will take place)

Problem:	Procedure:
47,678.339	47,678.339 +
−9,165.332	9,165.332 − */T
	38,513.007

Name _____

Class/Section _____

Score (Correct Answers ÷ No. of Assigned Problems) _____

PART 4   *Desktop Calculator*

Set the rounding switch at 5/4 for the following problems. Follow instructions below for setting the decimal selector.

Exercise 1

Use the add mode to complete the following problems.

$195.78	$52.38	$24.76	$87.91	$98.27	$19.22	$18.52
+2.16	+1.25	+3.64	+12.59	+26.19	+34.71	+93.28
1. _____	2. _____	3. _____	4. _____	5. _____	6. _____	7. _____

Complete the following problems, setting the decimal selector to round answers to whole numbers.

	7.528	4.331	17.846	24.627	55.228	98.352	17.436
	+2.11	+.634	+1.324	+7.124	+9.156	+13.936	+23.652
	8. _____	9. _____	10. _____	11. _____	12. _____	13. _____	14. _____

Complete the following problems, setting the decimal selector to avoid rounding answers.

15. $164.132 - 1.551 =$ _____
17. $164.225 - 18.363 =$ _____
19. $932.413 - 19.514 =$ _____
21. $639.462 - 86.139 =$ _____
23. $102.541 - 70.5221 =$ _____

16. $134.291 - 21.147 =$ _____
18. $553.916 - 28.136 =$ _____
20. $223.463 - 94.385 =$ _____
22. $152.221 - 10.558 =$ _____
24. $47.701 - 38.254 =$ _____

Add the following numbers. Set the decimal selector to round the answers to the thousandths place.

25. $16.4559 + 25.4$ _____
27. $39.6533 + 9.987$ _____
29. $108.679321 + 1,012.345299$ _____

26. $26.5579 + 101.443$ _____
28. $55.03 + 69.3575$ _____
30. $0.62991 + 3.5543 + 11.3456$ _____

Subtract the following numbers. Round all answers to the ten thousandths place.

31. $10,369.7934695 - 648,406.4902$ _____
32. $35,559.6711347 - 292,349.998329$ _____
33. $2.3202897 - 0.68830945$ _____
34. $1.0345445 - 0.3220114$ _____
35. $699.3 - 54.987606$ _____

Exercise 2

Strokes per Minute Score _____

Accuracy Score (Correct Strokes ÷ Total Strokes) _____

One-Minute Addition Timing (Keys 0 through 9 and Decimal Key; Add Mode)

(Optional: Your instructor may wish you to use Touch Key on the computer for all your timings. Check with your instructor before completing this exercise.)

Complete as many of the problems as possible in 1 minute by adding. Work quickly and accurately. The number preceding each closing parenthesis indicates the cumulative number of strokes for problems attempted. For example, if you complete Problems 1 through 3 in 1 minute, your strokes-per-minute score is 154. Optional: 3- to 5-minute timings.

Use the floating decimal setting. Remember, it is not necessary to key leading or trailing zeros.

1.	2.	3.	4.	5.	6.	7.	8.
0.60	1.110	0.87	8.29	9.17	6.32	99.39	4.471
1.82	2.895	0.281	8.032	88.19	8.20	6.63	4.30
34.14	4.23	0.14	3.60	74.518	58.21	74.10	7.82
1.26	5.29	9.10	20.30	2.10	5.827	69.31	1.91
8.8	2.228	0.524	13.337	8.13	2.529	3.632	2.094
2.8	5.12	0.6610	6.748	2.417	2.828	5.228	2.010
2.41	25.71	2.3	1.173	5.419	6.30	6.930	5.419
355.1	6.81	31.5	6.13	9.630	9.37	5.857	6.39
82.5	3.187	43.6	0.21	6.39	7.19	3.361	7.82
1.28	8.3	2.73	0.10	6.931	5.29	8.252	4.85
50)	105)	154)	209)	267)	321)	381)	436)

9. 1.7	10. 5.23	11. 10.2	12. 30.5	13. 53.9	14. 25.0	15. 18.9	16. 76.5
7.3	2.7	45.3	19.4	15.9	39.7	14.3	28.9
9.7	3.7	82.5	27.1	83.6	62.0	62.7	48.6
4.0	7.2	18.4	84.8	25.6	31.9	15.4	45.2
1.9	1.9	32.5	21.6	54.6	33.0	49.0	61.2
1.3	3.0	38.8	45.0	48.6	38.4	23.3	67.3
1.0	4.9	65.2	36.6	35.2	47.1	16.3	63.0
1.7	1.0	20.1	54.3	14.3	62.2	58.3	65.7
1.9	7.4	81.7	25.4	57.2	55.7	28.7	68.5
6.94	3.54	78.8	21.9	19.6	14.4	14.8	41.6
478)	521)	572)	623)	674)	725)	776)	827)

Use the add mode. It is not necessary to key decimals; however, it IS necessary to key trailing zeros.

17. 6.37	18. 6.52	19. 5.91	20. 4.39	21. 8.37	22. 9.12	23. 2.19	24. 2.14
5.69	8.20	8.64	5.45	2.24	8.29	4.53	5.28
8.60	1.57	4.37	2.40	6.10	5.39	8.38	8.35
7.35	5.29	6.20	7.53	7.67	4.72	6.69	1.40
1.26	7.27	2.50	8.60	8.53	6.59	3.58	4.52
2.24	9.49	5.30	3.16	1.70	3.61	1.35	7.60
5.57	6.60	9.50	1.86	9.46	1.50	7.50	3.18
8.29	5.69	3.58	9.96	4.54	7.20	9.27	6.23
9.39	3.53	7.38	5.74	2.20	2.30	5.15	9.30
4.34	4.37	6.63	8.25	8.21	8.59	5.49	5.16
869)	910)	951)	992)	1,033)	1,074)	1,115)	1,156)

25. 22.47	26. 31.28	27. 92.60	28. 21.30	29. 70.20	30. 89.29	31. 18.59	32. 97.37
25.41	25.19	57.40	15.63	52.37	23.26	88.25	94.60
36.59	48.63	46.59	14.26	70.43	26.38	74.15	91.38
65.60	21.49	51.17	10.59	80.18	24.50	40.14	92.67
68.50	26.51	58.23	50.69	90.51	85.42	78.13	93.43
12.59	89.62	52.38	62.67	10.29	87.10	79.35	95.60
29.64	35.13	59.67	60.63	20.32	49.57	76.31	98.53
45.51	42.20	96.62	85.30	30.16	43.59	73.36	48.25
62.43	50.25	98.53	20.37	40.59	41.53	72.26	42.56
69.63	65.34	33.62	30.31	50.48	45.60	75.34	26.39
1,207)	1,258)	1,309)	1,360)	1,411)	1,462)	1,513)	1,564)

CHAPTER 7 *Terminology Review*

Add mode
Decimal alignment
Decimal number
Decimal point
Floating decimal setting
Fraction
Hundred thousandths
Hundredths
Leading zero
Rounding switch
Ten thousandths
Tenths
Thousandths
Trailing zero

Insert the missing words to complete the following statements.

1. When adding or subtracting decimal numbers using pen and paper, correct _____ is essential.

2. To round to the _____ place, determine whether the digit in the ten thousandths place is 5 or greater.

3. A _____ separates the two parts of a _____.

4. A _____ and a _____ may both be used to represent a portion.

Questions 5 through 8 pertain to the desktop calculator.

5. Set the decimal selector on a desktop calculator at four to round answers at the _____ place.

6. To avoid keying decimals for columns of numbers with two decimal places when using the desktop calculator, use the _____.

7. The _____ should be used when rounding of answers is not desired.

8. It is necessary to key _____ when using the add mode.

Circle the answers below that best follow the instructions given in this chapter for recording decimal numbers.

9. *Decimal numbers less than one.* Write five tenths as a decimal number.
   a. .5   b. 0.5

10. *Trailing zeros.* Round 1.11022 to the thousandths place.
    a. 1.110   b. 1.11

11. *Unnecessary zeros.* Round 6.11008 to the thousandths place. Do not use unnecessary zeros in your answer.
    a. 6.110   b. 6.11

12. *Dollars and cents.* Round and record 6.7892 as a dollars and cents answer.
    a. 6.79   b. $6.79   c. $6.7892   d. 6.7892

13. *Dollars.* Round and record 187.9558 as whole dollars.
    a. 187.96   b. $187.96   c. $188   d. 187.96

14. *Rounding to the first digit.* Round 4,699 to the first digit.
    a. 5,000   b. 4,700

Name _____

Class/Section _____

Score (Correct Answers ÷ No. of Assigned Problems) _____

Chapter 7 Review Exercises
Exercise 1

Write the following numbers in words.

1. 96.9 _____

2. 115.89 _____

3. 8,339.336 _____

4. 25,004.5671 _____

5. 116,782.99852 _____

Exercise 2

Write the following numbers using Arabic numerals.

6. Thirty-three hundredths _____

7. Three hundred and sixty-five thousandths _____

8. One and five thousand one hundred sixty-two ten thousandths _____

9. Ten and forty-two thousand three hundred sixty-five hundred thousandths _____

10. Twelve and six hundred eleven thousand four hundred twelve millionths _____

Exercise 3

Round to dollars and cents. Be sure to put a dollar sign and decimal point in your answer.

11. 45.704 _____   12. 51.394 _____   13. 1.5006 _____   14. 6.7951 _____

Round to the tenths place.

15. 1,359.98 _____   16. 2,905.51 _____   17. 1,290.45 _____

Round to the thousandths place.

18. 19.886601 _____   19. 87.456289 _____   20. 511.32472 _____

21. 26.2671 _____   22. 104.86515 _____   23. 6.3356 _____   24. 19.58341 _____

Add the following numbers. Round the answers to whole numbers.

25. 86.45 + 5.4 _____   26. 19.579 + 10.43 _____   27. 3.63 + 9.7 _____

Subtract the following numbers. Round the answers to the hundredths place.

28. 55.131 − 9.37 _____   29. 8.21 − 1.399 _____   30. 19.9 − 9.321 _____

Write the following decimal numbers as fractions.

31. 0.5 _____   32. 0.65 _____   33. 0.75 _____   34. 0.122 _____

Multiplication and Division of Decimal Numbers, Conversion of Measurements

PART 1 *Speed and Accuracy Building Using Touch Key*

GOALS: Your speed goal is 7,000 strokes per hour.
Your accuracy target goal range is 95% to 100%.

With each repetition of the drill, try to improve your speed without lowering your accuracy score. If your percent-of-accuracy score falls below 95%, review your finger position and technique. Then try again.

Instructions: *Start Touch Key. Complete Drill 1, Parts A through E, One-Minute Timings. Write your scores for strokes per hour and percent of accuracy below.*

Touch Key Drill 1—The 0 through 9 keys, Three-digit numbers, One-Minute Timings

	Today's Date	Strokes per Hour	Percent of Accuracy
A.			
B.			
C.			
D.			
E.			

PART 2 *Business Math Skills*

MULTIPLYING DECIMAL NUMBERS

When multiplying decimal numbers, align the rightmost digits of the multiplicand, multiplier, and product. After multiplying, count the number of decimal places in the multiplicand and multiplier. The answer should contain this number of decimal places. Place the decimal point accordingly.

In Figure 8.1, there are three decimal places in the multiplicand and multiplier. This tells us that there must be three decimal places in the product. Has the decimal point been inserted correctly?

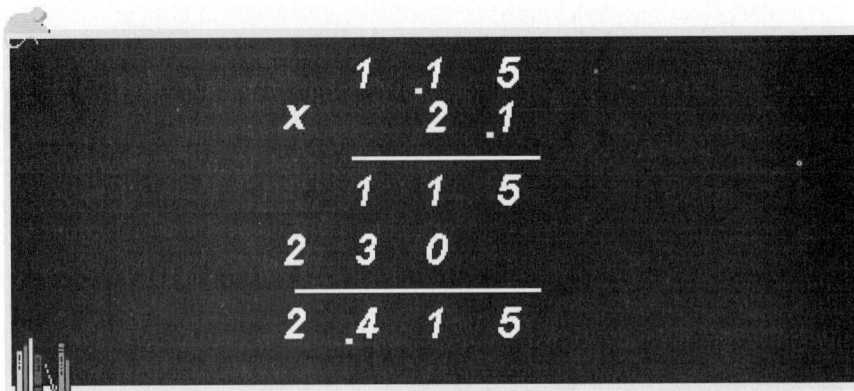

FIGURE 8.1

DIVIDING DECIMAL NUMBERS

In a division problem a dividend, divisor, or both may be a decimal number. When the dividend is a decimal number, be careful to align the decimal in the quotient vertically with the decimal in the dividend as shown in Figure 8.2.

Divide as usual as shown in Figure 8.3.

Add as many zeros to the dividend as necessary to carry the answer out to the desired number of decimal places or until there is no remainder (Figure 8.4).

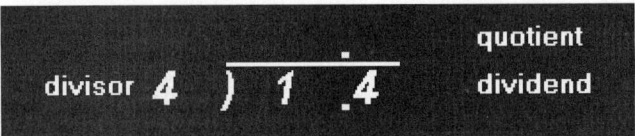

FIGURE 8.2

```
                    .3      quotient
divisor  4  )  1  .4        dividend
           -   1   2
               2
```

FIGURE 8.3

```
                    .3  5   quotient
divisor  4  )  1  .4  0
           -   1   2
                    2  0    partial dividend
               -    2  0
                    0
```

FIGURE 8.4

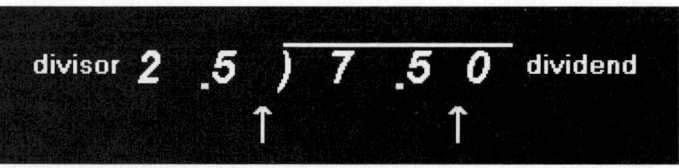

FIGURE 8.5

$$\begin{array}{r} 3.0 \quad \text{quotient} \\ \text{divisor } 2\ 5.\overline{)7\ 5.0} \quad \text{dividend} \\ -\ 7\ 5 \\ \hline 0 \\ 0 \\ \hline \end{array}$$

FIGURE 8.6

When the divisor contains one or more decimal places, move the decimal to the right enough places so that the divisor becomes a whole number. Move the decimal the same number of places in the dividend. In Figure 8.5 the divisor contains one decimal place. The decimal is moved one place to the right in both the divisor and the dividend.

Write the decimal in the quotient vertically aligned with the decimal in the dividend. Divide as usual.

Following are some examples of problems in which the decimal point should be moved before division occurs. Notice the placement of the decimal point in the quotient directly above the decimal point in the dividend.

Problem	*Rewrite as*	*Solution*
$.5\overline{)14.9}$	$5\overline{)149.0}$	$\overset{29.8}{5\overline{)149.0}}$
$6.09\overline{)900.8}$	$609\overline{)90,080.0}$	$\overset{147.91461}{609\overline{)90,080.00000}}$
$.3\overline{)99}$	$3\overline{)990.}$	$\overset{330.0}{3\overline{)990.0}}$
$3\overline{).21}$	$3\overline{).21}$	$\overset{.07}{3\overline{).21}}$

ROUNDING INFINITE NUMBERS

Sometimes the result of division is a **repeating decimal number** (an infinite number) such as .33333333 . . . , which is the result of $1 \div 3$. There are several ways to express an infinite number:

.3333   Round to *x* number of decimal places.

$.\overline{3}$ Place a bar over the decimal number to indicate a repeating decimal.

.33 1/3   Although used less frequently, this is the most accurate representation of the quotient of $1 \div 3$.

The result of $2 \div 3$ is .6666666 . . . ; it can be expressed as follows:

.6667   Round to *x* number of decimal places.

$.\overline{6}$ The bar over the number indicates a repeating decimal.

.66 2/3   Another representation of the quotient of $2 \div 3$.

ACCURACY IN MULTIPLYING AND DIVIDING DECIMAL NUMBERS

How accurate is accurate? How many decimal places are sufficient? When discrepancies of a tenth, a hundredth, a thousandth, and so on, occur, it is usually attributed to **rounding error**. Calculators and computers vary in the number of decimals that can be accommodated and also in the logic and tables used to comprise answers. Knowing this, what can we do to ensure consistency?

Certain rounding conventions are generally used. Some problems contain more than one multiplication or division operation. The results of all but the final operation are called **intermediate answers**. The result of the final operation is called the **final answer**.

EXAMPLE

Jane calculated an intermediate simple rate of 0.0125 monthly for an investment. If $1,000 is invested at this rate for 60 months, how much will be earned?

Correct	**Incorrect**
$0.0125 \times 60 = .75$	$0.013 \times 60 = .78$ The rate should not be rounded because it is an intermediate answer
$.75 \times 1,000 = \$750.00$	$.78 \times 1,000 = \$780.00$

If the calculation was for 20 years (240 months), what would the error be?

Correct	**Incorrect**
$0.0125 \times 240 \times 1,000 = \$3,000.00$	$0.013 \times 240 \times 1,000 = \$3,120.00$

Because the intermediate answer was rounded, a $120 error resulted.

To avoid rounding errors:

1. Watch for instructions that pertain to rounding final answers.
2. Do not round intermediate answers unless directed otherwise.
3. Round final dollars and cents answers to two places unless directed otherwise.

CONVERSIONS

Whether it's calculating how much punch will be needed for the office Christmas party, changing kilometers driven to miles driven, or budgeting for replacement carpet in an office building, a knowledge of **conversions** is essential. Many business activities involve converting one form of measurement to another, such as feet to yards, ounces to gallons, square inches to square feet, and so on. Begin by consulting the **conversion chart**. Becoming familiar with the more common conversions will give you confidence.

Number of feet may be indicated by placing a single quote mark to the right of a number. Number of inches may be indicated by placing a double quote mark to the right of a number. Some commonly used abbreviations are as follows:

inches	in	ounces	oz	seconds	sec
feet	ft	pounds	lb	minutes	min
yards	yd	grams	g	hours	hr
miles	mi	kilograms	kg	miles per hour	mph
square	sq	cups	c	miles per gallon	mpg
millimeters	mm	pints	pt	words per minute	wpm
centimeters	cm	quarts	qt	teaspoon	tsp
meters	m	gallons	gal	tablespoon	tbs
kilometers	km	liters	L		
tons	t	milliliters	ml		

Notice that the abbreviations for measurements are not followed by a period. However, the abbreviation for inches may be followed by a period (*in.*) if there is a chance of mistaking the abbreviation for the word *in*. The same abbreviation is used for both the singular and the plural forms of a unit of measurement.

Conversion Chart

Distance Measurements

To Convert . . .	Multiply . . .	To Convert . . .	Divide . . .
Feet to inches	Number of feet × 12″	Inches to feet	Number of inches ÷ 12″
Yards to feet	Number of yards × 3′	Feet to yards	Number of feet ÷ 3′
Yards to inches	Number of yards × 36″	Inches to yards	Number of inches ÷ 36″
Miles to feet	Number of miles × 5,280′	Feet to miles	Number of feet ÷ 5,280′
Millimeters to inches	Number of millimeters × 0.04	Inches to millimeters	Number of inches ÷ 0.04
Centimeters to inches	Number of centimeters × 0.39	Inches to centimeters	Number of inches ÷ 0.39
Meters to inches	Number of meters × 39.4	Inches to meters	Number of inches ÷ 39.4
Meters to feet	Number of meters × 3.28	Feet to meters	Number of feet ÷ 3.28
Meters to yards	Number of meters × 1.09	Yards to meters	Number of yards ÷ 1.09
Kilometers to miles	Number of kilometers × 0.62	Miles to kilometers	Number of miles ÷ 0.62

Weight Measurements

To Convert . . .	Multiply . . .	To Convert . . .	Divide . . .
Pounds to ounces	Number of pounds × 16 oz	Ounces to pounds	Number of ounces ÷ 16 oz
Tons to pounds	Number of tons × 2,000	Pounds to tons	Number of pounds ÷ 2,000
Grams to ounces	Number of grams × 0.04	Ounces to grams	Number of ounces ÷ 0.04
Kilograms to pounds	Number of kilograms × 2.2	Pounds to kilograms	Number of pounds ÷ 2.2

Liquid or Volume Measurements

To Convert . . .	Multiply . . .	To Convert . . .	Divide . . .
Cups to fluid ounces	Number of cups × 8 oz	Fluid ounces to cups	Number of ounces ÷ 8 oz
Pints to fluid ounces	Number of pints × 16 oz	Fluid ounces to pints	Number of ounces ÷ 16 oz
Quarts to fluid ounces	Number of quarts × 32 oz	Fluid ounces to quarts	Number of ounces ÷ 32 oz
Quarts to cups	Number of quarts × 4	Cups to quarts	Number of cups ÷ 4
Gallons to fluid ounces	Number of gallons × 128 oz	Fluid ounces to gallons	Number of ounces ÷ 128 oz
Pints to cups	Number of cups × 2	Cups to pints	Number of cups ÷ 2
Quarts to pints	Number of quarts × 2	Pints to quarts	Number of pints ÷ 2
Quarts to liters	Number of quarts × 1.06	Liters to quarts	Number of liters ÷ 1.06
Gallons to quarts	Number of gallons × 4	Quarts to gallons	Number of quarts ÷ 4
Gallons to liters	Number of gallons × 3.79	Liters to gallons	Number of liters ÷ 3.79

Time Measurements

To Convert . . .	Multiply . . .	To Convert . . .	Divide . . .
Minutes to seconds	Number of minutes × 60 sec	Seconds to minutes	Number of seconds ÷ 60 sec
Hours to minutes	Number of hours × 60 min	Minutes to hours	Number of minutes ÷ 60 min

For additional measurements, see Table of Measurements, The American Heritage College Dictionary, Houghton Mifflin Co., Boston, Massachusetts.

It is generally understood that the number of ounces in a pound refers to weight, and the number of ounces in a cup, pint, quart, or gallon refers to either liquid or volume.

VOLUME VERSUS WEIGHT

Some products, such as breakfast cereal, are sold by weight, not by volume, the amount of space the cereal occupies. Which is a more accurate measure of the amount? Suppose a box of cereal is full when it is packed, but after shipment, the customer opens it and finds that it is only three-fourths full? The cereal does not occupy as much space, but it still weighs the same as it did the day it was packed. Therefore, weight is a more accurate measure of the amount of a product that may settle. However, a bar of 3½″ by 12″ cold-rolled steel will not change shape or volume during shipment. A quart of orange juice will not change in volume during shipment. Therefore, whether a product is sold by weight or by volume depends on the type of product.

MATH STAR 8.1

BE A *Math*★ !

What To Do with Decimal Places

Let's see how to quickly multiply and divide numbers containing decimal places. We will combine this with some of the Math Star shortcuts you learned earlier. What a great opportunity to review!

Multiplying Decimal Numbers

Problem 1: 2.2 × 1.01.

22 × 101 = 2222 — **Step 1:** Disregard the three decimal places in the multiplicand and multiplier. Multiply.

2.222 — **Step 2:** Since there are three decimal places in the multiplicand and multiplier, place the decimal point so that there are three decimal places in the product.

Dividing Decimal Numbers

Problem 2: 48 ÷ 1.2.

48 ÷ 12 = 4 — **Step 1:** Disregard the decimal place in the divisor. Divide.

4 × 10 = 40 — **Step 2:** Because one decimal place was disregarded, multiply the result of step 1 by 10.

Problem 3: 480 ÷ 0.12

48 ÷ 12 = 4 — **Step 1:** Disregard the trailing zero and the two decimal places. Divide.

40 — **Step 2:** Replace the disregarded zero in the answer.

40 × 100 = 4,000 — **Step 3:** Since two decimal places were disregarded, multiply by 100.

Multiplying by 5 and 50

Instead of multiplying a number by 5, divide by 2 and then multiply by 10.

Problem 4: 25 × 5.

25 ÷ 2 = 12.5 — **Step 1:** Divide by 2.

125 — **Step 2:** Multiply by 10; that is, move the decimal point one place to the right.

Problem 5: 1.2 × 50

12 ÷ 2 = 6 — **Step 1:** Disregard the trailing zero and the decimal place. Divide by 2.

6 × 10 = 60 — **Step 2:** Multiply by 10.

600 — **Step 3:** Replace the disregarded zero.

60.0 — **Step 4:** Since one decimal place was disregarded, mark one decimal place in the answer.

(continued)

MATH STAR 8.1 *(continued)*

Dividing by 5

Conversely, instead of dividing by 5, it is possible to multiply by 2 and then move the decimal point one place to the left.

Problem 6: 42 ÷ 5

42 × 2 = 84   **Step 1:** Multiply by 2.

8.4   **Step 2:** Move the decimal point one place to the left; that is, multiply by .10.

Problem 7: 2.2 ÷ 5

22 × 2 = 44   **Step 1:** Disregard the decimal place. Multiply by 2.

4.4   **Step 2:** Move the decimal point one place to the left.

.44   **Step 3:** Since one decimal place was disregarded, move the decimal point one place to the left.

Problem 8: 4.2 ÷ 5

42 × 2 = 84   **Step 1:** Disregard the decimal place. Multiply by 2.

8.4   **Step 2:** Move the decimal point one place to the left.

.84   **Step 3:** Since one decimal place was disregarded, move the decimal point one place to the left.

Problem 9: 4.2 ÷ .5

42 × 2 = 84   **Step 1:** Disregard the two decimal places.* Multiply by 2.

8.4   **Step 2:** Move the decimal point one place to the left.

Because there is an equal number of decimal places in both the dividend and the divisor, the decimal places may be ignored.

Problem 10: 420 ÷ 50

42 × 2 = 84   **Step 1:** Disregard the trailing zero in both the dividend and the divisor.* Multiply by 2.

8.4   **Step 2:** Move the decimal point one place to the left.

Because there is an equal number of trailing zeros in both the dividend and the divisor, the decimal places may be ignored.

Try it for yourself!

1. 5.4 × 1.1
2. 3.1 × 10.1
3. 14 ÷ 5
4. 1.3 × 4
5. 360 ÷ .4
6. 3.4 × 5
7. 250 × 50
8. 900 ÷ 50

Answers: 1. 5.94 **2.** 31.31 **3.** 2.8 **4.** 5.2 **5.** 900 **6.** 17 **7.** 12,500 **8.** 18

PART 2 *Business Math Skills*

Exercise 1

Use shortcuts learned in Math Star 8.1 when applicable.

Multiply. Do not round answers.

12.5	90.6	9.5	62.4	89.1
×4.2	×0.3	×1.5	×1.2	×6.2

1. _____ 2. _____ 3. _____ 4. _____ 5. _____

6.125	5.02	22.3	2.5	1.2
×9.2	×0.134	×10.1	×5	×50

6. _____ 7. _____ 8. _____ 9. _____ 10. _____

Rewrite the following problems, moving the decimals as necessary. Divide. Round answers to hundredths.

11. $0.5\overline{)6.5}$ 12. $0.20\overline{)15.0}$ 13. $0.3\overline{)9.0}$

14. $0.15\overline{)6.5}$ 15. $2.6\overline{)4.29}$ 16. $3.5\overline{)7.95}$

Solve.

17. $6.5 \times 1.2 =$ _____   18. $65.00 \div 2.00 =$ _____

19. $2{,}200 \times 0.4 =$ _____   20. $48 \div 1.2 =$ _____

Convert. Round to tenths if necessary.

21. 2.25 gal to oz _____   22. 16.3 ft to yd _____

23. 5.5 qt to gal _____   24. 57 ft to in _____

25. 48 oz to pt _____   26. 11,000 ft to mi _____

27. 32 L to gal _____   28. 400,000 lb to t _____

29. 8.5 c to oz _____   30. 4.5 lb to oz _____

31. 360 min to hr _____   32. 60 t to lb _____

33. 16 pt to qt _____   34. 97 m to yd _____

Exercise 2

35. Bob's monthly insurance premium is $1.50 per $100 of coverage. If he purchases $2,200 of coverage, what will he pay for insurance each month? _____

36. If the price of a stock is $34.9 per share, how much will 100 shares of the stock cost? _____

PART 3 *The Pocket and Windows Calculators*

PROCEDURE

When multiplying or dividing decimal numbers, enter the decimals as written in the problem. If rounding is required, round mentally to the desired number of decimal places.

Problem 1	Procedure	Check
44.4 ÷ 0.9	44.4 ÷ .9 = $\boxed{49.3333333333}$ Round mentally to two decimal places—49.33	49.33 × .9 = $\boxed{44.397}$ Round mentally to one decimal place—49.4

Problem 2	Procedure	Check
12.375 × 0.1	12.375 × .1 = $\boxed{1.2375}$	÷ .1 = $\boxed{12.375}$

CALCULATOR FUN

Complete the following chart. Do not round. You will see an interesting mathematical phenomenon evolve.

1 ÷ 9 = .1111111	10 ÷ 9 = _____	100 ÷ 9 = _____
2 ÷ 9 = _____	20 ÷ 9 = _____	200 ÷ 9 = _____
3 ÷ 9 = _____	30 ÷ 9 = _____	300 ÷ 9 = _____
4 ÷ 9 = _____	40 ÷ 9 = _____	400 ÷ 9 = _____
5 ÷ 9 = _____	50 ÷ 9 = _____	500 ÷ 9 = _____
6 ÷ 9 = _____	60 ÷ 9 = _____	600 ÷ 9 = _____
7 ÷ 9 = _____	70 ÷ 9 = _____	700 ÷ 9 = _____
8 ÷ 9 = _____	80 ÷ 9 = _____	800 ÷ 9 = _____
9 ÷ 9 = _____	90 ÷ 9 = _____	900 ÷ 9 = _____

Now try some larger numbers in completing the following chart. Also use some numbers that are meaningful to you, such as the month of your mother's birthday, making sure the *dividend is smaller than the divisor.* You should see definite patterns emerge.

8 ÷ 999 = _____	The last two digits of your birth year ÷ 999 = _____
80 ÷ 999 = _____	The last three digits of your social security number ÷ 999 = _____
	(Remember the three digits must be smaller than 999)
800 ÷ 999 = _____	_____ ÷ 999 = _____
409 ÷ 999 = _____	_____ ÷ 999 = _____
622 ÷ 999 = _____	_____ ÷ 999 = _____
715 ÷ 999 = _____	_____ ÷ 999 = _____

Name _____

Class/Section _____

Score (Correct Answers ÷ No. of Assigned Problems) _____

 # PART 3 *Pocket or Windows Calculator*

Exercise 1

Multiply. Do not round answers.

12.3	27.4	15.6	17.8	39.2	2.459	8.164
×6	×8	×2.1	×6.2	×6.2	×0.1	×3.56
1. _____	2. _____	3. _____	4. _____	5. _____	6. _____	7. _____

Divide. Round to four places, if necessary.

8. 55.25 ÷ 16 = _____

9. 69.3 ÷ 1.3 = _____

10. 25.8 ÷ 2.44 = _____

11. 265.17 ÷ 12.9 = _____

12. 620 ÷ 10 = _____

13. 100.89 ÷ 2.25 = _____

14. 5,995 ÷ 7.75 = _____

15. 1,999.85 ÷ 4.5 = _____

Convert. Round to hundredths as necessary.

16. 25.5 qt to gal _____

17. 3.6 ft to in _____

18. 34 oz to lb _____

19. 5 yd to ft _____

20. 29.3 c to qt _____

21. 69 ft to yd _____

22. 325 oz to gal _____

23. 14,500 ft to mi _____

24. 1,200 oz to c _____

25. 3.2 mi to ft _____

26. 5 c to pt _____

27. 6,900 lb to t _____

Exercise 2

Complete the following sales report. Selling price for each model should be multiplied by the number of units sold. Find a grand total. Check your answers.

Frontier Log Home Kits
Yearly Sales Report

Model No.	Selling Price ($)	Units Sold	Totals
198A	89,798.98	15	28. _____
198B	69,799.99	12	29. _____
298A	75,898.88	26	30. _____
298B	150,989.99	18	31. _____
			32. _____

Exercise 3

33. A salesman in eastern Canada submitted mileage of 560 km on his expense report. The U.S. company for which he works pays $0.32 per mile. How much should he be reimbursed?_____

34. A group sold 1,600 cartons of Fund Raiser cookies. Each carton contained 12 boxes of cookies. The boxes sold for $3.15 each. Calculate total sales for the group._____

PART 3   *Review and Practice Using Business Math FUNdamentals*

GOAL: Complete 9 of the 10 problems correctly.

Instructions: *Start Business Math FUNdamentals. Complete Tutorials 19 and 20 and Drills 11 and 12. If you are not satisfied with your scores, repeat the drills. Write your scores below.*

Business Math FUNdamentals Drill 11

Today's Date	Score

Business Math FUNdamentals Drill 12

Today's Date	Score

PART 4 *The Desktop Calculator*

KEYSTROKING TECHNIQUE

Use the middle finger to key the double zero (00) key. Try to keep the little finger hovering over the plus key as you reach for the 00 key. Return fingers to the home row after pressing the double zero key. For numbers containing three zeros, develop the habit of keying the zero key first (with the thumb), then the double zero key (with the middle finger).

Add. Use the double zero key whenever possible. Check your answers.

1.	2.	3.	4.	5.	6.	7.	8.
9,064	4,801	7,000	2,700	1,700	3,002	3,009	7,100
5,002	9,000	8,400	3,200	1,800	2,005	9,003	3,300
1,804	2,003	9,004	9,100	1,800	2,001	1,900	8,200
7,006	2,700	7,001	3,300	1,002	2,004	3,001	9,100
5,500	9,005	2,900	3,700	1,003	2,006	3,002	6,400
8,005	1,000	7,005	7,800	1,700	2,500	2,005	1,300
4,190	8,004	2,003	7,300	1,900	3,300	3,003	4,600
5,100	9,001	3,900	1,003	3,005	3,100	5,007	6,600
5,000	5,700	7,300	2,000	3,006	1,900	6,001	5,200
7,700	5,500	2,300	1,200	3,001	2,009	5,200	5,500
58,371	56,714	56,813	41,303	19,917	23,827	41,131	57,300

PROCEDURE

When multiplying or dividing decimal numbers, enter the decimals as written in the problem.

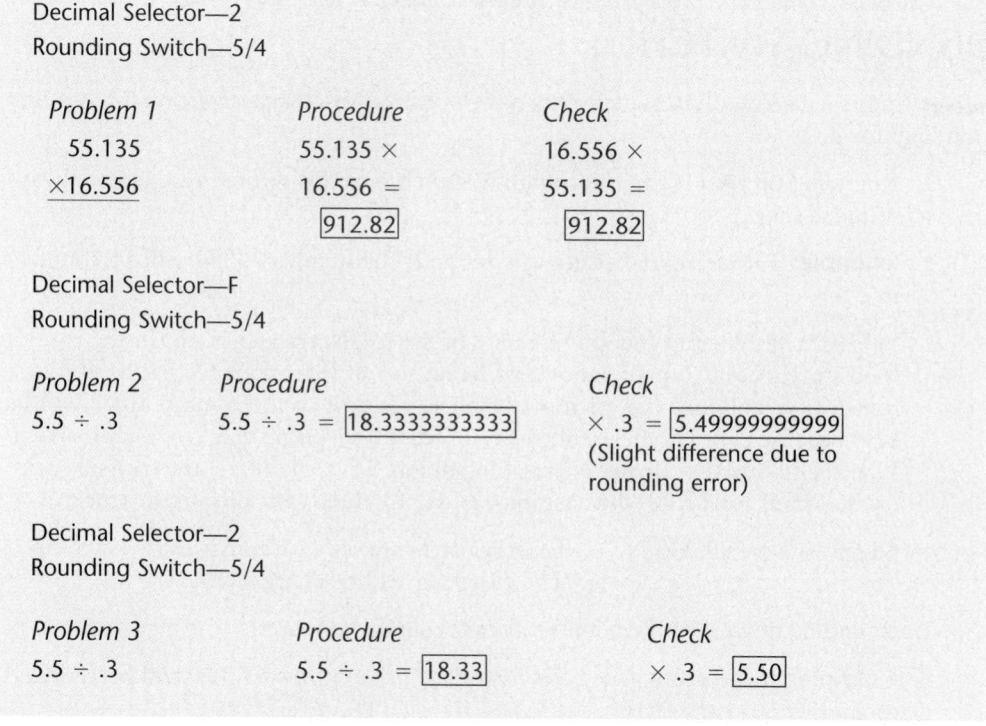

Decimal Selector—2
Rounding Switch—5/4

Problem 1	Procedure	Check
55.135	55.135 ×	16.556 ×
×16.556	16.556 =	55.135 =
	912.82	912.82

Decimal Selector—F
Rounding Switch—5/4

Problem 2 Procedure Check
5.5 ÷ .3 5.5 ÷ .3 = 18.3333333333 × .3 = 5.49999999999
(Slight difference due to rounding error)

Decimal Selector—2
Rounding Switch—5/4

Problem 3 Procedure Check
5.5 ÷ .3 5.5 ÷ .3 = 18.33 × .3 = 5.50

MACHINE SETUP FOR MULTIPLYING AND DIVIDING DECIMAL NUMBERS

Set the rounding switch on 5/4 unless directed otherwise. Use one of the following machine setups for determining the decimal selector setting to be used. Note that setups 1 and 2 should result in the same answer.

Machine Setup 1: If a specific number of decimal places is required, set the decimal selector accordingly. If the number of decimal places is not specified, count the number of decimal places in the problem and use that number of decimal places. As you key the problem, enter decimal points as they appear in the problem.

Example: Set decimal selector at 4: $100 \div 6 = 16.6667$.

Machine Setup 2: Set the decimal selector on F. As you key the problem, enter decimal points as they appear in the problem. If rounding is required, round mentally to the desired number of decimal places.

Example: Set decimal selector at F: $100 \div 6 = 16.6666666666$. Mentally round to four places. The answer is 16.6667.

Machine Setup 3: If the problem contains dollars and cents, set the decimal selector on two places. Alternatively, set the decimal selector on add mode and avoid keying the decimals in the problem. Remember, however, that when using add mode, you must enter trailing zeros so that the calculator can "count" the correct number of decimal places for positioning the decimal point.

Example: Set decimal selector on +: $100 \div 6 = 16.67$.

Machine Setup 4: Remember that intermediate answers should not be rounded. Set the decimal selector on F. (Rounding is not activated when the floating decimal setting is used.) When all arithmetic operations for the problem have been completed, mentally round the final answer.

MORE ON THE ROUNDING SWITCH

Two settings of the rounding switch that have not been discussed are **rounding up** and **rounding down**.

1. **Rounding up (▲):** When the rounding switch is at this setting, results are always rounded up.

   Example: If the decimal selector is set at 2, the number 2.334 will be rounded to 2.34.

   Cash registers and fuel pumps may be set to always round up. In the case of food store prices, tomato sauce may be on sale at three cans for $1.00. If a customer buys only one can of tomato sauce, the cost of the tomato sauce will be $.34 because the customer cannot pay 1/3 cent (there is no U.S. currency less than 1 cent) and the store owner is unwilling to lose 1/3 cent. To get the true sale price of three cans for $1.00, the customer must buy three cans of tomato sauce:

   $1.00 \div 3 = \$0.33333$ Cash registers are set to automatically round up. The customer will be charged $0.34.

2. **Rounding down (▼):** Results are always rounded down.

   Example: If the decimal selector is set at 2, the number 2.338 will be rounded to 2.33.

Sometimes rounding down is necessary when whole items are involved. If 84 pieces of candy are to be divided among 25 children, how many pieces of candy will each child receive? If we divided without rounding down, the result would be

$$84 \text{ pieces} \div 25 \text{ children} = 3\widehat{(36)}$$

Because we will be giving only whole pieces of candy, we need to know how many whole pieces to distribute. To round down to whole numbers, set the decimal selector on 0 and the rounding switch on ▼. Then the result is

$$84 \text{ pieces} \div 25 \text{ children} = 3$$

Name _____

Class/Section _____

Score (Correct Answers ÷ No. of Assigned Problems) _____

 # PART 4 *Desktop Calculator*

Exercise 1

Multiply. Set the machine to round to two decimal places.

612.3	9.554	91.56	2.9987	67.58	8.462	2.229
×5.56	×1.28	×12.291	×5.2	×4.46	×3.66	×0.25

1. _____   2. _____   3. _____   4. _____   5. _____   6. _____   7. _____

Divide. Set the machine to round to four decimal places.

8. $69.256 \div 0.59 =$ _____   9. $67.82 \div 3.5 =$ _____
10. $99.98 \div 2.74 =$ _____   11. $400.669 \div 5.9 =$ _____
12. $4,720 \div 0.10 =$ _____   13. $72.89 \div 0.12 =$ _____
14. $5,000 \div 700.75 =$ _____   15. $1,009.85 \div 400.3 =$ _____

Convert. Round to thousandths as necessary.

16. 36 oz to qt _____   17. 21,000 lbs to t _____
18. 19 oz to c _____   19. 486 oz to qt _____
20. 220 oz to lb _____   21. 486 oz to gal _____
22. 240 min to hr _____   23. 96 kg to lb _____

Exercise 2

24. Mrs. Levinsky's class had the following grades: 68, 54, 73, 75, 77, 72, 90, 89, and 88. Add the grades together and then divide by 9 to find the average grade. Set your machine to round down to whole numbers. _____

25. Terry sold 37 boxes of Fund Raiser cookies at $3.25 each. One customer paid for 3 boxes with a check. The other customers paid cash. How much cash did Terry receive for the cookies in addition to the check? Set the decimal selector at 2 and the rounding switch at 5/4. _____

26. What is the total amount of money received in Problem 25? _____

27. Does the answer change if you move the rounding switch to other positions as you work this problem? _____

Exercise 3

One-Minute Addition Timing (Keys 0 through 9; Add Mode)

(Optional: Your instructor may wish you to use Touch Key on the computer for all your timings. Check with your instructor before completing this exercise.)

Complete as many of the problems as possible in 1 minute by adding. Work quickly and accurately. The number preceding each closing parenthesis indicates the cumulative number of strokes for problems attempted. For example, if you complete Problems 1 through 4 in 1 minute, your strokes-per-minute score is 204. Optional: 3- to 5-minute timings.

1.	2.	3.	4.	5.	6.	7.	8.
6004	1001	8400	2006	5814	9200	3000	7001
5214	6500	5100	3002	9316	2500	6000	9003
1284	2305	7400	6001	1585	2100	1000	8002
1600	2876	1600	3003	7232	8400	3000	3001
5025	2745	9400	3004	7003	2006	3000	9004
2506	1002	1500	4005	8004	2005	2000	1002
4421	4571	2300	4003	6000	7003	3000	7007
5901	5631	7100	1003	3005	3004	5000	3004
5200	5994	4300	2001	5600	1006	6000	8005
2502	5300	5300	1002	9001	2006	5000	8003
51)	102)	153)	204)	255)	306)	357)	408)

9.	10.	11.	12.	13.	14.	15.	16.
1400	2900	7415	3502	3600	9722	1600	5004
7420	2700	2545	1002	8756	8734	3713	2600
6850	3956	5252	2005	3736	8965	3864	4000
4150	7002	8715	5008	2826	7936	3914	4870
1700	1000	9632	2796	3956	7835	3045	6002
1689	4702	3536	4502	2546	6731	2723	6003
1599	4005	2565	3046	3002	5741	2813	9514
7884	1002	1025	5213	1300	5962	9253	6787
1256	4008	5001	2001	5002	5854	9724	6412
6374	3005	4500	1600	1006	5014	1011	4600
459)	510)	561)	612)	663)	714)	765)	816)

Set decimal selector on add mode.

17.	18.	19.	20.	21.	22.	23.	24.
34.00	50.00	61.00	36.55	34.90	12.80	13.00	16.29
66.00	28.00	67.00	45.88	21.58	26.19	23.50	22.49
67.00	57.00	37.00	41.77	15.69	33.99	35.75	32.19
92.00	29.00	21.00	53.66	64.71	42.79	63.25	45.39
29.00	27.00	51.00	65.87	53.52	53.59	52.95	52.59
27.00	49.00	91.00	16.34	45.16	61.79	32.85	62.89
81.00	68.00	81.00	26.59	46.10	56.00	55.50	15.69
29.00	93.00	85.00	36.68	54.25	22.93	21.75	23.79
39.00	86.00	35.00	44.78	25.45	36.21	15.80	33.19
37.00	34.00	64.00	21.49	21.00	56.32	43.70	11.59
877)	938)	999)	1,060)	1,121)	1,182)	1,243)	1,304)

25.	26.	27.	28.	29.	30.	31.	32.
44.10	22.00	78.61	20.36	25.00	10.23	94.16	34.00
41.14	16.00	56.45	32.63	31.01	20.26	98.25	66.00
56.13	63.50	45.53	65.23	43.02	81.32	97.16	32.00
65.15	46.50	23.14	98.53	12.03	87.55	82.14	61.00
55.17	51.09	12.26	21.63	51.04	53.41	72.13	43.00
56.16	62.80	89.32	54.61	26.05	95.11	92.32	65.00
64.12	13.89	78.61	87.63	32.06	68.54	70.31	53.00
51.18	25.90	23.62	66.35	13.07	10.56	80.36	25.00
43.19	22.70	44.53	88.34	56.08	71.53	90.26	56.00
66.00	31.00	10.62	77.31	46.09	51.66	25.34	36.00
1,365)	1,426)	1,487)	1,548)	1,609)	1,670)	1,731)	1,792)

CHAPTER 8 *Terminology Review*

Conversion chart
Conversions
Final answer
Intermediate answers
Repeating decimal number
Rounding down
Rounding error
Rounding up

Insert the missing words to complete the following statements.

1. A(n) _____ is an answer that is usually not rounded.

2. An answer that, when checked, is found to be one hundredth of a point off may be the result of a(n) _____.

3. If a city and state tax rate results in a total of $88.1240, the customer will be charged $88.13 as a result of _____.

4. The _____ of a money problem should be rounded to two decimal places.

5. An infinite number is a(n) _____.

6. A number in which all decimals are dropped regardless of their value is a result of _____.

Answer with a sentence.

7. When dividing a dividend with a decimal point using pen and paper, place a decimal in the quotient where? _____

Answer true or false.

8. Add as many zeros to the dividend as necessary to carry the answer out to the desired number of decimal places (allowing for rounding) or until there is no remainder. T/F _____

9. When multiplying using pen and paper, David saw that there were three decimal places in the multiplicand and none in the multiplier. This indicated to David that there should be no decimal places in the product. T/F _____

10. When multiplying decimal numbers using pen and paper, always align the decimals in the multiplicand and the multiplier before beginning to multiply. T/F _____

11. When dividing, an equal number of decimal places in the divisor and in the dividend may be ignored without affecting the answer. T/F _____

Name _____

Class/Section _____

Score (Correct Answers ÷ No. of Assigned Problems) _____

Chapter 8 Review Exercises
Exercise 1

Multiply. Do not round.

15.125	10.58	57.35	81.6	100.5	8.759	280
×3.15	×2.24	×1.7	×7.2	×2.25	×3	×0.25
1. _____	2. _____	3. _____	4. _____	5. _____	6. _____	7. _____

Divide. Round to five places, as necessary.

8. $57.8 \div 0.9 =$ _____
9. $22.90 \div 0.5 =$ _____
10. $175.50 \div 2.5 =$ _____
11. $400 \div 5.2 =$ _____
12. $45.70 \div 1.50 =$ _____
13. $75.98 \div 2.2 =$ _____
14. $55.75 \div 7.5 =$ _____
15. $1,500 \div 5.8 =$ _____

Convert. Round to four places as necessary.

16. 62 oz to qt _____
17. 96.4 km to mi _____
18. 29.25 t to lb _____
19. 48 oz to c _____
20. 602 oz to lb _____
21. 69.3 ft to yd _____
22. 3.5 hr to min _____
23. 1.5 oz to g _____

Exercise 2

Better Bakers wishes to triple the following recipe. Can you help?

Original Italian Bread Recipe	Italian Bread Recipe (Ingredients Tripled)
8.5 oz water	24._____
0.5 oz olive oil	25._____
1.5 lb bread flour	26._____
2.5 tsp sugar	27._____
0.5 tsp salt	28._____
0.75 oz commercial yeast	29._____
1 egg white, beaten	30._____

Exercise 3

31. Randy walked 1.5 miles each day last week. If he walks the same number of miles for the next 12 weeks, how many miles will he have walked in all? _____
32. Joan can type 1,000 words in 10.75 minutes. How many words per minute does she type? Round the answer to two decimal places. _____
33. John bought lunch for five colleagues. Each had the lunch special at $9.95 (tax included). Each also had a soft drink at $1.75. How much did John spend for the meals? _____
34. An open-road race participant drives a truck that averages 2.8 miles per gallon. The race is 1,000 km long. How much gasoline will he need for the race? The answer should be rounded up to whole gallons. _____

Fractions, Word Problems

PART 1 *Speed and Accuracy Building Using Touch Key*

GOALS: Your speed goal is 7,500 strokes per hour.
Your accuracy target goal range is 95% to 100%.

With each repetition of the drill, try to improve your speed without lowering your accuracy score. If your percent-of-accuracy score falls below 95%, review your finger position and technique. Then try again.

Instructions: Start Touch Key. Complete Drill 1, Parts A and B, Three-Minute Timings. (Parts C through E are optional.) Write your scores for strokes per hour and percent of accuracy below.

Touch Key Drill 1—The 0 through 9 keys, Three-Digit Numbers, Three-Minute Timings

Today's Date	Strokes per Hour	Percent of Accuracy
A.		
B.		
C.		
D.		
E.		

PART 2 *Business Math Skills*

FRACTIONS

A **fraction** of an item is a part of that item. A fraction is formed by dividing one quantity into another. If an item has been divided into four equal parts and one of the parts has been sold, we can say that one fourth of the item was sold. The fraction one-fourth can be expressed by placing the number one (to represent the part that was sold) over the number four (to represent the total number of parts into which the item was divided). The two numbers should be separated by a horizontal line as in Figure 9.1. The top number of a fraction is the **numerator**. The bottom number of a fraction is the **denominator**. A fraction in which the numerator is smaller than the denominator is a **proper fraction**.

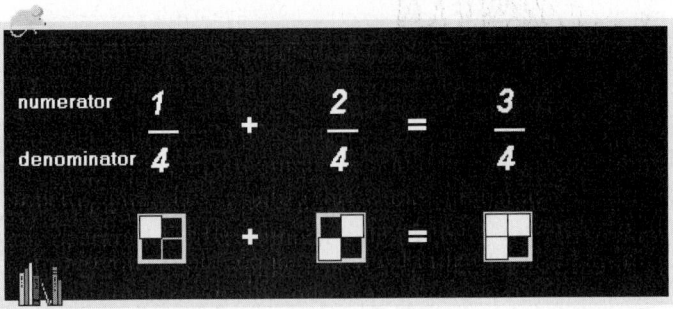

FIGURE 9.1

ADDING AND SUBTRACTING PROPER FRACTIONS

Just as it is possible to add or subtract like items (3 oranges plus 2 oranges = 5 oranges), it is possible to add or subtract fractions when the denominators are alike. Like denominators are referred to as **common denominators**. To add proper fractions with common denominators, add the numerators and place the sum over the same denominator. In Figure 9.1 one-fourth of a cake was placed on a tray. Later, an additional two-fourths of the cake was placed on the tray. One-fourth and two-fourths can be added to find that three-fourths of the cake now resides on the tray.

As stated earlier, fractions with common denominators can be subtracted. In the problem 7/8 − 6/8, subtract the two numerators and place the result over 8. The answer is 1/8:

$$\frac{7}{8} - \frac{6}{8} = \frac{1}{8}$$

EQUIVALENT FRACTIONS

Before two fractions with different denominators can be added or subtracted (see Figure 9.2), it is necessary to convert one or more of the fractions to **equivalent fractions** with common denominators. Equivalent fractions have the same value. The fractions 1/2, 2/4, and 8/16 are equivalent fractions—all equal 1/2 (see Figure 9.3).

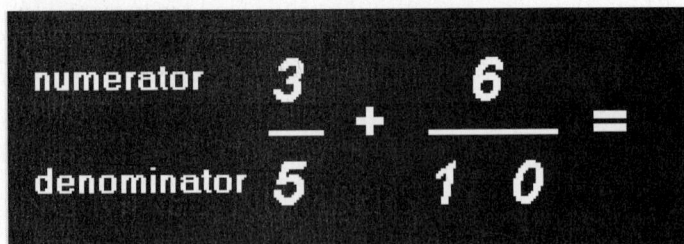

FIGURE 9.2

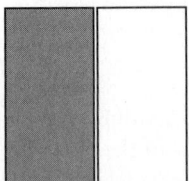 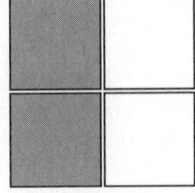 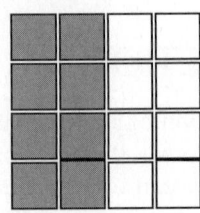

One of the two parts is red; 1/2 is red.   *Two of the four parts are red; 1/2 is red.*   *Eight of the 16 parts are red; 1/2 is red.*

FIGURE 9.3

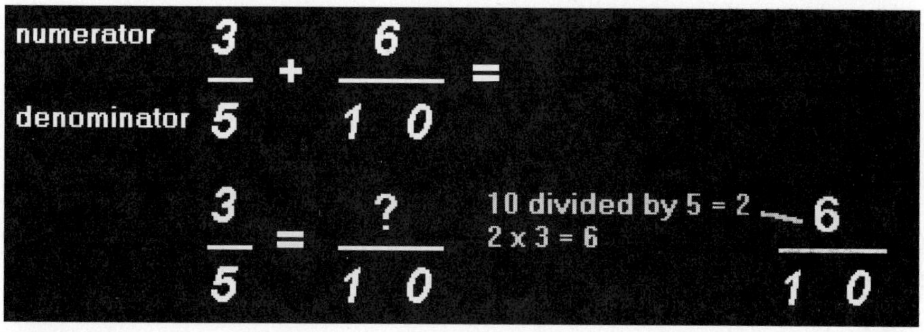

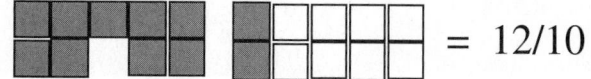

FIGURE 9.4

To convert a fraction to an **equivalent fraction of higher terms**, multiply both the numerator and the denominator by the same number. Refer to the problem in Figure 9.4.

First, note that the two denominators are 5 and 10, respectively. It is immediately apparent that 10 is evenly divisible by 5: $10 \div 5 = 2$.

Second, convert 3/5 to an equivalent fraction of higher terms by multiplying the numerator and the denominator by 2:

$$\frac{3 \times 2 = 6}{5 \times 2 = 10}$$

Third, replace 3/5 in the problem with the equivalent fraction of 6/10 (see Figure 9.5). Fourth, add the fractions: $6/10 + 6/10 = 12/10$.

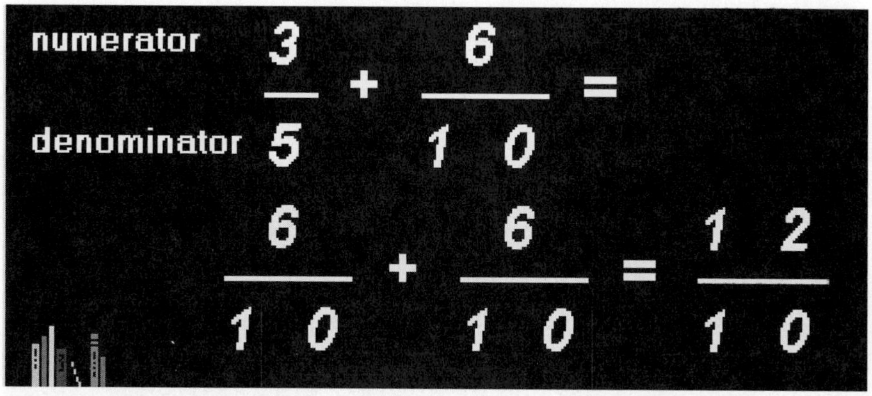

FIGURE 9.5

IMPROPER FRACTIONS

The result shown in Figure 9.5 (12/10) is an **improper fraction** because the numerator is larger than the denominator. Visualize this answer by drawing a picture (see Figure 9.6). The answer tells us that we have twelve tenths of something. Since ten-tenths represent one whole item, we have one item plus two parts of another item (two tenths) left over, or, $1\frac{2}{10}$. A number made up of both a whole number and a fraction, such as $1\frac{2}{10}$, is a **mixed number**.

$= 12/10$

FIGURE 9.6

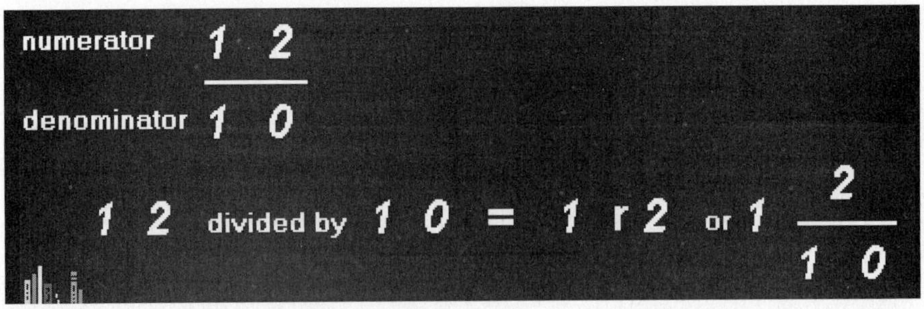

numerator   1 2
denominator 1 0

1 2   divided by   1 0 = 1 r 2   or 1 $\frac{2}{10}$

FIGURE 9.7

To convert 12/10 to a mixed number mathematically:

First, divide the numerator by the denominator mentally or using pen and paper (see Figure 9.7). The number of times the numerator can be divided by the denominator is the whole number portion of the mixed number.

Second, place the remainder over the denominator. This results in the fractional portion of the mixed number.

REDUCING FRACTIONS TO LOWEST TERMS

A fraction has been **reduced to lowest terms** when both the numerator and the denominator can no longer be divided evenly by any number except 1. As shown in Figure 9.8, both the numerator and the denominator of the fractional portion of 1²/₁₀ can be evenly divided by 2, resulting in an answer reduced to lowest terms: 1⅕.

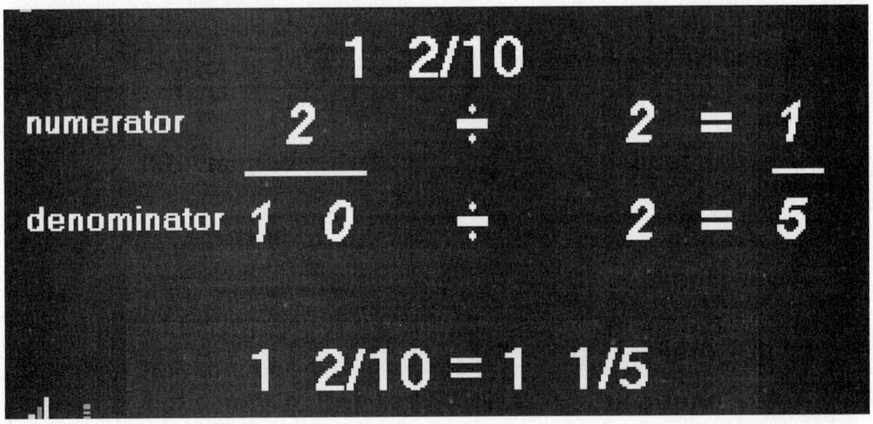

1 2/10

numerator   2 ÷ 2 = 1

denominator 1 0 ÷ 2 = 5

1 2/10 = 1 1/5

FIGURE 9.8

Reducing fractions to lowest terms makes them easier to understand. In Figure 9.9 the fraction 25/35 is easily reduced to lowest terms by dividing both the numerator and the

numerator   2 5 ÷ 5 = 5

denominator 3 5 ÷ 5 = 7

25/35 = 5/7

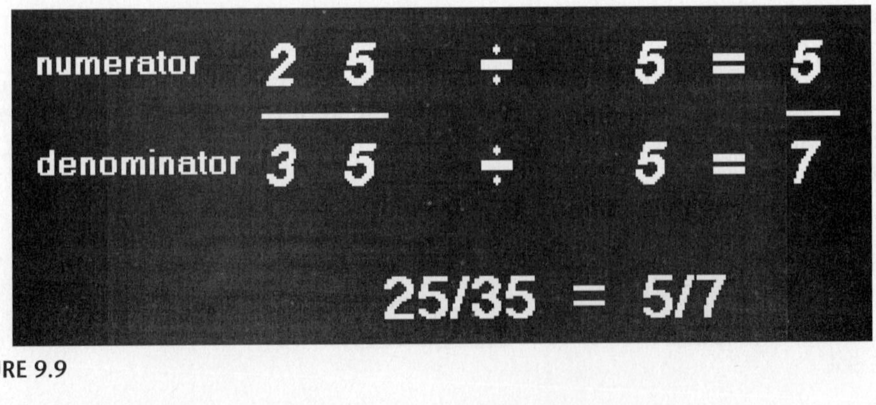

FIGURE 9.9

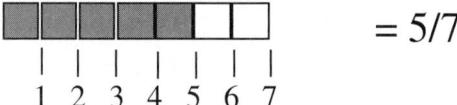

FIGURE 9.10

denominator by 5. The resulting fraction of 5/7 is much easier to visualize than 25/35 (see Figure 9.10).

Sometimes, as in Figure 9.11, the process of dividing the numerator and the denominator by a number may need to be repeated until the fraction has been reduced to lowest terms. After reducing 24/30 to 12/15, it is apparent that the fraction 12/15 may be further reduced by dividing the numerator and denominator by 3 for a result of 4/5.

$$\frac{24}{30} \div \frac{2}{2} = \frac{12}{15} \div \frac{3}{3} = \frac{4}{5}$$

FIGURE 9.11

DIVISIBILITY RULES

Table 9.1 contains some helpful rules for determining whether both the numerator and the denominator are evenly divisible by a number.

TABLE 9.1   Rules for Determining When a Number Is Evenly Divisible

Rule	Examples
A number is evenly divisible by	
2 if it ends in zero or an even number	20, 44, 282, 3,668
3 if the sum of the digits is divisible by 3	18, 39, 66, 285, 1,095
4 if the last two digits are both zeros, or if the last two digits are evenly divisible by 2	16, 48, 2300, 984
5 if it ends in zero or 5	15, 50, 65, 1,930
6 if it is even and the sum of the digits is divisible by 3	24, 78, 108, 2,730
9 if the sum of the digits is divisible by 9	27, 36, 135, 2,601
10 if it ends in zero	30, 500, 2,000, 99,000

LEAST COMMON DENOMINATOR

The **least common denominator** is the smallest number that can be evenly divided by all the denominators in a problem.

EXAMPLE

1/2 + 1/3 + 1/4. It is readily apparent that 12 is the smallest number that can be evenly divided by all the denominators in the problem. Convert each fraction to an equivalent fraction of higher terms with 12 as the denominator.

Figure 9.12 illustrates a counterclockwise motion to help you remember the procedure.

(continued)

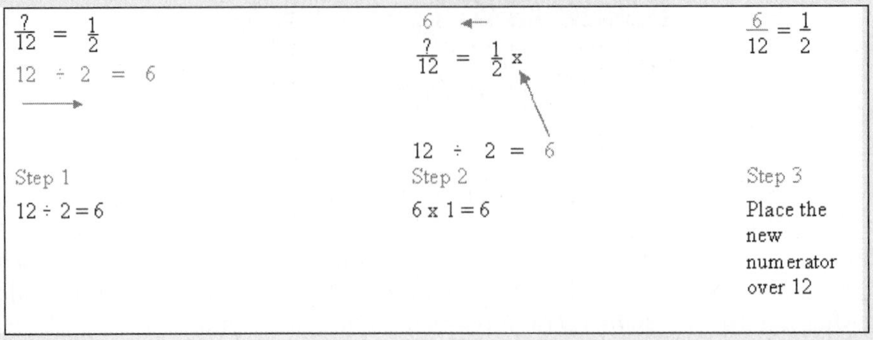

FIGURE 9.12

Convert

$$\frac{?}{12} = \frac{1}{2}, \qquad \frac{?}{12} = \frac{1}{3}, \qquad \frac{?}{12} = \frac{1}{4}$$

Repeat steps 1 through 3 to convert 1/3 and 1/4 to equivalent fractions with 12 as the denominator:

$$\frac{?}{12} = \frac{1}{3}: \qquad 12 \div 3 = 4; \qquad 4 \times 1 = 4; \qquad \text{Place 4 over 12}$$

$$\frac{?}{12} = \frac{1}{4}: \qquad 12 \div 4 = 3; \qquad 3 \times 1 = 3; \qquad \text{Place 3 over 12}$$

Add the numerators and place the result over 12: $6 + 4 + 3 = 13/12$.

Reduce to lowest terms: $13/12 = 1\frac{1}{12}$.

Whenever the least common denominator is not apparent, the prime number method can be used to determine the least common denominator. This method employs division of the denominators by prime numbers. A **prime number** is a number greater than 1 that can be divided evenly only by itself and 1. Prime numbers are 2, 3, 5, 7, 11, 13, 17, 19, 23, 29, 31, 37, 41, 43, 47, ...

PROBLEM

Find the least common denominator for one-sixth, one-fifth, and one-fourth using the prime number method and then add.

First, write the denominators (6, 5, and 4) in a row as in Figure 9.13.

Second, select the smallest prime number that will evenly divide some or all of the denominators. Write the prime number to the left of the row of denominators.

In this problem, 6 and 4 can be evenly divided by 2; therefore, the number 2 is written as the divisor.

Third, divide the denominators that are evenly divisible by the prime number and write the results and the remaining denominators in a new row.

Six is divided by 2 for a result of 3; 4 is divided by 2 for a result of 2. These two quotients are written on the next row. Five is not evenly divisible by 2; therefore, it is simply brought down to the next row with no change.

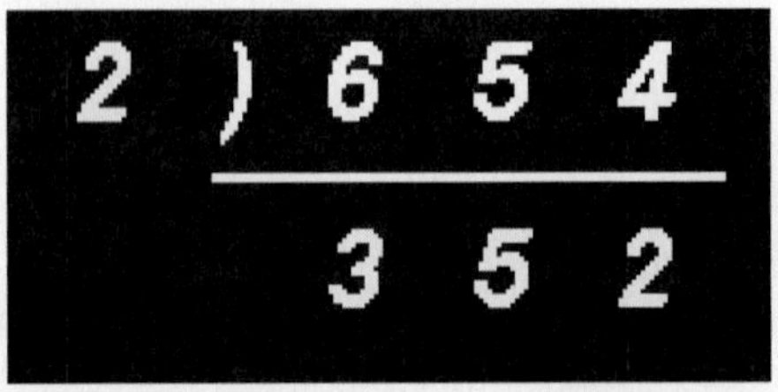

FIGURE 9.13

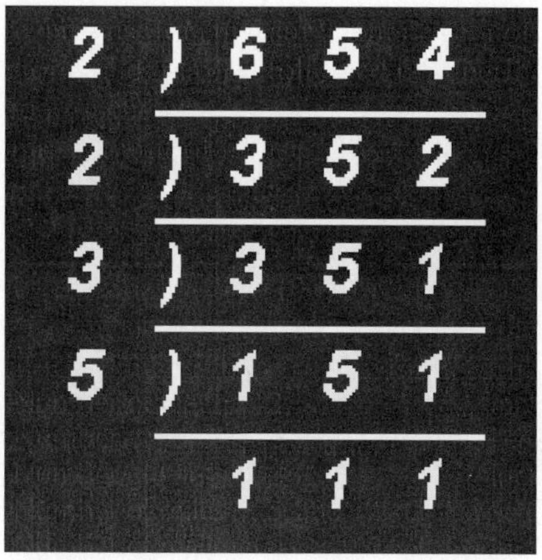

FIGURE 9.14

Fourth, continue dividing by the smallest prime numbers possible until all quotients are ones as in Figure 9.14.

In the second row, 2 is divided by the prime number 2 for a result of 1. The result and the numbers that were not divided in row 2 are written in row 3.

In the third row, 3 is divided by the prime number 3 for a result of 1. The result and the other two numbers are written in row 4.

In the fourth row, 5 is divided by 5 for a result of 1. All results are now 1; it is time for the next step.

Fifth, multiply all of the prime numbers that were used as divisors (see Figure 9.15).

The least common denominator for this problem is 60.

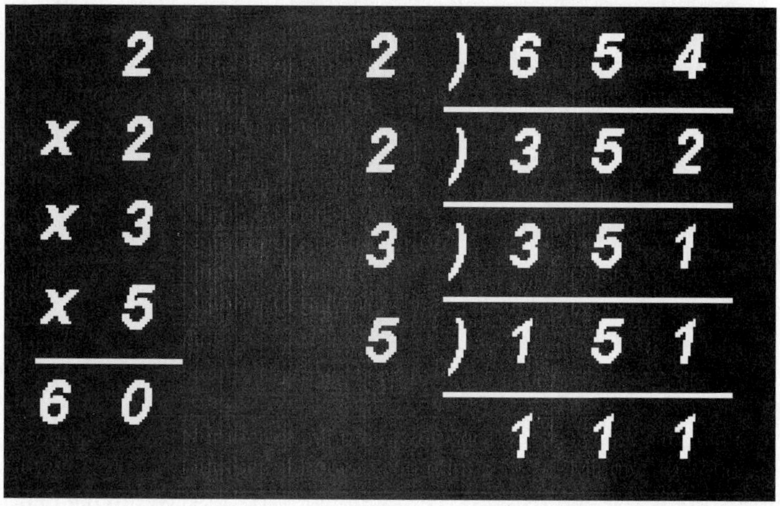

FIGURE 9.15

Sixth, convert 1/6, 1/5, and 1/4 to equivalent fractions with 60 as the denominator:

$$\frac{1}{6} = \frac{?}{60}; \quad 60 \div 6 = 10; \quad 10 \times 1 = 10; \quad \text{Place 10 over 60: 10/60}$$

$$\frac{1}{5} = \frac{?}{60}; \quad 60 \div 5 = 12; \quad 12 \times 1 = 12; \quad \text{Place 12 over 60: 12/60}$$

$$\frac{1}{4} = \frac{?}{60}; \quad 60 \div 4 = 15; \quad 15 \times 1 = 15; \quad \text{Place 15 over 60: 15/60}$$

Seventh, add the numerators: $10 + 12 + 15 = 37$. Place 37 over 60: 37/60.

MIXED NUMBERS

A **mixed number** is made up of a whole number and a fraction, such as 2⅚. Before performing arithmetic operations, mixed numbers should be converted to improper fractions. In the mixed number 2⅚, we may visualize the whole number as 2 items, each made up of 6 equal parts: 2 × 6 = 12 parts (Figure 9.16). The fractional portion of this mixed number, 5/6, may be visualized as 5 of 6 equal parts. Add the 12 parts plus the 5 parts and we have 17 parts.

 = 17/6

FIGURE 9.16

To convert a mixed number to an improper fraction mathematically:

First, multiply the whole number by the denominator of the fractional portion of the mixed number. Refer to Figure 9.17: 6 × 2 = 12.

Second, to this product add the numerator of the fraction: 12 + 5 = 17.

Third, write 17 as the numerator over the denominator, 6. The newly calculated improper fraction is 17/6.

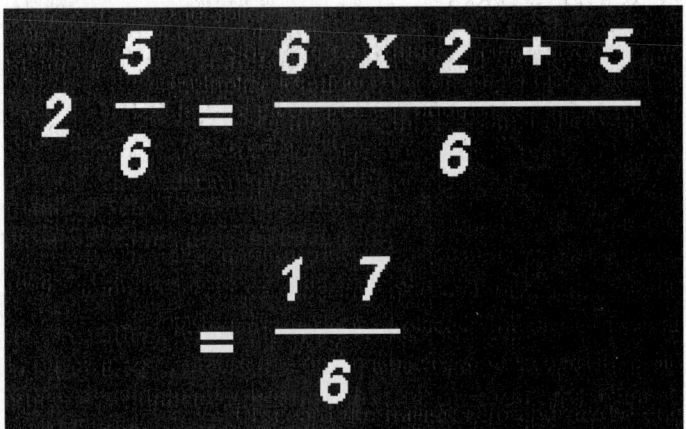

FIGURE 9.17

ADDING AND SUBTRACTING MIXED NUMBERS

To add or subtract mixed numbers, add or subtract the fractional portions first, and then add or subtract the whole numbers. If the fractional portions have unlike denominators, convert to equivalent fractions using the least common denominator before adding or subtracting. Reduce the answer to lowest terms.

In Figure 9.18, it is apparent that the least common denominator in the two fractions is 6.

First, convert 1/3 to an equivalent fraction with 6 as the denominator: 6 ÷ 3 = 2 and 2 × 1 (the numerator in the fraction 1/3) = 2. Place 2 over the denominator, 6. The equivalent fraction is 2/6.

Second, add the two fractions: 5/6 + 2/6 = 7/6.

Third, add the whole numbers: 2 + 1 = 3.

Fourth, reduce the mixed number 3⅞ to lowest terms by reducing 7/6, the fractional portion of the result, to 1⅙. Add 1⅙ to the whole number portion of the result: 3 + 1⅙ = 4⅙.

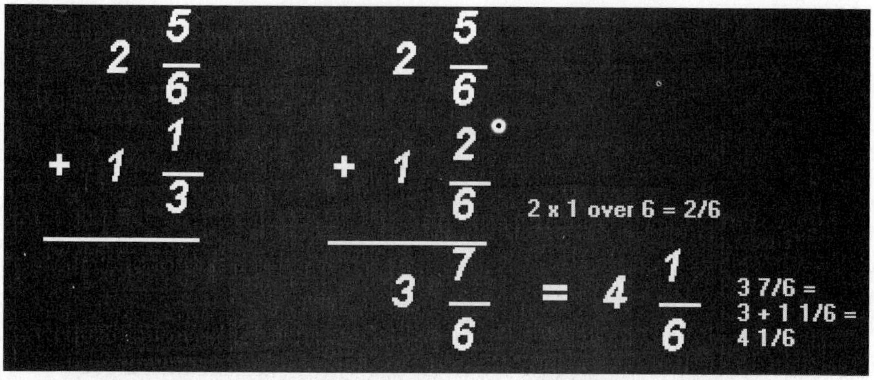

FIGURE 9.18

MIXED NUMBERS AND BORROWING

If it is necessary to borrow when subtracting the fractional portions of mixed numbers, borrow from the whole-number portions of the mixed numbers. Remember that the whole number 1 may be written as any fraction in which the numerator and the denominator are the same number, such as 4/4, 12/12, and 3/3, because any number divided by itself is 1 (see Figure 9.19).

In Figure 9.20, 1¾ is to be subtracted from 2¼.

First, it is necessary to borrow 1 from the whole-number portion of the minuend and convert it to 4/4. The whole number 2 is then equal to 1¼.

Second, add: 4/4 to 1/4 = 5/4.

Third, subtract the resulting fractional parts of the problem: 5/4 − 3/4 = 2/4.

Fourth, subtract the whole-number portions of the problem: 1 − 1 = 0.

Fifth, reduce the answer (2/4) to lowest terms: 1/2.

$$1 = 2/2$$
$$1 = 5/5$$
$$1 = 16/16$$

FIGURE 9.19

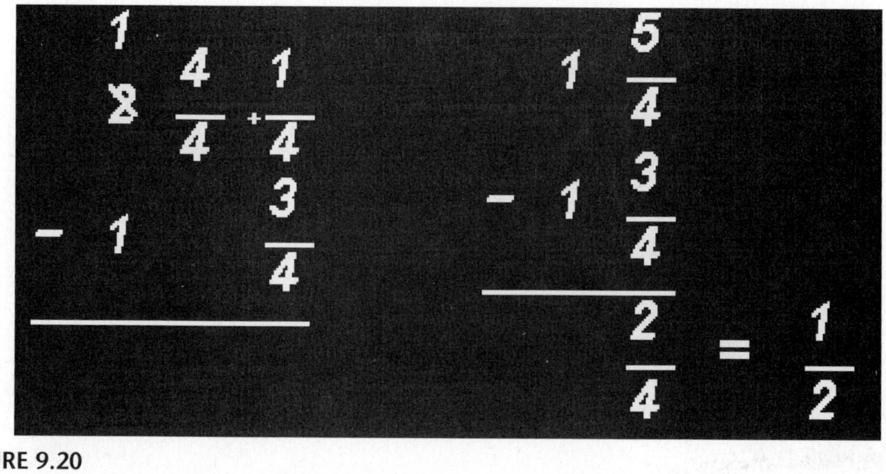

FIGURE 9.20

MULTIPLYING FRACTIONS

To multiply fractions:

First, multiply the numerators (sometimes called multiplying across the fractions).

Second, multiply the denominators. It is not necessary to have like denominators when multiplying.

Third, reduce the result to lowest terms. In Figure 9.21 the result of 3/12 can be reduced to 1/4 by dividing both the numerator and the denominator by 3.

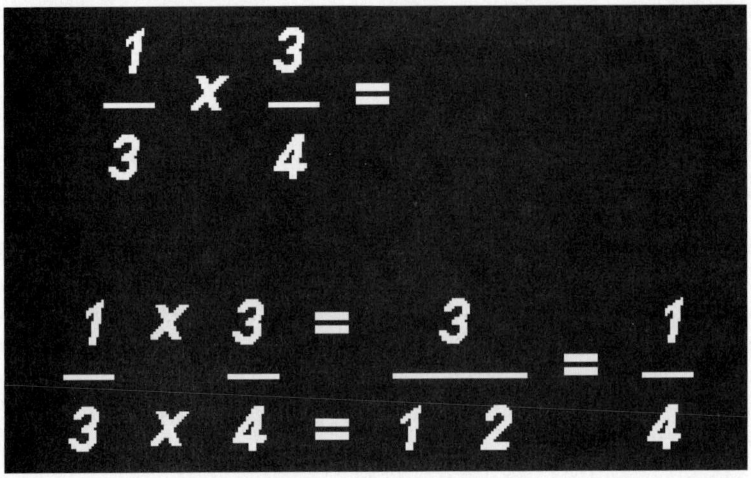

$$\frac{1}{3} \times \frac{3}{4} =$$

$$\frac{1 \times 3}{3 \times 4} = \frac{3}{1\,2} = \frac{1}{4}$$

FIGURE 9.21

MULTIPLYING A WHOLE NUMBER AND A FRACTION

Before multiplying a fraction and a whole number, the whole number must be converted to a fraction. Any whole number can be converted to a fraction by placing it over 1. In Figure 9.22, 2/5 is to be multiplied by 5.

First, place the whole number 5 over 1 because 5 divided by 1 also equals 5.

Second, multiply the numerators of the resulting fractions: $2 \times 5 = 10$.

Third, multiply the denominators: $1 \times 5 = 5$.

Fourth, reduce the resulting fraction (10/5) to lowest terms: 10/5 can be reduced by dividing the numerator by the denominator: $10 \div 5 = 2$.

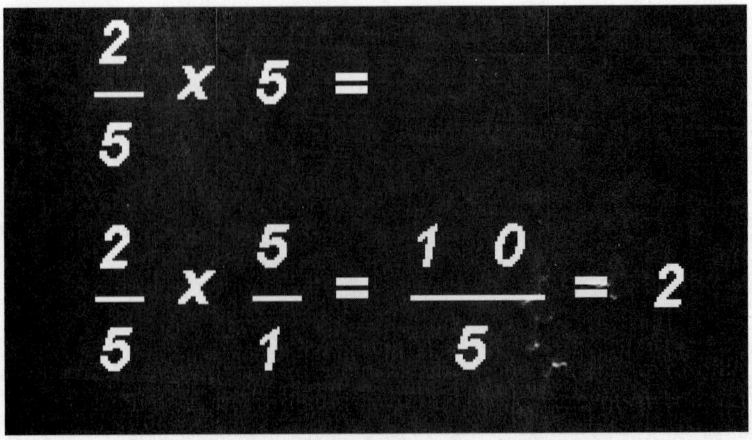

$$\frac{2}{5} \times 5 =$$

$$\frac{2}{5} \times \frac{5}{1} = \frac{1\,0}{5} = 2$$

FIGURE 9.22

MULTIPLYING MIXED NUMBERS

Before multiplying mixed numbers, convert the mixed numbers to improper fractions. Multiply numerators, then multiply denominators. Reduce the answer to lowest terms. In Figure 9.23, the mixed numbers 1½ and 2¼ must be converted to improper fractions.

First, convert 1½ to 3/2; then convert 2¼ to 9/4.

Second, multiply the two numerators: 3 × 9 = 27.

Third, multiply the two denominators: 2 × 4 = 8.

Fourth, write the resulting fraction: 27/8.

Fifth, reduce the result, 27/8, to 3⅜ by dividing: 27 ÷ 8 = 3 remainder 3. Three is the whole number portion of the mixed number. Place the remainder over 8 in the answer: 3⅜.

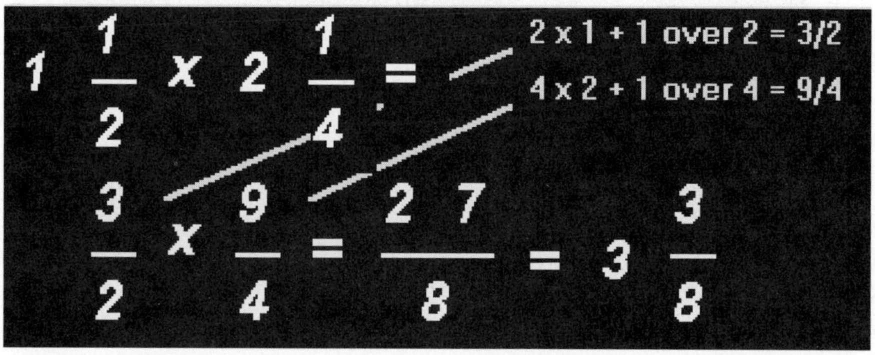

FIGURE 9.23

MULTIPLYING A MIXED NUMBER AND A WHOLE NUMBER

Before multiplying a mixed number and a whole number, convert the two numbers to improper fractions. Multiply as usual and reduce the answer to lowest terms. Refer to the problem in Figure 9.24, 1⅕ × 5.

First, convert 1⅕ to 6/5.

Second, convert 5 to a fraction by placing it over 1: 5/1.

Third, multiply the numerators: 6 × 5 = 30.

Fourth, multiply the denominators: 5 × 1 = 5.

Fifth, write the resulting fraction: 30/5.

Sixth, reduce the result, 30/5, to lowest terms: 6.

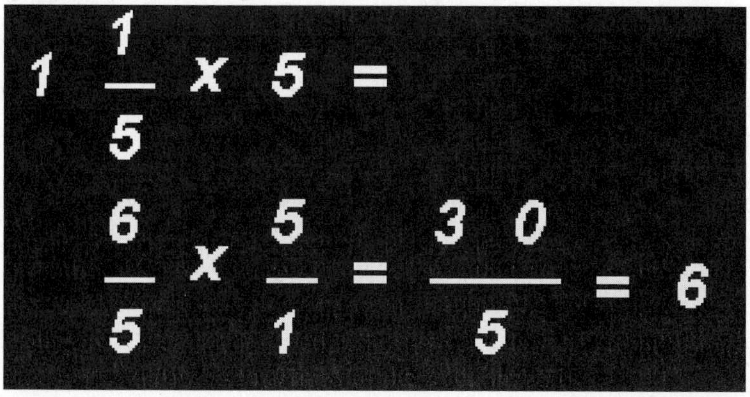

FIGURE 9.24

DIVIDING FRACTIONS

Before learning to divide by a fraction, an understanding of **reciprocals** is necessary. To write the reciprocal of a fraction, reverse the numerator and denominator, that is, write the denominator of the fraction as the numerator of the reciprocal and write the numerator of the fraction as the denominator of the reciprocal. As shown in Figure 9.25, a fraction times its reciprocal equals one: 2/3 × 3/2 = 6/6, which can be reduced to the whole number 1.

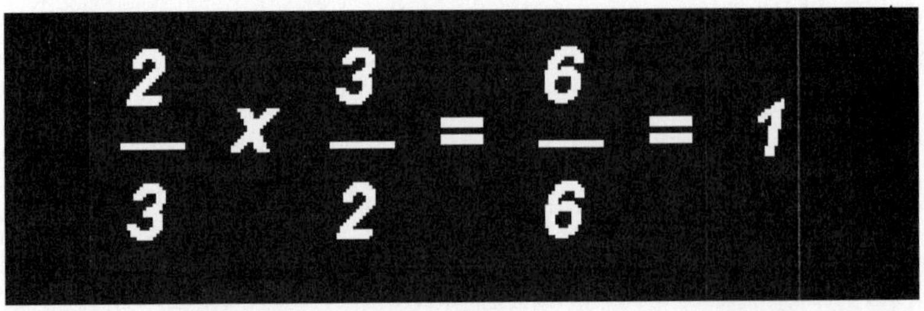

$$\frac{2}{3} \times \frac{3}{2} = \frac{6}{6} = 1$$

FIGURE 9.25

To divide fractions, multiply the dividend by the reciprocal of the divisor. Convert the answer to a whole or mixed number, if necessary. In Figure 9.26, 1/2 is to be divided by 1/3.

First, rewrite the problem using the reciprocal of the divisor and the multiplication sign instead of the division sign: 1/2 × 3/1.

Second, multiply the numerators: 1 × 3 = 3.

Third, multiply the denominators: 2 × 1 = 2.

Fourth, write the resulting fraction: 3/2.

Fifth, reduce the answer to lowest terms: 3/2 = 1½.

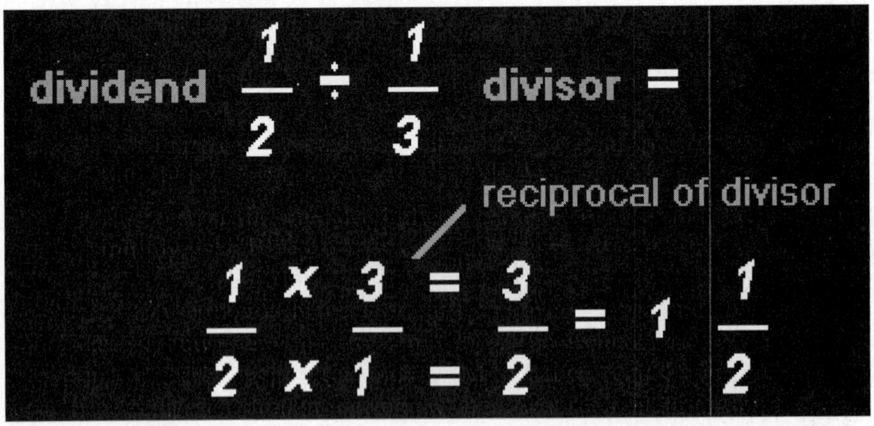

$$\text{dividend } \frac{1}{2} \div \frac{1}{3} \text{ divisor } =$$

reciprocal of divisor

$$\frac{1 \times 3 = 3}{2 \times 1 = 2} = 1\frac{1}{2}$$

FIGURE 9.26

FINDING THE RECIPROCAL OF A WHOLE NUMBER

As you learned earlier, any whole number can be converted to a fraction by placing the number over 1. Before dividing 1/3 by a whole number (3), convert the whole number to a fraction (3/1), and then find the reciprocal of the fraction (1/3). In Figure 9.27, we wish to prove that 3 × 1/3 will return the same answer as 3 ÷ 3.

First, convert the whole number 3, the dividend, to the fraction 3/1.

Second, write the reciprocal of 3/1 as the divisor (1/3) and change the sign to multiplication.

Third, multiply. The result is 3/3.

Fourth, reduce to lowest terms. The answer is 1.

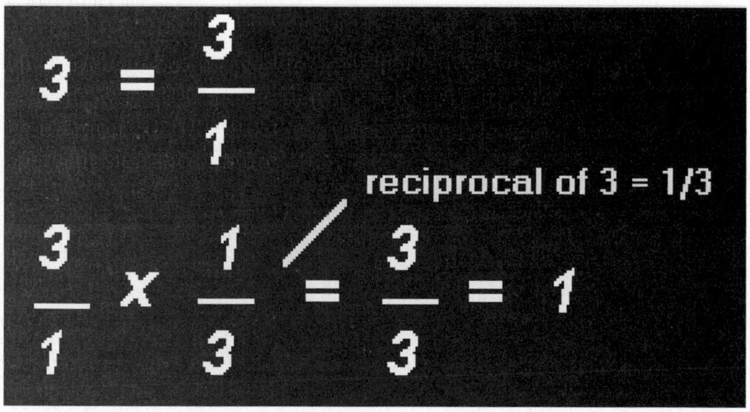

FIGURE 9.27

DIVIDING A FRACTION BY A WHOLE NUMBER

Remember: Before dividing a fraction by a whole number, convert the whole number to a fraction and find its reciprocal. Rewrite the problem, changing the sign to multiplication. Complete the problem.

Divide 1/4 by 5 as shown in Figure 9.28.

First, convert the whole number to a fraction (5 = 5/1).

Second, write the reciprocal of the fraction as the divisor and change the sign to multiplication (×1/5).

Third, multiply: $1/4 \times 1/5 = 1/20$. The answer is in lowest terms and cannot be reduced further.

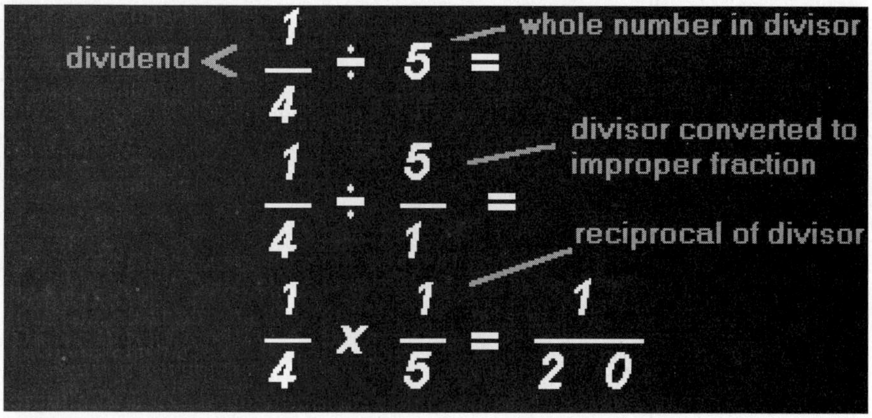

FIGURE 9.28

DIVIDING A WHOLE NUMBER BY A FRACTION

When the dividend is a whole number, convert it to a fraction by placing it over 1. When the divisor is a fraction, use its reciprocal and change the division sign to a multiplication sign. Complete the problem as usual.

PROBLEM

A carpenter has five pieces of wood. If he divides each piece in half, how many pieces of wood will he have?

$$5 \div 1/2 = \text{how many pieces of wood?}$$
$$5 \times 2/1 = 10$$

*Note: Always use the **reciprocal of the divisor** and change the sign to multiplication when dividing fractions. Do not use the reciprocal of the dividend.*

DIVIDING MIXED NUMBERS

Before dividing mixed numbers, convert the mixed numbers to improper fractions. Write the reciprocal of the divisor and change the sign to multiplication. Reduce the answer to lowest terms. Refer to the problem in Figure 9.29, $4\frac{1}{2} \div 1\frac{2}{3}$.

First, convert the dividend to an improper fraction: $4\frac{1}{2} = 9/2$

Second, convert the divisor to an improper fraction: $1\frac{2}{3} = 5/3$

Third, change the divisor to its reciprocal, 3/5, and change the division sign to a multiplication sign.

Fourth, multiply the numerators, then the denominators.

Fifth, reduce the result, 27/10, to lowest terms, $2\frac{7}{10}$.

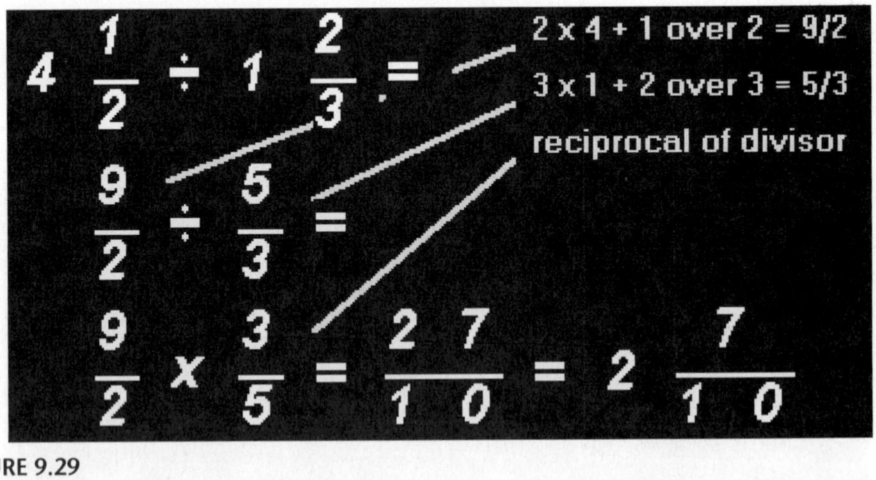

FIGURE 9.29

CHANGING FRACTIONS TO DECIMAL NUMBERS

A fraction can be converted into a decimal number by dividing the numerator by the denominator. In Figure 9.30, the fraction 3/4 is to be converted to a decimal number.

First, add a decimal and enough zeros to give the desired number of decimal places in the answer. (Remember to allow an extra place if rounding is necessary.)

Second, divide as usual. In this problem, we find that three-fourths is equal to seventy-five hundredths.

$$
\begin{array}{r}
.75 \\
4\,\overline{)\,3.00} \\
-\,2\,8 \\
\hline
2\,0 \\
-\,2\,0 \\
\hline
0
\end{array}
$$

FIGURE 9.30

CONVERTING MIXED NUMBERS TO DECIMAL NUMBERS

It is understood that the decimal point occurs after the whole-number portion of a mixed number and the fractional portion of the mixed number becomes the digits placed after the decimal point of a decimal number. Thus 25¾ can be converted to 25.75, since 3/4 = 0.75.

DECIMAL EQUIVALENTS OF FRACTIONS WORTH MEMORIZING

Figures 9.31 and 9.32 illustrate fractions and decimal equivalents that are encountered frequently in everyday business situations. Memorizing these fractions and decimal equivalents will help you work more smoothly and efficiently.

Note: The decimal equivalents for 1/3, 2/3, 1/6, and 5/6 are ***repeating decimal numbers*** *(see Chapter 8) and have been rounded to three places.*

$$\frac{1}{2} = .5 \quad \frac{3}{4} = .75 \quad \frac{2}{5} = .4 \quad \frac{4}{5} = .8$$

$$\frac{1}{4} = .25 \quad \frac{1}{5} = .2 \quad \frac{3}{5} = .6$$

FIGURE 9.31

$$\frac{1}{8} = .125 \quad \frac{5}{8} = .625 \quad \frac{1}{3} = .333 \quad \frac{1}{6} = .167$$

$$\frac{3}{8} = .375 \quad \frac{7}{8} = .875 \quad \frac{2}{3} = .667 \quad \frac{5}{6} = .833$$

FIGURE 9.32

MATH STAR 9.1

BE A *Math* ★ !

Wording to Watch: Examples of Word Problems

Carefully read word problems to determine what answer is required. Do not assume the problem will ask for a certain figure such as a total salary figure when a salary increase is desired. After underlining what the problem is asking you to calculate, underline all information given in the problem that is necessary to complete it. Briefly rewrite the problem you need to solve using information given in it. Substitute arithmetic operation signs for words where appropriate. Following are some typical examples of problems encountered daily in the business world. An analysis of each is given along with the solution.

Example 1: A coat has been advertised for one-fourth off the original price of $240. What is the amount of the reduction?

Analysis: Find the amount of the reduction. Find one-fourth of $240. Substitute a multiplication sign for the word "of," and complete the problem: $1/4 \times \$240 = \$60$, the amount of the reduction.

Example 2: A ring is on sale for $350, which is seven-eights of the original price. What was the original price?

Analysis: This is sometimes considered the most difficult type of fraction word problem, but careful analysis will show the problem to be quite easy. The information given states that $350 is seven-eighths of some number. To find the missing number (the original price in this case), substitute the division sign for the word "is": $\$350 \div 7/8 = $ _____. Remember, to divide by a fraction, rewrite the problem with a multiplication sign and the reciprocal of the divisor. Complete the problem: $\$350 \times 8/7 = \$400$.

Example 3: Tom's current salary is $29,500. He has been notified that he will receive an increase of 2/100 next year. Tom's salary will be how much next year?

Analysis: Tom's salary of $29,500 will be increased by 2/100. The problem asks for the amount of Tom's new salary, NOT the amount of the increase.

Method 1: Find the amount of the salary increase and then add the increase to Tom's original salary to find Tom's new salary.

Step 1: 2/100 of $29,500 = amount of increase. Replace the word "of" with a multiplication sign and multiply: $\frac{2}{100} \times \frac{\$29,500}{1} = ?$

Shortcut: Disregard an equal number of zeros in the numerator of the multiplicand and the dividend in the multiplier: $\frac{2}{1} \times \frac{\$295}{1} = \$590$ salary increase.

Step 2: Amount of increase + $29,500 = Tom's new salary.

$$\$590 + \$29,500 = \$30,090, \text{ Tom's new salary.}$$

Method 2: Before multiplying, add 1 to the fraction 2/100: $\$29,500 \times 1^2/_{100} = $ _____ , Tom's new salary. (Multiplying by 1 will return the same result as adding $29,500 to the amount of the reduction in a separate step.) Change the mixed number to an improper fraction: $\frac{29,500}{1} \times \frac{102}{100} = ?$

Shortcut: Disregard an equal number of zeros in the numerator of the multiplicand and the dividend of the multiplier before multiplying: $\frac{295}{1} \times \frac{102}{1} = \$30,090$, Tom's new salary.

Example 4: Matt decided to reduce his stock of 600 caps by 2/12. How many caps will remain in stock after the reduction?

Analysis: The problem is asking for the total number of caps remaining in stock, NOT the number of caps in the reduction.

Method 1: Find the number of caps in the reduction and then subtract that number from the original stock of 600 caps.

Step 1: The number of caps in the reduction = 2/12 of 600. Replace the word "of" with a multiplication sign: $2/12 \times 600 = 100$ caps in reduction.

(continued)

MATH STAR 9.1   *(continued)*

Step 2: Subtract to find the number of caps remaining in stock: $600 - 100 = 500$ caps remaining in stock.

Method 2: Taking the analysis of the problem a step further, if <u>2/12 of the caps are to be sold</u>, then <u>10/12 of the caps will remain in stock</u>. Therefore, the problem can be worked in one step: <u>10/12 of 600</u> = number of caps remaining in stock. Replace the word "of" with a multiplication sign and complete the problem: $10/12 \times 600 = 500$ caps remaining in stock.

Name _____

Class/Section _____

Score (Correct Answers ÷ No. of Assigned Problems) _____

PART 2 *Business Math Skills*

Exercise 1

Add.

$$\frac{1}{5} \qquad \frac{3}{8} \qquad \frac{1}{10} \qquad \frac{1}{12} \qquad \frac{2}{7}$$
$$+\frac{1}{5} \qquad +\frac{2}{8} \qquad +\frac{2}{10} \qquad +\frac{6}{12} \qquad +\frac{4}{7}$$

1. _____   2. _____   3. _____   4. _____   5. _____

Add. Reduce to lowest terms.

$$\frac{1}{4} \qquad \frac{4}{8} \qquad \frac{3}{10} \qquad 1\frac{5}{6} \qquad 2\frac{1}{4}$$
$$+\frac{1}{4} \qquad +\frac{2}{8} \qquad +\frac{2}{10} \qquad +\frac{1}{6} \qquad +3\frac{1}{2}$$

6. _____   7. _____   8. _____   9. _____   10. _____

Subtract. Reduce to lowest terms.

$$\frac{4}{5} \qquad 6\frac{1}{2} \qquad 7 \qquad 8\frac{4}{5} \qquad 2\frac{1}{2}$$
$$-\frac{2}{5} \qquad -1\frac{1}{6} \qquad -2\frac{10}{11} \qquad -1\frac{2}{10} \qquad -1\frac{3}{4}$$

11. _____   12. _____   13. _____   14. _____   15. _____

Multiply. Reduce to lowest terms.

$$\frac{1}{5} \times \frac{2}{3} \qquad \frac{1}{8} \times \frac{2}{3} \qquad 6\frac{1}{2} \times \frac{1}{2} \qquad 7 \times \frac{1}{3} \qquad 1\frac{1}{7} \times 2\frac{1}{4}$$

16. _____   17. _____   18. _____   19. _____   20. _____

Divide. Reduce to lowest terms.

$$\frac{10}{6} \div \frac{5}{4} \qquad \frac{25}{9} \div \frac{1}{2} \qquad 1\frac{2}{10} \div \frac{1}{3} \qquad 7 \div 1\frac{3}{4} \qquad 5\frac{1}{2} \div \frac{2}{5}$$

21. _____   22. _____   23. _____   24. _____   25. _____

Convert to decimal numbers. Round to thousandths as necessary.

$\frac{3}{4}$	$\frac{1}{3}$	$\frac{1}{9}$	$\frac{2}{8}$	$\frac{5}{12}$	$\frac{1}{10}$	$\frac{1}{6}$
26. _____	27. _____	28. _____	29. _____	30. _____	31. _____	32. _____

Exercise 2

33. If a 12′-long wooden plank is cut into 3/4″-long pieces, how many pieces will result? _____

34. If 25 pieces of 3/8″-long leather are needed, what length of leather should be purchased? Round up to the nearest whole inch. _____

35. Jan made a sample puzzle that is 5″ high. A marketing survey suggested a puzzle three-fourths this high would be more popular. How high will the new puzzle need to be? _____

36. A 3/4-carat diamond ring is on sale for $450 with a required down payment of one-fourth of the purchase price. How much is the down payment? _____

37. Biggs and Biggs Legal Services has billed $5,400, which is three-fourths of the amount agreed on for a current job. What is the total agreed-on amount? _____

38. Joan's current office budget of $95,000 is to be increased by 2/100 next year. What will be the amount of the new office budget? _____

39. One-third of the accounting-class students are men. There are 216 students in the class. How many are women? _____

40. During 2002 there were one-fifth fewer local robberies committed than in 2001. If there were 255 robberies in 2001, how many robberies were there in 2002? _____

 **PARTS 3 AND 4**   *The Pocket, Windows, and Desktop Calculators*

PROCEDURE

> The procedures for working with fractions on the various calculators are similar; therefore, Parts 3 and 4 are combined in this chapter.

It is easy to convert a fraction to a decimal number with a calculator. However, if you have memorized the frequently used decimal equivalents presented in Part 2 of this chapter, you can work many problems with one or more fewer steps, as shown in Problem 1 in the following chart (3/8 + 6.5322) and Problem 2 (456 ÷ 2/3). If you have memorized that 3/8 = .375 and that 2/3 = .667, simply enter the decimal numbers on your calculator as needed. This saves keystrokes because there is no need to convert the fractions to decimal numbers manually. Problem 3 illustrates the effort that can be saved by using memorized decimal equivalents whenever possible. The steps for working the problem without using decimal equivalents and for working the problem using decimal equivalents are shown (it is also a good review for subtracting fractions). Problem 4 demonstrates the two ways for working fraction problems for which the decimal equivalents are not known.

Note: Although the decimal equivalent for a fraction such as 1/2 appears in formal print and on calculator displays as 0.5, it is not necessary to key the zero before the decimal point. However, many instructors and the software that accompanies this book require that the zero be included in written answers.

Desktop Calculators

If no decimal selector setting is specified, set the decimal selector on F. Round the final answer according to instructions given with the problem. For the following problems, set the decimal selector on 6. Set the rounding switch on 5/4.

Problem 1	Pocket Calculator Procedure	Desktop Calculator Procedure	TAPE 1:
3/8 + 6.5322	.375 + 6.5322 = 6.9072	.375 + 6.5322 + */T 6.9072	$\begin{array}{rc} \mathbf{0 \cdot C} & \\ 0 \cdot 375000 & + \\ 6 \cdot 532200 & + \\ 6 \cdot 907200 & * \end{array}$

Problem 2	Procedure	Check	TAPE 2:
456 ÷ 2/3	456 ÷ .667 = 683.658171	× .667 = 456	$\begin{array}{rc} \mathbf{0 \cdot C} & \\ 456 \cdot & \div \\ 0 \cdot 667 & = \\ 683 \cdot 658171 & * \\ \\ 683 \cdot 658171 & \times \\ 0 \cdot 667 & = \\ 456 \cdot 000000 & * \end{array}$

Problem 3a	Convert to Equivalent Fractions	Subtraction Procedure	Convert Answer to a Decimal Number
5¼ − 2/3	12 is evenly divisible by both denominators 4 and 3 Convert 1/4: 12 ÷ 4 = 3 3 × 1 = 3 Place 3 over 12 Convert 2/3: 12 ÷ 3 = 4 4 × 2 = 8 Place 8 over 12	Rewrite problem using equivalent fractions with common denominators: $5^{3}/_{12} - 8/12$ Borrow 1 from 5, convert the 1 to 12/12, and add to 3/12: 12/12 + 3/12 = 15/12 Rewrite problem: $4^{15}/_{12} - 8/12 = 4^{7}/_{12}$	Convert the fraction portion of the mixed number to a decimal number. 7 ÷ 12 = 0.583333 Add the decimal number to the whole-number portion of the mixed number; the result is 4.583333

Problem 3b	Pocket Calculator Procedure	Desktop Calculator Procedure	TAPE 3:
Or, use memorized decimal equivalents	5.25 − .667 = 4.583*	5.25 + .667 − */T 4.583	$\begin{array}{rc} \mathbf{0 \cdot C} & \\ 5 \cdot 250000 & + \\ 0 \cdot 667000 & - \\ 4 \cdot 583000 & * \end{array}$

Note the slight difference in results because the procedure in Problem 3b used the decimal equivalent for 2/3 rounded to three places (.667), whereas the answer in Problem 3a was rounded to six places. Try Problem 3b again, using .666667 as the decimal equivalent for 2/3. Compare these results with those for Problem 3a.

When working a problem containing a fraction for which the decimal equivalent has not been memorized, you have two choices:

1. Leave the problem in fraction form. Write or visualize the problem as it would appear when working with pencil or paper. That is, when adding or subtracting fractions with unlike denominators, convert the fractions to equivalent fractions with common denominators and then perform the arithmetic operation in the problem (see Problem 4a in the following chart). When working multiplication or division problems with fractions, convert whole numbers to fractions and convert mixed numbers to improper fractions.

2. The second option is to convert the fractions in the problem to decimal numbers and then perform the arithmetic operations (see Problems 4b and 5).

Problem 4a	Convert to Equivalent Fractions	Addition Procedure Step 1	Convert Answer to a Decimal Number
925/8 + 15/16	16 is the least common denominator: 16 ÷ 8 = 2 2 × 925 = 1,850 Place 1,850 over 16	Add the numerators: 1,850 + 15 = 1,865 Place the result over 16: 1,865/16	Divide the numerator by the denominator: 1,865 ÷ 16 = 116.5625

Problem 4b	Convert Fractions to Decimal Numbers and Add	Display Answer	TAPE 4:
925/8 + 15/16	925 ÷ 8 = 115.625 Place this number in memory (M+) 15 ÷ 16 = .9375 Add to memory (M+)	Display the total in memory (MT) 116.5625	0 • C 925 • ÷ 8 • = 115 • 625000 * 115 • 625000 M+ 15 • ÷ 16 • = 0 • 937500 * 0 • 937500 M+ 116 • 562500 M*

Problem 5	Convert Fractions to Decimal Numbers and Subtract	Display Answer	TAPE 5:
120/293 − 16/34	120 ÷ 293 = .409556 M+ 16 ÷ 34 = .470588 M−	Display the total in memory (MT) −0.061032	0 • C 120 • ÷ 293 • = 0 • 409556 * 0 • 409556 M+ 16 • ÷ 34 • = 0 • 470588 * 0 • 470588 M− 0 • 061032 M*

PROBLEMS WITH FRACTIONS AND MULTIPLE ARITHMETIC OPERATIONS

To complete problems that contain more than one arithmetic operation, use features such as memory plus, memory minus, memory subtotal (memory recall), and memory total whenever possible to minimize keystrokes.

PROBLEM 6

(3/4 + 6/13) − (4/5 + 7/9).

If you are using a desktop calculator, set the decimal selector on 4. Set the rounding switch on 5/4. Turn the printer switch on.

First, complete calculations for any parts of the problem in parentheses. The first set of parentheses contains 3/4 + 6/13. We have memorized that 3/4 = .75.

Procedure	TAPE 6:
.75 M+ 6 ÷ 13 = 0.4615 M+ MT 1.2115	0 . C 0 . 7500 M+ 6 . ÷ 13 . = 0 . 4615 * 0 . 4615 M+ 1 . 2115 M*

The second set of parentheses contains 4/5 + 7/9.

Procedure	TAPE 7:
4 ÷ 5 = 0.8 M+ 7 ÷ 9 = 0.7778 M+ MS 1.5778	4 . ÷ 5 . = 0 . 8000 * 0 . 8000 M+ 7 . ÷ 9 . = 0 . 7778 * 0 . 7778 M+ 1 . 5778 M◊

Insert the values for the two sets of parentheses into the problem and complete: 1.2115 − 1.5778 [1.5778 is still stored in memory because we used memory subtotal (memory recall), not memory total in the previous step].

Pocket Calculator Procedure	Desktop Calculator Procedure	TAPE 8:
1.2115 − 1.5778 = −0.3663 or 1.2115 − MR = −0.3663	1.2115 + MT − */T −0.3663	1 . 2115 + 1 . 5778 M* 1 . 5778 − 0 . 3663 − *

 PARTS 3 AND 4 *Pocket, Windows, or Desktop Calculator*

Exercise 1

In the following exercises, do not use trailing (unnecessary) zeros.

Convert to decimal numbers. Round to thousandths as necessary.

$$\frac{5}{8} \qquad \frac{3}{13} \qquad \frac{1}{12} \qquad \frac{4}{6} \qquad \frac{6}{9}$$

1. _____ 2. _____ 3. _____ 4. _____ 5. _____

$$\frac{5}{7} \qquad \frac{10}{12} \qquad \frac{9}{16} \qquad \frac{7}{8} \qquad \frac{15}{100}$$

6. _____ 7. _____ 8. _____ 9. _____ 10. _____

Complete the following problems. If you are using a desktop calculator, set the decimal selector on F. Round final answer to hundredths.

$$\begin{array}{ccccc} \frac{1}{12} & \frac{22}{25} & \frac{13}{40} & 1\frac{1}{3} & 2\frac{1}{4} \\ +\frac{1}{60} & -\frac{2}{8} & \times\frac{5}{8} & \div\frac{1}{6} & \times3\frac{1}{2} \end{array}$$

11. _____ 12. _____ 13. _____ 14. _____ 15. _____

Complete the following problems. If you are using a desktop calculator, set the decimal selector on 4. Round the final answer to hundredths.

(1/5 + 4/6) + (2/3 − 1/8) (2/6 + 1/4) × (3/5 + 1/9)
    16. _____   17. _____

(12/10 + 2⅓) − (3⅔ − 3/9) (15/16 + 5¾) ÷ 1/4)
    18. _____   19. _____

(21/5 + 44/6) + (12/3 − 1/8)
    20. _____

Exercise 2

21. Last year a certain stock sold for 58⅛. Today the same stock is selling for 58.231. What is the amount of increase or decrease of the stock price? _____

22. Janey makes wire earrings. She needs 1⅞″ of wire for each earring. She received an order for 12 <u>pairs</u> of earrings. How much wire will she need to produce all the earrings? _____

23. Mike's gas tank holds 15½ gal. If gas costs $1.39 per gal, how much will it cost him to fill his tank? Round to dollars and cents. _____

24. Brandon places 5½ oz of barbeque on each adult plate served, and three-fourths of that amount on each child plate served. If he expects to serve 800 adult plates and 150 child plates this weekend, how much barbeque will he need? State your answer rounded to hundredths in ounces and in pounds. _____ _____

25. Josie made the following measurements for lengths of fabric needed for drapes in her office: 36⅛″, 45½″, 39⅜″, and 62¼″. How many yards of fabric should she buy? Round your answer up to whole inches and whole yards. _____ _____

26. A pair of shoes costing $65 has been reduced by one-fifth. What is the new sale price? _____
27. Johnnie's group had 15 boxes of Fund Raiser cookies left over after the cookie sale. If the 15 boxes represent 1/25 of the total number of boxes of cookies the group purchased for resale, with how many boxes did the group start? _____
28. The ABC Company has decided to reduce its inventory of $5,670,000 to $4,961,250. What is the amount of the reduction? _____ The inventory was reduced by what fraction? _____
    Hint: You will need the decimal equivalents you memorized.
29. The cost of 12 lamps is $180. The shop owner wishes to sell the lamps for $1\frac{5}{8}$ of cost. What is the total selling price for all the lamps? _____
30. Hailey estimates that three-fourths, or 354, of the shirts received for resale on May 10 will sell within 2 weeks. How many shirts were received May 10? _____

Exercise 3 for Desktop Calculators Only

Strokes per Minute Score _____

Accuracy Score (Correct Strokes ÷ Total Strokes) _____

One-Minute Addition Timing (Keys 0 through 9; Add Mode)

(Optional: Your instructor may wish you to use Touch Key on the computer for all your timings. Check with your instructor before completing this exercise.)

Complete as many of the problems as possible in 1 minute by adding. Work quickly and accurately. The number preceding each closing parenthesis indicates the cumulative number of strokes for problems attempted. For example, if you complete Problems 1 through 3 in 1 minute, your strokes-per-minute score is 183. Optional: 3- to 5-minute timings.

1.	2.	3.	4.	5.	6.	7.	8.
26,004	21,001	18,400	22,006	57,814	49,200	30,700	71,001
15,214	36,500	35,100	35,002	98,316	62,500	60,400	92,003
12,584	22,305	27,400	68,001	19,585	52,100	10,100	83,002
16,500	72,876	41,600	38,003	79,232	18,400	30,800	33,001
52,025	82,745	95,400	35,004	77,003	32,006	30,500	92,004
62,506	91,002	16,500	42,005	88,004	22,005	20,200	11,002
14,421	64,571	28,300	43,003	64,000	97,003	30,300	79,007
85,901	45,631	77,100	12,003	35,005	38,004	50,600	38,004
75,200	55,994	49,300	21,001	54,600	17,006	60,900	87,005
92,502	85,300	57,300	13,002	91,001	28,006	50,900	89,003
61)	122)	183)	244)	305)	366)	427)	488)

9.	10.	11.	12.	13.	14.	15.	16.
31,400	52,900	87,415	35,002	73,600	96,722	16,000	57,004
17,420	42,700	92,545	10,402	18,756	84,734	37,513	28,600
26,850	63,956	85,252	20,605	43,736	85,965	38,464	49,000
43,150	47,002	78,715	50,908	62,826	74,936	39,514	41,870
12,700	51,000	89,632	27,096	73,956	75,835	30,645	62,002
13,689	64,702	93,536	45,302	21,546	65,731	27,423	63,003
12,599	84,005	20,565	30,846	35,002	58,741	28,513	91,514
71,884	71,002	81,025	52,613	18,300	57,962	92,753	63,787
13,256	94,008	75,001	20,701	57,002	59,854	97,624	67,412
61,374	83,005	84,500	16,300	19,006	51,014	10,411	48,600
549)	610)	671)	732)	793)	854)	915)	976)

Set decimal selector on add mode.

17.	18.	19.	20.	21.	22.	23.	24.
534.00	150.00	961.00	136.55	634.90	162.80	183.00	136.29
166.00	328.00	867.00	545.88	821.58	256.19	773.50	252.49
267.00	257.00	737.00	641.77	715.69	343.99	395.75	362.19
192.00	129.00	921.00	453.66	464.71	462.79	653.25	485.39
129.00	327.00	951.00	965.87	953.52	543.59	562.95	592.59
327.00	249.00	891.00	716.34	845.16	641.79	312.85	672.89
381.00	168.00	781.00	126.59	746.10	556.00	515.50	175.69
129.00	393.00	985.00	836.68	354.25	242.93	231.75	283.79
139.00	286.00	735.00	944.78	125.45	376.21	145.80	393.19
237.00	334.00	964.00	321.49	121.00	586.32	463.70	191.59
1,037)	1,098)	1,159)	1,220)	1,281)	1,342)	1,403)	1,464)

PARTS 3 AND 4   *Review and Practice Using Business Math FUNdamentals*

GOAL: Complete 9 of the 10 problems correctly.

Instructions: *Start Business Math FUNdamentals. Complete Tutorials 21 through 26 and Drills 13 through 22. If you are not satisfied with your scores, repeat the drills. Write your scores below.*

Business Math FUNdamentals Drill 13

Today's Date	Score

Business Math FUNdamentals Drill 14

Today's Date	Score

Business Math FUNdamentals Drill 15

Today's Date	Score

Business Math FUNdamentals Drill 16

Today's Date	Score

Business Math FUNdamentals Drill 17

Today's Date	Score

Business Math FUNdamentals Drill 18

Today's Date	Score

Business Math FUNdamentals Drill 19

Today's Date	Score

Business Math FUNdamentals Drill 20

Today's Date	Score

Business Math FUNdamentals Drill 21

Today's Date	Score

Business Math FUNdamentals Drill 22

Today's Date	Score

CHAPTER 9 *Terminology Review*

Common denominators
Denominator
Equivalent fraction of higher terms
Equivalent fractions
Fraction
Improper fraction
Least common denominator
Mixed number
Numerator
Prime number
Proper fraction
Reciprocals
Reduced to lowest terms
Repeating decimal numbers

Fill in the blanks.

1. A(n) _____ consists of a whole number and a fraction.

2. A fraction and its _____ , when multiplied together, equal one.

3. A(n) _____ is a fraction in which the numerator is larger than the denominator.

4. A(n) _____ represents part of a whole number and is formed by dividing one number by another.

5. A(n) _____ is a whole number that can be divided evenly by the denominators in two or more fractions.

6. The _____ is the top number of a fraction.

7. A(n) _____ is a fraction in which the numerator is smaller than the denominator.

8. The _____ is the divisor of a fraction.

9. To convert a fraction to a(n) _____ of higher terms, multiply both the numerator and the denominator by the same number.

10. The numerator and the denominator of a fraction that has been _____ can no longer be divided evenly by any number except one.

Name _____

Class/Section _____

Score (Correct Answers ÷ No. of Assigned Problems) _____

Chapter 9 Review Exercises

Exercise 1

Convert improper fractions to mixed numbers. Convert mixed numbers to improper fractions.

	32/9		64/3		29/2		5¾		9²/₇
1. _____		2. _____		3. _____		4. _____		5. _____

Change to equivalent fractions as indicated.

2/5 = _____/35   6/14 = _____/7   3/69 = _____/23   1/4 = _____/12   4/6 = _____/18
6. _____   7. _____   8. _____   9. _____   10. _____

Add.

$$\frac{1}{9}$$ $$\frac{1}{8}$$ $$\frac{4}{11}$$ $$\frac{11}{25}$$ $$\frac{3}{27}$$
$$+\frac{4}{9}$$ $$+\frac{6}{8}$$ $$+\frac{6}{11}$$ $$+\frac{5}{25}$$ $$+\frac{4}{27}$$

11. _____   12. _____   13. _____   14. _____   15. _____

Add. Reduce to lowest terms.

$$\frac{9}{8}$$ $$\frac{2}{3}$$ $$\frac{13}{10}$$ $$4\frac{5}{7}$$ $$3\frac{3}{4}$$
$$+\frac{5}{8}$$ $$+\frac{1}{3}$$ $$+\frac{12}{10}$$ $$+\frac{2}{21}$$ $$+3\frac{1}{16}$$

16. _____   17. _____   18. _____   19. _____   20. _____

Subtract. Reduce to lowest terms.

$$\begin{array}{r} \frac{4}{15} \\ -\frac{2}{15} \\ \hline \end{array}$$
21. _____

$$\begin{array}{r} 6\frac{2}{3} \\ -2\frac{1}{6} \\ \hline \end{array}$$
22. _____

$$\begin{array}{r} 5 \\ -2\frac{1}{10} \\ \hline \end{array}$$
23. _____

$$\begin{array}{r} 55\frac{1}{5} \\ -41\frac{8}{20} \\ \hline \end{array}$$
24. _____

$$\begin{array}{r} 12\frac{1}{12} \\ -1\frac{3}{4} \\ \hline \end{array}$$
25. _____

Multiply. Reduce to lowest terms.

$\frac{3}{5} \times \frac{1}{3}$
26. _____

$\frac{7}{8} \times \frac{2}{3}$
27. _____

$9\frac{1}{2} \times \frac{8}{9}$
28. _____

$5 \times \frac{1}{16}$
29. _____

$2\frac{1}{4} \times 5\frac{1}{8}$
30. _____

Divide. Reduce to lowest terms.

$\frac{5}{6} \div \frac{1}{4}$
31. _____

$\frac{8}{9} \div \frac{1}{3}$
32. _____

$9\frac{2}{5} \div \frac{2}{3}$
33. _____

$8 \div 1\frac{1}{4}$
34. _____

$6\frac{1}{3} \div \frac{2}{9}$
35. _____

Convert to decimal numbers. Round to thousandths as necessary.

$\frac{29}{44}$
36. _____

$\frac{3}{11}$
37. _____

$\frac{1}{8}$
38. _____

$\frac{27}{100}$
39. _____

$\frac{8}{45}$
40. _____

$\frac{1}{16}$
41. _____

$\frac{3}{8}$
42. _____

Exercise 2

43. John is a partner in an accounting firm. The firm had profits of $9,466 in May. If John's share of the partnership is one-third, what is his share of the May profits? _____
44. If 1/6 oz of a certain chemical costs $6.21, how much does 4 oz of the chemical cost? _____
45. Chocolate cake orders for Tuesday included 5 sheet cakes, 9 quarter (1/4) sheet cakes, and 10 half (1/2) sheet cakes. Batter for how many whole chocolate cakes should be prepared? _____
46. The Sun is approximately 93 million miles from Earth. The Moon is approximately 250,000 miles from Earth. Complete the following statement using a fraction that has been reduced to lowest terms: The Moon is approximately _____ the distance of the sun from Earth.

Exercise 3

Better Bakers wishes to make one-fifth of the following recipe. Convert the recipe.

Lemon Pie Filling Mix	Lemon Pie Filling Mix (reduced to 1/5)
2½ c lemon drink mix, presweetened with sugar	47. _____
1¼ c cornstarch	48. _____
1¼ c sugar	49. _____
1 tsp salt	50. _____

CHAPTER 10

Working with Percents;
Sales Tax;
Sales, Ordering, and Shipping Forms

 PART 1 *Speed and Accuracy Building Using Touch Key*

GOALS: Your speed goal is 7,500 strokes per hour.
Your accuracy target goal range is 95% to 100%.

With each repetition of the drill, try to improve your speed without lowering your accuracy score. If your percent-of-accuracy score falls below 95%, review your finger position and technique. Then try again.

Instructions: *Start Touch Key. Complete Drill 1, Part A, Five-Minute Timing. (Parts B through E are optional.) Write your scores for strokes per hour and percent of accuracy below.*

Touch Key Drill 1—The 0 through 9 Keys, Three-Digit Numbers, Five-Minute Timing

Today's Date	Strokes per Hour	Percent of Accuracy
A.		
B.		
C.		
D.		
E.		

PART 2 *Business Math Skills*

PERCENTS

Using fractions to indicate portions of items, such as one-fourth cup of milk or one-half loaf of bread, has been discussed previously in this book. Percents are used to indicate a part or proportion of an item, as in the statement that 5% of the students were absent today.

WHAT IS A PERCENT?

First, we need to know that a **proportion** is a part of a whole. A **percent** is a way to represent a proportion of an amount in hundredths. A percent is represented by the percent (%) symbol. When working with percents, the whole is always represented as 100%.

Figure 10.1 illustrates that 100% represents all of the box. The box has been cut into fourths, and one-fourth of the box has been highlighted. Since 25 is one-fourth of 100, one piece of the box that has been cut into fourths is 25% of the box: 100% of the box ÷ 4 = 25%. Each of the four pieces of the box represents 25% of the entire box.

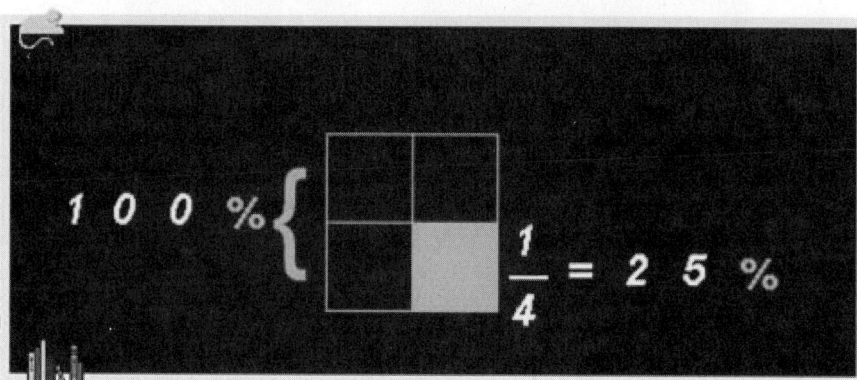

FIGURE 10.1

Percents can also be used to represent proportions of items that can be counted, such as buttons. Figure 10.2 illustrates a bin containing 3,000 buttons; 1,500 buttons are black and the other 1,500 buttons are white. By placing the number of black buttons (1,500) over the total number of buttons (3,000) to make a fraction and then dividing, it is found that 1/2 of the buttons are black. Because 100% divided by l/2 equals 50%, it may be said that 50% of the buttons are black.

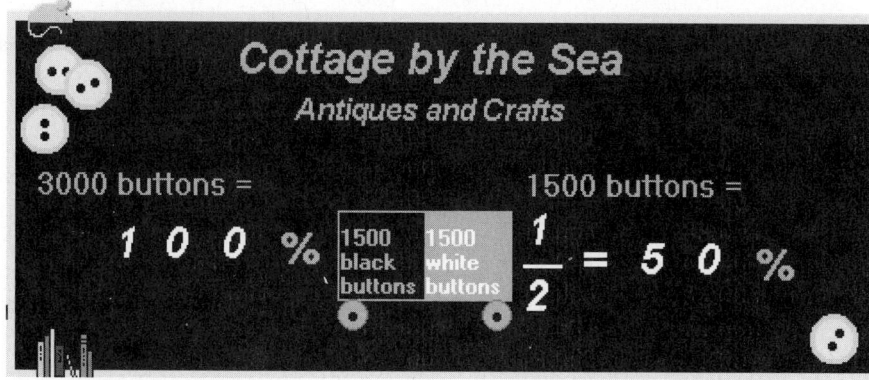

FIGURE 10.2

CONVERTING PERCENTS TO FRACTIONS AND DECIMAL NUMBERS

Any percent can be rewritten as a fraction by placing the percent over a denominator of 100 and removing the % sign. Figure 10.3 illustrates that 50% can be converted to the fraction 50/100 and 12% can be converted to the fraction 12/100.

Other examples are

$$10\% = 10/100 \qquad 25\% = 25/100$$
$$2\% = 2/100 \qquad 0.5\% = 0.5/100$$

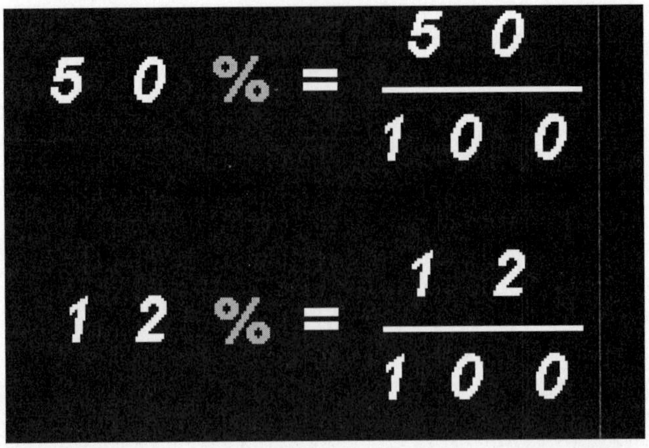

FIGURE 10.3

Some students become confused when a number is followed by a percent sign. This will not happen to you if you just remember that % means 1/100. With this in mind, it is possible to convert any percent to a fraction or decimal number. Look at the following examples. Each shows a percent converted to a fraction, and then a fraction converted to a decimal number.

Example 1: Multiply the whole number in 10% by 1/100. Remember that the whole number 10 can also be written as 10/1 to multiply it by a fraction:

$$10\% = \frac{10}{1} \times \frac{1}{100} = \frac{10}{100} = \frac{1}{10} = 0.1$$

Example 2: Multiply the fraction in 1/4% by 1/100:

$$1/4\% = \frac{1}{4} \times \frac{1}{100} = \frac{1}{400} = 0.0025$$

Example 3: Multiply the decimal number in 12.5% by 1/100:

$$12.5\% = \frac{12.5}{1} \times \frac{1}{100} = \frac{12.5}{100} = \frac{1}{8} = 0.125$$

Example 4: Convert the mixed number in 83⅓% to an improper fraction (83⅓ = 250/3). Multiply by 1/100:

$$83\frac{1}{3}\% = \frac{250}{3} \times \frac{1}{100} = \frac{5}{6} = 0.8333$$

Some prefer to use the following shortcut for converting percents to decimal numbers. In this shortcut, you must remember to simply move the decimal point two places to the left when removing the percent sign. It is understood that the decimal point follows the whole number in a percent even though it is not written. Consider Figure 10.4. Fifty percent is changed to a decimal number by simply moving the decimal point two places to the left and removing the percent sign. Will moving the decimal point two places to the left and removing the percent sign have the same result as multiplying the whole number by 1/100?

$$\frac{50}{1} \times \frac{1}{100} = \frac{50}{100} = \frac{1}{2} = 0.5$$

The result of using either method is 0.5.

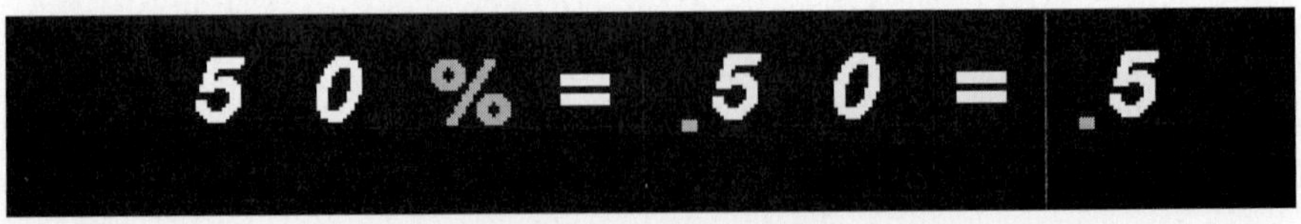

FIGURE 10.4

CONVERTING A FRACTION TO A PERCENT

A fraction such as 1/5 can be changed to a percent by converting it into an equivalent fraction of higher terms with 100 as the denominator. After converting 1/5 into 20/100, we can convert the fraction 20/100 into a percent by simply removing the denominator of 100 and adding a percent sign. See Figure 10.5.

$$\frac{1}{5} = \frac{20}{100} \quad \overset{100/5 \times 1}{} \quad = 20\%$$

FIGURE 10.5

CONVERTING A DECIMAL NUMBER TO A PERCENT

To convert a decimal number to a percent, move the decimal point two places to the right and add a percent sign.

Example 5: Convert 0.1 to a percent.

Note: It is necessary to add a zero after the 1 to move the decimal point two places to the right. Remember that it is understood that the decimal point follows the whole number in a percent.

$$0.10 = 10\%$$

Example 6: Convert 0.0025 to a percent:

$$0.0025 = 0.25\%$$

Example 7: Convert 0.125 to a percent:

$$0.125 = 12.5\%$$

Example 8: Convert 0.8333 to a percent:

$$0.8333 = 83.33\%$$

THE PERCENTAGE FORMULA

A **percentage** is a portion of a whole item and is always stated as an amount. Whenever a figure representing a whole is multiplied by a percent, the result is a percentage.

A **formula** is a statement of a rule, principle, or other factual information. Letters, numbers, and symbols may be used when writing the statement. Figure 10.6 illustrates the

Whole	x	Percent	=	Portion
Base	x	Rate	=	Percentage
B	x	R	=	P

FIGURE 10.6

most common formula for finding a percentage. Note the difference in terminology. In the percentage formula the whole is represented by **base**, percent is represented by **rate**, and portion is represented by **percentage**. For convenience these words are usually further shortened to single letters, resulting in the formula $B \times R = P$. The formula may also be stated as $P = B \times R$ without affecting the result.

The numbers from the button problem have been substituted for the words in the percentage formula in Figure 10.7. Three thousand buttons times 50% equal 1,500 buttons. In this problem, 1,500 is the percentage of buttons. To multiply by a percent when using pen and paper, the percent must first be converted to a decimal number. In this problem, 3,000 was multiplied by 0.5 (50% converted to 0.5).

Base   x Rate   = Percentage
3000   x 50%   = 1500
3000   x .50   = 1500

3000 buttons =   1500 buttons =
1 0 0 % |1500 black buttons | 1500 white buttons| *5 0 %*
of the buttons   of the buttons

FIGURE 10.7

PERCENT VERSUS PERCENTAGE

It is important to understand the difference between percent and percentage. A percent is a rate, such as 10%. **Rate** used in this manner refers to a number expressed as a proportion of a whole. Typical problems using rate in business involve calculating commission based on a rate and total sales, calculating percent of increase or decrease of sales between two periods of time, and calculating sales tax based on a rate and the amount of a sale. **Percentage** is an amount, that is, a number representing a part or portion of another number or amount. It is the result of multiplying an amount by a rate.

Try it. Figure 10.8 illustrates a typical word problem in which the rate and base are given and the percentage is to be calculated. Remember to convert the percent to a decimal number before multiplying. Your answer should be $200.

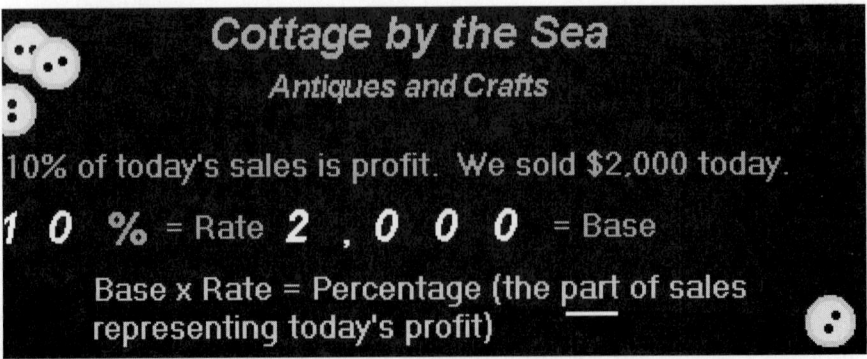

Cottage by the Sea
Antiques and Crafts

10% of today's sales is profit. We sold $2,000 today.

1 0 % = Rate *2 , 0 0 0* = Base

Base x Rate = Percentage (the <u>part</u> of sales
representing today's profit)

FIGURE 10.8

CALCULATING BASE

Sometimes rate and percentage are given in a problem and the base is not known.

PROBLEM 1

The button department had 25% of all company sales for this year (see Figure 10.9). The button department sold $75,000 worth of buttons. What were total company sales?

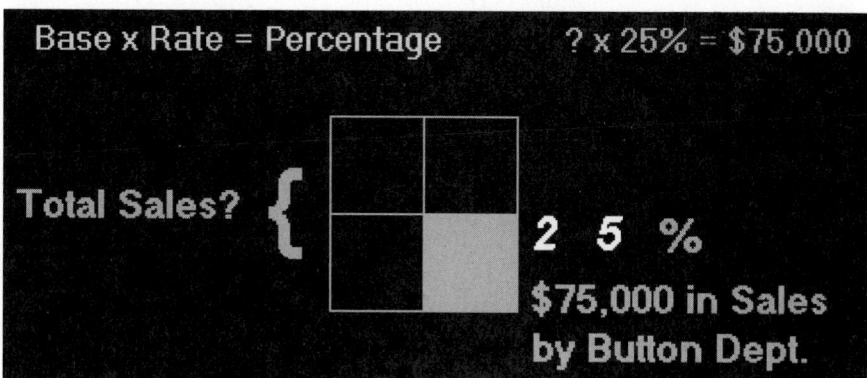

FIGURE 10.9

Begin by substituting the numbers that are given for corresponding words in the percentage formula. Substitute 25% for R and $75,000 for P. Convert 25% to the decimal number 0.25. We do not know total sales (base). We now have the formula (see Figure 10.10)

$$B \times 0.25 = \$75,000$$

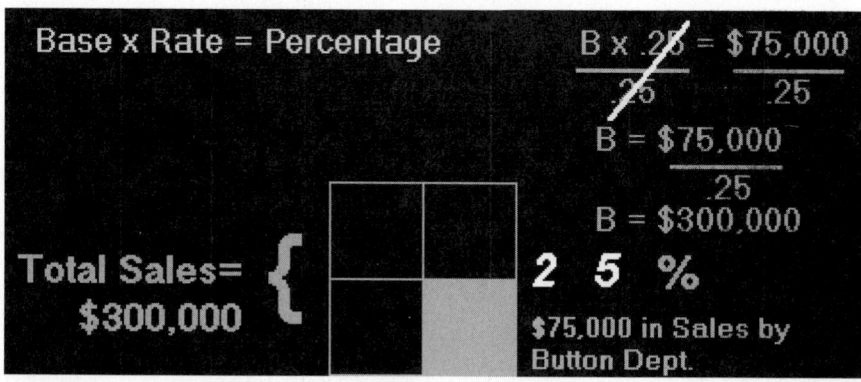

FIGURE 10.10

To find what B equals, we need to change the formula so that B is isolated on one side. One of the basic rules of algebra states that a variable may be isolated by performing the opposite arithmetic operation to both sides of a formula. Since the 0.25 to be multiplied needs to be removed from the left side of the formula, divide both sides of the formula by 0.25. Since 0.25 divided by 0.25 equals 1, we can cancel this fraction. The resulting formula, B = $75,000/0.25, can be readily solved. Total sales were $300,000.

Note: Learning to use this simple method for manipulating the percentage formula means that only the percentage formula must be memorized. It is not necessary to memorize two additional formulas to calculate rate and base.

CALCULATING RATE

If percentage and base are given in a problem, rate can also be calculated using the percentage formula.

PROBLEM 2

The Antiques Department of a company had $150,000 in sales. The company had $300,000 in total sales. What percent of total sales did the Antiques Department have?

Begin by filling in the percentage formula with the information given in the problem (see Figure 10.11).

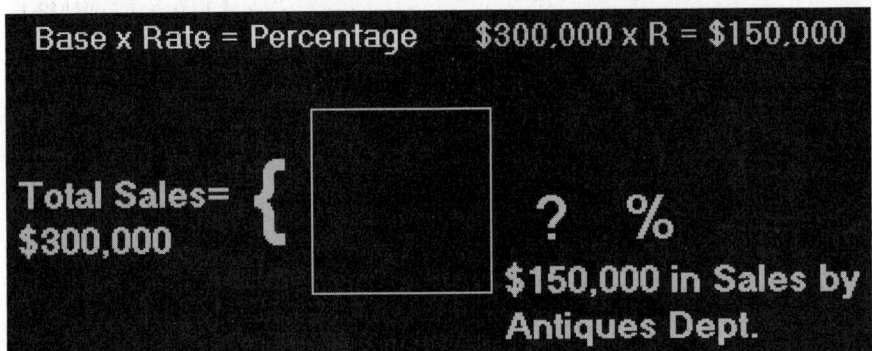

FIGURE 10.11

To find the rate, R must be isolated. Use the algebra rule discussed in the previous section to remove the multiple 300,000; that is, divide both sides of the formula by 300,000. Cancel the fraction 300,000/300,000 (see Figure 10.12). Rewrite the formula. Reduce the fraction 150,000/300,000 to lowest terms (1/2). Convert the fraction (1/2) to a decimal number (0.50). Convert the decimal number (0.50) to a percent by moving the decimal point two places to the right and adding a percent sign (50%).

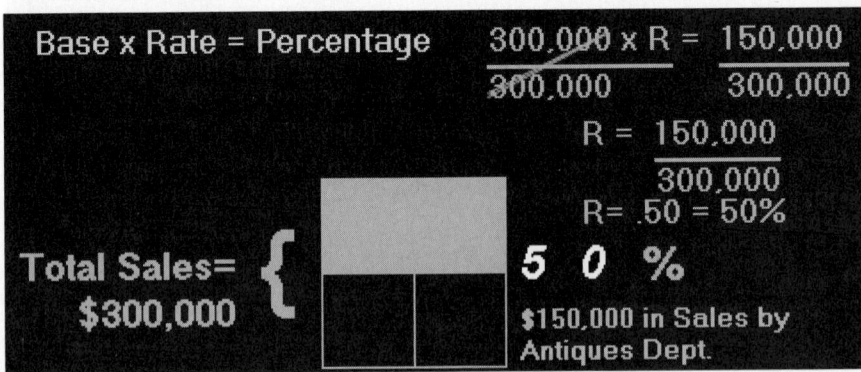

FIGURE 10.12

FOR VISUAL LEARNERS

Do the formulas have you baffled? Never fear, there is an easy way for the visual learner to remember all three of the percentage formulas. In the triangle shown in Figure 10.13, the horizontal line represents a fraction bar or division. The vertical line represents a multiplication sign. To use this triangle, cover the part representing what you wish to find. The uncovered part of the triangle reveals the formula required to find the missing element (the part you covered).

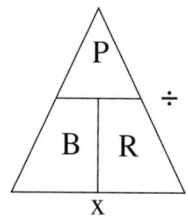

FIGURE 10.13

1. To find percentage, cover the section of the triangle containing P. The uncovered sections of the triangle reveal the formula to find percentage: B × R.
2. To find base, cover the B section of the triangle. The uncovered sections reveal the formula to find base: P ÷ R.
3. Similarly, to find rate, cover the R section of the triangle. The uncovered sections reveal the formula to find rate: P ÷ B.

MATH STAR 10.1

BE A *Math★* !

Wording to Watch: Examples of Word Problems

Example 9: If a safe-manufacturing company has five safes in inventory, the five safes make up 100% (the whole amount) of the company's inventory.

Example 10: If 80% of the company's inventory is made up of the less expensive model A, how much of the company's inventory is made up of the more expensive model B? Since 100% is the company's entire inventory, subtract 80% from 100% to find that 20% of the company's inventory is made up of model B.

It would also be correct to say that 80/100 of the company's inventory is made up of model A and 20/100 of the company's inventory is made up of model B. To find how many of the five safes represent 80/100, multiply,

$$\frac{5}{1} \times \frac{80}{100} = \frac{400}{100} = 4 \quad \text{Model A safes}$$

Example 11: To find how many of the five safes represent 20% of the company's five safes, multiply by 20/100:

$$\frac{5}{1} \times \frac{20}{100} = \frac{100}{100} = 1 \quad \text{Model B safe}$$

Example 12: It is also important to understand that some future amount of inventory can be computed. If the company wishes to increase inventory by 40% next year, we would need to either (1) calculate 40% of current inventory (the amount of inventory on hand today) and add it to 100% of current inventory, or (2) calculate next year's inventory in one step by multiplying by 140/100. The figure of 140 was obtained by adding 100%, representing current inventory, to 40%, representing the desired inventory increase. In other words, next year's inventory needs to be 140% of what it is today:

$$\frac{5}{1} \times \frac{140}{100} = \frac{700}{100} = 7 \quad \text{Next year's inventory}$$

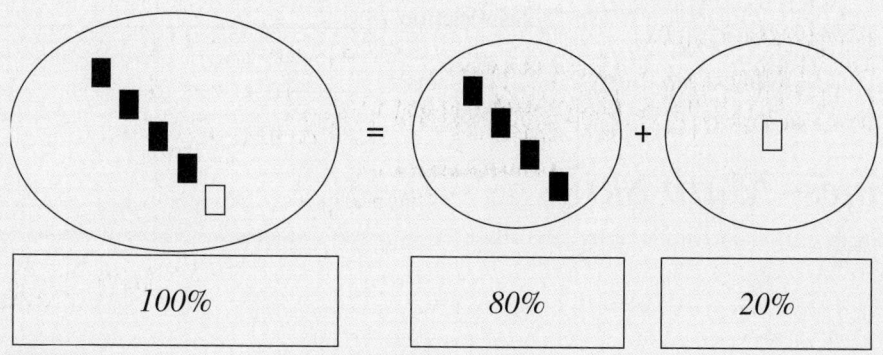

FIGURE 10.14

MATH STAR 10.2

BE A *Math* ★ !

You and your date are out for a night on the town. Your date has asked you to help with figuring the tips. No problem! And, you don't need a calculator!

Limo: The correct amount to tip the limo driver is 20%. Let's suppose the limo ride is $50.

First, find 10% of $50.00. Mentally move the decimal point in $50.00 one place to the left. 10% of 50.00 is 5.00:

$$50.00 \quad\quad 5.00$$
$$\leftarrow$$

To find 20% of $50.00, mentally multiply the $5.00 by 2:

$$5 \times 2 = 10$$

20% of $50.00 is $10.00.

Dining: The correct amount to tip the waiter or waitress is 15%. Suppose the bill is $63.50.

First, round the bill to $65.00 to make the following calculations super easy. Then, find 10% of $65.00 by moving the decimal point one place to the left. 10% of 65 is 6.50:

$$\$65.00 \quad\quad \$6.50$$
$$\leftarrow$$

Next, we need to find the additional 5% of the tip. If 6.50 is 10% of the bill, then we may divide 6.50 by 2 mentally to find the additional 5%. Break it into two steps if you like:

$$6.00/2 = 3.00$$
$$.50/2 = \underline{\quad .25}$$
$$3.25$$

Then add the $6.50 and $3.25. Use two steps if you like:

$$
\begin{array}{cc}
6 & .50 \\
\underline{+3} & \underline{+.25} \\
9 & .75
\end{array}
$$

15% of $65.00 is $9.75.

To calculate an exact 15% of $63.50, first find 10% by moving the decimal point: $6.35. Then find half of $6, or $3; and half of $.35, or $.175, which is rounded to $.18. So an exact 15% tip is $6.35 + $3.00 + $.18, or $9.53.

Name _____

Class/Section _____

Score (Correct Answers ÷ No. of Assigned Problems) _____

PART 2   *Business Math Skills*

Exercise 1

Convert the following percents to the equivalent decimal numbers and fractions. Reduce fractions to lowest terms. Round decimal numbers to the thousandths place as necessary. The first one has been completed for you.

Percent (%)	Decimal Number	Fraction	Lowest Terms
25	0.25	25/100	1/4
12.5	1. _____	2. _____	3. _____
.5	4. _____	5. _____	6. _____
50	7. _____	8. _____	9. _____
60	10. _____	11. _____	12. _____
33⅓	13. _____	14. _____	15. _____

Convert the following fractions to equivalent fractions, decimal numbers, and percents. Round percents to the tenths place as necessary. The first one has been done for you.

Fraction	Equivalent Fraction	Decimal Number	Percent (%)
3/4	75/100	.75	75
1/10	16. _____ /100	17. _____	18. _____
2/3	19. _____ /100	20. _____	21. _____
4/5	22. _____ /100	23. _____	24. _____
6/20	25. _____ /100	26. _____	27. _____
3/8	28. _____ /100	29. _____	30. _____

Calculate the missing ingredient for each problem below using the appropriate formula. Round answers to two places as necessary.

	Base	Rate	Percentage (%)
31.	7,000	20	_____
32.	400	5	_____
33.	10,000	_____	3,500
34.	1,500	_____	375
35.	_____	12	5,000
36.	_____	4	360

Exercise 2

37. A dress costing $189 was placed in a 25% off sale. How much should be subtracted from the original price to find the sale price? _____

38. Nancy had $12,000 in sales for the week. Her sales commission is 4% of sales. How much was her sales commission? _____

39. The M Company bought $215 in office supplies in March, which represented 4.5% of the total March budget. What was the total March budget rounded to whole dollars? _____

40. The Benton family spent $600 on food during May. The Benton's total monthly budget was $6,400. What percent of the family budget was spent on food? Round the answer to the hundredths place. _____

 **PART 3** *Pocket or Windows Calculator*

THE PERCENT KEY

When using a calculator to solve problems involving percents, it is not necessary to convert a percent to a decimal if the calculator has a percent key. However, some students find it confusing to switch between using a decimal number for percent when solving a problem manually and using the percent key when using a calculator. The choice is up to you and your instructor. Both methods are included in this section.

PROBLEM 1

Cottage by the Sea made a 10% profit on its sales of $2,000. How much was the profit?

Method A: Convert 10% to a decimal number (.10).

> *Note: Certain Windows calculators label the multiplication with an asterisk instead of an x. See Figure 10.15.*

$$2000 * 0.10 = \boxed{200}$$

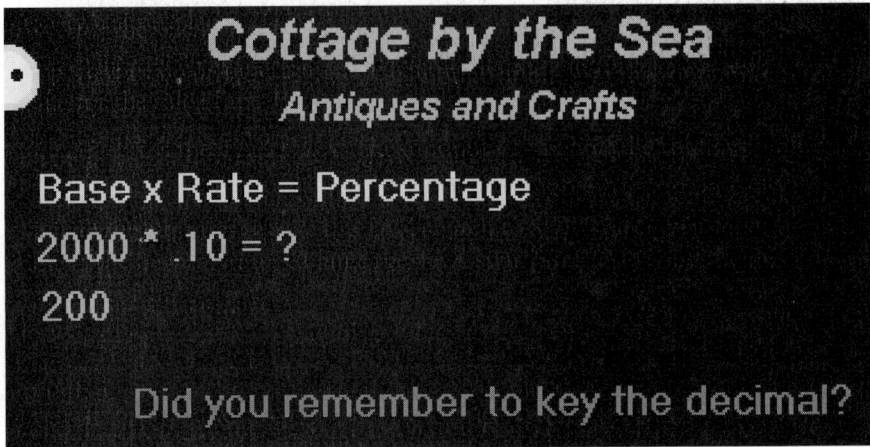

FIGURE 10.15

Method B: Instead of converting 10% to a decimal number, key 10 $\boxed{\%}$ (using the percent key) on the calculator. Do not press the equals key:

$$2,000 \times 10\% \boxed{200}$$

PROBLEM 2

The sales tax on a $2,000 item is 10%. What is the total amount due for the item? Enter the problem using the % key for the tax rate. Then press the + and = keys to add the tax and display the total amount due:

$$2,000 \times 10\% \boxed{200}$$
$$\boxed{+} \ \boxed{=} \ \boxed{2,200}$$

PROBLEM 3

Bob is buying a refrigerator for $1,200 plus a 10% delivery charge. What is the total amount due? To find the total due without displaying the amount of the delivery charge, use the plus key and the percent key as follows. The amount of the 10% delivery charge is calculated and added to the $1,200 and the total is displayed.

$$1,200 + 10\% \boxed{1,320}$$

> *Note: The amount of the delivery charge may be displayed by immediately pressing the − and = keys after completing the above problem. Although the answer displays as a negative number, the negative sign in front of 120 should be disregarded when using this shortcut:*

$$1,200 + 10\% \boxed{1,320} \ - \ = \ \boxed{-120}$$

PROBLEM 4

A beverage cooler that normally sells for $79.98 has been advertised for 25% off. What is the sale price? To find the sale price, use the minus key and the percent key as follows. Round answers to two places (dollars and cents):

79.99 − 25% $\boxed{59.99}$

Note: The amount of the discount may be displayed by immediately pressing the = key after completing the above problem:

79.99 − 25% $\boxed{59.99}$ = $\boxed{20.00}$

COMPLETING A SALES RECEIPT

A **sales receipt** is prepared when a sale is made at a store. It indicates the date, what was bought, the cost, and the amount paid or charged. A notation is made to indicate method of payment: cash, check, charge to account, or debit/credit card. Sales receipts may be handwritten (although a calculator is usually used to complete the calculations) or produced by a cash register. Following are instructions for completing a handwritten sales receipt.

To complete the calculations on a handwritten sales receipt, multiply the quantity by the price. Accumulate the amounts using the M+ key. Then, apply the tax rate to the total in memory. Round answers to two places (dollars and cents).

Complete the sales receipt in Figure 10.16. The sales tax rate is 7%.

 # 05632

Sales Receipt

Date *June 8, 2002*

Qty.	Item	Price	Amount
12 pc.	6′ SS 7/8″ tubing	33.99	407.88
2 pc.	30° round 7/8″ rail base	11.99	23.98
4 pc.	90° angle 7/8″ bow forms	11.99	47.96
	Pd cash		
		Subtotal	479.82
		Tax	33.59
		TOTAL	513.41

FIGURE 10.16

Procedure:

12 × 33.99 = $\boxed{407.88}$ M+
2 × 11.99 = $\boxed{23.98}$ M+
4 × 11.99 = $\boxed{47.96}$ M+
MT $\boxed{479.82}$ × 7% $\boxed{33.59}$ + =
$\boxed{513.41}$

A mechanically produced sales receipt may show store information as well as the date, items purchased, cost, tax rate, tax charged, method of payment, amount tendered, and change due. In Figure 10.17, the receipt shows that a DVD was purchased on December 18, 2001, for $18.44. The tax rate is 7.75%. The $1.43 of tax was added, resulting in a total of $19.87. The customer paid $19.87 (amount tendered) using a MasterCard (MCARD TEND). There was no change given (CHANGE DUE) to the customer.

```
          S U P E R C E N T E R
            WE SELL FOR LESS


           ARANSAS PASS, TEXAS
ST# 0458 OP# 00001694 TE# 67 TR# 00494
DVD             002519214692      18.44 J
                   SUBTOTAL       18.44
         TAX 1   7.750 %           1.43
                      TOTAL       19.87
               MCARD TEND         19.87

  ACCOUNT #0390-08/02
  APPROVAL #086290
  TRANS ID -
  VALIDATION -
  PAYMENT SERVICE - N
                CHANGE DUE         0.00

      # ITEMS SOLD 1

    TC# 7535 1087 9162 3482 4107
```

THE PRINCESS DIARIES, DECEMBER 18!
12/18/01   17:23:52

CUSTOMER COPY

FIGURE 10.17

BUDGET

When making plans, it is helpful to know what percent of the budget has been spent for various types of expenses. Consider a family budget. The total monthly budget (the total amount spent in 1 month) is the base. The amount spent for a given category, such as housing expense, is a percentage of the budget. To find the rate for a category, divide the category by the base or, in this case, total monthly budget.

After calculating the percents for each category of the budget, add the percents. The total should equal 100% or be within 0.1% to 0.2% of 100%, such as 99.9% or 99.8%. This allowance is made because of rounding.

PROBLEM

Complete the following budget. Round answers to the hundredths place. Check your answers with those provided.

Benton Family Budget

Month/Year: February 2003
Total Budget for Month: $4,500

Expense	Cost ($)	Percent of Total Monthly Budget
Housing (including insurance)	1,750	1. _____
Transportation (including insurance)	1,250	2. _____
Food	600	3. _____
Entertainment	80	4. _____
Clothing	70	5. _____
Medical (including insurance)	500	6. _____
Savings Plan	250	7. _____
	Total %	8. _____

Name _____

Class/Section _____

Score (Correct Answers ÷ No. of Assigned Problems) _____

 # PART 3   *Pocket or Windows Calculator*

Exercise 1

Convert the following percents to a decimal number.

Percent (%)	Decimal Number	Percent (%)	Decimal Number
53	1. _____	12.02	6. _____
1	2. _____	75½	7. _____
50	3. _____	10.90	8. _____
6	4. _____	62¼	9. _____
102	5. _____	125.26	10. _____

Calculate the missing ingredient for each problem below using the appropriate formula. <u>Convert percents in the formula to decimal numbers.</u> Round answers to the hundredths place as necessary.

	Base	Rate (%)	Percentage
11.	175,000	10	_____
12.	55,400	12¾	_____
13.	10,000	_____	400
14.	161,500	_____	30,750
15.	_____	9	15,000
16.	_____	5½	1,500

Calculate the missing ingredient for each problem below <u>using the percent key</u> and the appropriate formula. Round answers to the hundredths place as necessary.

	Base	Rate (%)	Percentage
17.	27,000	10.5	_____
18.	33,400	5.75	_____
19.	110,000	_____	112,000
20.	201,500	_____	115,000
21.	_____	4.5	25,000
22.	_____	14	2,500

Exercise 2

Complete the sales receipt in Figure 10.18 for a cash sale. The sales tax rate is 8.25%.

<table>
<thead>
<tr><th colspan="5"># 05632
Sales Receipt
Date _____</th></tr>
<tr><th>Qty.</th><th>Item</th><th>Price</th><th colspan="2">Amount</th></tr>
</thead>
<tbody>
<tr><td>7 pc</td><td>6°´ SS 7/8″ tubing</td><td>33.99</td><td>23.</td><td></td></tr>
<tr><td>4</td><td>30° round 7/8″ rail base</td><td>11.99</td><td>24.</td><td></td></tr>
<tr><td>14</td><td>90° angle 7/8″ bow forms</td><td>11.99</td><td>25.</td><td></td></tr>
<tr><td></td><td></td><td></td><td></td><td></td></tr>
<tr><td></td><td></td><td></td><td></td><td></td></tr>
<tr><td></td><td></td><td>Subtotal</td><td>26.</td><td></td></tr>
<tr><td></td><td></td><td>Tax</td><td>27.</td><td></td></tr>
<tr><td></td><td></td><td>TOTAL</td><td>28.</td><td></td></tr>
</tbody>
</table>

FIGURE 10.18

PART 3   *Review and Practice Using Business Math FUNdamentals*

GOAL: Complete 9 of the 10 problems correctly.

Instructions: Start Business Math FUNdamentals. Complete Tutorials 27 and 28 and Drill 23. If you are not satisfied with your scores, repeat the drills. Write your scores below.

Business Math FUNdamentals Drill 23

Today's Date	Score

PART 4   *The Desktop Calculator*

THE PAPERWORK TRAIL

Some forms used to track an order are prepared for company use only. These are internal documents. Other forms are sent to vendors, suppliers, or others outside the company. These are external documents. The following is a list of forms usually required for a typical purchase of supplies and their classification as internal or external documents.

1. **Purchase requisition** (internal document): a request to the purchasing department to order the needed supplies. The purchase requisition is prepared by the department needing the supplies, and must be approved by the head of the requesting department.
2. **Purchase order** (external document): an order for goods prepared in the purchasing department. Purchase orders must be approved by the person in charge of purchasing.
3. **Shipping list** (external document): an itemized list placed in a shipping container identifying the items contained in the shipment in fulfillment of a purchase order. Sometimes called a **packing slip** or shipping invoice, the shipping list does not list

prices and is not considered to be a bill. The shipping list may indicate how many cartons were used in the shipment and any items that were backordered or not in stock.

4. **Invoice** (external document): a bill prepared by the business office for items listed on the shipping invoice.

5. **Receiving report** (internal document): a list of items received as a result of a purchase order. A receiving report is prepared by the department that originally prepared the purchase requisition. Instead of a separate form, many companies either:
   a. place a checkmark beside each item received on a copy of the purchase requisition kept for this purpose, or
   b. make a notation of "received" and the date received beside each item as it is received on a copy of the shipping invoice.

   The report is then sent to the business office so that payment can be made for the items received.

6. **Payment** (external document): a check is prepared and signed by the company controller or business manager after verification has been made that the ordered items were received and properly billed. A completed transaction, ready for filing, should include a copy of the purchase requisition, a copy of the purchase order, a copy of the invoice, a copy of the receiving report, and a copy of the check issued in payment.

Department names and policies concerning authority for approvals vary slightly among companies, but the basics of good business practice should be maintained. Additional policies are required for the authorization of credit card use. Some companies maintain a petty cash fund for small cash purchases, and appropriate procedures for maintaining the petty cash fund should be developed and followed.

INVOICE

It is important to maintain company records dealing with buying, selling, shipping, and receiving goods in an orderly fashion. When an **invoice** (or bill) is prepared, it must contain information that will enable both the buyer and the seller to trace the paperwork concerning both the order and the invoice in case questions should arise; therefore, multiple copies of the invoice are prepared. Each invoice should be verified such that the items invoiced match the items on the purchase order and the items actually received. A paper tape should be made that verifies the amounts for items purchased, returned goods, applicable discounts, taxes, and shipping charges. (Returned goods, discount terms, and shipping terms that sometimes appear on invoices will be covered in later chapters.) The paper tape should be attached to the invoice. Only then should payment be approved and a check cut.

PURCHASE ORDER

A **purchase order** is prepared by the buyer when a company wishes to make a purchase. Purchase orders are numbered sequentially. When the purchase order is filled and the items shipped by the seller, an invoice is prepared by the seller that references the customer's purchase order number. A purchase order is not valid unless it has been approved and signed by the person in charge of purchase orders. Before an order is placed by telephone or via the Internet, an approved purchase order should be obtained.

CALCULATING TAX USING THE TAX SWITCH

Many of today's desktop calculators feature a special tax switch that allows the tax rate to be set and stored in one of the calculator's internal memory banks. The amount of tax can then be calculated and either added or subtracted using the TAX+ or TAX− keys. Set the decimal selector on 2 and the rounding switch on 5/4.

TAPE 10.1:

```
    14·98
     1·05▵
    16·03  *
```

TAPE 10.2:

```
    12·59
     0·88▵
    13·47  *
```

TAPE 10.3:

```
     0·00M*

      0·C

       65·  ×
     11·79  =
    766·35M+

       20·  ×
     35·81  =
    716·20M+

        2·  ×
     10·80  =
     21·60M+

        4·  ×
     14·99  =
     59·96M+

     49·99M+
        5·  ×
     29·99  =
    149·95M+

        4·  ×
     69·99  =
    279·96M+

    299·99M+
        5·  ×
     49·99  =
    249·95M+

  2›593·95M*

  2›593·95  ◇
    181·58▵
  2›775·53  *
```

Problem 1. In the city of Hope, the city and state sales tax rate is 7%. A customer bought a souvenir t-shirt for $14.98. Calculate the total amount of tax due for the sale (Tape 10.1).

> Set the TAX switch on SET. Key 7%.
>
> Set the TAX switch on CALC. Key 14.98.
>
> Press the TAX+ key. The amount of tax and the total amount due are displayed.

The tax rate of 7% has been stored and is available for any subsequent tax calculations requiring the 7% rate. The TAX+ and TAX− keys display the amount of tax and the total amount due, and also clear the machine for the next problem. It is not necessary to press the clear key between problems.

Problem 2. The next customer purchased an oscillating fan for $12.59. What was the total amount due for the sale (Tape 10.2)?

> Key 12.59. Press the TAX+ key. The amount of tax and the total amount due are displayed.

To change the tax rate, change the TAX switch to SET. The current tax rate setting will display. Enter the new tax rate. Change the TAX switch to CALC and the machine is ready for the next problem.

COMPLETING A PURCHASE ORDER OR INVOICE

Both purchase orders and invoices contain quantity and price. The amount column is used to record the result of multiplying quantity and price, and is referred to as the extension. The following problem illustrates how to calculate the extension, tax, and total on an invoice.

PROBLEM

The sales tax rate for the following invoice is 7%.

Make sure your calculator TAX feature is set to 7%. To complete the following invoice, multiply quantity and price to find amount (Tape 10.3). Use the memory feature to accumulate amounts and find a subtotal. Use the TAX+ feature to add the tax and find the total due. Note that in the fourth and eighth items it is not necessary to multiply by one. Simply key the single-item price and press the M+= key to add the price to memory.

Machine Setup	Decimal Selector—2
	Rounding Switch—5/4
	Tax Switch—CALC
	Printer Switch—ON

Procedure	Results
65 × 11.79 M+=	766.35
20 × 35.81 M+=	716.20
2 × 10.80 M+=	21.60
4 × 14.99 M+=	59.96
49.99 M+=	49.99
5 × 29.99 M+=	149.95
4 × 69.99 M+=	279.96
299.99 M+=	299.99
5 × 49.99 M+=	249.95
MT	2,593.95
TAX+	181.58
	2,775.53

INVOICE

Computers and More Direct
2290 Palmer Drive
Long Beach, CA 90800

SOLD TO:
Office Works, Inc.
PO Box 19
Victoria, TX 77900

INVOICE NUMBER 64592
INVOICE DATE May 14, 2002
PURCHASE ORDER NO. B3902229
TERMS
SALES PERSON J B
SHIPPED VIA
F.O.B.

SHIPPED TO:
Office Works, Inc.
200 S. Main
Victoria, TX 77901

QTY	DESCRIPTION	PRICE	AMOUNT
65 pkg.	Inkjet printer cartridges #BJ 1000 3/pkg.	11.79	766.35
20 boxes	Inkjet paper #P680, 10 reams per box	35.81	716.20
2 boxes	Black roller pens, #B15, 12 per box	10.80	21.60
4 ea.	Optical scrolling mouse, #L1320	14.99	59.96
1 ea.	Tool kit, #TK20	49.99	49.99
5 pkg.	20x Black Diamond CDR, #BD55, 50/pkg.	29.99	149.95
4 ea.	Desktop memory, 256MB, #DM 53	69.99	279.96
1 ea.	IPAQ color 3650, #I22	299.99	299.99
5 ea.	SmartMedia card, 128MB, #SM113	49.99	249.95

SUBTOTAL	2593.95
TAX RATE	7.00%
TAX	181.58
FREIGHT	0.00
$2,775.53	
TOTAL DUE	

THANK YOU FOR YOUR BUSINESS!

Name _____

Class/Section _____

Score (Correct Answers ÷ No. of Assigned Problems) _____

 PART 4   *The Desktop Calculator*

Exercise 1

Convert the following percents and fractions to decimal numbers. Round answers to the ten thousandths place as necessary.

Percent (%)	Decimal Number	Fraction	Decimal Number
12	1. _____	5/8	2. _____
7.5	3. _____	6/24	4. _____
16.75	5. _____	9/10	6. _____
6.20	7. _____	17/35	8. _____
155.12	9. _____	26/88	10. _____

Calculate the missing ingredient for each problem below using the appropriate formula. Round answers to the hundredths place as necessary.

	Base	Rate (%)	Percentage
11.	600	5	_____
12.	4,200	6.5	_____
13.	9,750	_____	2,450
14.	66,450	_____	9,655
15.	_____	35	445
16.	_____	$9\frac{3}{4}$	5,800

Exercise 2

Complete the following purchase order.

PURCHASE ORDER

Office Works, Inc.
PO Box 19
Victoria, TX 77900

TO:
[Computers and More Direct
2290 Palmer Drive
Long Beach, CA 90800]

P. O. NUMBER 56923
DATE June 7, 2002
REQUISITIONED BY AJ
SHIP BY June 10, 2002
SHIP VIA
F.O.B.
TERMS

SHIP TO:
Office Works, Inc.
200 S. Main St.
Victoria, TX 77901

Purchase order number must appear
on all forms relating to this order.

(continued)

QTY	UNIT	DESCRIPTION	PRICE	AMOUNT
6	each	Model # S69501 6-outlet surge strip	4.99	17. 29.94
4	each	Model # H55302 4-port USB hub	9.99	
2	kits	Model # NK649 Gear to Go notebook kits	12.99	19. 25.98
10	each	Model # #509sc Sound cards	11.99	
1	each	Model # M300549 17" TFT LCD	499.99	21. 499.99

SUBTOTAL		
FREIGHT		0.00
TAX RATE		7.000%
TAX		23. 50.80

TOTAL DUE

Jeremy Harrison   *June 7, 2002*

Authorized by   Date

Exercise 3

Strokes per Minute Score _____

Accuracy Score (Correct Strokes ÷ Total Strokes) _____

One-Minute Addition Timing (Keys 0 through 9; 00 Key; Add Mode)

(Optional: Your instructor may wish you to use Touch Key on the computer for all your timings. Check with your instructor before completing this exercise.)

Complete as many of the problems as possible in 1 minute by adding. Work quickly and accurately. The number preceding each closing parenthesis indicates the cumulative number of strokes for problems attempted. For example, if you complete Problems 1 through 4 in 1 minute, your strokes-per-minute score is 244. Optional: 3- to 5-minute timings.

1. 55,004	2. 87,001	3. 67,400	4. 65,006	5. 57,814	6. 49,200	7. 37,700	8. 18,001
56,214	98,500	69,100	57,002	48,316	84,500	70,400	19,003
89,584	89,305	65,400	58,001	49,585	74,100	80,100	71,002
96,500	72,876	64,600	59,003	74,232	46,400	90,800	91,001
43,025	78,745	76,400	95,004	77,003	47,006	60,500	81,004
51,506	79,002	86,500	85,005	48,004	71,005	50,200	41,002
32,421	97,571	59,300	75,003	64,000	72,003	40,300	51,007
12,901	98,631	57,100	56,003	45,005	73,004	11,600	61,004
31,200	96,994	58,300	45,001	54,600	17,006	14,900	21,005
13,502	68,300	57,300	54,002	94,001	27,006	17,900	24,003
61)	122)	183)	244)	305)	366)	427)	488)

175

9. 25,400	10. 92,900	11. 32,415	12. 90,002	13. 73,600	14. 20,722	15. 66,000	16. 50,004
27,420	24,700	23,545	10,402	83,756	21,734	30,513	52,600
26,850	72,956	34,252	20,605	93,736	25,965	38,464	29,000
23,150	82,002	43,715	50,908	39,826	24,936	39,514	27,870
32,700	92,000	35,632	60,096	30,956	26,835	96,645	28,002
27,689	62,702	53,536	36,302	20,546	27,731	69,423	63,003
72,599	88,005	30,565	63,846	10,002	28,741	63,513	81,514
71,884	33,002	20,025	37,613	18,300	29,962	69,753	82,787
81,256	31,008	70,001	73,701	57,002	60,854	97,624	92,412
61,374	13,005	80,500	38,300	19,006	51,014	90,411	72,600
549)	610)	671)	732)	793)	854)	915)	976)

Set decimal selector on add mode.

17. 524.00	18. 750.00	19. 561.00	20. 736.55	21. 829.90	22. 562.80	23. 483.00	24. 836.29
766.00	728.00	564.00	819.88	827.58	456.19	173.50	952.49
367.00	857.00	635.00	617.77	825.69	643.99	195.75	762.19
492.00	729.00	548.00	938.66	274.71	862.79	353.25	885.39
929.00	627.00	226.00	839.87	927.52	743.59	362.95	992.59
827.00	549.00	311.00	871.34	729.16	941.79	212.85	772.89
381.00	468.00	911.00	782.59	748.10	856.00	115.50	875.69
329.00	193.00	819.00	893.68	927.25	742.93	231.75	783.79
839.00	186.00	829.00	368.78	838.45	876.21	445.80	993.19
737.00	134.00	729.00	382.49	939.00	986.32	963.70	891.59
1,037)	1,098)	1,159)	1,220)	1,281)	1,342)	1,403)	1,464)

CHAPTER 10 *Terminology Review*

Base

Formula

Invoice

Packing slip

Payment

Percent

Percentage

Proportion

Purchase order

Purchase requisition

Rate

Receiving report

Sales receipt

Shipping list

Complete the following statements.

1. A _____ is a statement of a rule or principle.

2. To find a(n) _____, divide the percentage by the base.

3. When calculating percentage, the whole is represented by the word _____.

4. A(n) _____ is a portion of a whole and is always stated as an amount. It is the result of multiplying a whole by a rate.

5. A(n) _____ is part of a whole.

6. A(n) _____ is a proportion given in hundredths and is followed by a percent sign.

In the business office:

7. A(n) _____ is an internal request for a purchase order to be prepared.

8. A(n) _____ is a bill.

9. Before an order for goods is placed, a(n) _____ is prepared.

True or false:

10. Checks are usually prepared by the department that issued the purchase requisition. T/F _____

11. A receiving report is a list indicating which previously ordered items have arrived. T/F _____

12. A sales receipt indicates items purchased, cost of the items, and method of payment. T/F _____

13. A shipping invoice is a bill. T/F _____

Name _____

Class/Section _____

Score (Correct Answers ÷ No. of Assigned Problems) _____

Chapter 10 Review Exercises

Exercise 1

Convert the following percents to the equivalent decimal numbers and fractions. Reduce fractions to lowest terms.

Percent (%)	Decimal Number	Fraction	Lowest Terms
80	1. _____	2. _____	3. _____
15	4. _____	5. _____	6. _____
5	7. _____	8. _____	9. _____
94	10. _____	11. _____	12. _____
29.5	13. _____	14. _____	15. _____

Convert the following fractions to equivalent fractions, decimal numbers, and percents. Round answers to the hundredths place as necessary.

Fraction	Equivalent Fraction	Decimal Number	Percent (%)
1/5	16. _____ /100	17. _____	18. _____
9/10	19. _____ /100	20. _____	21. _____
2/4	22. _____ /100	23. _____	24. _____
5/25	25. _____ /100	26. _____	27. _____
8/50	28. _____ /100	29. _____	30. _____

Calculate the missing ingredient for each of the following problems using the appropriate formula. Round answers to the hundredths place as necessary.

	Base	Rate (%)	Percentage
31.	800	18	_____
32.	2,300	3.5	_____
33.	7,500	_____	200
34.	74,000	_____	12,375
35.	_____	1.75	15,000
36.	_____	5.4	925

Exercise 2

Round answers to the hundredths place as necessary.

37. JJC has an enrollment of 5,890 students. Of the students, 60% are female. How many female students are enrolled at JJC? _____

38. Use the information in Problem 37 to determine how many male students are enrolled at JJC. _____

39. If 30% of Wednesday's sales were cash sales, calculate the amount of cash sales if total sales were $5,400. _____

40. Vegetable and fruit spoilage is expected to be 15% at the Veggies Store this week. If the store has 6,600 pounds of produce, how much is expected to sell? _____

41. If three-fifths of music CD sales are made to teenagers, what percent of music CD sales are made to teenagers? _____

42. Manny's new vehicle had 15% better gas mileage than his old vehicle. If he was able to get 4 more miles per gallon, how many miles per gallon did he get with his old vehicle? _____

43. Johnny paid $200 down on a $1,359.98 refrigerator. What percent of the total price was the down payment? _____

44. Renee was able to buy a $5,000 item that had been discounted for a special sale for $4,150. What was the percent of the discount? _____

45. Sales of Brand A were 59% more than sales of Brand B. Total sales of Brand B were $10,250. What were total sales for both brands? _____

Exercise 3

Complete the following budget. Find the percent of total monthly budget for each advertising expense. The total dollar amount for the January 2003 budget is given. Round answers to the hundredths place.

Advertising Budget

Month/Year: January 2003
Total Advertising Budget for Month: Percent of Sales: 5%
Dollar Amount: $424,500

Medium	Specific Outlet (Name of Specific Newspaper or Magazine, etc.)	Frequency of Ads	Total Cost ($)	Percent of Total Monthly Budget
Newspaper	Daily News	Daily	65,000	46. _____
Magazine	Photo Monthly	Monthly	1,500	47. _____
Television	KCEM	5× daily	115,000	48. _____
Radio	KLRR	20× daily	120,000	49. _____
Internet	Isales.com	Not available	65,000	50. _____
Outdoor	Boards, Inc.	Not available	58,000	51. _____
			Total %	52. _____

UNIT II

Business Applications

CHAPTER 11

Simple Interest

 ## PART 1 *Speed and Accuracy Building Using Touch Key*

GOALS: Your speed goal is 8,000 strokes per hour.
Your accuracy target goal range is 95% to 100%.

With each repetition of the drill, try to improve your speed without lowering your accuracy score. If your percent-of-accuracy score falls below 95%, review your finger position and technique. Then try again.

Instructions: *Start Touch Key. Complete Lesson 8, Parts A through E. Write your scores for strokes per hour and percent of accuracy below.*

Touch Key Lesson 8—The 0 through 9 Keys, Four-Digit Numbers

	Today's Date	Strokes per Hour	Percent of Accuracy
A.			
B.			
C.			
D.			
E.			

PART 2 *Business Math Skills*

INTEREST

Interest is a fascinating subject because it has to do with the time value of money. It stands to reason that the longer money is invested in a savings account that pays interest, the more valuable the account will become as the interest is added to the account. On the other hand, if money has been borrowed, the longer the period of time for which the money is borrowed, the more interest will have to be paid.

What is interest and how is it earned? Consider a bank. Some of the services offered by a bank include checking accounts, savings accounts, and loans. Customers of the bank place money into checking and savings accounts at the bank for safekeeping. These accounts contain more money than is likely to be demanded or withdrawn by customers on any one day. Therefore, the bank may use these excess funds for making loans. The bank is, in effect, borrowing money from its customers. The bank may be asked for a loan by a customer. In return for being lent the money, the customer is expected to pay back the money borrowed plus an additional sum—interest. In this way the bank makes money.

On the other hand, if a customer places money in a savings account at the bank, the bank is expected to keep the money safe and to pay an additional sum into the account. This additional sum, called interest, is paid at a smaller rate than the interest the bank charges when it makes a loan. Thus, the bank makes more money in interest charged on loans than it pays out to savings account customers.

SIMPLE INTEREST

There are two types of interest—simple interest and compound interest. Credit unions may loan money at simple interest rates, whereas bank loans may be made at compound interest rates. It is up to the consumer to choose which type will be best for him or her. Compound interest will be covered in a later chapter.

As shown in the bank example, **interest** is the cost of borrowing money. **Simple interest** is the interest paid for one period, such as 1 year or 1 month, on money borrowed or invested. The amount of money borrowed or invested is the **principal**. **Rate** is the percent at which interest is charged on a loan or paid on an account. **Time** is the amount of time for which money has been borrowed or placed into an account.

THE SIMPLE INTEREST FORMULA

All four of these elements, interest, principal, rate, and time, are part of the formula for calculating simple interest. Although there are four elements instead of three, you will see some similarities between the simple interest formula and the percentage formula studied in the previous chapter.

To review, notice in Figure 11.1 that although some different words are used in the percentage formula, the meaning is the same. Percentage is an amount representing a portion of something. Base is an amount representing a whole item or whole amount. Rate is used in both formulas to represent the percent.

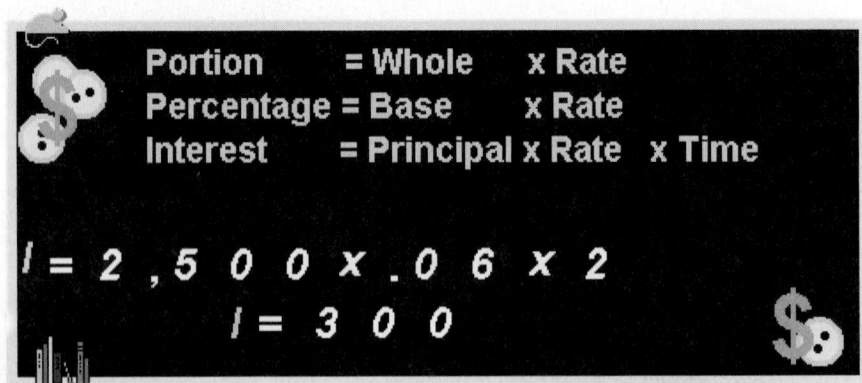

$$\text{Portion} = \text{Whole} \times \text{Rate}$$
$$\text{Percentage} = \text{Base} \times \text{Rate}$$
$$\text{Interest} = \text{Principal} \times \text{Rate} \times \text{Time}$$

$$I = 2,500 \times .06 \times 2$$
$$I = 300$$

FIGURE 11.1

Look at the third formula in Figure 11.1. The simple interest formula is **Interest = Principal × Rate × Time**. Compare the three formulas for similarities and differences. Interest is an amount representing a portion or percentage of some amount of dollars. Principal is the whole or base amount of money borrowed or invested. Rate is the percent at which interest will be paid, and is usually stated as the rate per year. Time is an additional factor present in the simple interest formula. It represents how long the principal has been borrowed or invested. Time is usually expressed in terms of years.

EXAMPLE 1

$2,500 was invested at 6% simple interest per year for 2 years. Thus, $2,500 is the principal, 6% is the rate, and 2 years is the time. Substituting the appropriate amounts for the terms in the formula, we have

I = 2,500 × 6% × 2	Before solving using pen and paper, convert the percent to a decimal number and rewrite the formula.
I = 2,500 × 0.06 × 2	Solve.
I = $300	Since interest always involves money, add the dollar sign to your answer.

It should be clear that whenever a loan is made by a person or business, an investment is being made by another person or business that is providing the money for the loan. Therefore, although most of the following problems deal with loans, the same techniques apply for calculating interest, principal, rate, or time for an investment.

I will <u>earn</u> 6% by making this loan of $2,500 for 1 year. Let's see. Hmmm. That's $300!

I will <u>pay</u> 6% for borrowing this $2,500 for 1 year. Let's see. Hmmm. That's $300!

FIGURE 11.2

MATURITY VALUE

As stated earlier, when <u>principal</u> is invested at a certain <u>rate</u> for a certain period of <u>time</u>, <u>interest</u> is earned. The principal invested and the interest earned, when added together, make up the **maturity value** of a loan. The maturity value formula is

$$\text{Maturity Value} = \text{Principal} + \text{Interest}$$

In Example 1, $2,500 was invested for 2 years at 6% and earned $300. The amount that the investor will receive at the end of 2 years (the maturity value) will be the $2,500 principal plus the $300 interest earned, or $2,800 (see Figure 11.3).

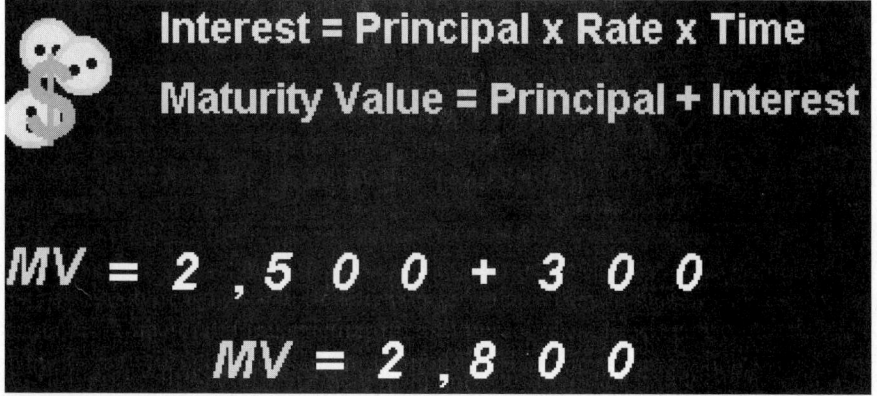

Interest = Principal x Rate x Time

Maturity Value = Principal + Interest

MV = 2,500 + 300

MV = 2,800

FIGURE 11.3

TIME EXPRESSED IN MONTHS

In Example 1, the principal was borrowed at a yearly rate for 2 full years. What if money is borrowed at 6% for a certain number of months? When time is expressed in months, 1 month is calculated as 1/12 of a year regardless of the number of days in the month.

EXAMPLE 2

$2,500 was invested at 6% simple interest for 6 months.

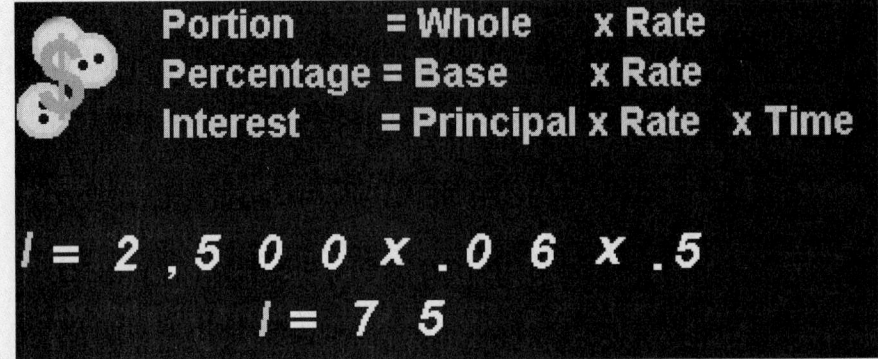

FIGURE 11.4

Substitute the appropriate amounts for the terms in the simple interest formula. Since the length of time for this loan is 6/12 or 1/2 year, you may wish to convert 1/2 year to a decimal number (0.5) before solving:

$$\text{Interest} = \text{Principal} \times \text{Rate} \times \text{Time}$$
$$I = 2,500 \times 0.06 \times 0.5$$
$$I = \$75$$

Add interest to principal to find the maturity value of the loan:

$$\text{Principal} + \text{Interest} = \text{Maturity Value}$$
$$\$2,500 + \$75 = \$2,575$$

ORDINARY VERSUS EXACT INTEREST

There are two methods for determining the amount of interest in the simple interest formula: ordinary interest and exact interest.

Ordinary Interest

If the **ordinary interest** (also known as banker's interest) method is used, interest is calculated as though every month has 30 days and every year has 360 days.

Ordinary Interest, Time Expressed in Months   A 4-month note signed January 3 would be due May 3. Count the months as follows:

January 3 to February 3	1
February 3 to March 3	2
March 3 to April 3	3
April 3 to May 3	4 months

A 3-month note signed August 31 would be due November 30 because there are only 30 days in November:

August 31 to September 30	1
September 30 to October 31	2
October 31 to November 30	3 months

Ordinary Interest, Time Expressed in Days   When using ordinary interest, a year is assumed to have 360 days. Therefore, time for a note of 45 days duration is stated as 45/360 of a year when the interest is calculated using the simple interest formula.

Exact Interest

If the **exact interest** method is specified in the terms of a loan, use 365 days per year (366 days for leap year). The exact time for a loan made May 1 and due July 22 is 82 days. Note in Figure 11.5 that the due date is NOT counted. Time in this case is stated as 82/365 for a non-leap year when using the simple interest formula.

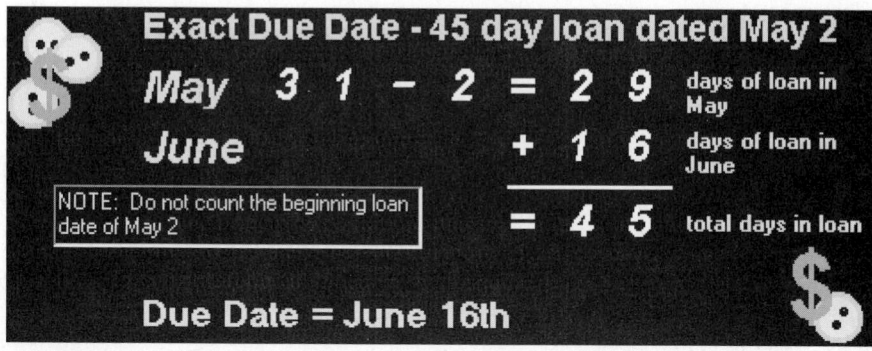

Exact Time - May 1 to July 22

May	3 1	days
June	3 0	days
July	2 1	days – DO NOT count the due date itself.
	8 2	days

FIGURE 11.5

CALCULATING THE DUE DATE OF A LOAN (EXACT INTEREST METHOD)

When the length of a loan or investment is stated in days, use the exact number of days when calculating the loan. Rather than counting the exact number of days on a calendar to find the due date of a loan, you can calculate the due date. Add the number of days in each month of the loan. A 45-day loan dated May 2 will be due on June 16 (see Figure 11.6).
   Note: May 2, the date the loan was made, is not counted.

Exact Due Date - 45 day loan dated May 2

May	3 1 – 2 = 2 9	days of loan in May
June	+ 1 6	days of loan in June
	= 4 5	total days in loan

NOTE: Do not count the beginning loan date of May 2

Due Date = June 16th

FIGURE 11.6

$31 - 2 = 29$	May has 31 days. Subtract both May 1 and May 2 from the 31 days in the month of May. Twenty-nine days from the month of May were covered by the loan.
$45 - 29 = 16$	However, the loan is for 45 days. Subtract the 29 days counted so far from 45 days. The loan also covers 16 days in the following month of June. The due date for the loan is June 16.

It is not enough to know that $2,500 was invested at 6% for 45 days. Before solving the problem, it must be ascertained whether the terms of the loan include ordinary interest or exact interest. To see the difference in the amount of interest due based on ordinary or exact interest, Example 3 will be solved using the ordinary interest method and Example 4 will be solved using the exact interest method.

EXAMPLE 3

$2,500 was invested at 6% for 45 days, ordinary interest.

Because ordinary interest is specified, a 360-day year will be used. Since the loan is for 45 days, which is only a fraction of a year, use a fraction for time (45/360). See Figure 11.7.

$I = 2,500 \times 0.06 \times 45/360$	Convert 6% to a decimal number before placing it into the simple interest formula.
$I = \$18.75$	(A calculator is suggested for convenience, or you may reduce 45/360 to lowest terms, 1/8, and use pen and paper for your calculations.) Add a dollar sign to your answer.

Ordinary Interest = Principal x Rate x Time

$$I = \frac{2,500 \times .06 \times 45}{360}$$

Hint: Calculate the numerator portion, then divide by the denominator using a calculator.

$$I = 18.75$$

FIGURE 11.7

EXAMPLE 4

$2,500 was invested at 6% for 45 days, exact interest.

Since exact interest is specified, a 365-day year will be used. Since the loan is for 45 days, which is only a fraction of a year, use a fraction for time (45/365). See Figure 11.8.

$I = 2,500 \times 0.06 \times 45/365$	Convert 6% to a decimal number before placing it into the simple interest formula.
$I = \$18.49$	(A calculator is suggested for convenience, or you may reduce 45/365 to lowest terms, 9/73, and use pen and paper for your calculations.) Add a dollar sign to your answer: $2,500 \times 0.06 \times 9 \div 73 = \$18.49$.

Which method, ordinary interest or exact interest, would be most advantageous to the borrower?

(continued)

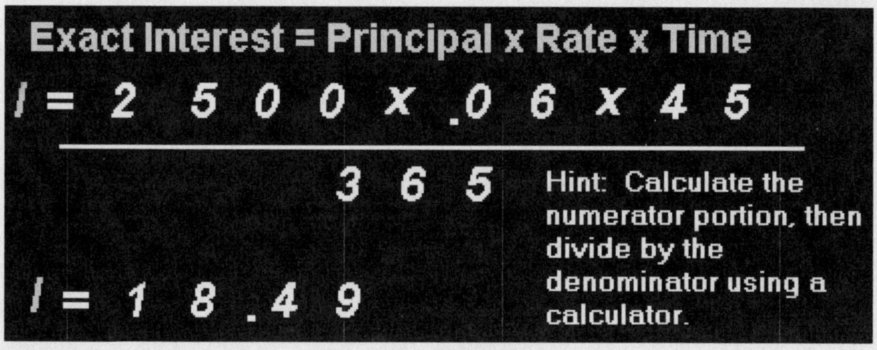

SIMPLE INTEREST

187

Exact Interest = Principal x Rate x Time

$$I = \frac{2\ 5\ 0\ 0\ X\ .0\ 6\ X\ 4\ 5}{3\ 6\ 5}$$

Hint: Calculate the numerator portion, then divide by the denominator using a calculator.

$$I = 1\ 8\ .4\ 9$$

FIGURE 11.8

Answer: The exact interest method would be most advantageous to the borrower because in this case the interest charged to the borrower, $18.49, is less than interest charged using the ordinary interest method.

CALCULATING PRINCIPAL

After you have memorized the simple interest formula, **Interest = Principal × Rate × Time**, you can manipulate the terms to find other elements of the formula in the same manner you manipulate the percentage formula to find elements other than percentage. In the simple interest formula, to find principal, isolate P on one side of the formula by dividing both sides by R × T. Since R × T divided by R × T equals 1, this part of the formula may be cancelled. This does two things: (1) it isolates P and (2) it moves R × T to the left side of the formula. The complete formula now states that **Interest divided by (Rate × Time) = Principal** (see Figure 11.9).

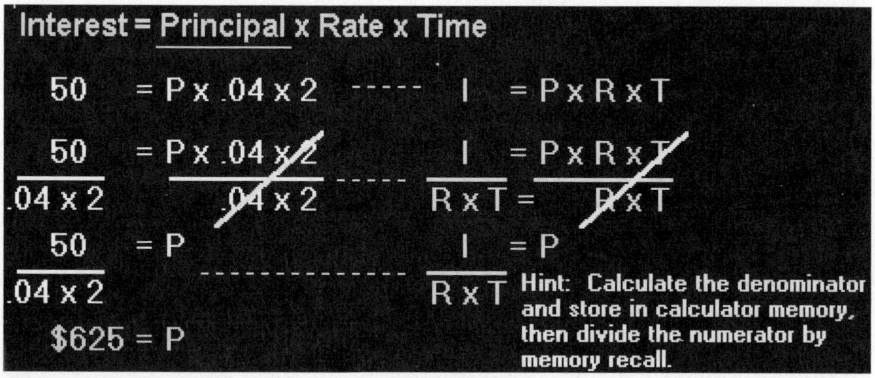

Interest = Principal x Rate x Time

$$50 = P \times .04 \times 2 \quad ----- \quad I = P \times R \times T$$

$$\frac{50}{.04 \times 2} = P \times \frac{.04 \times 2}{.04 \times 2} \quad ----- \quad \frac{I}{R \times T} = \frac{P \times R \times T}{R \times T}$$

$$\frac{50}{.04 \times 2} = P \quad ----- \quad \frac{I}{R \times T} = P$$

$$\$625 = P$$

Hint: Calculate the denominator and store in calculator memory, then divide the numerator by memory recall.

FIGURE 11.9

EXAMPLE 5

A total of $50 in interest was received on an investment made at 4% for 2 years. How much principal was originally invested?

Refer to Figure 11.9. Substitute the numbers in the problem for the terms in the formula. The interest is $50, the rate is 4% (change to a decimal number), and the time is 2 years. Solve to find the amount of principal:

$P = I \div (R \times T)$ Be sure to multiply rate × time before dividing

$P = 50 \div (.04 \times 2)$ Multiply: $0.04 \times 2 = 0.08$

Divide: $50 \div 0.08 = \$625$

Principal = $625

RULES, RULES, RULES . . .

Let us reiterate manipulating the simple interest formula. As you learned in Chapter 10:

1. A variable can be isolated by performing the opposite arithmetic operation to both sides of the formula.
2. Because principal is **multiplied** by both rate and time in the simple interest formula, it is possible to isolate P by **dividing** both sides of the formula by R $\times$ T because the opposite of multiplication is division.

CALCULATING RATE

To change the formula to solve for rate, isolate R (rate) by dividing both sides of the formula by P $\times$ T. Because P $\times$ T divided by P $\times$ T can be cancelled, the resulting formula is

$$\text{Interest} \div (\text{Principal} \times \text{Time}) = \text{Rate}$$

EXAMPLE 6

An investment of $3,500 earned $350 over a period of 2 years. What was the rate of interest earned?

Refer to Figure 11.10. Substitute the numbers in the formula for finding rate. In this problem, principal is $3,500, interest is $350, and time is 2 years:

$$350 \div (3,500 \times 2) = R \qquad \text{Multiply: } 3,500 \times 2 = 7,000$$
$$\text{Divide: } 350 \div 7,000 = 0.05$$

Convert the decimal number to a percent:

$$\text{Rate} = 5\%$$

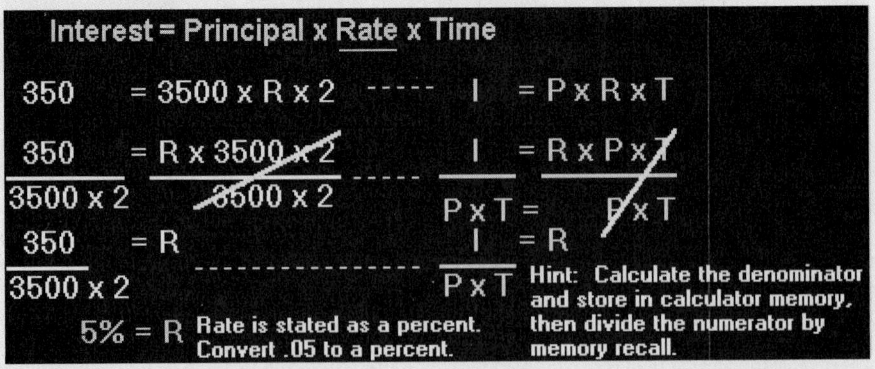

FIGURE 11.10

CALCULATING TIME

To change the formula to solve for time, isolate T (time) by dividing both sides of the formula by P $\times$ R. Because P $\times$ R divided by P $\times$ R can be cancelled, the resulting formula is I $\div$ (P $\times$ R) = T.

EXAMPLE 7

An investment of $3,500 earned $525 at 5% interest. What was the length of time of the investment?

Refer to Figure 11.11. Substitute the numbers in the formula for finding time. In this problem, principal is $3,500, interest is $525, and rate is 5%. Solve for time:

$$525 \div (3{,}500 \times 0.05) = T \qquad \text{Multiply: } 3{,}500 \times 0.05 = 175$$
$$\text{Divide: } 525 \div 175 = 3$$

$$\text{Time} = 3 \text{ years}$$

Interest = Principal x Rate x Time

$$525 = 3500 \times .05 \times T \text{ --- } I = P \times R \times T$$

$$\frac{525}{3500 \times .05} = \frac{3500 \times .05 \times T}{3500 \times .05} \text{ -- } \frac{I}{P \times R} = \frac{P \times R \times T}{P \times R}$$

$$\frac{525}{3500 \times .05} = T \text{ --------- } \frac{I}{P \times R} = T$$

$$3 \text{ yrs.} = T$$

Hint: Calculate the denominator and store in calculator memory, then divide the numerator by memory recall.

FIGURE 11.11

FOR VISUAL LEARNERS

Recognizing the similarities between the percentage formula and the simple interest formula can help you solve problems quickly using the visualization method (the triangle learned in the previous chapter). In the simple interest formula, interest (I) takes the place of percentage (P). Principal (P) takes the place of base (B). Rate continues to represent the percent in the problems. Only one major change is necessary to convert the percentage formula into the simple interest formula. Time (T) must be included as one of the factors necessary in solving for interest.

In the triangle shown in Figure 11.12, the horizontal line, which is similar to the horizontal line in a fraction, represents division. The vertical lines represent multiplication. To use this triangle, cover the part representing what you wish to find. The uncovered part of the triangle reveals the formula required to find the missing element (the part you covered).

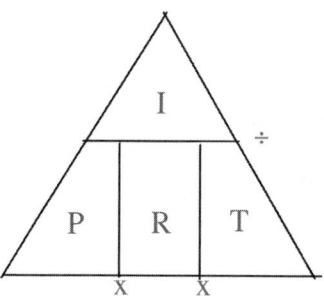

FIGURE 11.12

1. To find interest, cover the section of the triangle containing I. The uncovered sections of the triangle reveal the formula for finding interest: **Interest = Principal × Rate × Time.**
2. To find principal, cover the P section of the triangle. The uncovered sections reveal the formula for finding principal: P = I ÷ (R × T).
3. To find rate, cover the R section of the triangle. The uncovered sections reveal the formula for finding rate: R = I ÷ (P × T).
4. To find time, cover the T section of the triangle. The uncovered sections reveal the formula for finding time: T = I ÷ (P × R).

Note: Remember that T in the formula stands for time as stated in years. If days are specified, the days must be stated in the simple interest formula as a fraction of a year; such as 160/360 (ordinary interest) or 160/365 (exact interest). If time is stated in months, the months must also be stated in the simple interest formula as a fraction of a year, such as 5/12.

THE SIMPLE INTEREST NOTE

A simple interest note differs from other loans in that the interest is subtracted from the amount borrowed at the time the loan is made to a customer. A customer may borrow $7,000 for $500 in interest for 1 year. The bank will subtract the $500 in interest from the $7,000 before turning the remainder over to the customer. The customer will have use of only $6,500 of the $7,000 loan.

The simple interest formula can be used to calculate the interest charged for a simple interest note; however, there is a difference in terminology. The amount borrowed is the **face value** of the simple interest note. The amount of interest subtracted from the face value of the simple interest note is the **bank discount**. The remaining amount of money available for the customer's use is the **proceeds**.

EXAMPLE 8

Find the proceeds for a simple interest note for $5,000 at 8% ordinary interest for 1 year.

First, find the amount of the bank discount (interest) using the simple interest formula. Refer to Figure 11.13. Substitute amounts for the terms in the formula. Principal is $5,000, rate is 0.08, and time is 1 year:

$$\text{Bank Discount} = P \times R \times T$$
$$\text{Bank Discount} = 5,000 \times 0.08 \times 1$$
$$\text{Bank Discount} = \$400$$

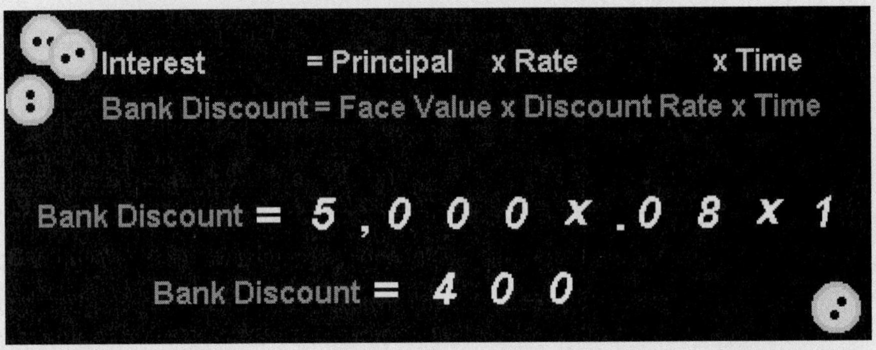

Interest = Principal x Rate x Time
Bank Discount = Face Value x Discount Rate x Time

Bank Discount = 5,000 X .08 X 1

Bank Discount = 400

FIGURE 11.13

Second, find the amount of proceeds by subtracting the bank discount from the face value of the simple interest note. Refer to Figure 11.14:

$$\text{Face Value} - \text{Bank Discount} = \text{Proceeds}$$
$$\$5,000 - \$400 = \$4,600$$

The customer will pay back the face value of the simple interest note ($5,000) on the due date (proceeds plus bank discount or interest).

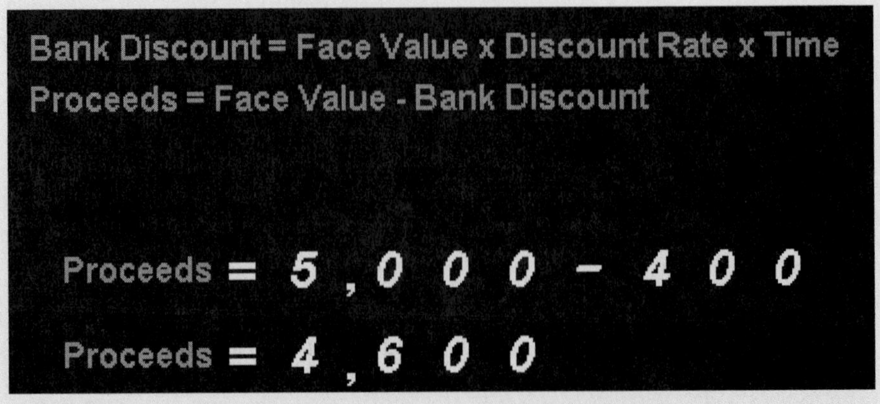

Bank Discount = Face Value x Discount Rate x Time
Proceeds = Face Value - Bank Discount

Proceeds = 5,000 - 400

Proceeds = 4,600

FIGURE 11.14

TREASURY BILLS

Treasury bills are a common type of bond sold in increments of $1,000 by the U.S. Government. Treasury bills (T-Bills) are short-term obligations that mature in 13, 26, or 52 weeks. Issuing (or selling) T-Bills is a way for the U.S. Government to borrow money. The interest rate is stated as a percent and the amount of interest is discounted from the face value of the T-Bill. The U.S. Government will receive the proceeds of the T-Bill. The proceeds are calculated by subtracting the discount amount from the face value of the T-Bill. The simple interest formula can be used to find the amount of the discount. Upon maturity, the holder of the T-Bill will receive the full face value when he or she redeems it.

EXAMPLE 9

If a T-Bill for $10,000 is purchased at a 5% discount, how much will the customer pay for it? What will be the proceeds to the government? How much will the customer receive when the T-Bill is redeemed at the end of the year?

First, use the simple interest formula to find the amount of interest or discount (see Figure 11.15). The face value (principal) of the T-Bill is $10,000, rate is 5%, and time is 1 year:

$$\text{Interest or Discount} = \$10,000 \times 0.05 \times 1 = \$500$$

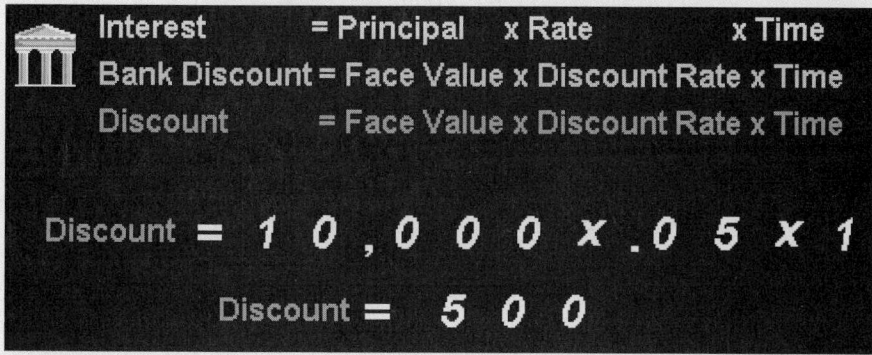

FIGURE 11.15

Second, subtract the amount of the interest or discount from the face value of the T-Bill to find how much the customer will pay for the T-Bill and how much the proceeds to the U.S. Government will be (refer to Figure 11.16):

Face Value − Discount = Proceeds to U.S. Government   (also equals amount customer will pay for the T-Bill)

$10,000 − $500 = $9,500

When the T-Bill is redeemed after one year, the customer will receive the face value of $10,000. For more information on T-Bills, visit www.publicdebt.treas.gov.

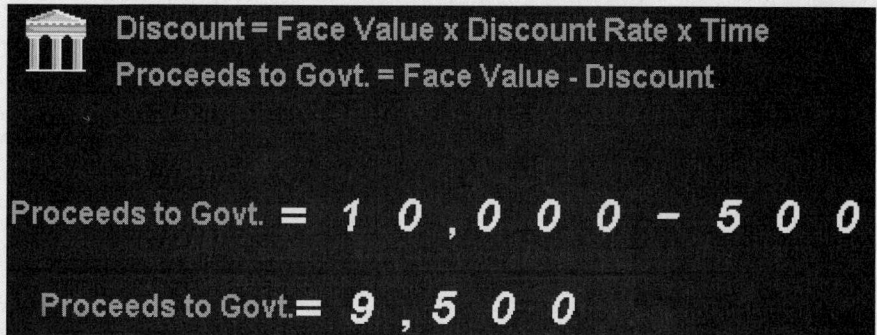

FIGURE 11.16

PROMISSORY NOTES AND THIRD-PARTY NOTES

A **promissory note** is a signed agreement in which a promise is made to pay an amount of money on a specified date. Businesses will sometimes accept promissory notes from customers for large-ticket items or services. The business accepting the promissory note for goods or services is the **holder** of the note (the holder of the note may also be referred to as the payee). The company that promises to pay is the **maker** of the note. The company holding the note may decide to sell the promissory note to a third party, such as a bank, to raise money. The third party will discount the note; that is, the third party will not pay the full value of the note to the holder. The third party will base the discount on the amount of time remaining on the note when it is purchased from the business. The amount of time remaining on the note is the discount time. The third party will also base the discount on a discount rate higher than the original rate of the promissory note. This is the discount rate. The third party is then responsible for collecting the full amount from the maker of the note on the due date. Following are the steps of a typical scenario involving a promissory note, and subsequently, a third-party note (refer to Figure 11.17).

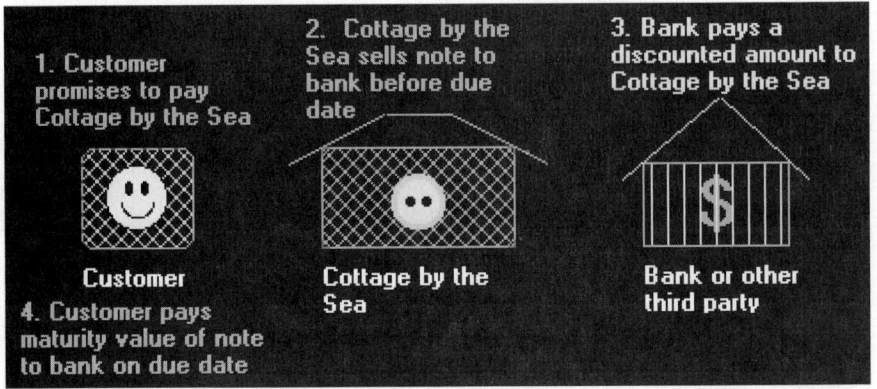

FIGURE 11.17

EXAMPLE 10

Step 1: Cottage by the Sea accepts a $2,500 promissory note from a customer on May 1 that is due July 22 at 10% exact interest.

Step 2: On May 10, Cottage by the Sea sells the promissory note to a third-party bank before the due date of the loan.

Step 3: The third-party bank buys the note at a discounted rate of 11% from Cottage by the Sea (the holder of the note).

Step 4: The bank collects the full value of the promissory note from the customer (the maker of the note) on the due date.

With the sequence of events firmly in mind, look at the math involved for the previous four steps. For convenience, the steps are reiterated below.

Step 1: Cottage by the Sea accepts a $2,500 promissory note from a customer on May 1 that is due July 22 at 10% exact interest.

Find the maturity value (principal plus interest) of the promissory note using the simple interest formula (refer to Figure 11.18). The principal is $2,500, the rate is 10%, and the time is the number of days between May 1 and July 22. How do you find the number of days between May 1 and July 22? You could count the number of days using a calendar, or you could list the

(continued)

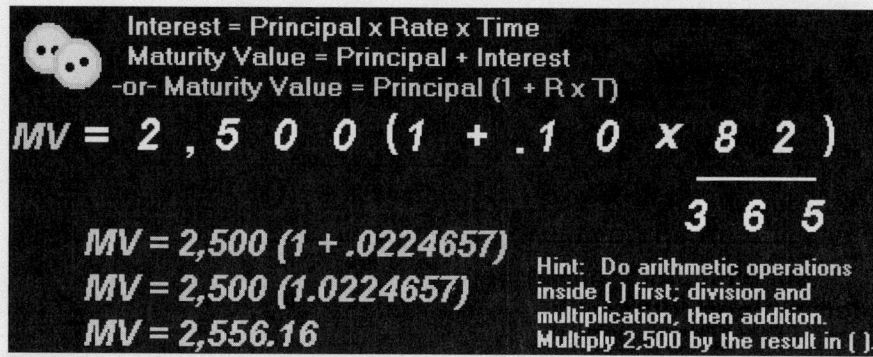

Interest = Principal x Rate x Time
Maturity Value = Principal + Interest
-or- Maturity Value = Principal (1 + R x T)

$$MV = 2,500 \left(1 + .10 \times \frac{82}{365}\right)$$

MV = 2,500 (1 + .0224657)
MV = 2,500 (1.0224657)
MV = 2,556.16

Hint: Do arithmetic operations inside ( ) first; division and multiplication, then addition. Multiply 2,500 by the result in ( ).

FIGURE 11.18

days included in the loan and then add:

May 1 to May 31	31 days
June 1 to June 30	30 days
July 1 to July 21*	21 days
	82 days total

Note: Do not count the due date.

The fraction 82/365 will be used for time in the simple interest formula because the loan is for 82 days at **exact** interest:

$$\text{Interest} = \text{Principal} \times \text{Rate} \times \text{Time}$$
$$I = 2,500 \times 0.10 \times 82 \div 365 = \$56.16$$

$$\text{Maturity Value (MV)} = \text{Principal} + \text{Interest}$$
$$MV = \$2,500 + \$56.16 = \$2,556.16$$

Alternatively, use the shortcut for finding maturity value as shown in Figure 11.18:

$$MV = \text{Principal} \times (1 + \text{Rate} \times \text{Time})$$
$$MV = \text{Principal} \times (1 + 0.10 \times 82 \div 365)$$

By multiplying the principal by **1 plus the rate** and then multiplying by time, the principal is added to the interest during the calculation, resulting in the amount of maturity value:

$MV = 2,500 \times (1 + 0.10 \times 82/365)$	Divide: $82 \div 365 = 0.2246575$
$MV = 2,500 \times (1 + 0.10 \times 0.2246575)$	Multiply: $0.10 \times 0.2246575 = 0.0224657$
$MV = 2,500 \times (1 + 0.0224657)$	Add: $1 + 0.0224657 = 1.0224657$
$MV = 2,500 \times 1.0224657$	Multiply: $2,500 \times 1.0224657 = \$2,556.16$
$MV = \$2,556.16$	

Rules, Rules, Rules . . .

1. When a formula contains parentheses, complete the calculations within the parentheses first.
2. When completing calculations within the parentheses, complete calculations involving division and multiplication before addition and subtraction.

Step 2: On May 11, Cottage by the Sea sold the promissory note to a third party (a bank) before the due date of the loan (July 22).

Find the amount of time remaining on the note after it was sold to the bank by Cottage by the Sea. The number of days from May 11 and the due date of the loan, July 22, is the discount time. The calculations in Figure 11.19 show the discount time to be 72 days.

Step 3: The third-party bank bought the note at a discounted rate of 11% from Cottage by the Sea (the holder of the note).

(continued)

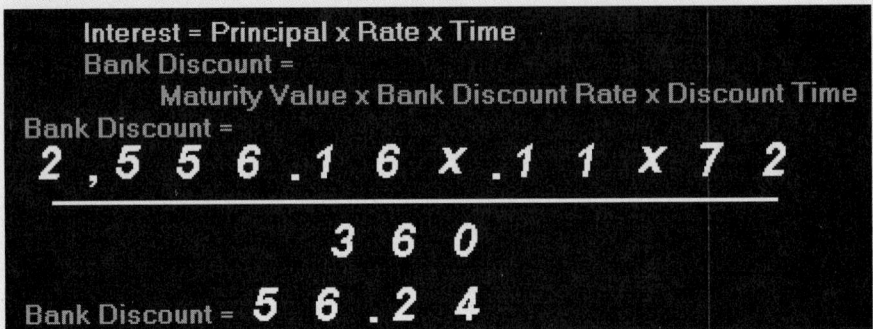

FIGURE 11.19

FIGURE 11.20

Calculate the amount of bank discount using the discount time (72 days) from step 2 and the discount rate of 11% (see Figure 11.20):

$$\text{Bank Discount} = \text{Maturity Value} \times \text{Discount Rate} \times \text{Discount Time}$$

Note: A 360-day year is used for ordinary or banker's interest.
We have

Bank Discount = \$2,556.16 × 0.11 × 72 ÷ 360	Multiply: 2,556.16 × 0.22 × 72 = 20,244.787
Bank Discount = 20,244.787 ÷ 360	Divide: 20,244.787 ÷ 360 = \$56.24
Bank Discount = \$56.24 (rounded)	

Subtract the amount of bank discount from the maturity value of the promissory note to find the proceeds that will be paid by the bank to Cottage by the Sea. As shown in Figure 11.21, proceeds paid to Cottage by the Sea were \$2,499.76.

Step 4: The bank collected the maturity value of the promissory note from the customer (the maker of the note) on the due date.

The maker of the note paid the full maturity value of the note, \$2,556.16, but it was paid to the third-party bank.

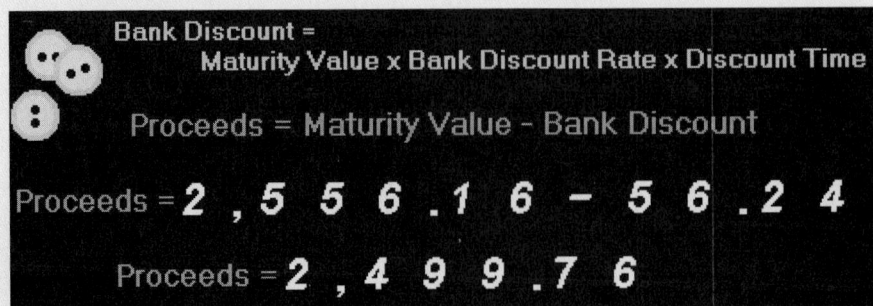

FIGURE 11.21

PART 2 *Business Math Skills*

Exercise 1: Simple Interest

Calculate amount of **ordinary** interest. Round answers to dollars and cents.

	Principal ($)	Rate (%)	Time	Interest ($)
1.	1,500	3	4 years	_____
2.	955.98	2.5	2 years	_____
3.	12,250	5	6 months	_____
4.	26,598	7	36 months	_____
5.	515.75	4.5	1/2 year	_____

Exercise 2: Exact Days of a Loan

Calculate the number of days of the following loans.

	Amount of Loan ($)	Interest Rate (%)	Beginning Date of Loan	Due Date of Loan	Number of Days of Loan
6.	5,000	6	April 4, 2000	May 4, 2000	_____
7.	300	8.5	March 15, 2001	June 8, 2001	_____
8.	2,555	3.25	October 31, 2001	February 20, 2002	_____
9.	5,879.59	4.75	January 1, 2002	August 31, 2002	_____
10.	69,995	5.3	September 5, 2002	September 29, 2002	_____

Using the information in Problems 6 through 10, calculate the amount of **exact** interest for each loan.

		Amount of Exact Interest ($)
11.	Amount of exact interest for Problem 6	_____
12.	Amount of exact interest for Problem 7	_____
13.	Amount of exact interest for Problem 8	_____
14.	Amount of exact interest for Problem 9	_____
15.	Amount of exact interest for Problem 10	_____

Using the information in Problems 6 through 10, calculate the amount of **ordinary** interest for each loan.

		Amount of Ordinary Interest
16.	Amount of ordinary interest for Problem 6	_____
17.	Amount of ordinary interest for Problem 7	_____
18.	Amount of ordinary interest for Problem 8	_____
19.	Amount of ordinary interest for Problem 9	_____
20.	Amount of ordinary interest for Problem 10	_____

Exercise 3: Calclulate Principal, Rate, and Time

Calculate principal. Round answers to dollars and cents.

	Principal ($)	Rate (%)	Time	Ordinary Interest ($)
21.	_____	4	4 years	96
22.	_____	6	2 years	150
23.	_____	4.5	6 months	290
24.	_____	7	36 months	750
25.	_____	8	45 days	45

Calculate rate. Round answers to hundredths as necessary.

	Principal ($)	Rate (%)	Time	Ordinary Interest ($)
26.	4,400	_____	4 years	385
27.	3,000	_____	2 years	175
28.	11,500	_____	6 months	505
29.	27,000	_____	36 months	722
30.	900	_____	45 days	60

Calculate time. Round years to tenths. Round days to whole numbers.

	Principal ($)	Rate (%)	Time	Ordinary Interest ($)
31.	500	2	_____ years	50
32.	1,500	4	_____ months	150
33.	7,700	6	_____ months	693
34.	4,800	8	_____ months	192
35.	500	5.5	_____ days	20.63

Exercise 4: Simple Interest Notes, Bank Discounts, Treasury Bills, Promissory and Third-Party Notes

36. A customer has qualified for a $10,000 simple interest note at 7½% interest for 2 years. Complete the following information for the loan:
    a. Amount of interest _____   b. Proceeds _____   c. Face value _____

37. Julie Brown bought eight U.S. Treasury Bills for $10,000 each at 1.5%. After 1 year, she redeemed the bills. Complete the following:
    a. Interest _____
    b. Amount Julie paid for the bills _____
    c. Proceeds to U.S. Government _____
    d. Face value of each of the bills _____
    e. Total amount received by Julie on redemption of the bills _____

38. On June 18, 2003, Shipyard Lumber Company promised to pay Hardwood Suppliers $45,000 plus 2% interest on December 10, 2003. Complete the following information:
    a. Maturity value _____

    On October 18, 2003, Hardwood Suppliers sold the note to Jamestown Bank & Trust at a discount rate of 4%. Calculate:

    b. Discount time _____
    c. Amount of bank discount _____
    d. Proceeds to Hardwood Suppliers _____
    e. Amount Jamestown Bank & Trust received from Shipyard Lumber on December 10, 2003 _____

PART 3 *Pocket or Windows Calculator*

SIMPLE INTEREST FORMULAS AND MATURITY VALUE

You can choose to solve simple interest problems by keying the decimal equivalent of the rate (percent) on the pocket or Windows calculator, or you can choose to use the percent key.

The memory key can be used to store the amount of principal. After interest is calculated, and while it is still in the display, simply add interest to memory using the M+ key, then recall the total in memory using the memory recall key or the memory clear key. The maturity value will appear in the display. Following are examples of problems and how to work them on the pocket or Windows calculator. Use the following formulas:

$$\text{Interest} = \text{Principal} \times \text{Rate} \times \text{Time}$$
$$\text{Maturity Value} = \text{Principal} + \text{Interest}$$

PROBLEM 1

A total of $2,500 was invested for 4 years at 3% simple interest.

    A. Calculate interest.

        1. Using the decimal equivalent for rate, obtain

$$2,500 \times 4 \times .03 = \boxed{300} \text{ interest}$$

        Principal—the decimal equivalent for rate—and time can be entered in any order.

        2. Using the percent key for rate, obtain

$$2,500 \times 4 \times 3 \boxed{\%} \boxed{300}$$

        Notice that the equals key is not pressed after the percent key in this example. Two other keying methods can be used with the pocket or Windows calculator:

$$2,500 \times 3 \boxed{\%} \times 4 = \boxed{300}$$
$$4 \times 3 \boxed{\%} \times 2,500 = \boxed{300}$$

        The keying method $3 \boxed{\%} \times 4 \times 2,500 = \boxed{0}$ **cannot** be used because a zero error will result. The percent key completes a calculation and returns an answer; therefore **do not** enter the rate (percent) portion of a problem on the pocket or Windows calculator **first**.

    B. Calculate maturity value for the foregoing problem.

        1. Using the decimal equivalent for rate, obtain

$$2,500 \boxed{M+} \times 4 \times .03 = \boxed{300} \boxed{M+} \boxed{MR} \boxed{2,800} \boxed{MC}$$

        2. Using the percent key for rate (check to be sure that memory is clear*), obtain

$$2,500 \boxed{M+} \times 4 \times 3 \boxed{\%} \boxed{300} \boxed{M+} \boxed{MR} \boxed{2,800} \boxed{MC}$$

    How does one know if memory needs to be cleared? Most calculators will display an **M when memory contains a number. Hint: Before "starting over" on a problem, always check that memory is cleared as well as the display.*

RULES, RULES, RULES . . .

The following are rules for efficiency for calculators with both a memory recall and a memory total or memory clear button:

      1. Use the memory recall button to display the current number or total in memory. Use the memory clear button to clear memory before starting the next problem.

Note: Pressing the ON/C key does NOT clear memory on most pocket calculators.

2. Some pocket calculators have a combination memory recall/clear (MRC) key. When pressed once, the key acts as a memory recall key. When pressed a second time, the MRC key clears memory.

    If your calculator has an MRC key, use the following order of entry:

    a. Using the decimal equivalent for rate, obtain

$$2{,}500 \boxed{\text{M+}} \times 4 \times .03 = \boxed{300} \boxed{\text{M+}} \boxed{\text{MRC}} \boxed{2{,}800}$$

    b. Using the percent key for rate (be sure to clear memory before starting a new problem by pressing the MRC key again), obtain

$$\boxed{\text{MRC}} \; 2{,}500 \boxed{\text{M+}} \times 4 \times 3 \boxed{\%} \boxed{300} \boxed{\text{M+}} \boxed{\text{MRC}} \boxed{2{,}800}$$
$$\boxed{\text{MRC}}$$

$$\textbf{Principal} \; = \; \textbf{Interest} \div (\textbf{Rate} \times \textbf{Time})$$

PROBLEM 2

A bank loaned a customer money for 2 years in exchange for $500 in interest. The bank charges 6% interest for its loans. How much was the principal of the loan?

    Refer to Figure 11.9 for a calculator hint. Whenever a calculation must be made in the denominator portion of a problem, calculate the denominator portion first and store the result in memory. Then calculate the numerator portion and divide the result by the amount recalled from memory.

    Substituting the amounts given in the problem for the variables in the formula for finding principal, we find

$$P = \$500 \div (6\% \times 2)$$

1. Using the decimal equivalent for rate (check to see that memory is clear), obtain

$$.06 \times 2 = \boxed{0.12} \boxed{\text{M+}} \; 500 \div \boxed{\text{MR}} = \boxed{4{,}166.67} \boxed{\text{MC}} \quad \text{(rounded to two decimal places)}$$

2. Using the percent key for rate (DO NOT enter the rate first), obtain

$$2 \times 6 \boxed{\%} \boxed{0.12} \boxed{\text{M+}} \; 500 \div \boxed{\text{MR}} = \boxed{4{,}166.67} \boxed{\text{MC}} \quad \text{(rounded to two decimal places)}$$

$$\textbf{Rate} \; = \; \textbf{Interest} \div (\textbf{Principal} \times \textbf{Time})$$

PROBLEM 3

Jonathan Brown borrowed $5,000 for a car from his local credit union for 39 months. The credit union is charging Jonathan $650 in interest. What is the rate of interest the credit union is charging Jonathan?

    Substitute the amounts given in the problem for the variables in the formula for finding rate. Be sure to state 39 months as a fraction. Calculate the amount in parentheses first, and then store the amount in memory:

$$\text{Rate} = \$650 \div \left(\$5{,}000 \times \frac{39}{12} \right)$$

Order of Entry:

$$5{,}000 \times 39 \div 12 = \boxed{16{,}250} \boxed{\text{M+}}$$

$$650 \div \boxed{\text{MR}} = \boxed{.04} \qquad \text{Convert the decimal number to a rate of 4\%}$$

Alternatively, use the % key instead of the equals key in the final step:

$$650 \div \boxed{\text{MR}} \boxed{\%} \boxed{4} \boxed{\text{MC}}$$

The answer is displayed as a percent and no conversion is necessary

$$\textbf{Time} \; = \; \textbf{Interest} \div (\textbf{Principal} \times \textbf{Rate})$$

PROBLEM 4

Robert Green borrowed $3,000 from his credit union at 3% interest. If the amount of interest is $375, what is the time of the loan stated in months?

Substitute the amounts given in the problem for the variables in the formula for finding time:

$$\text{Time} = 375 \div (3,000 \times 3\%)$$

Using the decimal equivalent for rate (check that memory is clear), obtain

$$3,000 \times .03 = 90 \text{ M+}$$

$375 \div \boxed{\text{MR}} = \boxed{4.16666666}$ The answer is displayed in years; because we wish time to be stated in months, multiply by 12; this may be done without clearing the display.

$\times 12 = \boxed{49.99999} \boxed{\text{MC}}$ Rounded to whole months: 50

Time = 50 months

PROCEEDS

When calculating proceeds, store the face value in memory. After calculating bank discount, simply press the M− key to subtract the discount from face value. Press the memory recall button to display the amount of proceeds:

$$\text{Bank Discount} = \text{Face Value} \times \text{Discount Rate} \times \text{Time}$$
$$\text{Proceeds} = \text{Face Value} - \text{Bank Discount}$$

PROBLEM 5

Find the amount of proceeds for a $10,000 loan at 6% ordinary interest for 27 months:

$$\text{Bank Discount} = 10,000 \times .06 \times \frac{27}{12}$$

Order of Entry:

$10,000 \boxed{\text{M+}} \times .06 \times 27 \div 12 = \boxed{1,350}$ Ten thousand has been stored in memory; the amount of bank discount is shown in the display.

$\boxed{\text{M−}} \boxed{1,350} \boxed{\text{MR}} \boxed{8,650} \boxed{\text{MC}}$ Press the M− key to subtract bank discount (the amount shown in the display) from the face value (which was stored in memory previously); press MR to display proceeds (the new memory total); press MC to clear memory.

THINK, THINK, THINK . . .

Many students think because the bank keeps the interest and gives only the proceeds to the customer at the beginning period of the loan, when the customer pays back the full face value, he or she is actually paying the interest twice. Can you find the fault with this logic?

PROMISSORY NOTES

$$\text{Maturity Value} = \text{Principal} + (\text{Principal} \times \text{Rate} \times \text{Time})$$

PROBLEM 6

Blue Water Distributors accepted a $5,000 promissory note from a customer on January 17, 2003, at 5% exact interest. The note was due on March 12, 2003. What is the maturity value of this note?

Before calculating the maturity value, the number of days in the loan must be determined. Make a chart of months and days in the loan and add the days:

January 17 to January 31	15 days	
February	28 days	
March 1 to March 12	11 days	(The due date is not counted.)
	54 days	

Substitute the amounts in the problem for the variables in the maturity value formula:

$$\text{Maturity Value} = 5,000 + \left(5,000 \times .05 \times \frac{54}{365}\right)$$

Order of Entry:

5,000 $\boxed{\text{M+}}$ × .05 × 54 ÷ 365 = $\boxed{36.986301}$

Display contains amount of interest (this number may be rounded to dollars and cents before being recorded on the customer's paperwork).

$\boxed{\text{M+}}$ $\boxed{36.986301}$ $\boxed{\text{MR}}$ $\boxed{5,036.99}$ $\boxed{\text{MC}}$

Use M+ to add the interest (shown in the display) to the principal (which has been stored in memory); press MR to display maturity value (the new total contained in memory); round to dollars and cents; use MC to clear memory.

THIRD-PARTY NOTES

Bank Discount = Maturity Value × Bank Discount Rate × Discount Time

Proceeds = Maturity Value − Bank Discount

PROBLEM 7

On February 1, 2003, Blue Water Distributors sold the promissory note described in Problem 6 to First National Bank at a discount rate of 7%. How much did Blue Water Distributors receive from the bank?

Before calculating the proceeds to Blue Water Distributors, it is necessary to find the discount time—the amount of time remaining on the loan. Prepare a chart of months and days remaining on the loan and add the days:

February 1 to 28	28 days	
March 1 to 12	11 days	(Do not count the due date.)
	39 days	= Discount Time

Substitute the amounts in the problem for the variables in the bank discount formula. Use 360 days for 1 year of discount time (ordinary interest method):

$$\text{Bank Discount} = 5,036.99 \times .07 \times \frac{39}{360}$$

Order of Entry:

5,036.99 $\boxed{\text{M+}}$ × .07 × 39 ÷ 360 = 38.197172

(Round to dollars and cents before recording the amount of interest)

| M− | 38.197172 | MR | 4,998.79 | MC |

The amount in the display is subtracted from memory using M−; the new total (the amount of proceeds to Blue Water Distributors) is displayed using MR; round the answer to dollars and cents.

PART 3 *Pocket or Windows Calculator*

There are no separate exercises for this section. Use your calculator as you complete the following Business Math FUNdamentals tutorials and drill.

PART 3 *Review and Practice Using Business Math FUNdamentals*

GOAL: Complete 9 of the 10 problems correctly.

Instructions: *Start Business Math FUNdamentals. Complete Tutorials 29 Simple Interest, Tutorial 30 Bank Discount and Proceeds, Tutorial 31 Treasury Bills, Tutorial 32 Discounting Commercial Notes (Third-Party Discounts), and Drill 24 Simple Interest, Bank Discounts, Third-Party Notes. If you are not satisfied with your score, repeat the drill. Write your scores below.*

Business Math FUNdamentals Drill 24

Today's Date	Score

PART 4 *The Desktop Calculator*

SIMPLE INTEREST AND MATURITY VALUE

To complete a simple interest problem using the desktop calculator, it is necessary either to enter the percent of interest as a decimal number or to use the percent key when entering or calculating the rate. Whichever method you choose should be used consistently to avoid confusion and errors.

$$\text{Interest} = \text{Principal} \times \text{Rate} \times \text{Time}$$
$$\text{Maturity Value} = \text{Principal} + \text{Interest}$$

Procedure

Machine setup (machine setup will remain the same for all simple interest problems in this chapter):

   Decimal Selector—F
   Rounding Switch—5/4
   Printer—On

TAPE 11.1:

```
4,000 · M+
4,000 ·   ×
0·07   ×
24 ·   ÷
12 ·   =
560 ·   *

560 · M+
4,560 · M*
```

PROBLEM 1

The Federal Credit Union loaned Bob Jones $4,000 for 24 months at 7% simple interest. How much interest will Bob pay?

Analyze the Problem: The principal is $4,000, time is 24 months, and rate is 7%. Interest needs to be calculated.

Order of Entry: Using the simple interest formula, Interest = Principal × Rate × Time, we can enter the items to be multiplied in any order (commutative property). Because the amount of time the money is loaned is stated in months, be sure to divide the product by 12 (because there are 12 months in a year). Memory will be used to store the principal, which will be added to the interest calculated in a later step. Before beginning a problem using memory, make sure memory is clear. An **M** in the display indicates memory is NOT clear. Press the memory total key to clear memory, if necessary.

Method A: Enter the problem using a decimal number for 7% (Tape 11.1).

$$4,000 \text{ M+} \times .07 \times 24 \div 12 = \boxed{560.00} \text{ (interest) M+ MT } \boxed{4,560} \text{ (maturity value)}$$

TAPE 11.2:

```
4,000 · M+
4,000 ·   ×
7·   %
280 ·   *

280 ·   ×
24 ·   ÷
12 ·   =
560 ·   *

560 · M+
4,560 · M*
```

Method B: Enter the problem using 7 and the percent key for 7% (Tape 11.2):

$$4,000 \times 7\% \times 24 \div 12 = \boxed{560.00} \text{ (interest) M+ MT } \boxed{4,560} \text{ (maturity value)}$$

Method C: Rearrange the order of the multiplied items to find the interest:

$$4,000 \times 24 \div 12 \times 7\% = \boxed{560.00} \quad \text{or} \quad 4000 \times 24 \div 12 \times .07 = \boxed{560.00}$$
$$24 \div 12 \times 4000 \times 7\% = \boxed{560.00} \quad \text{or} \quad 24 \times 4,000 \div 12 \times .07 = \boxed{560.00}$$

What order of entry will not work? Try entering the percent key in the wrong order, such as

$$4,000 \times 7 \times 24 \div 12\%$$

The answer (5,600,000.00) is clearly incorrect. As you can see, with so many choices, it would be best to pick an order-of-entry method, such as method A or B, and use it each time you need to calculate simple interest. A good habit such as this will help both your efficiency and accuracy in an office situation.

CALCULATING PRINCIPAL

$$\text{Principal} = \text{Interest} + (\text{Rate} \times \text{Time})$$

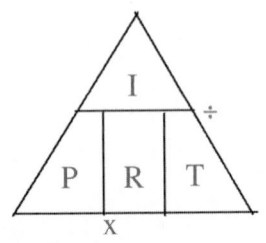

FIGURE 11.22

PROBLEM 2

Bill Johnson paid $30 in interest for a 45-day loan at 6% ordinary interest. How much did he borrow?

We are looking for the principal (the amount borrowed), so we will use our formula or visual aid for calculating principal. To use the visual aid in Figure 11.22, cover the P, which reveals the formula for calculating principal: I ÷ (R × T). Substitute the numbers in the problem for the letter symbols (variables) in the formula, and we have

$$\frac{30}{.06 \times \frac{45}{360}}$$

or

$$P = \$30 \div (.06 \times 45 \div 360)$$

Order of Entry: When working a problem in which a number must be divided by the quotient or product of two other numbers such as those contained in the denominator of this problem, it is better to calculate the denominator first and store the result in memory. Then enter the number to be

TAPE 11.3:

```
    0·06  ×
     45·  ÷
    360·  =
  0·0075  *

  0·0075 M+
     30·  ÷
  0·0075 M*
```

TAPE 11.4:

```
     45·  ×
      6·  %
     2·7  *

     2·7  ÷
    360·  =
  0·0075  *

  0·0075 M+
     30·  ÷
  0·0075 M*

  0·0075  =
  4,000·  *
```

TAPE 11.5:

```
   4,000·  ×
    0·06   ×
     45·   ÷
    360·   =
     30·   *
```

divided, the division sign, retrieve the stored number using memory total, and press the equals sign. Press the memory total key to clear memory, if necessary.

Method A: Enter the problem using a decimal number for percent (Tape 11.3):

$$\text{MT } .06 \times 45 \div 360 = \boxed{.0075} \text{ M+}$$
$$30 \div \text{MT} = \boxed{4,000}$$

Method B: Enter the rate using the percent key. Remember that the percent may NOT be entered as the first number in the order of entry (Tape 11.4):

$$45 \times 6\% \div 360 = \boxed{.0075} \text{ M+ } 30 \div \text{MT} = \boxed{4,000}$$

Check: Check the problem by substituting $4,000 for principal, .06 for rate, and 45/360 for time in the simple interest formula. If interest equals $30, then the $4,000 calculated for principal is correct (Tape 11.5):

$$I = 4,000 \times .06 \times 45/360$$
$$I = \$30$$

CALCULATING RATE

$$\text{Rate} = \text{Interest} + (\text{Principal} \times \text{Time})$$

PROBLEM 3

Jane Randolph borrowed $4,500 for 32 months. She paid $720 in interest. What was the rate of interest?

Analyze the Problem: The principal is $4,500, time is 32 months, and interest is $720. The problem is asking for the rate. To use the visual aid in Figure 11.22, cover R, which reveals the formula for rate: $I \div (P \times T)$. Substitute the numbers in the formula:

$$\frac{720}{4,500 \times \dfrac{32}{12}}$$

or

$$720 \div (4,500 \times 32 \div 12).$$

TAPE 11.6:

```
      0 · M*

 4,500 ·  ×
    32 ·  ÷
    12 ·  =
12,000 ·  *

12,000 · M+
   720 ·  ÷
12,000 · M*

12,000 ·  =
  0·06  *
```

TAPE 11.7:

```
 4,500 ·  ×
    32 ·  ÷
    12 ·  =
12,000 ·  *

12,000 · M+
   720 ·  ÷
12,000 · M*

12,000 ·  %
   6 ·  *
```

Order of Entry:

Method A: Use the equals key to find a decimal number for the rate (Tape 11.6). Convert to a percent mentally. Clear memory if necessary:

$$4{,}500 \times 32 \div 12 = \boxed{12{,}000}\ \text{M+}\ 720 \div \text{MT} = \boxed{0.06}$$

Convert to a percent: $0.06 = 6\%$.

Method B: Use the percent key instead of the equals key to find the rate stated as a percent (Tape 11.7):

$$4{,}500 \times 32 \div 12 = \boxed{12{,}000}\ \text{M+}\ 720 \div \text{MT}\ \boxed{\%}\ \boxed{6}$$

$$\text{Rate} = 6\%$$

CALCULATING TIME

$$\text{Time} = \text{Interest} + (\text{Principal} \times \text{Rate})$$

PROBLEM 4

Janet Lufton borrowed $5,000 at 4.5%. She paid $1,125 in interest. What was the length of time for this loan in years?

Analyze the Problem: The principal is $5,000, rate is 4.5%, and interest is $1,125. The problem asked for the time of the loan. To use the visual aid, in Figure 11.22 cover T, which reveals the formula for time: $I \div (P \times R)$. Substitute the terms in the problem for the variables in the formula for time:

$$\text{Time} = 1{,}125 \div (5{,}000 \times .045)$$

Order of Entry:

Method A: Using a converted decimal number for rate (Tape 11.8), obtain

$$5{,}000 \times .045 = \boxed{225}\ \text{M+}\ 1{,}125 \div \text{MT} = \boxed{5}\ \text{years}$$

Method B: Using percent and the percent key for rate (Tape 11.9), obtain

$$5{,}000 \times 4.5\ \boxed{\%}\ \boxed{225}\ \text{M+}\ 1{,}125 \div \text{MT} = \boxed{5}\ \text{years}$$

TAPE 11.8:

```
5,000·  x
0·045 =
225·  *

225·M+
1,125·  ÷
225·M*

225·  =
5·  *
```

TAPE 11.9:

```
5,000·  x
4·5 %
225·  *

225·M+
1,125·  ÷
225·M*

225·  =
5·  *
```

TAPE 11.10:

```
5,000·  x
0·045 ÷
360·  =
0·625 *

0·625M+
45·  ÷
0·625M*

0·625 =
72·  *
```

TAPE 11.11:

```
5,000·  x
4·5 %
225·  *

225·  ÷
360·  =
0·625 *

0·625M+
45·  ÷
0·625M*

0·625 =
72·  *
```

PROBLEM 5

Davey Jones borrowed $5,000 at 4.5% ordinary interest. He paid $45 in interest. What was the length of the loan in days?

Analyze the Problem: The principal is $5,000, rate is 4.5% ordinary interest, and amount of interest is $45. The problem is asking for the time of the loan in days. Since ordinary interest is specified, we will need to use 360 days per year in our formula.

Order of Entry:

Method A: Convert 4.5% to the decimal number .045 (Tape 11.10):

$$5,000 \times .045 \div 360 = \boxed{0.625} \text{ M+ } 45 \div \text{MT} = \boxed{72} \text{ days}$$

Method B: Use the percent key after entering the rate (Tape 11.11):

$$5,000 \times 4.5 \boxed{\%} \boxed{225} \div 360 = \boxed{.625} \text{ M+ } 45 \div \text{MT} = \boxed{72} \text{ days}$$

SIMPLE INTEREST NOTE

Bank Discount = Face Value × Rate × Time

Face Value − Bank Discount = Proceeds

PROBLEM 6

Jonathan Bates needed to borrow $7,200. He agreed to a simple interest note with his bank for 6.5% interest for 90 days ordinary interest.

Analysis: The face value of the simple note is $7,200, the rate is 6.5%, and time is 90/360. Substitute numbers in the problem for the variables in the formula for bank discount. Then continue by substituting numbers for the variables in the formula for proceeds:

$$\text{Bank Discount} = \$7,200 \times .065 \times 90 \div 360$$
$$\text{Proceeds} = \$7,200 - \text{Bank Discount}$$

Order of Entry (Tape 11.12):

$$7200 \text{ M+} \times .065 \times 90 \div 360 = \boxed{117} \text{ (bank discount) M− MT } \boxed{7,083} \text{ (proceeds)}$$

TAPE 11.12:

```
7,200·M+
7,200·  x
0·065 x
90·  ÷
360·  =
117·  *

117·M−
7,083·M*
```

PROMISSORY NOTE

$$\text{Interest} = \text{Principal} \times \text{Rate} \times \text{Time}$$
$$\text{Maturity Value} = \text{Principal} + \text{Interest}$$

PROBLEM 7

On February 28, 2003, ABC Mfg. Co. promised to pay Canton Supply Co. $12,000 at 5% exact interest. The due date of the note is April 14, 2003. What is the maturity value of the note?

TAPE 11.13:

```
    12,000.M+
    12,000. x
       0.05 x
         45. ÷
        365. =
  73.9726027397 *

  73.9726027397M+
 12,073.9726027M*
```

Analyze: The principal is $12,000, the rate is 5%. For time, the number of days of the loan must be calculated:

February 28	1 day	
March 1 to 31	31 days	
April 1 to 14	13 days	(Do not count due date.)
	45 days	

Next, substitute numbers in the problem for variables in the formulas:

$$12,000 \times .05 \times 45 \div 365 = \text{Interest}$$
$$12,000 + \text{Interest} = \text{Maturity Value}$$

Order of Entry (Tape 11.13):

12,000 M+ × .05 × 45 ÷ 365 = $\boxed{73.97\ldots}$ (interest) M+ MT $\boxed{12,073.97}$ (maturity value)

Answer has been rounded to dollars and cents.

THIRD-PARTY NOTES

PROBLEM 8

On August 1, 2003, Janis Oil Drilling Corp. promised to pay Osprey Oil Field Equipment Co. $67,500 on December 15, 2003, plus interest at a rate of 4%. On October 1, 2003, Osprey Oil Field Equipment sold the note to First National Bank at a discount rate of 10%. How much will Osprey Oil Field Equipment Co. receive for the note?

Analysis: The problem is asking for the proceeds of the third-party note. Before proceeds can be determined, the maturity value of the original promissory note must be calculated.

Step 1. Find the maturity value of the promissory note:

$$\text{Interest} = \text{Principal} \times \text{Rate} \times \text{Time} \qquad (\text{Time} = \text{number of days} \div 365)$$
$$\text{Maturity Value} = \text{Principal} + \text{Interest}$$

We know that the principal is $67,500 and that the rate is 4%. For time, the number of days in the loan must be calculated (Tape 11.14):

August 1 to 31	31 days	
September	30 days	
October	31 days	
November	30 days	
December 1 to 15	14 days	(Do not count the due date.)
	136 days	

$$\text{Time} = 136 \text{ days} \div 365$$

Substitute values for the variables in the formulas:

$$\text{Interest} = 67,500 \times .04 \times 136 \div 365$$
$$\text{Maturity Value} = 67,500 + \text{Interest}$$

Order of Entry:

$$67{,}500 \text{ M+} \times .04 \times 136 \div 365 = \boxed{1{,}006.027\ldots}\ \text{(interest)}$$

$$\text{M + MT}\ \boxed{68{,}506.03}\ \text{(maturity value) (rounded to dollars and cents) M+}$$

DO NOT clear display or memory.

Step 2. Find proceeds of the third-party note:

Bank Discount = Maturity Value × Bank Discount Rate × Time   (Time = number of days remaining in loan ÷ 360)

Proceeds = Maturity Value − Bank Discount

Before calculating proceeds, the amount of time remaining on the note must be determined (bank discount time):

October 1 to 31	31 days
November	30 days
December 1 to 15	14 days (Do not count due date.)
	75 days

Time = 75 days ÷ 360

Analyze the problem and substitute numbers in the formulas for bank discount and proceeds. We have calculated bank discount and have stored the amount in calculator memory: $68,506.03. From the problem we know that the bank discount rate is 10%. We have calculated the discount time as 75 days. Therefore, we are able to substitute these numbers for the variables in the formula:

$$\text{Bank Discount} = \$68{,}506.03 \times 0.10 \times 75 \div 360$$

$$\text{Proceeds} = \$68{,}506.03 - \text{Bank Discount}$$

Order of Entry: We continue entering the numbers for our problem assuming that $68,506.03 is still in memory. If you have cleared the memory, reenter this figure in memory before proceeding:

$$\times .10 \times 75 \div 360 = \boxed{1{,}427.208\ldots}\ \text{(bank discount) M− MT}\ \boxed{67{,}078.818\ldots}\ \text{(proceeds)}$$

Round the answer to dollars and cents: $67,078.82.

```
           0 • M*

          31 • +
          30 • +
          31 • +
          30 • +
          14 • +
         136 • *

     67 > 500 • M+
     67 > 500 • x
         0 • 04 x
         136 • ÷
         365 • =
 1 > 006 • 02739726 *

 1 > 006 • 02739726 M+
68 > 506 • 0273972 M*

68 > 506 • 0273972 M+
          31 • +
          30 • +
          14 • +
          75 • *

68 > 506 • 0273972 M◊
68 > 506 • 0273972 x
         0 • 10 x
          75 • ÷
         360 • =
 1 > 427 • 2089041 *

 1 > 427 • 2089041 M−
67 > 078 • 8184931 M*
```

Name _____

Class/Section _____

Score (Correct Answers ÷ No. of Assigned Problems) _____

 **PART 4** *Desktop Calculator*

Exercise 1: Simple Interest and Maturity Value

Calculate interest, principal, rate, and maturity value as required using ordinary interest.

	Interest ($)	Principal ($)	Rate (%)	Time	Maturity Value ($)
1.	_____	85,125	5	2 years	_____
2.	_____	51,721	4	5 years	_____
3.	4,080.00	_____	4.25	3 years	_____
4.	750.00	_____	6	2 months	_____
5.	1,482.29	63,130	____	8 months	_____
6.	3,005.39	97,144	____	9 months	_____
7.	531.30	35,420	6	days	_____
8.	196.60	22,972	5.135	days	_____
9.	448.50	19,995	4.65	days	_____

Calculate time. Round years to tenths. Round days and months to whole numbers.

	Principal ($)	Rate (%)	Time	Ordinary Interest ($)
10.	500	2	_____ years	40
11.	1,500	4	_____ months	200
12.	7,700	6	_____ months	577.50
13.	4,800	8	_____ months	544
14.	500	1	_____ days or years	25

Calculate due dates for the following non-leap-year loans.

15. $500 loaned on May 5 for 2 months _____
16. $1,200 loaned on August 31 for 3 months _____
17. $708 loaned on September 9 for 30 days _____
18. $1,200 loaned on April 6 for 60 days _____
19. $2,000 loaned on June 6 for 45 days _____
20. $5,400 loaned on January 15 for 180 days _____

Calculate bank discount and proceeds for the following simple interest notes using the ordinary interest method.

	Terms of Loan	Bank Discount	Proceeds
21.	$10,000 loaned for 4 years at 5%	_____	_____
22.	$5,700 loaned for 2 years at 4.5%	_____	_____
23.	$6,900 loaned for 6 months at 10%	_____	_____
24.	$10,000 loaned for 2 months at 7.25%	_____	_____
25.	$3,500 loaned for 60 days at 4.125%	_____	_____
26.	$9,120 loaned for 90 days at 5.55%	_____	_____
27.	$4,300 loaned for 270 days at 9.825%	_____	_____

Provide the requested information for the following promissory and third-party notes.

28. On May 5, Richard's Foods promised to pay Perkins Wholesalers $4,800 plus 8% interest on July 20 of the same year. On June 15, Perkins Wholesalers sold the promissory note to Elkhart Bank at a discount rate of 12%. What were the proceeds received by Perkins Wholesalers? _____

Exercise 2

Strokes per Minute Score _____

Accuracy Score (Correct Strokes ÷ Total Strokes) _____

One-Minute Addition Timing (Keys 0 through 9)

(Optional: Your instructor may wish you to use Touch Key on the computer for all your timings. Check with your instructor before completing this exercise.)

Complete as many of the problems as possible in 1 minute by adding. Work quickly and accurately. The number preceding each closing parenthesis indicates the cumulative number of strokes for problems attempted. For example, if you complete Problems 1 through 3 in 1 minute, your strokes-per-minute score is 213. Optional: 3- to 5- minute timings. If you complete Problems 1 through 15 in 5 minutes, your strokes-per-minute score is 213 (1065 ÷ 5).

Set decimal selector on add mode.

1.	2.	3.	4.	5.	6.	7.	8.
360.04	410.01	784.00	120.06	258.14	392.00	130.00	970.01
252.14	623.05	851.00	430.02	593.16	625.00	560.00	590.03
112.84	623.05	974.00	760.01	815.85	921.00	610.00	180.02
216.00	628.76	916.00	730.03	872.32	984.00	630.00	130.01
150.25	527.45	894.00	430.04	570.03	620.06	530.00	590.04
325.06	410.02	715.00	140.05	280.04	320.05	120.00	910.02

344.21	445.71	723.00	140.03	260.00	370.03	130.00	970.07
259.01	556.31	871.00	410.03	830.05	930.04	650.00	130.04
252.00	559.94	843.00	420.01	856.00	910.06	660.00	180.05
125.02	653.00	953.00	710.02	590.01	620.06	550.00	580.03
71)	142)	213)	284)	355)	426)	497)	568)

9. 140.01	10. 290.07	11. 741.58	12. 350.22	13. 360.01	14. 972.24	15. 160.06	16. 500.42
742.05	270.01	254.52	100.28	875.63	873.45	371.33	260.05
685.03	395.63	525.23	200.55	373.62	896.56	386.49	400.08
415.03	700.29	871.59	500.83	282.62	793.66	391.49	487.08
170.05	100.09	963.27	279.69	395.63	783.55	304.53	600.29
168.97	470.24	353.61	450.26	254.61	673.14	272.36	600.37
159.97	400.51	256.51	304.61	300.21	574.14	281.33	951.41
788.43	100.27	102.57	521.37	130.02	596.26	925.33	678.73
125.63	400.89	500.19	200.14	500.22	585.41	972.49	641.29
637.45	300.51	450.03	160.01	100.63	501.45	101.19	460.06
639)	710)	781)	852)	923)	994)	1,065)	1,136)

17. 534.00	18. 950.00	19. 961.00	20. 936.55	21. 334.90	22. 112.80	23. 113.00	24. 116.29
466.00	828.00	867.00	745.88	221.58	226.19	223.50	222.49
367.00	757.00	637.00	641.77	115.69	333.99	335.75	332.19
192.00	629.00	721.00	453.66	664.71	442.79	663.25	445.39
229.00	727.00	451.00	365.87	553.52	553.59	552.95	552.59
427.00	949.00	691.00	116.34	445.16	661.79	332.85	662.89
881.00	368.00	381.00	326.59	446.10	556.00	555.50	415.69
929.00	293.00	185.00	736.68	554.25	222.93	221.75	423.79
739.00	486.00	835.00	944.78	225.45	336.21	115.80	633.19
137.00	734.00	264.00	121.49	221.00	556.32	443.70	811.59
1,207)	1,278)	1,349)	1,420)	1,491)	1,562)	1,633)	1,704)

CHAPTER 11 *Terminology Review*

Bank discount
Exact interest
Face value
Holder
Interest
Maker
Maturity value
Ordinary interest
Principal
Proceeds
Promissory note
Rate
Simple interest
Time
Treasury bills

Fill in the blank with the appropriate terms.

1. _____ is the cost of borrowing money.

2. _____ _____ are short-term obligations issued by the U.S. Government.

3. Ordinary interest is also known as _____ _____.

4. On the due date of a simple interest loan, the borrower will pay the _____ _____ of the note.

5. _____ _____ is principal plus interest.

6. The money available to a customer to use after agreeing to a simple interest note is the _____.

7. _____ is the percent at which interest is paid.

8. Interest for a simple interest note is known as _____ _____.

9. A(n) _____ _____ is an agreement to pay a specified amount of money on a specified date.

10. The amount of money borrowed or invested is the _____.

11. _____ _____ is based on a 365-day year.

12. A business that accepts a promissory note for goods or services is the _____ of the note.

13. A business that promises to pay for goods or services at some future date is the _____ of a promissory note.

Answer true or false.

14. A person who purchases a T-Bill for $9,800 will receive $10,000 when the T-Bill is redeemed 1 year later. T/F _____

15. If a loan of $1,000 is made at 5% exact interest for 45 days, the time of the loan should be stated as 45/360. T/F _____

16. Proceeds of a U.S. Treasury bill are used by the purchaser of the bill. T/F _____

17. One reason the holder of a note might wish to sell the note to a third party for less than maturity value is to acquire needed cash. T/F _____

18. Company A accepted a promissory note from Company B for goods purchased. Company A later sold the note to First State Bank. Company B will pay the note off on the agreed-on due date, but not at full maturity value. T/F _____

Name _____

Class/Section _____

Score (Correct Answers ÷ No. of Assigned Problems) _____

Chapter 11 Review Exercises: Pen and Paper, Pocket Calculator, or Desktop Calculator

Exercise 1: Interest = Principal × Rate × Time

Calculate interest, principal, rate, time, and maturity value as required.

	Interest ($)	Principal ($)	Rate (%)	Time	Maturity Value (%)
1.	_____	5,600	3.25	6 months	_____
2.	_____	2,250	2.7	1 year	_____
3.	62.75	_____	4	4 months	_____
4.	1,211.00	_____	5	2 years	_____
5.	1,099.69	9,775	____	30 months	_____
6.	20,980.80	56,400	____	6 years	_____
7.	6,003.83	32,600	4.25	months	_____
8.	712.69	16,290	3.5	months	_____

Exercise 2: Due Dates

Calculate due date using exact interest.

	Amount of Loan ($)	Beginning Date of Loan	Number of Days of Loan	Due Date of Loan
9.	500	4-15-03	30	_____
10.	720	5-1-03	45	_____
11.	4,927	3-10-03	180	_____
12.	6,500	1-1-03	240	_____

Exercise 3: Simple Interest Notes and Treasury Bills

Calculate discount and proceeds.

	Face Value ($)	Discount Rate (%)	Time	Discount ($)	Proceeds ($)
13.	7,500	4	1 year	_____	_____
14.	9,200	3.5	2 years	_____	_____
15.	4,320	5	6 months	_____	_____
16.	1,690	4.5	9 months	_____	_____
17.	2,033	2.5	45 days	_____	_____
18.	10,000	3	28 months	_____	_____

Exercise 4: Promissory Notes

Calculate number of days of note, interest, and maturity value as required.

	Amount of Note ($)	Date of Note	Date Due	Rate (%)	Number of Days of Note	Interest ($)	Maturity Value ($)
19.	Note A 5,500	1-28-2003	6-17-2003	3	_____	_____	_____
20.	Note B 25,000	2-10-2003	10-15-2003	3.5	_____	_____	_____
21.	Note C 8,250	4-15-2003	7-20-2003	2.75	_____	_____	_____
22.	Note D 9,550	6-1-2003	12-15-2003	4	_____	_____	_____

Exercise 5: Third-Party Notes

Calculate discount time, bank discount, and proceeds for notes A through D in Problems 19 through 22, which have been sold to a third party.

	Maturity Value ($) (See Problems 19 to 22)	Date Note Was Sold to Third Party	Discount Rate (%)	Discount Time	Bank Discount ($)	Proceeds ($)
23.	Note A	3-15-2003	6.5	_____	_____	_____
24.	Note B	4-20-2003	8	_____	_____	_____
25.	Note C	5-1-2003	9	_____	_____	_____
26.	Note D	8-15-2003	7	_____	_____	_____

CHAPTER 12

Solving Equations; Equations for Area, Perimeter, Circumference, and Volume; Constructing Equations; Calculating Department and Store Square Footage

 **PART 1** *Speed and Accuracy Building Using Touch Key*

GOALS: Your speed goal is 8,000 strokes per hour.
Your accuracy target goal range is 95% to 100%.

With each repetition of the drill, try to improve your speed without lowering your accuracy score. If your percent-of-accuracy score falls below 95%, review your finger position and technique. Then try again.

Instructions: *Start Touch Key. Complete Drill 2, Parts A through E, One-Minute Timings. Write your scores for strokes per hour and percent of accuracy below.*

Touch Key Drill 2—The 0 through 9 Keys, Four-Digit Numbers, One-Minute Timings

Today's Date	Strokes per Hour	Percent of Accuracy
A.		
B.		
C.		
D.		
E.		

PART 2 *Business Math Skills*

WORKING WITH EQUATIONS

In the previous two chapters, formulas, or equations, were introduced for solving percentage and simple interest problems. In this chapter, additional information is discussed for writing and solving equations. Consider the simple interest formula (equation)

$$\text{Interest} = \text{Principal} \times \text{Rate} \times \text{Time} \quad \text{or} \quad I = P \times R \times T$$

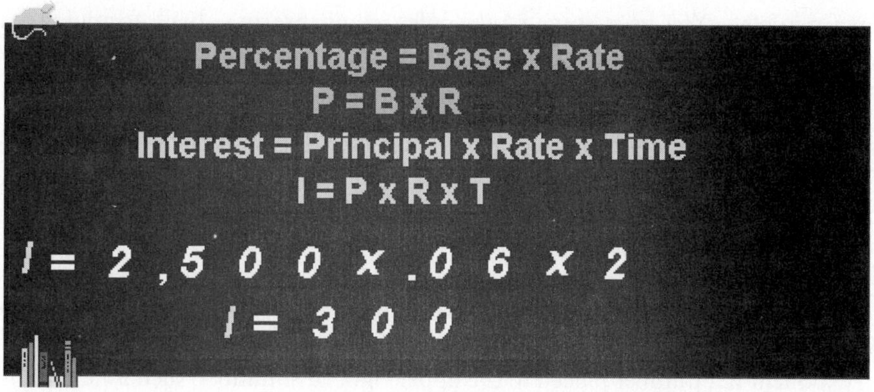

Percentage = Base x Rate
$$P = B \times R$$
Interest = Principal x Rate x Time
$$I = P \times R \times T$$
$$I = 2,500 \times .06 \times 2$$
$$I = 300$$

FIGURE 12.1

Notice that the letters and symbols in the equation are separated into left and right sides and are joined by an equal sign. The symbols on the left side of the equation make up a **mathematical expression**; the symbols on the right side of the equation make up a separate expression. The two expressions joined together with an equal sign make up an equation. Therefore, an **equation** is a statement asserting the equality of two expressions. Letters and symbols that take the place of missing information are called **variables**. A variable may be referred to as the "unknown." When all variables in an equation have been replaced with known values, a **solution** to the equation has been found. How is the checking of a solved problem accomplished? When a solution is found for an equation, the solution should be exchanged with the variable and the problem should be solved again. If the two sides of the equation are equal, the solution is probably correct. Refer to the interest problem in Figure 12.1. To check the problem, insert the amount that was found for interest, $300, in place of I in the formula and solve. Does $300 = 2,500 \times .06 \times 2$? Yes. The correct solution is $300.

You already know the signs for arithmetic operations $+$ for addition and $-$ for subtraction. You also know that the arithmetic operation of division may be indicated by $\div$ or $/$ or by writing a fraction with the number to be divided (the dividend) as the numerator and the number that you are dividing by (the divisor) as the denominator. For example, $24 \div 2$ can be written as $\frac{24}{2}$.

There are several ways to indicate when the arithmetic operation of multiplication is to take place within an equation. Refer to Figure 12.2. All of the examples indicate "three times what number equals 15?"

To ensure that correct solutions are obtained when solving equations, certain rules of algebra must be used. Algebra need not be scary. Algebra is simply arithmetic (adding, subtracting, multiplying, and dividing) in which symbols such as letters are used to indicate

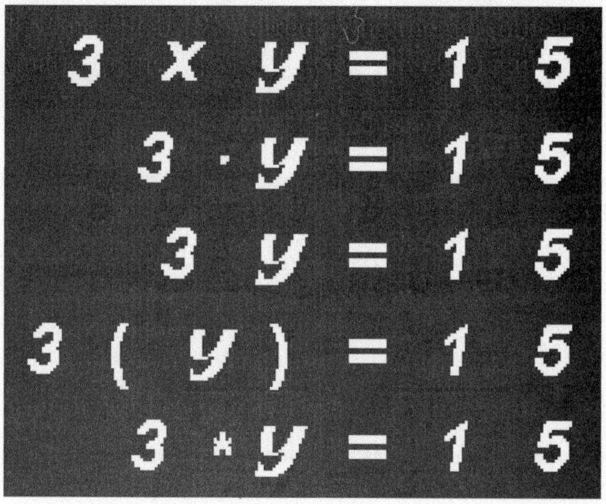

$$3 \times y = 15$$
$$3 \cdot y = 15$$
$$3\,y = 15$$
$$3(y) = 15$$
$$3 * y = 15$$

FIGURE 12.2

unknown numbers. You used some of the rules of algebra in solving formulas for percentage and simple interest in earlier chapters. Those rules and others are shown below. Do you recognize some of them?

Rule 1. Use the Standard Order of Operations when solving an equation. The Standard Order of Operations specifies that one should:

a. Solve for any values in parentheses.
b. Evaluate any numbers with exponents.
c. Work from left to right.
d. Solve all multiplication and division operations left to right, whichever comes first.
e. Solve all addition and subtraction operations left to right, whichever comes first.

An **exponent** is a number placed to the upper right of a number, such as 5^2; this is read "5 to the power of 2." The expression 5^2 indicates that 5 is to be multiplied by itself two times (the number shown in the exponent).

> **Example 1:** $5^2 = 5 \times 5 = 25$
> **Example 2:** $2^4 = 2 \times 2 \times 2 \times 2 = 16$

Note: A number with an exponent of 2 can also be read as that number "squared." A number with an exponent of 3 can also be read as that number "cubed."

PROBLEM 1

Figure 12.3 shows the equation $x = 2 + 3 \times 10 \div 5$.

a. To solve this equation correctly, we must apply Rule 1 and work from left to right, doing multiplication and division operations before addition and subtraction operations. The first multiplication or division operation is 3×10. Multiply. Recopy the equation on the next line substituting the number 30 for 3×10.

b. On examining the second line, we see that we must next solve the division operation of $30 \div 5$. Recopy the remaining portions of the equation on the third line, substituting 6 for $30 \div 5$.

c. Looking at the third line, you will see that arithmetic is the last operation. Adding $2 + 6$ results in the solution to the equation: $x = 8$.

```
Rule 1

x = 2 + 3 X 1 0 ÷ 5
      2 + 3 0 ÷ 5
      2 + 6
x = 8
```

FIGURE 12.3

Parentheses are used in equations to set off operations that should be completed before other operations in the equation. If an equation contains a set of parentheses, complete the arithmetic operations inside the parentheses first using the Standard Order of Operations. Then solve the remaining operations in the equation using Rule 1, Standard Order of Operations.

PROBLEM 2

In Figure 12.4 the equation to be solved is $x = 5 \div (9 \div 3 + 2)$.

Rule 1 cont.
$$x = 5 \div (9 \div 3 + 2)$$
$$x = 5 \div 5$$
$$x = 1$$

FIGURE 12.4

a. The parentheses indicate that 9 should be divided by 3 and then the quotient should be added to 2. Copy the remainder of the equation on the second line, substituting the value for the numbers in parentheses: 5.
b. Solve line 2 by dividing: $5 \div 5$.
c. $x = 1$.

Rule 2. The values of the left and right sides of the equation must be equal. To check the solutions to problems, substitute the solution for the variable in the problem and solve. Are both sides of the expression equal? If so, the solution is correct.

PROBLEM 3

In Figure 12.5 the problem $2 \times 3 = y$ is presented along with its solution: $6 = y$. To check this problem, substitute 6 for y in the equation and solve. Does $2 \times 3 = 6$? Yes. The solution is $y = 6$.

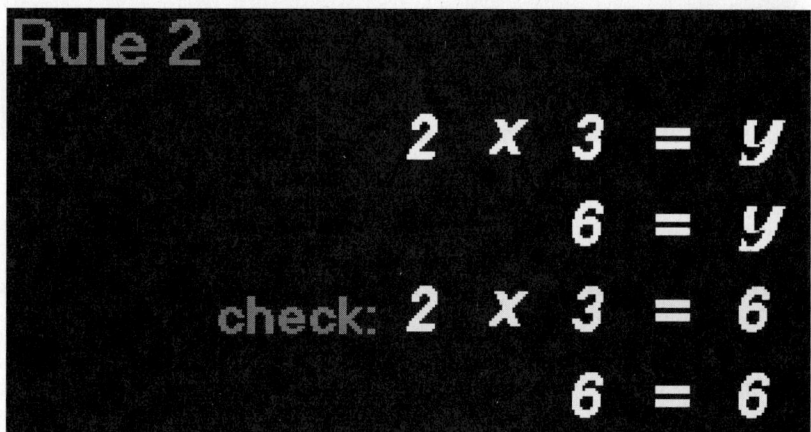

Rule 2
$$2 \times 3 = y$$
$$6 = y$$
$$\text{check: } 2 \times 3 = 6$$
$$6 = 6$$

FIGURE 12.5

Take a few moments to check the two problems worked previously. Are the solutions correct?

Check Problem 1. To check, substitute the result of 8 for x in the equation and solve again. Does $8 = 2 + 3 \times 10 \div 5$? Yes. The solution for x is correct.

Check Problem 2. Substitute 1 for x in the equation. Does $1 = 5 \div (9 \div 3 + 2)$? Yes. The solution to the equation is $x = 1$.

Rule 3. Simplify an equation so that only the variable remains on one side of the equation. The variable may be on either the left or the right side of the equation. Rules 4 through 6 may be used to help simplify equations. Figure 12.6 shows the equation $2 \times 4 = y + 2$. According to Rule 3, the variable y needs to be isolated on the right side of the equation. To do this, we turn to Rule 4 and its properties.

Rule 3

$$2 \times 4 = y + 2$$
$$2 \times 4 - 2 = y + 2 - 2$$
$$8 - 2 = y$$
$$6 = y$$

FIGURE 12.6

Rule 4. The same arithmetic operation may be performed on both sides of an equation without affecting the solution.

Addition Property: A number may be added to both sides of an equation.

PROBLEM 4

Figure 12.7 shows the equation $x - 10 = 30$. According to Rule 3, the first step is to isolate the variable x on the left side of the equation. Since the left side of the equation contains the expression $x - 10$, it is necessary to remove the -10. The opposite of subtraction is addition, so adding 10 to the left side of the equation will result in $x + 0$, or simply x. However, because of Rule 4, if **10 is added to the left side** of the equation, it must **also be added to the right side** of the equation.

$$x - 10 = 30$$
$$x - 10 + 10 = 30 + 10$$
$$x = 40$$

FIGURE 12.7

Copy the equation on the next line, placing $+10$ on each side of the equation. Solve. We now have $x = 30 + 10$. Solve: $x = 40$.

Check Problem 3. Substitute 40 for x in the equation. Does $40 - 10 = 30$? Yes. The solution is correct.

Quick Review: Refer to Figure 12.8 and the equation $2 \times 4 = y - 6$. Solve this equation using Rule 3 and **isolating the variable** y on the right side and the addition property to **add a number** (in this case, $+6$) **to both sides of the equation.**

Rule 4

$$2 \times 4 = y - 6$$
$$2 \times 4 + 6 = y - 6 + 6$$
$$8 + 6 = y$$
$$14 = y$$

FIGURE 12.8

$$y + 2 = 6$$
$$y + 2 - 2 = 6 - 2$$
$$y = 4$$

FIGURE 12.9

Check: Substitute the solution (14) for the variable (y):

$$2 \times 4 = 14 - 6$$
$$8 = 8$$

Subtraction Property: A number may be subtracted from both sides of an equation.

PROBLEM 5

Figure 12.9 shows the equation $y + 2 = 6$. To isolate the variable y, it will be necessary to subtract 2 from both sides of the equation as shown on line 2 of Figure 12.9. Solve.

Check Problem 4: Substitute 4 for y in the equation and solve. Does $4 + 2 = 6$? Yes.

Quick Review: Refer once again to Figure 12.6 and the equation $2 \times 4 = y + 2$. Solve this equation using Rule 3 to **isolate the variable** y on the right side and the subtraction property to **subtract a number** (in this case, -2) **from both sides of the equation.** Is your solution $6 = y$? Your answer should be yes.

Check: Substitute 6 for y and solve:

$$2 \times 4 = 6 + 2$$
$$8 = 8$$

Division Property: Both sides of an equation may be divided by the same number. In Figure 12.10, x is multiplied by 2 on the left side of the equation. The 2 in the expression $2x$ is known as the **coefficient** of x. A coefficient is the numerical part of an algebraic term. It is the number placed before a letter representing a variable. To isolate the variable x, both sides of the equation must be divided by 2. The 2 in the numerator and the 2 in the denominator on the left side of the equation may be cancelled,* leaving only x on the left side of the equation. Therefore, $x = 10/2$. The solution is $x = 5$.

*We say that the twos may be cancelled because $\dfrac{2x}{2} = 1x = x$.

$$2x = 10$$
$$\frac{2x}{2} = \frac{10}{2}$$
$$x = 5$$

FIGURE 12.10

$$\frac{y}{2} = 10$$

$$\frac{y}{2} \times 2 = 10 \times 2$$

$$y = 20$$

FIGURE 12.11

Multiplication Property: Both sides of an equation may be multiplied by the same number. In Figure 12.11, y is divided by 2 on the left side of the equation. To isolate the variable y, both sides of the equation must be multiplied by 2. Because the number 2 is the same as the fraction $\frac{2}{1}$, simply treat 2 as a numerator. The numerator 2 and the denominator 2 may then be cancelled on the left side of the equation.

*Note that this results in the the left side of the equation now equaling y. Therefore, $y = 10 \times 2$. The solution is $y = 20$.

**We say that the twos may be cancelled in this instance because* $\frac{y}{2} \times 2 = \frac{y}{2} \times \frac{2}{1} = y$.

Rule 5. When it is necessary to isolate a variable by using more than one arithmetic property, use the addition or subtraction property (or properties) first, then use the multiplication or division property (or properties). In the equation $5y - 6 = 69$ (Figure 12.12), it will be necessary to remove the -6 from the left side of the equation and also to remove the 5 that is multiplied by y on the left side of the equation to isolate the variable y.

Rule 5

$$5y - 6 = 69$$

$$5y - 6 + 6 = 69 + 6$$

$$\frac{5y}{5} = \frac{75}{5}$$

$$y = 15$$

FIGURE 12.12

According to Rule 5, the first step is to add 6 to both sides of the equation (see line 2 of Figure 12.12). Solve. The second step is to divide both sides of the equation by 5. See lines 3 and 4 of Figure 12.12. Solve. The solution is $y = 15$.

Rule 6. When solving an equation with more than one like variable, combine (add) the like variables before applying Rules 3 through 5. Refer to Figure 12.13. The equation contains two y variables. These are known as **like variables.** Rule 6 tells us to combine like variables; therefore, we will:

a. Add $y + 2y$. Recopy the equation on line 2, replacing $y + 2y$ with $3y$. The next step is to remove $+9$ to begin isolating the variable y.
b. Subtract 9 from both sides of the equation. Write the result on line 3: $3y = 12$.

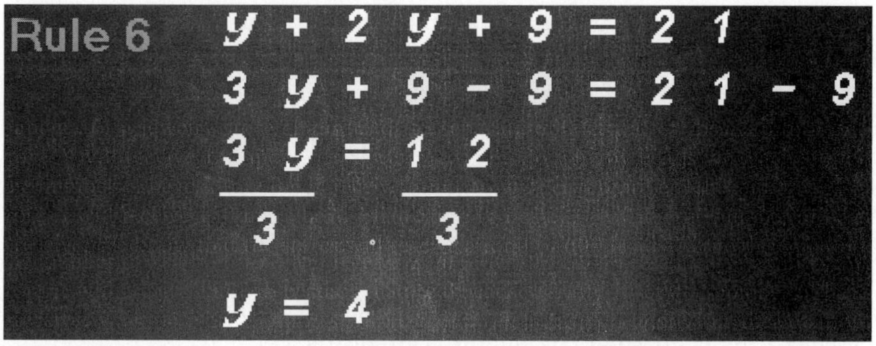

Rule 6

$$y + 2y + 9 = 21$$
$$3y + 9 - 9 = 21 - 9$$
$$3y = 12$$
$$\frac{3y}{3} = \frac{12}{3}$$
$$y = 4$$

FIGURE 12.13

c. To finish isolating y on the left side of the equation, divide both sides of the equation by 3. Solve. The solution is $y = 4$.

The *distributive property* allows an expression such as $3(6 + 2)$ to be worked two different ways. One might add first (Example A) or one might multiply both addends by the coefficient first (Example B) and get the same answer:

Example A	Example B
$3(6 + 2)$	$3(6 + 2)$
$3(8)$	$3 \times 6 + 3 \times 2$
24	$18 + 6$
	24

When we multiply first as in B, we **distribute the multiplication over the addition.** When the parentheses contain a variable as in the expression $4(y + 3)$ we should multiply all items within the parentheses by the coefficient first. That is, use the distributive property and remove the parentheses as in the following example:

$$4(y + 3)$$

Apply the distributive property and remove the parentheses:

$$4y + 4 \times 3$$
$$4y + 12$$

Thus, we have the following rule:

Rule 7. When solving an equation in which the **coefficient is placed before a set of parentheses** containing a variable, use the distributive property and remove the parentheses. Then follow Rules 1 through 6 as necessary. Refer to Figure 12.14 and the equation $9(y - 2) = 9$. According to Rule 7, the first step involves:

a. Multiplying both y and -2 by 9 and removing the parentheses. The result is that the left side of the equation is now $9y - 18$ (see line 2 of Figure 12.14).

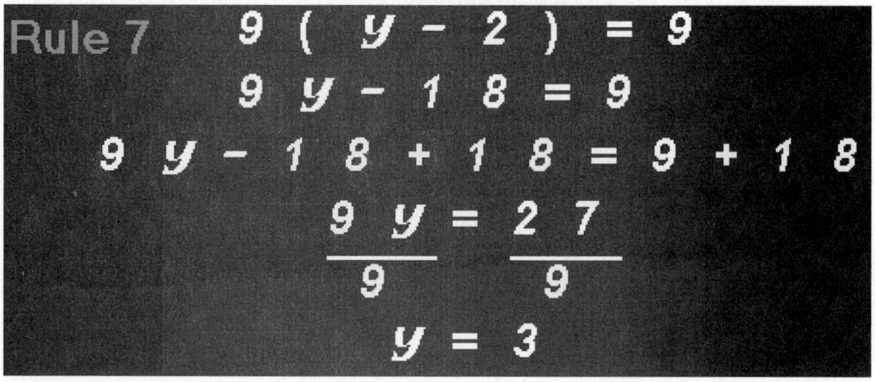

Rule 7

$$9(y - 2) = 9$$
$$9y - 18 = 9$$
$$9y - 18 + 18 = 9 + 18$$
$$9y = 27$$
$$\frac{9y}{9} = \frac{27}{9}$$
$$y = 3$$

FIGURE 12.14

b. The next step is to begin to isolate y on the left side of the equation by adding 18 to both sides of the equation, resulting in $9y = 27$ (see line 4 of Figure 12.14).

c. The next step in isolating y on the left side of the equation is to divide both sides of the equation by 9. Solve.

ONE FINAL NOTE: DISTRACTERS

Distracters are bits of information that are available but not needed to solve a problem. When solving a problem, watch for and disregard distracters.

COMMON EQUATIONS USED IN BUSINESS

It is often necessary to find area, length, and volume in business problems. Common problems, for example, are determining the number of square feet of carpet needed for an office, the amount of fabric needed to cover a round conference table, the length of fence to be placed around property, and the amount a container will hold. Though you may not need these equations every day, you may want to remember this section as a handy reference.

Although equations normally use letters and symbols, this chapter, as in the simple interest chapter, will use full words where appropriate to make the transition from word problem to equation easier. For example you may see Area = Length × Width as well as $a = lw$.

Squares and Rectangles

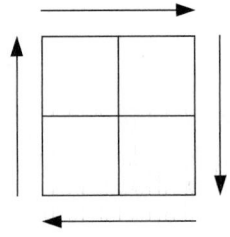

Picture the area of a square or a rectangle as the number of tiles, each 1 ft square, that would fit inside the square or rectangle. Picture the perimeter of a square or rectangle as the amount of rope that would be required if laid around its edge.

This square contains four squares that are all 1 ft on all sides. The area is therefore 4 sq ft. The perimeter (border), as indicated by the surrounding arrows, is 8 ft (the total of all sides of the large square). That is, Area = 4 sq ft and Perimeter = 8 ft.

Since all sides of a square are equal, the equations for area and perimeter can be shortened. However, since the equations for area and perimeter for rectangles can also be used for squares, equations for rectangles will be presented:

$$\text{Area of Rectangle} = \text{Length} \times \text{Width}$$

or

$$a = lw$$

length

area　　　　width

FIGURE 12.15

A room with dimensions of 12 ft × 10 ft has an area of

$$a = 12 \times 10$$
$$a = 120 \text{ square feet or } 120 \text{ ft}^2$$
$$\text{Perimeter of a Rectangle} = 2 \times \text{Length} + 2 \times \text{Width}$$

or

$$p = 2l + 2w \quad \text{or} \quad p = 2(l + w)$$

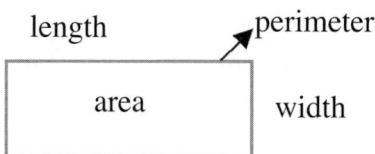

FIGURE 12.16

A 12 ft × 10 ft room has a perimeter of

$$p = 2(12 + 10)$$
$$p = 24 + 20 = 44 \text{ ft}$$

Circles

Before calculating the area of a circle, we must define some terms that apply to circles only.

The **circumference** is the length around a circle.

The **diameter** of a circle is the length across it.

The **radius** is half the length of the diameter:

$$\text{Radius} = \text{Diameter} \div 2$$

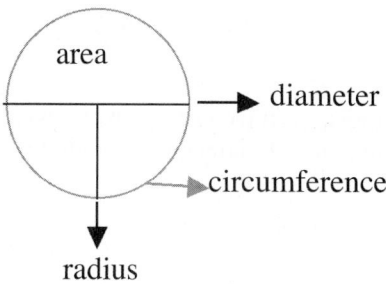

FIGURE 12.17

Pi is the name of the symbol π. This symbol designates the number 3.141592654, which is usually rounded to 3.14. Where ever you see the symbol π, insert the number 3.14 in the equation.

The area of a circle is given by

$$\text{Area} = \pi \times \text{Radius}^2 \qquad \text{or} \qquad a = \pi r^2$$

What is the area of a conference table that is 5 ft in diameter? Using the equation for the area of a circle, we see that we need to know the radius. We divide the diameter by 2 to find a radius of 2.5 ft. Then

$$\text{Area} = 3.14 \times 2.5^2$$

Begin by evaluating the exponent: $2.5 \times 2.5 = 6.25$. Then

$$\text{Area} = 3.14 \times 6.25$$
$$\text{Area} = 19.625 \text{ sq ft} \qquad \text{or} \qquad 19.625 \text{ ft}^2$$

The circumference is given by

$$\text{Circumference} = \pi \times \text{diameter} \qquad \text{or} \qquad c = \pi d$$

Find the circumference of the conference table. We have

$$\text{Circumference} = 3.14 \times 5 \, \text{ft}$$
$$\text{Circumference} = 15.7 \, \text{ft}$$

The diameter is given by

$$\text{Diameter} = \text{Circumference} \div \pi \quad \text{or} \quad d = c \div \pi$$

Find the diameter for a circle that has a circumference of 30 ft. We have

$$\text{Diameter} = 30 \, \text{ft} \div 3.14$$
$$\text{Diameter} = 9.554 \, \text{ft} \quad \text{Rounded to thousandths}$$

Volume of Four-Sided Figures

Picture volume as the number of 1-in. cubes (blocks that are 1-in. square on all sides) that an object can contain. It is often necessary to determine the amount or volume that a four-sided object such as a packing box will hold. For the dimensions of a four-sided figure, it is necessary to specify the height of the box as well as the length and the width:

$$\text{Volume} = \text{Length} \times \text{Width} \times \text{Height} \quad \text{or} \quad v = lwh$$

length   width

FIGURE 12.18

Find the volume of a packing box that is 24 in. high, 5 in. long, and 5 in. wide.

$$\text{Volume} = 5 \times 5 \times 24$$
$$\text{Volume} = 600 \, \text{cu in.} \quad \text{or} \quad 600 \, \text{in.}^3$$

Volume of Cylinders

To find the volume of a cylinder, such as a can, it is necessary to know the height of the can as well as either the radius or the diameter. If the diameter is known, remember that radius is 1/2 of the diameter. We have

$$\text{Volume} = \pi \times \text{Radius}^2 \times \text{Height} \quad \text{or} \quad v = \pi r^2 h$$

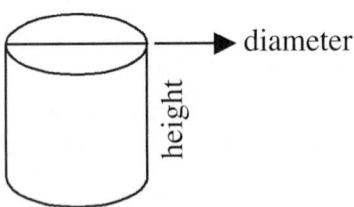

FIGURE 12.19

Find the volume of a can that has a diameter of 3.5 in. and is 8 in. tall.
Begin by dividing the diameter by 2 to find the radius: 3.5 in. ÷ 2 = 1.75 in.
Substitute the known values for π, the radius, and the height into the equation for the volume of a cylinder. We obtain

$$\text{Volume} = 3.14 \times 1.75^2 \times 8$$

Evaluate the exponent first: $1.75 \times 1.75 = 3.0625$. We have

$$\text{Volume} = 3.14 \times 3.0625 \times 8$$
$$\text{Volume} = 76.93 \, \text{cu in.} \quad \text{or} \quad 79.63 \, \text{in.}^3$$

CONSTRUCTING AN EQUATION

Until now the equations studied have represented formulas commonly used in business and examples of equations that have already been constructed for you. How are equations written to help solve word problems? It is necessary to correctly read the problem and translate it into mathematical expressions. Sometimes being able to write equations is a matter of being able to read and interpret problems correctly. Following are some examples of wordings and meanings of which to be aware. Remember, a letter should represent the unknown.

Wording	Resulting Mathematical Expression
A number increased by 4 = 8	$n + 4 = 8$
A number decreased by 7 = 3	$n - 7 = 3$
The product of a number and 5 = 20	$n \times 5 = 20$ or $5n = 20$
8 more than twice a number = 20	$2n + 8 = 20$
3 times the sum of a number + 1 = 12	$3(n + 1) = 12$
A number plus that number plus 40 = 200	$n + (n + 40) = 200$

PROBLEM 1

A company spent $750 total on three sizes of cartons during March. Small cartons cost $250, medium cartons cost $200. How much was paid for large cartons? Since we do not know the cost of large cartons, let this unknown be represented by the letter L. The problem tells us that the small cartons ($250) plus the medium cartons ($200) plus the large cartons cost $750. Write an equation:

$$\$250 + \$200 + L = \$750$$

Solve for L:

$$\$450 + L = \$750$$
$$\$450 - \$450 + L = \$750 - \$450 \qquad \text{(Apply subtraction property)}$$
$$L = \$300$$

Check the equation by substituting the solution in the equation and solving:

$$\$250 + \$200 + L = \$750$$
$$\$250 + \$200 + \$300 = \$750$$
$$\$750 = \$750$$

The equation checks.

PROBLEM 2

Two employees in the sales department drove 180 miles. Tom drove 80 miles more than Mike. How many miles did each drive?

What is unknown? The miles driven by each employee. However, we do know that Tom drove 80 PLUS whatever number of miles Mike drove and that together they drove 180 miles. Let the letter M represent the number of miles Mike drove. Since Tom drove 80 MORE MILES THAN MIKE, let $M + 80 = $ the miles driven by Tom. Since total miles $= 180$, then

$$\text{Miles Mike drove} + \text{miles Tom drove} = 180$$

or

$$M + (M + 40) = 180$$

Solve the equation by combining like variables, then use the subtraction property on both sides of the equation. Last, use the division property:

$$M + (M + 40) = 180$$

Combine like variables:

$$2M + 40 = 180$$

Use the subtraction property:

$$2M + 40 - 40 = 180 - 40$$
$$2M = 140$$

Use the division property:

$$\frac{2M}{2} = \frac{140}{2}$$

$M = 70$ Miles driven by Mike
$M + 40 = 70 + 40 = 110$ Miles driven by Tom

Check the problem by replacing variables with the solutions:

$$M + (M + 40) = 180$$
$$70 + (70 + 40) = 180$$
$$70 + 110 = 180$$
$$180 = 180$$

The equation checks.

PROBLEM 3

A skating rink is 150 ft long, which is two times the width less 5 ft. How wide is the skating rink?

The unknown is the width of the skating rink. Let width $= w$. The length is 150 ft, which is 2 times the width -5 ft; therefore,

$$2 \times \text{width} - 5 \text{ ft} = 150 \text{ ft}$$

or

$$2w - 5 \text{ ft} = 150 \text{ ft}$$

Then, using the addition property, we obtain

$$2w - 5 + 5 = 150 + 5$$

Using the division property, we find

$$\frac{2w}{2} = \frac{155}{2}$$

and

$$w = 77.5 \text{ ft}$$

The width of the skating rink is 77 ½ ft.

Check:

$$2w - 5 = 150$$
$$2 \times 77.5 - 5 = 150$$
$$155 - 5 = 150$$
$$150 = 150$$

The equation checks.

PROBLEM 4

The manager of a jewelry store chain needs to separate 600 strands of beads into two parts so that Store A will receive 150 more beads than Store B. How many beads will each store receive?

    The number of beads Store B will receive is unknown. Let B represent this unknown. We know that Store A will receive 150 more beads than Store B. Let $B + 150 =$ the number of beads Store A will receive. We know that the stores will receive a total of 600 beads. Write the equation:

$$\text{Store B beads} + (\text{Store B beads} + 150) = 600$$
$$B + (B + 150) = 600$$

Combine like variables:

$$2B + 150 = 600$$

Use the subtraction property:

$$2B + 150 - 150 = 600 - 150$$

Use the division property:

$$\frac{2B}{2} = \frac{450}{2}$$
$$B = 225$$

Check:

$$B + (B + 150) = 600$$
$$225 + 225 + 150 = 600$$
$$225 + 375 = 600$$
$$600 = 600$$

The equation checks.

Name _____

Class/Section _____

Score (Correct Answers ÷ No. of Assigned Problems) _____

PART 2 *Business Math Skills*

Exercise 1 Equations

Solve the following equations using the addition property. What is the value of the unknown represented by x?

    1. $x - 7 = 19$ _____
    2. $x - 13 = 52$ _____
    3. $x - 25 = 110$ _____
    4. $x - 12 = 30$ _____

Solve using the subtraction property.

    5. $x + 29 = 71$ _____
    6. $x + 13 + 12 = 90$ _____
    7. $x + 5 = 18$ _____
    8. $x + 9 = 32$ _____

Solve using the multiplication property.

9. $x \div 5 = 15$ _____
10. $x \div 19 = 2$ _____
11. $x \div 25 = 4$ _____
12. $x \div 90 = 3$ _____

Solve using the division property.

13. $3x = 30$ _____
14. $2x = 25$ _____
15. $21x = 63$ _____
16. $12x = 60$ _____

Solve using more than one property.

17. $2x - 8 = 16$ _____
18. $9 + 3x = 51$ _____
19. $x - 50 = 62$ _____
20. $3x \div 3 + 25 = 34$ _____

Solve combining like variables and using properties.

21. $2x - x + 10 = 14$ _____
22. $x + 9.2x = 51$ _____
23. $2x + 0.5x + 9 = 26.5$ _____
24. $3(x - 2) + 2 = 26$ _____

Solve using the distributive property.

25. $600(y - 4) = 3,600$ _____
26. $10 + (9y - 2) = 19$ _____
27. $\$10,000 \div 3(y + 5) = \$333.33$ _____
28. $4(x - 4) - 25 = 46.25$ _____

Exercise 2

Solve these common problems.

29. For a rectangle that is 25″ wide by 70″ in length, find area _____ and perimeter _____.
30. For a circle with a diameter of 12″, find radius _____, area _____, and circumference _____.
31. What is the volume of a box that is $5 \times 7 \times 11$″? _____
32. What is the volume of a cylinder that has a diameter of 2″ and a height of 6″? _____
33. Find the simple interest for a loan for $5,000 at 5% for 9 years. _____
34. Find the principal for a loan at 4.5% for 5 months for which $69 was paid in interest. _____

Write an equation for each problem, then solve. Use n for the unknown number.

35. ABC Co. owed $4,068.72 on an account. After making a payment of $525.20, how much did ABC Co. owe? Let n = amount owed. _____
36. Gladys paid $5.15 for 1/3 yd of fabric. How much would 1 yd of the same fabric cost? Let n = amount for 1 yard. _____
37. The length of a library table is twice its width. If the width is 36″, what is the length? Let n = length. _____
38. An SUV costs $32,500, which is $700 more than 12 times a certain number. What is the number? Let n = the number. _____
39. Roger and Don had $138. Don had three times as much as Roger. How much did each have? Let Roger's portion = n. _____
40. A playing field is 250′ in length. The width is one-fourth the length plus 26′. What is the width? Let n = the width. _____

PART 3   *The Pocket and Windows Calculators*

EQUATIONS

When solving equations and other business problems using a pocket calculator, numbers and arithmetic operations should be solved in the same order as when using paper and pencil. Make pencil notations of each step of the problem being solved to avoid confusion. The memory feature can be used to store values found in intermediate steps of solving equations in certain instances.

PROBLEM 1

Find the perimeter of a lot that is 320 ft × 625 ft.

$$\text{Perimeter} = 2 \times \text{Length} + 2 \times \text{Width}$$

The Standard Order of Operations specifies that the two multiplication operations must be accomplished, then the two products added together. Using the pocket calculator and the memory feature, first multiply, then add the result to memory. Solve the second multiplication operation and add that result to memory. Memory recall or memory total will display the solution to the equation. We have

$$\text{Perimeter} = 2 \times 625 \text{ ft} + 2 \times 320 \text{ ft}$$

Order of Entry:

$$2 \times 625 = \boxed{1.250} \text{ M+ } 2 \times 320 = \boxed{640} \text{ M+ MT } \boxed{1,890} \text{ sq ft}$$

PROBLEM 2

Find the area of a circle with a radius of 32 in. We have

$$\text{Area} = \pi \times \text{Radius}^2$$
$$\text{Area} = 3.14 \times 32^2$$

Order of Entry:

$$32 \times 32 = \boxed{1,024} \times 3.14 = \boxed{3,215.36} \text{ sq in.}$$

Note: If π will be used in several problems, you may wish to store 3.14 in memory and multiply by memory recall without clearing memory as follows:

$$3.14 \text{ M+ } 32 \times 32 = \boxed{1,024} \times \text{MR} = \boxed{3,215.36 \text{ sq in.}}$$

PROBLEM 3

Solve 2 + (8 − 2) × 6.

Following the Standard Order of Operations, first solve for the value in parentheses; second, complete the multiplication operation; and third, complete the addition operation.

Order of Entry:

$$8 - 2 = \boxed{6} \times 6 = \boxed{36} + 2 = \boxed{38}$$

PROBLEM 4

Solve $223 + 440 \div 2 + 25$.

Following the Standard Order of Operations, first complete the division operation, then complete the two addition operations working from left to right.

Order of Entry: (Check that memory is clear):

$$440 \div 2 = \boxed{220} + 223 + 25 = \boxed{468}$$

PROBLEM 5

Find the volume of a cylinder with a 35 in. diameter and a height of 45 in. We have

$$\text{Volume} = \pi \times \text{Radius}^2 \times \text{Height}$$

Find radius by dividing the diameter by 2:

$$35 \div 2 = \boxed{17.5} \quad \text{(Do not clear display)}$$

Thus

$$\text{Volume} = 3.14 \times 17.5^2 \times 45$$

Continue by evaluating the exponent, then multiply by π and by the height of the cylinder. The display should contain the number 17.5:

$$\times 17.5 \times 3.14 \times 45 = \boxed{43,273.125} \text{ cu in.} \quad \text{or} \quad 43,273.125 \text{ in.}^3$$

PART 3   *The Pocket or Windows Calculator*

There are no separate exercises for this section. Use your calculator as you complete the following Business Math FUNdamentals tutorials and drill.

PART 3   *Review and Practice Using Business Math FUNdamentals*

GOAL: Complete 9 of the 10 problems correctly.

Instructions: *Start Business Math FUNdamentals. Complete Tutorial 33 and Drill 25. If you are not satisfied with your scores, repeat the drills. Write your scores below.*

Business Math FUNdamentals Drill 25

Today's Date	Score

 PART 4   *The Desktop Calculator*

EQUATIONS

Following are some common business problems and equations and examples of how to key the problems on the desktop calculator following the rules of the Standard Order of Operations. Use the following machine setup for the problems:

Decimal Selector—F
Rounding Switch—5/4
Printer—On

PROBLEM 1

Solve $3,548 + (19 - 3) \times 2$.
 Find the value in parentheses, multiply, then add.

Order of Entry:

$$19 + 3 - T \boxed{16} \times 2 = \boxed{32} + 3,548 + T \boxed{3,580}$$

PROBLEM 2

Solve $3 \times (16 - 2) \div 2 + 125$.
 Find the value in parentheses, then multiply, then divide, then add.

Order of Entry:

$$16 + 2 - T \boxed{14} \times 3 \div 2 = \boxed{21} + 125 + T \boxed{146}$$

PROBLEM 3

Find perimeter of a room that is 27 ft × 15 ft.

$$\text{Perimeter} = 2 \times \text{Length} + 2 \times \text{Width}$$

 The answer should be labeled in feet.

Order of Entry:

$$2 \times 27 = \boxed{54} \text{ M+ } 2 \times 15 = \boxed{30} \text{ M+ MT } \boxed{84} \text{ ft}$$

PROBLEM 4

Find the area of a playground that is 300 ft wide and 700 ft long.

$$\text{Area} = \text{Length} \times \text{Width}$$

 The answer should be labeled in square feet.

Order of Entry:

$$300 \times 700 = \boxed{210,000} \text{ ft}^2$$

TAPE 12.1:   Problem 1

```
        19 ·  ÷
         3 ·  –
        16 ·  *

        16 ·  x
         2 ·  =
        32 ·  *

        32 ·  +
     3,548 ·  +
     3,580 ·  *
```

TAPE 12.2:   Problem 2

```
        16 ·  ÷
         2 ·  –
        14 ·  *

        14 ·  x
         3 ·  ÷
         2 ·  =
        21 ·  *

        21 ·  +
       125 ·  +
       146 ·  *
```

TAPE 12.3:   Problem 3

```
         2 ·  x
        27 ·  =
        54 ·  *

        54 · M+
         2 ·  x
        15 ·  =
        30 ·  *

        30 · M+
        84 · M*
```

TAPE 12.4:   Problem 4

```
       300 ·  x
       700 ·  =
   210,000 ·  *
```

```
      15·  ÷
       2·  =
     7·5   *

     7·5   x
     7·5   x
     3·14  =
   176·625 *
```

PROBLEM 5

Find the area and circumference of a circle that is 15 in. in diameter.
   Use

$$\text{Area} = \pi \times \text{Radius}^2$$

   Begin by finding the radius. Square the radius (7.5×7.5). Multiply the result by 3.14. Label the answer in square inches.

Order of Entry:

$$15 \div 2 = 7.5 \times 7.5 \times 3.14 = \boxed{176.625} \text{ in.}^2$$

Now,

$$\text{Circumference} = \pi \times \text{Diameter}$$

   Order of entry (label the answer in inches):

$$3.14 \times 15 = \boxed{47.1} \text{ in.}$$

```
   3·14  x
    15·  =
   47·1  *
```

PROBLEM 6

Find the volume of a box that is 15 in. high by 10 in. long by 4 in. wide.
   Use

$$\text{Volume} = \text{Height} \times \text{Length} \times \text{Width}$$

   Label the answer in cubic inches.

Order of Entry:

$$15 \times 10 \times 4 = \boxed{600} \text{ cu in.}$$

```
    0·C

    15·  x
    10·  x
     4·  =
   600·  *
```

PROBLEM 7

Find the volume of a drum (cylinder) that is 3 ft in height and has a diameter of 1.25 ft.

$$\text{Volume} = \pi \times \text{Radius}^2 \times \text{Height}$$

   Begin by finding the radius. Label the answer in cubic feet.

Order of Entry:

$$1.25 \div 2 = \boxed{0.625} \times .625 \times 3.14 \times 3 = \boxed{3.6796\ldots}$$

   Round answer to hundredths: 3.68 cu ft.

```
     1·25    ÷
      2·     =
    0·625    *

    0·625    x
    0·625    =
  0·390625   *

  0·390625   x
     3·14    =
 1·2265625   *

 1·2265625   x
      3·     =
 3·6796875   *
```

PROBLEM 8

Solve $3x + 101.2 = 110.8$.
   Begin simplifying the equation using the arithmetic property. Rewrite the problem as follows:

$$3x + 101.2 - 101.2 = 110.8 - 101.2$$

Order of Entry:

$$110.8 + 101.2 - \text{T} \boxed{9.6}$$

Rewrite the Problem:

$$3x = 9.6$$
$$3x \div 3 = 9.6 \div 3$$

Order of Entry:

$$9.6 \div 3 = \boxed{3.2}$$

Write the Solution:

$$x = 3.2$$

Check the problem by replacing the variable with the value of x. Are both sides of the equation equal (Tape 12.9)? We have

$$3(3.2) + 101.2 = 110.8$$

Order of Entry: Find a value for the left side of the equation:

$$3 \times 3.2 = \boxed{9.6} + 101.2 + T \boxed{110.8}$$

Rewrite the Equation:

$$110.8 = 110.8$$

TAPE 12.9: Problem 8

```
110·8 +
101·2 -
  9·6 *

  9·6 ÷
  3·  =
  3·2 *

  3·  x
  3·2 =
  9·6 *

  9·6 +
101·2 +
110·8 *
```

PROBLEM 9

Solve $3.625x + x + 8.875x = 27$.

Begin by combining like variables. To do this, add the three coefficients of x.

Order of Entry:

$$3.625 + 1 + 8.875 + T \boxed{13.5}$$

Rewrite the Problem:

$$13.5x = 27$$

Divide both sides of the equation by 13.5 to isolate the variable on the left side of the equation.

Rewrite the Problem:

$$13.5x \div 13.5 = 27 \div 13.5$$

Order of Entry:

$$27 \div 13.5 = \boxed{2}$$
$$x = 2$$

Check by replacing the variables in the equation with the value of x and solve:

$$3.625(2) + (2) + 8.875(2) = 27$$

Order of Entry:

$$3.625 \times 2 = \boxed{7.25} \, M+ \, 2 \, M+ \, 8.875 \times 2 = \boxed{17.75} \, M+ \, MT \boxed{27}$$

Rewrite the Equation:

$$27 = 27$$

TAPE 12.10: Problem 9

```
3·625 +
  1·  +
8·875 +
13·5  *

27·   ÷
13·5  =
 2·   *
```

TAPE 12.11: Problem 9

```
3·625 x
 2·   =
7·25  *

7·25 M+
 2· M+
8·875 x
 2·   =
17·75 *

17·75 M+
27· M*
```

CALCULATING DEPARTMENTAL AND STORE SQUARE FOOTAGE

TAPE 12.12: Comfy Steps

```
   30 •  ×
   35 •  =
1,050 •  *

1,050 • M+
   20 •  ×
   35 •  =
  700 •  *

  700 • M+
   20 •  ×
   30 •  =
  600 •  *

  600 • M+
   20 •  ×
   30 •  =
  600 •  *

  600 • M+
   10 •  ×
   30 •  =
  300 •  *

  300 • M+
3,250 • M*
```

PROBLEM

The following drawing shows the dimensions for the departments of the Comfy Steps shoe store. Calculate the square footage (area) for each department and the total square footage for the entire store. Begin by listing the dimensions for each department in the table provided. Keep a running total of square footage for the various departments using memory. After all department square footage has been calculated, press memory total to obtain the total square footage for the store.

Comfy Steps

30 ft — Ladies' Shoes	Men's Shoes — 20 ft	
	Boys' Shoes — 20 ft	
20 ft — Girls' Shoes	Infants — 10 ft	
35 ft	30 ft	

	Department	Dimensions (ft)	Sq Ft
1.	Ladies	30 × 35	1,050
2.	Girls	20 × 35	700
3.	Men's	20 × 30	600
4.	Boys	20 × 30	600
5.	Infants	10 × 30	300
6.		**Total Sq Ft**	3,250

Name _____

Class/Section _____

Strokes per Minute Score _____

Accuracy Score (Correct Strokes ÷ Total Strokes) _____

PART 4   *The Desktop Calculator*

Exercise 1

One-Minute Addition Timing (Four-Digit Numbers)

(Optional: Your instructor may wish you to use Touch Key on the computer for all your timings. Check with your instructor before completing this exercise.)

Complete as many of the problems as possible in 1 minute by adding. Work quickly and accurately. The number preceding each closing parenthesis indicates the cumulative number of strokes for problems attempted. For example, if you complete Problems 1 through 5 in 1 minute, your strokes-per-minute score is 255. Optional: 3- to 5-minute timings.

1.	2.	3.	4.	5.	6.	7.	8.
6104	1781	8415	2706	4814	9265	3656	7151
3214	6504	5125	3082	8316	2554	6353	9171
9784	4805	7435	6091	7585	2157	1252	8282
1652	9676	1645	3013	4232	8452	3151	3393
4025	2345	9455	3074	7003	2585	3858	9717
2996	1412	1565	4045	2004	2252	2454	1828
4681	9271	2375	4053	8000	7585	3757	7939
5871	1531	7185	1023	3665	3353	5959	3616
5290	1394	4395	2031	5640	1454	6353	8919
2532	5375	5355	1092	9481	2757	5252	8818
51)	102)	153)	204)	255)	306)	357)	408)

9.	10.	11.	12.	13.	14.	15.	16.
1100	2010	7015	3512	4100	9745	1628	4804
7470	2020	2505	1013	8751	8761	3730	2650
8850	3909	5250	2014	3761	8968	3832	4052
4450	7080	8710	5015	2871	7941	3934	4872
1770	1000	9632	2716	3981	7832	3036	6082
1688	4707	3530	4517	2591	6784	2738	6074
1599	4050	2560	3018	3122	5786	2840	9576
7884	1020	1020	5219	1360	5982	9242	6778
1255	4080	5000	2021	5032	5824	9744	6480
6377	3050	4505	1631	1046	5026	10146	4682
459)	510)	561)	612)	663)	714)	765)	816)

Set decimal selector on add mode.

17.	18.	19.	20.	21.	22.	23.	24.
44.12	50.06	61.29	36.59	34.98	12.89	43.00	22.29
64.00	38.42	67.39	45.89	21.58	26.19	43.50	24.49
87.14	57.43	37.99	41.79	15.69	33.99	35.70	35.19
82.00	89.57	21.98	53.69	64.79	42.79	63.20	48.39
49.16	87.95	51.00	65.89	53.58	53.59	52.90	57.59
27.00	49.97	91.97	16.39	45.19	61.79	32.80	69.89
61.18	68.98	81.96	26.58	46.19	56.59	55.50	75.69
49.00	63.89	85.89	36.69	54.29	22.99	21.70	83.79
49.20	86.00	35.79	44.79	25.49	36.29	15.80	93.19
67.22	84.79	64.78	21.49	21.00	56.39	43.70	91.59
877)	938)	999)	1,060)	1,121)	1,182)	1,243)	1,304)

CHAPTER 12 *Terminology Review*

Circumference
Coefficient
Diameter
Distracters
Equation
Exponent
Isolating the variable
Like variables

Mathematical expression

Radius

Solution

Variables

Write in the correct term.

1. When all variables in an equation have been replaced with known values, the equation is said to have a(n) _____.

2. The numerical part of an algebraic term such as $5x$ is known as the _____.

3. Letters and/or symbols used in an equation as a substitute for missing information are known as _____.

4. Manipulating an equation so that only the variable remains on one side of the equal sign is known as _____.

5. The symbols on either side of an equation make up a(n) _____.

6. A raised number indicating how many times the number to its left should be multiplied by itself is a(n) _____.

7. A statement of the equality of two expressions is a(n) _____.

8. Two algebraic terms such as $x + 3x$ in an equation are _____.

Name _____

Class/Section _____

Score (Correct Answers ÷ No. of Assigned Problems) _____

Chapter 12 Review Exercises

Exercise 1

Solve.

1. 4^2 _____
2. 3^4 _____
3. 2^3 _____
4. 5^2 _____
5. $2 \times 9 = x$ _____
6. $30 \div 5 = x$ _____
7. $45 - 15 = x$ _____
8. $29 + 3 = x$ _____
9. $6 + 3 \times 5$ _____
10. $9 \times 2 + 3$ _____
11. $2 + 6 \div 2$ _____
12. $(2 + 5) \times (2 + 3)$ _____
13. $2(3 + 2)$ _____
14. $5(x + 1)$ if $x = 3$ _____
15. $12 \div 2 + 3$ _____
16. $(5 + 9) \div 7$ _____
17. $3(x + 1) - 10 \div 2$ if $x = 6$ _____
18. $5(x - 3)$ if $x = 7$ _____
19. $32x + 2x - 10$ if $x = 2$ _____
20. $9x - x + 10$ if $x = 3$ _____
21. $y + 3 = 13$ _____
22. $y - 12 = 54$ _____
23. $2 + 10 = y - 2$ _____
24. $8 - 4 = y + 2$ _____
25. $6x = 18$ _____
26. $21x = 105$ _____

27. $\dfrac{45}{x} = 15$ _____

28. $60 \div x = 5$ _____

29. $\dfrac{n}{5} = 90$ _____

30. $n \div 17 = 3$ _____

31. $6y - 2 = 70$ _____

32. $5y + 9 = 84$ _____

33. $2(n - 8) = 6$ _____

34. $4(x + 2) = 16$ _____

Exercise 2

35. A shipping company charges an extra fee for boxes with outside dimensions greater than 200 in. Would the company charge the extra fee for a box 24 in. wide and 45 in. long? _____
36. A playground is 100 ft long and 32 ft wide. How many feet of fencing are needed to enclose the playground? _____
37. A compost bin is 4 ft high, 2 ft wide, and 3 ft long. When full, how many cubic feet of compost will be in the bin? _____
38. A warehouse floor needs to be painted. If the warehouse is 1,200 ft by 400 ft, paint will be required to cover how many square feet? _____
39. A barrel has a diameter of 23 in. and a height of 30 in. What is the volume in cubic inches? _____
40. The top of a cable spool is 42 in. in diameter. What is the circumference? _____
41. What is the area of the top of the cable spool described in Problem 40? _____

Exercise 3

Construct an equation for the following problems, then solve.

42. The Carpets-to-Go store installed 310 sq ft of carpet Wednesday morning and 295 sq ft Wednesday afternoon. How many square feet of carpet were installed Wednesday?
_____ _____

43. Jack was given an advance on his travel allowance of $500. He spent $190 Monday and $260 Tuesday. He spent the rest Wednesday. How much did he spend Wednesday?
_____ _____

44. A team of four brothers agreed to demolish a barn for $500. How much would each brother earn if the money were divided evenly?
_____ _____

45. Janet Barnes had $75 automatically deducted from her monthly paycheck and deposited in her savings account. How much was deducted at the end of 1 year?
_____ _____

46. Total sales for the two departments of a store were $53,961. Department A's sales were twice as much as those of Department B. What was the amount of sales for each department? Let b = Department B sales.
_____ _____Department B _____Department A

47. John and Bob together made 51 telephone sales calls. If Bob made 15 calls more than John, how many calls did each salesman make? Let j = the number of calls John made.
_____ _____John's calls _____Bob's calls

48. The landscaped portion of a building's grounds was 50 ft long and 8 ft wide. The width of the parking lot was 50 ft. The length of the parking lot was three times the width less 10 ft. What was the length of the parking lot?
_____ _____

49. A store sold 1,500 mugs, some red, some blue. Approximately three-fourths as many blue mugs sold as red mugs. How many of each color mug sold? Let r = number of red mugs sold.
_____ _____red mugs _____blue mugs

50. The quality control department reported that 5% of type B parts did not meet the manufacturing standards. If 5,100 of type B parts were manufactured, how many did not meet standard? Let p = number of type B parts.
_____ _____

Exercise 4

The following diagram illustrates the dimensions for a store. Calculate the area of each department and total square feet for the building. Complete the following table.

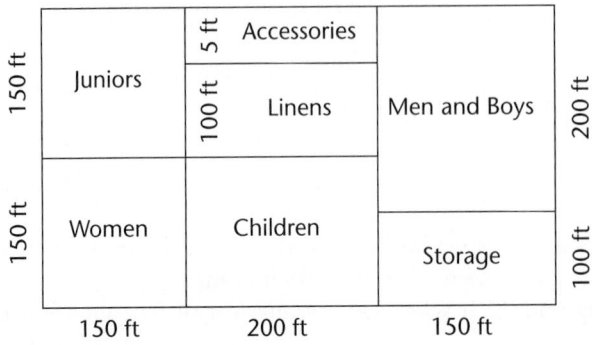

	Department	Dimensions	Sq Ft
1.	Juniors	_____	____
2.	Accessories	_____	____
3.	Linens	_____	____
4.	Women	_____	____
5.	Children	_____	____
6.	Men and Boys	_____	____
7.	Storage	_____	____
8.		**Total Sq Ft** _____	

Exercise 5

Calculate square footage for each department and total square footage for the following dimensions of the Sails A'Loft boating sports store.

Sails A'Loft

10 ft Shoes	10 ft Books and Maps	10 ft Safety
30 ft Clothing	20 ft Sailing Hardware / 10 ft Powerboat Hardware	30 ft Cleaners and Paints
40 ft Water Sports	40 ft Electrical	40 ft Plumbing
45 ft	80 ft	60 ft

50 ft Sail Loft (2nd floor)

	Department	Dimensions	Sq Ft
1.	Shoes		
2.	Clothing		
3.	Water Sports		
4.	Books and Maps		
5.	Sailing Hardware		
6.	Powerboat Hardware		
7.	Electrical		
8.	Safety		
9.	Cleaners and Paints		
10.	Plumbing		
11.	Sail Loft		
12.		**Total Sq Ft**	

CHAPTER 13

Percent of Increase or Decrease

 **PART 1** *Speed and Accuracy Building Using Touch Key*

GOALS: Your speed goal is 8,500 strokes per hour.
Your accuracy target goal range is 95% to 100%.

With each repetition of the drill, try to improve your speed without lowering your accuracy score. If your percent-of-accuracy score falls below 95%, review your finger position and technique. Then try again.

Instructions: *Start Touch Key. Complete Drill 2, Parts A and B, Three-Minute Timings. (Parts C through E are optional.) Write your scores for strokes per hour and percent of accuracy below.*

Touch Key Drill 2—The 0 through 9 Keys, Four-Digit Numbers, Three-Minute Timings

	Today's Date	Strokes per Hour	Percent of Accuracy
A.			
B.			
C.			
D.			
E.			

PART 2 *Business Math Skills*

In Chapter 10, percent and percentage were discussed. To review, percent is the rate, base is the whole, and percentage is a portion of that whole. Example: A bin contains 150 cups (150 is the whole). Ten percent of the cups are red (10% is the rate). Fifteen of the cups are red (15 is the portion or amount of cups that are red).

It is often necessary to compare large figures such as last year's sales compared to this year's sales. Some examples are as follows:

Last month's tax collections compared to collections for the same month last year

A TV show's ratings this season compared to those for last season

Budget increases or decreases this year compared to last year's budget

When comparing two large numbers, we might subtract the numbers to find the difference. However, the significance or meaning of the difference might not be readily apparent.

PROBLEM 1

A report contains sales information for Department A for 2 years (Figure 13.1).

Department A had sales of $286,543 in 1999. In 2000, its sales were $358,179. After subtracting, we find that Department A had an increase of sales of $71,636 in 2000. Although this figure indicates an increase in sales, the figure by itself does not convey an easily understood picture.

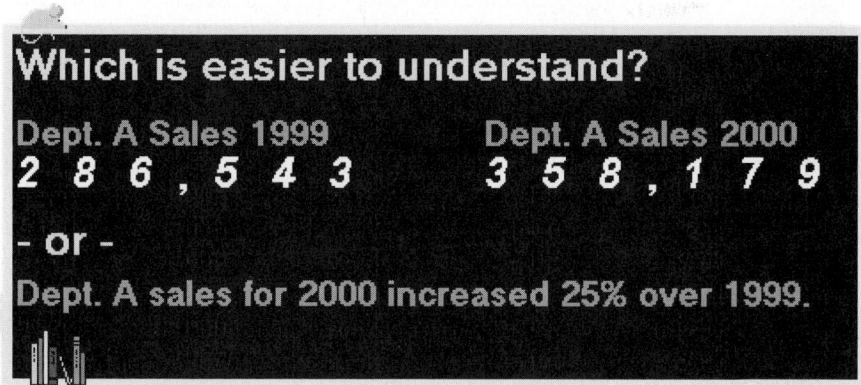

Which is easier to understand?

Dept. A Sales 1999   Dept. A Sales 2000
2 8 6 , 5 4 3   3 5 8 , 1 7 9

- or -

Dept. A sales for 2000 increased 25% over 1999.

FIGURE 13.1

However, if the increase of $71,636 is converted to a percent of increase of 25%, we can immediately grasp that sales were 25% greater in 2000 than in 1999. We can easily visualize the increase in 2000 sales over 1999 sales (Figure 13.2).

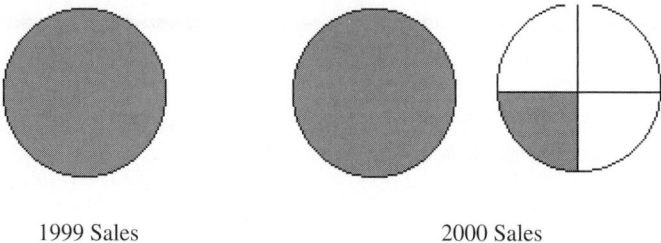

1999 Sales   2000 Sales

FIGURE 13.2

The figure shows that if we let sales for 1999 equal 100%, then sales for 2000 equaled 100% of sales for 1999 PLUS an additional 25%. Therefore, a **percent of increase** is the rate at which an amount has increased over a period of time. Conversely, a **percent of decrease** is the rate at which an amount has decreased over a period of time.

CALCULATING PERCENT OF INCREASE OR DECREASE

The equation for calculating percent of increase or decrease is

$$(\text{Amount} - \text{Base Amount}) \div \text{Base Amount} = \%\ \text{Increase (Decrease)}$$

In the above example, Department A sales for 1999 is the base amount. The **base amount** is the earlier figure and is the basis for comparison. That is, the sales figure for the year 2000 will be compared to the sales figure for 1999. **Amount** is the more recent figure being compared to the base amount. If the answer calculated using the above equation is positive, we have a **percent of increase**. If the answer is negative, the result is a percent of decrease. A **percent of decrease** is usually indicated by placing the result in parentheses.

PROBLEM 2

A pint of milk cost 52 cents. The price was raised to 69 cents during a milk shortage. What percent did the milk price increase?

In Figure 13.3 the amount of 69 cents and base amount of 52 are substituted in the percent-of-increase formula:

$(69 - 52) \div 52$ Subtract, and then remove parentheses.

$17 \div 52 = \boxed{0.326} = 33\%$ increase   Convert to 33%.

Alternatively, use the % key on the calculator:

$$17 \div 52 \boxed{\%} \boxed{33}$$

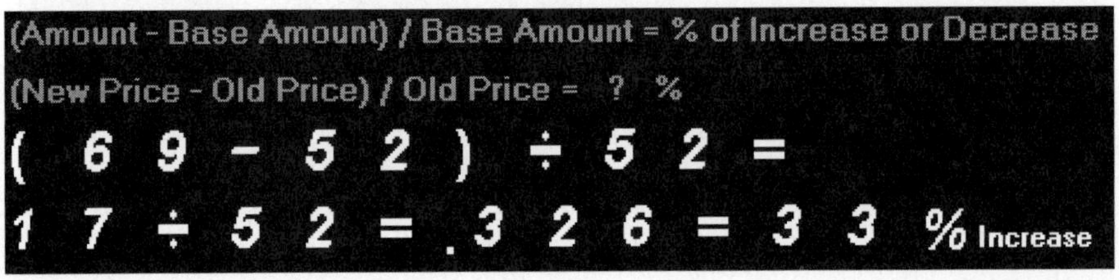

FIGURE 13.3

PROBLEM 3

The price of a pint of milk costing 52 cents was lowered to 50 cents. What is the percent of decrease of the milk price rounded to a whole number? Refer to Figure 13.4.

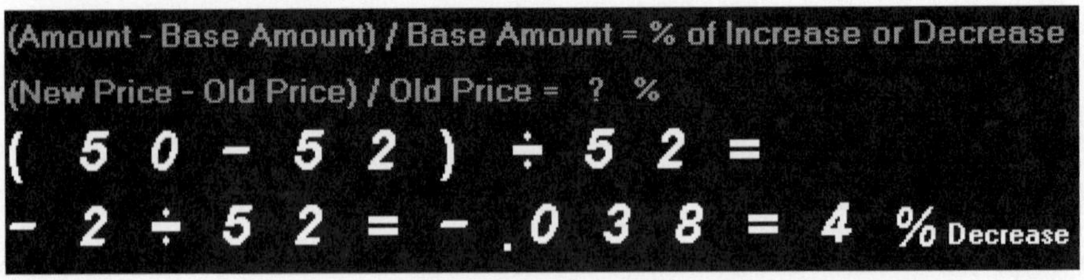

FIGURE 13.4

We have

$(50 - 52) \div 52 =$ Subtract, and then remove parentheses.

$-2 \div 52 = \boxed{-0.038}$ Round. Convert to −4% or (4%). Place the amount in parentheses to indicate a decrease.

Alternatively, use the % key on the calculator:

$-2 \div 52 \boxed{\%} \boxed{-3.8}$ Round. Place the amount in parentheses to indicate a decrease (4%).

Name _____

Class/Section _____

Score (Correct Answers ÷ No. of Assigned Problems) _____

 **PART 2** *Business Math Skills*

Exercise 1

Calculate the percent of increase or decrease for the following problems. Round answers to tenths.

1. Jamey earned $21,260 last year. He earned $22,390 this year. _____
2. The One-Stop Shop had 1,200 customers last week and 890 customers this week. _____
3. An accounting firm employed 32 employees last year and 37 employees this year. _____
4. A charter airline cut its number of employees from 860 to 720. _____
5. The newsstand price of a magazine published six times a year is $5.99 for each issue. A yearly subscription (six issues) is $16.97. What is the percent of increase or decrease of the subscription price compared to the newsstand price for a year's worth of issues? _____

Exercise 2

Calculate the percent of increase or decrease of sales for each department and for total sales.

	Department	2002	2003	Percent Increase (Decrease)
6.	A	$44,960	$49,960	
7.	B	$72,110	$89,050	
8.	C	$90,150	$110,290	
9.	D	$56,940	$54,950	
10.	E	$39,290	$28,110	
11.	Total sales			

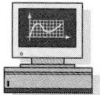 **PART 3** *Review and Practice Using Business Math FUNdamentals*

GOAL: Complete 9 of the 10 problems correctly.

Instructions: *Start Business Math FUNdamentals. Complete Tutorial 34 and Drill 26. If you are not satisfied with your scores, repeat the drill. Write your scores below.*

Business Math FUNdamentals Drill 26

Today's Date	Score

 **PART 4** *The Desktop Calculator*

CALCULATING PERCENT OF INCREASE OR DECREASE

PROBLEM 4

A tennis club had the following male and female membership in the years 2002 and 2003. Calculate the percent of increase or decrease for men and women. Also calculate the percent of increase or decrease for total membership. Round answers to tenths.

Membership	2002	2003	Percent Increase or Decrease (%)
Men	13,970	17,350	24.2
Women	15,668	16,970	8.3
Total membership	29,638	34,320	15.8

Procedure

To solve this problem, you will actually perform two procedures. You will first work across the table. Use memory to store the base amount. Subtract the base amount from the amount for 2003 and then divide by the base to find the percent of increase or decrease. Next, you will work down the columns using memory to store the total membership for the base year (2002). Find the difference between the total for 2003 and the total base amount. Divide the difference by the total base amount.

Remember that using the percent key instead of the equals key when dividing will result in an answer that has already been converted to a percent.

TAPE 13.1:
Part 1, Step 1

```
          0 · C

    17,350 · +
    13,970 · M+
    13,970 · -
     5,380 · ÷
    13,970 · M+

    13,970 · %
 24·194702934  %
```

MACHINE SETUP   Decimal Selector—F
Rounding Switch—5/4
Print Switch—On

Check that memory is clear.

Order of Entry:

Part 1: Working across the Rows

Step 1: Subtract the male membership base amount from the male membership for 2003. Divide the difference by the male membership base amount to find the percent increase. Round the answer:

$$17,350 + 13,970 \text{ M+} - \div \text{ MT } \boxed{\%} \quad \boxed{24.19...}$$

Step 2: Repeat the procedure in step 1 for the female membership figures:

$$16,970 + 15,668 \text{ M+} - \div \text{ MT } \boxed{\%} \quad \boxed{8.30...}$$

TAPE 13.2:
Part 1, Step 2

```
          0 · C

    16,970 · +
    15,668 · M+
    15,668 · -
     1,502 · ÷
    15,668 · M+

    15,668 · %
 8·309931009   %
```

Part 2: Working down the Columns

Add column 1. Store result (total base amount) in memory:

$$13,970 + 15,668 + \text{ T } \boxed{29,638} \text{ M+}$$

Add column 2. Subtract the total for column 1 (which was stored in memory) from the total of column 2. Since the base amount in memory will be used twice, you should use memory subtotal to recall the base amount without clearing memory. Divide the difference by the base amount (which is the total for column 1 stored in memory). Because this is the last time you will use the base amount in this problem, you may use the memory total key to display the total in memory and also clear memory. Mentally round the answer to tenths:

$$17,350 + 16,970 + \text{ T } \boxed{34,320} + \text{ MS } - \boxed{4,682}$$
$$\div \text{ MT } \boxed{\%} \boxed{15.79...}$$

THE PERCENT OF INCREASE/DECREASE $\boxed{\Delta\%}$ KEY

If your calculator has this key, calculating percent of increase/decrease is easy.

TAPE 13.3: **Part 2**

```
                    0 • C

            13,970 •   +
            15,668 •   +
            29,638 •   ÷

            29,638 • M+
            17,350 •   +
            16,970 •   +
            34,320 •   ÷

            34,320 •   +
            29,638 • MO
            29,638 •   -
             4,682 •   ÷
            29,638 • M÷

            29,638 •   %
    15•7972872663      ÷
```

PROBLEM 5

Calculate percent of increase/decrease for the club membership shown in Problem 4. Set decimal selector on 2:

$$13,970 \ \boxed{\Delta\%} \ 17,350 \ = \ \boxed{24.19}$$
$$15,668 \ \boxed{\Delta\%} \ 16,970 \ = \ \boxed{8.31}$$

Add the 2002 and 2003 columns and calculate percent of increase/decrease for the totals:

$$\text{MT } 13,970 + 15,668 + \text{T } 29,638$$
$$17,350 + 16,970 + \text{T } 34,320 \ \text{M+}$$
$$29,638 \ \boxed{\Delta\%} \ \text{MS} \ = \ \boxed{15.80}$$

Round to tenths mentally.

Name _____

Class/Section _____

Score (Correct Answers ÷ No. of Assigned Problems) _____

 ## PART 4 *Desktop Calculator*

Exercise 1

During the last quarter of 2003, the XYZ Company decreased its workforce in three departments. Calculate the percent of decrease in each of the three departments. Use the calculator memory function to speed your work. Round answers to tenths.

Department	Third Quarter 2003	Fourth Quarter 2003	Percent Increase (Decrease)
Shipping and Receiving	560	530	_____
Research and Development	28	25	_____
Maintenance	54	49	_____

Exercise 2

The personnel director has asked for a report comparing missed workdays on a monthly basis for the years 2002 and 2003. The missed workdays are summarized in the following report. Calculate the percent increase or decrease in missed workdays for each month. Also calculate total missed workdays for each year and the annual percent of increase or decrease. Round answers to tenths.

Month	Year 2002	Year 2003	Percent Increase (Decrease)
January	520	470	4. _____
February	450	488	5. _____
March	390	479	6. _____
April	395	463	7. _____
May	410	434	8. _____
June	362	412	9. _____
July	405	397	10. _____
August	299	403	11. _____
September	325	370	12. _____
October	360	375	13. _____
November	422	396	14. _____
December	490	492	15. _____
Yearly totals			16. _____

Exercise 3

Strokes per Minute Score _____

Accuracy Score (Correct Strokes ÷ Total Strokes) _____

One-Minute Addition Timing (Keys 0 through 9, Four-Digit Numbers)

(Optional: Your instructor may wish you to use Touch Key on the computer for all your timings. Check with your instructor before completing this exercise.)

Complete as many of the problems as possible in 1 minute by adding. Work quickly and accurately. The number preceding each closing parenthesis indicates the cumulative number of strokes for problems attempted. For example, if you complete Problems 1 through 5 in 1 minute, your strokes-per-minute score is 255. Optional: 3- to 5-minute timings.

1.	2.	3.	4.	5.	6.	7.	8.
5889	4000	6500	6690	9095	5880	9932	7225
7995	6339	5590	9795	1001	5008	6647	1495
4591	5125	4995	1315	8000	5119	9811	1598
5234	8629	8995	1516	9005	3519	2355	1999
8712	4977	7495	1918	1711	4995	5995	1000
4589	8132	9999	6588	6422	5266	7998	2555
2213	4225	8743	9115	1133	6455	7999	3133
2445	3587	3115	1995	3199	8211	1595	9133
8231	4971	1799	2995	6448	8344	2599	8422
7175	2325	8255	3550	1779	8110	1898	8311
51)	102)	153)	204)	255)	306)	357)	408)

9.	10.	11.	12.	13.	14.	15.	16.
2000	1694	1550	6195	8895	1695	6433	1799
4300	2000	2995	1300	2914	2000	1395	1500
8500	2001	4001	2500	3461	8400	1495	4130
9100	2002	2446	7994	9128	9700	1595	1499
3300	2003	3534	2456	2892	5500	7195	1500
1799	2004	9108	1378	3917	5200	8195	3500
1500	1999	8742	2165	8225	3200	9195	7344
2298	2998	6523	9821	8844	9800	1001	4600
1479	7915	9704	3121	4698	4500	1006	1800
1889	3492	3343	8762	4128	6900	2250	7755
459)	510)	561)	612)	663)	714)	765)	816)

Set decimal selector on add mode.

17.	99.21	18.	31.56	19.	40.34	20.	34.55	21.	69.98	22.	75.69	23.	55.95	24.	56.79
	86.51		75.25		61.35		13.95		34.99		35.50		66.00		20.00
	94.65		74.22		70.22		15.69		43.79		45.00		81.00		25.00
	90.12		92.66		27.81		75.99		29.95		69.50		89.55		33.00
	98.44		39.80		91.20		34.66		35.95		65.00		99.95		49.00
	88.54		42.56		94.63		89.19		20.99		99.45		10.00		56.00
	11.43		80.56		36.78		25.29		29.99		67.00		20.00		71.19
	45.63		90.23		93.36		39.39		49.99		13.35		50.00		25.50
	21.67		41.65		79.64		40.99		49.95		16.00		69.96		39.95
	33.41		73.50		18.50		69.79		65.99		15.99		44.90		79.95
877)		928)		989)		1,050)		1,111)		1,172)		1,233)		1,294)	

CHAPTER 13 *Terminology Review*

Amount
Base amount
Percent of decrease
Percent of increase

Briefly, describe each of the following.

1. Percent of increase. _____
2. Percent of decrease. _____
3. The formula for calculating percent of increase. _____

Name _____

Class/Section _____

Score (Correct Answers ÷ No. of Assigned Problems) _____

Chapter 13 Review Exercises
Exercise 1

Round answers to tenths.

1. James Washington's salary rose from $42,769 in 2003 to $48,890 in 2004. What was the percent of increase/decrease? _____
2. The research and development department of the ABC Co. found that Foam A withstood 50,000 compressions. After modifications, Foam A was able to withstand 62,000 compressions. What was the percent of increase of durability after the modifications? _____
3. Yearly income of Management Partners, Inc., was $1,125,000 in 2002 and $987,000 in 2003. Calculate percent of increase/decrease. _____

Exercise 2

Following are the mileage figures for sales representatives who worked in four territories for a distributing company for the years 2000 and 2003. Calculate the percent increase/decrease in mileage.

Territory/Salesman	2000	2003	Percent Increase (Decrease)
Northwest			
John Brown	14,025	16,900	4. _____
Tom Jones	15,609	13,799	5. _____
Bill Smith	12,090	15,400	6. _____
Total Northwest mileage			7. _____
Northern California			
Alfred Gonzalez	13,000	13,540	8. _____
Gloria Monroe	16,220	17,555	9. _____
Steve Rainwater	12,500	14,030	10. _____
Total Northern California mileage			11. _____
Southern California			
Sam Travers	11,600	10,032	12. _____
April Indeo	10,045	10,855	13. _____
Frances Lopez	8,790	9,433	14. _____
Total Southern California mileage			15. _____
Arizona/Nevada			
Jill Lassiter	9,000	8,545	16. _____
Kenneth Walls	8,650	7,950	17. _____
Franklin Alvarez	7,432	6,790	18. _____
Total Arizona/Nevada mileage			19. _____
Total mileage, all territories			20. _____

CHAPTER 14

Understanding Data; Mean, Median, Mode, and Range

 PART 1 *Speed and Accuracy Building Using Touch Key*

GOALS: Your speed goal is 8,500 strokes per hour.
Your accuracy target goal range is 95% to 100%.

With each repetition of the drill, try to improve your speed without lowering your accuracy score. If your percent-of-accuracy score falls below 95%, review your finger position and technique. Then try again.

Instructions: *Start Touch Key. Complete Drill 2, Part A, Five-Minute Timing. (Parts B through E are optional.) Write your scores for strokes per hour and percent of accuracy below.*

Touch Key Drill 2—The 0 through 9 Keys, Four-Digit Numbers, Five-Minute Timing

Today's Date	Strokes per Hour	Percent of Accuracy
A.		
B.		
C.		
D.		
E.		

 PART 2 *Business Math Skills*

UNDERSTANDING AND USING DATA

For a business to make money, it needs to provide goods or services that are needed or wanted. The marketplace is said to have a demand for such products. A product line that is not selling well may need to be changed or replaced with products that will better meet the needs of the marketplace.

One way a business can determine marketplace demand is to collect data using surveys. A group of values such as the group illustrated in Figure 14.1 is referred to as a **data set**. One company conducted worldwide taste tests of its soft drink and a competitor's soft drink. Records were kept of the number of participants and their preferences. The total

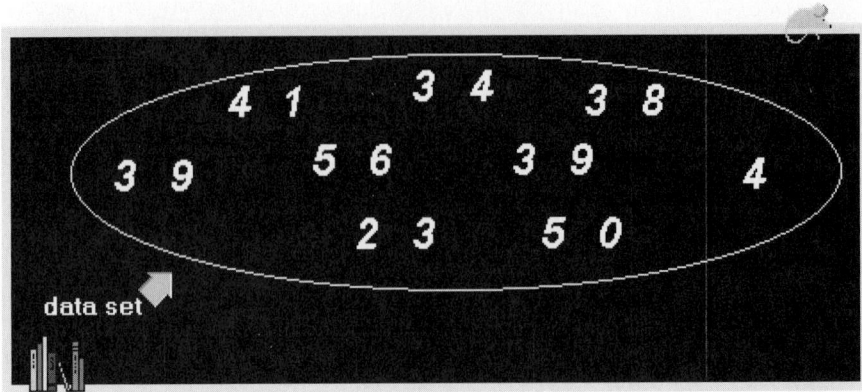

FIGURE 14.1

number of participants made up the data set for this survey. A **marketing survey** consists of questions(s) asked of a certain group of people, such as people who drink soft drinks in the case previously discussed. A company selling home alarm systems might want to limit its survey to homeowners only.

Another way a company gathers data is by looking at records of its own activities such as sales statistics. The **statistics** is a collection of numerical data. Analysis of these data may help the company make better marketing decisions.

After data have been collected, certain values can be derived from the data such as mean, median, mode, and range. It might be helpful to a real estate agency in Atlanta to know the average age of persons who purchased homes in Atlanta during the last 5 years. Statistically, an average is known as the **mean**. To find the mean, add the values in the data set, then divide the total by the number of values.

Teachers often need to know statistics about class performance. Finding the average test score is a common problem.

PROBLEM 1

A data set contains the following group of values: 41, 34, 38, 39, 56, 39, 4, 23, and 50. Find the mean.

Add the values, and then divide by the number of values. See Figure 14.2.

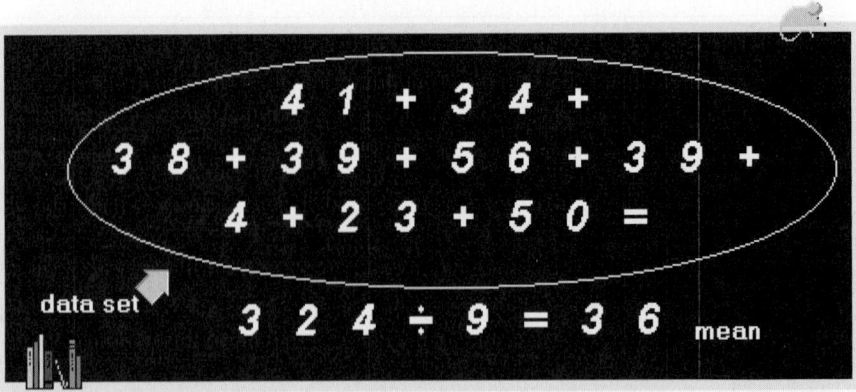

FIGURE 14.2

The **median** is the middle number occurring in a data set. To find median, arrange the group of numbers in a data set in numerical order (highest to lowest or lowest to highest). Mark the middle number. See Figure 14.3, data set 1.

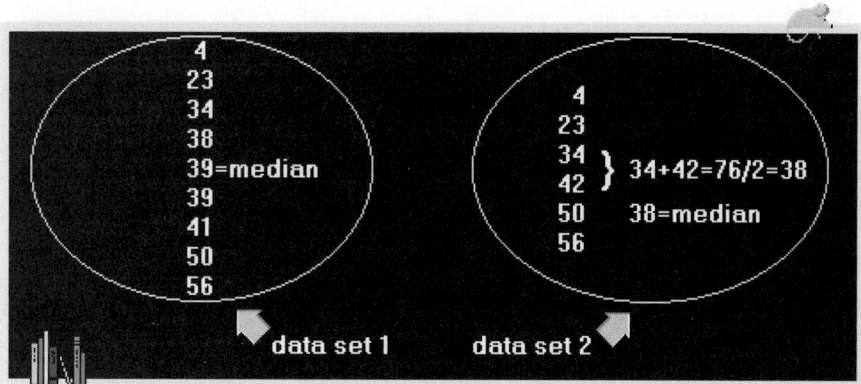

FIGURE 14.3

If a list has an even number of values, find the average of the two middle values. See Figure 14.3, data set 2. The average of the two middle values is the median.

PROBLEM 2

A data set contains the following group of values: 29, 35, 40, 29, 53, 36, 38, 34, and 56. What is the median?

   Arrange the numbers in order and mark the middle number:

1. 29
2. 29
3. 34
4. 35
5. 36—median
6. 38
7. 40
8. 53
9. 56

The median is 36.

PROBLEM 3

Class test scores were 59, 80, 95, 98, 70, 75, 90, 82, 74, and 88. What is the median?

   Arrange the scores in order. Since there is an even number of scores, average the two middle numbers:

1. 59
2. 70
3. 74
4. 75
5. 80—average the two middle numbers to find the median
6. 82—(80 + 82) ÷ 2 = 81 median
7. 88
8. 90
9. 95
10. 98

The **mode** is the number in a data set that appears most often. Again, the data set values should be listed in numerical order. Mark the number that appears most often in the list. See Figure 14.4, data set 1.

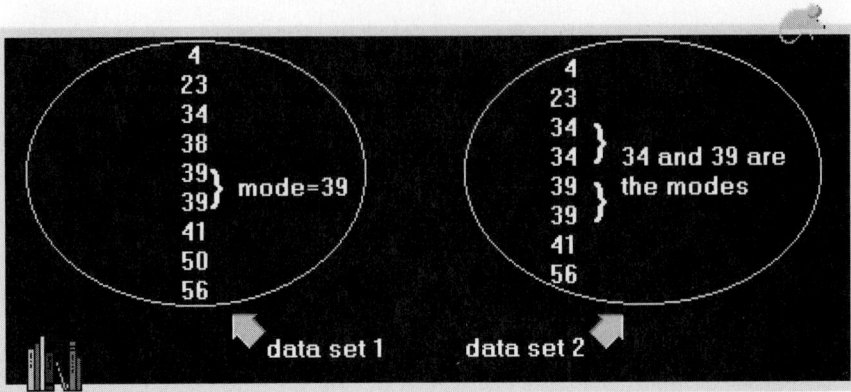

FIGURE 14.4

A data set may have more than one mode if more than one number occurs with the same frequency. In Figure 14.4, data set 2, the modes are 34 and 39 because each occurs twice in the data set and no other number occurs more than twice.

PROBLEM 4

The ages of the members in a tour group are 55, 60, 58, 65, 70, 72, 65, 64, 59, 61, 65, and 64 years. What is the mode?

Arrange the values of the data set in numerical order. Mark the age that occurs most frequently:

55
58
59
60
61
64
64
65—
65—
65—
70
72

The mode is 65 years.

PROBLEM 5

The ages in a junior tour group are 13, 13, 15, 16, 14, 13, 14, 14, 15, and 16 years. What is the mode?

Arrange the ages in numerical order and mark the mode(s).

13—
13—
13—
14—
14—
14—
15
15
16
16

There are two modes, ages 13 and 14 years, because each appears three times.

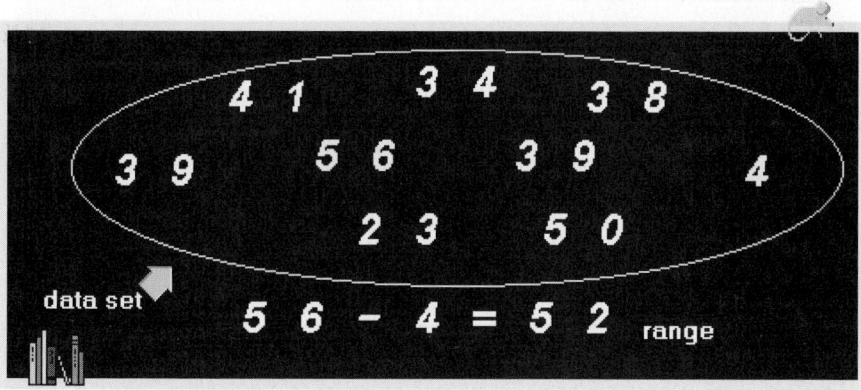

FIGURE 14.5

The **range** is the difference between the smallest and largest numbers in a data set. In Figure 14.5, the smallest number in the data set is 4. The largest number in the data set is 56. Subtracting the smallest from the largest number results in a range of 52. If all values are similar, the range is small. A large range indicates that there is much variation in the data set. If the range is large, the mean can be affected and thus be less meaningful in describing the data set. For example, if the age of those who preferred soft drink A over soft drink B ranged from 2 years to 90 years, the large variation in ages might spark a new advertising campaign for soft drink A that targets several generations of people.

WHEN IS MEAN NOT A GOOD DESCRIPTOR?

A wide variation in data can affect the mean. It is important to consider median, mode, and range as well as mean when making a decision. Look at the following data set of scores, which have been arranged in numerical order. The mean is 78.5, the median is 85, the mode is 90, and the range is 90:

10
55
70
75
——mean 78.5
79
80
85—median
90—mode
90—mode
94
95
98
100

The range of 90 is large and should alert one to look at more than the mean when analyzing these data. Marking where the mean lies in the arranged scores is helpful. If the mean is not near the middle of the arranged data, look for the reason. Because 9 of the 13 scores, or 69%, are above the mean, the extremely low score is affecting the mean downward. In this case the median of 85 gives a better description of the majority of the scores. The median or the mode might be more descriptive and reveal more accurate information than the mean when the variation is large.

Confused? Consider the following extreme example. If the boss at a business makes $500,000 and the nine employees each makes $40,000, would the mean salary of $86,000 give an accurate description of most of the salaries? Perhaps mode ($40,000) would give a more accurate picture of the salaries.

PROBLEM 6

Two commercials for milk were shown to a group of survey participants. The ages of those who liked the commercials are shown below.

1. Which commercial had the widest range? The range for commercial A is 15.
2. Using the data from this survey, how would you plan to use the commercials?

Use commercial A during children's and teen's programming and commercial B during programming appropriate for the young adult, age 21 to 35 years.

Commercial A	Commercial B
5	21
5	21
6	21
6	22
7	22
7	26
10	29
12	30
13	32
14	33
14	33
14	34
15	34
15	
16	
16	
16	
17	
17	
20	

3. For commercial A, find mean 12, median 13.5, mode 14, and range 15. Which of these descriptors would be most helpful in determining which ages to target specifically with commercial A? It appears the median and mode would be more characteristic of those who liked commercial A, ages 13 and 14 years.

Name _____

Class/Section _____

Score (Correct Answers ÷ No. of Assigned Problems) _____

PART 2   *Business Math Skills*

Exercise 1

1. Calculate the mean for the following numbers:
   45, 60, 95, 50, 75, 80. _____
2. What is the median of the following data set?
   20, 25, 32, 34, 26, 19. _____
3. What is the mode of the following data set?
   15, 18, 15, 16, 14, 13, 17, 16, 15, 18. _____
4. What is the range of the following data set?
   1,000; 3,500; 1,750; 2,750; 2,000; 1,500; 2,500; 1,500. _____

Exercise 2

Use the following data set to answer Questions 5 through 10:

28,000	105,000	30,000	32,000	27,000
32,000	75,000	40,000	25,000	36,000
29,000	60,000	32,000	28,000	28,000
26,000	40,000	23,000	30,000	28,000
22,000	29,000	31,000	33,000	24,000

5. Would the range for these salaries be considered large or small? _____
6. What is the mean? _____
7. Does the mean of the data set represent the average salary of most of the employees? _____
8. Why or why not? _____
9. What salary appears most often as the mode? _____
10. Compare the mean, median, and mode for this data set. Which is more descriptive of the data set? _____

PART 3 *Review and Practice Using Business Math FUNdamentals*

GOAL: Complete 9 of the 10 problems correctly.

Instructions: *Start Business Math FUNdamentals. Complete Tutorial 35 and Drill 27. If you are not satisfied with your scores, repeat the drills. Write your scores below.*

Business Math FUNdamentals Drill 27

Today's Date	Score

Name _____

Class/Section _____

Strokes per Minute Score _____

Accuracy Score (Correct Strokes ÷ Total Strokes) _____

 PART 4 *Desktop Calculator*

Exercise 1

One-Minute Addition Timing (Keys 0 through 9, Four-Digit Numbers)

(Optional: Your instructor may wish you to use Touch Key on the computer for all your timings. Check with your instructor before completing this exercise.)

Complete as many of the problems as possible in 1 minute by adding. Work quickly and accurately. The number preceding each closing parenthesis indicates the cumulative number of strokes for problems attempted. For example, if you complete Problems 1 through 5 in 1 minute, your strokes-per-minute score is 255. Optional: 3- to 5-minute timings.

1.	2.	3.	4.	5.	6.	7.	8.
4440	8090	3445	6896	2690	6670	6611	2001
4795	6187	3540	4896	4567	3350	6178	2003
5661	7182	8450	7896	7890	4690	3178	1999
1312	7357	8717	4796	9151	4210	2198	1998
8283	8191	1519	4159	9461	4611	4159	2004
8978	8128	1418	4258	2198	5589	6187	2005
4512	5282	1417	4159	2298	8213	6258	2010
6123	7147	1312	4339	3000	8343	4973	1997
2548	4645	1615	4541	4200	7791	7364	1989
4262	4432	1413	1213	4800	1155	7330	1988
51)	102)	153)	204)	255)	306)	357)	408)

9.	10.	11.	12.	13.	14.	15.	16.
7751	7749	8512	3133	2288	2288	1699	1028
8870	5666	7489	9751	4866	3345	1995	1045
9551	4599	9782	3199	4686	1255	2995	2950
9789	5822	8192	5713	2446	4992	4885	4005
8843	7633	8131	7713	4688	9396	3445	4007
4589	7151	8542	7513	3151	9778	8950	4681
4580	9144	3391	9755	8824	9461	3660	8339
6121	8711	7521	3599	2495	1659	9660	8357
4872	9422	4977	1995	8899	8959	3669	2008
6971	9433	1179	5773	7135	3996	1939	3009
459)	510)	561)	612)	663)	714)	765)	816)

Set decimal selector on add mode.

17.	18.	19.	20.	21.	22.	23.	24.
49.95	57.67	35.00	24.55	21.77	99.95	45.00	30.58
50.50	58.28	26.00	46.90	84.66	78.49	58.00	69.70
60.00	61.31	89.00	84.70	28.90	52.90	66.00	25.60
10.20	92.52	47.00	92.54	27.14	69.57	79.00	45.00
25.25	97.77	45.00	63.41	15.32	62.20	44.11	69.77
64.40	73.25	21.00	75.95	69.90	49.68	25.50	58.22
41.99	62.44	56.00	14.20	34.12	52.19	36.65	15.74
42.89	86.82	99.00	29.55	58.11	45.29	49.89	45.18
43.79	86.46	83.00	45.65	49.13	36.90	60.45	29.95
46.89	45.34	89.00	23.79	67.14	42.25	33.20	39.95
877)	938)	999)	1,060)	1,121)	1,182)	1,243)	1,304)

CHAPTER 14 *Terminology Review*

Data set

Marketing Survey

Mean

Median

Mode

Range

Statistics

Write the correct term next to the appropriate description.

1. _____ A collection of numerical data.
2. _____ Questions asked of a certain group of people.
3. _____ The difference between the smallest and largest numbers in a data set.
4. _____ The average of the values in a data set.
5. _____ The middle number occurring in a data set.
6. _____ A group of values.

Name _____

Class/Section _____

Score (Correct Answers ÷ No. of Assigned Problems) _____

Chapter 14 Review Exercises
Exercise 1

Last week a small dealership sold automobiles at the following prices. Calculate mean, median, mode, and range.

$30,000	$16,500
$52,000	$18,400
$28,000	$18,400
$20,000	$22,000
$21,000	$35,000

1. mean _____ 2. median _____ 3. mode_____ 4. range _____

A teacher's class had the following scores on a math test. Calculate mean, median, mode, and range.

45	68	72	76	86	95
40	70	73	79	76	92
75	88	74	76	78	76
90	85	85	78	80	85
98	81	83	85	95	85

5. mean _____ 6. median _____ 7. mode _____ 8. range _____
9. Calculate mean _____, median _____, mode _____, and range _____ for the following data set:

$1.4 million	$1 million	$800,000	$800,000	$850,000

10. Compare mean, median, and mode for Problem 9. Which is (are) more descriptive of the data? _____ Why? _____

CHAPTER 15

Presenting Data, Tables and Charts, Software-Generated Charts

 **PART 1** *Speed and Accuracy Building Using Touch Key*

GOALS: Your speed goal is 9,000 strokes per hour.
Your accuracy target goal range is 95% to 100%.

With each repetition of the drill, try to improve your speed without lowering your accuracy score. If your percent-of-accuracy score falls below 95%, review your finger position and technique. Then try again.

Instructions: *Start Touch Key. Complete Lesson 9, Parts A through E. Write your scores for strokes per hour and percent of accuracy below.*

Touch Key Lesson 9—The 0 through 9 Keys, Five-Digit Numbers

	Today's Date	Strokes per Hour	Percent of Accuracy
A.			
B.			
C.			
D.			
E.			

 **PART 2** *Business Math Skills*

TABLES

As discussed in Chapter 14, data sets are groups of values such as expenses, mileage records, data from surveys, and so on. The types of data sets you may encounter are quite numerous.

Whatever the type of data that have been collected, they need to be organized into an easily understood form, such as a **table**. The table shown in Figure 15.1 illustrates Susan's basic living expenses for January 1997 by category and the percent each category is relative to her total monthly expenses. Sometimes called a frequency distribution table, a table organizes data so that patterns become visible. Data can then be shown visually in graphs or charts using data from the table.

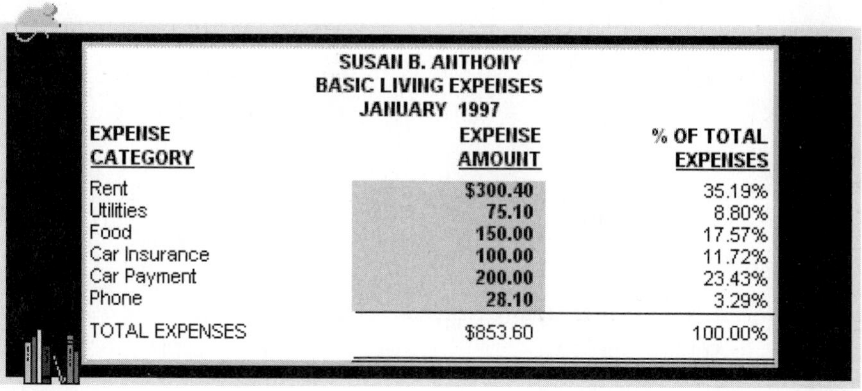

SUSAN B. ANTHONY
BASIC LIVING EXPENSES
JANUARY 1997

EXPENSE CATEGORY	EXPENSE AMOUNT	% OF TOTAL EXPENSES
Rent	$300.40	35.19%
Utilities	75.10	8.80%
Food	150.00	17.57%
Car Insurance	100.00	11.72%
Car Payment	200.00	23.43%
Phone	28.10	3.29%
TOTAL EXPENSES	$853.60	100.00%

FIGURE 15.1

Because many businesses use spreadsheet software such as Microsoft Excel to prepare tables, you should be familiar with the parts of a table and the terms used in completing a table. Tables begin with a **heading**, which should include a short descriptive name and a date, if appropriate.

Each blank rectangle of a spreadsheet is a **cell**. The horizontal lines of data are **rows**, which have **labels** with numbers in ascending order (1, 2, 3, . . .). The vertical lines of data are **columns**, which are labeled with letters in alphabetical order (A, B, C, . . .). If a spreadsheet table requires more than 26 columns, the labels continue as AA, BB, CC, ... Columns usually have **column headings** that identify the contents of the columns accurately.

Each cell in a spreadsheet has a **cell address**. The cell address is composed of the labels of the column and the row that intersect at the cell. The address of the highlighted cell in Figure 15.2 is B2; that is, column B, row 2.

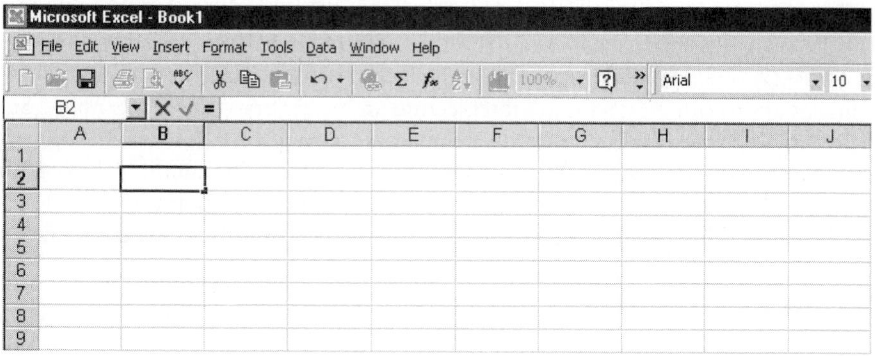

FIGURE 15.2

Either alphabetical or numerical data can be entered in a cell. Thus, each individual value from the data set can be entered in a cell as well as the table name, individual row names, column headings, and other necessary identifiers.

Tables can also be prepared using word processing software such as Microsoft Word.

CHARTS

Once a table has been prepared using software such as Excel or Word, the software can generate charts automatically that illustrate the point of a table to the reader at a glance. You may wish to prepare a chart the traditional way with pen and paper.

Whichever methods you use, **charts** are used to further organize and summarize information for clarification in a graphic form. The object of preparing a chart should be to present information in a clear, concise, and effective manner. Charts should include a descriptive title and a date, if appropriate. All charts except the pie chart have a horizontal

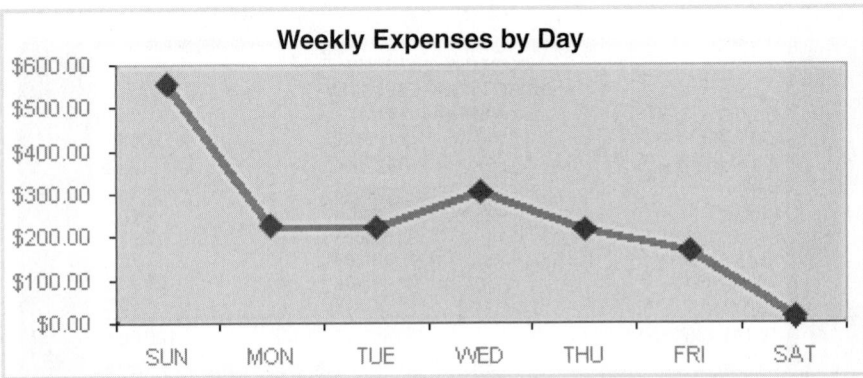

FIGURE 15.3

axis across the top or bottom and a vertical axis down the left or right side. Each should be divided into appropriate units. Labels should be placed incrementally on the two axes to identify their units. In Figure 15.3, the horizontal axis is labeled with days of the week and the vertical axis is labeled with increments of $100,000 beginning with zero.

Specific types of charts are used to illustrate certain types of information.

LINE CHARTS

A **line chart** is the most accurate of all graphs. It is used to show changes in data *over a period of time*. Data are plotted on a line chart by placing a dot where the horizontal and vertical axes intersect.

In Figure 15.3, the following daily expenses are plotted: Sunday $555.68, Monday $227.08, Tuesday $221.52, Wednesday $304.28, Thursday $218.63, Friday $166.46, and Saturday $15.12. Since Sunday expenses are $555.68, a dot is placed on an imaginary horizontal line at approximately $555.68 intersecting an imaginary vertical line above Sunday. Since Monday expenses are $227.08, another dot is plotted on a horizontal line running across from approximately $227.08 and intersecting a vertical line running above Monday. After all the points are plotted, a line is then drawn from point to point to indicate the rise or fall of expenses. How steeply the line in a line chart rises or falls is called the line's **slope**.

Preparing a Line Chart

PROBLEM 1

Weekend magazine sales at JV's #10 (a convenience store) for week 20 of 2003 are as follows for the different categories of magazines. Prepare a line chart illustrating sales.

Category	Sales ($)
Business	65.00
Women's/Home	227.50
Men's	97.50
Auto	97.50
Health	162.50

Select a title. Divide the horizontal and vertical axes into equal units and label them appropriately. In Figure 15.4, five units of $50 each, beginning with zero and ending with $250, are used for the vertical axis. The horizontal axis is divided into five equal units, one for each of the five magazine categories. Plot the points indicating amount of sales for each magazine category. Draw a line to connect the points.

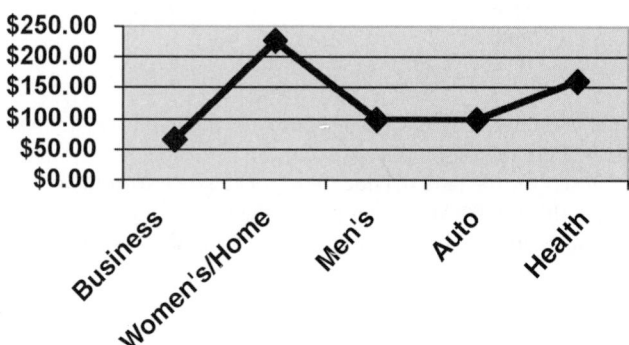

JV's #10, Weekend Magazine Sales, Week 20, 2003

FIGURE 15.4

BAR CHARTS

A **bar chart** is used to compare quantities of like data *at the same point in time*. The various lengths of bars on a graph make comparisons easy for the reader. The bars used in a bar chart may be vertical or horizontal. Beginning with a base level of zero makes comparisons easier.

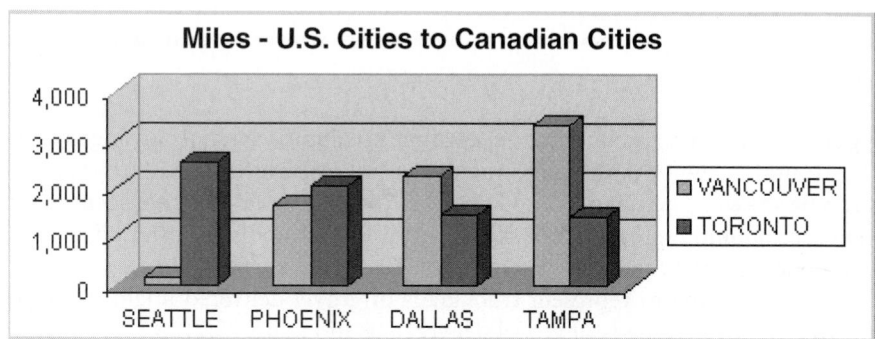

Miles - U.S. Cities to Canadian Cities

FIGURE 15.5

Figure 15.5 illustrates the distance in miles between Vancouver, British Columbia (represented by the first bar in each set), and several U.S. cities as well as the distance in miles between Toronto (represented by the second bar in each set) and the same U.S. cities. From this chart it can be seen that a Canadian manufacturing company wishing to do business primarily in the southern United States should place its facilities in Toronto because mileage from Toronto to Tampa and Dallas is less than mileage from Vancouver to Tampa and Dallas. However, if the same company wished to do business with the U.S. West/Southwest, it should place its facilities in Vancouver.

Preparing a Bar Chart

PROBLEM 2

Weekend magazine sales at JV's #10 (a convenience store) for week 20 of 2003 are again shown in the following chart. Prepare a bar chart illustrating sales for the five categories of magazines.

Category	Sales ($)
Business	65.00
Women's/Home	227.50
Men's	97.50
Auto	97.50
Health	162.50

To draw the bar chart, select a title. Choose colors for the five bars that will represent the five categories of magazines. Prepare a legend identifying the five categories of magazine sales and the five colors you have chosen for the bars. Divide the vertical axis into equal units appropriate to the sales figures beginning with zero. Because the top sales figure in this problem is $227.50, three units of $100 each would be appropriate. Draw the bars, estimating their position by closely referencing the scale (see Figure 15.6).

JV's #10
Weekend Magazine Sales, Week 20,
2003

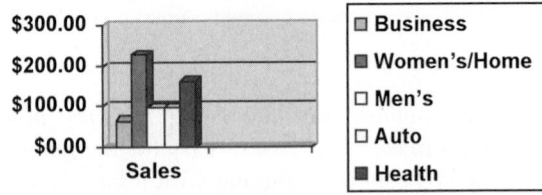

FIGURE 15.6

PICTOGRAPHS

A **pictograph** is similar to a bar chart except that it contains symbols arranged in a vertical or horizontal fashion that relate to the data being presented in a chart. Approximate figures can be shown. The symbols used in the pictograph should be consistent in size and shape and each should represent the same quantity. The symbols used should be explained in a legend. Pictographs cannot be generated by Excel.

A company wishing to represent truckloads of gravel delivered might let each truck symbol represent 100 carloads of gravel delivered as in Figure 15.7.

Heavy Haulers, Inc.			
1st Quarter Gravel Deliveries, 2003			
400			🚚
300	🚚		🚚
200	🚚	🚚	🚚
100	🚚	🚚	🚚
	January	February	March
🚚	= 100 loads of 3 cu yd (300 cu yd of gravel)		

FIGURE 15.7

PIE CHARTS

Also known as a circle graph, a **pie chart** should be used when it is necessary to compare portions to each other and to the whole. Figure 15.8 illustrates the data contained in the table of Figure 15.1. The relationship of each individual expense to total basic living expenses is shown. In a pie chart, a circle represents 100% of something. The portions that represent parts of the whole resemble wedges of pie; thus the name, pie chart. Each wedge should be sized and labeled as a percent of the whole. The percents, when totaled, must equal 100%. A key or legend should be used to explain color coding, if used.

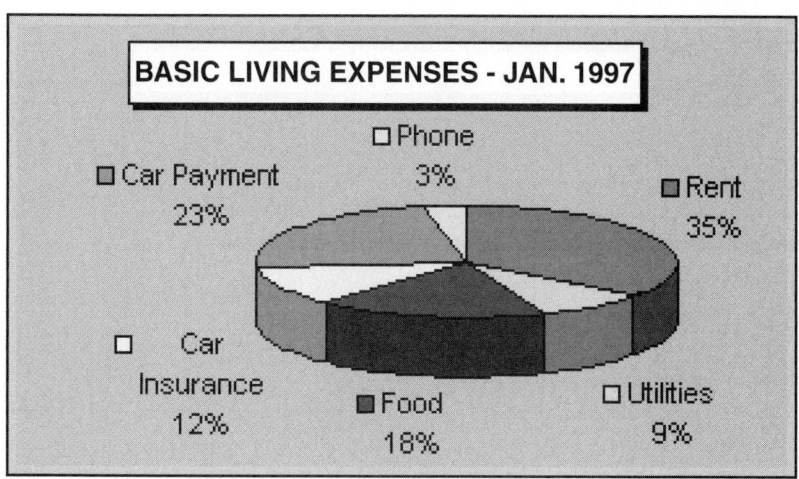

FIGURE 15.8

A complete circle is 360°. Each portion of a circle is a portion of 360°; therefore, 50% of a circle is 180°:

50%	$0.5 \times 360° = 180°$
25%	$0.25 \times 360° = 90°$
2%	$0.02 \times 360° = 7.2°$

Preparing a Pie Chart

PROBLEM 3

Weekend magazine sales at JV's #10 (a convenience store) for week 20 of 2003 are shown below. This time, prepare a pie chart illustrating sales for each category of magazine sales.

Category	Sales ($)	Percent (%)	Degrees
Business	65.00	10	36
Women's/Home	227.50	35	126
Men's	97.50	15	54
Auto	97.50	15	54
Health	162.50	25	90
Total	650.00	100	360

Select a title for the chart. Choose colors to represent each category of magazine sales and prepare a legend containing this information. Begin the calculations by finding total sales, and then find the percent of total sales for each category. Multiply the percent of total sales for each category by 360° to find the number of degrees for each section of the pie chart, and then draw the pie chart (see Figure 15.9).

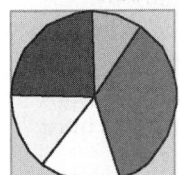
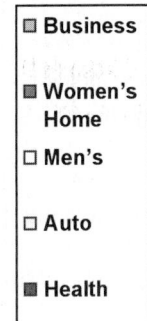

**JV's #10
Magazine Sales,
Week 20, 2003**

☐ Business

■ Women's
  Home

☐ Men's

☐ Auto

■ Health

FIGURE 15.9

Example: $65 ÷ $650 = .10
                     0.10 × 360° = 36°.

Remember that the degrees, when added, must equal 360°.

Pie charts may also be generated using the software mentioned earlier.

Name _____

Class/Section _____

Score (Correct Answers ÷ No. of Assigned Problems) _____

PART 2   *Business Math Skills*

Exercise 1

Jeri Franco compiled a chart of U.S. recreational boat deaths per year for the years 1985 to 2001 based on information she received from the U.S. Coast Guard. Answer the following questions about information contained in the chart shown in Figure 15.10.

1. What year were recreational boat fatalities the highest? _____
2. Were fatalities in 1999 greater or less than 750? _____

Recreational Boating Fatalities, 1985-2001

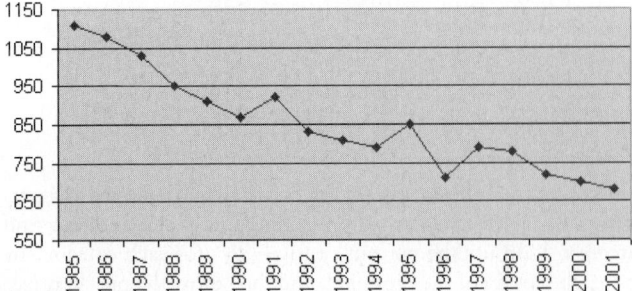

FIGURE 15.10

3. What year had the fewest deaths? _____
4. If 8 of 10 people who died in boating accidents in 1988 were not wearing life jackets, what was the total number of people who died in 1988 who were not wearing life jackets? _____
5. If the number of accidental boating deaths was exactly 701 in 2000 and 681 in 2001, what was the percent of increase/decrease? _____

Exercise 2

For practice in entering table data using Excel spreadsheet software, turn to Part 4 of the Touch Key manual in Appendix A. You will also need the Touch Key CD and a data disk. Follow the instructions to open a partially completed spreadsheet, enter table data, and view related charts.

   a. Select mileage.xls to view a bar chart
   b. Select budget.xls to view a pie chart
   c. Select sales.xls to view a chart that indicates sales levels on a U.S. map.

Exercise 3

Complete the following line chart using Excel.
   Open Excel (samples are from Microsoft Office 2000).

   1. In the first cell type **LW Marina Slip Rentals, 2003**.
   2. On the second row, type the months of the year, one month in each cell, beginning with the month of January in cell A2. Increase the width of the cells in row 2 by highlighting all the cells containing the months of the year. (To highlight cells, point to the first cell, hold the left mouse button, and drag the mouse across the cells to be highlighted. When the desired cells have been selected, release the left mouse button.) Select Format, Column, Width, Column Width: 10.
   3. On the third row, type the amount of revenue for each month of 2003 as shown in Figure 15.11.

	A	B	C	D	E	F	G	H	I	J	K	L
1	LW Marina Slip Rentals, 2003											
2	January	February	March	April	May	June	July	August	September	October	November	December
3	22,500	23,000	24,500	35,000	50,000	60,000	65,000	55,000	45,000	35,000	25,000	30,000

FIGURE 15.11

   4. Save the spreadsheet as **marina1.xls** on your data disk (A:).

To generate the line chart:

   1. Select the Sheet 2 tab at the bottom of the spreadsheet screen. A blank spreadsheet will appear.
   2. Select Insert, Chart, Chart Type: Line, Chart Sub-Type: 1st chart on 2nd row—Line w/markers displayed at each data value, Next.
   3. Click in the Data Range text box, then click on the Sheet 1 tab at the bottom of the spreadsheet screen. Highlight all the cells containing data in rows 2 and 3. (Do not select the title.) Select Next.
   4. Type **LW Marina Slip Rentals, 2003** in the Chart Title text box.
   5. Type **Months of the Year** in the Category (X) Axis text box.
   6. Type **U.S. Dollars** in the Value (Y) Axis text box.
   7. Select the Save as Object in Sheet 2 option. Select Finish. A chart will appear on Sheet 2 of your spreadsheet similar to Figure 15.12.

Optional: Improve the appearance of the chart with some of the following options.

   1. Click on the Series 1 box and delete it, since it is not needed.
   2. Right click on the title. Select Format Chart Title. Select from the options given, such as pick a light color for Area and a Font size of 14.

   Note: When picking colors, always check that there is enough contrast between the text or the plotted line and the background colors to make for easy reading.

   3. Right click on the labels on the Y-axis. Select Format Axis, Number tab, Currency, OK.
   4. Right click on the labels on the Y-axis. Select Format Axis, Font, Bold.

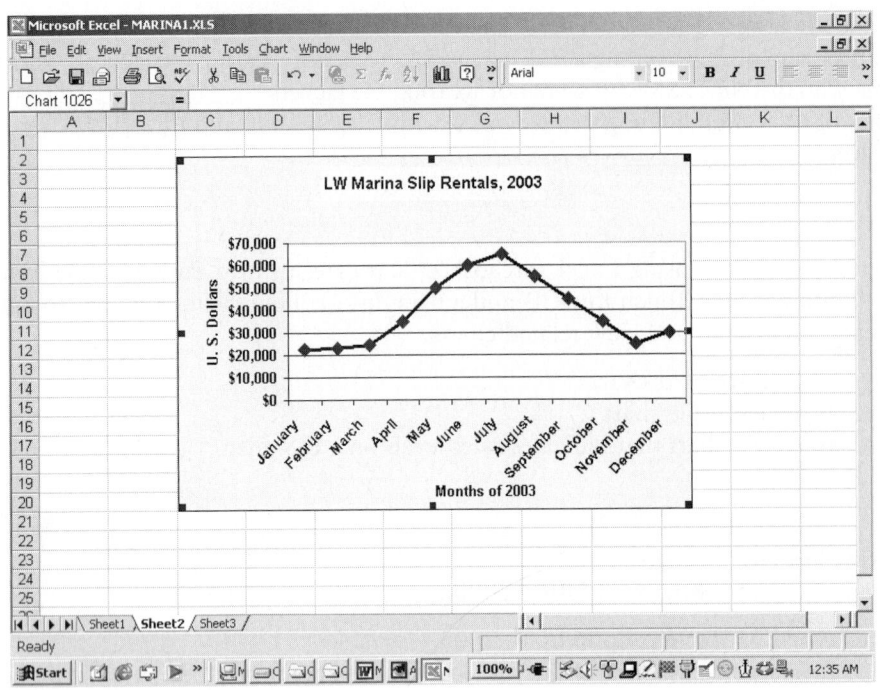

FIGURE 15.12

5. Repeat step 4 for the X-axis.
6. Right click on the shaded area of the chart. Select Format Plot Area and choose a light color for the area.
7. Right click on the plotted line. Select Format Data Series. Under Line, Weight, select a thicker line.
8. Make the chart larger by dragging one or more of the corners outward.
9. Right click on a blank area of the chart. Select Format Chart area and a medium color.
10. To print the chart, first use the Preview button to determine whether the chart will print correctly (Figure 15.13). If necessary make the chart smaller, move it to the left by clicking and dragging the chart, and so on. Preview again. When satisfied that the preview is correct, select the chart by clicking, and then select Print.

Note: If colors are used, a greater degree of contrast is necessary between text and background for printed material than for material viewed on screen. Generally, use very light colors for background and dark, bold colors for text and the plotted line.

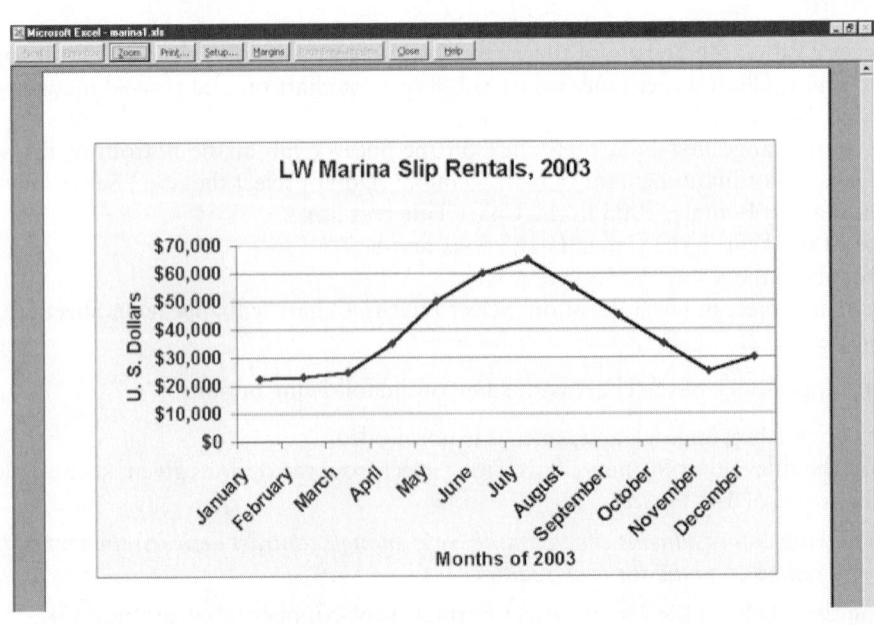

FIGURE 15.13

264

PART 3 *Review and Practice Using Business Math FUNdamentals*

GOAL: Complete 9 of the 10 problems correctly.

Instructions: *Start Business Math FUNdamentals. Complete Tutorial 36 and Drill 28. If you are not satisfied with your scores, repeat the drills. Write your scores below.*

Business Math FUNdamentals Drill 28

Today's Date	Score

Name _____

Class/Section _____

Strokes per Minute Score _____

Accuracy Score (Correct Strokes ÷ Total Strokes) _____

 ## PART 4 *Desktop Calculator*

Exercise 1

One-Minute Addition Timing (0 through 9 Keys, Five-Digit Numbers)

(Optional: Your instructor may wish you to use Touch Key on the computer for all your timings. Check with your instructor before completing this exercise.)

Complete as many of the problems as possible in 1 minute by adding. Work quickly and accurately. The number preceding each closing parenthesis indicates the cumulative number of strokes for problems attempted. For example, if you complete Problems 1 through 5 in 1 minute, your strokes-per-minute score is 305. Optional: 3- to 5-minute timings.

1. 37,556	2. 10,024	3. 76,544	4. 29,006	5. 77,850	6. 94,200	7. 30,000	8. 17,001
78,341	76,932	75,350	30,902	45,500	28,500	60,000	19,003
23,890	62,009	74,800	60,701	34,650	23,100	10,000	18,002
13,657	97,545	15,600	44,603	69,995	87,400	30,000	13,001
75,987	86,041	97,400	30,104	57,359	21,006	30,000	19,004
83,524	19,000	19,500	40,405	34,229	23,005	20,000	71,002
91,093	64,788	24,300	24,003	67,899	79,003	30,000	77,007
76,835	54,921	76,100	51,003	45,775	36,004	50,000	83,004
90,569	53,896	40,300	82,001	54,900	14,006	60,000	38,005
53,870	11,009	53,300	91,002	34,556	25,006	50,000	48,003
61)	122)	183)	244)	305)	366)	427)	488)

	9.	10.	11.	12.	13.	14.	15.	16.
	41,400	76,900	56,987	44,779	43,450	90,661	16,000	95,004
	66,420	42,677	20,122	53,100	29,995	89,000	37,013	82,600
	55,850	63,553	60,455	20,666	41,995	79,885	38,064	64,000
	66,150	76,998	70,004	35,350	27,229	69,655	39,014	34,870
	77,700	88,565	22,999	55,555	30,759	76,444	30,045	96,002
	88,689	74,322	59,000	33,886	60,999	67,111	27,023	16,003
	99,599	97,659	65,880	76,772	37,577	56,741	28,013	89,514
	66,884	22,100	10,432	72,250	20,659	52,962	92,053	46,787
	17,256	25,000	11,119	40,495	45,695	59,854	97,024	36,412
	99,374	35,575	33,980	32,495	20,000	56,014	10,011	54,600
	549)	610)	671)	732)	793)	854)	915)	976)

	17.	18.	19.	20.	21.	22.	23.	24.
	88,900	95,995	36,100	13,655	22,349	15,120	26,213	16,290
	69,100	92,110	76,700	45,880	66,215	12,261	23,500	22,499
	55,800	59,900	93,700	41,770	54,156	91,339	20,435	32,199
	72,300	28,300	32,100	53,660	11,647	85,429	35,163	45,399
	98,500	99,500	95,100	65,870	21,535	74,559	79,452	52,599
	11,500	54,900	49,100	16,340	32,451	62,179	88,432	62,895
	76,600	62,000	58,100	26,590	31,460	45,600	61,255	15,695
	27,200	90,000	88,500	36,680	77,545	29,573	25,721	23,795
	78,900	86,500	63,500	44,780	46,245	32,331	30,115	33,195
	35,000	34,600	16,490	21,490	84,100	56,232	26,543	11,595
	1,037)	1,098)	1,159)	1,220)	1,281)	1,342)	1,403)	1,464)

CHAPTER 15 *Terminology Review*

Bar chart
Cell
Cell address
Charts
Column headings
Columns
Heading
Labels
Line chart
Pictograph
Pie chart
Rows
Slope
Table

Write the correct term next to the appropriate description

1. _____ Used to compare portions or percents to each other and to the whole.

2. _____ Data organized into rows and columns for ease of understanding.

3. _____ Names of columns and rows in a spreadsheet such as A, B, and C and 1, 2, and 3; also, names of units on the horizontal and vertical axes in a chart.

4. _____ Similar to a bar chart but uses symbols instead of bars to represent amounts of data.

5. _____ Descriptive title and date of a table.

6. _____ Composed of the labels of the row and the column that intersect at a cell.

7. _____ A graph used to show changes in data over a period of time.

8. _____ Each block of a table or spreadsheet where a row and a column intersect.

9. _____ Used to visually compare data at a point in time.

10. _____ Lines of data running horizontally in a table.

11. _____ Present data from a table in graphic form.

12. _____ Lines of data running vertically in a table.

13. _____ The amount the line in a line chart rises or falls over time indicating increases or decreases, respectively.

Name _____

Class/Section _____

Score (Correct Answers ÷ No. of Assigned Problems) _____

Chapter 15 Review Exercises

Exercise 1

Joe Browning's portfolio of investments is represented by the pie chart in Figure 15.14. Answer the questions by referring to the chart.

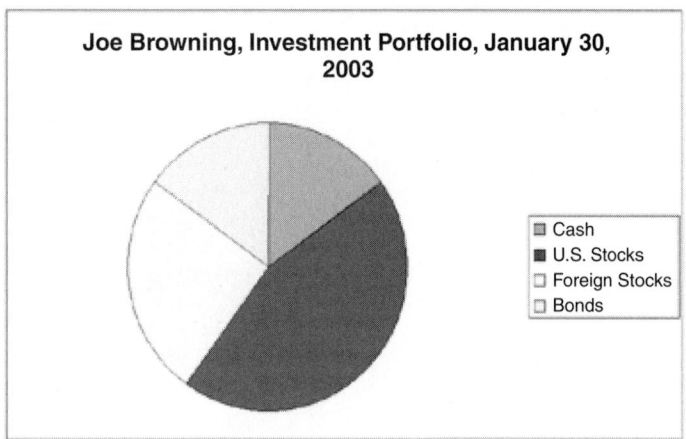

FIGURE 15.14

1. Which investments constitute approximately 25% of Joe's portfolio? _____

2. Which two investments are approximately equal in value? _____

3. Joe has decided that his portfolio should consist of 50% U.S. stocks. To achieve this goal, should he increase or decrease his U.S. stocks? _____

Exercise 2

Complete a bar chart indicating total sales for each model of Frontier Log Home. Selling price for each model should be multiplied by the number of units sold.

Frontier Log Home Kits 2003 Yearly Sales Report

Model No.	Selling Price ($)	Units Sold	Totals
198A	89,798.98	15	
198B	69,799.99	12	
298A	75,898.88	26	
298B	150,989.99	18	

Exercise 3

Prepare a pie chart using data from the table in Exercise 2 indicating the percent of total sales for each model home.

CHAPTER 16

Bank Checking Accounts

 ## PART 1 *Speed and Accuracy Building Using Touch Key*

GOALS: Your speed goal is 9,000 strokes per hour.
Your accuracy target goal range is 95% to 100%.

With each repetition of the drill, try to improve your speed without lowering your accuracy score. If your percent-of-accuracy score falls below 95%, review your finger position and technique. Then try again.

Instructions: *Start Touch Key. Complete Drill 3, Parts A through E, One-Minute Timings. Write your scores for strokes per hour and percent of accuracy below. Repeat Lesson 9 four more times. Write your scores below.*

Touch Key Drill 3—The 0 through 9 Keys, Five-Digit Numbers, One-Minute Timings

Today's Date	Strokes per Hour	Percent of Accuracy
A.		
B.		
C.		
D.		
E.		

 ## PART 2 *Business Math Skills*

AN OVERVIEW OF CHECKING ACCOUNTS

In today's business world, few businesses operate on a cash-only basis. It is inconvenient and risky to keep large amounts of cash on hand for monetary transactions. Handling transactions with cash does not provide proof that payments, loans, and so on were made.

Both personal and business **checking accounts** are services offered by banks. It is important to always keep business and personal money separate. Customers of the bank place money into their account by making a **deposit**. Although banks may invest part of the money deposited in their safekeeping, the bank must keep enough cash on hand for cash withdrawals and other transactions made by customers. The Federal Deposit Insurance Corporation (**FDIC**) is an independent agency of the U.S. Government created by an act of Congress in 1933. Depositor's accounts in FDIC insured institutions are insured up to $100,000 each. A depositor may have more than one account that is FDIC insured. Most banks are FDIC insured institutions.

A customer (the **maker**) may write a **check**, which is an order to the bank (the **payer**) to use cash in the customer's account to pay the amount specified on the check to the person or business (the **payee**) named on the check. Checks are also referred to as **bank drafts**. Banks also offer a **debit card**, also known as a **check card**, which is a check-writing alternative. However, the amount of a payment made by a debit card is electronically deducted from the customer's checking account immediately; whereas the amount of a payment made by check is deducted from the customer's checking account when the check clears (is paid by) the bank, usually in 1 to 4 days. The amount of time it takes for a check to clear a bank is the **float time**.

The **canceled check** indicates that payment by check has been processed by the bank. Debit cards may be used in place of writing checks. The amount of the payment is withdrawn from the checking account at the time of purchase. An electronic record of the transaction is kept by the bank.

When a customer opens a business or a personal checking account at a bank, a **signature card** must be completed on which the signature of the person responsible for approving and signing checks is placed. The bank then keeps the signature card so that the bank may compare the signature on a check with that on the signature card. Money is placed into the account and a number is assigned to the account. This account number must appear on all deposit slips and checks to access the account. If a debit card (check card) is issued, a separate personal identification number (**PIN**) is issued to the customer who can then access his or her account at an automatic teller machine (**ATM**) and use the debit card in stores that have point-of-sale (**POS**) debit/credit card machines at the checkout counters to pay for purchases.

Some debit cards may also be used as credit cards. When presented at stores without POS debit machines, the card may be treated in the same way as any other credit card (store policies vary). Some POS debit machines also have a credit button that may be used when the holder wishes to use the card as a credit card instead of a debit card.

Many banks also offer **on-line access** to checking accounts. Customers may direct bill paying, check the account balance, and see lists of transactions affecting their account on-line. Usually an additional password is required for access to an account on-line that includes bill-paying privileges.

Electronic deposit allows checks received on a regular basis such as payroll and Social Security checks to be deposited automatically in the recipient's checking account and is considered to be much safer and more cost efficient than paper checks. **Automatic drafts** allow the customer to direct the bank to pay regular monthly bills.

Other services may be especially helpful to business customers. Electronic funds transfer (**ETF**) allows a business to credit an employee's checking account for payroll or to collect recurring money from accounts receivables, membership dues, and payments from credit card companies. The credit card and debit card service allows a business to accept certain credit cards and ATM/debit cards in payment of goods and services. **Positive pay** is a feature offered by banks to help protect checking accounts and simplify checking account reconciliation. An electronic report of issued checks from the business is matched daily with the cleared transactions from the bank.

Once the account has been opened, the account holder receives a checkbook with checks, deposit tickets (also called deposit slips), and one of the following: check stubs, a check register, or the means to make carbon-less check copies. Because canceled checks and deposit tickets may serve as legal records that certain transactions have been made, care should be taken to complete each legibly and accurately.

Banks provide a monthly bank statement that summarizes all the activities of the checking account during that month.

PREPARING CHECKS

Along with the business name, address, and customer account number, bank identification numbers and bank routing numbers are printed on each check. The magnetic numbers at the bottom of the check identify the bank, the customer account, and the check number. The numbers just below the check number (6534 in Figure 16.1) in the top right corner are

Susan B. Anthony   **6534**
2200 Dollar Drive   25-80/440
Four Bits, Texas 77666   DATE _____

PAY TO THE
ORDER OF
_____ $ _____

_____ DOLLARS

Lotsa Money Federal Bank

MEMO _____   _____

⑆122345667⑆ ⑈77 51234⑈ 6534

FIGURE 16.1

the American Bankers Association (ABA) transit or routing numbers. These numbers are used to help trace lost checks. In Figure 16.1 the first routing number, 25-80, identifies the city or state and the specific bank. The next number, 440, identifies the Federal Reserve District where the check will be cleared. Checks are numbered sequentially. Checks are printed with six blanks to be completed by the maker with the following information:

1. Date of the check
2. Recipient of the check (payee)
3. Amount of check in numerals
4. Amount of check in words
5. Purpose of check (optional)
6. Signature of maker

PREPARING DEPOSIT SLIPS

A deposit slip (see Figure 16.2) should contain the checking account number to which the deposit is being made, the date of the deposit, the amount of cash being deposited, and the check number and amount of each check being deposited. After the currency, coins, and checks are listed, the amount is totaled.

A personal deposit slip (Figure 16.3) has a space for customers to request cash. If cash is to be withdrawn, deduct the amount of the cash withdrawal and write the remainder (the amount to be deposited) on the deposit slip.

Personal checks may be deposited or cashed, but to maintain proper records, a deposit slip should be prepared for all checks received by a business. Remember to keep personal and

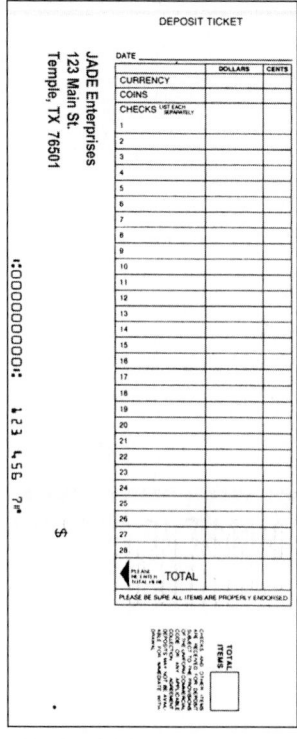

FIGURE 16.2

DEPOSIT TICKET   SH ▶

                                     7-87   CHECKS

JD's RESTAURANT
101 MAIN ST.
CUERO, TX 77954

DATE_____

DEPOSITS MAY NOT BE AVAILABLE FOR IMMEDIATE WITHDRAWAL

                                             SUBTOTAL ▶
SCHEDULE OF CASH RECEIVED FROM DEPOSIT

                                             LESS CASH ▶

FIRST NATIONAL BANK
CUERO, TEXAS   NET DEPOSIT $

⑆ 13102552 ⑈ 71   9596⑈

FIGURE 16.3

```
┌─────────────────────────────────────────┐
│ ENDORSE HERE                              │
│                                           │
│ X_____ │
│                                           │
│                                           │
│                                           │
│                                           │
│                                           │
│                                           │
│ DO NOT WRITE, STAMP, OR SIGN BELOW THIS LINE │
│ _____ │
│                                           │
└─────────────────────────────────────────┘
```

FIGURE 16.4

business money separate. All checks that have been received by the business and are to be deposited must have an **endorsement** (be signed) on the back of the check in the space indicated (see Figure 16.4). There are several methods for endorsing checks.

BLANK ENDORSEMENT

A **blank endorsement** is usually used on personal checks only, and should only be used on checks that are to be carried into the bank and deposited or cashed in person. After a blank endorsement is placed on a check, anyone can cash it. It is obvious, therefore, that the check should be endorsed only at the time of deposit. Types of blank endorsement are as follows:

1. The payee must sign his or her name exactly as written on the front of the check.
2. A stamp may be used to endorse the back of a check with a signature or a business name.

RESTRICTED ENDORSEMENT

A **restricted endorsement** provides extra security for checks to be deposited through the mail or an **ATM** machine or to sign a check over to another party:

1. To ensure checks are deposited into the payee's account, the words "for deposit only," the account number, and the payee's signature or the business name are placed on the back of the check. For security, this type of endorsement should be made as soon as a business receives a check.
2. Some cash registers are equipped with a printing slot for endorsing checks. The check is inserted into the slot and the appropriate information is printed on the endorsement area of the check.
3. To sign the check over to another party, write the words "pay to the order of" and write the name of the party you wish to receive the funds for the check followed by the original payee's signature.

WHAT IF A BUSINESS RECEIVES MANY, MANY CHECKS EACH DAY?

Some businesses such as large supermarkets may receive hundreds of checks each day or each shift. How are these deposited? Instead of writing lists of checks on deposit slips, two employees each prepares an adding machine tape of the amounts of all checks received for the day or shift. The totals of the two tapes must match. The total is written on a deposit slip. The deposit slip, the two adding machine tapes, and all checks are placed in a bank bag for deposit.

CURRENCY

Depending on company policy, currency to be deposited by financial institutions may be itemized as shown on the bottom of the deposit slip in Figure 16.5. If space is not provided on the deposit slip, the cash can be itemized on a separate sheet of paper and included with the deposit. Count the number of bills of each denomination and note the number. Multiply the number of bills by the denomination. Add the products. The sum should equal your total cash.

Alternately, two persons may be required to count the currency, bundle it by denomination, and keep a calculator tape of the number of bills in each bundled denomination. When the two tapes match, each person signs his or her calculator tape and places the tapes in the deposit envelope.

The amount of currency is written in the space on the front of the deposit slip.

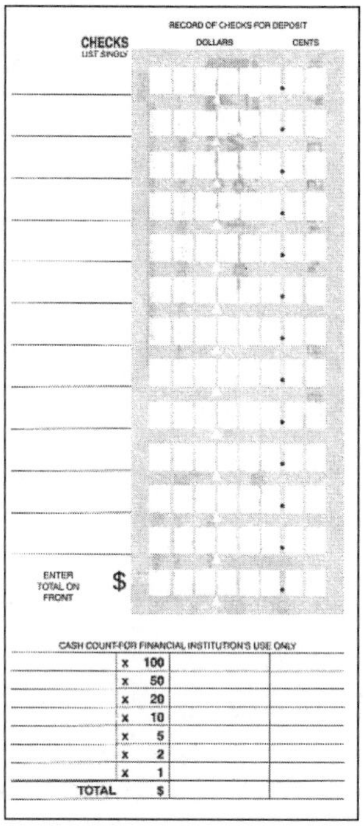

COINS

Separate and count coins to be deposited by denomination. Itemize the coins on paper or by calculator tape and find a total using the same method as with currency. Write the amount in the space for coins on the front of the deposit slip.

If separate spaces are not provided for currency and coins, add the two together and place the total in the space for cash as shown in Figure 16.3.

FIGURE 16.5

DEBIT AND CREDIT MEMOS

If an error on the deposit slip is detected by the bank personnel, the bank will correct the error and issue a **credit memo** if the correction increases the customer's account and a **debit memo** if the correction decreases the customer's account.

UNDERSTANDING DEBIT AND CREDIT

Let's look at debit and credit from the *bank's point of view*. Because money deposited in a bank by a customer is still the customer's money and is payable to the customer on demand, the bank records the deposit on its records as a credit. Thus, bank customers' accounts normally have a credit balance. On the other hand, any withdrawals from the account are recorded by the bank as a debit to the account. The debit decreases the credit balance. Note the partial bank statement in Figures 16.9A and 16.9B. Deposits are listed under the heading Credits. Point-of-sale debit (DEB) automatic payments made by the bank when the customer uses a debit card and the bank service charge are listed under Debits.

Note: This is not to be confused with the way a transaction is recorded in the business records of a customer that will reflect the point of view of the customer's business. *The cash account of a business normally has a debit balance. Cash received is debited to the cash account, increasing the debit balance. Cash spent is credited to the cash account. Credits are subtracted from the debit balance.*

CHECK REGISTER AND CHECK STUB

Figure 16.6 shows a typical **check stub**; Figure 16.7 shows a typical **check register**. It is important to keep an accurate listing of all deposits and withdrawals from a bank account in the check register or on the check stubs. It may not be easy to remember to record all

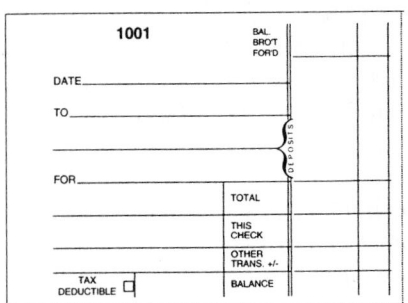

NUMBER	DATE	TRANSACTION DESCRIPTION	PAYMENT DEBIT	CODE	FEE	DEPOSIT CREDIT	$

FIGURE 16.6   **FIGURE 16.7**

electronic transfers of funds (ETFs), debit card purchases, ATM transactions, and automatic payments, but it is necessary to do so. The check stub allows checks, deposits, and other transactions to be recorded. A space is provided for writing the current balance of the checkbook. The space for other transactions is limited. If you have many electronic transactions, it may be necessary to keep an additional register of **all** transactions that affect your checking account. Notice that the check register has a Code column. Identifying transactions by code makes sense with today's many ways to access the checking account. Codes that may be used include the following

    D: Deposit

    DP: Debit card purchase

    ATM CD: ATM cash deposit

    ATM CW: ATM cash withdrawal

    AP: Automatic payment

    EFT: Electronic funds transfer

    I: Interest earned

    SC: Service charge

    TD: Tax-deductible

The check register may have either a Fee column like the one shown in Figure 16.7 or a column marked with a checkmark (✓). When reconciling statements, use this column to indicate with a checkmark those items that appear on the bank statement or to record applicable fees. The first space in the last column is used to record the balance brought forward. The remaining spaces in the last column are used to keep a **running balance**. That is, as each item is recorded in the check register, the new balance should be calculated so that the check register is continually updated. Note the running balance shown in Figure 16.8.

ITEM NO. OR TRANS. CODE	DATE	TRANSACTION DESCRIPTION	SUBTRACTIONS AMOUNT OF PAYMENT OR WITHDRAWAL (-)	ADDITIONS AMOUNT OF DEPOSIT OR INTEREST (+)	BALANCE
					$275.23
Ck. # 2213	4/20	Wal-Mart	$19.64		$255.59
ATM w/d	4/25	A.B.B. cash	$100.00		$155.59
Deposit	4/30	A.B.B. paycheck		$531.94	$687.53
Ck. # 2214	4/30	First Card	$168.53		$519.00

FIGURE 16.8

BANK STATEMENT RECONCILIATION

A bank statement summarizes all the checking account activity for the preceding month (see Figures 16.9A and 16.9B). Although the bank statement is provided by the bank, it is up to you to ensure that the bank statement is correct by comparing it to your check register or stubs. To compare, place a checkmark beside each item in the check register or check stubs that appears on the bank statement. Items without checkmarks will need to be added to or subtracted from the bank statement balance. Place a checkmark beside items on the bank statement that appear in the check register or check stubs. Items without checkmarks on the bank statement should be added or subtracted from the checkbook balance.

After adjusting the **bank statement** balance and the check register balance at the end of the month, the two balances should be equal. This process is called **bank statement reconciliation**. Note that the balance in the check register is $519.00. If the bank statement for April 30 shows a balance of $1,000, we must account for the difference and bring the two into balance. Most bank statements have a form printed on the back that guides the customer through bank statement reconciliation. Figure 16.10 uses the simple form of placing items affecting the bank statement balance on the left side of the "chalkboard" and items affecting the check register balance on the right side of the "chalkboard." Following are some occurrences that might require adjusting the bank statement and checkbook balances.

We begin with items that can affect the bank statement balance. The code is included where applicable.

1. A deposit recorded in the checkbook may not have been made in time to appear on the bank statement (Figure 16.10). Such deposits are called **deposits in transit**. In this case the deposit in transit was for $280. Deposits in transit must be ADDED to the bank statement balance—D.

```
                        CHECKING ACCOUNTS

              WHEN USING YOUR DEBIT CARD, PLEASE BE SURE TO SUBTRACT TRAN-
              SACTIONS FROM YOUR RECORDS IMMEDIATELY.  TRANSACTIONS WILL
              REDUCE YOUR AVAILABLE BALANCE AT THE TIME THEY ARE PERFORMED


    1ST CLASS CHECKING                   Number of Enclosures              1
    Account Number                       Statement Dates  4/10/03 thru  5/11/03
    Previous Balance           373.45    Days in statement period         32
         2 Deposits/Credits  1,291.94    Average Ledger             1,039.74
         7 Checks/Debits       444.63    Average Collected            918.20
    Total Account Charges       11.00
    Interest Paid                 .00
    Current Balance          1,209.76


    ------------------------------- CREDITS -------------------------------------
    DATE     DESCRIPTION                                   AMOUNT
     4/11    Deposit                                       972.31 CR
     5/09    TAX REFUND US TREASURY 220                    319.63 CR
             PPD

    ------------------------------- DEBITS --------------------------------------
    DATE     DESCRIPTION                                   AMOUNT
     4/11    D/C SET 0833 04/09/03 40104099                 59.34
             USCELL DC04         RC8
             6701 E 41ST STREET
             18889449400  OK
     4/14    POS DEB 1517 04/13/03 747783                   55.36
             FAMILY CENTER IGA
             416 SOUTH ALISTER ST
             PORT ARANSAS TX
```

FIGURE 16.9A

1ST CLASS CHECKING   (Continued)

```
------------------------------- DEBITS -----------------------------------
DATE      DESCRIPTION                              AMOUNT
4/15      POS DEB 1427 04/15/03 824682             56.70
          FAMILY CENTER IGA
          416 SOUTH ALISTER ST
          PORT ARANSAS TX
4/18      Automatic Cash Reserve Payment           61.89
4/21      POS DEB 1901 04/19/03 526365             90.12
          WAL-MART #0490
          10241 SOUTH PADRE ISL D
          CORPUS CHRIS TX
4/28      POS DEB 1431 04/26/03 11643103           67.12
          HEB HEB #333
          101 Goodnight
          Aransas Pass TX
5/02      POS DEB 2153 05/01/03 700692             54.10
          FAMILY CENTER IGA
          416 SOUTH ALISTER ST
          PORT ARANSAS TX
5/09      Total Account Charges                    11.00 SC

----------------------- SERVICE CHARGE SUMMARY ---------------------------
DATE      DESCRIPTION                              AMOUNT
5/09      Service Charge                           11.00

----------------------- DAILY BALANCE INFORMATION ------------------------
DATE      BALANCE        DATE      BALANCE        DATE      BALANCE
4/10      373.45         4/15      1,174.36       4/28      955.23
4/11      1,286.42       4/18      1,112.47       5/02      901.13
4/14      1,231.06       4/21      1,022.35       5/09      1,209.76
```

* *

FIGURE 16.9B

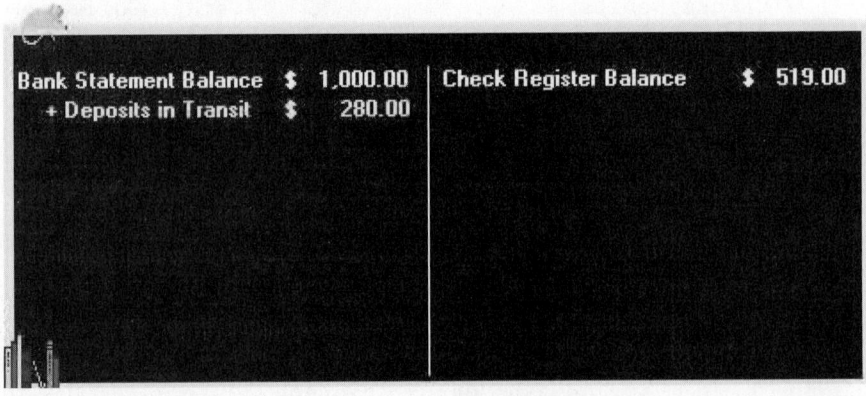

FIGURE 16.10

    2. Some of the checks you have written may not have cleared the bank and may not appear on your bank statement (Figure 16.11). Such checks are called **outstanding checks.** The amounts of all outstanding checks should be added together and the total subtracted from the bank statement balance. In this case, $40 of outstanding checks must be SUBTRACTED from the bank statement balance—Check #.

Bank Statement Balance	$ 1,000.00	Check Register Balance	$ 519.00
+ Deposits in Transit	+ 280.00		
- Outstanding Checks	- 40.00		

FIGURE 16.11

3. Recent withdrawals made at ATM machines may not appear on the bank statement and should be subtracted from the bank statement balance (Figure 16.12). In this case $100 was withdrawn from an ATM and should be SUBTRACTED from the bank statement balance—ATM CW.

Bank Statement Balance	$ 1,000.00	Check Register Balance	$ 519.00
+ Deposits in Transit	+ 280.00		
- Outstanding Checks	- 40.00		
- ATM Withdrawals	- 100.00		

FIGURE 16.12

4. Recent transfers to other accounts might include:
   a. Transferring money from the checking account to a savings account at a bank, ATM, or on-line (Figure 16.13). In this case $500 was transferred to another account and should be SUBTRACTED from the bank statement balance—EFT.
   b. Recent purchases made with the checking account debit card—DP.
   c. Recent on-line bill paying using funds from the checking account—AP.

Bank Statement Balance	$ 1,000.00	Check Register Balance	$ 519.00
+ Deposits in Transit	+ 280.00		
- Outstanding Checks	- 40.00		
- ATM Withdrawals	- 100.00		
- Transfers to other Acct.	- 500.00		

FIGURE 16.13

Now we will look at items that can affect the check register balance:

1. Items that should be DEDUCTED from the check register balance are bank service fees, such as a monthly charge for the checking account; charges for preprinted checks; **returned checks** and charges associated with them (Figure 16.14). Returned checks are checks given to you by another party that cannot be paid because the party who gave the check to you has stopped payment or does not have enough money in his or her account to cover the check.

Bank Statement Balance	$ 1,000.00	Check Register Balance	$ 519.00
+ Deposits in Transit	+ 280.00	- Service Charge	- 15.00
- Outstanding Checks	- 40.00	- Returned Checks	- 100.00
- ATM Withdrawals	- 100.00	- Returned Check Fee	- 15.00
- Transfers to other Acct.	- 500.00	- Check Printing Charge	- 10.00
Adjusted Bank Statement Balance	$ 640.00		

FIGURE 16.14

In this case the customer had a bank service charge of $15 (SC), returned checks of $100, a returned check fee of $15, and a check printing charge of $10, all of which must be SUBTRACTED from the check register balance.

2. **Nonsufficient funds** (NSF) fees are charged by the bank for checks written by you without sufficient funds in your account to cover them. NSF fees must be DEDUCTED

from the check register balance. Because the check was written but not paid, the check should be canceled in the cash register or check stubs by drawing a line through the check entry and ADDING the amount of the check to the checkbook balance. You must then make other arrangements to pay the payee of the NSF check.

3. Debit memos issued by the bank to notify you of an error that decreases the amount in your bank account should be SUBTRACTED from the check register balance.

4. Items that should be ADDED to the check register balance are transfers from other accounts, such as from a savings account to a checking account; interest earned on the account, if any; notes collected by the bank; other electronic or automatic deposits to the account; and credit memos issued by the bank (Figure 16.15). In this case, a transfer of $60 from another account, interest earned of $1, and notes collected by the bank of $200 were ADDED to the check register balance.

Bank Statement Balance	$	1,000.00	Check Register Balance	$	519.00
+ Deposits in Transit	+	280.00	- Service Charge	-	15.00
- Outstanding Checks	-	40.00	- Returned Checks	-	100.00
- ATM Withdrawals	-	100.00	- Returned Check Fee	-	15.00
- Transfers to other			- Check Printing Charge	-	10.00
Accounts	-	500.00	+ Transfers from other	+	60.00
			Accounts		
Adjusted Bank Statement			+ Interest Earned	+	1.00
Balance	$	640.00	+ Notes Collected by		
			Bank	+	200.00

FIGURE 16.15

The new balances are called the **adjusted bank statement balance** and **adjusted check register balance**, respectively. After the adjustments have been made correctly, the two adjusted balances must match (Figure 16.16).

Bank Statement Balance	$	1,000.00	Check Register Balance	$	519.00
+ Deposits in Transit	+	280.00	- Service Charge	-	15.00
- Outstanding Checks	-	40.00	- Returned Checks	-	100.00
- ATM Withdrawals	-	100.00	- Returned Check Fee	-	15.00
- Transfers to other			- Check Printing Charge	-	10.00
Accounts	-	500.00	+ Transfers from other	+	60.00
Adjusted Bank Statement			Accounts		
Balance	$	640.00	+ Interest Earned	+	1.00
			+ Notes Collected by		
			Bank	+	200.00
			Adjusted Check Register	$	640.00

FIGURE 16.16

Name _____

Class/Section _____

Score (Correct Answers ÷ No. of Assigned Problems) _____

PART 2　*Business Math Skills*

Exercise 1

Write a check in the name of Susan B. Anthony to Computers, Etc. for $206.75 on February 2, 2004, for laser ink cartridges (see Figure 16.17).

Susan B. Anthony   6534
2200 Dollar Drive
Four Bits, Texas 77666   DATE _____

PAT TO THE
ORDER OF _____ $ _____

_____ DOLLARS

Lotsa Money Federal Bank

MEMO _____   _____

⑈⑈1234567⑈ ⑈⑈77 51234⑈ 6534

FIGURE 16.17

Exercise 2

Record the check written in Exercise 1 and record the new balance in Susan B. Anthony's check register.

Date	Check No.	Description	✓	Debit	Credit	Balance $3,895.64

Exercise 3

Record check #7001 written on January 10, 2004, to Anderson Property Mgt. for $609.00 for rent on the check stub. The balance to be brought forward is $5,598.65. An ATM deposit of $200.00 was also made on January 10, 2004. Complete the check stub.

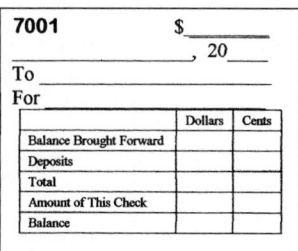

Exercise 4

Complete a deposit slip (Figure 16.18) dated May 10, 2004, $440.00 in cash (currency) and the following checks: Check #79832 from Mary Anderson for $59.67, Check #1009 from Annette Lowry for $275.34, and Check #3211 from ABC Co. for $357.69.

Exercise 5

Properly endorse a check using your name as though you will cash the check and the check is made out to your full name.

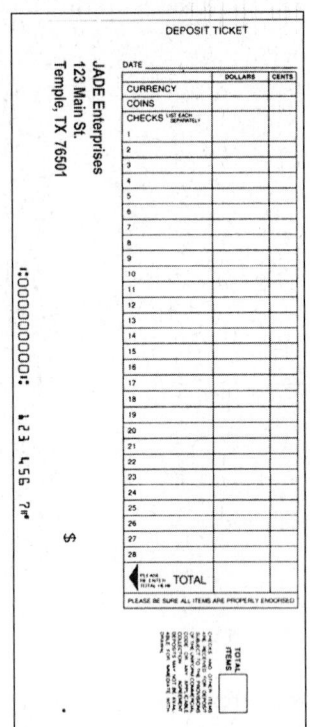

FIGURE 16.18

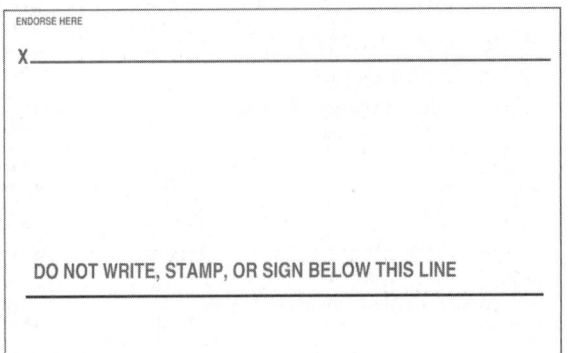

Exercise 6

Use a restrictive endorsement on a check so that the check must be deposited in your account #1067555222. The check is made out to your first and last name.

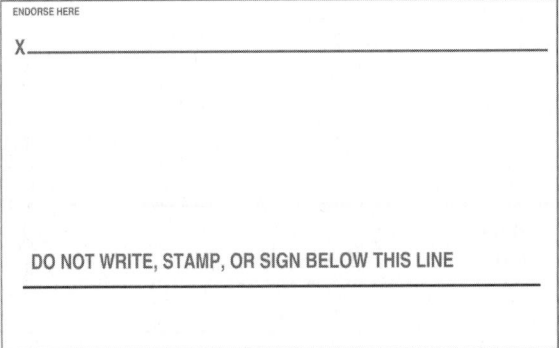

Exercise 7

Complete a bank statement reconciliation for January 30, 2004. The bank statement showed a balance of $4,559.42. The checkbook showed a balance of $5,699.01. On comparison of the bank statement and the check register, you discover:

Outstanding deposits of $690.12 and $253.64

Outstanding checks: #1790 for $55.69, #1795 for $75.90, #1796 for $104.35, and #1799 for $68.00

A bank service charge of $12.00

Returned checks of $390.87 and $56.90

Returned check fees of $40.00

What is the amount of the adjusted bank statement and checkbook balances? _____

	CHECKS OUTSTANDING		
	NO.	AMOUNT	

THIS IS PROVIDED TO HELP YOU BALANCE YOUR BANK STATEMENT

BANK BALANCE
SHOWN ON THIS STATEMENT $_____

ADD + (IF ANY)
DEPOSITS NOT SHOWN
ON THIS STATEMENT   _____

SUBTOTAL   _____

SUBTRACT - (IF ANY)
CHECKS OUTSTANDING   _____

BALANCE $_____
SHOULD AGREE WITH YOUR CHECKBOOK BALANCE

THIS IS PROVIDED TO HELP YOU BALANCE YOUR BANK STATEMENT

CHECKBOOK BALANCE
AT STATEMENT DATE $_____

SUBTRACT - (IF ANY)
ACTIVITY CHARGES   _____

SUBTOTAL   _____

SUBTRACT - (IF ANY)
OTHER BANK CHARGES   _____

TOTAL

BALANCE $_____
SHOULD AGREE WITH YOUR CHECKBOOK BALANCE

PART 3 *Review and Practice Using Business Math FUNdamentals*

GOAL: Complete 9 of the 10 problems correctly.

Instructions: *Start Business Math FUNdamentals. Complete Tutorial 37 and Drill 29. If you are not satisfied with your scores, repeat the drills. Write your scores below.*

Business Math FUNdamentals Drill 29

Today's Date	Score

Name _____

Class/Section _____

Strokes per Minute Score _____

Accuracy Score (Correct Strokes ÷ Total Strokes) _____

 ## PART 4 *Desktop Calculator*

Exercise 1

One-Minute Addition Timing (0 through 9 Keys, Five-Digit Numbers)

(Optional: Your instructor may wish you to use Touch Key on the computer for all your timings. Check with your instructor before completing this exercise.)

Complete as many of the problems as possible in 1 minute by adding. Work quickly and accurately. The number preceding each closing parenthesis indicates the cumulative number of strokes for problems attempted. For example, if you complete Problems 1 through 3 in 1 minute, your strokes-per-minute score is 183. Optional: 3- to 5-minute timings.

1. 37,229	2. 35,024	3. 91,544	4. 11,006	5. 27,850	6. 94,200	7. 50,000	8. 87,001
78,877	76,562	75,920	30,672	48,500	28,100	67,000	11,003
23,651	62,000	74,807	60,703	34,950	23,128	10,800	18,002
13,324	87,545	83,600	27,971	69,915	91,400	30,010	13,501
75,256	86,811	97,930	68,104	57,355	21,836	30,003	19,064
83,117	91,000	19,788	40,195	94,229	23,007	10,000	71,008
91,339	64,533	67,300	24,008	68,899	51,003	32,000	17,007
76,541	54,514	76,460	47,003	45,975	36,284	50,800	85,004
90,471	53,736	40,303	82,591	54,980	14,007	60,090	38,905
77,870	11,829	18,300	91,009	34,557	32,006	50,004	48,053
61)	122)	183)	244)	305)	366)	427)	488)

9. 81,400	10. 46,900	11. 66,987	12. 14,779	13. 40,450	14. 90,061	15. 96,000	16. 67,004
65,420	46,677	22,122	52,100	29,005	89,400	36,013	32,600
55,750	63,853	60,455	20,356	41,990	79,005	38,564	62,000
66,110	76,928	70,014	35,357	20,229	60,005	39,064	34,370
77,706	88,561	22,992	55,000	30,059	76,004	30,044	96,022
28,689	34,322	19,000	30,886	60,909	60,001	47,023	16,001
93,599	99,659	63,880	76,002	37,570	57,741	25,013	19,514
66,784	22,756	10,132	72,258	50,659	52,962	92,653	43,787
17,216	95,000	11,139	40,495	40,695	59,004	97,054	36,212
99,372	36,575	33,982	50,495	20,990	56,002	10,016	54,613
549)	610)	671)	732)	793)	854)	915)	976)

17. 18,900	18. 27,995	19. 45,100	20. 21,848	21. 87,349	22. 61,120	23. 76,213	24. 76,290
62,100	92,280	76,120	49,880	66,855	12,681	28,500	28,499
55,340	59,929	93,713	41,480	54,198	91,361	20,938	32,899
72,546	37,300	78,100	53,647	46,647	85,462	75,163	45,379
28,500	99,380	95,890	67,870	21,875	69,559	71,452	52,596
18,500	54,939	49,145	16,680	32,423	62,639	88,632	92,895
76,370	19,000	23,100	26,569	31,000	45,606	61,285	75,695
27,219	90,180	88,210	84,680	70,005	76,573	25,729	28,795
17,900	86,517	89,500	44,810	40,045	32,731	97,115	33,895
35,270	19,600	28,490	21,483	80,100	56,272	26,873	11,575
1,037)	1,098)	1,159)	1,220)	1,281)	1,342)	1,403)	1,464)

CHAPTER 16 *Terminology Review*

Adjusted bank statement balance

Adjusted check register balance

ATM

Automatic drafts

Bank drafts

Bank statement

Bank statement reconciliation

Blank endorsement

Canceled check

Check

Check card

Check register

Check stub

Checking accounts

Credit memo

Debit card

Debit memo

Deposit

Deposits in transit

Electronic deposit

Endorsement

ETF

FDIC

Float time

Maker

Nonsufficient funds
On-line access
Outstanding checks
Payee
Payer (drawee)
PIN
POS
Positive pay
Returned checks
Restricted endorsement
Running balance
Signature card

Write the correct term next to the appropriate description.

1. _____ Used at stores to pay for purchases instead of writing a check. The amount of the purchase is removed from the checking account electronically at the time of the sale.

2. _____ Used to ensure that checks are deposited in the payee's account or to sign a check over to another party.

3. _____ Issued by the customer's bank and decreases the customer's checking account balance.

4. _____ Issued by the customer's bank and increases the customer's checking account balance.

5. _____ A service offered by banks that provides a way for a business to buy and sell without using cash by honoring orders by the customer to pay money.

6. _____ One who is to receive the funds specified on a check.

7. _____ A form containing the signature of the person(s) responsible for approving and signing checks used by a bank to verify signatures on checks.

8. _____ An order to a bank to use cash in the customer's account to pay a specified amount to a payee.

9. _____ Money placed into a checking account.

10. _____ A signature or stamp with a signature or business name of the payee of a check.

11. _____ Checks given by another party that cannot be paid because the party has stopped payment or does not have enough money in the account to cover the check.

12. _____ The checkbook balance after bank statement reconciliation.

13. _____ The bank statement balance after reconciliation.

14. _____ The person writing and signing a check.

15. _____ A summary of all checking account activities, usually for 1 month.

16. _____ or _____ Used to record written checks and other activities affecting the checking account.

17. _____ The process of adjusting the bank statement balance and the checkbook balance so that they are in agreement.

18. _____ The customer does not have enough cash in his or her checking account to cover one or more checks that have been written.

19. _____ A purchase made using a debit card.

20. _____ Transfer of funds electronically.

Chapter 16 Review Exercises

Exercise 1

1. Write a check in the name of Susan B. Anthony for $65.70 dated December 15, 2003, to Barnes Jewelry on account (see Figure 16.19).

FIGURE 16.19

2. Complete a check stub using the information in Problem 1. The balance brought forward is $611.15.

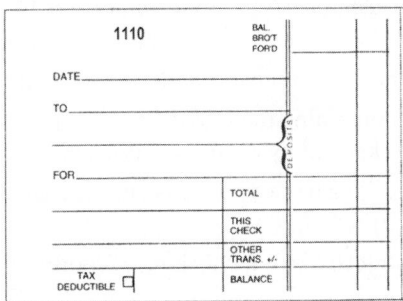

Exercise 2

3. Write a check in the name of Susan B. Anthony for $135.70 dated December 16, 2003, to Bill's Auto Service for a muffler (see Figure 16.20).

FIGURE 16.20

4. Make an entry in the check register for check #1111. The balance brought forward is $579.58.

NUMBER	DATE	TRANSACTION DESCRIPTION	PAYMENT DEBIT	CODE	FEE	DEPOSIT CREDIT	$	

Exercise 3

5. Complete a deposit ticket for the three checks shown in Figures 16.21 through 16.23. Use the date January 12, 2003.

Anne's Decorating Service
1250 N. Main St.
Victoria, TX 77901

12905

DATE 1/8/2004

PAY TO THE
ORDER OF Biltmore Wholesale Co. $ 350.76

Three hundred fifty dollars and 76/100   DOLLARS

First National Bank

MEMO   Anne McDermott

⑆123456789⑉⑆00 12345⑊12905

FIGURE 16.21

Johnson Hardware
1122 James Ave.
Victoria, TX 77901

2551

DATE 1/11/2004

PAY TO THE
ORDER OF Biltmore Wholesale Co. $ 775.44

Seven hundred seventy-five and 44/100   DOLLARS

First National Bank

MEMO   Mary Lou Carter

⑆ 123456789 ⑉⑆77 12345⑊ 2551

FIGURE 16.22

The Marketplace
2200 N. Windsor
San Antonio, 70001

2295

DATE 1/10/2004

PAY TO THE
ORDER OF Biltmore Wholesale Co. $ 490.68

Four hundred ninety dollars and 68/100   DOLLARS

Lotsa Money Federal Bank

MEMO   Robert M. Biltmore

⑆122345667⑉⑆77 51234⑊2295

FIGURE 16.23

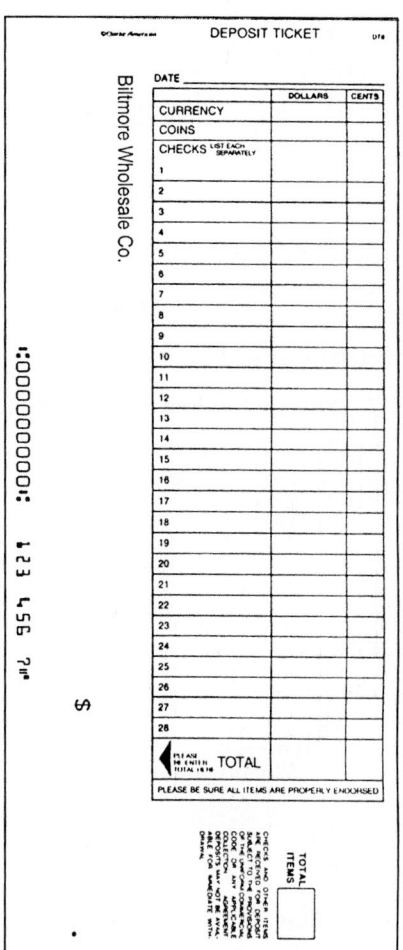

285

6. Endorse the checks shown in Problem 5 using a restrictive endorsement to ensure deposit in business checking account #1234567.

```
ENDORSE HERE
X_____




_____
DO NOT WRITE, STAMP, OR SIGN BELOW THIS LINE
_____
```

```
ENDORSE HERE
X_____




_____
DO NOT WRITE, STAMP, OR SIGN BELOW THIS LINE
_____
```

```
ENDORSE HERE
X_____




_____
DO NOT WRITE, STAMP, OR SIGN BELOW THIS LINE
_____
```

Exercise 4

7. You are Mildred E. Schaefer and you have received a check that you wish to cash. Endorse the check appropriately.

```
ENDORSE HERE
X_____




_____
DO NOT WRITE, STAMP, OR SIGN BELOW THIS LINE
_____
```

Exercise 5

8. The Island Wearables checkbook shows the following entries for September 2004. Codes used by the business to identify transactions are:

D: Deposit

DP: Debit card purchase

ATM CD: ATM cash deposit

ATM CW: ATM cash withdrawal

AP: Automatic payment

EFT: Electronic funds transfer

I: Interest earned

SC: Service charge

Date	Check Number or Code	Payment/Debit (−) in Dollars ($)	Deposit/Credit (+) in Dollars ($)	Balance ($)
2004				3,569.84
9-3	17531	121.59		
9-3	17532	1650.00		
9-3	17333	349.00		
9-4	D		4395.00	
9-7	17334	89.90		
9-8	DP	145.00		
9-9	17335	295.47		
9-9	17336	348.92		
9-12	17337	2091.08		
9-15	17338	592.80		
9-15	17339	648.20		
9-16	ATM CD		3452.81	
9-20	17340	40.00		
9-22	DP	129.00		
9-25	17341	1050.95		
9-26	17342	50.45		
9-30	17343	598.42		
9-30	17344	644.93		
9-30	D		3,200.15	
9-30	Adjustments:			

The September bank statement showed a balance of $14,970.83. After comparing the check register and the September bank statement, it is found that the following checks did not appear on the bank statement: 17334, 17341, 17342, 17343, and 17344. The following deposit did not appear on the bank statement: 9-30 D $3,200.15. The bank statement indicated a POS debit of $414.92 on September 13 that was not recorded in the check register, a bank service charge of $25, a returned check of $119.00, and a returned check fee of $15. An EFT payment from MC of $6,025.92 was deposited to the account on September 20. The bank made two automatic payments of $150 and $320 for the customer on September 25.

Prepare a bank statement reconciliation using the form provided. What is the adjusted checkbook balance?

_____

September Bank Statement Reconciliation

Bank Statement Balance	$_____	Checkbook Balance	$_____

CHAPTER 17

Employee Payroll, Payroll Forms

 **PART 1** *Speed and Accuracy Building Using Touch Key*

GOALS: Your speed goal is 9,500 strokes per hour.
Your accuracy target goal range is 95% to 100%.

With each repetition of the drill, try to improve your speed without lowering your accuracy score. If your percent-of-accuracy score falls below 95%, review your finger position and technique. Then try again.

Instructions: Start Touch Key. Complete Drill 3, Parts A and B, Three-Minute Timings. (Drill 3, Parts C through E are optional.) Write your scores for strokes per hour and percent of accuracy below.

Touch Key Drill 3—The 0 through 9 Keys, Five-Digit Numbers, Three-Minute Timings

	Today's Date	Strokes per Hour	Percent of Accuracy
A.			
B.			
C.			
D.			
E.			

 **PART 2** *Business Math Skills*

EMPLOYEE PAYROLL

Employees of a business must be paid. It seems simple, but important record keeping is required. Federal and state governments require that certain deductions must be withheld from employees' pay. A business needs to know how much is being spent on salaries and wages. It is, therefore, necessary for the business to keep records on each employee including the amount of work performed, the amount earned, deductions made from the amount earned, the amount paid each pay period, and the year-to-date earnings. The amount earned by an employee is **gross pay**. After the deductions are made from gross pay, the amount remaining is **net pay**.

Let us begin by looking at the different methods used to calculate employee pay.

ANNUAL SALARY

Salaried employees are promised a certain amount of pay per year. The annual amount is then divided by the number of pay periods in a year, usually monthly, to determine gross pay for each pay period. Overtime is generally not paid to salaried employees.

PROBLEM 1

A new employee was hired by JADE Enterprises at $24,000 per year. Pay periods at this company are monthly. Calculate gross pay per pay period. Refer to Figure 17.1. Divide the $24,000 annual salary by 12 pay periods per year for a quotient of $2,000 gross pay per month.

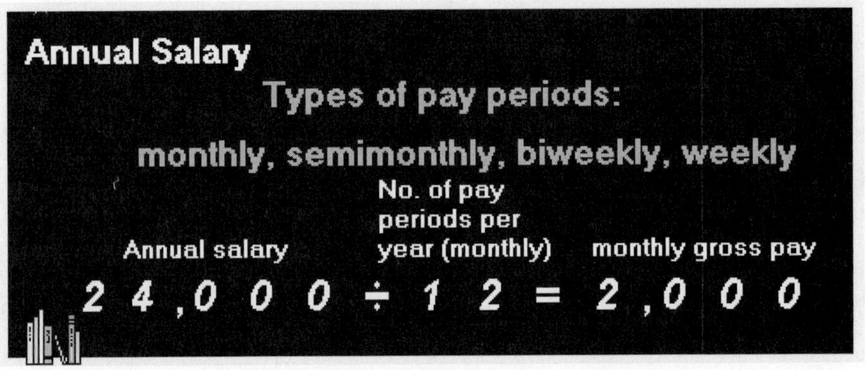

FIGURE 17.1 Converting annual salary to monthly salary.

HOURLY WAGE

Employment laws vary from state to state, but most companies are subject to federal law, which requires that most employees classified as hourly employees be paid overtime for hours more than 40 per week. However, union contracts and other circumstances can require a multitude of hourly pay rates based on holidays, time of day, risk, and other factors. Companies may have multiple levels of overtime rates.

Hourly wage employees are paid a stated amount for each hour worked, usually up to 40 hours per week. These hours are referred to as **regular hours**. If more than 40 hours are worked per week, hours over 40 are referred to as **overtime hours**. As stated earlier, an overtime rate (usually 1.5 times the regular rate) is paid for overtime hours. Overtime hours over a certain number per week and holidays may be paid at 2 times the regular rate.

To calculate gross pay based on an hourly wage for each pay period:

1. Multiply regular hours by the regular pay per hour.
2. Multiply overtime hours by the overtime pay per hour.
3. Multiply double-time hours by double-time pay per hour.
4. Total the products.

PROBLEM 2

Renee Olson, an employee of American Realty, worked 44 hours during week 18 of 2003. Her regular pay is $5.75 per hour. Overtime at American Realty is time-and-a-half (1.5 times regular pay). Calculate Renee's gross pay for week 18 using steps 1, 2, and 4 above (see Figure 17.2).

Step 1: Begin by multiplying $5.75 regular pay per hour by 40 regular hours per week.

Step 2: Multiply $5.75 × 1.5 to find the overtime rate. Multiply the overtime rate by the 4 hours of overtime Renee worked.

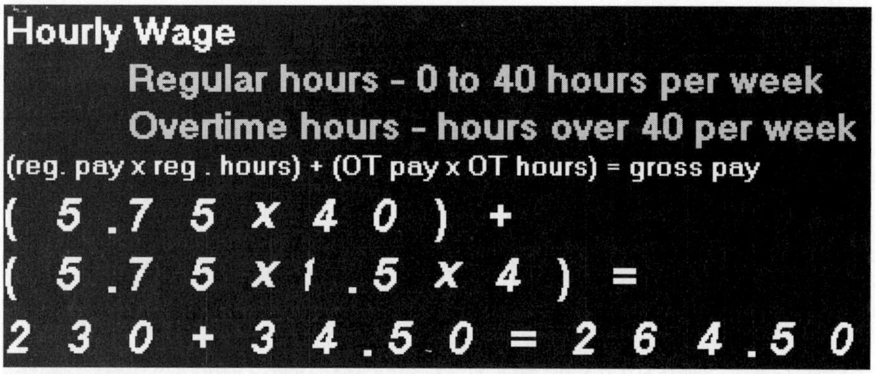

Hourly Wage

Regular hours – 0 to 40 hours per week

Overtime hours – hours over 40 per week

(reg. pay x reg . hours) + (OT pay x OT hours) = gross pay

$$(\ 5.75 \ X \ 40 \ ) \ +$$

$$(\ 5.75 \ X \ 1.5 \ X \ 4 \ ) \ =$$

$$230 + 34.50 = 264.50$$

FIGURE 17.2   Gross pay calculation based on hourly wage.

Step 3: Add the two results to find gross pay for week 18.

Calculator Procedure

MC 5.75 $\times$ 40 = $\boxed{230}$ M+ 5.75 $\times$ 1.5 $\times$ 4 = $\boxed{34.5}$ M+ MR $\boxed{264.50}$

COMMISSIONS

There are several types of commissions. We will discuss three types: straight commission, commission plus salary, and sliding scale commissions. We begin with straight commission, that is, commission only.

A **commission** is an amount paid based on a percent of sales. For example, a used-car salesman earns 8% on each car sold. If he sells a car for $10,000, his commission is $800. How do we know this? In the percentage formula, the car sales figure ($10,000) is the base, the commission percent (8%) is the rate, and the result of multiplying base times rate is the percentage, or in this case the salesman's commission ($800).

PROBLEM 3

Don Danvers had furniture sales of $120,000 during a biweekly (2 week) pay period. If his commission rate is 2%, how much did he earn in commissions? See Figure 17.3.

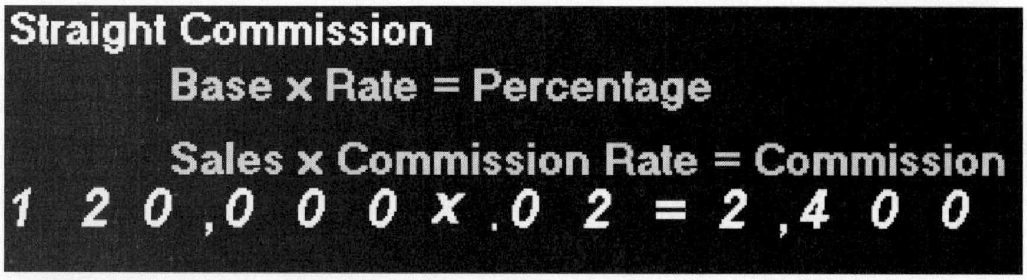

Straight Commission

Base x Rate = Percentage

Sales x Commission Rate = Commission

$$120,000 \ X \ .02 = 2,400$$

FIGURE 17.3   Calculation of straight commission.

SALARY PLUS COMMISSION

The **salary plus commission** method involves paying an employee a base salary plus a commission on all sales over a given quota. A **quota** is the amount of sales a salesperson must make before any commission is paid.

PROBLEM 4

Robert Copeland earns a base monthly salary of $2,000 plus a 1% commission on all sales over $100,000. In January he had sales of $120,000. Calculate Robert's gross pay for January (see Figure 17.4).

Salary plus Commission
Base salary + (sales above quota x commission rate) = gross pay

$$2,000 + (120,000 -$$
$$100,000) \times .01 =$$
$$2,000 + 200 = 2,200$$

FIGURE 17.4   Calculation of gross pay based on salary plus commission.

Begin by calculating how much his sales were above his quota:

$120,000 in sales $-$ $100,000 quota $=$ $20,000 sales over quota

Multiply the sales over quota by his commission rate of 1% converted to a decimal number:

$20,000 $\times$ .01 $=$ $200

Add the base salary and his commission to find gross pay:

$20,000 $+$ $200 $=$ $2,200

Pocket Calculator Procedure

MC 2,000 M+ 120,000 $-$ 100,000 $=$ $\boxed{20,000}$ $\times$ .01 $=$ $\boxed{200}$ + MR $=$ $\boxed{2,200}$

Desktop Calculator Procedure

MT 2,000 M+ 120,000 + 100,000 $-$ $\boxed{20,000}$ $\times$ 1% $\boxed{200}$ M+ MT $\boxed{2,200}$

SLIDING SCALE COMMISSION

In the **sliding scale commission** method commissions are paid on a graduated basis. As sales pass certain levels, the commission rate changes. In Figure 17.5 the sliding scale shows that employees earn 5% on the first $10,000 in sales, 6% on the next $10,000 in sales, and 7% on the next $10,000 in sales.

PROBLEM 5

Using the scale in Figure 17.5, calculate Tom Grey's commission on sales of $28,000 in March.
    Begin by multiplying the amount of sales on each level by the specified rate. Tom had $10,000 in sales at the 5% level, $10,000 in sales at the 6% level, and $8,000 in sales at the 7% level. Add together the commissions for the three levels to find gross pay as shown in Figure 17.5.

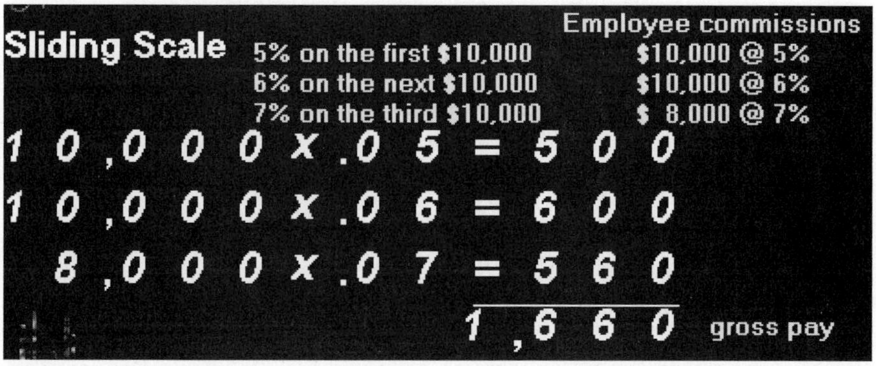

FIGURE 17.5   Calculation of gross pay based on a sliding scale commission.

Calculator Procedure

MC 10,000 × .05 = $\boxed{500}$ M+ 10,000 × .06 = $\boxed{600}$ M+ 8,000 × .07 = $\boxed{560}$ M+ MR $\boxed{1,660}$

PIECE RATE

Employees may be paid based on how much they produce. Medical transcribers may be paid on how many pages they type. Crafters may be paid for the number of pieces they complete, which is also referred to as "piecework." Two piecework methods will be discussed here: piece rate and differential piecework rate. An employee paid by the **piece rate** method earns a certain amount for each piece produced.

PROBLEM 6

Employees of Moore Fabricators earn $.10 for each piece. Calculate the gross pay for an employee who produces 6,000 pieces. See Figure 17.6.

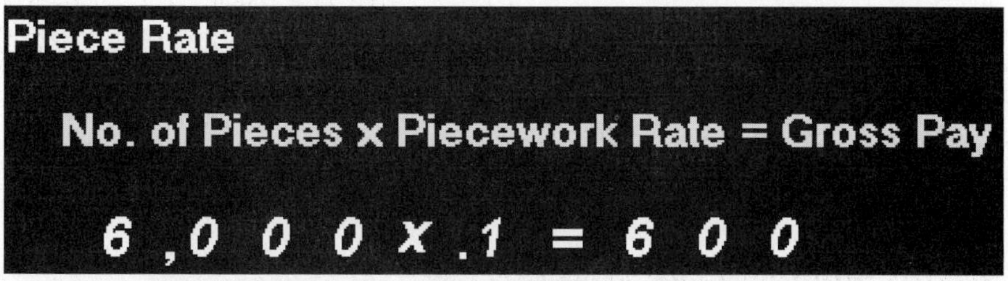

FIGURE 17.6   Calculation of gross pay based on a piece rate.

DIFFERENTIAL PIECEWORK RATE

A scale is used to calculate pay for an employee paid on the **differential piecework rate** method. The scale in Figure 17.7 shows that for the first 500 pieces produced, $1.50 is paid for each piece; for the next 100 pieces, $1.60 is paid for each piece; and for the next 100 pieces, $1.70 is paid for each piece.

PROBLEM 7

Tober Products uses the scale in Figure 17.7 to pay its workers using the differential piecework rate method. Calculate gross pay if Anna Smith, a Tober Products employee, produced 650 pieces.

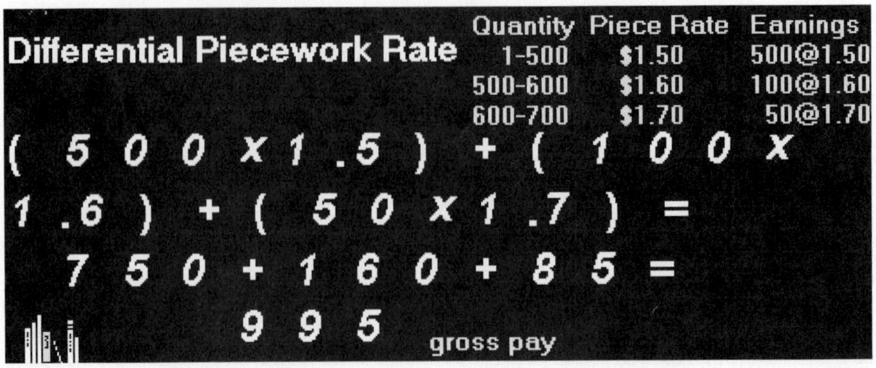

FIGURE 17.7 Calculation of gross pay based on a differential piecework rate.

Begin by calculating the amount to be paid for each level of the scale and then add the products to find gross pay. Anna produced 500 pieces at the $1.50 rate, 100 pieces at the $1.60 rate, and 50 pieces at the $1.70 rate. Therefore, she earned

$750 for the first 500 pieces	$500 \times \$1.50$
$160 for the next 100 pieces	$100 \times \$1.60$
$85 for the last 50 pieces	$50 \times \$1.70$

for a gross pay of $995.00.

Calculator Procedure

MC 500 × 1.5 = 750 M+ 100 × 1.6 = 160 M+ 50 × 1.7 = 85 M+ MR 995 gross pay.

NET PAY

As stated earlier, net pay equals gross pay minus deductions (see Figure 17.8). **Deductions** are amounts withheld from the employee's pay by the employer at the direction of the government or the employee. Typical deductions include federal income tax, Social Security, Medicare, health insurance premiums, union dues, employee savings, and employee retirement plans. Some states also require that state income taxes be deducted from employee pay. Some cities have a city income tax.

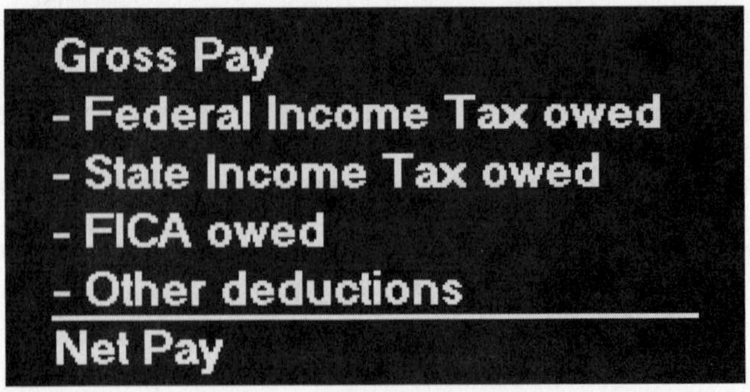

FIGURE 17.8 Sample net pay formula.

When an employee is hired, he or she must complete certain forms. These include a W-4 form, which guides the employer in determining how much income tax to deduct from gross pay each pay period. Form W-4 Employee's Withholding Allowance Certificate and the accompanying worksheet are shown in Figures 17.9 and 17.10.

(*Note: All Internal Revenue Service [IRS] forms in this chapter are from IRS Publication 15-T New Withholding Tables for Wages Paid Through December 2004.*)

Form W-4 (2003)

Purpose. Complete Form W-4 so that your employer can withhold the correct Federal income tax from your pay. Because your tax situation may change, you may want to refigure your withholding each year.

Exemption from withholding. If you are exempt, complete only lines 1, 2, 3, 4, and 7 and sign the form to validate it. Your exemption for 2003 expires February 16, 2004. See **Pub. 505,** Tax Withholding and Estimated Tax.

Note: *You cannot claim exemption from withholding if: (a) your income exceeds $750 and includes more than $250 of unearned income (e.g., interest and dividends) and (b) another person can claim you as a dependent on their tax return.*

Basic instructions. If you are not exempt, complete the **Personal Allowances Worksheet** below. The worksheets on page 2 adjust your withholding allowances based on itemized deductions, certain credits, adjustments to income, or two-earner/two-job situations. Complete all worksheets that apply. **However, you may claim fewer (or zero) allowances.**

Head of household. Generally, you may claim head of household filing status on your tax return only if you are unmarried and pay more than 50% of the costs of keeping up a home for yourself and your dependent(s) or other qualifying individuals. See line **E** below.

Tax credits. You can take projected tax credits into account in figuring your allowable number of withholding allowances. Credits for child or dependent care expenses and the child tax credit may be claimed using the **Personal Allowances Worksheet** below. See **Pub. 919,** How Do I Adjust My Tax Withholding? for information on converting your other credits into withholding allowances.

Nonwage income. If you have a large amount of nonwage income, such as interest or dividends, consider making estimated tax payments using **Form 1040-ES,** Estimated Tax for Individuals. Otherwise, you may owe additional tax.

Two earners/two jobs. If you have a working spouse or more than one job, figure the total number of allowances you are entitled to claim on all jobs using worksheets from only one Form W-4. Your withholding usually will be most accurate when all allowances are claimed on the Form W-4 for the highest paying job and zero allowances are claimed on the others.

Nonresident alien. If you are a nonresident alien, see the **Instructions for Form 8233** before completing this Form W-4.

Check your withholding. After your Form W-4 takes effect, use Pub. 919 to see how the dollar amount you are having withheld compares to your projected total tax for 2003. See Pub. 919, especially if your earnings exceed $125,000 (Single) or $175,000 (Married).

Recent name change? If your name on line 1 differs from that shown on your social security card, call 1-800-772-1213 for a new social security card.

Personal Allowances Worksheet (Keep for your records.)

A Enter "1" for **yourself** if no one else can claim you as a dependent . . . . **A** _____

B Enter "1" if:
- You are single and have only one job; or
- You are married, have only one job, and your spouse does not work; or
- Your wages from a second job or your spouse's wages (or the total of both) are $1,000 or less.

B _____

C Enter "1" for your **spouse.** But, you may choose to enter "-0-" if you are married and have either a working spouse or more than one job. (Entering "-0-" may help you avoid having too little tax withheld.) . . . . **C** _____

D Enter number of **dependents** (other than your spouse or yourself) you will claim on your tax return . . . . . **D** _____

E Enter "1" if you will file as **head of household** on your tax return (see conditions under **Head of household** above) . **E** _____

F Enter "1" if you have at least $1,500 of **child or dependent care expenses** for which you plan to claim a credit . **F** _____

(**Note:** *Do not include child support payments. See* **Pub. 503,** *Child and Dependent Care Expenses, for details.*)

G **Child Tax Credit** (including additional child tax credit):
- If your total income will be between $15,000 and $42,000 ($20,000 and $65,000 if married), enter "1" for each eligible child plus **1 additional** if you have three to five eligible children or **2 additional** if you have six or more eligible children.
- If your total income will be between $42,000 and $80,000 ($65,000 and $115,000 if married), enter "1" if you have one or two eligible children, "2" if you have three eligible children, "3" if you have four eligible children, or "4" if you have five or more eligible children. **G** _____

H Add lines A through G and enter total here. **Note:** *This may be different from the number of exemptions you claim on your tax return.* ▶ **H** _____

For accuracy, complete all worksheets that apply.
- If you plan to **itemize or claim adjustments to income** and want to reduce your withholding, see the **Deductions and Adjustments Worksheet** on page 2.
- If you have **more than one job** or are **married and you and your spouse both work** and the combined earnings from all jobs exceed $35,000, see the **Two-Earner/Two-Job Worksheet** on page 2 to avoid having too little tax withheld.
- If **neither** of the above situations applies, **stop here** and enter the number from line H on line 5 of Form W-4 below.

- **Cut here and give Form W-4 to your employer. Keep the top part for your records.** - - - - - - - - - - - - - - - - -

Form **W-4**
Department of the Treasury
Internal Revenue Service

Employee's Withholding Allowance Certificate

▶ **For Privacy Act and Paperwork Reduction Act Notice, see page 2.**

OMB No. 1545-0010

20**03**

1 Type or print your first name and middle initial	Last name	2 Your social security number

Home address (number and street or rural route)

3 ☐ Single ☐ Married ☐ Married, but withhold at higher Single rate.
Note: *If married, but legally separated, or spouse is a nonresident alien, check the "Single" box.*

City or town, state, and ZIP code

4 If your last name differs from that shown on your social security card, check here. You must call 1-800-772-1213 for a new card. ▶ ☐

5	Total number of allowances you are claiming (from line **H** above **or** from the applicable worksheet on page 2)	5	
6	Additional amount, if any, you want withheld from each paycheck	6	$
7	I claim exemption from withholding for 2003, and I certify that I meet **both** of the following conditions for exemption:		

- Last year I had a right to a refund of **all** Federal income tax withheld because I had **no** tax liability **and**
- This year I expect a refund of **all** Federal income tax withheld because I expect to have **no** tax liability.

If you meet both conditions, write "Exempt" here . . . . ▶ | 7 | |

Under penalties of perjury, I certify that I am entitled to the number of withholding allowances claimed on this certificate, or I am entitled to claim exempt status.

Employee's signature
(Form is not valid unless you sign it.) ▶ _____ Date ▶ _____

8 Employer's name and address (Employer: Complete lines 8 and 10 only if sending to the IRS.)	9 Office code (optional)	10 Employer identification number

Cat. No. 10220Q

FIGURE 17.9 Front of Form W-4.

The income tax deduction is based on gross pay, marital status, and the number of dependents claimed. An employee is allowed to claim a **withholding allowance** (an exemption from paying a certain amount of taxes) for himself or herself, his or her spouse, and each child, elderly person, or other dependent that he or she supports. The dependents can be claimed only once. For example, if a husband and wife of a household with two children both work, only one of them may claim any one dependent in the household. Following are the choices that could be made by the couple:

1. One spouse may elect to claim himself or herself and one child; the other spouse may elect to claim himself or herself and one child.

Form W-4 (2003)   Page **2**

Deductions and Adjustments Worksheet

Note: *Use this worksheet **only** if you plan to itemize deductions, claim certain credits, or claim adjustments to income on your 2003 tax return.*

1 Enter an estimate of your 2003 itemized deductions. These include qualifying home mortgage interest, charitable contributions, state and local taxes, medical expenses in excess of 7.5% of your income, and miscellaneous deductions. (For 2003, you may have to reduce your itemized deductions if your income is over $139,500 ($69,750 if married filing separately). See **Worksheet 3** in Pub. 919 for details.) . . **1** $ _____

2 Enter:
   $7,950 if married filing jointly or qualifying widow(er)
   $7,000 if head of household
   $4,750 if single
   $3,975 if married filing separately   . . . . **2** $ _____

3 **Subtract** line 2 from line 1. If line 2 is greater than line 1, enter "-0-" . . . . **3** $ _____
4 Enter an estimate of your 2003 adjustments to income, including alimony, deductible IRA contributions, and student loan interest **4** $ _____
5 **Add** lines 3 and 4 and enter the total. Include any amount for credits from **Worksheet 7** in Pub. 919 . **5** $ _____
6 Enter an estimate of your 2003 nonwage income (such as dividends or interest) . . . . **6** $ _____
7 **Subtract** line 6 from line 5. Enter the result, but not less than "-0-" . . . . **7** $ _____
8 **Divide** the amount on line 7 by $3,000 and enter the result here. Drop any fraction . . . . . . **8** _____
9 Enter the number from the **Personal Allowances Worksheet**, line H, page 1 . . . . . . **9** _____
10 **Add** lines 8 and 9 and enter the total here. If you plan to use the **Two-Earner/Two-Job Worksheet**, also enter this total on line 1 below. Otherwise, **stop here** and enter this total on Form W-4, line 5, page 1 . **10** _____

Two-Earner/Two-Job Worksheet

Note: *Use this worksheet **only** if the instructions under line H on page 1 direct you here.*

1 Enter the number from line H, page 1 (or from line 10 above if you used the **Deductions and Adjustments Worksheet**) **1** _____
2 Find the number in **Table 1** below that applies to the **lowest** paying job and enter it here . . . . . **2** _____
3 If line 1 is **more than or equal to** line 2, subtract line 2 from line 1. Enter the result here (if zero, enter "-0-") and on Form W-4, line 5, page 1. **Do not** use the rest of this worksheet . . . . **3** _____

Note: *If line 1 is **less than** line 2, enter "-0-" on Form W-4, line 5, page 1. Complete lines 4–9 below to calculate the additional withholding amount necessary to avoid a year-end tax bill.*

4 Enter the number from line 2 of this worksheet . . . . **4** _____
5 Enter the number from line 1 of this worksheet . . . . **5** _____
6 **Subtract** line 5 from line 4 . . . . **6** _____
7 Find the amount in **Table 2** below that applies to the **highest** paying job and enter it here . . . . **7** $ _____
8 **Multiply** line 7 by line 6 and enter the result here. This is the additional annual withholding needed . . **8** $ _____
9 Divide line 8 by the number of pay periods remaining in 2003. For example, divide by 26 if you are paid every two weeks and you complete this form in December 2002. Enter the result here and on Form W-4, line 6, page 1. This is the additional amount to be withheld from each paycheck . . . . **9** $ _____

Table 1: Two-Earner/Two-Job Worksheet

Married Filing Jointly				All Others			
If wages from **LOWEST** paying job are—	Enter on line 2 above	If wages from **LOWEST** paying job are—	Enter on line 2 above	If wages from **LOWEST** paying job are—	Enter on line 2 above	If wages from **LOWEST** paying job are—	Enter on line 2 above
$0 - $4,000	0	44,001 - 50,000	8	$0 - $6,000	0	75,001 - 100,000	8
4,001 - 9,000	1	50,001 - 60,000	9	6,001 - 11,000	1	100,001 - 110,000	9
9,001 - 15,000	2	60,001 - 70,000	10	11,001 - 18,000	2	110,001 and over	10
15,001 - 20,000	3	70,001 - 90,000	11	18,001 - 25,000	3		
20,001 - 25,000	4	90,001 - 100,000	12	25,001 - 29,000	4		
25,001 - 33,000	5	100,001 - 115,000	13	29,001 - 40,000	5		
33,001 - 38,000	6	115,001 - 125,000	14	40,001 - 55,000	6		
38,001 - 44,000	7	125,001 and over	15	55,001 - 75,000	7		

Table 2: Two-Earner/Two-Job Worksheet

Married Filing Jointly		All Others	
If wages from **HIGHEST** paying job are—	Enter on line 7 above	If wages from **HIGHEST** paying job are—	Enter on line 7 above
$0 - $50,000	$450	$0 - $30,000	$450
50,001 - 100,000	800	30,001 - 70,000	800
100,001 - 150,000	900	70,001 - 140,000	900
150,001 - 270,000	1,050	140,001 - 300,000	1,050
270,001 and over	1,200	300,001 and over	1,200

FIGURE 17.10 Back of Form W-4.

2. One spouse may elect to claim himself or herself and two dependents; the other spouse may elect to claim only himself or herself.
3. One spouse may elect to claim all four of the dependents in the household and the other spouse would then claim no deductions.
4. Sometimes when the two salaries are combined, a couple finds themselves in a higher tax bracket and owes taxes at the end of the year. To avoid this, some couples take none or only part of their allowed withholding allowances, which results in more taxes being withheld from their paychecks and less taxes being owed at the end of the year. Another option is to direct the employer to withhold additional federal income tax each pay period.

CALCULATING DEDUCTIONS

Federal Income Tax Withholding

As stated previously, **federal income tax** is based on gross pay, marital status, and withholding allowances (exemptions) claimed by the employee. Tables are provided for married and single employees for weekly, biweekly, monthly, annual, and so on, periods. The most recent tables are available at www.irs.gov. A partial IRS tax table for Single Persons—Weekly Payroll Period is shown in Figure 17.11.

SINGLE Persons—WEEKLY Payroll Period
(For Wages Paid Through December 2004)

If the wages are—		And the number of withholding allowances claimed is—										
At least	But less than	0	1	2	3	4	5	6	7	8	9	10
		The amount of income tax to be withheld is—										
$0	$55	$0	$0	$0	$0	$0	$0	$0	$0	$0	$0	$0
55	60	1	0	0	0	0	0	0	0	0	0	0
60	65	1	0	0	0	0	0	0	0	0	0	0
65	70	2	0	0	0	0	0	0	0	0	0	0
70	75	2	0	0	0	0	0	0	0	0	0	0
75	80	3	0	0	0	0	0	0	0	0	0	0
80	85	3	0	0	0	0	0	0	0	0	0	0
85	90	4	0	0	0	0	0	0	0	0	0	0
90	95	4	0	0	0	0	0	0	0	0	0	0
95	100	5	0	0	0	0	0	0	0	0	0	0
100	105	5	0	0	0	0	0	0	0	0	0	0
105	110	6	0	0	0	0	0	0	0	0	0	0
110	115	6	0	0	0	0	0	0	0	0	0	0
115	120	7	1	0	0	0	0	0	0	0	0	0
120	125	7	1	0	0	0	0	0	0	0	0	0
125	130	8	2	0	0	0	0	0	0	0	0	0
130	135	8	2	0	0	0	0	0	0	0	0	0
135	140	9	3	0	0	0	0	0	0	0	0	0
140	145	9	3	0	0	0	0	0	0	0	0	0
145	150	10	4	0	0	0	0	0	0	0	0	0
150	155	10	4	0	0	0	0	0	0	0	0	0
155	160	11	5	0	0	0	0	0	0	0	0	0
160	165	11	5	0	0	0	0	0	0	0	0	0
165	170	12	6	0	0	0	0	0	0	0	0	0
170	175	12	6	0	0	0	0	0	0	0	0	0
175	180	13	7	1	0	0	0	0	0	0	0	0
180	185	13	7	1	0	0	0	0	0	0	0	0
185	190	14	8	2	0	0	0	0	0	0	0	0
190	195	14	8	2	0	0	0	0	0	0	0	0
195	200	15	9	3	0	0	0	0	0	0	0	0
200	210	16	9	3	0	0	0	0	0	0	0	0
210	220	18	10	4	0	0	0	0	0	0	0	0
220	230	19	11	5	0	0	0	0	0	0	0	0
230	240	21	12	6	1	0	0	0	0	0	0	0
240	250	22	13	7	2	0	0	0	0	0	0	0
250	260	24	15	8	3	0	0	0	0	0	0	0
260	270	25	16	9	4	0	0	0	0	0	0	0
270	280	27	18	10	5	0	0	0	0	0	0	0
280	290	28	19	11	6	0	0	0	0	0	0	0
290	300	30	21	12	7	1	0	0	0	0	0	0
300	310	31	22	13	8	2	0	0	0	0	0	0
310	320	33	24	15	9	3	0	0	0	0	0	0
320	330	34	25	16	10	4	0	0	0	0	0	0
330	340	36	27	18	11	5	0	0	0	0	0	0
340	350	37	28	19	12	6	0	0	0	0	0	0

FIGURE 17.11 Partial IRS Tax Table, Single Persons—Weekly Payroll Period.

PROBLEM 8

Jean Riley's gross pay for week 10 is $346.57. Jean is single and has claimed one withholding allowance on her W-4 Form filed with her employer. How much federal income tax should be withheld from her pay?

Look at the data in Figure 17.11. The bottom row of the first two columns of the tax table indicates the range of wages of at least $340 but less than $350. Jean's wages fall within this range. The next three columns indicate the amount of income tax to be withheld for that wage if the number of withholding allowances claimed is 0, 1, 2, and so on. Because she claims 1 dependent, the amount of income tax to be withheld is $28.

State and Local Income Tax Withholding

State and local income taxes are collected by some states and cities. Some states have an income tax that consists of a percentage of the federal income tax. Some states, such as New York State, have a set of tables that indicate the amount of taxes to withhold. Some cities, such as New York City, use the state income tax tables; others, such as Yonkers, use a percentage of state income tax. Figure 17.12 indicates that Yonkers has a city income tax of 0.05 times the New York State income tax. For example, if a person's New York State income tax is $78, multiply the tax by 0.05 to find Yonker's city income tax:

$$\$78 \times 0.05 = \$3.90$$

The amount of the **standard deduction** (a deduction that everyone gets) and the amount for each exemption may vary. Examples of New York State (NYS), New York City, and Yonkers income taxes are shown in Figure 17.12. The examples indicate the taxes to be withheld from a single person who claims one exemption and has an annual salary of $26,251.42.

New York State Income Tax	
Single, 1 exemption	
Annual Salary	26,251.42
Standard Deduction	-6,975.00
Exemption Amount for each Withholding Allowance	-1,000.00
Taxable Income	18,276.42
Total Annual Tax (from NYS tax table)	*871.31
*Divide tax by number of pay periods per year	
New York City Income Tax	
Single, 1 exemption	
Annual Salary	26,251.42
Standard Deduction	-5,000.00
Exemption Amount for each Withholding Allowance	-1,000.00
Taxable Income	20,251.42
Total Annual Tax (from NYS tax table)	*560.30
*Divide tax by number of pay periods per year	
Yonkers City Income Tax	
Single, 1 exemption	
Total Annual NY State Income Tax (from NYS tax return)	871.31
Tax Rate	x 0.05
Annual Yonkers City Income Tax	*43.57
*Divide tax by number of pay periods per year	
Note: Yonkers City tax is .05 of New York State income tax.	

FIGURE 17.12   Examples of New York State, New York City, and Yonkers income taxes.

PROBLEM 9

Jean Riley's state has a state income tax rate of 12% of *federal income tax*. If her federal income tax for the week is $28, calculate the amount of state income tax to be withheld.

Use the percentage formula, $\$28 \times .12 = \$3.36$, to find the amount to be deducted from her gross pay for state income tax.

Social Security (FICA)

The Federal Insurance Contributions Act (FICA) is commonly known as **Social Security**. Social Security pays a monthly benefit after an employee retires or is disabled as well as certain other benefits. In this book we will use a Social Security tax rate of 6.2% of the first $87,000 of annual gross pay (the FICA ceiling). Once an employee earns more than $87,000 in one year, Social Security tax is no longer collected. The **year-to-date earnings** amount is a running total of an employee's gross earnings for the current year. Always check the employee's pay record for year-to-date earnings before calculating Social Security to see whether the employee has reached the Social Security ceiling. The rate and ceiling are subject to change, so check for up-to-date information each year.

Medicare

Medicare helps to pay the medical expenses of those age 65 years or older. The Medicare tax rate used in this book is 1.45% of all gross pay. There is no gross pay ceiling for Medicare. Again, check annually for any changes in the Medicare tax rate.

PROBLEM 10

Jean Riley has earned $4,080 so far this year. Her gross weekly pay is $346.57. Calculate the FICA and Medicare deductions.

FICA	
346.57 x .062 =	21.49
MediCare	
346.57 x .0145 =	5.03
Total FICA deduction	26.52

FIGURE 17.13 Calculation of Social Security and Medicare deductions.

Multiply the gross pay by 6.2% (or the decimal equivalent, .062).

Multiply gross pay by 1.45% (or the decimal equivalent, .0145).

Other Deductions

Along with the deductions for taxes, an employer may elect to deduct amounts specified by the employee for other items such as health insurance premiums, savings, retirement plans, union dues, and so on.

PROBLEM 11

Jean's health insurance premiums are paid by her company as an employee benefit. Therefore no deductions are made for health insurance premiums. However, Jean has an automatic payroll deduction made to her savings account of $35 weekly (other deductions). Calculate Jean's net pay using the deductions calculated beginning with Problem 8.

$346.57	Gross Pay
-28.00	-Federal Income Tax Deduction
-3.36	-State Income Tax Deduction
-21.49	- Social Security Deduction
-5.03	-Medicare Deduction
-35.00	-Other Deductions
$253.69	Net Pay

FIGURE 17.14 Calculation of net pay.

After subtracting all amounts to be withheld from Jean's weekly pay, her net pay is $253.69. Her paycheck will be written for this amount.

PERCENTAGE METHOD OF WITHHOLDING

Sometimes employers use the percentage method instead of the table method described previously when calculating federal income tax deductions. The **percentage method of withholding** is an alternate method used to calculate federal income tax to be deducted from an employee's gross pay. It is a two-part process:

1. A table is consulted to determine the amount of one withholding allowance for a specified type of pay period such as weekly, monthly, and so on.
2. A second table is consulted to determine how much income should be multiplied by what rate to find the income tax deduction.
3. Federal income tax is calculated.

PROBLEM 12

Use Jean as an example again—she is single, claims one exemption, is paid weekly, and her gross pay this week is $346.57. Calculate the amount of her federal income tax deduction.

Step 1: Consult the IRS Table 1. Percentage Method—Amount for One Withholding Allowance (shown in Figure 17.15). Look at the Weekly line to find the amount for one withholding allowance for a weekly payroll period. Subtract this amount from gross pay: $346.57 − $59.62 = $286.95.

Note: If a person has more than one withholding allowance, simply multiply the amount for one withholding allowance by the number of withholding allowances claimed by the employee.

Table 1. Percentage Method—Amount for One Withholding Allowance

Payroll Period	One Withholding Allowance
Weekly	$59.62
Biweekly	119.23
Semimonthly	129.17
Monthly	258.33
Quarterly	775.00
Semiannually	1,550.00
Annually	3,100.00
Daily or miscellaneous (each day of the payroll period)	11.92

FIGURE 17.15

Step 2: After the amount for withholding allowances has been subtracted from gross pay, consult the IRS Tables for Percentage Method of Withholding, Table 1—Weekly Payroll Period for Single Person shown in Figure 17.16.

Tables for Percentage Method of Withholding
(For Wages Paid Through December 2004)

TABLE 1—WEEKLY Payroll Period

(a) SINGLE person (including head of household)—

If the amount of wages (after subtracting withholding allowances) is: Over—	But not over—	The amount of income tax to withhold is:	of excess over—
Not over $51		$0	
$51	—$187	10%	—$51
$187	—$592	$13.60 plus 15%	—$187
$592	—$1,317	$74.35 plus 25%	—$592
$1,317	—$2,860	$255.60 plus 28%	—$1,317
$2,860	—$6,177	$687.64 plus 33%	—$2,860
$6,177		$1,782.25 plus 35%	—$6,177

(b) MARRIED person—

If the amount of wages (after subtracting withholding allowances) is: Over—	But not over—	The amount of income tax to withhold is:	of excess over—
Not over $154		$0	
$154	—$429	10%	—$154
$429	—$1,245	$27.50 plus 15%	—$429
$1,245	—$2,270	$149.90 plus 25%	—$1,245
$2,270	—$3,568	$406.15 plus 28%	—$2,270
$3,568	—$6,271	$769.59 plus 33%	—$3,568
$6,271		$1,661.58 plus 35%	—$6,271

FIGURE 17.16

Note the text above the first two columns: "If the amount of wages (after subtracting withholding allowances) is:". This refers to the adjusted gross income figure that was determined in the first step, $286.95. The first two columns read "Over—" and "But not over—." Find the line with the pay range in which Jean's adjusted gross income falls. In this case the income falls between $187 and $502. The third and fourth columns on this line tell us that the amount of income tax to withhold is $13.60 *plus* 15% of adjusted gross income over $187.

Therefore, before applying the 15% tax, subtract $187 from the adjusted gross income: $286.95 − $187 = $99.95. Multiply the difference by 15%: $99.95 × .15 = $14.99. Add to $13.60. The amount of income tax to be withheld from the employee's pay is 13.60 + 14.99 = $28.59. Round to $29 (see Figure 17.17).

```
  $346.57   Gross Pay
   -59.62   1 withholding allowance for weekly pay period
   286.95   Adjusted Gross Income
  -187.00   Subtract to find excess over $187
    99.95
    x .15   Find 15% of excess over $187
    14.99
 +  13.60
    28.59   Federal Income Tax to be withheld (Round to $29)
```

FIGURE 17.17   Calculation of FIT using the percentage method of withholding.

AUTOMATED PAYROLL SYSTEMS

Formula tables for percentage-method withholding and alternatives for automated payroll systems are also available in IRS Publication T-15.

ROUNDING WITHHOLDING AMOUNTS

When businesses use the percentage method or an alternative method of calculating income tax withholding, the tax for the pay period may be rounded to the nearest dollar. If rounding is used, it must be used consistently. Amounts less than 50 cents should be dropped, and amounts of 50 cents or more should be increased to the next higher dollar.

Name _____

Class/Section _____

Score (Correct Answers ÷ No. of Assigned Problems) _____

PART 2   *Business Math Skills*

Exercise 1   Calculating Gross Pay

Calculate gross pay according to the specified method for each of the employees in the following problems. No employee has reached the Social Security ceiling of $87,000.

1. Karen Koto's yearly salary is $40,250. How much did she earn last month? _____
2. Last week James Robinson worked 40 regular hours, 12 hours overtime at time and a half, and 3 hours overtime at double time. His hourly wage is $8.95 per hour. _____

3. Sandra Brown finished 900 pieces last week at the piecework rate of $0.30 each. _____
4. John Reyna finished 345 pieces last week on the following piecework differential scale: 1 to 200 pieces, $2.59; 201 to 300 pieces, $2.65; and 301 to 400 pieces, $2.90. How much did he earn? _____
5. Ron Bakti is paid a 2% commission on all sales. Last month he sold $160,000. _____
6. January Baker earns $2,000 per month plus 1% on all sales over $80,000. Last month her sales totaled $225,000. _____
7. Kara Jenkins earns a commission on sales based on the following sliding scale: $1 to $30,000, 5%; $30,001 to $60,000, 6%; $60,001 to $100,000, 7.5%. What did she earn if her sales last month were $75,000? _____

Exercise 2   Calculating Net Pay

Use the information in Problems 1 through 7 to calculate net pay for the employees in the following problems. None of the employees has reached the Social Security ceiling. Use the tables to find the amount of the federal income tax deductions. Use 6.2% for Social Security and 1.45% for Medicare deductions.

8. Karen Kato (Problem 1) is married and claims one withholding allowance. _____
9. James Robinson (Problem 2) is married and claims three withholding allowances. _____
10. Sandra Brown is single and claims one withholding allowance. _____
11. John Reyna is single and claims two withholding allowances. _____
12. Ron Bakti is married and claims four withholding allowances. _____
13. January Baker is married and claims two withholding allowances. _____
14. Kara Jenkins is single and claims one withholding allowance. _____

Exercise 3

Use the percentage method to calculate federal income tax for the following employees. Round answers to whole dollars.

15. Mary Keller earned $750 during a biweekly payroll period. She is single and claims three withholding allowances. _____
16. Jeffrey Lewis earns a yearly salary of $39,855. He is married and claims two withholding allowances. What was his federal income tax for March? _____
17. Todd Lambert earns $910.85 weekly. He is single and claims no withholding allowances. _____
18. Jay Monroe earns $1,225.74 each biweekly pay period. He is married and claims two withholding allowances. _____
19. Mary Smith is married and claims one withholding allowance. She earns $890 weekly. _____
20. Jay Leonard earns $50,000 per year. He is paid semimonthly. He is single and claims one withholding allowance. _____

PART 3   *Review and Practice Using Business Math FUNdamentals*

GOAL: Complete 9 of the 10 problems correctly.

Instructions: *Start Business Math FUNdamentals. Complete Tutorials 38 and 39 and Drill 30. If you are not satisfied with your score, repeat the drill. Write your scores below.*

Business Math FUNdamentals Drill 30

Today's Date	Score

 PART 4   *The Desktop Calculator*

EMPLOYEE TIME CARD

Hourly employees have a time card for each pay period. Along with the employee's name and employee number, the dates and hours worked are given as handwritten, stamped, punched by a time clock, or computer generated.

At the end of the pay period, time cards are collected and the payroll clerk then calculates regular and overtime hours for each day. Some time cards contain an area where the payroll clerk can calculate total regular hours and total overtime hours for the entire pay period. Another section may be included for the computation of regular pay, overtime pay, and total gross pay. Other businesses may use a separate work sheet, payroll register, or payroll journal for recording the hourly wage information.

PROBLEM

The weekly time card in Figure 17.18 must be completed. The times that the employee reported in and out for work each day are shown on the time card. Pay is computed as follows:

Regular pay: 40 hours per week worked Monday through Friday.

Overtime pay at time and a half: hours more than 40 worked Monday through Saturday.

Overtime pay at double time: hours worked on Sundays and holidays.

John Jones' regular pay rate is $12.80.

<table>
<tr><td colspan="9" align="center">ABC Co. Weekly Time Card</td></tr>
<tr><td colspan="4">Pay Period Ending 8/10/2003</td><td colspan="3">Employee Name Jones, John</td><td colspan="2">Employee No. 98</td></tr>
<tr><td></td><td>Date</td><td>In</td><td>Out</td><td>In</td><td>Out</td><td>Hours Worked</td><td>Regular Hours</td><td>Overtime Hours</td></tr>
<tr><td>M</td><td>8/4</td><td>8:00</td><td>11:00</td><td>2:00</td><td>5:00</td><td></td><td></td><td></td></tr>
<tr><td>T</td><td>8/5</td><td>8:00</td><td>12:00</td><td>1:00</td><td>6:00</td><td></td><td></td><td></td></tr>
<tr><td>W</td><td>8/6</td><td>8:00</td><td>12:00</td><td>1:00</td><td>5:00</td><td></td><td></td><td></td></tr>
<tr><td>T</td><td>8/7</td><td>8:00</td><td>12:00</td><td>1:00</td><td>6:00</td><td></td><td></td><td></td></tr>
<tr><td>F</td><td>8/8</td><td>8:00</td><td>12:00</td><td>1:00</td><td>6:00</td><td></td><td></td><td></td></tr>
<tr><td>S</td><td>8/9</td><td>8:00</td><td>12:00</td><td></td><td></td><td></td><td></td><td></td></tr>
<tr><td>S</td><td>8/10</td><td></td><td></td><td></td><td></td><td></td><td></td><td></td></tr>
</table>

<table>
<tr><td colspan="4">For office use:</td></tr>
<tr><td></td><td></td><td colspan="2">Employee Pay Rate _____</td></tr>
<tr><td></td><td>Hours Worked</td><td>Rate</td><td>Gross Pay</td></tr>
<tr><td>Regular Hours</td><td></td><td></td><td></td></tr>
<tr><td>Overtime Hours @ 1.5</td><td></td><td></td><td></td></tr>
<tr><td>Overtime Hours @ 2</td><td></td><td></td><td></td></tr>
<tr><td>Totals</td><td></td><td></td><td></td></tr>
</table>

FIGURE 17.18

1. Begin by writing the number of regular and overtime hours worked each day (Figure 17.19). Calculate Monday's time as follows:

$$11 + 8 - T \boxed{3} M + 5 + 2 - T \boxed{3} M + MT \boxed{6}$$

		Date	In	Out	In	Out	Hours Worked	Regular Hours	Overtime Hours
				ABC Co. Weekly Time Card					
		Pay Period Ending 8/10/2003 Employee Name Jones, John					Employee No. _98_		
M		8/4	8:00	11:00	2:00	5:00	6	6	
T		8/5	8:00	12:00	1:00	6:00	9	9	
W		8/6	8:00	12:00	1:00	5:00	8	8	
T		8/7	8:00	12:00	1:00	6:00	9	9	
F		8/8	8:00	12:00	1:00	6:00	9	8	1
S		8/9	8:00	12:00			4		4
S		8/10	8:00	10:00			2		2

FIGURE 17.19

2. After the hours worked column has been completed, write the number of regular hours and overtime hours in the appropriate columns. In the ABC Co., once an employee has worked 40 hours Monday through Friday, overtime is paid. On Friday, the employee reached 41 hours worked for the week. Therefore, 8 hours are placed under regular hours and 1 hour is placed under overtime hours. Saturday and Sunday hours are overtime hours:

$$6 + 9 + 8 + 9 + 9 + T \boxed{41} + \boxed{40} - T \boxed{1}$$

For Office Use

			Employee Pay Rate _$12.80_
	Hours Worked	Rate ($/hr)	Gross Pay ($)
Regular hours	40	12.80	512.00
Overtime hours @ 1.5	5	19.20	96.00
Overtime hours @ 2	2	25.60	51.20
Totals	47		659.20

3. Complete the bottom section of the time card. Write the employee pay rate for regular hours. Transfer the number of regular hours to the hours worked column, multiply by the regular pay rate, and write the result in the gross pay column:

$$6 + 9 + 8 + 9 + 8 \, T \boxed{40} \times 12.80 = \boxed{\$512}$$

4. Transfer the number of overtime hours to be paid at time and a half to the hours-worked column. Multiply the regular pay rate by 1.5 and write the result in the rate column. Multiply by the overtime hours and write the result in the gross pay column:

$$12.8 \times 1.5 = \boxed{19.20} \times 5 = \boxed{96}$$

5. Repeat step 4 for overtime hours to be paid at 2 times the regular pay rate:

$$12.8 \times 2 = 25.6 \times 2 = \boxed{51.20}$$

6. Complete the hours worked and gross pay columns:

$$40 + 5 + 2 + T \boxed{47}$$
$$512 + 96 + 51.2 + T \boxed{659.2}$$

Payroll Register

Another type of record used is the payroll register. The hourly employees are listed along with total hours worked and regular pay rate for each employee. This information is used to calculate gross pay for each employee.

PROBLEM

A partial payroll register is shown below. Marital status is abbreviated to M/S and withholding allowances is abbreviated as W.A.

Payroll Register

Employee Number	Employee Name	M/S	W.A.	Gross Pay ($)	Year-to-Date Earnings ($)	Deductions ($) Federal	Social Security	Medicare	Other	Total Deductions ($)	Net Pay ($)
									For Week Ending August 16, 2005		
1981	Troy, L.	Single	0	1,150	37,950				85.50		

Reading across the payroll register, we see that Employee #1981 is single and claims no withholding allowance. He has $85.50 deducted for other deductions.

1. Using the IRS tables located at the end of this chapter, find the federal income tax to be withheld. In the Single Persons—Weekly Payroll table, find the line containing the gross pay of $1,150. On the same line under 0 withholding allowances, find the amount of tax to withhold: $215.00. Write this in the Federal column.

2. Find Social Security tax to be withheld. The year-to-date earnings column indicates that this employee has not reached the Social Security ceiling of $87,000. Multiply the gross pay by 6.2% and write the result in the Social Security column:

$$1,150 \text{ M+} \times .062 = \boxed{71.30}$$

Place gross pay in memory because it will be used again in steps 3 and 4.

3. Find Medicare tax to be withheld. Multiply gross pay by 1.45% and write the result in the Medicare column:

$$\text{MR} \boxed{1,150} \times .0145 = \boxed{16.675}$$

Round to hundredths: 16.68.

The payroll register should now look as follows:

Payroll Register

Employee Number	Employee Name	M/S	W.A.	Gross Pay ($)	Year-to-Date Earnings ($)	Deductions ($) Federal	Social Security	Medicare	Other	Total Deductions ($)	Net Pay ($)
									For Week Ending August 16, 2005		
1981	Troy, L.	Single	0	1,150	37,950	215.00	71.30	16.68	85.50		

4. Find net pay. Add all the deductions and write the result in the total deductions column. Subtract total deductions from gross pay. Write the difference in the net pay column:

$$215 + 71.30 + 16.68 + 85.50 + \text{T} \boxed{388.48} \text{ M− MR} \boxed{761.52}$$

DIFFERENTIAL PIECEWORK SCALE WORKSHEET

PROBLEM

M. Lee is an employee who is paid on the following differential piecework scale for items produced weekly:

1 to 600 pieces, $.55 each

601 to 800 pieces, $.65 each

801 to 999 pieces, $.75 each

When calculating gross pay using a sliding or differential piecework scale, setting up a worksheet is very helpful. A partial worksheet is shown below. M. Lee completed 810 pieces.

1. Place the number of pieces that were completed at each rate level in the appropriate columns: 600 pieces at .55, 200 pieces at .65, and 10 pieces at .75.

Employee Name	Total Pieces	1 to 600 Pieces @ 0.55		601 to 800 Pieces @ 0.65		801 to 999 Pieces @ 0.75		Gross Pay
Lee, M.	810	600	$_____	200	$_____	10	$_____	$____

2. Multiply the number of pieces in each level of the chart by the rate for that level and write the result in the appropriate column. Accumulate the totals to find gross pay:

$$600 \times .55 = \boxed{330} \ M+ \ 200 \times .65 = \boxed{130} \ M+ \ 10 \times .75 = \boxed{7.5} \ M+ \ MR \ \boxed{467.50}$$

Your table should now resemble the following:

Employee Name	Total Pieces	1 to 600 Pieces @ 0.55		601 to 800 Pieces @ 0.65		801 to 999 Pieces @ 0.75		Gross Pay
Lee, M.	810	600	$330.00	200	$130.00	10	$7.50	$467.50

Name _____

Class/Section _____

Score (Correct Answers ÷ No. of Assigned Problems) _____

 PART 4 *Desktop Calculator*

Exercise 1

Complete the following time card for Edward Jones, Employee #350. His hourly pay rate is $13.60. His is paid time and a half for hours over 40 per week Monday through Friday, time and a half for Saturday, and double time for Sundays and holidays. Half-hours are counted, quarter-hours are not.

ABC Co. Biweekly Time Card

	Date	In	Out	In	Out	Regular Hours	Overtime Hours
Pay Period Ending	*9/27/2005* Employee Name _____ Employee Number _____						
M	9/14	6:00	12:00	1:00	3:30	1. _____	_____
T	9/15	6:30	12:00	1:00	4:00	2. _____	_____
W	9/16	7:00	12:00	1:30	5:00	3. _____	_____
T	9/17	8:00	12:30	1:30	5:00	4. _____	_____
F	9/18	8:00	12:00	1:00	5:15	5. _____	_____
S	9/19	7:00	11:00			6. _____	_____
S	9/20			2:30	9:30	7. _____	_____
M	9/21	8:00	12:00	1:00	6:00	8. _____	_____
T	9/22	6:00	11:00	1:00	4:00	9. _____	_____
W	9/23	7:00	12:00	1:00	4:00	10. _____	_____
T	9/24	7:00	12:30	1:30	4:30	11. _____	_____
F	9/25	7:00	12:00	1:00	4:30	12. _____	_____
S	9/26	7:00	10:00			13. _____	
S	9/27					14. _____	

Employee Hourly Pay Rate _____

	Hours Worked	Gross Pay
Regular Hours		15. _____
Overtime hours @ 1.5		16. _____
Overtime hours @ 2		17. _____
Totals		18. _____

Exercise 2

Complete the following payroll register. Here, S indicates single, M indicates married, and YTD signifies year to date.

Payroll Register

						For Week Ending August 16, 2005						
							Deductions ($)					
	Employee Number	Employee Name	M/S	W.A.	Gross Pay ($)	YTD Earnings ($)	Federal	Social Security	Medicare	Other	Total Deductions ($)	Net Pay ($)
19.	1981	Brown, L.	S	0	950.98	28,529.40	____	____	____	55.50	____	____
20.	2222	Chaney, S.	M	2	1002.35	30,070.50	____	____	____	29.70	____	____
21.	2527	Taylor, S.	M	4	750.56	22,516.80	____	____	____	28.12	____	____
22.	2679	Sung, L.	M	3	832.21	24,966.30	____	____	____	15.90	____	____
23.	2780	Maybrey, I.	S	5	587.00	17,610.00	____	____	____	22.00	____	____
24.	2781	Canfield, J.	S	1	398.74	11,962.20	____	____	____	15.33	____	____

Exercise 3

Complete the following worksheet listing employees who are paid on the following differential piecework scale for items produced weekly. The total pieces for each employee are given.

1 to 600 pieces, $.55 each

601 to 800 pieces, $.65 each

801 to 999 pieces, $.75 each

	Employee Name	Total Pieces	1 to 600 Pieces @ 0.55		601 to 800 Pieces @ 0.65		801 to 999 Pieces @ 0.75		Gross Pay
25.	Lee, M.	810	600	$330.00	200	$130.00	10	$7.50	$467.50
26.	Johns, D.	790	___	____	___	____	___	____	____
27.	Gaylor, K.	698	___	____	___	____	___	____	____
28.	Curry, T.	910	___	____	___	____	___	____	____

Exercise 4

Strokes per Minute Score _____

Accuracy Score (Correct Strokes ÷ Total Strokes) _____

One-Minute Addition Timing (0 through 9 Keys, Five-Digit Numbers)

(Optional: Your instructor may wish you to use Touch Key on the computer for all your timings. Check with your instructor before completing this exercise.)

Complete as many of the problems as possible in 1 minute by adding. Work quickly and accurately. The number preceding each closing parenthesis indicates the cumulative number of strokes for problems attempted. For example, if you complete Problems 1 through 4 in 1 minute, your strokes-per-minute score is 244. Optional: 3 to 5-minute timings.

1. 43,556	2. 85,079	3. 16,544	4. 91,006	5. 11,850	6. 14,200	7. 36,000	8. 87,001
78,561	16,932	72,350	30,812	45,220	68,889	62,000	99,003
23,878	67,009	74,300	60,771	34,633	83,100	14,000	88,002
78,657	97,845	15,630	72,603	77,995	47,400	33,000	73,001
75,987	86,091	97,402	30,824	57,889	41,006	34,000	69,004
12,524	19,007	19,789	40,483	34,299	63,005	26,000	41,002
91,193	14,788	78,300	19,003	64,899	69,003	38,000	87,007
76,828	52,921	76,910	51,183	45,645	96,004	59,000	33,004
90,536	53,396	40,345	82,017	54,965	94,006	67,000	58,005
18,870	11,031	53,313	91,023	34,566	75,006	59,000	28,003
61)	122)	183)	244)	305)	366)	427)	488)

9. 81,400	10. 16,900	11. 36,987	12. 84,779	13. 74,450	14. 87,779	15. 76,000	16. 45,004
69,420	22,677	26,122	55,100	49,995	79,000	38,013	85,600
55,950	63,553	60,995	20,266	47,995	78,885	38,964	64,600
66,170	16,998	70,034	35,320	27,729	69,755	39,074	34,840
77,709	18,565	22,996	55,558	30,749	76,484	30,048	96,006
48,689	34,322	59,009	53,886	60,991	67,119	77,023	46,003
95,599	97,659	15,880	78,772	17,577	76,741	28,013	85,514
66,666	32,100	20,432	72,250	40,659	58,962	92,953	46,687
47,256	15,000	13,119	40,455	47,695	59,954	97,074	36,512
59,374	35,575	33,380	32,498	20,100	56,078	10,019	54,656
549)	610)	671)	732)	793)	854)	915)	976)

17. 18,900	18. 25,995	19. 96,100	20. 10,000	21. 72,349	22. 12,120	23. 76,213	24. 10,000
62,100	95,110	76,400	45,000	68,215	12,200	28,500	42,499
55,300	59,500	93,750	65,770	54,996	13,339	20,735	35,199
72,312	28,320	32,106	53,460	11,747	85,139	35,183	45,699
38,500	59,500	45,100	65,856	21,585	13,559	79,459	52,549
21,500	14,900	45,100	56,340	32,497	12,179	98,432	62,896
71,123	62,000	58,600	46,590	78,460	32,600	67,255	45,695
37,200	90,500	88,540	66,680	77,885	29,213	29,789	25,795
38,900	86,580	63,505	45,780	46,278	32,000	70,115	33,695
32,000	34,602	36,496	21,690	84,199	56,000	28,543	11,546
1,037)	1,098)	1,159)	1,220)	1,281)	1,342)	1,403)	1,464)

CHAPTER 17 *Terminology Review*

Commissions

Deductions

Differential piecework rate

Federal income tax

Gross pay

Hourly wage employees

Medicare

Net pay

Overtime hours

Percentage method of withholding

Piece rate

Quota

Regular hours
Salary plus commission
Sliding scale commissions
Social Security
Standard deduction
Withholding allowance
Year-to-date earnings

Write the correct term next to the appropriate description.

1. _____ The amount of an employee's earnings.
2. _____ An alternate method for calculating federal income tax withholding.
3. _____ An exemption from paying income taxes that an employee may claim for himself or herself or for a dependent.
4. _____ are paid a stated amount for each hour worked, usually up to 40 per week.
5. _____ The amount of sales required before a commission is paid.
6. _____ Helps pay medical expenses of those age 65 years or older.
7. _____ Commissions are paid on a graduated basis.
8. _____ Gross pay less deductions.
9. _____ Paying an employee a base salary plus a percent of sales over a given quota.
10. _____ A certain amount is paid for each piece produced by an employee.
11. _____ A running balance of an employee's earnings updated each pay period.
12. _____ Amounts paid employees based on a percent of sales.
13. _____ Pays a monthly retirement and other benefits.
14. _____ A graduated scale is used to pay an employee for the pieces produced.
15. _____ A stated number of hours worked each week at the employee's stated pay rate per hour.
16. _____ Tax collected by the federal government based on an employee's gross earnings and withholding allowances.
17. _____ Hours worked above the number of regular hours per week.
18. _____ Amounts withheld from an employee's pay by the employer at the direction of the government or the employee.

Name _____

Class/Section _____

Score (Correct Answers ÷ No. of Assigned Problems) _____

Chapter 17 Review Exercises

Exercise 1 Gross Pay

Calculate gross pay for each of the following employees for week 12 of 2005. Employees earn overtime at the rate of 1.5 for any hours above 40.

	Number	Name	Hours Worked	Regular Hours	Regular Hourly Rate ($)	Overtime Hours	Gross Pay ($)
1.	97	Balley, J.	45	_____	12.80	_____	_____
2.	104	King, M.	48	_____	16.50	_____	_____
3.	125	Moore, S.	40	_____	22.90	_____	_____
4.	152	Williams, B.	38	_____	15.45	_____	_____

Exercise 2   Net Pay

Complete the following pay register for Riley's. The six employees and their gross pay, marital status (M/S), withholding allowances (W. A.), and amount of other deductions are already listed for the week of August 10 to 16, 2005. Here, S indicates single, M indicates married, and YTD signifies year to date.

Payroll Register

							For Week Ending August 16, 2005					
								Deductions ($)				
	Employee Number	Employee Name	M/S	W.A.	Gross Pay ($)	YTD Earnings ($)	Federal	Social Security	Medicare	Other	Total Deductions ($)	Net Pay ($)
5.	101	Ross, J.	S	0	1,200	45,000	_____	_____	_____	15.50	_____	_____
6.	222	Perez, T.	M	2	800	24,000	_____	_____	_____	25.70	_____	_____
7.	303	Douglas, S.	M	4	495	14,850	_____	_____	_____	8.00	_____	_____
8.	309	Cain, E.	M	6	580	17,400	_____	_____	_____	0	_____	_____
9.	310	Smith, W.	S	5	540	16,200	_____	_____	_____	12.00	_____	_____
10.	320	Jones, B.	S	1	657	19,710	_____	_____	_____	10.33	_____	_____

Exercise 3

11. Joan Baize packed 922 boxes this week. She receives $.50 for each box up to and including 500. She receives $.55 for each box over 500. She is married and claims three withholding allowances. She has $14 weekly deducted for insurance premiums. What is her net pay for the week? _____

12. Bill Bartok earns 4.5% commission on all sales over $20,000. In May his sales were $75,500. He is married and claims four withholding allowances. He has $100 placed in a retirement plan each month. What is his net pay for the month? _____

13. Jerry Smith worked 95 hours in 2 weeks. He is paid $14 per hour. The regular work week at his company is 36 hours. After that an overtime rate of 1.6 is paid. What is Jerry's gross pay for the 2-week period? _____

14. Leonard Kruptka earns $36,584 per year. He is single and claims one exemption. He has $25 deducted for insurance and $100 deducted for a retirement plan each month. What is his net pay for January? _____

15. Tawnia Talley earns $2,000 per month plus 1% commission on all sales. She is married and claims two withholding allowances. Monthly she has $225 placed in a retirement account and $85 deducted for insurance premiums. Her sales were $165,000 this month. What is her gross monthly pay? _____ Net pay? _____

16. Ben Reynolds worked 48 hours last week. His regular pay rate is $15 per hour. He receives 1.5 times the regular rate for hours over 40 per week. He is single and claims one exemption. Calculate his gross pay for the week. _____

Exercise 4

Susan Lee pays her employees on the following piecework scale for items produced weekly:

1 to 200, pieces $.85 each

201 to 300 pieces, $.95 each

301 to 400 pieces, $1.05 each

401 to 500 pieces, $1.60 each

Calculate gross pay, federal income tax, Social Security, and Medicare deductions and net pay for each of the following employees. Marital status (M/S), withholding allowance (W. A.), and other deductions are as shown. None of the employees has reached the Social Security ceiling. Here, S indicates single, and M indicates married.

	Name	M/S	W.A.	Pieces	Gross Pay ($)	Federal ($)	Social Security ($)	Medicare ($)	Other ($)	Net Pay ($)
17.	Lee, J.	M	4	410	_____	_____	_____	_____	10.40	_____
18.	Tucker, L.	S	2	380	_____	_____	_____	_____	8.50	_____
19.	Chu, K.	S	1	250	_____	_____	_____	_____	0	_____
20.	Chen, L.	S	0	455	_____	_____	_____	_____	0	_____

SELECTED IRS WITHHOLDING TABLES

See Figures 17.20 through 17.22.

Table 1. Percentage Method—Amount for One Withholding Allowance

Payroll Period	One Withholding Allowance
Weekly	$59.62
Biweekly	119.23
Semimonthly	129.17
Monthly	258.33
Quarterly	775.00
Semiannually	1,550.00
Annually	3,100.00
Daily or miscellaneous (each day of the payroll period)	11.92

FIGURE 17.20

Tables for Percentage Method of Withholding
(For Wages Paid Through December 2004)

TABLE 1—WEEKLY Payroll Period

(a) SINGLE person (including head of household)—

If the amount of wages (after subtracting withholding allowances) is: The amount of income tax to withhold is:

Not over $51 . . . . . $0

Over—	But not over—		of excess over—
$51	—$187	10%	—$51
$187	—$592	$13.60 plus 15%	—$187
$592	—$1,317	$74.35 plus 25%	—$592
$1,317	—$2,860	$255.60 plus 28%	—$1,317
$2,860	—$6,177	$687.64 plus 33%	—$2,860
$6,177	. . . . . .	$1,782.25 plus 35%	—$6,177

(b) MARRIED person—

If the amount of wages (after subtracting withholding allowances) is: The amount of income tax to withhold is:

Not over $154 . . . . $0

Over—	But not over—		of excess over—
$154	—$429	10%	—$154
$429	—$1,245	$27.50 plus 15%	—$429
$1,245	—$2,270	$149.90 plus 25%	—$1,245
$2,270	—$3,568	$406.15 plus 28%	—$2,270
$3,568	—$6,271	$769.59 plus 33%	—$3,568
$6,271	. . . . . .	$1,661.58 plus 35%	—$6,271

TABLE 2—BIWEEKLY Payroll Period

(a) SINGLE person (including head of household)—

If the amount of wages (after subtracting withholding allowances) is: The amount of income tax to withhold is:

Not over $102 . . . . $0

Over—	But not over—		of excess over—
$102	—$373	10%	—$102
$373	—$1,185	$27.10 plus 15%	—$373
$1,185	—$2,635	$148.90 plus 25%	—$1,185
$2,635	—$5,719	$511.40 plus 28%	—$2,635
$5,719	—$12,354	$1,374.92 plus 33%	—$5,719
$12,354	. . . . . .	$3,564.47 plus 35%	—$12,354

(b) MARRIED person—

If the amount of wages (after subtracting withholding allowances) is: The amount of income tax to withhold is:

Not over $308 . . . . $0

Over—	But not over—		of excess over—
$308	—$858	10%	—$308
$858	—$2,490	$55.00 plus 15%	—$858
$2,490	—$4,540	$299.80 plus 25%	—$2,490
$4,540	—$7,137	$812.30 plus 28%	—$4,540
$7,137	—$12,542	$1,539.46 plus 33%	—$7,137
$12,542	. . . . . .	$3,323.11 plus 35%	—$12,542

TABLE 3—SEMIMONTHLY Payroll Period

(a) SINGLE person (including head of household)—

If the amount of wages (after subtracting withholding allowances) is: The amount of income tax to withhold is:

Not over $110 . . . . . $0

Over—	But not over—		of excess over—
$110	—$404	10%	—$110
$404	—$1,283	$29.40 plus 15%	—$404
$1,283	—$2,854	$161.25 plus 25%	—$1,283
$2,854	—$6,196	$554.00 plus 28%	—$2,854
$6,196	—$13,383	$1,489.76 plus 33%	—$6,196
$13,383	. . . . . .	$3,861.47 plus 35%	—$13,383

(b) MARRIED person—

If the amount of wages (after subtracting withholding allowances) is: The amount of income tax to withhold is:

Not over $333 . . . . $0

Over—	But not over—		of excess over—
$333	—$929	10%	—$333
$929	—$2,698	$59.60 plus 15%	—$929
$2,698	—$4,919	$324.95 plus 25%	—$2,698
$4,919	—$7,731	$880.20 plus 28%	—$4,919
$7,731	—$13,588	$1,667.56 plus 33%	—$7,731
$13,588	. . . . . .	$3,600.37 plus 35%	—$13,588

TABLE 4—MONTHLY Payroll Period

(a) SINGLE person (including head of household)—

If the amount of wages (after subtracting withholding allowances) is: The amount of income tax to withhold is:

Not over $221 . . . . . $0

Over—	But not over—		of excess over—
$221	—$808	10%	—$221
$808	—$2,567	$58.70 plus 15%	—$808
$2,567	—$5,708	$322.55 plus 25%	—$2,567
$5,708	—$12,392	$1,107.80 plus 28%	—$5,708
$12,392	—$26,767	$2,979.32 plus 33%	—$12,392
$26,767	. . . . . .	$7,723.07 plus 35%	—$26,767

(b) MARRIED person—

If the amount of wages (after subtracting withholding allowances) is: The amount of income tax to withhold is:

Not over $667 . . . . . $0

Over—	But not over—		of excess over—
$667	—$1,858	10%	—$667
$1,858	—$5,396	$119.10 plus 15%	—$1,858
$5,396	—$9,838	$649.80 plus 25%	—$5,396
$9,838	—$15,463	$1,760.30 plus 28%	—$9,838
$15,463	—$27,175	$3,335.30 plus 33%	—$15,463
$27,175	. . . . . .	$7,200.26 plus 35%	—$27,175

FIGURE 17.21

SINGLE Persons—**WEEKLY** Payroll Period

(For Wages Paid Through December 2004)

If the wages are-		And the number of withholding allowances claimed is-										
At least	But less than	0	1	2	3	4	5	6	7	8	9	10
		The amount of income tax to be withheld is-										
200	210	16	9	3	0	0	0	0	0	0	0	0
210	220	18	10	4	0	0	0	0	0	0	0	0
220	230	19	11	5	0	0	0	0	0	0	0	0
230	240	21	12	6	1	0	0	0	0	0	0	0
240	250	22	13	7	2	0	0	0	0	0	0	0
250	260	24	15	8	3	0	0	0	0	0	0	0
260	270	25	16	9	4	0	0	0	0	0	0	0
270	280	27	18	10	5	0	0	0	0	0	0	0
280	290	28	19	11	6	0	0	0	0	0	0	0
290	300	30	21	12	7	1	0	0	0	0	0	0
300	310	31	22	13	8	2	0	0	0	0	0	0
310	320	33	24	15	9	3	0	0	0	0	0	0
320	330	34	25	16	10	4	0	0	0	0	0	0
330	340	36	27	18	11	5	0	0	0	0	0	0
340	350	37	28	19	12	6	0	0	0	0	0	0
450	460	54	45	36	27	18	11	5	0	0	0	0
460	470	55	46	37	29	20	12	6	0	0	0	0
470	480	57	48	39	30	21	13	7	1	0	0	0
480	490	58	49	40	32	23	14	8	2	0	0	0
490	500	60	51	42	33	24	15	9	3	0	0	0
500	510	61	52	43	35	26	17	10	4	0	0	0
510	520	63	54	45	36	27	18	11	5	0	0	0
520	530	64	55	46	38	29	20	12	6	0	0	0
530	540	66	57	48	39	30	21	13	7	1	0	0
540	550	67	58	49	41	32	23	14	8	2	0	0
650	660	90	75	66	57	48	39	30	21	13	7	1
660	670	93	78	67	59	50	41	32	23	14	8	2
670	680	95	80	69	60	51	42	33	24	16	9	3
680	690	98	83	70	62	53	44	35	26	17	10	4
690	700	100	85	72	63	54	45	36	27	18	11	5
900	910	153	138	123	108	93	78	68	59	50	41	32
910	920	155	140	125	110	95	81	69	60	51	42	33
920	930	158	143	128	113	98	83	71	62	53	44	35
930	940	160	145	130	115	100	86	72	63	54	45	36
940	950	163	148	133	118	103	88	74	65	56	47	38
1,050	1,060	190	175	160	145	130	116	101	86	72	63	54
1,060	1,070	193	178	163	148	133	118	103	88	74	65	56
1,070	1,080	195	180	165	150	135	121	106	91	76	66	57
1,080	1,090	198	183	168	153	138	123	108	93	78	68	59
1,090	1,100	200	185	170	155	140	126	111	96	81	69	60
1,150	1,160	215	200	185	170	155	141	126	111	96	81	69
1,160	1,170	218	203	188	173	158	143	128	113	98	83	71
1,170	1,180	220	205	190	175	160	146	131	116	101	86	72
1,180	1,190	223	208	193	178	163	148	133	118	103	88	74
1,190	1,200	225	210	195	180	165	151	136	121	106	91	76
1,200	1,210	228	213	198	183	168	153	138	123	108	93	79
1,210	1,220	230	215	200	185	170	156	141	126	111	96	81
1,220	1,230	233	218	203	188	173	158	143	128	113	98	84
1,230	1,240	235	220	205	190	175	161	146	131	116	101	86
1,240	1,250	238	223	208	193	178	163	148	133	118	103	89

FIGURE 17.22

MARRIED Persons—WEEKLY Payroll Period

360	370	21	15	9	3	0	0	0	0	0	0	0
370	380	22	16	10	4	0	0	0	0	0	0	0
380	390	23	17	11	5	0	0	0	0	0	0	0
390	400	24	18	12	6	0	0	0	0	0	0	0
400	410	25	19	13	7	1	0	0	0	0	0	0
470	480	34	26	20	14	8	2	0	0	0	0	0
480	490	36	27	21	15	9	3	0	0	0	0	0
490	500	37	28	22	16	10	4	0	0	0	0	0
500	510	39	30	23	17	11	5	0	0	0	0	0
510	520	40	31	24	18	12	6	0	0	0	0	0
540	550	45	36	27	21	15	9	3	0	0	0	0
550	560	46	37	29	22	16	10	4	0	0	0	0
560	570	48	39	30	23	17	11	5	0	0	0	0
570	580	49	40	32	24	18	12	6	0	0	0	0
580	590	51	42	33	25	19	13	7	1	0	0	0
790	800	82	73	65	56	47	38	29	22	16	10	5
800	810	84	75	66	57	48	39	30	23	17	11	6
810	820	85	76	68	59	50	41	32	24	18	12	7
820	830	87	78	69	60	51	42	33	25	19	13	8
830	840	88	79	71	62	53	44	35	26	20	14	9
940	950	105	96	87	78	69	60	51	42	33	25	20
950	960	106	97	89	80	71	62	53	44	35	26	21
960	970	108	99	90	81	72	63	54	45	36	27	22
970	980	109	100	92	83	74	65	56	47	38	28	23
980	990	111	102	93	84	75	66	57	48	39	29	24

SINGLE Persons—MONTHLY Payroll Period

2,880	2,920	406	341	295	256	218	179	140	101	63	35	10
2,920	2,960	416	351	301	262	224	185	146	107	69	39	14
2,960	3,000	426	361	307	268	230	191	152	113	76	43	18
3,000	3,040	436	371	313	274	236	197	158	119	81	47	22
3,040	3,080	446	381	319	280	242	203	164	125	87	51	26
4,280	4,320	756	691	627	562	498	433	368	311	273	234	195
4,320	4,360	765	701	637	572	508	443	378	317	279	240	201
4,360	4,400	776	711	647	582	518	453	388	324	285	246	207
4,400	4,440	786	721	657	592	528	463	398	334	291	252	213
4,440	4,480	796	731	667	602	538	473	408	344	297	258	219

MARRIED Persons—MONTHLY Payroll Period

2,440	2,480	209	171	132	102	76	50	24	0	0	0	0
2,480	2,520	215	177	138	106	80	54	28	3	0	0	0
2,520	2,560	221	183	144	110	84	58	32	7	0	0	0
2,560	2,600	227	189	150	114	88	62	36	11	0	0	0
2,600	2,640	233	195	156	118	92	66	40	15	0	0	0
3,040	3,080	299	261	222	183	144	110	84	59	33	7	0
3,080	3,120	305	267	228	189	150	114	88	63	37	11	0
3,120	3,160	311	273	234	195	156	118	92	67	41	15	0
3,160	3,200	317	279	240	201	162	124	96	71	45	19	0
3,200	3,240	323	285	246	207	168	130	100	75	49	23	0
3,280	3,320	335	297	258	219	180	142	108	83	57	31	5
3,320	3,360	341	303	264	225	186	148	112	87	61	35	9
3,360	3,400	347	309	270	231	192	154	116	91	65	39	13
3,400	3,440	353	315	276	237	198	160	121	95	69	43	17
3,440	3,480	359	321	282	243	204	166	127	99	73	47	21
3,480	3,520	365	327	288	249	210	172	133	103	77	51	25
3,520	3,560	371	333	294	255	216	178	139	107	81	55	29
3,580	3,600	377	339	300	261	222	184	145	111	85	59	33
3,600	3,640	383	345	306	267	228	190	151	115	89	63	37
3,640	3,680	389	351	312	273	234	196	157	119	93	67	41

FIGURE 17.22 Continued

CHAPTER 18

Employer Payroll Taxes

 ## PART 1   *Speed and Accuracy Building Using Touch Key*

GOALS: Your speed goal is 9,500 strokes per hour.
Your accuracy target goal range is 95% to 100%.

With each repetition of the drill, try to improve your speed without lowering your accuracy score. If your percent-of-accuracy score falls below 95%, review your finger position and technique. Then try again.

Instructions: *Start Touch Key. Complete Drill 3, Part A, Five-Minute Timing. (Parts B through E are optional.) Write your scores for strokes per hour and percent of accuracy below.*

Touch Key Drill 3—The 0 through 9 Keys, Five-Digit Numbers, Five-Minute Timing

Today's Date	Strokes per Hour	Percent of Accuracy
A.		
B.		
C.		
D.		
E.		

 ## PART 2   *Business Math Skills*

PAYROLL TAX RETURNS

In the previous chapter, federal income tax, Social Security tax, and Medicare tax that the employer must withhold from employee paychecks were discussed. Along with the taxes withheld from employee paychecks, the employer's share of Social Security and Medicare taxes must be deposited by mailing or delivering a check, money order, or cash to an institution that is an authorized depository for federal taxes or by using the Electronic Federal Tax Payment System (**EFTPS**).

This deposit for Social Security, Medicare, and withheld income taxes is made either monthly or semiweekly, depending on the deposit schedule of the business. (See IRS Publication 15, Circular E, Employer's Tax Guide, "When to Deposit," for more information.)

However, if the federal tax accumulated during the quarter is less than $2,500, payment may be made in full when Form 941, Employer's Quarterly Federal Tax Return, is filed at the end of each calendar quarter using Form 941-V, Payment Voucher. Form 941 is shown in Figure 18.1. Form 941-V is shown in Figure 18.2. Forms and publications are available from www.irs.gov.

Form **941**
(Rev. January 2002)
Department of the Treasury
Internal Revenue Service (99)

Employer's Quarterly Federal Tax Return

▶ See separate instructions revised January 2002 for information on completing this return.

Please type or print.

Enter state code for state in which deposits were made **only** if different from state in address to the right ▶ (see page 2 of instructions).

		OMB No. 1545-0029
Name (as distinguished from trade name)	Date quarter ended	T
Trade name, if any	Employer identification number	FF
Address (number and street)	City, state, and ZIP code	FD
		FP
		I
		T

If address is different from prior return, check here ▶ ☐

IRS Use

1 1 1 1 1 1 1 1 1 1 2 3 3 3 3 3 3 3 3 4 4 4 5 5 5

6 7 8 8 8 8 8 8 8 8 9 9 9 9 9 10 10 10 10 10 10 10 10 10 10

If you do not have to file returns in the future, check here ▶ ☐ and enter date final wages paid ▶

If you are a seasonal employer, see **Seasonal employers** on page 1 of the instructions and check here ▶ ☐

1	Number of employees in the pay period that includes March 12th . ▶ 1			
2	Total wages and tips, plus other compensation		2	
3	Total income tax withheld from wages, tips, and sick pay		3	
4	Adjustment of withheld income tax for preceding quarters of calendar year		4	
5	Adjusted total of income tax withheld (line 3 as adjusted by line 4—see instructions)		5	
6	Taxable social security wages 6a	× 12.4% (.124) =	6b	
	Taxable social security tips 6c	× 12.4% (.124) =	6d	
7	Taxable Medicare wages and tips . . . 7a	× 2.9% (.029) =	7b	
8	Total social security and Medicare taxes (add lines 6b, 6d, and 7b). Check here if wages are not subject to social security and/or Medicare tax . . . ▶ ☐		8	
9	Adjustment of social security and Medicare taxes (see instructions for required explanation) Sick Pay $ ______ ± Fractions of Cents $ ______ ± Other $ ______ =		9	
10	Adjusted total of social security and Medicare taxes (line 8 as adjusted by line 9—see instructions)		10	
11	**Total taxes** (add lines 5 and 10)		11	
12	Advance earned income credit (EIC) payments made to employees		12	
13	Net taxes (subtract line 12 from line 11). **If $2,500 or more, this must equal line 17, column (d) below (or line D of Schedule B (Form 941))**		13	
14	Total deposits for quarter, including overpayment applied from a prior quarter		14	
15	**Balance due** (subtract line 14 from line 13). See instructions		15	

16 **Overpayment.** If line 14 is more than line 13, enter excess here ▶ $ ______
and check if to be: ☐ Applied to next return **or** ☐ Refunded.

- **All filers:** If line 13 is less than $2,500, you need not complete line 17 or Schedule B (Form 941).
- **Semiweekly schedule depositors:** Complete Schedule B (Form 941) and check here . . . ▶ ☐
- **Monthly schedule depositors:** Complete line 17, columns (a) through (d), and check here. . . ▶ ☐

17 Monthly Summary of Federal Tax Liability. Do not complete if you were a semiweekly schedule depositor.

(a) First month liability	**(b)** Second month liability	**(c)** Third month liability	**(d)** Total liability for quarter

Third Party Designee
Do you want to allow another person to discuss this return with the IRS (see separate instructions)? ☐ **Yes.** Complete the following. ☐ **No**
Designee's name ▶ **Phone no. ▶** ( ) Personal identification number (PIN) ▶

Sign Here
Under penalties of perjury, I declare that I have examined this return, including accompanying schedules and statements, and to the best of my knowledge and belief, it is true, correct, and complete.
Signature ▶ **Print Your Name and Title ▶** **Date ▶**

For Privacy Act and Paperwork Reduction Act Notice, see back of Payment Voucher. Cat. No. 17001Z Form **941** (Rev. 1-2002)

FIGURE 18.1

▼ Detach Here and Mail With Your Payment ▼ Form **941-V** (2002)

Form **941-V** Department of the Treasury Internal Revenue Service (99)	**Payment Voucher** ▶ **Do not staple or attach this voucher to your payment.**		OMB No. 1545-0029 **2002**
1 Enter your employer identification number	2 **Enter the amount of the payment**	Dollars	Cents
3 Tax period: ○ 1st Quarter ○ 3rd Quarter ○ 2nd Quarter ○ 4th Quarter	4 Enter your business name (individual name if sole proprietor) Enter your address Enter your city, state, and ZIP code		

FIGURE 18.2

EMPLOYER TAX LIABILITY

The employer must also pay federal unemployment taxes (**FUTA**) on employees. Different forms are used for filing and paying federal unemployment taxes and are discussed later in the chapter.

Most states require that state unemployment taxes (**SUTA**) be paid on all employees. Check with your state government for information about exempt employees, rates, and how to submit state unemployment taxes.

Income tax withheld, both employer and employee Social Security and Medicare taxes, FUTA, and SUTA, comprise the **employer's tax liability**, which is the amount of tax the employer must deposit with federal and state governments.

SOCIAL SECURITY AND MEDICARE TAXES

The employer must match the employee contributions for Social Security and Medicare.

PROBLEM 1

The ABC Co. withheld \$89.52 in Social Security and Medicare from employee paychecks during the first quarter of 2003.

a. How much Social Security and Medicare does the employer owe?
b. How much Social Security and Medicare does the employer need to deposit with Form 941 Employer's Quarterly Federal Tax Return?

Solution:

a. Because the employer must match the employee contributions for Social Security and Medicare, the employer also owes \$89.52.
b. The employer will need to deposit \$89.52 × 2 at the end of the quarter for Social Security and Medicare (see Figure 18.3).

Total FICA and MediCare deducted from employees' paychecks x 2 = amount to be deposited by employer this quarter for FICA and MediCare.

89.52 x 2 = 179.04

FIGURE 18.3

Note that Form 941 in Figure 18.1 directs the employer to multiply taxable Social Security wages and tips by 12.4% (6.2% × 2) and to multiply taxable Medicare wages and tips by 2.9% (1.45% × 2). Both methods give the same result.

Self-employed persons must pay both the employee and the employer share of Social Security and Medicare taxes, 12.4% of taxable Social Security earnings and 2.9% of taxable Medicare earnings.

AMOUNT OF QUARTERLY DEPOSIT

To find the total amount the employer must deposit at the end of a quarter, add the amount of federal income tax (FIT) withheld for all employees, the Social Security deducted from employee paychecks, the employer's matching amount of Social Security, the Medicare tax deducted from employee paychecks, and the employer's matching amount for Medicare as shown in Figure 18.4.

> FIT withheld for all employees
> FICA paid by all employees
> FICA matching amount to be paid by employer
> MediCare paid by all employees
> MediCare matching amount to be paid by employer
>
> **Amount of Quarterly Deposit**

FIGURE 18.4

UNEMPLOYMENT TAXES

Unemployment taxes are used to pay benefits to those who have recently become unemployed. It is a federal program administered by the states. The amount and the duration of the benefit payments vary by state. Some states provide additional benefits not provided by federal law. The federal government often varies benefits based on current economic conditions.

There are two unemployment taxes:

1. Federal unemployment tax (FUTA)
2. State unemployment tax (SUTA)

FUTA is 6.2% of the first $7,000 earned by an employee each year minus the employer's SUTA (up to 5.4%). For problems in this book, a SUTA rate of 5.4% of the first $7,000 earned by an employee each year will be used. Therefore, FUTA is 6.2% − 5.4% = .8% or .008 converted to a decimal number. Be sure to note the decimal in .8%. It is easy to overlook!

Be sure to check with your state as to the exact base and rate to use for SUTA. In this book we will use 5.4% for SUTA.

Note: There is a special credit for successor employers. A successor employer is one who acquired a business from an employer who was required to file Form 940 or Form 940EZ. See page 2 of the Form 940EZ instructions (available from www.irs.gov).

PROBLEM 2

The Cottage by the Sea employees earned a total of $6,700 this quarter. None of the employees has $7,000 or more year-to-date earnings. How much does Cottage by the Sea need to deposit for FUTA and SUTA taxes this quarter?

Multiply $6,700 by 0.8%, or 0.008, to find FUTA.
Multiply $6,700 by 5.4%, or 0.054, to find SUTA.

Calculator Procedure

$$6,700 \times .8 \boxed{\%} \boxed{53.6}$$
$$6,700 \times 5.4 \boxed{\%} \boxed{361.8}$$

Figure 18.5 illustrates the FUTA and SUTA calculations with the percents converted to decimal numbers.

The company must know when an employee has reached $7,000 in earnings so as not to continue to pay unemployment tax. For this reason, each employee's year-to-date earnings should be recorded each pay period.

Employee Quarterly earnings = $6,700 (no employee has reached the $7,000 ceiling for FUTA and SUTA

FUTA = 6.2% – up to 5.4% SUTA = .8%

$$6,700 \times .008 = 53.60$$

SUTA = 5.4% (usually)

$$6,700 \times .054 = 361.80$$

FIGURE 18.5

DEPOSITING AND FILING FUTA

If FUTA for the quarter is $100 or less, the tax does not have to be deposited at the end of that quarter. Instead, it can be carried over and added to the FUTA owed the next quarter. If the FUTA owed for the next quarter including the amount carried over is still less than $100, the FUTA may again be carried over to the next quarter, and so on until the end of the calendar year. At the end of the year, if the FUTA for the fourth quarter, including any amounts carried over from previous quarters, is $100 or less, the FUTA may be paid when Form 940 or Form 940EZ, Employer's Annual Federal Unemployment (FUTA) Tax Return, is filed. Pages 1 and 2 of Form 940 are shown in Figures 18.6 and 18.7, respectively. The deadline for payment is January 31.

If the FUTA tax liability for any calendar quarter is over $100, including any amount(s) carried over from previous quarter(s), the tax must be deposited by EFTPS or in an authorized financial institution using Form 8109, Federal Tax Deposit Coupon.

PROBLEM 3

A family business has two employees. Each earns $400 per week. When should the FUTA deposits be made?

Calculate the amount of FUTA and record it for each pay period of the quarter. Total the FUTA each quarter. If the tax is more than $100, make a deposit. If the tax is $100 or less, carry the tax over to the next quarter. Refer to the employees' pay records to complete a FUTA worksheet.

Note: YTD, year to date.

Employee A: First Quarter				Employee B: First Quarter			
Week Number	Earnings	– YTD Earnings	FUTA	Week Number	Earnings	YTD Earnings	FUTA
1	400	400	3.20	1	400	400	3.20
2	400	800	3.20	2	400	800	3.20
3	400	1,200	3.20	3	400	1,200	3.20
4	400	1,600	3.20	4	400	1,600	3.20
5	400	2,000	3.20	5	400	2,000	3.20
6	400	2,400	3.20	6	400	2,400	3.20
7	400	2,800	3.20	7	400	2,800	3.20
8	400	3,200	3.20	8	400	3,200	3.20
9	400	3,600	3.20	9	400	3,600	3.20
10	400	4,000	3.20	10	400	4,000	3.20
11	400	4,400	3.20	11	400	4,400	3.20
12	400	4,800	3.20	12	400	4,800	3.20
13	400	5,200	3.20	13	400	5,200	3.20

Employee A: Second Quarter				Employee B: Second Quarter			
Week Number	Earnings	YTD Earnings	FUTA	Week Number	Earnings	YTD Earnings	FUTA
14	400	5,600	3.20	14	400	5,600	3.20
15	400	6,000	3.20	15	400	6,000	3.20
16	400	6,400	3.20	16	400	6,400	3.20
17	400	6,800	3.20	17	400	6,800	3.20
18	400	7,200	*1.60	18	400	7,200	*1.60
19	400		0	19	400		0
20	400		0	20	400		0
21	400		0	21	400		0
22	400		0	22	400		0
23	400		0	23	400		0
24	400		0	24	400		0
25	400		0	25	400		0
26	400		0	26	400		0

*7,000 – 6,800 = 200 taxable income for pay period 18: $200 × 0.8% = 1.60.

No FUTA is collected after the employees' gross earnings reach $7,000.

FUTA Worksheet

First Quarter		Second Quarter		Third Quarter		Fourth Quarter	
		Amount Carried Over:	83.20	Amount Carried Over:		Amount Carried Over:	
Pay Period	FUTA	Pay Period	FUTA	Pay Period	FUTA	Pay Period	FUTA
1	6.40	14	6.40				
2	6.40	15	6.40				
3	6.40	16	6.40				
4	6.40	17	6.40				
5	6.40	18	3.20				
6	6.40	19	0				
7	6.40	20	0				
8	6.40	21	0				
9	6.40	22	0				
10	6.40	23	0				
11	6.40	24	0				
12	6.40	25	0				
13	6.40	26	0				
Total:	83.20	Total:	118.40	Total:	0	Total:	0

One deposit of $118.40 for FUTA must be made at the end of the second quarter.

Form **940**

Department of the Treasury
Internal Revenue Service   (99)

**Employer's Annual Federal
Unemployment (FUTA) Tax Return**

► **See separate Instructions for Form 940 for information on completing this form.**

OMB No. 1545-0028

20**02**

T	
FF	
FD	
FP	
I	
T	

**You must
complete
this section.** ▶

Name (as distinguished from trade name)

Calendar year

Trade name, if any

Address and ZIP code

Employer identification number

A   Are you required to pay unemployment contributions to only one state? (If "No," skip questions B and C) .   ☐ **Yes**   ☐ **No**

B   Did you pay all state unemployment contributions by January 31, 2003? ((1) If you deposited your total FUTA
tax when due, check "Yes" if you paid all state unemployment contributions by February 10, 2003. (2) If a 0%
experience rate is granted, check "Yes." (3) If "No," skip question C.) .   .   .   .   ☐ **Yes**   ☐ **No**

C   Were all wages that were taxable for FUTA tax also taxable for your state's unemployment tax? .   .   .   .   .   ☐ **Yes**   ☐ **No**

If you answered "No" to any of these questions, you must file Form 940. If you answered "Yes" to all the
questions, you may file Form 940-EZ, which is a simplified version of Form 940. (Successor employers, see
Special credit for successor employers on page 2 of the instructions.) You can get Form 940-EZ by calling
1-800-TAX-FORM (1-800-829-3676) or from the IRS Web Site at **www.irs.gov.**

If you will not have to file returns in the future, check here (see **Who Must File** in separate instructions) **and
complete and sign the return** .   .   .   .   ▶ ☐

If this is an Amended Return, check here (see **Amended Returns** on page 2 of the separate instructions) .   .   .   .   ▶ ☐

Part I	Computation of Taxable Wages

1   Total payments (including payments shown on lines 2 and 3) during the calendar year for
services of employees **1**

2   Exempt payments. (Explain all exempt payments, attaching additional
sheets if necessary.) ▶ --
--   **2**

3   Payments of more than $7,000 for services. Enter only amounts over the
first $7,000 paid to each employee. (see separate instructions) Do not
include any exempt payments from line 2. The $7,000 amount is the
Federal wage base. Your state wage base may be different. **Do not use
your state wage limitation**. **3**

4   Add lines 2 and 3 .   .   .   .   **4**

5   **Total taxable wages** (subtract line 4 from line 1) .   .   .   .   ▶ **5**

Be sure to complete both sides of this form, and sign in the space provided on the back.

For Privacy Act and Paperwork Reduction Act Notice, see separate instructions.   ▼ **DETACH HERE** ▼   Cat. No. 11234O   Form **940** (2002)

Form **940-V**

Department of the Treasury
Internal Revenue Service

Form 940 Payment Voucher

Use this voucher only when making a payment with your return.

OMB No. 1545-0028

20**02**

Complete boxes 1, 2, and 3. Do not send cash, and do not staple your payment to this voucher. Make your check or money order payable to the
"United States Treasury." Be sure to enter your employer identification number, "Form 940," and "2002" on your payment.

1   Enter your employer identification number.

2

Enter the amount of your payment. ▶

Dollars	Cents

3   Enter your business name (individual name for sole proprietors).

Enter your address.

Enter your city, state, and ZIP code.

FIGURE 18.6

Form 940 (2002)   Page **2**

Part II	**Tax Due or Refund**

1	Gross FUTA tax. (Multiply the wages from Part I, line 5, by .062)	**1**	
2	Maximum credit. (Multiply the wages from Part I, line 5, by .054)	**2**	

3 Computation of tentative credit (**Note:** *All taxpayers must complete the applicable columns.*)

(a) Name of state	(b) State reporting number(s) as shown on employer's state contribution returns	(c) Taxable payroll (as defined in state act)	(d) State experience rate period		(e) State experience rate	(f) Contributions if rate had been 5.4% (col. (c) x .054)	(g) Contributions payable at experience rate (col. (c) x col. (e))	(h) Additional credit (col. (f) minus col.(g)) If 0 or less, enter -0-.	(i) Contributions paid to state by 940 due date
			From	To					

3a	Totals . . . ▶			
3b	**Total tentative credit** (add line 3a, columns (h) and (i) only—for late payments, also see the instructions for Part II, line 6) . . . . ▶	**3b**	
4			
5			
6	**Credit:** Enter the smaller of the amount from Part II, line 2 or line 3b; or the amount from the worksheet on page 5 of the separate instructions	**6**	
7	**Total FUTA tax** (subtract line 6 from line 1). If the result is over $100, also complete Part III	**7**	
8	Total FUTA tax deposited for the year, including any overpayment applied from a prior year . .	**8**	
9	**Balance due** (subtract line 8 from line 7). Pay to the "United States Treasury." If you owe more than $100, see **Depositing FUTA Tax** on page 3 of the separate instructions . . . . . . ▶	**9**	
10	**Overpayment** (subtract line 7 from line 8). Check if it is to be: ☐ **Applied to next return** or ☐ **Refunded** . . . . ▶	**10**	

Part III	**Record of Quarterly Federal Unemployment Tax Liability** (Do not include state liability.) **Complete only if line 7 is over $100.** See page 6 of the separate instructions.

Quarter	First (Jan. 1–Mar. 31)	Second (Apr. 1–June 30)	Third (July 1–Sept. 30)	Fourth (Oct. 1–Dec. 31)	Total for year
Liability for quarter					

Third Party Designee	Do you want to allow another person to discuss this return with the IRS (see instructions page 6)? ☐ **Yes. Complete the following.** ☐ **No**
	Designee's name ▶ Phone no. ▶ ( ) Personal identification number (PIN) ▶ ☐☐☐☐☐

Under penalties of perjury, I declare that I have examined this return, including accompanying schedules and statements, and, to the best of my knowledge and belief, it is true, correct, and complete, and that no part of any payment made to a state unemployment fund claimed as a credit was, or is to be, deducted from the payments to employees.

Signature ▶   Title (Owner, etc.) ▶   Date ▶

✱   Form **940** (2002)

FIGURE 18.7

Name _____

Class/Section _____

Score (Correct Answers ÷ No. of Assigned Problems) _____

PART 2 *Business Math Skills*

Exercise 1

1. The AVC Co. has five employees. Their federal income tax, Social Security, and Medicare contributions are shown below. Calculate the amount of the employer's tax deposit. _____

Employee Number	Federal Income Tax ($)	Social Security ($)	Medicare ($)
60	150	180	15
39	210	309	29
15	175	211	21
40	85	190	16
28	40	151	13

Exercise 2

Calculate FUTA and SUTA taxes on the following employees. The FUTA rate is 0.8% on the first $7,000 earned. The SUTA rate is 5.4% on the first $7,000 earned.

	Gross Earnings ($)	FUTA	SUTA
2.	6,070	_____	_____
3.	14,090	_____	_____
4.	8,003	_____	_____
5.	7,050	_____	_____
6.	4,339	_____	_____

Exercise 3

Complete the following partial pay register. The Social Security rate is 6.2% on the first $87,000 earned. The Medicare rate is 1.45%.

	Employee Number	Gross Earnings ($)	YTD Earnings ($)	Social Security	Medicare	FUTA	SUTA
7.	25	2950.45	14752.25	_____	_____	_____	_____
8.	46	3040.91	6081.82	_____	_____	_____	_____
9.	30	5092.84	25464.20	_____	_____	_____	_____
10.	12	3541.92	17709.60	_____	_____	_____	_____
11.	47	3809.55	3809.55	_____	_____	_____	_____
12.			Totals				

Calculate the employer's total tax liability for:

13. Social Security _____
14. Medicare _____
15. FUTA _____
16. SUTA _____

Exercise 4

Erin McClaine earned $14,721.52 last month. His year-to-date earnings are $103,050.64. What is the employer's tax liability for this employee?

17. Social Security _____
18. Medicare _____
19. FUTA _____
20. SUTA _____

 **PART 3** *Review and Practice Using Business Math FUNdamentals*

GOAL: Complete 9 of the 10 problems correctly.

Instructions: *Start Business Math FUNdamentals. Complete Tutorial 40 and Drill 31. If you are not satisfied with your score, repeat the drill. Write your scores below.*

Business Math FUNdamentals Drill 31

Today's Date	Score

 **PART 4**   *Desktop Calculator*

EMPLOYEE PAY RECORD

Employers are required to keep a pay record for each employee detailing all of that employee's earnings and deductions from pay.

The procedure for completing an employee pay record is as follows.

PROBLEM 3

Kenneth Lowden earns $82,000 per year. He is married and claims three withholding allowances. He has $65 deducted each pay period for health insurance premiums. Use the following rates: Social Security 6.2% for the first $87,000; Medicare 1.45%; FUTA 0.8% on the first $7,000; and SUTA 5.4% on the first $7,000.

1. Calculate gross earnings for each week. Divide Kenneth's annual salary by 52 and enter the result ($1,576.92) under gross earnings for pay period 1.
2. The year-to-date earnings will be the same as gross earnings for pay period 1. For each pay period thereafter, add $1,576.92 to the previous year-to-date earnings figure.
3. Use the table method to calculate the federal income tax withholding for pay period 1.
4. Calculate Social Security using the rate of 6.2% and Medicare using the rate of 1.45%.
5. Total the four deductions for pay period 1. Write the total under total deductions.
6. Subtract total deductions from gross pay and write the difference under net pay.

TAPE 18.1:

```
 82,000. ÷
      52. =
 1,576.92 *

 1,576.92 +
 1,576.92 ×
     6.2 %
   97.77 *

 1,576.92 +
 1,576.92 ×
    1.45 %
   22.87 *

  110.00 +
   97.77 +
   22.87 +
   65.00 +
  295.64 *

  295.64 M-
1,281.28 M*
```

Employee Name Kenneth Lowden				Employee Number #103				Year 2005	
					Deductions ($)				
Pay Period	Pay Period Ending	Gross Earnings ($)	Year-to-Date Earnings ($)	Federal Income Tax	Social Security	Medicare	Insurance Premiums	Total Deductions ($)	Net Pay ($)
1	1/5	1,576.92	1,576.92	110.00	97.77	22.87	65.00	295.64	1,281.28
2	1/12								
3	1/19								

$$82,000 \div 52 = \boxed{1,576.92} \; M+ \; \times \; 6.2\% \; \boxed{97.77}$$
$$MS \times 1.45\% \; \boxed{22.87}$$
$$110 + 97.77 + 22.87 + 65 + T \; \boxed{295.64} \; M - MT \boxed{1,281.28}$$

To calculate the employer's tax liability for an employee over a specified period of time such as a month or a quarter:

1. Federal income tax: Total the federal income tax column. Place total in memory.
2. Social Security: Total the Social Security column; multiply by 2. Add to memory.
3. Medicare: Total the Medicare column; multiply by 2. Add to memory.
4. FUTA: Multiply year-to-date earnings by 0.8%. Add to memory.
5. SUTA: Multiply year-to-date earnings by 5.4%. Add to memory.
6. Use memory recall or memory subtotal to see the results of steps 1 through 5 added together.

Name _____

Class/Section _____

Score (Correct Answers ÷ No. of Assigned Problems) _____

 PART 4 *Desktop Calculator*

Exercise 1

Complete pay periods 2 through 14 for Kenneth Lowden's pay record. Kenneth Lowden earns $82,000 per year. He is married and claims three withholding allowances. He has $65 deducted each pay period for health insurance premiums. Use the following rates: Social Security 6.2% for the first $87,000 earned; Medicare 1.45%; FUTA 0.8% on the first $7,000 earned; and SUTA 5.4% on the first $7,000 earned.

				Deductions ($)					
Employee Name Kenneth Lowden				**Employee Number #103**				**Year 2005**	
Pay Period	Pay Period Ending	Gross Earnings ($)	Year-to-Date Earnings ($)	Federal Income Tax	Social Security	Medicare	Insurance Premiums	Total Deductions ($)	Net Pay ($)
1	1/5	1,576.92	1,576.92	110.00	97.77	22.87	65.00	295.64	1,281.28
2	1/12								
3	1/19								
4	1/26								
5	2/6								
6	2/2								
7	2/9								
8	2/16								
9	2/23								
10	3/2								
11	3/9								
12	3/16								
13	3/23								
14	3/30								
15	First quarter totals								

Calculate the employer's tax liability for the first quarter of the year for the following:

16. Federal income tax _____
17. Social Security _____
18. Medicare _____
19. FUTA _____
20. SUTA _____

Exercise 2

Strokes per Minute Score _____

Accuracy Score (Correct Strokes ÷ Total Strokes) _____

One-Minute Addition Timing (0 through 9 Keys, Five-Digit Numbers)

(Optional: Your instructor may wish you to use Touch Key on the computer for all your timings. Check with your instructor before completing this exercise.)

Complete as many of the problems as possible in 1 minute by adding. Work quickly and accurately. The number preceding each closing parenthesis indicates the cumulative number of strokes for problems attempted. For example, if you complete Problems 1 through 3 in 1 minute, your strokes-per-minute score is 183. Optional: 3- to 5-minute timings.

1. 17,556	2. 90,024	3. 71,544	4. 19,006	5. 97,850	6. 94,209	7. 30,393	8. 17,141
72,341	70,932	75,250	32,902	48,500	28,880	60,363	19,171
23,390	62,909	74,830	60,301	34,750	93,100	10,585	18,414
13,647	97,585	15,604	44,643	69,965	88,400	30,252	13,474
75,985	86,047	57,400	30,105	57,355	21,706	30,282	19,717
13,524	69,000	16,500	60,405	94,229	23,065	20,939	71,747
92,093	65,788	24,700	25,003	69,899	79,005	30,696	77,411
76,335	54,421	76,180	51,403	45,075	46,004	50,828	83,711
90,549	53,836	40,309	82,031	54,990	13,006	60,528	38,477
53,875	11,002	53,311	91,002	34,558	25,216	50,639	48,147
61)	122)	183)	244)	305)	366)	427)	488)

9. 41,987	10. 96,900	11. 46,987	12. 64,779	13. 73,450	14. 30,661	15. 82,000	16. 31,004
66,979	93,677	25,122	55,100	24,995	36,000	85,013	32,600
55,979	63,553	60,655	20,466	41,995	39,885	28,064	34,000
66,878	96,998	70,074	35,353	27,229	69,633	39,614	33,870
77,797	98,565	22,998	25,555	30,471	76,433	30,735	31,002
88,789	94,322	99,000	31,886	76,999	97,111	37,023	32,003
99,898	93,659	60,880	76,172	37,777	57,731	38,013	13,514
66,884	23,100	10,932	72,220	67,659	73,962	93,053	23,787
17,877	23,000	11,189	40,493	78,695	59,734	96,023	32,412
99,987	33,575	33,987	32,494	73,000	71,014	13,011	33,600
549)	610)	671)	732)	793)	854)	915)	976)

17. 28,900	18. 15,995	19. 31,100	20. 23,312	21. 82,349	22. 75,120	23. 96,213	24. 56,290
29,100	12,110	72,700	47,808	86,215	17,261	28,500	22,499
52,800	19,900	93,700	46,770	58,156	91,739	28,435	82,199
22,300	18,300	32,100	64,660	18,647	85,479	36,163	85,399
28,500	91,500	93,100	64,870	81,535	74,557	39,452	52,522
12,500	51,900	39,100	14,340	82,451	72,179	28,432	62,825
26,600	61,000	38,100	76,590	51,460	48,600	61,615	15,635
22,200	91,000	28,500	76,680	57,545	29,773	28,781	83,785
28,900	82,500	23,500	74,780	56,245	32,931	30,485	33,185
25,000	33,600	16,492	71,490	86,100	56,932	26,983	18,585
1,037)	1,098)	1,159)	1,220)	1,281)	1,342)	1,403)	1,464)

CHAPTER 18 *Terminology Review*

Employer's tax liability

EFTPS

FUTA

SUTA

1. Define employer's tax liability. What is included in the employer's tax liability? Why do you think it is often miscalculated? Give some examples.
   _____

2. Give an example of a situation in which FUTA and/or SUTA taxes may be used to pay benefits. _____

3. What is the SUTA rate and base (amount of earnings for which tax is paid) for your state? You may use the Internet or contact your local tax office. If SUTA varies by business, check with a local business to find its SUTA tax rate and base. _____

Chapter 18 Review Exercises
Exercise 1

Complete the partial pay register and then calculate the employer's tax liability for this pay period. Marital status and withholding allowances are indicated with abbreviations such as M-2 for married with two withholding allowances and S-1 for single with one withholding allowance.

	Employee	Status and W.A.	Earnings ($)	YTD Earnings ($)	Federal Income Tax ($)	Social Security ($)	Medicare ($)	FUTA ($)	SUTA ($)
1.	G. Mauldin	M-1	2,090.41	_____	_____	_____	_____	_____	_____
2.	J. Mauldin	M-1	5,060.10	_____	_____	_____	_____	_____	_____
3.	J. Mauldin, Jr.	S-1	680.45	_____	_____	_____	_____	_____	_____
4.				Totals	_____	_____	_____	_____	_____

5. The employer's total tax liability for the above three employees is _____.

Exercise 2

Complete the following partial employee pay records and the FUTA worksheet. At the end of which quarter will the employer need to deposit FUTA? The two employees are Amy Clarendon, who earns $1,500 per month, and Rose Rodriguez, who earns $1,990 per month. Both employees have worked for the company since the beginning of the year.

Amy Clarendon

	Month	Earnings	YTD Earnings	FUTA
1.	January	_____	_____	_____
2.	February	_____	_____	_____
3.	March	_____	_____	_____
4.	April	_____	_____	_____
5.	May	_____	_____	_____
6.	June	_____	_____	_____
7.	July	_____	_____	_____
8.	August	_____	_____	_____
9.	September	_____	_____	_____
10.	October	_____	_____	_____
11.	November	_____	_____	_____
12.	December	_____	_____	_____

Rose Rodriguez

Month	Earnings	YTD Earnings	FUTA
January	_____	_____	_____
February	_____	_____	_____
March	_____	_____	_____
April	_____	_____	_____
May	_____	_____	_____
June	_____	_____	_____
July	_____	_____	_____
August	_____	_____	_____
September	_____	_____	_____
October	_____	_____	_____
November	_____	_____	_____
December	_____	_____	_____

FUTA Worksheet

	First Quarter		Second Quarter Amount Carried Over:		Third Quarter Amount Carried Over:		Fourth Quarter Amount Carried Over:	
	Month	FUTA	Month	FUTA	Month	FUTA	Month	FUTA
13.	January	_____	April	_____	July	_____	October	_____
14.	February	_____	May	_____	August	_____	November	_____
15.	March	_____	June	_____	September	_____	December	_____
16.	Total	_____	Total	_____	Total	_____	Total	_____

17. A deposit of FUTA will need to be made at the end of quarter(s) _____.
18. The employer's total FUTA tax liability for the year is _____.

Exercise 3

19. Ken Barry is a self-employed carpenter. He earned $979.85 last week. What is his Social Security liability? _____ What is his Medicare liability? _____

20. Renee Sorenson owns a catering business. Last year she paid her manager $59,543. She has two additional employees. She paid Amy Carson $9,012 and Roseann Robinson $15,039. She withheld $32,532 from the three employees' pay for federal income tax. Calculate her tax liability for the three employees for Social Security _____, Medicare _____, FUTA _____, and SUTA _____. What was the total employer tax liability? _____

Trade Discounts

PART 1 *Speed and Accuracy Building Using Touch Key*

GOALS: Your speed goal is 10,000 strokes per hour.

Your accuracy target goal range is 95% to 100%.

With each repetition of the drill, try to improve your speed without lowering your accuracy score. If your percent-of-accuracy score falls below 95%, review your finger position and technique. Then try again.

Instructions: *Start Touch Key. Complete Lesson 10, Parts A through E. Write your scores for strokes per hour and percent of accuracy below.*

Touch Key Lesson 10—The 0 through 9 and Decimal Keys, Six-Digit Numbers

Today's Date	Strokes per Hour	Percent of Accuracy
A.		
B.		
C.		
D.		
E.		

PART 2 *Business Math Skills*

TRADE DISCOUNTS

How are goods that are produced by a manufacturer distributed to the consumer? In most cases, the **pattern of distribution of goods** is as shown in Figure 19.1.

Manufacturer, Wholesaler, or Supplier	
↓	sells to
Retailer	
↓	sells to
Consumer	

FIGURE 19.1

Suppliers such as manufacturers and wholesalers sometimes offer incentives to their customers, who may be dealers or retailers, as a way to increase sales. One such incentive is the **trade discount.** How are trade discounts used? Suppliers print catalogs listing prices for each item. The catalog price is referred to as the **list price.** The prices may be labeled as the suggested retail price. The trade discount is a discount applied to the list price. The price of an item after the trade discount has been taken from the list price is the **net price.** Storeowners or retailers pay the net price.

Using a trade discount has several advantages: (1) Discounts may be easily quoted or changed by means of a printed flyer, fax, e-mail, or a telephone call. The entire catalog does not have to be reprinted to reflect a change in prices. (2) A manufacturer's sales representative who wishes to quote greater discounts to large-volume buyers may do so easily. The advantages of this are readily apparent if we consider a potential order for quantities of 10,000 of 25 different items. It is much quicker and easier to quote a 10% discount than to calculate new individual prices for 25 items during a brief sales call.

SINGLE TRADE DISCOUNT

Using the percentage formula, base × rate = percentage, we can apply a single trade discount to the list price in a catalog or other printed medium to find the amount of the trade discount. The trade discount is subtracted from the list price to find the new (net) price.

PROBLEM 1

Calculate the trade discount amount for an item listed at $1,200 for which a 25% trade discount has been quoted.

This problem can be worked in one of two ways:

1. Two-step method: Use to find trade discount and net price (Figure 19.2).

Pocket Calculator Procedure

1,200 × .25 = $\boxed{300}$ trade discount amount

1,200 − 300 = $\boxed{900}$ net price

---

2. One-step method: Use to find net price (Figure 19.3).

The one-step method uses the complement of the trade discount rate. A **complement** is the difference of a percent and 100% or the difference of a decimal number and 1. The complement of 12% is 88% because 100% − 12% = 88%. The complement of 0.12 is 0.88 because 1 − 0.12 = 0.88.

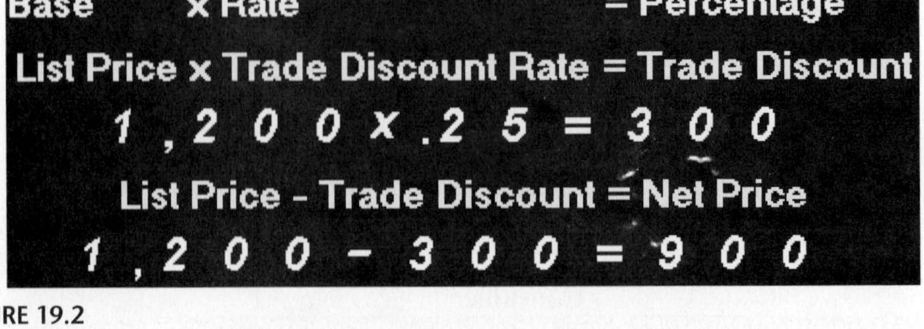

Base   x Rate   = Percentage

List Price x Trade Discount Rate = Trade Discount

$$1,200 \times .25 = 300$$

List Price − Trade Discount = Net Price

$$1,200 - 300 = 900$$

FIGURE 19.2

Shortcut:

To find the complement of 25%:

$$100\% - 25\% = 75\%$$

List Price x complement of discount rate = net price

$$1,200 \times .75 = 900$$

FIGURE 19.3

Solve Problem 1 using the one-step method.

If 25% is the amount of the trade discount, then 75% of the list price is the net price. Therefore, the list price times the complement of the trade discount rate (100% − 25%) equals the net price:

75% of $1,200 is the net price ($900)

Read carefully when solving a trade discount problem. Watch for words that will help you determine whether you need to solve for the amount of the trade discount or for the net price.

CALCULATING LIST PRICE AND TRADE DISCOUNT RATE

The percentage formula can be used to find rate and list price. Substitute **trade discount amount** for percentage, list price for base, and trade discount percent for rate as shown in Figure 19.4.

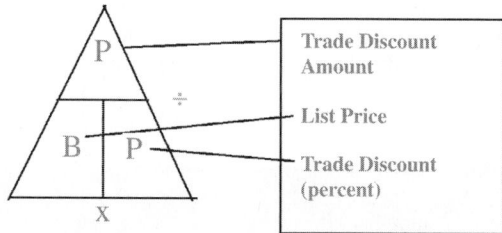

FIGURE 19.4

PROBLEM 2

Robert Bland, a car dealer, received a trade discount offer of 5%, which was $2,000 off the list price of a vehicle. What was the manufacturer's list price for the new vehicle?

1. To find the list price, use the percentage formula for base, Base = Percentage ÷ Rate, substituting appropriate terms: List Price = Trade Discount Amount ÷ Trade Discount Percent.
2. Substitute numbers for the terms in the formula and solve:

$$\text{List price} = \$2,000 \div 5\%$$
$$\text{List price} = \$40,000$$

PROBLEM 3

A restaurant chain wished to purchase new glassware. They can get the glassware for $31,000 less a $4,000 discount from company A, and they can get the glassware for $34,000 less a $5,500 discount from company B. What are the trade discount percents offered by the two companies?

Company A: Use the percentage formula for rate, Rate = Percentage ÷ Base, substituting appropriate terms: Trade Discount Percent = Trade Discount Amount ÷ List Price. Substitute numbers for the terms and solve:

$$\text{Trade discount percent} = 4{,}000 \div 31{,}000$$
$$\text{Trade discount percent} = 12.9\%$$

Company B:

$$\text{Trade discount percent} = 4{,}500 \div 34{,}000$$
$$\text{Trade discount percent} = 13.24\% \quad \text{(answer rounded to hundredths)}$$

TRADE DISCOUNT SERIES

Rather than a single trade discount, a manufacturer may elect to give additional discounts using two or more discount rates known as a **trade discount series**. A trade discount series may also be referred to as a **chain discount**. An example of a trade discount series is 20/10/15, where the numbers refer to percents. The discounts in the trade discount series are applied to the list price in order, first to last.

PROBLEM 4

Apply the trade discount 20/10/10 to the list price of $1,200 to find net price. Beginning with the first discount in the series, find the 20% discount and subtract it from $1,200. To the difference ($960), apply the second discount of 10%. Subtract the discount amount from $960. To this difference ($864), apply the third discount, which is also 10%. Subtract the discount amount from $864. The net price is $777.60. See Figure 19.5.

Trade Discount Series 20/10/10 (chain discount)
$1,200 x .20 = 240 $1,200 - 240 = 960
$960 x .10 = 96 $960 - 96 = 864
$864 x .10 = 86.40 $864 - 86.40 = 777.60

FIGURE 19.5

Pocket Calculator Procedure
1,200 − 20 % 960 − 10 % 864 − 10 % 777.60

Net price can also be found by multiplying list price by the complement of each discount in the series, which would allow the skipping of the subtraction step.

3. _____ The price of an item after a trade discount has been subtracted from the list price.

4. _____ The discount applied to a list price in a catalog.

5. _____ More than one discount applied in order, first to last, to a list price in a catalog.

6. _____ The result of multiplying a series of discounts that have been converted to decimal numbers.

7. _____ Wholesalers, manufacturers, and suppliers sell to retailers who sell to consumers.

8. _____ Another name for trade discount series.

9. _____ The dollar amount of a trade discount.

Name _____

Class/Section _____

Score (Correct Answers ÷ No. of Assigned Problems) _____

Chapter 19 Review Exercises
Exercise 1

Find the trade discount amount for the following:

	List Price ($)	Trade Discount (%)	Trade Discount Amount ($)
1.	35.95	16	_____
2.	79.59	22	_____
3.	3,457.49	35	_____
4.	339.45	12	_____
5.	65.72	8	_____

Exercise 2

Find the net price using the complement of the trade discount. Round to hundredths.

	List Price ($)	Trade Discount (%)	Net Price ($)
6.	698.00	26	_____
7.	4,529.90	25	_____
8.	53.67	29	_____
9.	195.00	12	_____
10.	0.25	15	_____

Exercise 3

Find the net price.

	List Price ($)	Trade Discount Series (%)	Net Price ($)
11.	54.00	15/10/10	_____
12.	39.95	25/20/5	_____
13.	2.59	35/10/2	_____
14.	10.59	24/10/10	_____
15.	33.99	10/9/8	_____

Exercise 4

Find the net decimal equivalent.

	Trade Discount Series (%)	Net Decimal Equivalent
16.	5/4/4	_____
17.	10/7/5	_____
18.	15/20/9	_____
19.	10/5/5	_____
20.	5/2	_____

Exercise 5

Find the net price using the net decimal equivalent.

	List Price ($)	Trade Discount Series (%)	Net Decimal Equivalent	Net Price ($)
21.	5.95	5/3/2	_____	_____
22.	16.57	10/8/4	_____	_____
23.	0.29	15/20/10	_____	_____
24.	312.11	25/10/5	_____	_____
25.	15.43	20/10/3	_____	_____

Exercise 6

Find the trade discount amount using the complement of the net discount equivalent.

	List Price ($)	Trade Discount Series (%)	Net Discount Equivalent	Complement of Net Discount Equivalent	Trade Discount Amount ($)
26.	1,300	12/5/3	_____	_____	_____
27.	6,950	10/8/5	_____	_____	_____
28.	3,004	9/8/4	_____	_____	_____
29.	2,559	12/10/8	_____	_____	_____
30.	10,000	10/9/5	_____	_____	_____

Exercise 7

1. Krajak's Lamps has selected $1,750 worth of goods from a supplier's catalog. The supplier is offering a 30% trade discount. What is the net price of the order? _____

2. A piece of equipment lists for $45,496 with a trade discount of 28%. What is the net price? _____

3. A supplier discounts merchandise at 25/10/15. The list price of the merchandise needed by a store manager is $6,908. What is the net price? _____

4. A dinette set lists for $2,112. If the manufacturer offers a 63% trade discount, what is the amount of the discount? _____ What is the net price? _____

5. A selection of shoes lists at $1,580. A trade discount of 20/10/10 is offered by the manufacturer. What is the net price? _____ What is the amount of the trade discount? _____

6. A computer lists at $1,600. The discount amount is $300. What is the trade discount rate rounded to hundredths? _____

7. A storeowner wishing to purchase merchandise was quoted a trade discount amount of $500 or 15%. What is the list price? _____

8. A supplier offers a trade discount of 15/12/10. What would the net price be on merchandise that lists at $522.89? _____ What is the trade discount amount? _____

9. A school supply company lists small desks at $59.59 each. If the trade discount is 10/8, what is the net price? _____

10. If an order for school desks exceeds $5,000, the trade discount is 10/8/8 for the entire order. What is the net price for an order of $6,550? _____

CHAPTER 20

Cash Discounts, Invoices with Terms

PART 1 *Speed and Accuracy Building Using Touch Key*

GOALS: Your speed goal is 10,000 strokes per hour.
Your accuracy target goal range is 95% to 100%.

With each repetition of the drill, try to improve your speed without lowering your accuracy score. If your percent-of-accuracy score falls below 95%, review your finger position and technique. Then try again.

Instructions: *Start Touch Key. Complete Drill 4, Parts A through E, One-Minute Timings. Write your scores for strokes per hour and percent of accuracy below.*

Touch Key Drill 4—The 0 through 9 and Decimal Keys, Six-Digit Numbers, One-Minute Timings

Today's Date	Strokes per Hour	Percent of Accuracy
A.		
B.		
C.		
D.		
E.		

PART 2 *Business Math Skills*

CASH DISCOUNTS

Chapter 19 illustrated the pattern of distribution of goods from a manufacturer, wholesaler, or supplier to the retailer and then to the consumer. The use of trade discounts as an incentive to buyers was discussed. Once the sale to the retailer has been made, it is to the benefit of the seller to collect payment for the merchandise as soon as possible to maintain the cash flow of the business. The receipt of cash from sales of goods and services and the disbursement of cash to pay for goods and expenses is referred to as **cash flow**. An adequate cash flow is imperative for the business to meet its obligations. The seller may offer a **cash discount**, which is an incentive to the buyer to pay the invoice promptly. After a sale is made, an invoice (bill) is prepared that itemizes the goods sold, prices, and **terms** of the sale including cash discounts, date payment is expected, and freight charges, if any. On the invoice in Figure 20.1 the seller gave a trade discount, so

Gordon's Gift Supply

1300 N. Eldon St.
Cranston, NJ 10001
100-555-1234
Fax: 100-555-1235

INVOICE

SOLD TO:		
Janie's Gifts	INVOICE NUMBER	50321
1001 First St.	INVOICE DATE	May 15, 2004
Corpus Christi, TX 78001	PURCHASE ORDER NO.	JG200031
	TERMS	2/10,n30
	SALES PERSON	S. Brown
	SHIPPED VIA	Yellow Freight
	F.O.B.	Shipping point

SHIPPED TO:

Janie's Gifts
1001 First St.
Corpus Christi, TX 78001

QTY	DESCRIPTION	PRICE	AMOUNT
12	#1289 Vase Assortment	129.50	1554.00
30	#8911 Jewelry Boxes	12.80	384.00
12	#6780 Assorted Party Favor Packages	8.70	104.40
	Prices reflect terms of 30/10/10.		
	THANK YOU FOR YOUR BUSINESS!		
		SUBTOTAL	2042.40
		TAX	0.00
		FREIGHT	69.00
		$2,111.40	
		TOTAL DUE	

FIGURE 20.1

the amounts shown are the **net prices**—in other words, the seller has already calculated the trade discount. An invoice may or may not list the trade discount terms.

READING AND INTERPRETING CASH DISCOUNT TERMS

2/10,n30

A typical designation for a cash discount is written 2/10,n30 (see upper right portion of the invoice in Figure 20.1). It is read "two 10 net 30," and means that a 2% discount will be applied to the total net price if the invoice is paid within 10 days of the date of the invoice. The date of the invoice in Figure 20.1 is May 15, 2004. A cash discount of 2% will be taken if the seller receives the invoice payment by May 25, 2004. Net price minus the cash discount equals the **net amount**. Note that the payment must be in the seller's hands within the **cash discount period**; a postmark within 10 days of the invoice date is generally not acceptable for granting cash discounts. Cash discounts are applied to the amounts for merchandise only. Discounts are not applied to freight charges.

The n30 part of the term means that if the invoice is not paid within 10 days of the date of the invoice, the total invoice amount is due 30 days from the date of the invoice. Penalties may be charged by the seller if the invoice is not paid by the due date.

PROBLEM 1

An invoice dated May 1 for $1,200 with terms of 2/15,n30 was paid before May 14. Does a cash discount apply? What is the net amount to be paid?

Because the bill was paid during the 15-day discount period, the 2% cash discount can be taken. To find the amount to pay, multiply $1,200 by the complement of 2%:

$$1{,}200 \times .98 = \$1{,}176 \text{ net amount}$$

CASH DISCOUNT PERIOD

Some companies have a policy of taking advantage of all cash discounts. It is certainly to the advantage of the company to do so if the necessary cash is available. Some companies will even borrow money to take advantage of cash discounts when the cost of borrowing money is less than the amount of the cash discount received. Consider an invoice dated May 30 and terms are 2/15,n30. The terms tell us that the discount period is 15 days from the date of the invoice. To determine the last day of the discount period, refer to Figure 20.2.

Step 1: Add 15 days to May 30.

Step 2: There are 31 days in May, so 31 days are subtracted from the 45 days found in step 1.

Step 3: The remaining 14 days fall within June. The last day to take advantage of the 2% cash discount is June 14.

May	3	0	Date of invoice
+	1	5	Number of days in discount period
	4	5	
−	3	1	Number of days in May
	1	4	Last day in June discount may be taken

FIGURE 20.2

MORE TERMS

2/10,1/20,n30

Another frequently used cash discount term gives different discounts for two or more discount periods. The term 2/10,1/20,n30 is an example. It is read "two 10, one 20, net 30" and means that a 2% discount will be taken if the invoice is paid within 10 days of the invoice date, a 1% discount will be taken if the invoice is paid on days 11 through 20 after the invoice date, and the full amount is due by the day 30 after the invoice date.

PROBLEM 2

An invoice dated March 3 for $900 with terms of 2/10,1/20,n30 is being paid March 18. Is a cash discount allowed, and if so, how much is the cash discount?

Begin by calculating the number of days that have elapsed since the invoice date as shown in Figure 20.3. Fifteen days have passed since the date of the invoice. A 1% cash discount can be taken.

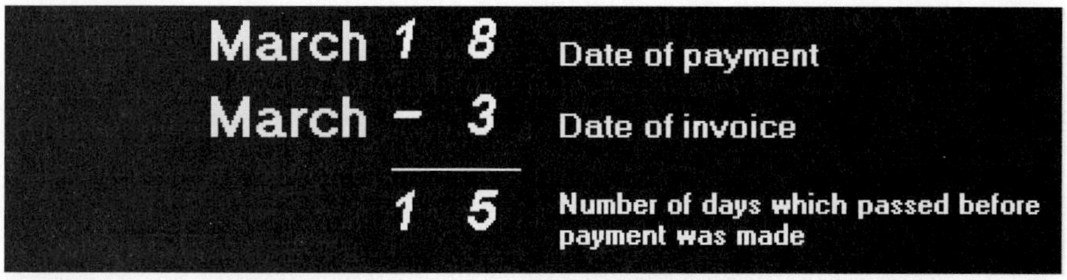

March 1 8 Date of payment
March – 3 Date of invoice
1 5 Number of days which passed before payment was made

FIGURE 20.3

To find the net amount, multiply the total net price by the complement of 1%:

$$\text{Net Price} \times \text{Complement of Cash Discount Rate} = \text{Net Amount}$$
$$\$900 \times 0.99 = \$891$$

1/10EOM,n30EOM

The term 1/10EOM,n30EOM is read "one 10 end of month, net 30 end of month" and indicates that a buyer can take a 1% discount if the invoice is paid within 10 days after the end of the current month. The full amount is due 30 days after the end of the current month. The last day of the discount period of an invoice dated June 20, 2004, is July 10, 2004. The full amount is due July 30, 2004.

Exception

If an invoice with terms of 1/10EOM,n30EOM is dated on or after the 26th, the buyer can take a 1% discount if the invoice is paid by the 10th of the month after next. The last day of the discount period of an invoice dated June 26, 2004, is August 10, 2004. The due date for full payment is the 30th of the month after next (August 30, 2004).

PROBLEM 3

The terms of an invoice dated February 5 for $545 are 1/10EOM. The invoice was paid before March 10, the end of the discount period (see Figure 20.4). What was the net amount?

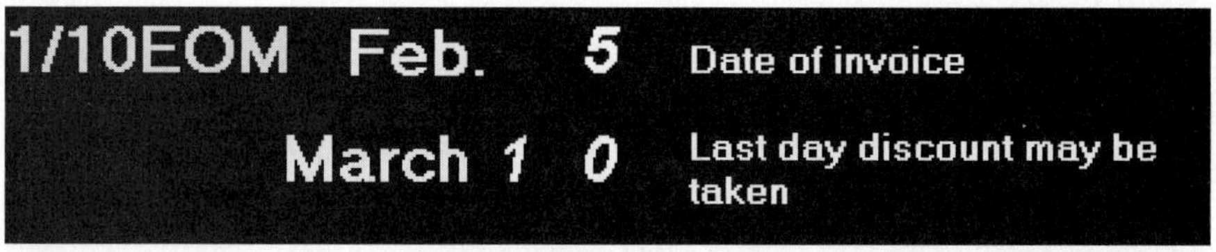

1/10EOM Feb. 5 Date of invoice
March 1 0 Last day discount may be taken

FIGURE 20.4

Multiply total net price by the complement of the 1% cash discount to find the net amount:

$$\$545 \times 0.99 = \$539.55$$

PROBLEM 4

An invoice for $545 is dated February 27 with terms of 1/10EOM. What is the ending date of the discount period? What is the net amount if the invoice is paid April 1?

Because the invoice date of February 27 is after the 26th of the month, the exception that states that the buyer has until the 10th day of the month after next is used to determine the discount period as shown in Figure 20.5. March is the next month after February, and April is the month after that. April 10 is the last day the 1% cash discount can be taken.

1/10EOM	Feb. 2 7	Since the invoice date is on or after the 26th, the buyer has until the 10th of the month
	Mar.	after next to take advantage of the discount
	Apr. 1 0	Last day discount may be taken

FIGURE 20.5

The invoice was paid April 1, so the net amount is $545 \times .99 = \$539.55$ (Amount of Invoice $\times$ Complement of 1% = Net Amount).

22/10ROG,n30ROG

The term 2/10ROG,n30ROG is read "two 10 receipt of goods, (net 30 receipt of goods)" and indicates that the buyer can take a 2% discount if the invoice is paid within 10 days after the receipt of goods. The full amount of the invoice is due 30 days after the goods are received.

Knowing the date goods are received is necessary to determine the last day this type of cash discount can be taken and to determine the due date of the full amount of the invoice if cash discounts are not taken. The receiving department should stamp the paperwork for all merchandise received with a date-received stamp. Some receiving departments date stamp the packing slip and send it to the accounting department to be matched with the purchase order and with the invoice when it arrives from the seller. Other receiving departments make it a practice to match the packing slip with a copy of the purchase order, date stamp the purchase order, and send it to accounting to be matched with the invoice when the invoice arrives from the seller.

PROBLEM 5

Merchandise was received on December 12. An invoice of $650 for these goods was dated December 10 with terms of 2/10ROG. What is the last day of the discount period? What is the net amount if the invoice is paid within the discount period?

The discount period runs from December 12, the date the goods were received, until December 22, 10 days after the goods were received (Figure 20.6). If the invoice were paid within the discount period, the net price would be $637, the net price multiplied by the complement of the cash discount:

$$\$650 \times 0.98 = \$637 \text{ net amount}$$

| 2/10ROG | Dec. 1 2 | Date goods were received |
| | Dec. 2 2 | Last day discount may be taken |

FIGURE 20.6

PARTIAL PAYMENTS AND CASH DISCOUNTS

Cash flow problems may prevent a business from paying the full amount of an invoice within the discount period. However, if a business can pay part of the invoice within the discount period, it may take a discount on the **partial payment**. The cash discount in this case is given as a credit on the partial payment itself. In other words, if a cash discount of 2% is offered, a partial payment of $100 within the discount period is worth more than $100. Using the percentage formula where the partial payment is the percentage, the complement of the discount rate is the rate, and the amount to be credited to the buyer's account is the base, we have

$$\$100 \div 0.98 = \$102.04$$

The visual reminder in Figure 20.7 illustrates the percentage formula when used to find the amount to credit a buyer's account after a partial payment has been made during a cash discount period.

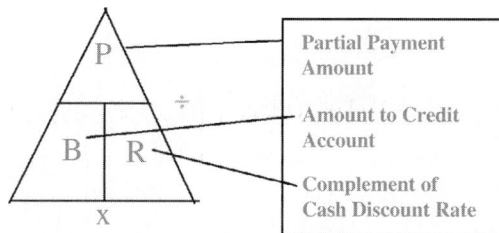

FIGURE 20.7

An **outstanding balance** is the amount owed on an account after partial payments have been made. After calculating the amount to be credited, subtract it from the invoice total to find the outstanding balance.

PROBLEM 6

An invoice for $900 with terms of 2/15,n45 was received January 5. A partial payment of $450 was made before January 20. Find the amount to be credited to the buyer's account as a result of the partial payment.

Step 1: The partial payment divided by the complement of the cash discount rate equals the amount to credit the buyer's account. Substitute numbers into the formula as shown in Figure 20.8.

Step 2: Subtract the result of step 1 ($459.18) from the amount of the invoice to find the outstanding balance ($440.82).

Percentage / Rate = Base
Partial payment / Complement of Rate = Amount to be credited
$$450 \div .98 = 459.18$$
Invoice amount - Amount to be credited = Outstanding balance
$$900 - 459.18 = 440.82$$

FIGURE 20.8

FREIGHT TERMS

Freight refers to the method of shipping goods. As mentioned earlier in this chapter, discounts do not apply to freight charges. When calculating the amount of a cash discount, do not include the cost of freight in the net price even if the freight charge is included on the invoice.

There are three typical freight terms. Two freight terms include the acronym **FOB**, which means free on board. **FOB shipping point** means that the seller has the responsibility and expense for moving the merchandise to the shipping point. That is, the buyer pays all shipping from the shipping point to the destination of the merchandise. **FOB destination** means that the seller has the responsibility and expense for moving the merchandise to its destination. That is, the shipping costs will be paid by the seller. A third freight term, **prepay** or **prepay and bill** specifies that the seller will pay the freight charges and will later bill the buyer for the freight costs (Figure 20.9).

Note: Many invoices simply include a space for SHIPPING. If an amount other than zero is shown in this space, the shipping charge is to be paid by the buyer.

FOB shipping point—buyer pays freight

FOB destination—seller pays freight

Prepay—seller pays freight; then bills buyer for freight costs

FIGURE 20.9

PROBLEM 7

An invoice for $500 including a $50 freight charge was dated April 4. Terms of the invoice were 2/10,n30. If the bill is paid on April 10, calculate total amount to be submitted in payment of the invoice.

1. Begin by subtracting the freight charge from the amount of the invoice as shown in Figure 20.10.

(Invoice - Shipping) x Complement of discount rate = Net amount for goods

$$500 - 50 = 450$$

$$450 \times .98 = 441$$

Net amount for goods + shipping cost = total payment to submit

$$441 + 50 = 491$$

FIGURE 20.10

2. The invoice was paid within the cash discount period. Use the complement of the cash discount rate to find the net amount.
3. Add the freight charge to the net amount to find the total payment for the invoice.

Calculator Procedure

500 − 50 = $\boxed{450}$ × .98 = $\boxed{441}$ + 50 = $\boxed{491}$

MERCHANDISE RETURNS

Defective or damaged merchandise may be returned to the buyer. A **credit voucher** will be issued by the seller for the dollar amount of the returned merchandise. Before paying an invoice or calculating a cash discount, subtract the dollar amount for the returned merchandise from the net price.

Name _____

Class/Section _____

Score (Correct Answers ÷ No. of Assigned Problems) _____

 PART 2 *Business Math Skills*

Exercise 1

Calculate the last day of the discount period(s) and the last day to pay the invoice.

	Date of Invoice	Terms	Last Day of Discount Period(s)	Last Day to Pay Invoice
1.	December 10	2/10,n30	_____	_____
2.	April 9	2/20,1/30,n60	_____	_____
3.	March 29	2/10EOM,n30EOM	_____	_____
4.	March 22	3/15,2/25ROG,n45ROG (goods received March 20)	_____	_____
5.	October 10	3/10,2/15,1/20,n30	_____	_____

Exercise 2

Complete the following worksheet detailing several invoices received. What is the last day of the discount period(s)? What is the complement of the cash discount rate if *all invoices were paid within the first discount period*? What is the net amount for each invoice? There were no freight charges or merchandise returns.

	Invoice Date	Invoice Amount ($)	Terms	Last Day of Discount Period(s)	Complement of Cash Discount Rate to be Used	Net Amount ($)
6.	April 10	459.82	3/15,n30	_____	_____	_____
7.	August 1	751.25	2/10,1/20,n30	_____	_____	_____
8.	July 28	140.79	1/15EOM,n30EOM	_____	_____	_____
9.	April 15	77.49	3/10ROG,n30ROG (goods received April 10)	_____	_____	_____
10.	July 13	32.51	2/10EOM,n30EOM	_____	_____	_____

Exercise 3

Complete the following worksheet listing invoices received. What is the last day of the discount period(s)? What is the complement of the cash discount rate to be used to calculate net amount? What is the net amount for each invoice? There were no freight charges or merchandise returns.

	Invoice Amount ($)	Invoice Date	Terms	Date Paid	Last Day of Discount Period(s)	Complement of Cash Discount Rate to be Used	Net Amount ($)
11.	690.13	January 20	2/10,n30	January 24	_____	_____	_____
12.	3,055.57	March 28	2/10EOM,n30EOM	May 12	_____	_____	_____
13.	2,510.50	April 15	2/10,1/15,n30	April 26	_____	_____	_____
14.	359.12	March 6	3/10,1/30,n45	April 1	_____	_____	_____
15.	1,325.19	April 4	3/20ROG,n30ROG (goods received April 10)	April 28	_____	_____	_____

Exercise 4

Calculate the amount to be credited to the buyer's account for each of the partial payments below. All partial payments were made within the first cash discount period.

	Invoice Date	Terms	Partial Payment ($)	Amount to Credit Account ($)
16.	July 9	3/10,n30	425	_____
17.	August 10	2/10EOM	605	_____
18.	July 25	2/10,1/15,n30	1,350	_____
19.	April 1	2/10ROG (goods received March 31)	870	_____
20.	April 16	2/15,1/25,n45	900	_____

PART 3 *Review and Practice Using Business Math FUNdamentals*

GOAL: Complete 9 of the 10 problems correctly.

Instructions: Start Business Math FUNdamentals. Complete Tutorials 42 through 44, and Drills 33 through 35. If you are not satisfied with your score, repeat the drill. Write your scores below.

Business Math FUNdamentals Drill 33

Today's Date	Score

Business Math FUNdamentals Drill 34

Today's Date	Score

Business Math FUNdamentals Drill 35

Today's Date	Score

 PART 4 *Desktop Calculator*

CALCULATING NET AMOUNT

PROBLEM

Use the desktop calculator to calculate the amount to pay for an invoice dated May 25 for $690 with terms of 2/10,n30. The invoice is paid June 1.

MACHINE SETUP Decimal Selector—F
Rounding Switch—5/4
Printer Switch—On

Procedure: Begin by determining whether the invoice was paid within the cash discount period.

1. Add 10 days to the date of the invoice, May 25.
2. There are 31 days in May, so 31 should be subtracted from the total calculated in step 1. The difference, 4, is carried into June. The last day to receive a cash discount is June 4.

May   25
        +10
       ‾‾‾‾
         35

        −31   Number of days in May
June   4

$$25 + 10 + T\ \boxed{35} + 31 - T\ \boxed{4}$$

The invoice was paid June 1, so the cash discount is applied to the net price of the invoice, $690, to find the net amount:

$$690 \times .98 = \boxed{676.2}$$

The desktop calculator feature that allows a percent to be calculated and subtracted easily and efficiently may be used when both the cash discount amount and the net amount is required:

$$690 \times 2\ \boxed{\%}\ \boxed{13.8} - \boxed{676.2}$$

The cash discount amount is $13.80. The net amount is $676.20.

TAPE 20.1:

```
       0 · C


25 · 00   ÷
10 · 00   +
35 · 00   *


35 · 00   +
31 · 00   −
 4 · 00   *
```

TAPE 20.2:

```
     0 · C


690 ·     ×
  2 ·     %
 13 · 8   *

676 · 2 - %
```

CHECKING AN INVOICE

PROBLEM

The prices on the invoice should reflect a trade discount (see Figure 20.11). Check the invoice carefully and calculate the net price if the invoice is paid within the discount period.

TERMS 2/10,n30			
QTY	DESCRIPTION	PRICE	AMOUNT
12	#1289 Vase Assortment	129.50	1554.00
30	#8911 Jewelry Boxes	12.80	384.00
12	#6780 Assorted Party Favor Packages	8.70	104.40
	Prices reflect terms of 30/10/10.		
	THANK YOU FOR YOUR BUSINESS!		
		SUBTOTAL	2042.40
		TAX	0.00
		FREIGHT	69.00
		$2,111.40	
		TOTAL DUE	

FIGURE 20.11

TAPE 20.4:

```
    228·4  x
   0·567  =
  129·50  *

  129·50  x
     12·  =
1,554·00  *

1,554·00 M+
  22·57  x
  0·567  =
  12·80  *

  12·80  x
    30·  =
 384·00  *

 384·00 M+
  15·34  x
  0·567  =
   8·70  *

   8·70  x
    12·  =
 104·40  *

 104·40 M+
2,042·40 M*

2,042·40  x
   0·98  =
2,001·55  *

2,001·55  +
  69·00  +
2,070·55  *
```

The list prices for the items on the invoice are as follows:

#1289 Vase assortment	$228.40
#8911 Jewelry boxes	$22.57
#6780 Assorted party favor packages	$15.34

1. Begin by calculating the net decimal equivalent for the trade discount series 30/10/10:

$$.7 \times .9 \times .9 = \boxed{.567}$$

MACHINE SETUP Decimal selector—2
Rounding Switch—5/4
Printer Switch—On

Check that memory is clear.

2. Multiply each list price by the net decimal equivalent to check the net price listed on the invoice. Multiply by the quantity to check the **extension**—the price for a single item multiplied by the quantity ordered. Store each in memory. Recall memory total to find the invoice subtotal:

$$228.40 \times .567 = \boxed{129.50} \times 12 = \boxed{1,554} \text{ M+}$$
$$22.57 \times .567 = \boxed{12.80} \times 30 = \boxed{384} \text{ M+}$$
$$15.34 \times .567 = \boxed{8.70} \times 12 = \boxed{104.40} \text{ M+ MT } \boxed{2,042.40}$$

3. Multiply the subtotal, which is still in the calculator display, by the complement of the cash discount to find the net amount. Note the net amount on the invoice:

$$\boxed{2,042.40} \times .98 \text{ T } \boxed{2,001.55}$$

4. Add the freight charges to the net amount to find the total due. Note the total due on the invoice:

$$\boxed{2,001.55} + 69 + \text{T } \boxed{2,070.55}$$

TAPE 20.3:

```
   0·C

   0·7  x
   0·9  x
   0·9  =
 0·567  *
```

 PART 4 *Desktop Calculators*

Exercise 1

Calculate the last day of the discount period(s), the cash discount amount, and the net amount for each invoice.

	Net Price ($)	Invoice Date	Terms	Date of Invoice Payment	Amount of Cash Discount	Last Day of Discount Period(s)	Net Amount ($)
1.	700	June 10	2/10,1/20,n30	June 25	_____	_____	_____
2.	450	May 20	2/10,1/15,n30	May 28	_____	_____	_____
3.	1,112	July 15	2/20ROG,n30ROG (goods received July 10)	August 1	_____	_____	_____
4.	5,960	August 30	1/10EOM,n30EOM	September 30	_____	_____	_____
5.	680	September 25	2/10EOM,n30EOM	October 5	_____	_____	_____

Exercise 2

Calculate the last day of the discount period(s) and the amount to credit the account for each invoice.

	Net Price ($)	Invoice Date	Terms	Date of Payment	Last Day of Discount Period (s)	Amount of Partial Payment ($)	Amount to Credit Account ($)
6.	500	July 11	2/10,1/20,n30	July 25	_____	300	_____
7.	650	May 20	2/10,1/15,n30	June 1	_____	350	_____
8.	790	March 4	3/15ROG,n30ROG (goods received March 6)	March 15	_____	400	_____
9.	8,000	March 26	2/15,n30	April 1	_____	6,000	_____
10.	2,500	March 9	2/10EOM,n30EOM	April 15	_____	2,000	_____

Exercise 3

Check the invoice shown in Figure 20.12 from A-1 Automotive Suppliers to Gene's Auto Shop for errors. A trade discount of 20/10/10 is allowed by Automotive Suppliers, Inc. The purchase order shows the following merchandise order:

Quantity	Part Number	List Price ($)
12	36905	59.29
20	20001	169.25
10	39607	65.05
5	37991	112.72

1. Mark any corrections necessary on the invoice.
2. Calculate the amount of payment if the invoice is paid on January 30. _____
3. If the manager decided to pay only $1,500 on the invoice on January 30, calculate the amount to be credited and the outstanding balance. _____, _____

A-1 Automotive Suppliers, Inc.

101 Main St.
Dallas, TX 75000
*   100-555-1234*
Fax: 100-555-1235

INVOICE

SOLD TO:

Gene's Auto Shop

PO Box 67001

San Antonio, TX 76000

INVOICE NUMBER	67008
INVOICE DATE	January 17, 2004
PURCHASE ORDER NO.	65332
TERMS	3/10,2/20,n30
SALES PERSON	S. Brown
SHIPPED VIA	UPS
F.O.B.	Shipping point

SHIPPED TO:

Gene's Auto Shop

1200 N. Rio Grande

San Antonio, TX 76000

QTY	DESCRIPTION	PRICE	AMOUNT
12	Part #36905	59.29	711.48
20	Part #20001	169.25	3385.00
10	Part #39607	65.05	650.50
5	Part # 37991	112.72	563.60
	Prices reflect terms of 20/10/10.		
	THANK YOU FOR YOUR BUSINESS!		
		SUBTOTAL	5310.58
		TAX	0.00
		FREIGHT	125.00
			5435.58
			TOTAL DUE

FIGURE 20.12

Exercise 4

Strokes per Minute Score _____

Accuracy Score (Correct Strokes ÷ Total Strokes) _____

One-Minute Addition Timing (0 through 9 Keys, Six-Digit Numbers)

(Optional: Your instructor may wish you to use Touch Key on the computer for all your timings. Check with your instructor before completing this exercise.)

Complete as many of the problems as possible in 1 minute by adding. Work quickly and accurately. The number preceding each closing parenthesis indicates the cumulative number of strokes for problems attempted. For example, if you complete Problems 1 through 3 in 1 minute, your strokes-per-minute score is 213. Optional: 3- to 5-minute timings.

1. 137,556	2. 910,024	3. 776,544	4. 729,006	5. 477,850	6. 694,200
478,341	676,932	475,350	830,902	545,500	628,500
723,890	362,009	174,800	960,701	634,650	323,100
301,657	297,545	215,600	544,603	169,995	187,400
275,987	586,041	897,400	630,104	257,359	321,006
583,524	819,000	519,500	440,405	334,229	223,005
891,093	164,788	624,300	124,003	107,899	109,003
276,835	454,921	976,100	251,003	745,775	700,004
390,569	753,896	340,300	382,001	854,900	314,006
653,870	101,009	303,300	101,002	934,556	325,006
71)	142)	213)	284)	355)	426)

7. 730,000	8. 917,001	9. 341,400	10. 976,900	11. 656,987	12. 444,779
860,000	819,003	266,420	942,677	420,122	753,100
910,000	718,002	155,850	563,553	660,455	120,666
430,000	413,001	266,150	876,998	570,004	135,350
530,000	519,004	177,700	788,565	622,999	155,555
620,000	671,002	388,689	874,322	459,000	733,886
130,000	377,007	299,599	797,659	565,880	476,772
250,000	283,004	366,884	822,100	410,432	472,250
360,000	138,005	317,256	825,000	411,119	740,495
950,000	948,003	199,374	735,575	633,980	732,495
497)	568)	639)	710)	781)	852)

13. 543,450	14. 690,661	15. 916,000	16. 295,004	17. 388,900	18. 495,995
629,995	389,000	937,013	582,600	369,100	492,110
241,995	679,885	838,064	864,000	355,800	459,900
627,229	969,655	739,014	234,870	372,300	528,300
830,759	376,444	730,045	296,002	298,500	599,500
360,999	367,111	827,023	816,003	211,500	654,900
137,577	656,741	828,013	589,514	276,600	562,000
920,659	652,962	792,053	246,787	127,200	490,000
845,695	959,854	797,024	836,412	178,900	486,500
220,000	956,014	910,011	254,600	135,000	434,600
923)	994)	1,065)	1,136)	1,207)	1,278

19. 836,100	20. 100,655	21. 622,349	22. 100,120	23. 126,213	24. 120,290
876,700	145,880	366,215	800,261	800,500	220,499
793,700	141,770	354,156	791,339	200,435	320,199
832,100	253,660	911,647	185,429	350,163	450,399
795,100	265,870	921,535	974,559	790,452	520,599
749,100	216,340	632,451	362,179	880,432	620,895
958,100	326,590	631,460	145,600	610,255	150,695
988,500	136,680	977,545	829,573	250,721	230,795
963,500	144,780	946,245	832,331	300,115	330,005
916,490	321,490	384,100	356,232	260,543	110,000
1,349)	1,420)	1,491)	1,562)	1,633)	1,704)

CHAPTER 20 *Terminology Review*

Cash discount

Cash discount period

Cash flow

Credit voucher
Extension
FOB
FOB destination
FOB shipping point
Freight
Net amount
Net prices
Outstanding balance
Partial payment
Prepay
Prepay and bill
Terms

Write the correct term next to the appropriate description.

1. _____ A payment less than the net amount of an invoice.
2. _____ Seller pays for shipping and later bills the buyer for it.
3. _____ The receipt and expenditure of cash in a business.
4. _____ Indicate any cash discount, cash discount period, and due date for full payment of invoice.
5. _____ Buyer pays for shipping.
6. _____ Invoice amount minus partial payment(s).
7. _____ Net price minus cash discount(s).
8. _____ A discount stated on an invoice that is applicable if the invoice is paid within a specified number of days.
9. _____ Seller pays shipping.
10. _____ Shipping charges.
11. _____ A cash discount is allowed if payment of an invoice is made during these dates.

Name _____

Class/Section _____

Score (Correct Answers ÷ No. of Assigned Problems) _____

Chapter 20 Review Exercises
Exercise 1

Calculate the last day of the discount period(s) and the last day to pay the invoice.

	Date of Invoice	Terms	Last Day of Discount Period(s)	Last Day to Pay Invoice
1.	March 22	3/15,n30	_____	_____
2.	June 26	2/10,1/15,n30	_____	_____
3.	April 12	3/30,1/45,n90	_____	_____
4.	August 25	1/10,2/20EOM,n30EOM	_____	_____
5.	February 20, 2004 (leap year)	2/10,n30	_____	_____

Exercise 2

Complete the following worksheet detailing several invoices received. What is the last day of the discount period(s)? What is the complement of the cash discount rate if *all invoices were paid within the first discount period*? What is the net amount for each invoice? There were no freight charges or merchandise returns.

	Invoice Date	Invoice Amount ($)	Terms	Last Day of Discount Period(s)	Complement of Cash Discount Rate	Net Amount ($)
6.	March 22	768.90	2/10,n30	_____	_____	_____
7.	July 20	1,102.91	2/10,1/20,n30	_____	_____	_____
8.	June 30	139.20	1/10EOM,n30EOM	_____	_____	_____
9.	March 30	82.56	2/10ROG,n30ROG (goods received March 15)	_____	_____	_____
10.	September 21	69.25	1/20ROG,n30ROG (goods received September 19)	_____	_____	_____

Exercise 3

Complete the following worksheet listing invoices received. What is the last day of the discount period(s)? What is the complement of the cash discount rate to be used to calculate the net amount? What is the net amount for each invoice? There were no freight charges or merchandise returns.

	Invoice Amount ($)	Invoice Date	Terms	Date Paid	Last Day of Discount Period(s)	Complement of Cash Discount Rate to be Used	Net Amount ($)
11.	12,080.56	March 10	2/10,1/20,n30	March 25	_____	_____	_____
12.	16,895.90	March 20	2/10EOM,n30EOM	April 1	_____	_____	_____
13.	10,168.59	March 5	3/10,n30	March 9	_____	_____	_____
14.	15,670.98	April 2	3/10EOM,n30EOM	May 1	_____	_____	_____
15.	21,658.79	April 10	2/15EOM,n30EOM	May 14	_____	_____	_____

Exercise 4

Calculate the amount to be credited to the buyer's account for each of the partial payments below. All partial payments were made within the first cash discount period.

	Invoice Date	Terms	Partial Payment ($)	Amount to Credit Account ($)
16.	August 5	2/10,n30	55,000	_____
17.	August 30	2/10EOM	13,600	_____
18.	June 22	3/10EOM	7,900	_____
19.	June 5	3/10ROG (goods received June 10)	21,000	_____
20.	September 20	4/10,3/15,n30	5,000	_____

Exercise 5

21. An invoice dated June 1 for $714.90 with terms of 2/10,n30 included $24 for freight. A credit voucher was issued by the seller for $80 in returned merchandise. The invoice was paid June 9. For what amount should the check be written? _____

22. An invoice for $9,069.71 was dated March 28. Terms were 2/15ROG,n30ROG. Freight charges of $110 were included on the invoice. The goods were received March 31. Defective goods of $229 were returned to the seller. The invoice was paid on April 14. What is the last day of the discount period? _____ For what amount should the check be written? _____

23. An invoice for $850.42 dated January 18, 2003, with terms of 3/10,2/15,1/20,n45 was paid February 7. A shipping charge of $50 was included on the invoice. What is the last day to take advantage of the 2% cash discount? _____ For what amount should the check be written? _____ What is the last day to pay the total invoice? _____ What would be the amount to pay if the invoice were paid January 27? _____

24. An invoice dated June 1 with terms of 2/20ROG,n30ROG for $1,209.64 was received June 4 for goods received May 30. A partial payment of $400 was made June 8. What is the amount to be credited to the buyer's account? _____ What is the outstanding balance? _____

25. A partial payment of $750 was made on February 1 for Invoice #60009 for $2,019.92 dated January 23. The terms of the invoice were 3/10,n30. A credit voucher of $325 for damaged goods was received January 26. A shipping charge of $69.85 was included on the invoice. What amount should be credited to the buyer's account for the partial payment? _____ What is the outstanding balance?_____

CHAPTER 21

Markup Based on Cost, Markup Based on Selling Price

 **PART 1** *Speed and Accuracy Building Using Touch Key*

GOALS: Your speed goal is 10,500 strokes per hour.
Your accuracy target goal range is 95% to 100%.

With each repetition of the drill, try to improve your speed without lowering your accuracy score. If your percent-of-accuracy score falls below 95%, review your finger position and technique. Then try again.

Instructions: *Start Touch Key. Complete Drill 4, Parts A and B, Three-Minute Timings. (Parts C through E are optional.) Write your scores for strokes per hour and percent of accuracy below.*

Touch Key Drill 4—The 0 through 9 and Decimal Keys, Six-Digit Numbers, Three-Minute Timings

	Today's Date	Strokes per Hour	Percent of Accuracy
A.			
B.			
C.			
D.			
E.			

 **PART 2** *Business Math Skills*

MARKUP

When a manufacturer, wholesaler, or retailer (store owner) prices merchandise, he or she must set the price high enough to cover the costs for manufacturing or purchasing the merchandise; employee salaries, building rent, utilities, and other overhead expenses; and to make a profit. Therefore, the **selling price** (the price at which an item is sold) must be set a certain amount above **cost** (the dollar amount needed to manufacture or purchase an item for resale). The difference between cost and selling price is the **markup**. Therefore,

$$\text{Cost} + \text{Markup} = \text{Selling Price}$$
$$\text{Selling Price} - \text{Cost} = \text{Markup}$$
$$\text{Selling Price} - \text{Markup} = \text{Cost}$$

There are two kinds of markup rates that may be used. Manufacturers often choose to use a markup rate based on the cost of an item, whereas retailers often choose to use a markup rate based on the selling price of an item, although either method may be used. Each method will be explained in this chapter.

CALCULATING MARKUP: MARKUP RATE BASED ON COST

To find markup based on cost, the cost must be known as well as the desired **markup rate based on cost**. It is helpful to compare the calculation for finding markup to the percentage formula, where cost is the base, markup rate based on cost is the rate, and markup is the percentage, as illustrated in Figure 21.1:

$$\text{Cost} \times \text{Markup Rate Based on Cost} = \text{Markup}$$

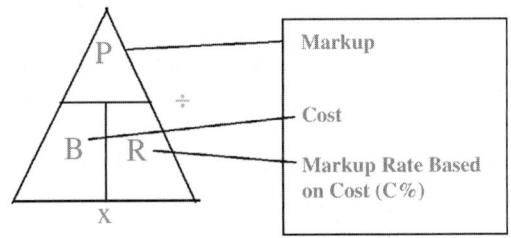

FIGURE 21.1

It may be helpful to use symbols as memory joggers for the formula as follows:

C for Cost
C% for Markup Rate Based on Cost
M for Amount of Markup

Thus

$$C \times C\% = M$$

The selling price for a markup of 20% based on cost can be stated in percentages as follows:

$$\text{Cost} = 100\%, \qquad \text{Markup} = 20\%, \qquad \text{Selling Price} = 100\% + 20\% = 120\%$$

CALCULATING SELLING PRICE: MARKUP RATE BASED ON COST

To find the selling price of an item, add cost plus markup. Let selling price equal S in the formula

$$C + M = S$$

PROBLEM 1

A lamp cost a retailer $40. He wishes to use a markup rate based on cost of 20%. Find the markup and the selling price.

To find the markup, multiply $40 by 20% or the decimal equivalent. To find the selling price, add the markup to the cost. Figure 21.2 shows the figures substituted into the formula for markup based on cost, $C \times C\% = M$, and the formula for selling price, $C + M = S$.

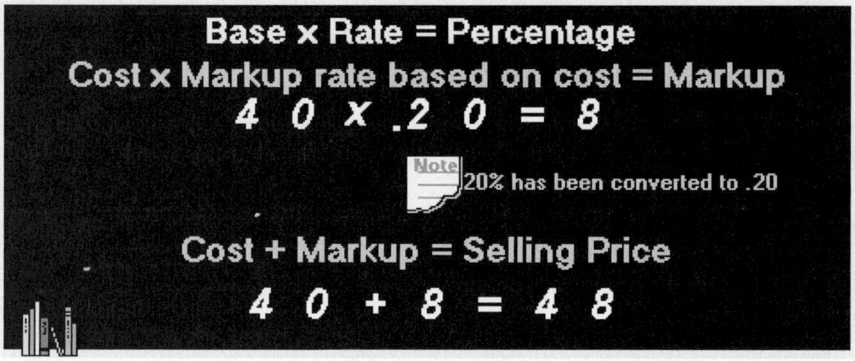

Base x Rate = Percentage
Cost x Markup rate based on cost = Markup
4 0 X .2 0 = 8

Note 20% has been converted to .20

Cost + Markup = Selling Price
4 0 + 8 = 4 8

FIGURE 21.2

A shortcut can be used to calculate the selling price in one operation instead of two. Multiply cost times one plus the markup rate based on cost. Using the above example, substitute numbers into the formula using a decimal number for the rate of markup based on cost:

$$\text{Cost} \times (1 + \text{Markup Rate Based on Cost}) = \text{Selling Price}$$
$$C \times (1 + C\%) = S$$
$$40 \times 1.20 = \$48 \text{ selling price}$$

Pocket Calculator Procedure

$$40 + 20 \boxed{\%} \boxed{48}$$

CALCULATING MARKUP RATE: MARKUP RATE BASED ON COST

If cost and markup are known, the markup rate based on cost can be determined using the percentage formula for rate where cost is the base and markup is the percentage. The markup rate based on cost is given by markup divided by cost (Figure 21.3).

PROBLEM 2

A chair cost a retailer $40. If the markup on the chair is $8, what is the markup rate based on cost?

$$\text{Markup} \div \text{Cost} = \text{Markup Rate Based on Cost (Figure 21.3)}$$
$$M \div C = C\%$$
$$\$8 \div \$40 = 20\%$$

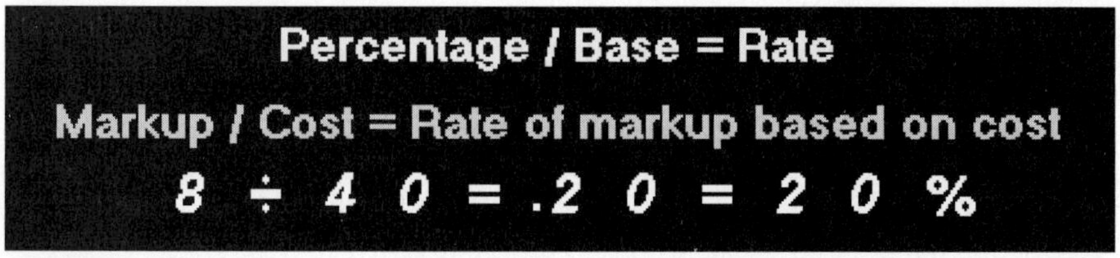

Percentage / Base = Rate
Markup / Cost = Rate of markup based on cost
8 ÷ 4 0 = .2 0 = 2 0 %

FIGURE 21.3

CALCULATING COST: MARKUP RATE BASED ON COST

If the markup rate based on cost and markup are known, cost can be calculated using the percentage formula with markup as the percentage and markup rate based on cost as the rate.

PROBLEM 3

The markup on a book is $25.00. If the bookstore uses a standard markup of 40% based on cost, what is the cost of the book?

Substitute values for the formula and solve:

$$M \div C\% = C$$
$$25 \div 40 = .625$$

Convert to 62.5%.

Pocket Calculator Procedure

$$25 \div 40 \boxed{\%} \; 62.5\%$$

CALCULATING COST: MARKUP RATE BASED ON SELLING PRICE

Some stores use a method for calculating markup based on selling price. Let S% represent **markup rate based on selling price**.

PROBLEM 4

A pair of shoes sells for $48. The markup rate based on cost is 20%. What is the cost of the shoes to the retailer? Using the percentage formula, let (see Figure 21.4)

Selling Price (S) = Percentage

Cost (C) = Base

Markup Rate Based on Selling Price (S%) =
Markup Rate Based on Cost (C%) + 100% = Rate   100% + 20% = 120%

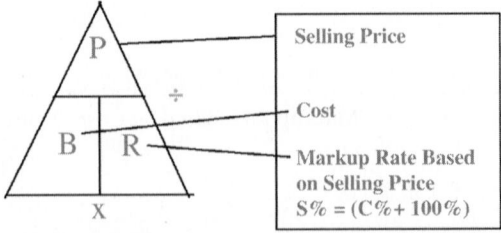

FIGURE 21.4

1. Find the markup rate based on selling price. Because cost is the base, or 100%, adding the markup rate based on cost (20%) to the base (100%) results in the markup rate based on selling price (120%), which is used for the rate in the formula:

    $$C\% + 100\% = S\%$$
    $$20\% + 100\% = 120\% \quad \text{rate of markup based on selling price}$$

Percentage / Rate = Base

Selling price / Markup rate based on selling price = Cost

$$48 \div 1.20 = 40$$

Note 120% has been converted to 1.20

FIGURE 21.5

2. Find the cost using the percentage formula. Selling price ($48) divided by markup rate based on selling price (120%) equals cost ($40). See Figure 21.5.

Pocket Calculator Procedure

$$48 \div 120 \boxed{\%} \boxed{40}$$

Desktop Calculator Procedure

See Explanation in Part 4:

$$50 \boxed{GPM} 20 = \boxed{62.50}$$

CALCULATING SELLING PRICE: MARKUP RATE BASED ON SELLING PRICE

To find the selling price when the cost and the markup rate based on selling price are known, we use the complement of the markup rate based on selling price (see Figure 21.6).

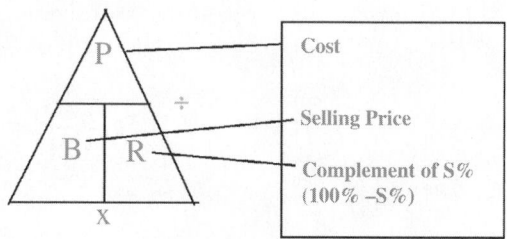

FIGURE 21.6

PROBLEM 5

A backpack cost the retailer $50. He uses a 20% markup based on selling price. What is the selling price of the backpack?

Use the percentage formula (shown in Figure 21.7) with

Cost = Percentage

Selling Price = Base

Complement of Markup Rate Based on Selling Price =
Base − Markup Rate Based on Selling Price = Rate   100% − 20% = 80%

Here, 20% of the selling price represents the amount of markup, 80% of the selling price equals the cost, and 100% equals the selling price.

Percentage / Rate = Base

Cost / Complement of markup rate = Selling price

$$50 \div .80 = 62.50$$

FIGURE 21.7

Pocket Calculator Procedure

50 ÷ 80 [%] [62.50]

Once the selling price has been determined, the cost can be subtracted from the selling price to find the amount of markup as shown in Figure 21.8.

Selling price – Cost = Markup

$$62.50 - 50 = 12.50$$

FIGURE 21.8

MARKUP RATE BASED ON SELLING PRICE

If the markup and the selling price are known, the rate of markup based on selling price can be calculated by dividing the markup by the selling price as shown in Figure 21.9.

Percentage / Base = Rate

Markup / Selling price = Rate of markup based on selling price

$$12.50 \div 62.50 = .20$$

(Convert answer to 20%)

FIGURE 21.9

Pocket Calculator Procedure

12.50 ÷ 62.50 [%] [20]

CONVERTING A MARKUP RATE BASED ON SELLING PRICE TO A MARKUP RATE BASED ON COST

Sometimes a markup rate based on selling price must be converted to a markup rate based on cost. A business may change markup methods, or wish to compare its markup rate to that of a business that uses a different method of markup.

PROBLEM 6

A store manager regularly marks items up 25% based on selling price. A competitor uses a 30% markup rate based on cost. To determine whether her markup rate is competitive, the manager wishes to convert her 25% markup rate based on selling price to a markup rate based on cost.

To convert to a markup rate based on cost, divide the markup rate based on selling price by the complement of the markup rate based on selling price as shown in Figure 21.10. Use the formula $S\% \div (100\% - S\%) = C\%$.

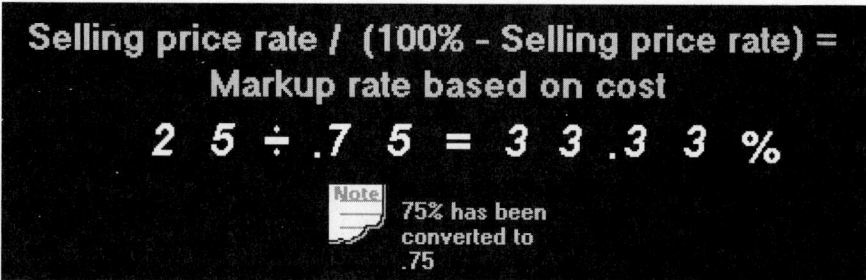

FIGURE 21.10

CONVERTING A MARKUP RATE BASED ON COST TO A MARKUP RATE BASED ON SELLING PRICE

PROBLEM 7

What is the markup rate based on selling price for an item that is marked up 30% based on cost?

To convert a markup rate based on cost to a markup rate based on selling price, divide the markup rate based on cost (30%) by 100% plus the markup rate based on cost (130%). Use the formula $C\% \div (100\% + C\%) = S\%$ as shown in Figure 21.11:

$$30 \div (100 + 30) = 23\%$$

Markup rate based on cost / (100% + Markup rate based on cost) = Markup rate based on selling price
$3\ 0 \div (\ 1\ 0\ 0 + 3\ 0\ ) =$
$.2\ 3$ (Convert answer to 23%)

FIGURE 21.11

Pocket Calculator Procedure

$$30 \div 130 \boxed{\%} \boxed{23}$$

MARKUP FORMULAS QUICK REFERENCE

Symbols used:

$$C = \text{Cost}$$
$$S = \text{Selling Price}$$
$$M = \text{Markup}$$
$$C\% = \text{Markup Rate Based on Cost}$$
$$S\% = \text{Markup Rate Based on Selling Price}$$

Markup, Cost, and Selling Price

$$\text{Selling Price} - \text{Cost} = \text{Markup}, \qquad S - C = M$$
$$\text{Selling Price} - \text{Markup} = \text{Cost}, \qquad S - M = C$$
$$\text{Cost} + \text{Markup} = \text{Selling Price}, \qquad C + M = S$$

Markup and Selling Price Using Markup Rate Based on Cost

$$\text{Cost} \times C\% = M$$
$$\text{Cost} \times (100\% + C\%) = S$$

Selling Price Using Markup Rate Based on Selling Price

$$\text{Cost} \div (100\% - S\%) = \text{Selling Price}$$

(Note: $100\% - S\% = $ Complement of $S\%$)

Markup Rate Based on Cost

$$\text{Markup} \div \text{Cost} = C\%$$

Markup Rate Based on Selling Price

$$\text{Markup} \div \text{Selling Price} = S\%$$

Cost Using Markup Rate Based on Selling Price

$$\text{Selling Price} \times (100\% - S\%) = \text{Cost}$$

Conversion Formulas

Converting Markup Rate Based on Selling Price to Markup Rate Based on Cost (S% to C%)

$$S\% \div (100\% - S\%) = C\%$$

Converting Markup Rate Based on Cost to Markup Rate Based on Selling Price (C% to S%)

$$C\% \div (100\% + C\%) = S\%$$

MATH STAR 21.1

BE A *Math★* !

Sometimes being a math star is simply a matter of being able to recognize patterns. Look at the following markup formulas and try to spot any patterns.

Section A: Formulas Involving Markup Based on Cost: Cost = $100, C% = 20%	*Memory Joggers*	*Examples*
Cost × Markup Rate Based on Cost = Markup	C × C% = M	100 × 20% = 20
Cost + Markup = Selling Price	C + M = SP	100 + 20 = 120
Cost × (100% + Markup Rate Based on Cost) = Selling Price[1]	C × (100% + C%) = S	100 × (100% + 20%) = 144
Markup ÷ Cost = Markup Rate Based on Cost	M ÷ C = C%	20 ÷ 100 = 20%
Markup ÷ Markup Rate Based on Cost = Cost	M ÷ C% = C	20 ÷ 20% = 100

Section B: Formulas Involving Markup Based on Selling Price: Cost = $100, S% = 15%	*Memory Joggers*	*Examples*
Selling Price[2] × (100% − Percent of Markup Based on Selling Price) = Cost	S × (100% − S%) = C	117.65 × 85% = 100
Cost[3] ÷ (100% − Percent of Markup Based on Selling Price) = Selling Price	C ÷ (100% − S%) = S	100 ÷ (100% − 15%) = 117.65
Selling Price − Cost = Markup	S − C = M	117.65 − 100 = 17.65
Markup ÷ Selling Price = Markup Rate Based on Selling Price	M ÷ S = S%	17.65 ÷ 117.65 =15%

Section C: Formulas to Convert One Type of Markup Rate to Another	*Memory Joggers*	*Examples*
Percent of Markup Based on Cost[4] ÷ (100% + Percent of Markup Based on Cost = Percent of Markup Based on Selling Price	C% ÷ (100% + C%) = S%	20% ÷ 120% = 16.67%
Percent of Markup Based on Selling Price[5] ÷ (100% − Percent of Markup Based on Selling Price) = Percent of Markup Based on Cost	S% ÷ (100% − S%) = C%	15% ÷ 85% = 17.65%

Hints

Selling Price Based on Cost. Because the cost is the base, the cost is 100%.

Explanation: If the markup based on the cost of an item is 40%, then the cost of the item is 100%, and 100% + 40% is equal to selling price because cost plus markup equals selling price.

Check: An item with the above markup costs $300. What is the selling price (remember, $300 is 100% of the cost)?

$$\$300 (100\% + 40\%) = \$420 \text{ (selling price)}$$

[1] *To cover expenses and make a profit, the selling price is **greater** than the cost, so it is easy to remember to multiply the cost by a rate **greater** than 100% (100% + C%) to find the selling price C(100% + C%).*

Cost Based on Selling Price. Because the selling price is the base, the selling price is 100%.

(continued)

MATH STAR 21.1 *(continued)*

Explanation: If the markup based on the selling price is 40%, then the selling price is 100%, and 100% − S% = Cost because Selling Price − Markup = Cost.

Check: An item with the above markup sells for $200. How much did the item cost (remember, $200 is 100% of the selling price)?

$$200 \times (100\% - 40\%) = \$120 \text{ (cost)}$$

[2] *Because the cost is* **smaller** *than the selling price, remember to multiply the selling price by a rate* **smaller** *than 100%(100% − S%) to find the cost, or S(100 − S%).*

Selling Price When Cost and S% Are Known

[3] *When the cost and the rate of markup based on the selling price are known, remember to* **divide** *the cost by (100% − S%) to find the larger selling price, or C ÷ (100% − S%).*

Converting Markup Rates. The markup rate based on cost must be larger than the markup rate based on selling price to find the **same** amount of markup.

Check: The markup on an item that cost $55 is $25. What is the markup rate based on cost?

$$\text{Markup} \div \text{Cost} = \text{Markup Rate Based on Cost}$$
$$25 \div 55 = \mathbf{45.45\%}$$

What is the markup rate based on the selling price?

$$\text{Cost} \times (100\% + C\%) = \text{Selling Price}$$
$$55(100\% + 45.45\%) = \$80.00$$
$$\text{Markup} \div \text{Selling Price} = \text{Markup Rate Based on Selling Price}$$
$$25 \div 80 = \mathbf{31.25\%}$$

[4] *When converting C% to S%, divide C% by* **(100% + C%)**.
[5] *When converting S% to C%, divide S% by* **(100% − S%)**.

Name _____

Class/Section _____

Score (Correct Answers ÷ No. of Assigned Problems) _____

PART 2 *Business Math Skills*

Exercise 1

Calculate the selling price.

	Cost ($)	Markup Rate Based on Cost (%)	Selling Price ($)
1.	35	30	_____
2.	79	25	_____
3.	220	40	_____
4.	105	60	_____

Exercise 2

Calculate the missing components. Round percents to hundredths.

	Cost	Markup Rate Based on Cost (%)	Markup ($)	Selling Price ($)
5.	1.59	25	_____	_____
6.	25.99	30	_____	_____
7.	22.50	____	10.00	_____
8.	_____	15	22.00	_____
9.	30.00	____	7.00	_____
10.	_____	75	1,200.00	_____

Exercise 3

Calculate the missing components.

	Cost ($)	Markup Rate Based on Selling Price (%)	Selling Price ($)
11.	399	15	_____
12.	139	40	_____
13.	1,200	____	1,599
14.	769	____	1,200
15.	_____	25	95
16.	_____	35	1,096

Exercise 4

Convert markup rate based on cost to markup rate based on selling price. Round answers to hundredths.

	Markup Rate Based on Cost (%)	Markup Rate Based on Selling Price
17.	35	_____
18.	25	_____
19.	18	_____
20.	30	_____
21.	75	_____

Exercise 5

Convert markup rate based on selling price to markup rate based on cost.

	Markup Rate Based on Selling Price (%)	Markup Rate Based on Cost
22.	29	_____
23.	25	_____
24.	50	_____
25.	40	_____

PART 3 *Review and Practice Using Business Math FUNdamentals*

GOAL: Complete 9 of the 10 problems correctly.

Instructions: *Start Business Math FUNdamentals. Complete Tutorials 45 through 47 and Drills 36 through 38. If you are not satisfied with your score, repeat the drill. Write your scores below.*

Business Math FUNdamentals Drill 36

Today's Date	Score

Business Math FUNdamentals Drill 37

Today's Date	Score

Business Math FUNdamentals Drill 38

Today's Date	Score

PART 4 *Desktop Calculator*

GROSS PROFIT MARGIN KEY

If your calculator has a gross profit margin (GPM) key, you may easily calculate selling price when cost and percent of markup based on selling price (S%) are known.

PROBLEM

Calculate the selling price for an item that cost $50. Use a 40% markup based on selling price. Set the decimal selector on 2.

Procedure:

$$50 \boxed{\text{GPM}} \ 40 \ = \ \boxed{108.33}$$

 PART 4 *Desktop Calculator*

Exercise 1

One-Minute Addition Timing (0 through 9 Keys, Six-Digit Numbers)

(Optional: Your instructor may wish you to use Touch Key on the computer for all your timings. Check with your instructor before completing this exercise.)

Complete as many of the problems as possible in 1 minute by adding. Work quickly and accurately. The number preceding each closing parenthesis indicates the cumulative number of strokes for problems attempted. For example, if you complete Problems 1 through 3 in 1 minute, your strokes-per-minute score is 213. Optional: If you complete Problems 1 through 16 in 5 minutes, your strokes-per-minute score is 227.

1. 537,556	2. 670,024	3. 476,544	4. 579,006	5. 677,850	6. 454,200	7. 130,765	8. 717,001
258,341	566,932	575,350	560,902	545,500	458,500	260,564	369,003
226,890	255,009	267,800	750,701	534,650	153,100	210,276	417,002
513,657	457,545	457,600	684,603	469,995	767,400	230,755	313,001
265,987	476,041	657,400	680,104	757,359	671,006	430,586	249,004
583,524	679,000	569,500	768,405	634,229	453,005	420,003	275,002
491,093	674,788	464,300	500,003	567,899	567,003	330,005	677,007
576,835	464,921	456,100	581,003	745,775	836,004	150,006	453,004
490,569	473,896	540,300	682,001	454,900	714,006	160,005	436,005
245,870	561,009	453,300	591,002	434,556	625,006	450,004	548,003
71)	142)	213)	284)	355)	426)	497)	568)

9. 121,400	10. 176,900	11. 956,987	12. 944,779	13. 943,450	14. 990,661	15. 916,000	16. 195,004
564,420	422,677	700,122	753,100	869,995	700,000	737,013	212,600
455,320	363,553	350,455	560,666	741,995	989,885	838,064	314,000
166,150	576,998	477,004	635,350	527,229	679,655	539,014	514,870
427,700	358,565	500,999	555,555	630,759	686,444	630,045	136,002
383,689	674,322	759,000	833,886	860,999	997,111	337,023	326,003
499,599	197,659	965,880	396,772	937,577	800,741	618,013	514,514
356,884	513,100	610,432	772,250	820,659	788,962	562,053	132,787
517,656	225,000	511,119	940,495	945,695	890,854	197,024	142,412
599,374	335,575	833,980	732,495	720,000	300,014	522,011	114,600
639)	710)	781)	852)	923)	994)	1,065)	1,136)

17. 418,900	18. 600,995	19. 432,100	20. 112,559	21. 398,331	22. 115,120	23. 300,213	24. 316,290
642,100	152,110	142,700	315,880	920,215	932,261	200,500	842,499
130,800	125,900	433,700	851,770	320,156	892,339	120,435	735,199
800,300	100,300	120,100	313,660	901,647	785,129	715,163	145,399
121,500	142,500	142,100	211,872	312,535	974,529	971,452	712,599
421,500	142,900	142,100	132,308	632,451	862,173	288,432	961,895
200,600	132,000	153,100	521,504	531,460	245,600	821,255	215,695
421,200	142,000	123,500	311,685	477,545	329,573	822,721	833,795
214,900	143,500	321,500	124,783	846,245	432,331	330,115	354,195
142,000	121,600	301,490	200,441	504,100	556,232	736,543	111,595
1,207)	1,278)	1,349)	1,420)	1,491)	1,562)	1,633)	1,704)

CHAPTER 21 *Terminology Review*

Cost
Markup
Markup rate based on cost
Markup rate based on selling price
Selling price

Write the correct term next to the appropriate description.

1. _____ Difference between selling price and cost.
2. _____ A percent applied to the cost of an item to find the markup.
3. _____ The amount to manufacture or purchase an item for resale.
4. The markup rate based on the selling price plus the complement of the markup rate based on the selling price equals _____.
5. _____ The price at which an item is sold.

Name _____

Class/Section _____

Score (Correct Answers ÷ No. of Assigned Problems) _____

Chapter 21 Review Exercises

Exercise 1

Calculate the missing components. Round answers to hundredths.

	Cost ($)	Markup ($)	Selling Price ($)
1.	35.00	10.00	_____
2.	165.00	38.00	_____
3.	129.00	_____	150.00
4.	157.00	_____	187.00
5.	_____	59.00	160.00
6.	_____	75.00	210.00

Exercise 2

Calculate the markup and the selling price for items manufactured by the Island Candy Shop if a standard 60% markup rate based on cost is used.

	Item	Cost per Pound ($)	Markup ($)	Selling Price ($)
7.	Fudge	3.00	_____	_____
8.	Pralines	3.25	_____	_____
9.	Caramels	2.75	_____	_____
10.	Pecan clusters	3.50	_____	_____
11.	Almond bark	3.10	_____	_____
12.	Jelly beans	2.19	_____	_____

Exercise 3

Calculate the markup rate based on the selling price for these items sold by J&J Crafts. Round answers to whole numbers.

	Item	Cost ($)	Markup Rate Based on Selling Price (%)	Selling Price ($)
13.	Tie-dye T-shirt, adult size	1.50	_____	9.95
14.	Tie-dye dresses, adult size	2.50	_____	14.95
15.	Tie-dye T-shirt, child size	1.00	_____	5.95

Exercise 4

Calculate cost.

	Selling Price ($)	Markup Rate Based on Selling Price (%)	Cost ($)
16.	39.95	40	_____
17.	152.39	35	_____
18.	19.95	50	_____

Exercise 5

Calculate the selling price.

	Cost ($)	Markup Rate Based on Selling Price (%)	Selling Price ($)
19.	55.00	40	_____
20.	5.95	60	_____

Exercise 6

Calculate the selling price based on cost.

	Cost ($)	Markup Rate Based on Cost (%)	Selling Price ($)
21.	29.00	120	_____
22.	35.00	65	_____

Exercise 7

23. Uptown Sportswear Manufacturers can produce a line of suits for $159.00 each. If the markup is 40% based on cost, what is the selling price for each unit? _____
24. Jayne was instructed to price a shipment of items that cost $4.99 each. The store uses a standard markup rate of 35% based on selling price. What price should she place on the items? _____
25. Michael was asked to calculate the cost of a dining table that sells for $2,779.95. The furniture store uses a standard markup rate of 55% based on selling price. What was the cost of the table? _____

CHAPTER 22

Markdown, Pricing of Seasonal and Perishable Goods

 ## PART 1 *Speed and Accuracy Building Using Touch Key*

GOALS: Your speed goal is 10,500 strokes per hour.
Your accuracy target goal range is 95% to 100%.

With each repetition of the drill, try to improve your speed without lowering your accuracy score. If your percent-of-accuracy score falls below 95%, review your finger position and technique. Then try again.

Instructions: Start Touch Key. Complete Drill 4, Part A, Five-Minute Timing. (Parts B through E are optional.) Write your scores for strokes per hour and percent of accuracy below.

Touch Key Drill 4—The 0 through 9 and Decimal Keys, Six-Digit Numbers, Five-Minute Timing

	Today's Date	Strokes per Hour	Percent of Accuracy
A.			
B.			
C.			
D.			
E.			

PART 2 *Business Math Skills*

MARKDOWN AND SALE PRICE

A **markdown** is a reduction in selling price. It is used to give discounts, for sale prices, or for special prices. The **markdown rate** is stated as a percent of the selling price; therefore, markdowns are calculated after the markups and the selling price have been calculated. Selling price minus markdown equals **sale price**.

PROBLEM 1

An item with a selling price of $80 was advertised at 25% off during a special sale. What was the new selling price (sale price)?

First, find the amount of the markdown. Use the percentage formula with selling price (S) the base, markdown rate (M%) the rate, and markdown (M) the percentage. A visual representation of this formula is shown in Figure 22.1:

$$\text{Selling Price} \times \text{Markdown Rate} = \text{Markdown}$$
$$80 \times .25 = 20$$

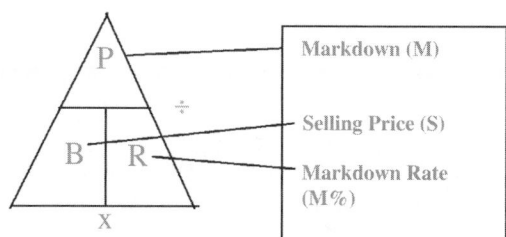

FIGURE 22.1

Second, subtract the markdown from the selling price to find the sale price. That is, $S - M = $ Sale Price (see Figure 22.2).

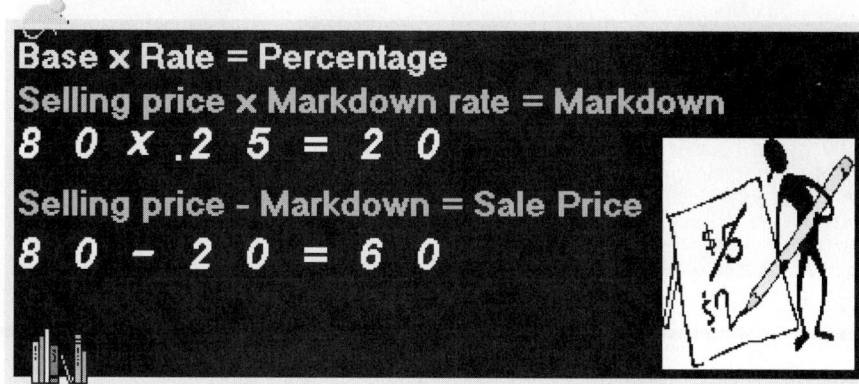

FIGURE 22.2

Alternatively, use the complement of the markdown rate to find the sale price in one arithmetic operation (see Figure 22.3):

$$S \times (100\% - M\%) = \text{Sale Price}$$
$$80 \times .75 = 60$$

Selling price x Complement of markdown = New Sale price

8 0 X .7 5 = 6 0

FIGURE 22.3

When using a calculator with a % key, it is not necessary to use the complement method.

Pocket Calculator Procedure	Desktop Calculator Procedure
To find sale price: 80 − 25 %̄ 60̄	80 × 25 %̄ − 60̄
To find amount of markdown: 80 × 25 %̄ 20̄	80 × 25 %̄ 20̄

CALCULATING THE MARKDOWN RATE

If the original selling price and the sale price are known, the markdown rate can be calculated.

PROBLEM 2

A lamp originally sold for $80. The new selling price is $60. Calculate the markdown rate.

Subtract the sale price from the selling price to find the amount of markdown. Use the percentage formula with selling price the base and percentage the markdown to find the markdown rate. Alternatively, M ÷ S = M%, where M = Markdown, S = Selling Price, and M% = Markdown Rate. Calculations are shown in Figure 22.4.

Selling price − New selling price = Markdown
8 0 − 6 0 = 2 0

Percentage / Base = Rate

Markdown / Selling Price = Markdown Rate
2 0 ÷ 8 0 = .2 5

(Convert answer to 25%)

FIGURE 22.4

BEFORE AND AFTER SALES

Sometimes an item is marked down for a special sale. After the special sale is over, the item may be marked up (see Chapter 21, Markup), but not marked up to the original selling price (Figure 22.5).

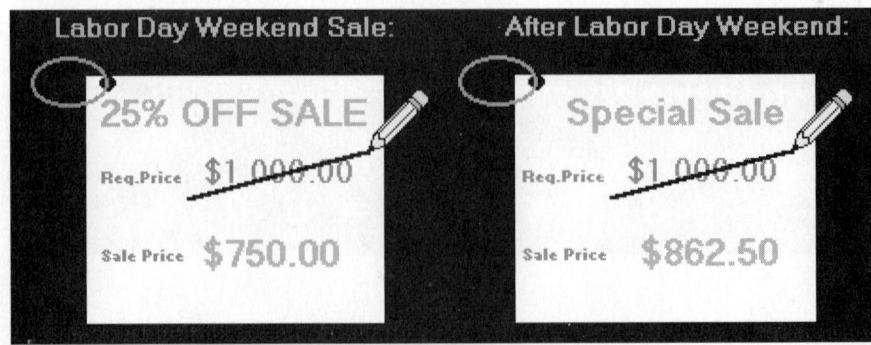

FIGURE 22.5

When calculating a **series of markups and markdowns**, calculate each subsequent markup or markdown on the previous selling or sale price as shown in Figure 22.6.

	Markdown/markup Series	Formula	Result
1.	1st markdown	Original selling price − markdown %	1st sale price
2.	1st markup	1st sale price + markup %	2nd sale price
3.	2nd markdown	2nd sale price − markdown %	3rd sale price
4.	2nd markup	3rd sale price + markup %	4th sale price

FIGURE 22.6

PROBLEM 3

The selling price of an antique chest is $1,000. It was marked down 25% for a Labor Day weekend sale. After Labor Day weekend, the chest was marked up 15%. What is the latest selling price?

Begin by multiplying the selling price by the markdown rate. Subtract the markdown from the selling price to find the sale price:

$$S \times M\% = M$$
$$1,000 \times .25 = 250$$
$$S - M = \text{sale price}$$
$$1,000 - 250 = 750$$

Alternatively, use the complement method shown in Figure 22.7.

$$S \times (100\% - M\%) = \text{Sale Price}$$

After the sale, multiply the sale price by the markup rate and add the markup to the sale price:

$$\text{Sale Price} \times \text{Markup Rate} = \text{Markup}$$
$$750 \times .15 = 112.50$$
$$\text{Sale Price} + \text{Markup} = \text{Final Selling Price}$$
$$750 + 112.50 = 862.50$$

Alternatively, use the complement method shown in Figure 22.7:

$$\text{Sale Price} \times (100\% + C\%) = \text{Final Selling Price}$$

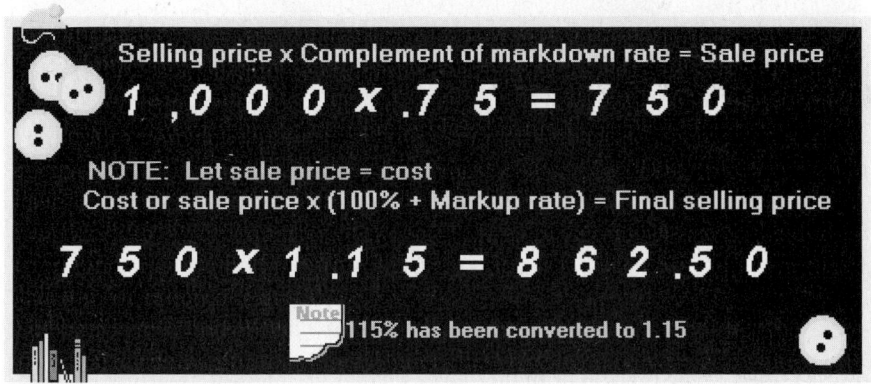

FIGURE 22.7

Pocket Calculator Procedure	Desktop Calculator Procedure
1,000 − 25 % 750	1,000 × 25 % − 750
750 + 15 % 862.50	750 × 15 % + 862.50

SEASONAL AND PERISHABLE GOODS

Sometimes goods purchased for sale have to be marked down. Fashions go out of style. **Seasonal goods** such as patio and lawn furniture, outdoor grills, kites, seasonal decorations, and gifts that do not sell during the appropriate season may be marked down for quick sale. **Perishable goods** such as fruits and vegetables that spoil must be discarded. Slightly damaged goods may be marked down; heavily damaged goods must be discarded.

A business will use past experience and figures to estimate the amount of certain goods that are usually marked down or discarded. Using historical figures, a manager or storeowner can estimate the portion of goods purchased that will sell at full price. The manager must then set a selling price on the goods expected to sell that is high enough to cover the cost of all goods purchased, whether they sell or not, and to cover the desired profit on the goods. Setting a selling price is demonstrated in the next problem.

PROBLEM 4

A grocer paid $.40 per pound for 100 pounds of apples. His store normally experiences a 10% spoilage rate on apples. What is the selling price per pound of apples if the grocer needs a 120% markup on cost?

There are three steps involved in solving this problem.

Step 1: Find the cost, the markup, and the selling price for the total amount of apples (Figure 22.8):

Cost per Pound ($.40) × Quantity (100 lb) = Cost ($40) for All the Apples

Markup Rate (120%) × Cost ($40) = Markup ($48)

Cost ($40) + Markup ($48) = Selling Price for 100 lb of Apples ($88)

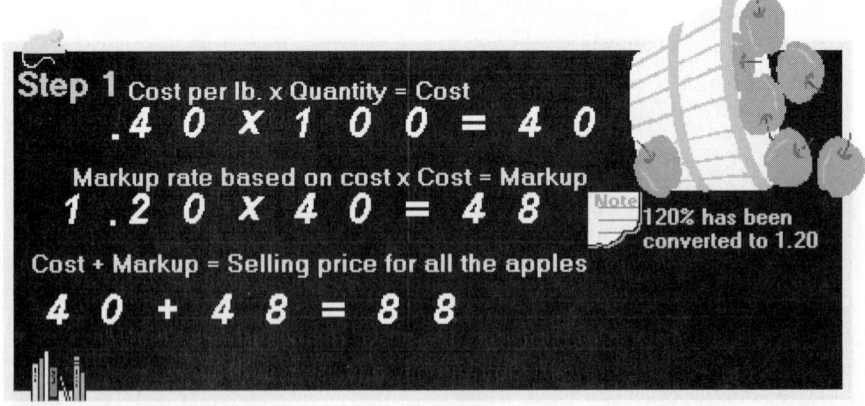

FIGURE 22.8

However, the grocer expects some of the apples will not sell and will spoil. The next step is necessary to find the selling price for the apples that **will** sell. That is, the apples that will sell should be priced slightly higher to make up for the losses due to the spoiled apples.

Step 2: Find the quantity of apples expected to sell.

Quantity (100 lb) × Complement of Spoilage Rate (.90) = Quantity Expected to Sell (90 lb)

Step 3: Find the selling price per pound.

Divide the selling price for all the apples from step 1 ($88) by the quantity expected to sell from step 2 (90 lb) to find the selling price per pound ($.98; Figure 22.9).

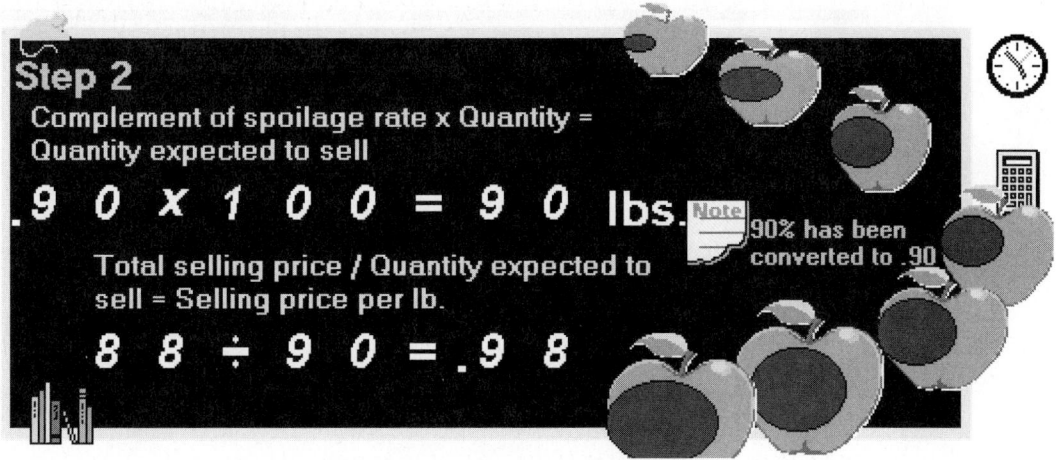

FIGURE 22.9

Pocket Calculator Procedure	Desktop Calculator Procedure
Check that memory is clear (MC)	Check that memory is clear (MT)
Step 1: 100 × 40 % 40 + 120 % 88	100 × 40% 40 × 120 % + 88
Step 2: 100 − 10 % 90 M+	100 × 10 % − 90 M+
Step 3: 88 ÷ MR = .98 MC	88 + MT = .98

WATCH THE WORDING...

Sales clerks and managers are often asked questions about the sale price of items that have been discounted. Sometimes a subtle difference in wording can make a large difference in the amount to charge the customer. Placing a sign on a table or a rack rather than changing the price on all the goods individually may discount an entire table or rack of goods. A further discount may then be offered either on the already reduced prices or on the original prices of the items. The difference is demonstrated in the following two problems.

PROBLEM 5

A rack of shirts was marked 50% off. "Early-bird" customers were given coupons for an additional *10% off already reduced prices*. A customer selected a shirt marked $45 off the sale rack. She also had an early-bird coupon. What is the final sale price of the shirt?

    First take the 50% discount off the original price of $45. Then reduce the sale price by 10%.

Pocket Calculator Procedure	Desktop Calculator Procedure
45 − 50 % 22.50 − 10 % 20.25	45 × 50 % − 22.50 × 10 % − 20.25

PROBLEM 6

A T-shirt selling for $16.00 was reduced to $14.00 A sign on the rack advertised *25% off the original price*. What is the correct sale price of the shirt?

    The discount must be calculated on the original price ($16), **not** on the sale price of $14.

Pocket Calculator Procedure	Desktop Calculator Procedure
16 − 25 % 12 —**NOT**	16 × 25 % − 12 —**NOT**
14 − 25 % 10.50	14 × 25 % − 10.50

Name _____

Class/Section _____

Score (Correct Answers ÷ No. of Assigned Problems) _____

PART 2   *Business Math Skills*

Exercise 1

Calculate the markdown and the sale price.

	Selling Price ($)	Markdown Rate (%)	Markdown ($)	Sale Price ($)
1.	45.59	15	_____	_____
2.	1,223.50	5	_____	_____
3.	69.95	25	_____	_____
4.	129.67	20	_____	_____
5.	101.50	10	_____	_____

Exercise 2

Calculate the sale price.

	Selling Price ($)	Markdown Rate (%)	Sale Price ($)
6.	5,923.60	12	_____
7.	7,500.25	15	_____
8.	16,780.22	20	_____
9.	1,567.90	5	_____
10.	235.12	18	_____

Exercise 3

Calculate the markdown rate. Round answers to hundredths.

	Selling Price ($)	Sale Price ($)	Markdown Rate (%)
11.	59.95	56.59	_____
12.	3.19	2.69	_____
13.	39.95	35.00	_____
14.	299.59	259.99	_____
15.	679.00	655.99	_____

Exercise 4

Calculate the selling price, the sale price, and the new selling price for the following markup and markdown series.

	Cost ($)	First Markup (%)	Selling Price ($)	First Markdown (%)	Sale Price ($)	Second Markup (%)	New Selling Price ($)
16.	890	30	_____	15	_____	10	_____
17.	1,285	50	_____	30	_____	20	_____
18.	500	150	_____	25	_____	15	_____
19.	0.39	200	_____	50	_____	15	_____
20.	229.75	75	_____	33	_____	18	_____

Exercise 5

Calculate the cost, the total selling price, the quantity expected to sell, and the selling price.

	Cost per Item	Quantity	Total Cost ($)	Markup (%)	Total Selling Price ($)	Spoilage Rate (%)	Quantity Expected to Sell	Selling Price per Item ($)
21.	$1.19/lb	25 lb	_____	60	_____	20	_____	_____
22.	$.45/lb	30 lb	_____	25	_____	10	_____	_____
23.	$.15/lb	112 lb	_____	15	_____	5	_____	_____
24.	$2.99 each	50	_____	35	_____	12	_____	_____
25.	$1.59 each	25	_____	40	_____	8	_____	_____

PART 3 Review and Practice Using Business Math FUNdamentals

GOAL: Complete 9 of the 10 problems correctly.

Instructions: *Start Business Math FUNdamentals. Complete Tutorials 48 through 50 and Drills 39 through 41. If you are not satisfied with your score, repeat the drill. Write your scores below.*

Business Math FUNdamentals Drill 39

Today's Date	Score

Business Math FUNdamentals Drill 40

Today's Date	Score

Business Math FUNdamentals Drill 41

Today's Date	Score

 PART 4 *Desktop Calculator*

Exercise 1

One-Minute Addition Timing (0 through 9 Keys, Six-Digit Numbers)

(Optional: Your instructor may wish you to use Touch Key on the computer for all your timings. Check with your instructor before completing this exercise.)

Complete as many of the problems as possible in 1 minute by adding. Work quickly and accurately. The number preceding each closing parenthesis indicates the cumulative number of strokes for problems attempted. For example, if you complete Problems 1 through 5 in 1 minute, your strokes-per-minute score is 355.

1.	137,556	2.	110,024	3.	376,544	4.	329,006	5.	177,850	6.	494,200
	278,341		176,932		375,350		330,902		145,500		128,500
	223,890		262,009		274,800		360,701		134,650		123,100
	113,657		297,545		115,600		144,603		369,995		187,400
	275,987		186,041		197,400		130,104		257,359		421,006
	283,524		119,000		219,500		140,405		234,229		423,005
	291,093		264,788		224,300		224,003		267,899		279,003
	176,835		154,921		276,100		251,003		345,775		236,004
	190,569		153,896		140,300		382,001		354,900		314,006
	253,870		111,009		153,300		391,002		134,556		325,006
71)		142)		213)		284)		355)		426)	

7.	130,000	8.	417,001	9.	541,400	10.	476,900	11.	456,987	12.	344,779
	260,000		319,003		566,420		442,677		420,122		453,100
	210,000		418,002		455,850		263,553		360,455		520,666
	230,000		413,001		466,150		276,998		470,004		535,350
	430,000		219,004		477,700		388,565		522,999		455,555
	420,000		271,002		388,689		374,322		459,000		433,886
	330,000		177,007		399,599		497,659		565,880		376,772
	150,000		483,004		366,884		522,100		510,432		372,250
	160,000		438,005		517,256		525,000		411,119		340,495
	450,000		348,003		499,374		435,575		533,980		532,495
497)		568)		639)		710)		781)		852)	

13.	643,450	14.	690,661	15.	716,000	16.	795,004	17.	588,900	18.	695,995
	269,995		589,000		537,013		682,600		669,100		792,110
	441,995		679,885		638,064		764,000		855,800		859,900
	527,229		669,655		539,014		634,870		872,300		628,300
	430,759		476,444		530,045		596,002		798,500		599,500
	560,999		567,111		727,023		616,003		811,500		754,900
	637,577		556,741		628,013		589,514		776,600		862,000
	420,659		652,962		192,053		446,787		827,200		890,000
	545,695		459,854		597,024		536,412		778,900		786,500
	220,000		356,014		510,011		654,600		735,000		734,600
923)		994)		1,065)		1,136)		1,207)		1,278)	

19.	20.	21.	22.	23.	24.
836,100	563,655	722,349	815,120	926,213	916,290
776,700	845,880	566,215	912,261	823,500	822,499
793,700	841,770	554,156	891,339	820,435	732,199
632,100	753,660	711,647	785,429	735,163	845,399
695,100	865,870	721,535	974,559	979,452	752,599
749,100	716,340	832,451	862,179	988,432	962,895
758,100	626,590	831,460	845,600	861,255	915,695
788,500	636,680	777,545	729,573	825,721	823,795
563,500	544,780	646,245	832,331	730,115	933,195
716,490	521,490	584,100	756,232	726,543	911,595
1,349)	1,420)	1,491)	1,562)	1,633)	1,704)

CHAPTER 22 *Terminology Review*

Markdown
Markdown rate
Perishable goods
Sale price
Seasonal goods
Series of markups and markdowns

Write the correct terms next to the appropriate description.

1. _____ Multiple markups or markdowns sometimes associated with a special holiday sale.
2. _____ A reduction in selling price.
3. _____ A percent of selling price.
4. Selling price times the complement of the markdown rate equals _____.
5. _____ Selling price minus markdown.
6. Baked goods are an example of _____.
7. Halloween masks are an example of _____.

Name _____

Class/Section _____

Score (Correct Answers ÷ No. of Assigned Problems) _____

Chapter 22 Review Exercises
Exercise 1

A 25%-off white sale was announced in January at a department store. Calculate the sale price for each item.

	Item	Selling Price ($)	Sale Price ($)
1.	Wash cloth	2.99	_____
2.	Hand towel	6.99	_____
3.	Bath towel	9.99	_____
4.	Bath sheet	15.99	_____
5.	Contour bath rug	13.99	_____
6.	Lid cover	7.99	_____
7.	Rectangular bath rug	20.99	_____
8.	Percale sheets, twin	29.99	_____
9.	Percale sheets, double	39.99	_____
10.	Percale sheets, queen	49.99	_____
11.	Percale sheets, king	59.99	_____
12.	Comforter, king	269.59	_____
13.	Bed ruffle, king	35.99	_____
14.	Mattress pad, queen	35.98	_____
15.	Mattress pad, king	39.98	_____

Exercise 2

Calculate the markdown and the markdown rate.

	Selling Price ($)	Sale Price ($)	Markdown ($)	Markdown Rate (%)
16.	1,200	999	_____	_____
17.	789	720	_____	_____
18.	159.98	99.98	_____	_____
19.	2,999.95	2,759.95	_____	_____
20.	560.94	498.94	_____	_____

Exercise 3

21. A rack of shirts priced at $45 each was marked 20% off. A customer had a newspaper coupon that offered an additional 10% off previously reduced prices. How much should the customer be charged for one of the shirts? _____

22. A dishwasher priced at $799 was advertised at $679. What was the markdown and the rate of markdown? _____

23. Fifty artificial Christmas trees can be purchased for resale at a cost of $1,943. A markup rate of 120% of cost is needed. The manager expects 95% of the trees to sell at full price. What is the selling price for each tree? _____

24. A trampoline priced at $1,600 was marked down to $1,299. Calculate the markdown rate. _____

25. A store advertised a free coffeepot with the purchase of four 1-lb cans of Morning Goodness coffee. The store requires a 20% markup on cost. The coffee costs the store $0.75 per 1-lb can and the coffeepot costs $3.50. To cover costs and markup, what should the store charge for each can of coffee? _____

UNIT III

Business Mathematics for Accounting

CHAPTER 23

Depreciation

PART 1   *Speed and Accuracy Building Using Touch Key*

GOALS: Your speed goal is 11,000 strokes per hour.
Your accuracy target goal range is 95% to 100%.

With each repetition of the drill, try to improve your speed without lowering your accuracy score. If your percent-of-accuracy score falls below 95%, review your finger position and technique. Then try again.

Instructions: *Start Touch Key. Complete Lesson 11, Parts A through E. Write your scores for strokes per hour and percent of accuracy below.*

Touch Key Lesson 11—The 0 through 9, Decimal, and Minus Keys, Six-Digit Numbers

	Today's Date	Strokes per Hour	Percent of Accuracy
A.			
B.			
C.			
D.			
E.			

PART 2   *Business Math Skills*

DEPRECIATION

The topic of items purchased for resale was discussed in Chapters 21 and 22. Businesses also purchase items that will be used by the employees of the business—items that will *not* be resold as merchandise. Some of the items, such as furniture, manufacturing equipment, tools, and computers, will be used by the business for many years before the items wear out. Such items are assets of the business as long as the items have cash value.

Depreciation is the decline in value that occurs as a piece of equipment ages and becomes worn. This wear and tear causes the equipment to **depreciate** in value. The years of expected usefulness of a piece of equipment is referred to as its **useful life**, or life. Businesses are allowed to claim depreciation expense during each year of the equipment's useful life, which spreads the cost of the equipment over this period. Depreciation expense is deducted from sales (also referred to as revenue), reducing the amount of income, thereby reducing the amount of income tax paid. **Accumulated depreciation** is all the depreciation that has been claimed from the time the asset was purchased to the current date. The yearly depreciations are added together over time to find the accumulated depreciation. **Salvage value** is the amount an item is worth once its useful life is over. Records must be kept reflecting the depreciation and value of equipment. The cost of an item minus its salvage value (if any) plus accumulated depreciation equals the item's **book value**.

Most tangible property, such as buildings, machinery, vehicles, furniture, and equipment, may be depreciated. However, land may not be depreciated. Certain intangible property, such as patents, copyrights, and computer software, may also be depreciated. For a business owner to depreciate property, the property to be depreciated must be owned by the person, be used in his or her business, have a determinable useful life, and must be expected to last more than 1 year.

There are several types of depreciation methods, including straight-line, units-produced, sum-of-the-years'-digits, and declining-balance depreciation, the accelerated cost recovery system (ACRS), and the modified accelerated cost recovery system (MACRS).

STRAIGHT-LINE DEPRECIATION

The **straight-line depreciation method** allows an equal amount to be depreciated each year of the life of the equipment. Cost minus salvage value is divided by life to find the amount of yearly depreciation.

PROBLEM 1

A desktop computer and monitor were purchased by ABC Real Estate Co. for $2,000. The computer is expected to have a useful life of 5 years and a salvage value of $100. What is the yearly depreciation expense for the computer?

Use the straight-line depreciation formula

$$(\text{Cost} - \text{Salvage Value}) \div \text{Life} = \text{Yearly Depreciation}$$

as shown in Figure 23.1:

$$(\$2,000 - \$100) \div 5 = \$380$$

$$\frac{\text{Cost} - \text{Salvage value}}{\text{Life}} = \text{Depreciation per year}$$

$$\frac{2,000 - 100}{5} = 380$$

FIGURE 23.1 Straight-line depreciation formula.

PREPARING A STRAIGHT-LINE DEPRECIATION SCHEDULE

A straight-line depreciation schedule should be prepared listing each year of the life of the equipment, the depreciation each year, the accumulated depreciation, and the book value at the end of each year. A straight-line depreciation schedule for the desktop computer is

Straight-Line Depreciation Schedule

Year	Depreciation	Accumulated Depreciation	End-of-Year Book Value
1	380	380	1,620
2	380	760	1,240
3	380	1,140	860
4	380	1,520	480
5	380	1,900	100

FIGURE 23.2   Straight-line depreciation schedule.

shown in Figure 23.2. To prepare the schedule, add the depreciation each year to find accumulated depreciation. Subtract depreciation from cost to find book value for the end of year 1. Subtract depreciation from the previous year's book value to find book value for the end of years 2 through 5.

If the schedule is prepared correctly, book value at the end of year 5 (the end of the computer's useful life) should equal salvage value—in this case, $100.

Also, at the end of year 5, accumulated depreciation plus the book value should equal the original cost of the computer—$1,900 + $100 = $2,000.

UNITS-PRODUCED METHOD OF DEPRECIATION

The **units-produced depreciation method** involves depreciating a piece of equipment based on the number of units produced, miles driven, or hours used.

PROBLEM 2

Seaside Campground purchased an ATV for $4,200. The ATV is expected to have a salvage value of $500 after being driven 29,200 miles. The ATV was driven 3,000 miles the first year. What was the annual depreciation for year 1?

To find annual depreciation using the units-produced method:

1. Find the amount the equipment depreciates for each unit produced, mile driven, or hour used by dividing cost minus salvage value by expected units, miles, or hours over the life of the equipment as shown in Figure 23.3:

$$(\$4,200 - \$500) \div \$29,200 = 0.13$$

First, find depreciation per mile:

Cost – Salvage value / Units produced during life = Depreciation per unit

$$\frac{4,200 - 500}{29,200} = .13$$

FIGURE 23.3   Units-produced depreciation method, step 1.

2. Multiply depreciation per unit, mile, or hour by units produced, miles driven, or hours used during the year to find annual depreciation as shown in Figure 23.4:

$$0.13 \times \$3,000 = \$390$$

Second, find annual depreciation:

Depreciation per unit x Units produced in 1 year = Annual depreciation

.1 3 x 3 , 0 0 0 = 3 9 0

FIGURE 23.4 Units-produced depreciation method, step 2.

Note that with the units-produced method of depreciation, annual depreciation will *vary* each year according to the amount of use the equipment receives.

SUM-OF-THE-YEARS'-DIGITS METHOD OF DEPRECIATION

The **sum-of-the-years'-digits depreciation method** allows greater depreciation during the early years of the life of an asset. This method gets its name because the digits of all the years in the life of the equipment are added (summed). The sum of the years' digits for 3 years is 1 + 2 + 3 = 6. The depreciable value of an asset is multiplied by the years remaining in the life of the asset and divided by the sum of the years' digits. Notice in Figure 23.5 that the fraction of remaining life divided by the sum of the years' digits declines each year: 5/15, 4/15, 3/15, ...

Depreciable value = $1,500 - $200 = $1,300

Sum of year's digits = 1 + 2 + 3 + 4 + 5 = 15

(Years remaining in life / Sum of years' digits in life) x Depreciable value = Annual depreciation

Year 1 Dep. = 5/15 x 1300 = .333333 x 1300 = $433.33

Year 2 Dep. = 4/15 x 1300 = .266666 x 1300 = $346.67

Year 3 Dep. = 3/15 x 1300 = .2 x 1300 = $260.00

Year 4 Dep. = 2/15 x 1300 = .133333 x 1300 = $173.33

Year 5 Dep. = 1/15 x 1300 = .066666 x 1300 = $ 86.67

FIGURE 23.5 Sum-of-the-years'-digits depreciation method.

PROBLEM 3

ABC Real Estate Co. purchased a color laser printer with an expected life of 5 years and a salvage value of $200. The printer cost $1,500. What is annual depreciation for years 1 through 5?

To find depreciation for each year, divide the years remaining in the life of the equipment by the sum of the years' digits. Multiply the result by the **depreciable value**, which is the cost ($1,500) minus salvage value ($200). Figure 23.5 indicates that the depreciable value of the printer is $1,300. The sum of the years' digits is 15.

Year 1: The years remaining in life (5) divided by the sum of the years' digits (15) equals 0.333333. This result multiplied by the depreciable value ($1,300) is equal to $433.33 annual depreciation for year 1.
Alternately, multiply remaining years of life (5) by the depreciable value ($1,300) and divide by sum of the years' digits (15).

Year 2: The years remaining in life (4) divided by the sum of the years' digits (15) equals 0.266666. This result multiplied by the depreciable value ($1,300) is equal to $346.67 annual depreciation for year 2.
Alternately, multiply remaining years of life (4) by the depreciable value ($1,300) and divide by sum of the years' digits (15).

Repeat for years 3 through 5, with the years remaining in life declining each year.

POCKET CALCULATOR PROCEDURE

$5 \times 1{,}300 \div 15 = \boxed{433.33}$ M+ depreciation for first year
$4 \times 1{,}300 \div 15 = \boxed{346.67}$ M+
$3 \times 1{,}300 \div 15 = \boxed{260.00}$ M+
$2 \times 1{,}300 \div 15 = \boxed{173.33}$ M+
$1 \times 1{,}300 \div 15 = \boxed{86.67}$ M+ MR $\boxed{1{,}300}$

Add the annual depreciation for years 1 through 5. The sum should equal the depreciable value of the equipment ($1,300).

DECLINING-BALANCE METHOD OF DEPRECIATION

Like the sum-of-the-years'-digits method, the **declining-balance depreciation method** also allows for accelerated depreciation in the early years of useful life of an asset. In this method a rate of depreciation is used. Rates that may be used include:

1. **Straight-line rate.** To find the straight-line rate, divide 1 by the number of years of useful life.
2. **Double-declining rate.** The double-declining rate, also known as the 200% rate, is the straight-line rate multiplied by 2.
3. **150% rate.** The 150% rate is the straight-line rate multiplied by 1.5.

Figure 23.6 shows examples of these rates calculated for an item with a useful life of 5 years.

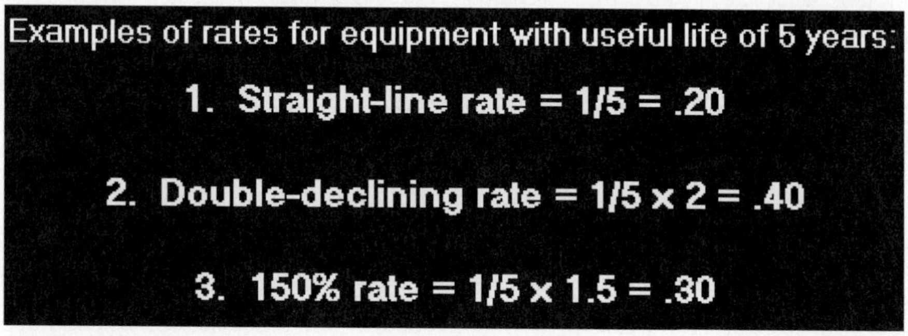

Examples of rates for equipment with useful life of 5 years:

1. Straight-line rate = 1/5 = .20

2. Double-declining rate = 1/5 × 2 = .40

3. 150% rate = 1/5 × 1.5 = .30

FIGURE 23.6 Declining-balance depreciation examples.

The rate is applied to the book value each year until the book value equals the salvage value. In later years of equipment life, depreciation may have to be adjusted to ensure that the book value does not fall below the salvage value.

Note that in the declining-balance method of depreciation *salvage value is not* subtracted from cost before calculating depreciation.

PROBLEM 4

Prepare a schedule of depreciation for a color laser printer that cost $1,500, using the double-declining rate. The estimated salvage value is $200. Estimated useful life of the printer is 5 years.

Find the double-declining rate (straight-line rate $\times$ 2):

$$1 \div 5 \text{ years} = 0.20 \times 2 = 0.40$$

Year 1: Multiply the cost of the printer ($1,500) by the double-declining rate (0.40) to find the depreciation ($600). Subtract the depreciation ($600) from the cost ($1,500) to find the book value ($900).

Years 2 through 4: Multiply the previous year's book value by the double-declining rate to find the depreciation. Subtract depreciation from the previous book value to find the book value for the current year.

Example:

Year 2:　900 × .40 = 360

　　　　　900 − 360 = 540

Notice in Figure 23.7 that depreciation for year 4 must be adjusted so that the book value does not fall below $200.

Adjust depreciation to $124.00 so that book value equals $200.00 (salvage value).

Schedule of Depreciation for Color Laser Printer
Double-Declining Balance Method

Year	Book Value x Rate	Depreciation	Book Value
1	$1,500 x .40	$600	$900
2	$ 900 x .40	$360	$540
3	$ 540 x .40	$216	$324
4	$ 324 x .40	$129.00 $124	$194.40 $200

FIGURE 23.7　Double-declining balance schedule of depreciation with year 4 adjustment.

Year 5: No depreciation is calculated for year 5 because the book value cannot be less than the salvage value of $200.

POCKET CALCULATOR PROCEDURE

If your calculator has a reverse key, $+/-$, you can save time when completing depreciation schedules such as the one shown above. The reverse key allows you to change the sign of the displayed number:

$$1 \div 5 = \boxed{.2} \times 2 = \boxed{.4}$$

Year 1: 1,500 M+ × .4 = $\boxed{600}$ $\boxed{+/-}$ $\boxed{-600}$ + MR = $\boxed{900}$ MC M+
Year 2: ×.4 = $\boxed{360}$ $\boxed{+/-}$ $\boxed{-360}$ + MR = $\boxed{540}$ MC M+
Year 3: ×.4 = $\boxed{216}$ $\boxed{+/-}$ $\boxed{-216}$ + MR = $\boxed{324}$ MC M+
Year 4: ×.4 = $\boxed{129.60}$ $\boxed{+/-}$ $\boxed{-129.60}$ + MR = $\boxed{194.40}$ MC

Adjust the depreciation for year 4 so that book value is equal to salvage value ($200):

$$324 - 200 = \boxed{124} \text{ depreciation for year 4}$$

ACCELERATED COST RECOVERY SYSTEM

The **ACRS** is another method used to depreciate assets for tax purposes. It was used for property placed in service after 1980 but before 1987. The placed-in-service date is the date that depreciable property was actually turned over to the business for its use. Some features of the ACRS are shown in Figure 23.8. For more information, consult IRS Publication 534, Depreciating Property Placed in Service Before 1987.

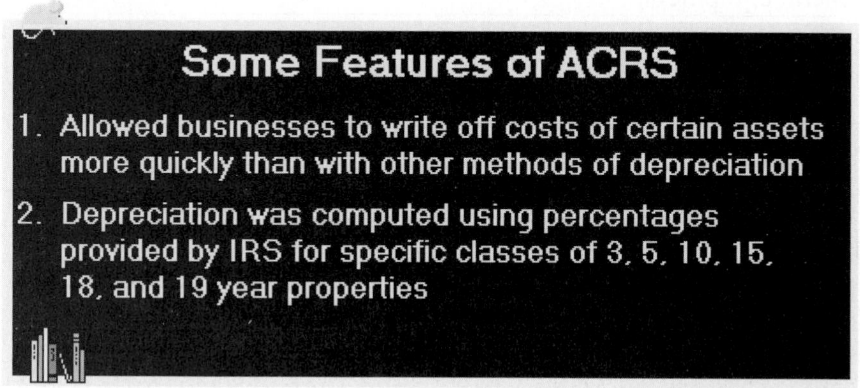

Some Features of ACRS

1. Allowed businesses to write off costs of certain assets more quickly than with other methods of depreciation

2. Depreciation was computed using percentages provided by IRS for specific classes of 3, 5, 10, 15, 18, and 19 year properties

FIGURE 23.8 ACRS features.

A depreciation schedule was prepared at the time property was placed in service. The schedule is used instead of calculating depreciation each year of the property's remaining life. A 19-year property placed in service in 1986 will be depreciated using ACRS rates until the end of its 19-year life in 2005.

MODIFIED ACCELERATED COST RECOVERY SYSTEM

The **MACRS** is used for tax purposes in the recovery of costs for most property placed in service after 1986. MACRS consists of two depreciation systems, the General Depreciation System (GDS) and the Alternative Depreciation System (ADS). Generally, the GDS is used by businesses and is the method discussed in this book. Three depreciation systems are allowed under GDS, which are calculated for the appropriate GDS recovery period (allowable life under GDS):

1. The 200% declining-balance method
2. The 150% declining-balance method
3. The straight-line rate method

Depreciation may be calculated with or without the use of an IRS percentage table that incorporates the applicable convention and depreciation method. Figure 23.9 lists the nine property classes (allowable life for the property) under the GDS and examples of the types of property included in each class, taken from IRS Publication 946, How To Depreciate Property.

For a complete list of properties, see Table of Class Lives and Recovery Periods of IRS Publication 946.

	Property Classes Under GDS and Examples of Such Properties	Recovery Period
1)	**3-year property.**	
	a) Tractor units for over-the-road use.	3
	b) Any race horse over 2 years old when placed in service.	3
	c) Any other horse over 12 years old when placed in service.	3
	d) Qualified rent-to-own property.	3
2)	**5-year property.**	
	a) Automobiles, taxis, buses, and trucks.	5
	b) Computers and peripheral equipment.	5
	c) Office machinery (such as typewriters, calculators, and copiers).	5
	d) Any property used in research and experimentation.	5
	e) Breeding cattle and dairy cattle.	5
	f) Appliances, carpets, furniture, etc., used in a residential rental real estate activity.	5
3)	**7-year property.**	
	a) Office furniture and fixtures (such as desks, files, and safes).	7
	b) Agricultural machinery and equipment.	7
	c) Any property that does not have a class life and has not been designated by law as being in any other class.	7
4)	**10-year property.**	
	a) Vessels, barges, tugs, and similar water transportation equipment.	10
	b) Any single purpose agricultural or horticultural structure.	10
	c) Any tree or vine bearing fruits or nuts.	10
5)	**15-year property.**	
	a) Certain improvements made directly to land or added to it (such as shrubbery, fences, roads, and bridges).	15
	b) Any retail motor fuels outlet, such as a convenience store.	15
	c) Any municipal wastewater treatment plant.	15
6)	**20-year property.**	
	This class includes farm buildings (other than single purpose agricultural or horticultural structures.	20
7)	**25-year property.** This class is water utility property, which is either of the following	
	a) Property that is an integral part of the gathering, treatment, or commercial distribution of water, and that, without regard to this provision, would be 20-year property.	25
	b) Any municipal sewer.	25
8)	**Residential rental property.**	27.5
9)	**Nonresidental real property.**	39

FIGURE 23.9   MACRS GDS property classes.

Cost or Basis

The depreciable amount is referred to as the **basis**. The basis of a property is its cost plus amounts paid for the item such as sales tax, freight charges, installation, and testing fees multiplied by the percent of business use. The cost or basis includes the amount paid in cash, debt obligations, if any, and other property or services offered in exchange for the property.

An **adjusted basis** is a result of certain increases and decreases to property cost after it was acquired but before it was placed in service, such as addition of utility lines or a loss due to theft.

The **unadjusted basis** is the original basis less any Section 179 deduction claimed or any special depreciation allowances claimed.

Special Depreciation Allowances

Special depreciation allowances may be allowed in some years to recover an extra portion of the cost of qualified property. In 2002 a special Liberty Zone depreciation allowance and a **special depreciation allowance** of 30% were allowed. The special depreciation allowance is allowed only in the year property is placed in service. It may be taken after any Section 179 deduction and before regular depreciation is calculated.

Section 179 Deduction

Under Section 179 of the Internal Revenue Code, one may choose to recover all or part of the cost of certain property used for business purposes (up to $25,000 as of 2003) by deducting it in the year the property is placed in service. This **Section 179 deduction** is taken in place of recovering the cost by taking depreciation deductions. The $25,000 may be allocated in any way among qualifying property. The entire $25,000 does not have to be claimed.

The total amount deducted under Section 179 may not exceed taxable income for the year. It may not be used as part of a net loss. Any cost not deductible in one year because of this limit may be carried to the next year. Records must be kept that show the specific identification of each piece of qualifying Section 179 property, reflecting how the property was acquired, from whom it was acquired, and when it was placed in service. Estates and trusts may not elect the Section 179 deduction.

MACRS CONVENTIONS

MACRS conventions are used to determine how many months a property may be depreciated the year it is placed in service and the year it is taken out of service. There are three conventions.

1. The midmonth convention is used for residential rental and nonresidential real property. All property placed in service during a month is treated as though it were placed in service at the midpoint of the month. One-half month of depreciation is allowed for the month the property is placed in or taken out of service.

2. The midquarter convention is used (a) for MACRS property that does not fall under the midmonth convention and (b) if the depreciable basis of such property placed in service during the last 3 months of the year is more than 40% of the total depreciable basis of all such MACRS property placed in service during the entire year. Treat all property placed in service during any quarter of the tax year as placed in service at the midpoint of that quarter. One and one-half months of depreciation is allowed for the quarter the property is placed in or taken out of service.

3. The half-year convention is used for depreciating property if neither the midmonth nor the midquarter convention applies. Under the MACRS half-year convention, treat all property placed in service during a tax year as placed in service or disposed of at the midpoint of the year. This means that a half-year of depreciation is allowed for the year the property is placed in service or is taken out of service. For a 3-year property, rates for year 1 and year 4 reflect depreciation for only half a year. Figure 23.10 shows rates to be used for property placed in service at midyear. IRS Publication 946 contains tables for property placed in service at other times during the year.

IRS Table 4-1 from Publication 946, shown in Figure 23.11, shows which depreciation method should be used when depreciating various types of property and lists some of the benefits of each method. An accountant should be consulted when choosing which depreciation method to use. (For the curious, notice that property that is *required* to be depreciated under the ADS is listed in the ADS using SL row.)

MACRS Cost Recovery Factors				
Year	3-Yr. Class	5-Yr. Class	7-Yr. Class	10-Yr. Class
1	0.3333	0.2000	0.1429	0.1000
2	0.4445	0.3200	0.2449	0.1800
3	0.1481	0.1920	0.1749	0.1440
4	0.0741	0.1152	0.1249	0.1152
5		0.1152	0.0893	0.0922
6		0.0576	0.0892	0.0737
7			0.0893	0.0655
8			0.0446	0.0655
9				0.0655
				...

FIGURE 23.10   MACRS rates for property placed in service at midyear.

Table 4-1. **Depreciation Methods**

Note. The declining balance method is abbreviated as DB and the straight line method is abbreviated as SL.		
Method	**Type of Property**	**Benefit**
GDS using 200% DB	• Nonfarm 3-, 5-, 7-, and 10-year property	• Provides a greater deduction during the earlier recovery years • Changes to SL when that method provides an equal or greater deduction
GDS using 150% DB	• All farm property (except real property) • All 15- and 20-year property • Nonfarm 3-, 5-, 7-, and 10-year property	• Provides a greater deduction during the earlier recovery years • Changes to SL when that method provides an equal or greater deduction[1]
GDS using SL	• Nonresidential real property • Residential rental property • Trees or vines bearing fruit or nuts • Water utility property • All 3-, 5-, 7-, 10-, 15- and 20-year property[2]	• Provides for equal yearly deductions (except for the first and last years)
ADS using SL	• Listed property used 50% or less for business • Property used predominantly outside the U.S. • Tax-exempt property • Tax-exempt bond-financed property • Farm property used when an election not to apply the uniform capitalization rules is in effect • Imported property[3] • Any property for which you elect to use this method[2]	• Provides for equal yearly deductions
[1] The MACRS percentage tables in Appendix A have the switch to the straight line method built into their rates		
[2] Elective method		
[3] See section 168(g)(6) of the Internal Revenue Code		

FIGURE 23.11   MACRS depreciation methods to use when depreciating various properties.

In summary, to use the MACRS system, the following items must be known about a property before depreciation can be calculated:

1. Type of depreciation system under MACRS: ADS or GDS (all of the problems in this book will use GDS).
2. Under GDS, the depreciation method: 200% declining-balance, 150% declining balance, or straight-line rate method.
3. The convention to be used: midmonth, midquarter, or half-year convention.
4. Property class (refer to the table of property classes in Figure 23.9 for a partial list).
5. Recovery period (from the table of property classes in Figure 23.9).
6. Month or quarter placed in service.
7. Unadjusted basis.

USING MACRS TABLES

Once these determinations have been made, depreciation may be calculated using IRS tables for the unadjusted basis only. Do not use tables if the basis has been adjusted for any reason other than depreciation. Also, MACRS tables may not be used unless the company was in business the entire year.

To use MACRS tables, refer to IRS Chart 1, a portion of which is shown in Figure 23.12, to find the correct rate table to use for property other than residential rental and nonresidental real property. Use Chart 2, a portion of which is shown in Figure 23.13, to find the correct rate for residential rental and nonresidental real property (land is not depreciable, but buildings and improvements are). Complete charts are included at the end of this chapter.

Chart 1. *Use this chart to find the correct percentage table to use for any property other than residential rental and nonresidential real property. Use Chart 2 for residential rental and nonresidential real property.*

MACRS System	Depreciation Method	Recovery Period	Convention	Class	Month or Quarter Placed in Service	Table
GDS	200%	GDS/3, 5, 7, 10 (Nonfarm)	Half-Year	3, 5, 7, 10	Any	A-1
GDS	200%	GDS/3, 5, 7, 10 (Nonfarm)	Mid-Quarter	3, 5, 7, 10	1st Qtr 2nd Qtr 3rd Qtr 4th Qtr	A-2 A-3 A-4 A-5
GDS	150%	GDS/3, 5, 7, 10	Half-Year	3, 5, 7, 10	Any	A-14

FIGURE 23.12   MACRS rate tables to use for certain properties.

Chart 2. *Use this chart to find the correct percentage table to use for residential rental and nonresidential real property. Use Chart 1 for all other property.*

MACRS System	Depreciation Method	Recovery Period	Convention	Class	Month or Quarter Placed in Service	Table
GDS	SL	GDS 27.5	Mid-Month	Residential Rental	Any	A-6
GDS	SL SL	GDS/31.5 GDS/39	Mid-Month	Nonresidential Rental	Any	A-7 A-7a

FIGURE 23.13   MACRS rate tables to use for residential rental and nonresidential real properties.

PROBLEM 5

Michael Brown placed a 7-year property that cost $30,000 in service November 2002. He plans to claim a Section 179 deduction of $24,000 and the special depreciation allowance (30%). He uses the 200% declining-balance method and the half-year convention. Calculate the following:

A. Special depreciation allowance
B. Unadjusted basis
C. MACRS depreciation

Solution:

a. From the cost of the equipment, subtract the Section 179 deduction. Multiply the difference by 30% to find the special depreciation allowance:

$$\$30,000 - \$24,000 = \$6,000$$
$$\$6,000 \times .30 = \$1,800$$

b. Subtract the special depreciation allowance from $6,000 to find the depreciable amount:

$$\$6,000 - \$1,800 = \$4,200$$

c. Consult Figure 23.12 to find the table to use. Row one indicates that the rate for a 7-year property using GDS, 200% declining-balance method, and half-year convention, will be found in Table A-1 (located at the end of this chapter). The rate given in Table A-1 for the first year of a 7-year property is 14.29%. Multiply the basis for depreciation ($4,200) by the rate (14.29%) to find the amount to deduct for depreciation for year 1:

$$\$4,200 \times .1429 = \$600.18$$

PROBLEM 6

Office machinery costing $10,000 was purchased for use by a business and placed in service September 10, 2002. The business uses the GDS, the 200% declining-balance method, and the half-year convention. No Section 179 deduction or special depreciation allowances were taken. Calculate the following:

1. Unadjusted basis
2. Depreciation for each year of the recovery period of the property:
    2002
    2003
    2004
    2005
    2006
    2007

Solution:

a. The unadjusted basis is the cost, $10,000.
b. 1. The property classes table indicates that office machinery is a 5-year property.
    2. Chart 1 indicates that for a 5-year property using GDS, 200% declining-balance method, and the half-year convention, Table A-1 should be used.
    3. Using the rates in Table A-1 for a 5-year property multiplied by the basis ($10,000) results in the following amounts of yearly depreciation:

Year	Basis ($)	Rate (%)	Depreciation ($)
1	10,000	20	2,000
2	10,000	32	3,200
3	10,000	19.20	1,920
4	10,000	11.52	1,152
5	10,000	11.52	1,152
6	10,000	5.76	576

Check: The listed percents should equal 100%:

$$20\% + 32\% + 19.20\% + 11.52\% + 11.52\% + 5.76\% = 100\%$$

The yearly depreciation amounts should equal the basis:

$$\$2,000 + \$3,200 + \$1,920 + \$1,152 + \$1,152 + \$576 = \$10,000$$

POCKET CALCULATOR PROCEDURE

10,000 M+ × 20 % 2,000

MR × 32 % 3,200

MR × 19.20 % 1,920

MR × 11.52 % 1,152

MR × 11.52 % 1,152

MR × 5.76 % 576

PROBLEM 7

A business wishing to expand purchased a building for $200,000 and land for $55,500 on February 10 to be used as nonresidential real property. The business uses GDS. Calculate the following:

A. Unadjusted basis (land is not depreciable)
B. Depreciation deduction for year 1 and year 2

Solution:

a. The unadjusted basis is the cost of the building, $200,000.
b. 1. The property classes table indicates that nonresidential real property has a 39-year recovery period.
    2. Chart 2 indicates that for GDS, straight-line rate method, 39-year recovery period, nonresidential real property, use Table A-7a. The midmonth convention is used for nonresidential real property.
    3. Table A-7a indicates that the depreciation rate for the second month (the property was purchased in February) of the first year is 2.247%. The rate for year 2 is 2.564%.
    4. Multiply rate by basis:

$$\text{Year 1 Depreciation} = \$200{,}000 \times .02247 = \$4{,}494$$
$$\text{Year 2 Depreciation} = \$200{,}000 \times .02564 = \$5{,}128$$

PROBLEM 8

During the last quarter of 2001, research equipment was placed in service that cost $50,000. No Section 179 deduction or special depreciation allowance were taken. This was the only business equipment placed in service this year. The company uses GDS. What are the following:

A. The property class
B. The convention to be used
C. The depreciation for year 1 and year 2

Solution:

a. The property classes table indicates research equipment is a 5-year property.
b. Because this property was placed in service during the last quarter of the year and was the only property placed in service in 2001, the midquarter convention should be used for calculating depreciation.
c. 1. Chart 1 indicates that under GDS, midquarter convention, 5-year property placed in service during the fourth quarter, midquarter convention, Table A-5 should be used.
    2. Table A-5 indicates the depreciation rate for year 1 for a 5-year property placed in service during the fourth quarter is 5%. The depreciation rate for year 2 is 38%.
    3. Multiply basis by the rate for years 1 and 2 to find depreciation to be deducted:

$$\text{Year 1 Depreciation} = \$50{,}000 \times .05 = \$2{,}500$$
$$\text{Year 2 Depreciation} = \$50{,}000 \times .38 = \$19{,}000$$

PROBLEM 9

Jane Smithwick bought and placed in service the following items for her business. Jane did not take a Section 179 deduction or special depreciate allowance. She uses GDS.

Item	Cost/Basis ($)	Placed in Service Date
Office furniture	2,000	February 2002
Office safe	1,000	March 2002
Computers	5,500	October 2002

A. Does Jane need to use the midquarter convention for these items? Yes.
Why or why not? The cost of depreciable property placed in service during the last quarter was more than 40% of the depreciable property placed in service during the entire year.

B. Use the following worksheet to calculate the depreciation for year 1 for each item of equipment.

Quarter Placed in Service	Item	Cost/Basis	Property Class	Table to Use	First-Year Rate	Depreciation for Year 1
___	___	___	___	___	___	___
___	___	___	___	___	___	___

Solution:

a. First determine if the last-quarter depreciable property cost was more than 40% of the depreciable property for the year. Divide the last-quarter depreciable property cost by the total depreciable property costs for the year to find the percent fourth-quarter depreciable property cost to depreciable property costs for the entire year:

$$\$5,500 \div \$8,500 = 65\%$$

The fourth-quarter percent of depreciable property costs to depreciable costs for the entire year is greater than 40%, so Jane must use the midquarter convention for all three items.

b. 1. The table of property classes indicates that the furniture and the safe are 7-year properties and the computer is a 5-year property.

2. Chart 1 indicates that under the midquarter convention we should use Table A-2 for the property placed in service in the first quarter and Table A-5 for property placed in service the fourth quarter.

3. Multiply the basis of each item by the appropriate depreciation rate for the first year:

Furniture $\$2,000 \times .25 = \$500$
Safe $\$1,000 \times .25 = \$250$
Computers $\$5,500 \times .05 = \$275$

The completed worksheet should look as follows:

Quarter Placed in Service	Item	Cost/Basis ($)	Property Class	Table to Use	First-Year Rate (%)	Depreciation for Year 1 ($)
First	Furniture	2,000	7-year	A-2	25	500
First	Safe	1,000	7-year	A-2	25	250
Fourth	Computers	5,500	5-year	A-5	5	275

DEPRECIATING PASSENGER AUTOMOBILES UNDER MACRS

There is a depreciation limit for passenger automobiles. As of 2002, the total Section 179 and depreciation deductions cannot be more than $7,660* the first year, $4,900 the second year, $2,950 the third year, and $1,775 the fourth year and each year thereafter if a Section 179 or the special depreciation allowance is claimed.

Note: If a Section 179 or special depreciation allowance is not claimed, the first year depreciation limit is $3,060. See IRS Publication 946, Maximum Depreciation Deduction for Passenger Automobile, for years prior to 1995.

PROBLEM 5

What is the depreciation each year for a $12,000 car placed in service at midyear? No Section 179 or special depreciation allowance was taken.

Step 1: Consult the excerpt of Classes of Property Used for MACRS shown in Figure 23.9 to find the allowed recovery period for cars (5 years).

Step 2: Consult the excerpt of MACRS Cost Recovery Factors shown in Figure 23.10. Multiply the rate for year 1 (0.2) by the total cost of the property ($12,000). Salvage value is not used in calculating depreciation using MACRS as shown in Figure 23.14. Note that depreciation for years 1 and 2 do not exceed the depreciation limit for passenger automobiles for which no special depreciation allowance was claimed.

	From tables: Car is a 5-yr. property. MACRS rate for mid-yr. placement, year 1=.20; year 2=.32		
Year	Rate x Depreciable Value	Depreciation	Book Value
1	.20 x $12,000	$2,400.00	$9,600.00
2	.32 x $12,000	1,228.80	8,371.20

FIGURE 23.14   MACRS years 1 and 2 depreciation for a car with no special allowances claimed.

The next problem demonstrates how to handle depreciation of a car for which a special depreciation allowance is claimed and depreciation deductions are reduced under the passenger automobile limits.

PROBLEM 6

Calculate depreciation each year for a $16,000 car placed in service at midyear. The car is used 100% for business purposes. No Section 179 deduction was taken. A special depreciation allowance of $4,800 ($16,000 × 30%) was claimed.

Complete a schedule of depreciation.

Step 1: Same as step 1 in Problem 5. Recovery period is 5 years.

Step 2: Consult the excerpt of MACRS Cost Recovery Factors shown in Figure 23.10. Multiply the rate for year 1 (0.2) by the remaining cost of the property to find the MACRS depreciation:

$$\$16,000 - \$4,800 = \$11,200$$
$$\$11,200 \times .2 = \$2,240$$

Add the special depreciation allowance and the MACRS depreciation together to find total depreciation for year 1. Check that it does not exceed the first-year depreciation limit of $7,660:

$$\$4,800 + \$2,240 = \$7,040$$

Repeat step 2 to find the appropriate rate for each of the remaining years of life.

Step 3: Complete a schedule of depreciation as shown in Figure 23.15. The Allowed Depreciation column reflects the amount of depreciation actually subtracted from the book value.

a.   Notice that 6 years are listed for a 5-year property placed in service at midyear because years 1 and 6 each reflects half a year of depreciation. In this case, the car was fully depreciated in 4 years because of the special depreciation allowance taken in year 1. Also notice that the passenger automobile limits were less than the calculated depreciation for years 2 and 3, and in year 4 the book value was less than the calculated depreciation and the limit.

b.   Total all the amounts for annual depreciation. The result should be the total cost of the car ($16,000).

c.   To calculate book value:

Year 1: Subtract depreciation from cost of the car.

Years 2 through 6: Subtract depreciation from the previous year's book value.

Schedule of Depreciation for Car (MACRS)					
Year	Rate X Cost	Amount	Limit	Allowed Depreciation	Book Value
1	.30 x $16,000 + .20 x 11,200	$7,040	$7,660	$7,040	8,960
2	.32 x 16,000	5,120	$4,900	4,900	4,060
3	.1920 x 16,000	3,072	2,950	2,950	1,110
4	.1152 x 16,000	1,843	1,775	1,110	0
5	.1152				
6	.0576				

FIGURE 23.15 MACRS schedule of depreciation for a car with a special allowance claimed and passenger auto depreciation limits in effect.

The next problem demonstrates how to treat the unrecovered basis of a car when a car has not been fully depreciated at the end of 5 years.

PROBLEM 7

Calculate depreciation each year for a $30,000 car placed in service at midyear. The car was used 100% for business purposes. No Section 179 or special depreciation allowance was taken. The car was taken out of service at the end of year 8. Complete a schedule of depreciation.

Step 1: Same as step 1 in Problem 6. Recovery period is 5 years.

Step 2: Same as step 2 in Problem 6. The rate for year 1 is 0.2.

Repeat step 2 to find the appropriate rate for each of the remaining years of life (years 1 through 6).

Step 3: Multiply the rate for each year by the cost of the car. Compare to the passenger automobile limits and write the lesser amount in the Allowed Depreciation column.

    a. The limit for year 1 is $3,060 because no Section 179 or special depreciation allowance was taken.

    b. Total all the amounts for annual depreciation. The result should be the total cost of the car ($30,000).

    c. To calculate book value:

        Year 1: Subtract the allowed depreciation from cost of the car.

        Years 2 through 6: Subtract the depreciation from the previous year's book value.

As you can see in Figure 23.16, at the end of year 6 an unrecovered basis or book value of $13,812 exists. If the car remains in 100% use at the business, it may be depreciated each year at $1,775 or the car's unrecovered basis, whichever is less, until the car is taken out of service.

MACRS WITHOUT USING TABLES

Let us calculate depreciation using the straight-line rate as described earlier in this chapter. For the 200% declining-balance method divide 2 (the decimal equivalent of 200%) by the number of years in the MACRS recovery period to find the depreciation rate. Multiply the basis by this rate the first year. For succeeding years, subtract the previous year's depreciation from the basis to find the adjusted basis for the current year. Switch to the straight-line rate when the depreciation equals or exceeds that

Schedule of Depreciation for Car (MACRS)

Year	Rate X Cost	Amount	Limit	Allowed Depreciation	Book Value
1	.20 x $30,000	$6,000	$3,060	$3,060	$26,940
2	.32 x 30,000	9,600	$4,900	4,900	22,040
3	.1920 x 30,000	5,760	2,950	2,950	19,090
4	.1152 x 30,000	3,456	1,775	1,775	17,315
5	.1152 x 30,000	3,456	1,775	1,775	15,540
6	.0576 x 30,000	1,728	1,775	1,728	13,812
7			1,775	1,775	12,037
8			1,775	1,775	10,262

FIGURE 23.16 MACRS schedule of depreciation for a car with an unrecovered basis after 5 years.

resulting from the 200% declining-balance method. The procedure for the 150% declining-balance rate is the same except that we divide 1.5 (150%) by the number of years in the recovery period.

Use the MACRS recovery periods and conventions. For example, if the half-year convention is used, deduct only half the depreciation the first year of the recovery period.

PROBLEM 8

Use the 200% declining-balance rate and half-year convention to calculate depreciation for a 3-year property with a basis of $2,000. Complete the following worksheet.

Depreciation Worksheet for $2,000, 3-Year Property

Year	Method	Basis ($)	Rate (%)	Formula Used to Find Rate	Depreciation ($)	Half-Year Depreciation ($)	Check Method to Be Used
Year 1	200% declining balance	2,000	66.67	2 ÷ 3 = .6667	1,333.40	666.70	✓
	Straight line	2,000	33.33	1 ÷ 3 = .3333	666.60	333.30	
Year 2	200% declining balance	1,333.33	66.67		888.93	_____	✓
	Straight line	1,333.33	40	1 ÷ 2.5	533.33	_____	
Year 3	200% declining balance	444.40	66.67		296.28	_____	
	Straight line	444.40	66.67	1 ÷ 1.5	296.28	_____	✓*
Year 4	200% declining balance	148.12	66.67		98.75	49.38	
	Straight line	148.12	100	**	148.12	74.06	✓

*Note: Notice that in year 3 the depreciations resulting from the declining-balance method and the straight-line rate method are equal, so you should switch to the straight-line method when calculating the depreciation for the remaining years. Although it is no longer necessary to calculate depreciation using the declining-balance method, the completion of the worksheet confirms that the amount calculated using the declining-balance method is smaller from this point forward.

**Note: There is less than 1 year remaining in the recovery period, so the rate for year 4 is 100%.

Year 1: Declining-balance method. Divide 2 by 3 years to find the rate to use (66.67%). Multiply the rate by the basis ($2,000). Divide the result by 2 to find the half-year depreciation ($666.70).

Straight-line rate. Divide 1 by 3 to find the rate to use (33.33%). Multiply the rate by the basis ($2,000). Divide the result by 2 to find the half-year depreciation ($333.30).

The depreciation using the declining balance method ($666.70) is larger, so it is the depreciation amount deducted.

Year 2: Declining-balance method. Subtract the first-year depreciation from the basis. Multiply difference ($1,333.33) by 66.67% to find the second-year depreciation ($888.93).

Straight-line rate. Calculate the rate by dividing 1 by 2.5, the years remaining in the recovery period: $1 \div 2.5 = .4$, or 40%. Subtract the first-year depreciation from the basis to find the adjusted basis for year 2. Multiply by rate: $1,333.33 \times .4 = \$533.33$.

The depreciation using the declining balance method ($888.93) is larger, so it is the depreciation amount deducted.

Years 3 and 4: Repeat the procedures to calculate the depreciation for the remaining years.

Note: Calculations made without the use of tables may differ slightly from those obtained using tables.

FINANCIAL STATEMENTS VERSUS TAX RECORDS

Some companies use different depreciation methods for financial statements and for calculating taxes. Take a moment to look at the purposes of each.

Financial statements are used to measure company income accurately and consistently from year to year. In addition to reporting the company's condition, financial statements are audited and, for publicly held corporations, are available to the general public. Once a depreciation method is chosen for a certain asset, it is usually used until the useful life of the equipment expires, in the interest of consistency.

Tax records, on the other hand, are intended to meet the federal income tax code. The federal government may use tax law to stimulate economic activity, job growth, and so on, by allowing companies to quickly depreciate assets, thereby receiving a larger tax write-off in the early years of the equipment life. Tax law does not necessarily agree with accounting financial reporting. State and local taxes, just like federal taxes, change on a continual basis. Each may use a different method of accounting for certain expenses such as depreciation and inventory.

Name _____

Class/Section _____

Score (Correct Answers ÷ No. of Assigned Problems) _____

PART 2 *Business Math Skills*

Exercise 1

Calculate the annual depreciation for each item using the straight-line method.

	Asset	Cost ($)	Salvage Value ($)	Estimated Useful Life (Years)	Annual Depreciation
1.	Building	375,000	25,000	30	_____
2.	Furniture	80,000	15,000	15	_____
3.	Computer network	28,000	1,000	3	_____
4.	SUV	51,000	5,500	5	_____
5.	Van	35,000	5,500	5	_____

Exercise 2

Prepare a schedule of depreciation for a tractor that cost $85,000. The tractor is expected to have a useful life of 8 years and a salvage value of $20,000. Use the straight-line depreciation method.

Asset _____ **Cost** _____ **Life** _____
Salvage Value _____

	Year	Depreciation	Accumulated Depreciation	End-of-Year Book Value
6.	1	_____	_____	_____
7.	2	_____	_____	_____
8.	3	_____	_____	_____
9.	4	_____	_____	_____
10.	5	_____	_____	_____
11.	6	_____	_____	_____
12.	7	_____	_____	_____
13.	8	_____	_____	_____

Exercise 3

A piece of equipment, Asset #322, was purchased for $32,000. It is expected to produce 600,000 units of an item and have no salvage value.

1. Calculate depreciation per unit, rounding the decimal number to seven figures. _____
2. What is the depreciation for year 1 if 72,000 units were produced? _____

Complete the following schedule of depreciation.

Asset #322 Cost $32,000 Estimated Unit Production 600,000
Salvage Value $0 Depreciation per Unit _____

	Year	Units Produced	Depreciation	Accumulated Depreciation	End-of-Year Book Value
16.	1	72,000	_____	_____	_____
17.	2	75,000	_____	_____	_____
18.	3	67,500	_____	_____	_____
19.	4	75,250	_____	_____	_____
20.	5	72,300	_____	_____	_____
21.	6	78,250	_____	_____	_____
22.	7	82,300	_____	_____	_____
23.	8	77,400	_____	_____	_____

Exercise 4

A piece of equipment, Asset #500, was purchased for $15,590. It is expected to have a useful life of 6 years and a salvage value of $300. Complete a depreciation schedule using the sum-of-the-years'-digits method.

Asset _____ **Cost** _____ **Life** _____
Salvage Value _____

	Year	Depreciation	Accumulated Depreciation	End-of-Year Book Value
24.	1	_____	_____	_____
25.	2	_____	_____	_____
26.	3	_____	_____	_____
27.	4	_____	_____	_____
28.	5	_____	_____	_____
29.	6	_____	_____	_____

Exercise 5

Use the declining-balance method to complete a depreciation schedule for each of the following assets.

Asset #230 Cost $2,000 Life 5 Years Salvage Value $100 Rate Straight Line

	Year	Depreciation	Accumulated Depreciation	End-of-Year Book Value
30.	1	_____	_____	_____
31.	2	_____	_____	_____
32.	3	_____	_____	_____
33.	4	_____	_____	_____
34.	5	_____	_____	_____

Asset #560 Cost $5,150 Life 3 Years Salvage Value $500 Rate Double Declining

	Year	Depreciation	Accumulated Depreciation	End-of-Year Book Value
35.	1	_____	_____	_____
36.	2	_____	_____	_____
37.	3	_____	_____	_____

Asset #340 Cost $3,755 Life 3 Years Salvage Value $800 Rate 150%

	Year	Depreciation	Accumulated Depreciation	End-of-Year Book Value
38.	1	_____	_____	_____
39.	2	_____	_____	_____
40.	3	_____	_____	_____

Exercise 6

A business purchased office machines for $16,000. The business uses GDS and the half-year convention. Prepare a schedule of depreciation for the office machinery using MACRS tables.

Asset _____ Cost $_____ Class _____

	Year	Rate	Depreciation	Accumulated Depreciation	End-of-Year Book Value
41.	1	___	_____	_____	_____
42.	2	___	_____	_____	_____
43.	3	___	_____	_____	_____
44.	4	___	_____	_____	_____
45.	5	___	_____	_____	_____
46.	6	___	_____	_____	_____

Exercise 7

Calculate first-year depreciation for the following equipment and passenger automobile purchased by XYZ Co. The company uses GDS, half-year convention. No Section 179 or special depreciation allowance was taken. Use the MACRS tables.

47. Research equipment, $15,000 _____
48. Light truck, $45,000 _____

Calculate the first-year depreciation for the following equipment using GDS and the MACRS tables and the 200% midquarter convention.

49. Office furniture, $3,000, purchased January 13, 2002 _____
50. Appliances to be used in residential rental property, $12,000, purchased October 2, 2002 _____

PART 3 *Review and Practice Using Business Math FUNdamentals*

GOAL: Complete 9 of the 10 problems correctly.

Instructions: *Start Business Math FUNdamentals. Complete Tutorials 51 through 55 and Drills 42 and 43. If you are not satisfied with your score, repeat the drill. Write your scores below.*

Business Math FUNdamentals Drill 42

Today's Date	Score

Business Math FUNdamentals Drill 43

Today's Date	Score

PART 4 *Desktop Calculator*

Following are some sample problems and how to work them using the desktop calculator.

MACHINE SETUP Decimal selector—2
Rounding switch—5/4
Printer—On

STRAIGHT-LINE DEPRECIATION METHOD

PROBLEM

Prepare a schedule of depreciation for a forklift that cost $35,000 that has an expected useful life of 8 years and a salvage value of $2,000.

Asset _____ Cost $_____ Life _____ Salvage Value $_____

Year	Depreciation	Accumulated Depreciation	End-of-Year Book Value
1	_____	_____	_____
2	_____	_____	_____
3	_____	_____	_____
4	_____	_____	_____
5	_____	_____	_____
6	_____	_____	_____
7	_____	_____	_____
8	_____	_____	_____

```
35,000 .  +
 2,000 .  -
33,000 .  *

35,000 .  ÷
    8 .  =
 4,125 .  *

 4,125 . M+
 4,125 .  +
 4,125 . M◊
 4,125 .  +
 8,250 .  *

 8,250 .  +
 4,125 . M◊
 4,125 .  +
12,375 .  *

12,375 .  +
 4,125 . M◊
 4,125 .  +
16,500 .  *

16,500 .  +
 4,125 . M◊
 4,125 .  +
20,625 .  *

20,625 .  +
 4,125 . M◊
 4,125 .  +
24,750 .  *

24,750 .  +
 4,125 . M◊
 4,125 .  +
28,875 .  *

28,875 .  +
 4,125 . M◊
 4,125 .  +
33,000 .  *
```

1. Fill in the asset information portion at the top of the depreciation schedule.

2. Calculate the *annual depreciation* using the straight-line depreciation formula, (Cost − Salvage Value) ÷ Life = Annual Depreciation. Add the annual depreciation amount to memory.

Procedure: Clear memory, if necessary.

$$35,000 + 2,000 - T \boxed{33,000} \div 8 = \boxed{4,125} \; M+$$

Enter this amount for each year of depreciation on the depreciation schedule.

3. Enter 4,125 for the first year of *accumulated depreciation*. Then add the second-year annual depreciation to the first year's accumulated depreciation. Add the third-year annual depreciation to the second year's accumulated depreciation and so on through year 8.

Procedure: 4,125 should still be on the desktop calculator display.

$$+MS + T \boxed{8,250}$$
$$+MS + T \boxed{12,375}$$
$$+MS + T \boxed{16,500}$$
$$+MS + T \boxed{20,625}$$
$$+MS + T \boxed{24,750}$$
$$+MS + T \boxed{28,875}$$
$$+MS + T \boxed{33,000}$$

4. Subtract the annual depreciation from the cost to find the *end-of-year book value* for year 1.

Subtract the annual depreciation from the year 1 end-of-year book value to find end-of-year book value for year 2, and so on for the remaining years.

Procedure: 4,125 should still be stored in memory.

$$35,000 + MS - T \boxed{30,875}$$
$$+ MS - T \boxed{26,750}$$
$$+ MS - T \boxed{22,625}$$
$$+ MS - T \boxed{18,500}$$
$$+ MS - T \boxed{14,375}$$
$$+ MS - T \boxed{10,250}$$
$$+ MS - T \boxed{6,125}$$
$$+ MS - T \boxed{2,000}$$

Your completed depreciation schedule should resemble the following one.

Asset <u>Forklift</u> Cost <u>$35,000</u> Life <u>8 Years</u> Salvage Value <u>$2,000</u>

Year	Depreciation ($)	Accumulated Depreciation ($)	End-of-Year Book Value ($)
1	4,125	4,125	30,875
2	4,125	8,250	26,750
3	4,125	12,375	22,625
4	4,125	16,500	18,500
5	4,125	20,625	14,375
6	4,125	24,750	10,250
7	4,125	28,875	6,125
8	4,125	33,000	2,000

Notice that the accumulated depreciation for year 8 equals the depreciable value of the equipment ($35,000 − $2,000 = $33,000 depreciable value), and that the end-of-year book value for year 8 equals the salvage value of the equipment.

SUM-OF-THE-YEARS'-DIGITS DEPRECIATION METHOD

PROBLEM

A piece of equipment, Asset #361, purchased for $3,000 has an expected useful life of 3 years and a salvage value of $100. Complete a depreciation schedule using the sum-of-the-years'-digits method.

1. Complete the asset information section at the top of the schedule.
2. Calculate the depreciable value of the equipment (cost minus salvage value).

Procedure (Tape 23.3A): Clear memory.

$$MT\ 3{,}000\ +\ 100\ -\ T\ \boxed{2{,}900}$$

3. Add the year's digits:

$$1 + 2 + 3 + T\ \boxed{6}$$

Year 1:

Asset _____	Cost $_____	Life _____	Salvage Value $_____
Year	Depreciation	Accumulated Depreciation	End-of-Year Book Value
1	_____	_____	_____
2	_____	_____	_____
3	_____	_____	_____

4. Multiply the depreciable value ($2,900) by the years remaining in life (3 years) and then divide by sum-of-the-years' digits (6) to find the depreciation. Add to memory. Write the result in the Depreciation and Accumulated Depreciation columns for year 1.

Procedure (Tape 23.3B):

$$2{,}900 \times 3 \div 6 = \boxed{1{,}450}\ M+$$

5. Subtract the depreciation for year 1 from the depreciable value of the asset to find the book value for year 1. Write the difference in the End-of-Year Book Value column.

$$2{,}900 + MT - T\ \boxed{1{,}450}$$

TAPE 23.3A:

```
    4,125.M*

    3,000.  +
      100.  -
    2,900.  *

        1.  +
        2.  +
        3.  +
        6.  *

    2,900.  ×
        3.  ÷
        6.  =
    1,450.  *

    1,450.M+
    2,900.  ÷
    1,450.M*

    1,450.  -
    1,450.  *
```

TAPE 23.3B:

```
           0.C

         0.00M*

       2,900.  ×
           2.  ÷
           6.  =
      966.67  *

      966.67M+
    1,450.00  ÷
      966.67M*
      966.67  +
    2,416.67  *

    1,450.00  +
      966.67M*

      966.67  -
      483.33  *

       2,900.  ×
           1.  ÷
           6.  =
      483.33  *

      483.33M+
    2,416.67  +
      483.33M*
      483.33  ÷
    2,900.00  *
```

TAPE 23.2:

```
    35,000.  +
     4,125.Mo
     4,125.  -
    30,875.  ÷

    30,875.  +
     4,125.Mo
     4,125.  -
    26,750.  *

    26,750.  +
     4,125.Mo
     4,125.  -
    22,625.  *

    22,625.  +
     4,125.Mo
     4,125.  -
    18,500.  *

    18,500.  +
     4,125.Mo
     4,125.  -
    14,375.  *

    14,375.  +
     4,125.Mo
     4,125.  -
    10,250.  *

    10,250.  +
     4,125.Mo
     4,125.  -
     6,125.  *

     6,125.  +
     4,125.Mo
     4,125.  -
     2,000.  *
```

TAPE 23.3C:

```
483.33  +
483.33 M*

483.33  -
  0.00  *
```

Year 2 (see Tape 23.3B)

6. Multiply the depreciable value by remaining life (2 years) and divide by the sum-of-the-years' digits (6). Add to memory. Write the result in the Depreciation column.

$$2{,}900 \times 2 \div 6 = \boxed{966.67}\, M+$$

7. Add the result to accumulated depreciation for year 1. Write the total in the Accumulated Depreciation column for year 2.

$$1{,}450 + MS + T \;\boxed{2{,}416.67}$$

8. Subtract the year 2 depreciation from the year 1 book value. Write the difference in the End-of-Year Book Value column.

$$1{,}450 + MT - T \;\boxed{483.33}$$

9. Calculate depreciation, accumulated depreciation, and book value for year 3.

$$2900 \times 1 \div 6 = \boxed{483.33}\, M+$$
$$2{,}416.67 + MS + T \;\boxed{2{,}900}$$
$$483.33 - MT - T \;\boxed{0} \qquad \text{(see Tape 23.3c)}$$

When calculated correctly, the total depreciation should equal the original cost of the asset minus the salvage value.

Your completed depreciation schedule should resemble the following one.

TAPE 23.4:

```
       1.   ÷
       3.   =
    0.33    *

6,000.00 M+
6,000.00    x
   0.33    =
1,980.00    *

1,980.00    -÷
6,000.00 M*
6,000.00    +
4,020.00    *

4,020.00    x
   0.33    =
1,326.60    *

1,326.60    ÷
1,980.00    +
3,306.60    *

3,306.60    -+
6,000.00 M*
6,000.00    +
2,693.40    *

2,693.40    x
   0.33    =
 888.82    *

 888.82    +
3,306.60    +
4,195.42    *
4,195.42    -+
6,000.00 M*

6,000.00    +
1,804.58    *
```

Asset #361 Cost $3,000 Life 3 Years
Salvage Value $100

Year	Depreciation ($)	Accumulated Depreciation ($)	End-of-Year Book Value ($)
1	1,450	1,450.00	1,450
2	966.67	2,416.67	483.33
3	483.33	2,900.00	0*

Note: Sometimes rounding errors will cause a difference of a few cents in the last year of the book value. If this is the case, add the difference to the depreciation for the last year. This adjustment should cause the end-of-year book value to be zero the last year of the asset's life.

DECLINING-BALANCE DEPRECIATION METHOD

PROBLEM

Use the declining-balance method to complete a depreciation schedule for the following asset.

Asset #500 Cost $6,000 Life 3 Years Salvage Value $100
Rate Straight Line

Year	Depreciation ($)	Accumulated Depreciation ($)	End-of-Year Book Value ($)
1	_____	_____	_____
2	_____	_____	_____
3	_____	_____	_____

1. Calculate the straight-line rate. $1/3 = \boxed{.33}$
2. Add the original cost to memory and multiply by the straight-line rate to find the first-year depreciation. Place the result in the Depreciation and Accumulated Depreciation columns for year 1. Repeat for years 2 and 3.

Procedure:

$$6,000 \text{ M+} \times .33 = \boxed{1,980} \text{ +/−} \boxed{-1.980} + \text{MS} + \text{T} \boxed{4,020}$$
$$\times .33 = \boxed{1,326.60} + 1,980 + \text{T} \boxed{3,306.60} \text{ +/−} \boxed{-3,306.60} + \text{MS} + \text{T} \boxed{2,693.40}$$
$$\times .33 = \boxed{888.82} + 3,306.60 + \text{T} \boxed{4,195.42} \text{ +/−} \boxed{-4,195.42} + \text{MT} + \text{T} \boxed{1,804.58}$$

Your completed depreciation schedule should resemble the following one.

Asset #500 Cost $6,000 Life 3 Years Salvage Value $100 Rate Straight Line

Year	Depreciation ($)	Accumulated Depreciation ($)	End-of-Year Book Value ($)
1	1,980	1,980	4,020
2	1,326.60	3,306.60	2,693.40
3	888.82	4,195.42	1,804.58

UNITS-OF-PRODUCTION DEPRECIATION METHOD

PROBLEM

Equipment was purchased for $50,000. It is expected to produce 20,000 units and have no salvage value.
Calculate the depreciation per piece produced. <u>0.00375</u>
Complete the following schedule of depreciation.

Asset #122 Cost _____ Estimated Unit Production _____ Salvage Value _____

Year	Units Produced	Depreciation ($)	Accumulated Depreciation ($)	End-of-Year Book Value ($)
1	4,505	_____	_____	_____
2	5,650	_____	_____	_____
3	6,600	_____	_____	_____
4	3,245	_____	_____	_____

Procedure (Tape 23.5A): Set the decimal selector at 6. Clear memory, if necessary.
Depreciation per piece:

$$50,000 \div 20,000 = \boxed{2.50} \text{ M+}$$

Year 1:

$$4,505 \times \text{MS} = \boxed{11,262.50} \quad \text{depreciation and accumulated depreciation}$$
$$-50,000 + \text{T} \boxed{38,737.50} \quad \text{end-of-year book value}$$

Year 2:

$$5,650 \times \text{MS} = \boxed{14,125.00} \quad \text{depreciation}$$
$$+11,262.50 + \text{T} \boxed{25,387.50} \quad \text{accumulated depreciation}$$
$$+50,000 + \text{T} \boxed{24,612.50} \quad \text{end-of-year book value}$$

Year 3 (Tape 23.5B):

$$6,600 \times \text{MS} = \boxed{16,500.00} + 25,387.50 + \text{T} \boxed{41,887.50} - 50,000 + \text{T} \boxed{8,112.50}$$

Year 4:

$$3,245 \times \text{MT} = \boxed{8,112.50} + 41,887.50 + \text{T} \boxed{50,000} - 50,000 + \text{T} \boxed{0.00}$$

TAPE 23.5A:

50,000.
20,000.
2.50

2.50 M
4,505.
2.50 M
2.50
11,262.50

11,262.50
50,000.00
38,737.50

5,650.
2.50 M
2.50
14,125.00

14,125.00
11,262.50
25,387.50

25,387.50
50,000.00
24,612.50

TAPE 23.5B:

6,600. ×
2.50 M
2.50 =
16,500.00 ÷

16,500.00 +
25,387.50 +
41,887.50 ×

41,887.50 −
50,000.00 ÷
8,112.50 ÷

3,245. ×
2.50 M

2.50 =
8,112.50 ×

8,112.50 ÷
41,887.50 +
50,000.00 ×

50,000.00 −
50,000.00 ÷
0.00 ×

Your completed schedule of depreciation should resemble the following schedule.

Asset #122 Cost $50,000 Estimated Unit Production 20,000
Salvage Value $0

Year	Units Produced	Depreciation ($)	Accumulated Depreciation ($)	End-of-Year Book Value ($)
1	4,505	11,262.50	11,262.50	38,737.50
2	5,650	14,125.00	25,387.50	24,612.50
3	6,600	16,500.00	41,887.50	8,112.50
4	3,245	8,112.50	50,000.00	0

Name _____

Class/Section _____

Score (Correct Answers ÷ No. of Assigned Problems) _____

 PART 4 *Desktop Calculator*

Exercise 1

Prepare a schedule of depreciation for bookshelves that cost $2,500 with an estimated life of 7 years and a salvage value of $100 using straight-line depreciation.

Asset _____ Cost _____ Life _____
Salvage Value _____

	Year	Depreciation ($)	Accumulated Depreciation ($)	End-of-Year Book Value ($)
1.	1	_____	_____	_____
2.	2	_____	_____	_____
3.	3	_____	_____	_____
4.	4	_____	_____	_____
5.	5	_____	_____	_____
6.	6	_____	_____	_____
7.	7	_____	_____	_____

Prepare a schedule of depreciation for an office computer that cost $2,200, has an expected life of 5 years, and a salvage value of $100. Use the sum-of-the-years'-digits depreciation method.

	Year	Annual Depreciation ($)	Accumulated Depreciation ($)	Book Value ($)
8.	8	_____	_____	_____
9.	9	_____	_____	_____
10.	10	_____	_____	_____
11.	11	_____	_____	_____
12.	12	_____	_____	_____

Complete the first 4 years of a depreciation schedule for an asset using the units-of-production method. Round the cost per hour to six decimal places.

Asset #200 Cost $150,000 Estimated Hours of Production 15,000
Salvage Value $500

	Year	House of Use	Depreciation ($)	Accumulated Depreciation ($)	End-of-Year Book Value ($)
13.	1	3,000	_____	_____	_____
14.	2	2,900	_____	_____	_____
15.	3	3,200	_____	_____	_____
16.	4	5,500	_____	_____	_____

Prepare a depreciation schedule for equipment, Asset #119, that cost $7,000 and has an estimated life of 4 years and a salvage value of $300. Use the declining-balance method and the straight-line rate.

Asset _____ Cost _____ Salvage Value _____
Declining-Balance Rate _____

	Year	Rate	Depreciation ($)	Accumulated Depreciation ($)	End-of-Year Book Value ($)
17.	1	_____	_____	_____	_____
18.	2	_____	_____	_____	_____
19.	3	_____	_____	_____	_____
20.	4	_____	_____	_____	_____

Exercise 2

Strokes per Minute Score _____

Accuracy Score (Correct Strokes ÷ Total Strokes) _____

One-Minute Addition Timing (0 through 9, Decimal, and Minus Keys, Six-Digit Numbers)

(Optional: Your instructor may wish you to use Touch Key on the computer for all your timings. Check with your instructor before completing this exercise.)

Complete as many of the problems as possible in 1 minute by adding. Work quickly and accurately. The number preceding each closing parenthesis indicates the cumulative number of strokes for problems attempted. For example, if you complete Problems 1 through 5 in 1 minute, your strokes-per-minute score is 415.

1.	2.	3.	4.	5.	6.	7.	8.
452.556	920.024	4.76544	3500.76	4.70050	3442.00	−5132.12	9.17001
−89.6321	30.5932	7.75350	7890.62	4.45500	7251.00	76450.3	7.89003
23.1321	−18.6209	−12.8100	4770.41	7.92050	6231.68	−100.341	−9.18772
13.0057	320.545	48.6300	−8790.83	8.69995	2491.56	900.437	4.13006
14.0987	400.041	390.400	−9310.94	3.50059	3310.06	3500.79	1.89004
5002.24	7.19000	−20.5005	8240.55	−9.34229	3257.05	2071.00	−7.74002
9.81093	−6.64788	75.3006	7100.63	5.00316	5737.03	3001.00	1.77607
185.835	8.54921	6.06100	6200.43	3.40075	3360.21	50009.1	9.83074
−84.3269	460.896	130.300	4800.81	−1.54900	−8840.06	60.7939	5.38009
43.1170	9.11009	200.300	2800.62	2.30056	−9261.06	500.671	2.48503
83)	166)	249)	332)	415)	498)	581)	664)

9.	4,158.61	10.	1.61285	11.	−300.987	12.	2247.79	13.	61.3451	14.	900.661	15.	176.905	16.	85.0048
	66,429.1		3.42661		720.002		−9431.79		20.2995		453.802		431.813		−8286.17
	29,850.8		9.54553		−800.455		8206.90		40.1395		−679.811		538.019		81.0006
	66,340.9		7.76628		170.514		4300.50		20.7249		−229.655		−200.014		34.8203
	−77,708.1		3.88567		922.990		311.555		30.0755		873.344		930.175		96.0083
	−88,689.6		3.54322		459.968		−955.385		80.0999		867.009		827.021		−84.0031
	31,599.9		1.91359		266.780		5347.72		37.7577		300.741		398.013		89.8542
	66,614.5		8.21092		910.495		7726.11		−20.6659		252.162		−899.753		46.7886
	17,257.9		−3.50415		841.119		8974.95		40.5595		859.825		697.062		87.4124
	31,374.1		−4.67575		238.480		8326.55		−20.0946		776.014		3610.011		54.8809

747)   830)   913)   996)   1,079)   1,162)   1,245)   1,328)

CHAPTER 23 *Terminology Review*

Accumulated depreciation
ACRS
Adjusted basis
Basis
Book value
Declining-balance depreciation method
Depreciable value
Depreciate
Depreciation
Financial statements
MACRS
MACRS conventions
Salvage value
Section 179 deduction
Special depreciation allowance
Straight-line depreciation method
Sum-of-the-years'-digits depreciation method
Tax records
Unadjusted basis
Units-produced depreciation method
Useful life

Write the correct term next to the appropriate description.

1. _____ The original basis less any Section 179 deduction claimed or any special depreciation allowances claimed.

2. _____ The depreciable amount for a property under MACRS.

3. _____ The result of certain increases and decreases to property cost after it was acquired but before it was placed in service.

4. _____ An allowance of 30% that is allowed only in the year property is placed in service. It may be taken after any Section 179 deduction and before regular depreciation is calculated.

5. _____ Allows one to recover all or part of the cost of certain property used for business purposes (up to $25,000 as of 2003) by deducting it in the year the property is placed in service.

6. _____ The declining value that occurs as a piece of equipment ages and becomes worn.

7. _____ The years of expected usefulness of a piece of equipment.

8. _____ All the depreciation that has been claimed from the time the asset was purchased to the current date.

9. _____ The amount an item is worth once its useful life is over.

10. _____ The cost of an item minus its salvage value (if any) and accumulated depreciation.

11. _____ Using this depreciation method, cost minus salvage value is divided by life to find the amount of yearly depreciation.

12. ____ _____ Involves depreciating a piece of equipment based on the number of units produced, miles driven, or hours used.

13. _____ With this method, the depreciable value of an asset is multiplied by the years remaining in the life of the asset and divided by the sum of the years' digits.

14. _____ The cost of a depreciable item minus its salvage value.

15. _____ In this method a rate of depreciation is used. Rates that may be used include the straight-line rate, the double-declining rate, and the 150% rate.

16. _____ A method used to depreciate assets for tax purposes. It was used for property placed in service after 1980 but before 1987.

17. _____ Is used for tax purposes in the recovery of costs for most property placed in service after 1986.

18. _____ Are used to determine how many months a property may be depreciated the year it is placed in service and the year it is taken out of service.

19. _____ Are used to measure company income accurately and consistently from year to year.

20. _____ Are intended to meet the federal income tax code.

Name _____

Class/Section _____

Score (Correct Answers ÷ No. of Assigned Problems) _____

Chapter 23 Review Exercises
Exercise 1

1. Beeman and Co. purchased counters and fixtures for $58,000. The company estimates useful life of the counters and fixtures to be 11 years with a salvage value of 15% of cost. Using the straight-line depreciation method, calculate salvage value _____, annual depreciation _____, and book value at the end of year 2 _____.

2. A business purchased a van for $40,000. It is estimated that the van can be driven 50,000 miles and that it will have a salvage value of $5,000. The van was driven 12,250 miles the first year and 9,665 miles the second year. Using the units-of-production method, calculate depreciation for year 1 _____ and year 2 _____.

3. AVC Manufacturing Co. purchased furniture for its reception area for $12,950. The furniture is expected to last 7 years and have a salvage value of $1,200. Using the sum-of-the-years'-digits method, calculate depreciation for year 1 _____ and year 2 _____.

4. Machinery was purchased by XYZ Manufacturing Co. for $75,000. The life of the machinery is estimated to be 25 years. Salvage value is estimated to be $12,000. Use the declining-balance method to find the depreciation for year 1 using:

a. Straight-line rate _____

b. Double-declining rate _____

c. 150% rate _____

5. John Brown purchased furniture and appliances for his rental property for $37,000. It was placed in service January 2, 2002. Using MACRS and the 200% half-year convention, calculate the rates, depreciation, accumulated depreciation, and book value for the first 3 years.

Asset _____ **Cost $** _____ **Class** _____

Year	Rate	Depreciation ($)	Accumulated Depreciation ($)	End-of-Year Book Value ($)
1	_____	_____	_____	_____
2	_____	_____	_____	_____
3	_____	_____	_____	_____

Exercise 2

A printing press was purchased for $175,000 with a salvage value of $15,000 and an expected life of 20 years. For each depreciation method, calculate (a) depreciation for year 1 and (b) book value at the end of year 1.

6. Straight-line method:

   a. _____
   b. _____

7. Sum-of-the-years'-digits method:

   a. _____
   b. _____

8. Double declining-balance method (200% rate):

   a. _____
   b. _____

9. Units-of-production method. It is estimated the printer will last through 50,000 hours of printing. The printer was used 3,000 hours the first year.

   a. _____
   b. _____

10. MACRS. The GDS, 200% half-year convention is used. A printing press is a 7-year property.

    a. _____
    b. _____

Exercise 3

John Klein purchased office calculators to be used in his business for $2,000. The machines were placed in service in January 2002. He uses the half-year convention and the 200% declining-balance method. He does not use tables to calculate depreciation. Complete the following depreciation worksheet.

Depreciation Worksheet for _____

Year	Method	Basis	Rate	Formula Used to Find Rate	Depreciation	Half-Year Depreciation	Check Method to Be Used	
Year 1	200% declining balance Straight line	____	____	_____	_____	_____	_____	11.
Year 2	200% declining balance Straight line	____	____	_____	_____	_____	_____	12.
Year 3	200% declining balance Straight line	____	____	_____	_____	_____	_____	13.
Year 4	200% declining balance Straight line	____	____	_____	_____	_____	_____	14.
Year 5	200% declining balance Straight line	____	____	_____	_____	_____	_____	15.
Year 6	200% declining balance Straight line	____	____	_____	_____	_____	_____	16.

MACRS TABLES

Property Classes under GDS and Examples of Such Properties	Recovery Period
1. **3-year property**	
(a) Tractor units for over-the-road use	3
(b) Any race horse over 2 years old when placed in service	3
(c) Any other horse over 12 years old when placed in service	3
(d) Qualified rent-to-own property	3
2. **5-year property**	
(a) Automobiles, taxis, buses, and trucks	5
(b) Computers and peripheral equipment	5
(c) Office machinery (such as typewriters, calculators, and copiers)	5
(d) Any property used in research and experimentation	5
(e) Breeding cattle and dairy cattle	5
(f) Appliances, carpets, furniture, etc., used in a residential rental real estate activity	5
3. **7-year property**	
(a) Office furniture and fixtures (such as desks, files, and safes)	7
(b) Agricultural machinery and equipment	7
(c) Any property that does not have a class life and has not been designated by law as being in any other class	7
4. **10-year property**	
(a) Vessels, barges, tugs, and similar water transportation equipment	10
(b) Any single-purpose agricultural or horticultural structure	10
(c) Any tree or vine bearing fruits or nuts	10
5. **15-year property**	
(a) Certain improvements made directly to land or added to it, such as shrubbery, fences, roads, and bridges	15
(b) Any retail motor fuels outlet, such as a convenience store	15
(c) Any municipal wastewater treatment plant	15
6. **20-year property.** This class includes farm buildings other than single-purpose agricultural or horticultural structures	20
7. **25-year property.** This class is water utility property, which is either of the following:	
(a) Property that is an integral part of the gathering, treatment, or commercial distribution of water, and that, without regard to this provision, would be 20-year property	25
(b) Any municipal sewer	25
8. **Residential rental property**	27.5
9. **Nonresidental real property**	39

Chart 1. Finding the Correct Percentage Table to Use for Any Property Other Than Residential Rental and Nonresidential Real Property

MACRS System	Depreciation Method	Recovery Period	Convention	Class	Month or Quarter Placed in Service	Table
GDS	200%	GDS/3, 5, 7, 10 (Nonfarm)	Half-Year	3, 5, 7, 10	Any	A-1
GDS	200%	GDS/3, 5, 7, 10 (Nonfarm)	Midquarter	3, 5, 7, 10	First	A-2
					Second	A-3
					Third	A-4
					Fourth	A-5
GDS	150%	GDS/3, 5, 7, 10	Half-Year	3, 5, 7, 10	Any	A-14
GDS	150%	GDS/3, 5, 7, 10	Midquarter	3, 5, 7, 10	First	A-15
					Second	A-16
					Third	A-17
					Fourth	A-18
GDS	150%	GDS/15, 20	Half-Year	15 & 20	Any	A-1
GDS	150%	GDS/15, 20	Midquarter	15 & 20	First	A-2
					Second	A-3
					Third	A-4
					Fourth	A-5
GDS ADS	SL	GDS ADS	Half-Year	Any	Any	A-8
GDS ADS	SL	GDS ADS	Midquarter	Any	First	A-9
					Second	A-10
					Third	A-11
					Fourth	A-12
ADS	150%	ADS	Half-Year	Any	Any	A-14
ADS	150%	ADS	Midquarter	Any	First	A-15
					Second	A-16
					Third	A-17
					Fourth	A-18

Note: Use Chart 2 for residential rental and nonresidential real property.

Chart 2. Finding the Correct Percentage Table to Use for Residential Rental and Nonresidential Real Property

MACRS System	Depreciation Method	Recovery Period	Convention	Class	Month or Quarter Placed in Service	Table
GDS	SL	GDS/27.5	Midmonth	Residential rental	Any	A-6
GDS	SL	GDS/31.5	Midmonth	Nonresidential real	Any	A-7
	SL	GDS/39				A-7a

Note: Use Chart 1 for all other property.

Table A-1. 3-, 5-, 7-, 10-, 15-, and 20-Year Property
Half-Year Convention

	Depreciation Rate for Recovery Period					
Year	3-Year	5-Year	7-Year	10-Year	15-Year	20-Year
1	33.33%	20.00%	14.29%	10.00%	5.00%	3.750%
2	44.45	32.00	24.49	18.00	9.50	7.219
3	14.81	19.20	17.49	14.40	8.55	6.677
4	7.41	11.52	12.49	11.52	7.70	6.177
5		11.52	8.93	9.22	6.93	5.713
6		5.76	8.92	7.37	6.23	5.285
7			8.93	6.55	5.90	4.888
8			4.46	6.55	5.90	4.522
9				6.56	5.91	4.462
10				6.55	5.90	4.461
11				3.28	5.91	4.462
12					5.90	4.461
13					5.91	4.462
14					5.90	4.461
15					5.91	4.462
16					2.95	4.461
17						4.462
18						4.461
19						4.462
20						4.461
21						2.231

Table A-2. 3-, 5-, 7-, 10-, 15-, and 20-Year Property Midquarter
Convention Placed in Service in First Quarter

	Depreciation Rate for Recovery Period					
Year	3-Year	5-Year	7-Year	10-Year	15-Year	20-Year
1	58.33%	35.00%	25.00%	17.50%	8.75%	6.563%
2	27.78	26.00	21.43	16.50	9.13	7.000
3	12.35	15.60	15.31	13.20	8.21	6.482
4	1.54	11.01	10.93	10.56	7.39	5.996
5		11.01	8.75	8.45	6.65	5.546
6		1.38	8.74	6.76	5.99	5.130
7			8.75	6.55	5.90	4.746
8			1.09	6.55	5.91	4.459
9				6.56	5.90	4.459
10				6.55	5.91	4.459
11				0.82	5.90	4.459
12					5.91	4.460
13					5.90	4.459
14					5.91	4.460
15					5.90	4.459
16					0.74	4.460
17						4.459
18						4.460
19						4.459
20						4.460
21						0.557

Table A-5. 3-, 5-, 7-, 10-, 15-, and 20-Year Property Midquarter Convention Placed in Service in Fourth Quarter

Year	Depreciation Rate for Recovery Period					
	3-Year	5-Year	7-Year	10-Year	15-Year	20-Year
1	8.33%	5.00%	3.57%	2.50%	1.25%	0.938%
2	61.11	38.00	27.55	19.50	9.88	7.430
3	20.37	22.80	19.68	15.60	8.89	6.872
4	10.19	13.68	14.06	12.48	8.00	6.357
5		10.94	10.04	9.98	7.20	5.880
6		9.58	8.73	7.99	6.48	5.439
7			8.73	6.55	5.90	5.031
8			7.64	6.55	5.90	4.654
9				6.56	5.90	4.458
10				6.55	5.91	4.458
11				5.74	5.90	4.458
12					5.91	4.458
13					5.90	4.458
14					5.91	4.458
15					5.90	4.458
16					5.17	4.458
17						4.458
18						4.459
19						4.458
20						4.459
21						3.901

Table A-6. Residential Rental Property Midmonth Convention Straight Line—27.5 Years

Year	Month Property Placed in Service											
	1	2	3	4	5	6	7	8	9	10	11	12
1	3.485%	3.182%	2.879%	2.576%	2.273%	1.970%	1.667%	1.364%	1.061%	0.758%	0.455%	0.152%
2–9	3.636	3.636	3.636	3.636	3.636	3.636	3.636	3.636	3.636	3.636	3.636	3.636
10	3.637	3.637	3.637	3.637	3.637	3.637	3.636	3.636	3.636	3.636	3.636	3.636
11	3.636	3.636	3.636	3.636	3.636	3.636	3.637	3.637	3.637	3.637	3.637	3.637
12	3.637	3.637	3.637	3.637	3.637	3.637	3.636	3.636	3.636	3.636	3.636	3.636
13	3.636	3.636	3.636	3.636	3.636	3.636	3.637	3.637	3.637	3.637	3.637	3.637
14	3.637	3.637	3.637	3.637	3.637	3.637	3.636	3.636	3.636	3.636	3.636	3.636
15	3.636	3.636	3.636	3.636	3.636	3.636	3.637	3.637	3.637	3.637	3.637	3.637
16	3.637	3.637	3.637	3.637	3.637	3.637	3.636	3.636	3.636	3.636	3.636	3.636
17	3.636	3.636	3.636	3.636	3.636	3.636	3.637	3.637	3.637	3.637	3.637	3.637
18	3.637	3.637	3.637	3.637	3.637	3.637	3.636	3.636	3.636	3.636	3.636	3.636
19	3.636	3.636	3.636	3.636	3.636	3.636	3.637	3.637	3.637	3.637	3.637	3.637
20	3.637	3.637	3.637	3.637	3.637	3.637	3.636	3.636	3.636	3.636	3.636	3.636
21	3.636	3.636	3.636	3.636	3.636	3.636	3.637	3.637	3.637	3.637	3.637	3.637
22	3.637	3.637	3.637	3.637	3.637	3.637	3.636	3.636	3.636	3.636	3.636	3.636
23	3.636	3.636	3.636	3.636	3.636	3.636	3.637	3.637	3.637	3.637	3.637	3.637
24	3.637	3.637	3.637	3.637	3.637	3.637	3.636	3.636	3.636	3.636	3.636	3.636
25	3.636	3.636	3.636	3.636	3.636	3.636	3.637	3.637	3.637	3.637	3.637	3.637
26	3.637	3.637	3.637	3.637	3.637	3.637	3.636	3.636	3.636	3.636	3.636	3.636
27	3.636	3.636	3.636	3.636	3.636	3.636	3.637	3.637	3.637	3.637	3.637	3.637
28	1.97	2.273	2.576	2.879	3.182	3.485	3.636	3.636	3.636	3.636	3.636	3.636
29							0.152	0.455	0.758	1.061	1.364	1.667

Table A-7. Nonresidential Real Property Midmonth Convention
Straight Line—31.5 Years

	Month Property Placed in Service											
Year	1	2	3	4	5	6	7	8	9	10	11	12
1	3.042%	2.778%	2.513%	2.249%	1.984%	1.720%	1.455%	1.190%	0.926%	0.661%	0.397%	0.132%
2–7	3.175	3.175	3.175	3.175	3.175	3.175	3.175	3.175	3.175	3.175	3.175	3.175
8	3.175	3.174	3.175	3.174	3.175	3.174	3.175	3.175	3.175	3.175	3.175	3.175
9	3.174	3.175	3.174	3.175	3.174	3.175	3.174	3.175	3.174	3.175	3.174	3.175
10	3.175	3.174	3.175	3.174	3.175	3.174	3.175	3.174	3.175	3.174	3.175	3.174
11	3.174	3.175	3.174	3.175	3.174	3.175	3.174	3.175	3.174	3.175	3.174	3.175
12	3.175	3.174	3.175	3.174	3.175	3.174	3.175	3.174	3.175	3.174	3.175	3.174
13	3.174	3.175	3.174	3.175	3.174	3.175	3.174	3.175	3.174	3.175	3.174	3.175
14	3.175	3.174	3.175	3.174	3.175	3.174	3.175	3.174	3.175	3.174	3.175	3.174
15	3.174	3.175	3.174	3.175	3.174	3.175	3.174	3.175	3.174	3.175	3.174	3.175
16	3.175	3.174	3.175	3.174	3.175	3.174	3.175	3.174	3.175	3.174	3.175	3.174
17	3.174	3.175	3.174	3.175	3.174	3.175	3.174	3.175	3.174	3.175	3.174	3.175
18	3.175	3.174	3.175	3.174	3.175	3.174	3.175	3.174	3.175	3.174	3.175	3.174
19	3.174	3.175	3.174	3.175	3.174	3.175	3.174	3.175	3.174	3.175	3.174	3.175
20	3.175	3.174	3.175	3.174	3.175	3.174	3.175	3.174	3.175	3.174	3.175	3.174
21	3.174	3.175	3.174	3.175	3.174	3.175	3.174	3.175	3.174	3.175	3.174	3.175
22	3.175	3.174	3.175	3.174	3.175	3.174	3.175	3.174	3.175	3.174	3.175	3.174
23	3.174	3.175	3.174	3.175	3.174	3.175	3.174	3.175	3.174	3.175	3.174	3.175
24	3.175	3.174	3.175	3.174	3.175	3.174	3.175	3.174	3.175	3.174	3.175	3.174
25	3.174	3.175	3.174	3.175	3.174	3.175	3.174	3.175	3.174	3.175	3.174	3.175
26	3.175	3.174	3.175	3.174	3.175	3.174	3.175	3.174	3.175	3.174	3.175	3.174
27	3.174	3.175	3.174	3.175	3.174	3.175	3.174	3.175	3.174	3.175	3.174	3.175
28	3.175	3.174	3.175	3.174	3.175	3.174	3.175	3.174	3.175	3.174	3.175	3.174
29	3.174	3.175	3.174	3.175	3.174	3.175	3.174	3.175	3.174	3.175	3.174	3.175
30	3.175	3.174	3.175	3.174	3.175	3.174	3.175	3.174	3.175	3.174	3.175	3.174
31	3.174	3.175	3.174	3.175	3.174	3.175	3.174	3.175	3.174	3.175	3.174	3.175
32	1.720	1.984	2.249	2.513	2.778	3.042	3.175	3.174	3.175	3.174	3.175	3.174
33							0.132	0.397	0.661	0.926	1.190	1.455

Table A-7a. Nonresidential Real Property Midmonth Convention
Straight Line—39 Years

	Month Property Placed in Service											
Year	1	2	3	4	5	6	7	8	9	10	11	12
1	2.461%	2.247%	2.033%	1.819%	1.605%	1.391%	1.177%	0.963%	0.749%	0.535%	0.321%	0.107%
2–39	2.564	2.564	2.564	2.564	2.564	2.564	2.564	2.564	2.564	2.564	2.564	2.564
40	0.107	0.321	0.535	0.749	0.963	1.177	1.391	1.605	1.819	2.033	2.247	2.461

Table A-8. Straight-Line Method Half-Year Convention

							Recovery Periods in Years						
Year	2.5	3	3.5	4	5	6	6.5	7	7.5	8	8.5	9	9.5
1	20.0%	16.67%	14.29%	12.5%	10.0%	8.33%	7.69%	7.14%	6.67%	6.25%	5.88%	5.56%	5.26%
2	40.0	33.33	28.57	25.0	20.0	16.67	15.39	14.29	13.33	12.50	11.77	11.11	10.53
3	40.0	33.33	28.57	25.0	20.0	16.67	15.38	14.29	13.33	12.50	11.76	11.11	10.53
4		16.67	28.57	25.0	20.0	16.67	15.39	14.28	13.33	12.50	11.77	11.11	10.53
5				12.5	20.0	16.66	15.38	14.29	13.34	12.50	11.76	11.11	10.52
6					10.0	16.67	15.39	14.28	13.33	12.50	11.77	11.11	10.59
7						8.33	15.38	14.29	13.34	12.50	11.76	11.11	10.52
8								7.14	13.33	12.50	11.77	11.11	10.53
9										6.25	11.76	11.11	10.52
10												5.56	10.53

Table A-8. (Continued)

							Recovery Periods in Years						
Year	10	10.5	11	11.5	12	12.5	13	13.5	14	15	16	16.5	17
1	5.0%	4.76%	4.55%	4.35%	4.17%	4.0%	3.85%	3.70%	3.57%	3.33%	3.13%	3.03%	2.94%
2	10.0	9.52	9.09	8.70	8.33	8.0	7.69	7.41	7.14	6.67	6.25	6.06	5.88
3	10.0	9.52	9.09	8.70	8.33	8.0	7.69	7.41	7.14	6.67	6.25	6.06	5.88
4	10.0	9.53	9.09	8.69	8.33	8.0	7.69	7.41	7.14	6.67	6.25	6.06	5.88
5	10.0	9.52	9.09	8.70	8.33	8.0	7.69	7.41	7.14	6.67	6.25	6.06	5.88
6	10.0	9.53	9.09	8.69	8.33	8.0	7.69	7.41	7.14	6.67	6.25	6.06	5.88
7	10.0	9.52	9.09	8.70	8.34	8.0	7.69	7.41	7.14	6.67	6.25	6.06	5.88
8	10.0	9.53	9.09	8.69	8.33	8.0	7.69	7.41	7.15	6.66	6.25	6.06	5.88
9	10.0	9.52	9.09	8.70	8.34	8.0	7.69	7.41	7.14	6.67	6.25	6.06	5.88
10	10.0	9.53	9.09	8.69	8.33	8.0	7.70	7.40	7.15	6.66	6.25	6.06	5.88
11	5.0	9.52	9.09	8.70	8.34	8.0	7.69	7.41	7.14	6.67	6.25	6.06	5.89
12			4.55	8.69	8.33	8.0	7.70	7.40	7.15	6.66	6.25	6.06	5.88
13					4.17	8.0	7.69	7.41	7.14	6.67	6.25	6.06	5.89
14							3.85	7.40	7.15	6.66	6.25	6.06	5.88
15									3.57	6.67	6.25	6.06	5.89
16										3.33	6.25	6.06	5.88
17											3.12	6.07	5.89
18													2.94

Table A-9. Straight-Line Method Midquarter Convention
Placed in Service in First Quarter

	Recovery Periods in Years												
Year	2.5	3	3.5	4	5	6	6.5	7	7.5	8	8.5	9	9.5
1	35.0%	29.17%	25.00%	21.88%	17.5%	14.58%	13.46%	12.50%	11.67%	10.94%	10.29%	9.72%	9.21%
2	40.0	33.33	28.57	25.00	20.0	16.67	15.38	14.29	13.33	12.50	11.77	11.11	10.53
3	25.0	33.33	28.57	25.00	20.0	16.67	15.39	14.28	13.33	12.50	11.76	11.11	10.53
4		4.17	17.86	25.00	20.0	16.67	15.38	14.29	13.33	12.50	11.77	11.11	10.53
5				3.12	20.0	16.66	15.39	14.28	13.34	12.50	11.76	11.11	10.52
6					2.5	16.67	15.38	14.29	13.33	12.50	11.77	11.11	10.53
7						2.08	9.62	14.28	13.34	12.50	11.76	11.11	10.52
8								1.79	8.33	12.50	11.77	11.12	10.53
9										1.56	7.35	11.11	10.52
10												1.39	6.58

Table A-9. (*Continued*)

	Recovery Periods in Years												
Year	10	10.5	11	11.5	12	12.5	13	13.5	14	15	16	16.5	17
1	8.75%	8.33%	7.95%	7.61%	7.29%	7.0%	6.73%	6.48%	6.25%	5.83%	5.47%	5.30%	5.15%
2	10.00	9.52	9.09	8.70	8.33	8.0	7.69	7.41	7.14	6.67	6.25	6.06	5.88
3	10.00	9.52	9.09	8.70	8.33	8.0	7.69	7.41	7.14	6.67	6.25	6.06	5.88
4	10.00	9.53	9.09	8.69	8.33	8.0	7.69	7.41	7.14	6.67	6.25	6.06	5.88
5	10.00	9.52	9.09	8.70	8.33	8.0	7.69	7.41	7.14	6.67	6.25	6.06	5.88
6	10.00	9.53	9.09	8.69	8.34	8.0	7.69	7.41	7.14	6.67	6.25	6.06	5.88
7	10.00	9.52	9.09	8.70	8.33	8.0	7.69	7.41	7.14	6.67	6.25	6.06	5.88
8	10.00	9.53	9.09	8.69	8.34	8.0	7.69	7.41	7.15	6.66	6.25	6.06	5.88
9	10.00	9.52	9.09	8.70	8.33	8.0	7.70	7.40	7.14	6.67	6.25	6.06	5.88
10	10.00	9.53	9.10	8.69	8.34	8.0	7.69	7.41	7.15	6.66	6.25	6.06	5.88
11	1.25	5.95	9.09	8.70	8.33	8.0	7.70	7.40	7.14	6.67	6.25	6.06	5.88
12			1.14	5.43	8.34	8.0	7.69	7.41	7.15	6.66	6.25	6.06	5.89
13					1.04	5.0	7.70	7.40	7.14	6.67	6.25	6.06	5.88
14							0.96	4.63	7.15	6.66	6.25	6.06	5.89
15									0.89	6.67	6.25	6.06	5.88
16										0.83	6.25	6.07	5.89
17											0.78	3.79	5.88
18													0.74

Table A-14. 150% Declining-Balance Method
Half-Year Convention

Recovery Periods in Years

Year	2.5	3	3.5	4	5	6	6.5	7	7.5	8	8.5	9	9.5
1	30.0%	25.0%	21.43%	18.75%	15.00%	12.50%	11.54%	10.71%	10.00%	9.38%	8.82%	8.33%	7.89%
2	42.0	37.5	33.67	30.47	25.50	21.88	20.41	19.13	18.00	16.99	16.09	15.28	14.54
3	28.0	25.0	22.45	20.31	17.85	16.41	15.70	15.03	14.40	13.81	13.25	12.73	12.25
4		12.5	22.45	20.31	16.66	14.06	13.09	12.25	11.52	11.22	10.91	10.61	10.31
5				10.16	16.66	14.06	13.09	12.25	11.52	10.80	10.19	9.65	9.17
6					8.33	14.06	13.09	12.25	11.52	10.80	10.19	9.64	9.17
7						7.03	13.08	12.25	11.52	10.80	10.18	9.65	9.17
8							6.13		11.52	10.80	10.19	9.64	9.17
9										5.40	10.18	9.65	9.17
10												4.82	9.16

Table A-14. *(Continued)*

Recovery Periods in Years

Year	10	10.5	11	11.5	12	12.5	13	13.5	14	15	16	16.5	17
1	7.50%	7.14%	6.82%	6.52%	6.25%	6.00%	5.77%	5.56%	5.36%	5.00%	4.69%	4.55%	4.41%
2	13.88	13.27	12.71	12.19	11.72	11.28	10.87	10.49	10.14	9.50	8.94	8.68	8.43
3	11.79	11.37	10.97	10.60	10.25	9.93	9.62	9.33	9.05	8.55	8.10	7.89	7.69
4	10.02	9.75	9.48	9.22	8.97	8.73	8.51	8.29	8.08	7.70	7.34	7.17	7.01
5	8.74	8.35	8.18	8.02	7.85	7.69	7.53	7.37	7.22	6.93	6.65	6.52	6.39
6	8.74	8.35	7.98	7.64	7.33	7.05	6.79	6.55	6.44	6.23	6.03	5.93	5.83
7	8.74	8.35	7.97	7.64	7.33	7.05	6.79	6.55	6.32	5.90	5.55	5.39	5.32
8	8.74	8.35	7.98	7.63	7.33	7.05	6.79	6.55	6.32	5.90	5.55	5.39	5.23
9	8.74	8.36	7.97	7.64	7.33	7.04	6.79	6.55	6.32	5.91	5.55	5.39	5.23
10	8.74	8.35	7.98	7.63	7.33	7.05	6.79	6.55	6.32	5.90	5.55	5.39	5.23
11	4.37	8.36	7.97	7.64	7.32	7.04	6.79	6.55	6.32	5.91	5.55	5.39	5.23
12			3.99	7.63	7.33	7.05	6.78	6.55	6.32	5.90	5.55	5.39	5.23
13					3.66	7.04	6.79	6.56	6.32	5.91	5.54	5.38	5.23
14							3.39	6.55	6.31	5.90	5.55	5.39	5.23
15									3.16	5.91	5.54	5.38	5.23
16										2.95	5.55	5.39	5.23
17											2.77	5.38	5.23
18													2.62

CHAPTER 24

Ratios and Proportions

PART 1 *Speed and Accuracy Building Using Touch Key*

GOALS: Your speed goal is 11,000 strokes per hour.
Your accuracy target goal range is 95% to 100%.

With each repetition of the drill, try to improve your speed without lowering your accuracy score. If your percent-of-accuracy score falls below 95%, review your finger position and technique. Then try again.

Instructions: *Start Touch Key. Complete Drill 5, Parts A through E. Write your scores for strokes per hour and percent of accuracy below*

Touch Key Drill 5—The 0 through 9, Decimal, and Minus Keys, Six-Digit Numbers, One-Minute Timings

	Today's Date	Strokes per Hour	Percent of Accuracy
A.			
B.			
C.			
D.			
E.			

PART 2 *Business Math Skills*

RATIOS

Ratios are used to compare one item to another. If roses cost twice as much as daisies, the ratio of the cost of roses to the cost of daisies is 2 to 1, usually written 2:1. Ratios can be written as fractions, as shown in the following problem.

PROBLEM 1

The ratio of sales of chocolate milk to sales of 2% milk was 1 to 25. Written as a fraction, sales of chocolate milk were 1/25 of sales of 2% milk.

Fractions representing ratios can be reduced.

PROBLEM 2

There are 12 girls and 6 boys in a Spanish class. The ratio is written 12:6. As a fraction, it is written as 12/6 and can be reduced to 2/1 (Figure 24.1).

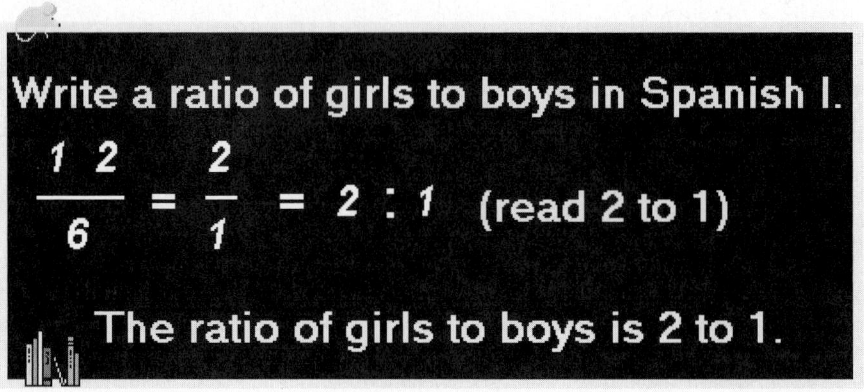

Write a ratio of girls to boys in Spanish I.

$$\frac{1\,2}{6} = \frac{2}{1} = 2 : 1 \quad \text{(read 2 to 1)}$$

The ratio of girls to boys is 2 to 1.

FIGURE 24.1

Do not reduce an improper fraction representing a ratio to a mixed number.

PROBLEM 3

Sales of pantyhose to knee-highs were 3 to 1. Written as a fraction, sales of pantyhose were 3/1 over sales of knee-highs.

When comparing measurements, money, and time, convert to like items.

PROBLEM 4

Write the following as ratios:

1 dollar to 5 quarters	1:1.25 dollars	Quarters converted to dollars
1 dollar to 5 quarters	4/5 = 4:5 quarters	Dollars converted to quarters
30 minutes to 2 hours	30/120 = 1/4 = 1:4	Hours converted to minutes
30 minutes to 2 hours	0.5/2 = 1/4 = 1:4	Minutes converted to hours
9 yards to 45 feet	27/45 = 3/5 = 3:5	Yards converted to feet
9 yards to 45 feet	9/15 = 3/5 = 3:5	Feet converted to yards

PROPORTIONS

Proportions are made up of two sets of equal ratios. To determine if two sets of ratios are equal, a technique called **cross-multiplying** is used. In cross-multiplying, the numerator of the first fraction is multiplied by the denominator of the second fraction, then the denominator of the first fraction is multiplied by the numerator of the second fraction. The product of the two cross-multiplications should be equal. To illustrate, let us evaluate the proportion 1:4 :: 25:100, which is read "1 is to 4 as 25 is to 100."

1. Write as a fractional proportion (1/4 = 25/100) and then cross-multiply:

$$\frac{1}{4} \diagdown\!\!\!\!\!\diagup \frac{25}{100}$$

$$1 \times 100 = 4 \times 25$$

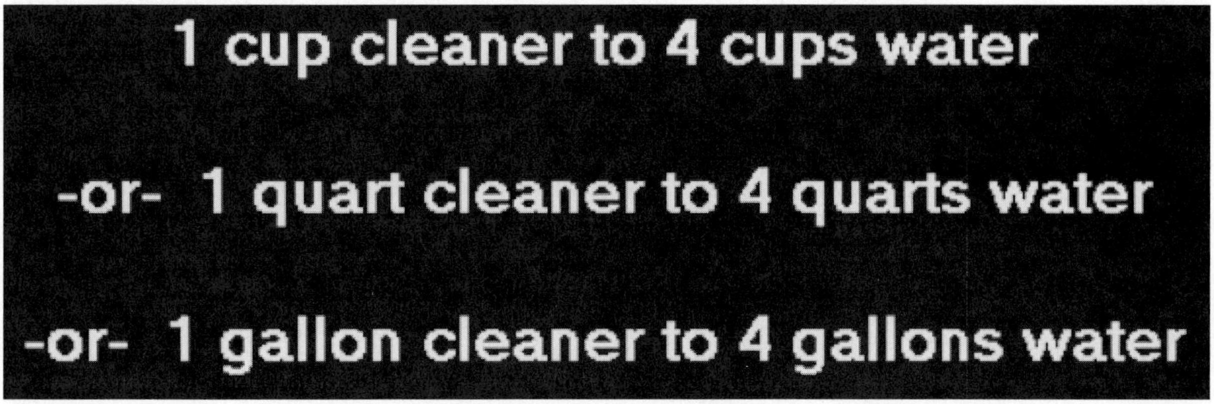

> # 1 cup cleaner to 4 cups water
>
> ## -or- 1 quart cleaner to 4 quarts water
>
> ## -or- 1 gallon cleaner to 4 gallons water

FIGURE 24.2

  2. Solve the equation:

$$100 = 100$$

  3. The proportion is correct.

A common business use for ratios is to give instructions for mixing compounds of various amounts. A small business might need 1 quart of mixed cleaning solution; an industrial complex might need barrels of mixed cleaning solution. Mixing instructions for a cleaning solution might call for 1 part cleaning solution to 4 parts water, or a 1:4 ratio. This could be translated to 1 capful of cleaner to 4 capfuls of water, and similarly with other measures. See Figure 24.2.

A proportion may be written with a variable. You may then solve for the unknown beginning with cross-multiplication.

PROBLEM 5

A school worker needs a minimum of 16 cups of cleaning solution per week. Using a cleaner-to-water ratio of 1:4, calculate how much cleaner should be added to 16 cups of water.

  1. Begin by writing the proportion using x as the unknown:

$1:4 :: x:16$ "1 is to 4 as ? is to 16"

  2. Write as a fractional proportion and then cross-multiply:

$$\frac{1}{4} = \frac{x}{16}$$
$$1 \times 16 = 4x$$

  3. Solve the equation by dividing both sides by 4:

$$\frac{16}{4} = \frac{4x}{4}$$
$$4 = x$$

To 16 cups of water, add 4 cups of cleaner to mix the cleaning solution correctly.

Check: Write the new proportion:

$$1:4 :: 4:16$$

Write as a fractional proportion and reduce:

$$1/4 = 4/16$$
$$1/4 = 1/4$$

The proportion is correct.

PROBLEM 6

A store sells party favors at 3 for $1.15. Amy is expecting 18 guests at her office party. What will 18 party favors cost?

1. Set up the proportion using a symbol for the unknown. (Think, "If 3 sell for $1.15, 18 will sell for how much?"):

$$\frac{3}{1.15} = \frac{18}{x}$$

2. Cross-multiply:

$$3x = 1.15 \times 18$$
$$3x = 20.7$$

3. Solve the equation by dividing both sides by 3:

$$\frac{3x}{3} = \frac{20.70}{3}$$
$$x = \$6.90$$

SOLVING PERCENT PROBLEMS USING PROPORTIONS

Proportions can be used to solve for percentage, rate (percent), and base. Using proportions to solve percent problems is sometimes referred to as the algebraic method, whereas using the percent formulas discussed in the chapter on percentages is referred to as the business method.

Solve for Percentage

Set the base, such as total sales, over 100 because total sales is equal to 100% of sales. Set the unknown over the rate because x equals a certain percentage of sales.

PROBLEM 7

The Bartek Mfg. Co. budgets 15% of each year's sales for research and development the following year. Last year, sales were $3,150,000. What amount was budgeted for research and development this year?

Think, "$3,150,000 is to 100% as $\times$ is to 15%."

1. Write the proportion:

$$3,150,000:100 :: x:15$$

2. Write the proportion using fractions:

$$\frac{3,150,000}{100} = \frac{x}{15}$$

3. Cross-multiply:

$$3,150,000 \times 15 = 100x$$
$$47,250,000 = 100x$$

4. Solve the equation:

$$472,500 = x$$

$472,500 was budgeted for research and development in the current year.

Check using the business formula for percentage: P = B × R:

$$\$3,150,000 \times .15 = \$472,500$$

The answer is the same as found using the proportion method.

Solve for Percent

Again set the base, such as total income, over 100 because the base is equal to 100%. Set the percentage, such as amount spent, over x because the amount spent equals "what %."

PROBLEM 8

Bartek Mfg. Co. spent $35,000 on office supplies last year. What percent of total sales ($3,150,000) was spent on office supplies?

   Think, "$3,150,000 is to 100% as $35,000 is to what %?"

1. Write the proportion:

$$3,150,000:100 :: 35,000:x$$

2. Write the proportion as fractions:

$$\frac{3,150,000}{100} = \frac{35,000}{x}$$

3. Cross-multiply:

$$3,150,000x = 100 \times 35,000$$
$$3,150,000x = 3,500,000$$

4. Solve the equation:

$$\frac{3,150,000x}{3,150,000} = \frac{3,500,000}{3,150,000}$$
$$x = 1.11\%$$

Check:

$$\text{Rate} = \text{Percentage} \div \text{Base}$$
$$R = 35,000 \div 3,150,000$$
$$R = 1.11\%$$

Solve for Base

Because the base is not known, place an x over 100 because we do not know what number is 100%. Set the percentage over the rate.

PROBLEM 9

Roscoe Harrison has 5% or $210 automatically deducted from his paycheck and placed in a savings account each month. What is the amount of his monthly paycheck?

   Think "what number is to 100% as $210 is to 5%?"

   Write the proportion as fractions, cross-multiply, and solve the resulting equation:

$$\frac{x}{100} = \frac{210}{5}$$
$$5x = 21,000$$
$$x = \$4,200 \qquad \text{amount of Roscoe's monthly paycheck}$$

Check:

$$\text{Base} = \text{Percentage} \div \text{Rate}$$
$$B = 210 \div .05 \quad \text{or} \quad B = 210 \div 5\%$$
$$B = \$4,200$$

PART 2 *Business Math Skills*

Exercise 1

Write the following ratios as fractions.

1. 5/5 to 2
2. 4 to 9
3. 5 dollars to 20 quarters
4. 25 feet to 9 yards
5. 45 minutes to 3 hours

Exercise 2

Write the following proportions as fractions and solve for the unknown.

6. 4:5 :: x:100
7. 800:100 :: 25:x
9. 100:x :: 6:9
10. x:25 :: 4:5

Exercise 3

Write the fractional proportion for each problem and solve. Round answers to hundredths.

11. Sales tax on a $29.95 purchase was $3. What would sales tax be on a $98.99 purchase? Set up as 3:29.95 :: x:98.99.
12. John paid $1.89 in tax for office supplies. The sales tax rate in his city is 8.25%. How much did he spend for office supplies less sales tax? Set up as .0825:1 :: 1.89:x.
13. A map scale is 1.5 inches to 100 miles. The distance on the map between two cities measures 3.25 inches. How many miles are between the two cities? Set up as 1.5:100 :: 3.25:x.
14. Bob knows the distance between two cities is 85 miles. What is the length in inches between the two cities on a road map with a scale of 1 inch to 10 miles? Set up as 1:10 :: x:85.
15. A bed and breakfast charges $490 for 3 days. At the same rate, how much would it cost to stay for 5 days? Set up as 3:490 :: 5:x.

PART 3 *Review and Practice Using Business Math FUNdamentals*

GOAL: Complete 9 of the 10 problems correctly.

Instructions: *Start Business Math FUNdamentals. Complete Tutorial 56 and Drill 44. If you are not satisfied with your score, repeat the drill. Write your scores below.*

Business Math FUNdamentals Drill 44

Today's Date	Score

 PART 4   *Desktop Calculator*

Exercise 1

One-Minute Addition Timing (0 through 9, Decimal, and Minus Keys, Six-Digit Numbers)

(Optional: Your instructor may wish you to use Touch Key on the computer for all your timings. Check with your instructor before completing this exercise.)

Complete as many of the problems as possible in 1 minute by adding. Work quickly and accurately. The number preceding each closing parenthesis indicates the cumulative number of strokes for problems attempted. For example, if you complete Problems 1 through 3 in 1 minute, your strokes-per-minute score is 255.

1. 347.556	2. 910.024	3. 765.544	4. 12,900.6	5. 77,850.7	6. 6.94200	7. −5,300.00	8. 3.17001
758.541	−576.932	751.350	−73,090.2	−45,500.2	928.500	6,609.00	61.9003
263.987	−462.009	746.800	−46,070.1	−34,650.1	12.3100	4,100.00	−318.002
113.657	397.545	−150.600	64,460.3	−69,995.6	−48.7400	9,300.00	8,130.01
735.987	886.041	972.400	53,010.4	−57,359.1	82.1006	−1,300.00	−91,900.4
883.524	719.000	199.500	−34,040.5	34,229.9	−2.23005	−1,200.00	67,100.2
−991.093	164.788	240.300	92,400.3	67,899.1	5.79003	5,300.00	477.007
−706.835	654.921	−764.100	15,100.3	45,775.4	−6.36004	1,250.00	−3.83004
−920.569	−453.896	−403.300	−88,200.1	54,900.3	51,400.6	−5,600.00	−23,800.5
−563.870	−211.009	−535.300	79,100.2	34,556.8	−32,500.6	9,500.00	−2,480.03
85)	170)	255)	340)	425)	510)	595)	680)

9. 94.1400	10. 7,690.01	11. 7.56987	12. 14,477.9	13. 143.450	14. 49,066.1	15. 16.0036	16. 950.049
−86.6420	44.2677	22.0122	153.100	29.9957	78,900.9	63.7013	826.002
−75.5850	36.3553	−16.0455	120.666	41.9951	67,988.5	73.8064	640.003
76.6150	−776.998	−1.70004	135.350	27.2293	96,965.5	83.9014	348.708
−67.7700	−5,885.65	322.999	155.555	−30.7594	17,644.4	53.0045	960.024
98.8689	−1,743.22	−2590.00	133.886	−60.9992	26,711.1	62.7023	160.039
99.9599	−39,765.9	2658.80	176.772	−37.5771	35,674.1	82.8013	895.145
86.6884	8,221.00	−110.432	1,722.50	−20.6594	45,296.2	99.2053	467.876
−81.7256	8,250.00	31.1119	1,404.95	45.6951	55,985.4	59.7024	364.127
79.9374	935.575	4.33980	23,249.5	120.000	85,601.4	61.0011	546.009
765)	850)	935)	1,010)	1,101)	1,182)	1,263)	1,344)

CHAPTER 24 *Terminology Review*

Formulas

$$\frac{\text{Base}}{100} = \frac{x}{\text{Percent}}$$

$$\frac{\text{Base}}{100} = \frac{\text{Percentage}}{x}$$

$$\frac{x}{100} = \frac{\text{Percentage}}{\text{Percent}}$$

Terms

Cross-multiplying
Proportion method
Proportions
Ratios

Write the correct term or formula next to the appropriate description.

1. _____ Used to compare one item to another.
2. _____ The fractional proportion for finding the base.
3. _____ Can be used to solve percent problems.
4. _____ The fractional proportion for finding the rate (percent).
5. _____ Are made up of two sets of equal ratios.
6. _____ Used to determine if two ratios are equal and for solving for an unknown in a set of ratios.
7. _____ The fractional proportion for finding percentage (part).

Name _____

Class/Section _____

Score (Correct Answers ÷ No. of Assigned Problems) _____

Chapter 24 Review Exercises

Exercise 1

Write the following ratios as fractions.

1. 2:1 _____
2. 5:9 _____
3. 1/5:2 _____
4. 70:2 _____
5. 4:32 _____

Solve for the unknown. Round answers to hundredths as necessary.

6. $7/x = 9/3$ _____
7. $3/4 = 9/x$ _____
8. $x/2 = 50/80$ _____
9. $5/12 = x/60$ _____
10. $3/90 = 4/x$ _____

Exercise 2

Set up the following percent problems as proportions and solve.

11. Base equals $5,000 and rate equals 15%. Find percentage. _____
12. After a tune-up, a car's gas mileage improved 2%. If the car was getting 15 miles per gallon before the tune-up, what is the improvement in miles per gallon? _____
13. Sales tax on a purchase of $195.59 is 7.5%. What is the amount of tax? _____
14. A stockbroker reported that a certain account of $5,000 earned $359 last year. What is the rate of earnings? _____
15. An investor earned 8%, or $1,500, on his investment last year. How much was invested? _____

Exercise 3

Solve the following proportion problems. Round answers to hundredths as necessary.

16. David's truck can go 200 miles on 15 gallons of gas. How far can the truck go on 75 gallons of gas? _____
17. A stationers is having a sale on pens, 3 for $2.29. How much do 2 pens cost? _____
18. If fertilizer is to be spread at 1 pound to 25 square feet, how much fertilizer is needed to cover 750 square feet? _____
19. If 2 gallons of wall paint will cover a room that has 320 sq ft of wall space, how much wall space will 8 gallons of the paint cover? _____
20. If 2 gallons of wall paint will cover a room that has 300 sq ft of wall space, how much paint will be required to paint six rooms the same size? _____
21. If peaches cost $.89 per pound and there are 4 peaches in a pound, what do 15 peaches cost? _____
22. Joe's Smokin' Grill can serve 20 barbeque meals from 7 pounds (before cooking) of brisket. How much brisket should be purchased to provide barbeque for a party of 45? _____
23. Otto's Ag Business plants 25% of its 1,250 acres in corn. How many acres are planted in corn? _____
24. Dry-land grazing requires 10 acres of land for each cow/calf pair. How many pairs will 675 acres support? _____
25. On a map with a scale of 1 1/8 inches = 100 miles, the distance between Miami, Florida, and Hope Town, Bahamas, measures 1 15/16 inches. What is the distance between the two cities in miles? _____

CHAPTER 25

Merchandise Inventory, Raw Materials Inventory, Cost of Goods Sold

PART 1   Speed and Accuracy Building Using Touch Key

GOALS: Your speed goal is 11,500 strokes per hour.
Your accuracy target goal range is 95% to 100%.

With each repetition of the drill, try to improve your speed without lowering your accuracy score. If your percent-of-accuracy score falls below 95%, review your finger position and technique. Then try again.

Instructions: *Start Touch Key. Complete Drill 5, Parts A and B, Three-Minute Timings. (Parts C through E are optional.) Write your scores for strokes per hour and percent of accuracy below.*

Touch Key Drill 5—The 0 through 9, Decimal, and Minus Keys, Six-Digit Numbers, Three-Minute Timings

Today's Date	Strokes per Hour	Percent of Accuracy
A.		
B.		
C.		
D.		
E.		

PART 2   Business Math Skills

MERCHANDISE INVENTORY VERSUS RAW MATERIALS INVENTORY

In earlier chapters both cost and pricing of goods purchased or produced for resale were discussed. **Merchandise** is made up of the goods purchased or produced for resale. **Raw materials inventory** is made up of the materials used to produce goods for resale. All the goods purchased or produced for resale that have not yet been sold constitute **merchandise inventory**. This chapter will focus on merchandise inventory, although the methods can be used for both raw materials and merchandise inventory.

Beginning inventory is the amount of merchandise on hand at the beginning of the accounting period. **Ending inventory** is the amount of merchandise on hand at the end of the accounting period. Careful records of inventory must be maintained for various reasons. A company must know when stock is low in order to reorder in a timely fashion (Figure 25.1). Inventory is an asset of the company and the value of inventory must be accurately reflected in accounting and tax records.

FIGURE 25.1

In addition to paper and computer records of inventory purchased and sold, a physical inventory is usually made at least once at the end of the year. A **physical inventory** is an actual count of the units on hand in the warehouse and stockroom and on store shelves. Some companies may still find it necessary to close for end-of-year inventory, but hand-held barcode readers make taking a physical inventory of merchandise quicker and easier so that a closing may no longer be necessary.

Various methods are used to account for inventory, including the perpetual inventory method, the weighted-average method, the first-in, first-out method, the last-in, first-out method, and the lower-of-cost-or-market method. In addition, the retail **inventory method** can be used to estimate the cost of inventory.

PERPETUAL INVENTORY METHOD

When the **perpetual inventory method** is used, a continuous count is maintained of all items in inventory. Items are added to or subtracted from inventory as they are received or sold, resulting in a current record of unit costs and units on hand. Because a count is maintained of individual items, the perpetual inventory method is also known as the **specific identification method**. Companies selling high-cost items often use this system. Each item is assigned a code number. The exact cost of the item and date of purchase are recorded as shown in Figure 25.2. In addition, a physical inventory is made and compared to the company records at least once a year.

FIGURE 25.2

PROBLEM 1

Complete the following inventory to find current cost.

Inventory Number	Date Purchased	Date Sold	Cost of Addition to Inventory ($)	Cost to Be Subtracted from Inventory ($)	Inventory Balance ($)
33389	9-1-1999	_____	9,750	_____	_____
33390	9-1-1999	_____	8,549	_____	_____
33389	_____	9-2-1999	_____	_____	_____
33391	9-5-1999	_____	10,559	_____	_____
33390	_____	9-6-1999	_____	_____	_____
33392	9-10-1999	_____	7,659	_____	_____

Add the cost of inventory purchases to inventory balance. Subtract the cost of merchandise sold from inventory balance as shown below. Answers are in bold print.

Inventory Number	Date Purchased	Date Sold	Cost of Addition to Inventory ($)	Cost to Be Subtracted from Inventory ($)	Inventory Balance ($)
33389	9-1-1999	_____	9,750	_____	**9,750**
33390	9-1-1999	_____	8,549	_____	**18,299**
33389	_____	9-2-1999	_____	**9,750**	**8,549**
33391	9-5-1999	_____	10,559	_____	**19,108**
33390	_____	9-6-1999	_____	**8,549**	**10,559**
33392	9-10-1999	_____	7,659	_____	**18,218**

WEIGHTED-AVERAGE INVENTORY METHOD

When the **weighted-average method** of accounting for inventory is used, the costs of the units on hand for an item are averaged. The average cost is used as the value of each unit.

PROBLEM 2A

Calculate the unit cost using the weighted-average method for the following purchases of Door Hinge Model #332.

On January 20, 110 hinges were purchased at $.50 each.

On April 10, 120 hinges were purchased at $.45 each.

On June 22, 90 units were purchased at $.52 each.

1. Begin by calculating the total cost of each purchase:

January 20	110 × $.50	= $55.00
April 10	120 × $.45	= $54.00
June 22	90 × $.52	= $46.80

2. Total the number of units purchased:

   $$110 + 120 + 90 = 320 \text{ units}$$

3. Find total cost of all the units purchased:

   $$\$55 + \$54 + \$46.80 = \$155.80$$

4. Divide total cost by total units to find average cost per unit (Figure 25.3):

   $$\$155.80 \div 320 = \$0.49 \text{ average cost per unit}$$

Total cost of units / Number of units = Ave. cost per unit

$$155.80 \div 320 = .49 \quad \boxed{\begin{array}{c}.486875 \\ \text{rounded}\end{array}}$$

Total units x Ave. cost per unit = Ending inv. at ave. cost

$$320 \times .49 = 156.80$$

FIGURE 25.3

PROBLEM 2B

Find ending inventory if none of the door hinges have sold.

Multiply total units by the average cost per unit to find the amount of ending inventory using the weighted-average method (Figure 25.3):

$$320 \times \$0.49 = \$156.80 \text{ ending inventory}$$

FIRST-IN, FIRST-OUT INVENTORY METHOD

The **first-in, first-out** (FIFO) method of computing inventory assumes that units received first were sold first and that items remaining in inventory were received most recently. Therefore, the costs for the most recently received units are used in computing inventory value.

PROBLEM 3

Figure 25.4 shows that there were 10 boxes of cereal purchased at $1 each in beginning inventory on January 1. On January 10, 10 boxes of cereal were purchased at $2 per box. There were 6 boxes on hand when ending inventory was taken on January 31. Using the FIFO inventory method, what was the cost of the 6 boxes on hand (the amount of ending inventory)?

Because the FIFO method assumes the boxes purchased at the earlier date were sold first, the 6 boxes in ending inventory were part of the second purchase. Each box of cereal purchased January 10 cost $2. Therefore, ending inventory is equal to 6 × $2, or $12.

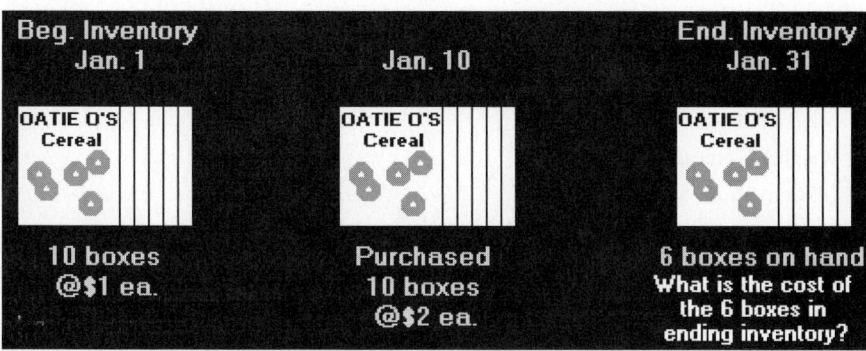

FIGURE 25.4

LAST-IN, FIRST-OUT INVENTORY METHOD

The **last-in, first-out** (LIFO) method of computing inventory assumes that units received last (most recently) are sold first. This means that inventory on hand consists of the units received first (at the earlier date).

PROBLEM 4

Using the information shown in Figure 25.4, what was the cost of the 6 boxes of cereal on hand if the LIFO inventory method was used to calculate ending inventory?

Because LIFO assumes that items received most recently were sold first, the 6 boxes of cereal on hand were part of the boxes in beginning inventory on January 1 that cost $1 each. Therefore, ending inventory using the LIFO method is equal to 6 × $1, or $6.

COMPARING INVENTORY METHODS

Take a moment to compare the weighted-average method with the LIFO and FIFO inventory methods.

PROBLEM 5

Using the information shown in Figure 25.4, what is ending inventory using the weighted-average method?

1. Find total cost of each purchase:

   January 1   10 × $1 = $10
   January 20   10 × $2 = $20

2. Find total units purchased:

$$10 + 10 = 20$$

3. Find total cost of units:

$$\$10 + \$20 = \$30$$

4. Divide total cost by total number of units.

$$30 \div 20 = \$1.50 \text{ average cost per unit}$$

5. Multiply ending inventory units by average cost per unit:

$$6 \times \$1.50 = \$9.00 \text{ ending inventory using weighted-average method}$$

Comparison of ending inventory values using the three methods reveals the following:

FIFO method: $12

Weighted-average method: $9

LIFO method: $6

From this comparison we can conclude that if merchandise purchased to replace stock is usually purchased at a higher price due to inflation and so on, it would be to the company's advantage to use the LIFO inventory method because of state and local end-of-year taxes on inventory.

Note: LIFO is considered to be more accurate from an accounting standpoint because it more accurately matches current revenues with current costs.

LOWER-OF-COST-OR-MARKET INVENTORY METHOD

Computing inventory using the **lower-of-cost-or-market** (LCM) method is a two-step process. In the first step, inventory cost is computed based on one of the three methods discussed previously: FIFO, LIFO, or weighted average. In the second step, the cost of inventory computed in the first step is compared to the market value of inventory. Whichever of the two figures is lower is used for inventory valuation.

PROBLEM 6

The coats that wouldn't sell. Figure 25.5 illustrates the case of six coats, Style 202, and the drop in inventory value using the lower-of-cost-or-market inventory valuation method.

The weighted-average cost of each of the six coats in inventory on September 1, 1999, was $150. The market value of each coat on December 30, 1999, was $200. Comparing these two figures, we see that the lower-of-cost-or-market-value figure was $150. Multiplying $150 by 6 results in an ending inventory valuation of $900.

By December 30, 2000, the market value of the coats had dropped to $75 each. Comparing the lower of cost ($150) or market value ($75) results in an inventory value of $75 for each coat. Multiplying $75 × 6 results in an inventory valuation for the six coats of $450.

The drop in inventory value reflects the drop in market value of the coats.

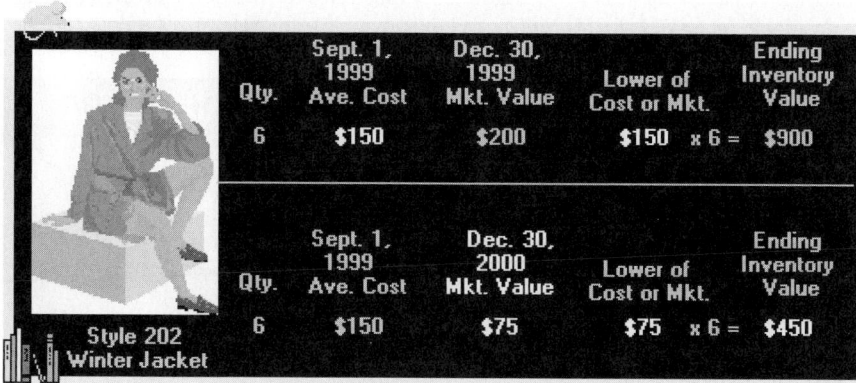

FIGURE 25.5

COST OF GOODS SOLD

Periodically, a business will need to calculate the cost of goods that have been sold by the business. The **cost of goods sold** (COGS) is simply the amount paid for goods that have been removed from inventory as the goods were sold. Any purchases of merchandise are added to beginning inventory. At the end of the period, the amount of ending inventory is subtracted, and the result is the cost of goods sold.

PROBLEM 7

On May 1, inventory was valued at $50,000. During the month, $80,000 in merchandise was purchased. Ending inventory on May 30 was $40,000. What was COGS for the month? Figure 25.6 illustrates the use of the formula, Beginning Inventory + Purchases − Ending Inventory = COGS ($90,000).

Beginning inventory	5 0 , 0 0 0
+ Purchases	8 0 , 0 0 0
- Ending inventory	4 0 , 0 0 0
= Cost of goods sold	9 0 , 0 0 0

FIGURE 25.6

RETAIL INVENTORY METHOD

The **retail inventory method** can be used to estimate the cost of inventory periodically rather than performing an actual count of inventory. In this method the sales for the period are multiplied by the *cost* of goods available for sale. The product is then divided by the *retail value* of goods available for sale.

PROBLEM 8

Estimate COGS for April if sales were $400, cost of goods available for sale was $500, and the retail value of goods available was $700. Figure 25.7 illustrates the use of the formula, Sales $\times$ Cost of Goods Available for Sale $\div$ Retail Value of Goods Available for Sale $=$ COGS ($286).

COGS = Sales x (Cost of goods available for sale / retail value of goods available for sale)

$$COGS = \frac{400 \times 500}{700} = 286 \text{ rounded}$$

FIGURE 25.7

The cost of ending inventory can also be calculated. Subtract retail sales ($400) from the retail value of inventory ($700). Multiply the difference ($300) by the cost of goods available for sale divided by retail value of goods available for sale ($500 ÷ 700).

Note: You may want to calculate the percent for cost of goods available for sale divided by the retail value of goods available for sale and store the result in memory because it will be needed for both formulas. Do not round the percent or decimal equivalent.

POCKET CALCULATOR PROCEDURE

a. Percent of cost of goods available for sale divided by the retail value of goods available for sale:

500 ÷ 700 = 0.7142857 M+

b. COGS

400 × MR = 285.71   (or $286 rounded)

c. Cost of ending inventory

700 − 400 = 300 × MR = 214.29   (or $214 rounded)

PART 2 *Business Math Skills*

Exercise 1

1. On April 15, 2002, an equipment company had in inventory Asset #405, which cost $14,600; Asset #508, which cost $5,400; and Asset #410, which cost $17,200. During April, Asset #411, which cost $5,100, and Asset #412, which cost $500, were purchased. Assets #508, 410, and 411 were sold during April. What was the amount of ending inventory on April 30 if the perpetual inventory (specific identification) method is used? _____

2. Beginning inventory at I LOVE TOYS on October 1 was $55,100. Purchases were made on October 5 of $5,600 and October 20 of $12,115. Ending inventory on October 31 was $46,000. What was cost of goods sold (COGS) as of October 31? _____

Exercise 2

Calculate the total cost of each purchase, the total quantity, the total cost of available merchandise, and the weighted average for the following widget purchases.

Date	Item Number	Quantity	Cost/Each ($)	Total Cost per Item ($)	
March 10	210	5,000	1.29		3.
March 20	210	5,250	1.31		4.
March 29	210	4,500	1.32		5.
	Totals				6.
			Weighted average		7.

8. Use the information in the above table to complete this problem. Beginning inventory on March 1 was $15,000. If 12,000 of Item #210 sold during March, what was ending inventory on March 30? _____

Exercise 3

Use the FIFO inventory method to calculate the cost of goods sold for Item #66 if there were 75 units in ending inventory. On June 1, there were 55 units of Item #66 in beginning inventory. The dates of purchase and costs are shown below.

Date of Purchase	Quantity	Cost ($)	Total Cost ($)	
May 15	16	2.25	_____	9.
May 30	50	2.27	_____	10.
June 15	50	2.29	_____	11.
June 29	45	2.30	_____	12.

13. Beginning inventory _____
14. +Purchases _____
15. −Ending inventory _____
16. Cost of goods sold _____

Exercise 4

Use the last-in, first-out method to calculate the cost of goods sold in January for Item #322. On January 1, 790 units were on hand. On January 31, 400 units were on hand.

Date of Purchase	Quantity	Cost ($)	Total Cost ($)
December 10	500	3.20	17. _____
December 20	520	3.25	18. _____
January 13	610	3.33	19. _____
January 22	650	3.30	20. _____
January 28	650	3.45	21. _____

22. Beginning inventory _____
23. +Purchases _____
24. −Ending inventory _____
25. Cost of goods sold _____

Exercise 5

26. What is the weighted average for the January purchases of Item #322 as shown in Exercise 4? _____

Calculate COGS using the weighted-average method if beginning inventory was $5,000 and 1,300 of Item #322 (from Exercise 4) sold during January.

27. Beginning inventory _____
28. +Purchases _____
29. −Cost of goods sold _____
30. Ending inventory _____

Exercise 6

Use the retail inventory method to estimate the cost of goods sold in February. The retail value of beginning inventory was $3,000. The retail value of purchases made during February was $35,000.

31. Calculate retail value of goods available for sale. _____

The cost of goods available for sale was $29,000.

32. Calculate the percent of cost of goods to retail value of goods. _____

Sales during February were $32,000.

33. Calculate the retail value of ending inventory. _____
34. Calculate the cost of ending inventory. _____
35. Calculate the cost of goods sold. _____

PART 3 Review and Practice Using Business Math FUNdamentals

GOAL: Complete 9 of the 10 problems correctly.

Instructions: *Start Business Math FUNdamentals. Complete Tutorial 57 and Drill 45. If you are not satisfied with your score, repeat the drill. Write your scores below.*

Business Math FUNdamentals Drill 45

Today's Date	Score

 **PART 4** *Desktop Calculator*

INVENTORY

Formulas to remember:

Beginning Inventory **+** Purchases **−** Ending Inventory **=** Cost of Goods Sold

Beginning Inventory **+** Purchases **−** Cost of Goods Sold **=** Ending Inventory

Following are sample inventory problems and how to solve them using the desktop calculator.

PROBLEM

The table below shows a partial inventory record for Item #c300. *Records indicate that 751 of the items were sold during the month.* Complete the extensions and the total merchandise available for sale in units and in dollar amount.

TAPE 25.1:

```
     170·  ×
    3·98  =
  676·60  ＊

  676·60 M+
    150·  ×
    1·20  =
  180·00  ＊

  180·00 M+
    160·  ×
    5·98  =
  956·80  ＊

  956·80 M+
    212·  ×
     7·9  =
1,674·80  ＊

1,674·80 M+
    180·  ×
    5·69  =
1,024·20  ＊

1,024·20 M+
4,512·40 M＊
```

Date	Inventory	Quantity	Unit Cost ($)	Total Cost ($)	
June 1	Beginning inventory	170	3.98	1. _____	
June 8	Purchases	150	1.20	2. _____	
June 13	Purchases	160	5.98	3. _____	
June 24	Purchases	212	7.90	4. _____	
June 29	Purchases	180	5.69	5. _____	
	Total merchandise available for sale			6. _____	

Using the information in the table, calculate cost of goods sold for each method.

7. Specific identification method. (Records show that all merchandise has been sold except 21 units of the June 24 purchases and 100 units of the June 29 purchases.) $3,777.50

8. Weighted-average method $3,882.67

9. FIFO method $3,823.91

10. LIFO method $4,030.82

Begin by calculating the extensions for total cost for lines 1 through 5. As total cost is figured for each line item, add to memory:

$$170 \times 3.98 = \boxed{676.60} \text{ M+}$$
$$150 \times 1.20 = \boxed{180} \text{ M+}$$
$$160 \times 5.98 = \boxed{956.80} \text{ M+}$$
$$212 \times 7.90 = \boxed{1,674.80} \text{ M+}$$
$$180 \times 5.69 = \boxed{1,024.20} \text{ M+}$$

MT $\boxed{4,512.40}$ (Cost of total merchandise available for sale, line 6)

Check: Total the Total Cost column. The result should match the amount that was stored in memory in the above calculation, line 6.

Total the quantity column to find total merchandise available for sale in units, line 6:

$$170 + 150 + 160 + 212 + 180 + \text{T } \boxed{872}$$

Your table should look like the one below.

TAPE 25.2:

```
  170·00  ÷
  150·00  ÷
  160·00  ÷
  212·00  ÷
  180·00  ÷
  872·00  ＊
```

Date	Inventory	Quantity	Unit Cost ($)	Total Cost ($)	
June 1	Beginning inventory	170	3.98	**676.60**	1.
June 8	Purchases	150	1.20	**180.00**	2.
June 13	Purchases	160	5.98	**956.80**	3.
June 24	Purchases	212	7.90	**1,674.80**	4.
June 29	Purchases	180	5.69	**1,024.20**	5.
	Total merchandise available for sale	**872**		**4,512.40**	6.

TAPE 25.3:

```
         21 ·   x
          7·9   =
     165·90     *

     165·90M+
        100·    x
          5·69  =
     569·00      *

     569·00M+
   4,512·40      +
     734·90M*

     734·90      -
   3,777·50      *
```

TAPE 25.4:

```
   4,512·4   ÷
      872·   =
        5·17  *

        5·17  x
      751·   =
   3,882·67   *
```

7. To calculate cost of goods sold using the specific identification method, calculate the cost of the specific unsold units, store in memory, and subtract the amount from total merchandise available for sale:

    June 24   21 units × 7.90 = $\boxed{165.90}$ M+

    June 29   100 units × 5.69 = $\boxed{569.00}$ M+

    4,512.40 + MT $\boxed{734.90}$ − T $\boxed{3,777.50}$

8. To calculate cost of goods sold using the weighted-average method:

  a. Begin by dividing the total cost of all merchandise available for sale by the total number of units available for sale to find the average cost per unit:

    4,512.40 ÷ 872 = $\boxed{5.17}$ (rounded)

  b. Multiply the units sold (751) by the average cost per unit (5.17):

    751 × 5.17 = $\boxed{3,882.67}$

9. To calculate cost of goods sold using the FIFO method, calculate the total cost of the first 751 units purchased (and assumed sold first). To do this:

  a. Begin by calculating units needed from beginning inventory and from the earlier purchases until a total of 751 is reached. Note that only 59 units from the June 29 purchases are needed:

    170 + 150 + 160 + 212 + T $\boxed{692}$ M+

    751 + MT − T $\boxed{59}$

  b. Calculate the cost of the 59 units purchased June 29:

    59 × 5.69 = $\boxed{335.71}$

  c. Calculate the total cost for the units sold. It may be helpful to make a list of units to include in the cost of goods sold total as shown below. See Tape 25.5B.

Beginning inventory	170	$676.60
Purchases made June 8	150	$180.00
Purchases made June 13	160	$956.80
Purchases made June 24	212	$1,674.80
Plus 59 of the units purchased June 24	59 × $5.69	$335.71
	751	$3,823.91

676.60 + 180 + 956.80 + 1,674.80 + 335.71 + T $\boxed{3,823.91}$

TAPE 25.5A:

```
   170·00   +
   150·00   +
   160·00   +
   212·00   +
   692·00   *

   692·00M+
   751·00   ÷
   692·00M*

   692·00   -
    59·00   *

    59·00   x
     5·69   =
   335·71   *
```

TAPE 25.5B:

```
     676·60   +
     180·00   +
     956·80   +
   1,674·80   +
     335·71   +
   3,823·91   *
```

10. To calculate cost of goods sold using the LIFO method:

a. Begin by calculating units needed from most recent purchases until a total of 751 is reached. Note that only 49 units from beginning inventory are needed:

$$180 + 212 + 160 + 150 + \text{T} \boxed{702} \text{ M+}$$
$$751 + \text{MT} - \text{T} \boxed{49}$$

b. Calculate the cost of the 49 units from beginning inventory:

$$49 \times 3.98 = \boxed{195.02}$$

c. Calculate the total cost for the units sold. The units and costs to be used are listed below.

Purchases made June 29	180	$1,024.20
Purchases made June 24	212	$1,674.80
Purchases made June 13	160	$956.80
Purchases made June 8	150	$180.00
Plus 49 units from beginning inventory	49 × $3.98	$195.02
	751	$4,030.82

$$1{,}024.20 + 1{,}674.8 + 956.8 + 180 + 195.02 + \text{T} \boxed{4{,}030.82}$$

To find ending inventory for Problems 7 through 10, subtract the cost of goods sold from total goods available for sale.

TAPE 25.6:

```
180·00 +
212·00 +
160·00 +
150·00 +
702·00 ✳

702·00 ✳
751·00 +
702·00 ✳

702·00 −
 49·00 ✳

 49·00 ×
  3·98 =
195·02 ✳

1,024·20 +
1,674·80 +
  956·80 +
  180·00 +
  195·02 +
4,030·82 ✳
```

Name _____

Class/Section _____

Score (Correct Answers ÷ No. of Assigned Problems) _____

 # PART 4 *Desktop Calculator*

Exercise 1

The table below shows a partial inventory record for Model #43cx electric coffee pots. Complete the extensions and the total merchandise available for sale in units and in dollar amount.

Date	Inventory	Quantity	Unit Cost ($)	Total Cost ($)
January 1	Beginning inventory	75	10.98	1. _____
March 8	Purchases	250	11.20	2. _____
May 13	Purchases	100	11.98	3. _____
August 8	Purchases	150	11.90	4. _____
November	Purchases	100	12.19	5. _____
Total merchandise available for sale				6. _____

Using the information in the table, calculate ending inventory and cost of goods sold for each method. *Records indicate that 600 of the items were sold during the year.*

7. Specific identification method (records show that all merchandise has been sold except 50 units of the August 24 purchases and 25 units of the November 29 purchases).

Ending inventory _____ Cost of goods sold _____

8. Weighted-average method

   Ending inventory _____ Cost of goods sold _____

9. FIFO method

   Ending inventory _____ Cost of goods sold _____

10. LIFO method

    Ending inventory _____ Cost of goods sold _____

Exercise 2

Strokes per Minute Score _____

Accuracy Score (Correct Strokes ÷ Total Strokes) _____

One-Minute Addition Timing (0 through 9, Decimal, and Minus Keys, Six-Digit Numbers)

(Optional: Your instructor may wish you to use Touch Key on the computer for all your timings. Check with your instructor before completing this exercise.)

Complete as many of the problems as possible in 1 minute by adding. Work quickly and accurately. The number preceding each closing parenthesis indicates the cumulative number of strokes for problems attempted. For example, if you complete Problems 1 through 3 in 1 minute, your strokes-per-minute score is 249.

1.	192.556	2.	110.024	3.	3.76544	4.	2900.76	5.	2.77750	6.	1942.00
	−13.6321		76.5932		2.75350		3090.62		3.45500		7285.00
	23.1001		−22.6209		−74.8100		6070.41		5.34650		6231.00
	13.1657		197.545		15.6300		−4460.83		6.69995		8874.00
	75.4987		869.041		297.400		−3010.94		9.57359		4210.06
	8322.24		9.19000		−19.5005		4040.55		−1.34229		3230.05
	1.81093		−1.64788		24.3006		2400.63		5.67899		5790.03
	736.835		1.54921		7.06100		5100.43		3.45775		3360.04
	−90.3269		535.896		430.300		8200.81		−8.54900		−2140.06
	43.0070		3.11009		536.300		9100.62		1.34556		−9250.06
83)		166)		249)		332)		415)		598)	

7.	−3000.12	8.	5.17001	9.	4,140.61	10.	1.76985	11.	−356.987	12.	9447.79
	60000.3		7.19003		66,420.9		3.42677		720.122		−9447.79
	−100.561		−9.18002		55,850.8		6.63553		−860.455		8206.66
	300.437		4.13001		66,150.9		7.76998		170.004		4353.50
	3000.79		8.19004		−77,700.1		3.88565		922.999		955.555
	2001.00		−7.71002		−88,689.3		9.74322		359.968		−955.555
	3008.00		1.77007		99,599.9		1.97659		265.880		6767.72
	50000.1		9.83004		66,884.5		8.21002		910.432		7722.50
	60.7989		5.38005		17,256.2		−4.50005		511.119		9404.95
	500.679		6.48003		99,374.1		−4.35575		233.980		8324.95
581)		664)		747)		830)		913)		996)	

13.	60.3451	14.	150.661	15.	346.905	16.	19.0048
	20.9995		458.902		437.013		−82.6008
	40.1995		−679.885		538.064		64.0006
	20.7229		−469.655		−939.014		34.8703
	30.0759		876.444		930.045		96.0029
	60.0999		867.111		227.023		−16.0031
	30.7577		356.741		328.013		89.5142
	−20.0659		252.962		−892.053		46.7871
	40.5695		859.854		697.024		36.4124
	−20.0986		956.014		810.011		54.6009
1,079)		1,162)		1,245)		1,328)	

CHAPTER 25 *Terminology Review*

Beginning inventory
Cost of goods sold
Ending inventory
First-in, first-out method
Last-in, first-out method
Lower-of-cost-or-market method
Merchandise
Merchandise inventory
Raw materials inventory
Retail inventory method
Perpetual inventory method
Physical inventory
Specific identification method
Weighted-average method

Write the correct term next to the appropriate description.

1. _____ Goods purchased or produced for resale.

2. _____ Materials used to produce goods for resale.

3. _____ All the goods purchased or produced for resale but that have not yet been sold.

4. _____ Merchandise on hand at the beginning of the accounting period.

5. _____ Merchandise on hand at the end of the accounting period.

6. _____ An actual count of the merchandise units on hand.

7. _____ With this method items are added to or subtracted from inventory as they are received or sold.

8. _____ The perpetual inventory method is also known as this.

9. _____ With this method the costs of the units on hand for an item are averaged.

10. _____ Assumes that units received first were sold first and that items remaining in inventory were received most recently.

11. _____ In the second step of this method, the cost of inventory computed in the first step is compared to the market value of the inventory. Whichever of the two figures is lower is used for inventory valuation.

12. _____ Used to estimate the cost of inventory periodically rather than performing an actual count of inventory. In this method the sales for the period are multiplied by the *cost* of goods available for sale. The product is then divided by the *retail value* of goods available for sale.

13. _____ Assumes that units received last (most recently) are sold first.

14. _____ The amount paid for goods that have been removed from inventory as the goods were sold.

Chapter 25 Review Exercises

Exercise 1

Complete the extensions in the following table. Then use the information about units in inventory to answer questions in this exercise. Records show that 215 units were sold during May.

Date	Inventory	Quantity	Unit Cost ($)	Total Cost ($)
May 1	Beginning inventory	35	2.98	1. _____
May 8	Purchases	100	3.20	2. _____
May 13	Purchases	74	1.98	3. _____
May 24	Purchases	15	3.90	4. _____
May 28	Purchases	25	2.69	5. _____

Calculate ending inventory using the following inventory methods.

6. Weighted average _____
7. FIFO _____
8. LIFO _____
9. Calculate cost of goods sold if the FIFO method was used. _____

Exercise 2

10. A sporting goods store had a beginning merchandise inventory of $78,955. Purchases of $361,290 were made, and the ending inventory for the year was $36,710. Calculate cost of goods sold. _____

Exercise 3

Calculate the lower of cost or market value for each inventory item below.

Inventory Number	Quantity on Hand	Unit Cost ($)	Retail Value ($)	Lower of Cost or Market Value
C56	56	.39	1.25	11. _____
D759	44	1.50	4.50	12. _____
C311	27	3.95	8.65	13. _____
D32	20	6.19	12.90	14. _____
D12	12	.59	.29	15. _____

Exercise 4

Jazzwear Stores had the following records for Shirt Style #50B for January. Beginning inventory showed 14 shirts at $10.50 each. Fifteen shirts were purchased at $11.00 each on January 5. Twelve shirts were purchased at $11.25 each on January 20. There were 9 shirts in ending inventory at the end of the month. Calculate ending inventory and cost of goods sold for each method.

16. FIFO: ending inventory _____ cost of goods sold _____
17. Weighted average: ending inventory _____ cost of goods sold _____
18. LIFO: ending inventory _____ cost of goods sold _____
19. If the store wishes cost of goods to be high (for tax purposes), which inventory method should be adopted by the store? _____

Exercise 5

20. The Styles for Curves store wishes to estimate COGS using the retail inventory method for the first quarter of the year. Sales were $116,000. Cost of goods available for sale was $32,000. The retail value of goods available for sale was $135,000. What is the estimate for COGS? _____

CHAPTER 26

Overhead Expense

 ## PART 1   *Speed and Accuracy Building Using Touch Key*

GOALS: Your speed goal is 12,000 strokes per hour.
Your accuracy target goal range is 95% to 100%.

With each repetition of the drill, try to improve your speed without lowering your accuracy score. If your percent-of-accuracy score falls below 95%, review your finger position and technique. Then try again.

Instructions: Start Touch Key. Complete Drill 5, Part A, Five-Minute Timing. (Parts B through E are optional.) Write your scores for strokes per hour and percent of accuracy below.

Touch Key Drill 4—The 0 through 9, Decimal, and Minus Keys, Six-Digit Numbers, Five-Minute Timing

	Today's Date	Strokes per Hour	Percent of Accuracy
A.			
B.			
C.			
D.			
E.			

 ## PART 2   *Business Math Skills*

ALLOCATING OVERHEAD

In recent chapters certain items for which a business must pay were discussed. A business purchases items to be used within the business itself, such as furniture and equipment. Businesses that offer goods for sale must purchase merchandise. In this chapter overhead expense will be discussed.

   Overhead expense refers to costs such as rent, electricity and other utilities, insurance, taxes, managerial salaries, cleaning, and maintenance. These are the expenses of the business that are not related to any one department. The **allocation of overhead expense** is the sharing of overhead expense among the departments of the business. Two methods often used include allocation based on sales and allocation based on floor space.

ALLOCATION OF OVERHEAD BASED ON SALES

This method can be used by a business that has several departments. The allocation of overhead is made according to the sales figures for each department. The department with the largest sales will bear the greatest amount of the overhead expense.

To find the amount of departmental overhead based on sales, find a departmental rate by dividing the department sales by total sales. Multiply the departmental rate by total overhead.

PROBLEM 1

During a slow month, Cottage by the Sea had a total overhead expense of $6,000. The antique department had $2,000 in sales. The craft department had $8,000 in sales (see Figure 26.1).

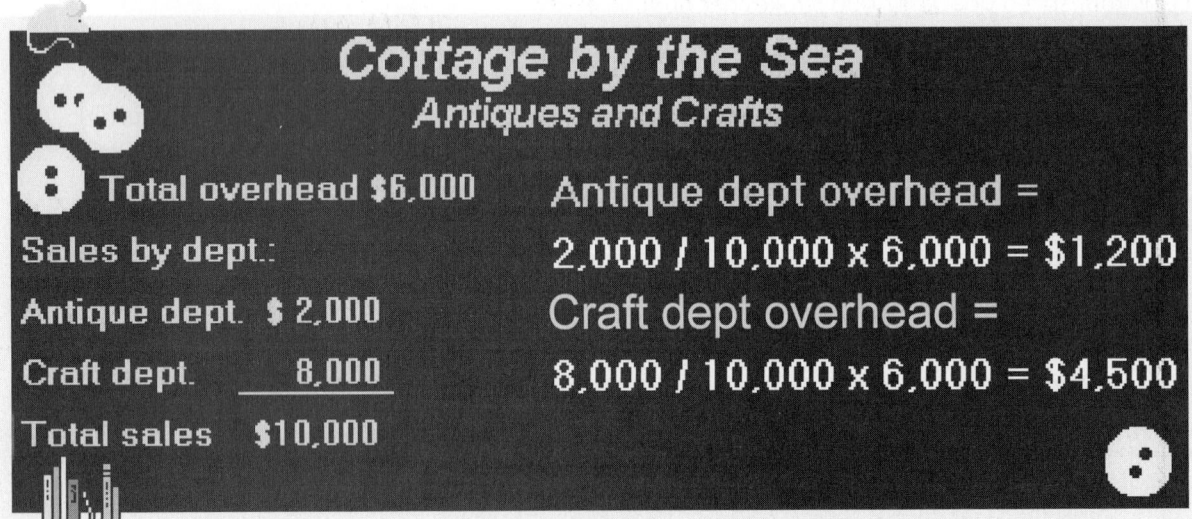

FIGURE 26.1

The pocket calculator procedure is as follows:

1. Calculate total sales.

$$2,000 + 8,000 = \boxed{10,000}$$

2. Calculate the departmental rate for each department. Use the formula Percentage ÷ Base = Rate, where a department's sales figure is the percentage and total sales is the base.
3. Multiply total overhead expense by the departmental rate to find the amount of departmental overhead:

$$2,000 \div 10,000 = \boxed{0.2} \times 6,000 = \boxed{1,200} \quad \text{antique department overhead}$$
$$8,000 \div 10,000 = \boxed{0.8} \times 6,000 = \boxed{4,500} \quad \text{craft department overhead}$$

ALLOCATION OF OVERHEAD BY SQUARE FEET

In this method, each department's share of overhead is calculated according to the number of square feet occupied by the department. To find the amount of departmental overhead based on square feet, find a departmental rate by dividing the number of square feet occupied by a department by total square feet. Multiply the departmental rate by total overhead as shown in Figure 26.2.

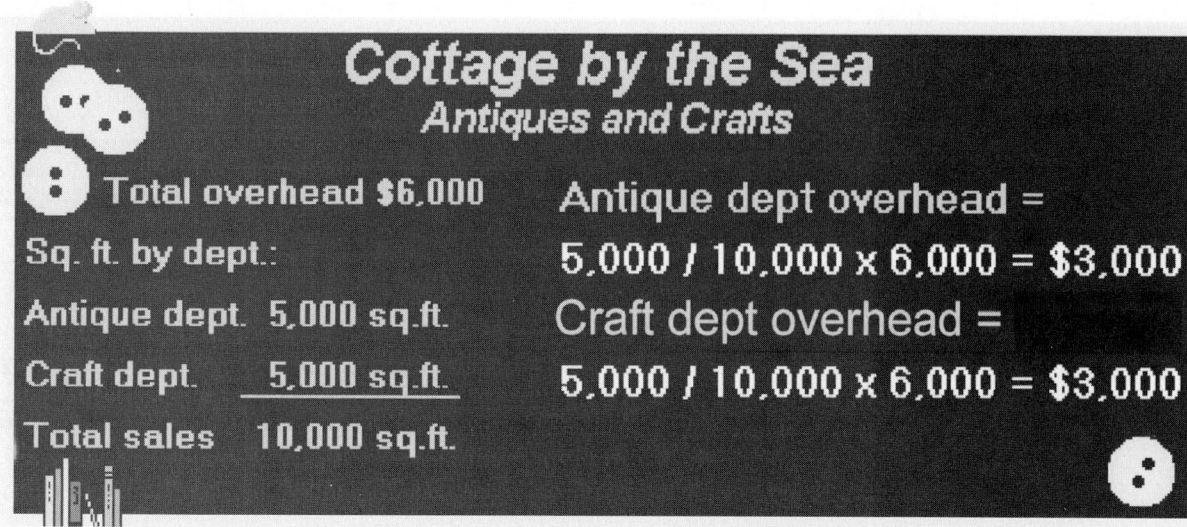

FIGURE 26.2

PROBLEM 2

Calculate departmental overhead based on square feet for Cottage by the Sea. Each of the two departments occupies 5,000 sq ft of floor space.

The pocket calculator procedure is as follows:

1. Calculate total square footage:

$$5,000 + 5,000 = \boxed{10,000}$$

2. Divide departmental square footage by total square footage to find the departmental rate. Because both departments occupy the same amount of space, only one calculation need be made.

3. Multiply by total overhead expense:

$$5,000 \div 10,000 = \boxed{0.5} \quad \text{(departmental rate)}$$

$$\times \ 6,000 = \boxed{\$3,000} \quad \text{(amount of overhead for each department)}$$

ALLOCATION OF OVERHEAD BY SQUARE FEET USING STATED RATES

A business may state departmental rates rather than calculate them. In this case, total overhead is multiplied by the stated departmental rate. The stated rates, when totaled, should equal 100%. The total departmental overhead amounts should equal total overhead expense.

PROBLEM 3

ABC Company had $45,000 in overhead expenses. The stated rates for each department are as follows: Department A, 13%; Department B, 39%; Department C, 48%. Calculate the amount of overhead for which each department is responsible.

Department A	$45,000 \times 0.13 = $5,850
Department B	$45,000 \times 0.39 = $17,550
Department C	$45,000 \times 0.48 = $21,600

Check:

$$13\% + 39\% + 48\% = 100\%$$
$$\$5,580 + \$17,550 + \$21,600 = \$45,000$$

	Pocket Calculator Procedure	Desktop Calculator Procedure: Set Decimal Selector at 2
Department A	MC 45,000 M+ ×13% 5,850	MT 45,000 M+ × 13% 5,850
Department B	MR × 39% 17,550	MS × 39% 17,550
Department C	MR × 48% 21,600 MC	MS × 48% 21,600 MT
Check	5,850 + 17,550 + 21,600 = 45,000	5,850 + 17,550 + 21,600 + T 45,000

Name _____

Class/Section _____

Score (Correct Answers ÷ No. of Assigned Problems) _____

PART 2   *Business Math Skills*

Exercise 1

Compare the amount of overhead each department will pay based on sales versus square feet. The company's total monthly overhead is $8,000.

	Department	Sales ($)	Overhead Based on Sales	Square Feet	Overhead Based on Square Feet
1.	230	15,000		12,500	
2.	231	22,000		16,200	
3.	233	7,000		6,500	
4.	Totals				

Exercise 2

Calculate the amount of departmental overhead using the stated rate based on the square-foot method. The company's total overhead is $72,000. Check your work.

	Department	Stated Rate (%)	Amount of Overhead
5.	A	29	
6.	B	37	
7.	C	18	
8.	D	16	
9.	Totals		

Exercise 3

Calculate the departmental overhead based on sales for a company with an overhead of $14,000. Sales for each department were as follows:

Department	Sales ($)	Departmental Overhead
212	35,000	10.
213	40,100	11.
214	12,500	12.
215	22,000	13.
216	19,000	14.
Totals		15.

PART 3 Review and Practice Using Business Math FUNdamentals

GOAL: Complete 9 of the 10 problems correctly.

Instructions: *Start Business Math FUNdamentals. Complete Tutorial 58 and Drill 46. If you are not satisfied with your score, repeat the drill. Write your scores below.*

Business Math FUNdamentals Drill 46

Today's Date	Score

Name _____

Class/Section _____

Strokes per Minute Score _____

Accuracy Score (Correct Strokes ÷ Total Strokes) _____

PART 4 Desktop Calculator

Exercise 1

One-Minute Addition Timing (0 through 9, Decimal, and Minus Keys, Six-Digit Numbers)

(Optional: Your instructor may wish you to use Touch Key on the computer for all your timings. Check with your instructor before completing this exercise.)

Complete as many of the problems as possible in 1 minute by adding. Work quickly and accurately. The number preceding each closing parenthesis indicates the cumulative number of strokes for problems attempted. For example, if you complete Problems 1 through 3 in 1 minute, your strokes-per-minute score is 249. Optional: 3- and 5-minute timings.

1. 45.8236	2. 452.024	3. 4.76544	4. 8900.76	5. 7.77750	6. 3942.00	7. −6000.12	8. 8.17001
−90.6321	765.781	2.55350	7090.62	6.45500	7685.00	6900.03	7.79003
93.1001	−890.209	−7.46100	8070.41	9.34650	6251.00	−1075.61	−9.16002
83.1657	197.390	1.56700	−7460.83	1.69995	8876.00	3009.37	4.13501
33.4987	356.041	2.97480	−9010.94	4.57359	4210.76	8000.79	8.19044
83.9824	919.819	−1.95009	8040.55	−8.34229	3230.58	2401.00	−7.71004
48.7693	−238.816	9.43006	6400.63	4.67899	3790.03	3068.00	3.77007
1073.68	731.921	7.86100	5700.43	6.45775	3260.04	5002.01	9.23004
−90.3213	535.001	4.37300	8800.81	−8.54900	−2110.06	6079.09	5.31005
43.5629	311.321	5.36600	9899.62	3.34556	−9233.06	5006.72	6.48193
83)	166)	249)	332)	415)	598)	581)	664)

9. 1140.61	10. 576.985	11. −756.987	12. 9400.79	13. 4004.51	14. 565.661	15. 200.905	16. 3420.48
6621.09	346.677	760.122	−9400.79	1300.95	454.012	100.013	−8242.08
5585.31	663.753	−865.455	8200.66	4009.95	−679.867	520.064	4780.06
4115.09	776.988	170.403	4300.50	2072.29	−469.140	−900.014	3483.43
−7742.01	988.565	922.939	9500.55	3007.59	876.442	180.045	9602.45
−8868.43	984.322	359.962	−9500.55	6009.99	865.111	227.128	−1433.31
5159.99	197.759	165.880	6700.72	3005.77	356.341	328.990	2952.42
6662.45	621.002	920.432	7700.50	−2006.59	252.966	−100.053	1678.71
1725.61	−440.005	513.119	9400.95	4006.95	329.854	623.024	3431.24
4137.41	−434.575	233.480	8300.95	−2009.86	952.814	867.711	5461.19
747)	830)	913)	996)	1,079)	1,162)	1,245)	1,328)

CHAPTER 26 *Terminology Review*

Allocation of overhead expense
Overhead expense

Write the correct term next to the appropriate description.

1. _____ Refers to costs such as rent, electricity and other utilities, insurance, taxes, managerial salaries, cleaning, maintenance, and other expenses of the business that are not related to any one department.

2. _____ The division of overhead expense among departments.

Answer true or false.

3. When allocating overhead using stated percents, the square feet of each department is multiplied by the stated rate for the department. T/F _____

4. Allocating overhead based on departmental sales always results in higher overhead per department than when using allocation based on square feet. T/F _____

5. To calculate the departmental rate based on sales, divide departmental sales by total sales. T/F _____

Chapter 26 Review Exercises

Exercise 1

Calculate departmental overhead based on sales. Total overhead expense is $22,000.

Department	Sales ($)	Departmental Overhead
A	15,000	1.
B	24,500	2.
C	18,200	3.
D	22,000	4.
E	31,200	5.
Totals		6.

Exercise 2

Calculate departmental overhead based on square feet. Total overhead expense is $15,000.

Department	Square Feet	Departmental Overhead
A	39,250	7.
B	41,210	8.
C	37,500	9.
D	25,900	10.
E	43,280	11.
Totals		12.

Exercise 3

Calculate departmental overhead based on a stated percent. Total overhead is $12,500.

Department	Rate (%)	Departmental Overhead
A	22	13.
B	24.5	14.
C	18	15.
D	12	16.
E	23.5	17.
Totals		18.

Exercise 4

19. Moore Manufacturing Company had monthly overhead expense of $45,000. Allocation of overhead expense is accomplished according to floor space occupied by each department. Calculate departmental overhead for each: painting 24,220 sq ft, welding 13,350 sq ft, bending 45,000 sq ft, and finishing 20,000 sq ft.

    Painting _____   Welding _____   Bending _____   Finishing _____

20. The PRX store sells prescription pharmaceuticals, seasonal goods, health and beauty items, cards and publications, and school/office supplies. The overhead last month was $36,000. Allocate overhead according to departmental sales.

    Pharmacy sales were $65,000. _____   Seasonal goods sales were $2,000. _____

    Health and beauty sales were $52,000. _____

    Greeting card, book, and magazine sales were $2,000. _____

    Office and school supply sales were $1,500. _____

CHAPTER 27

Financial Statements,
Financial Statement Analysis,
Financial Statement Ratios

PART 1   *Speed and Accuracy Building Using Touch Key*

GOALS: Your speed goal is 12,000 strokes per hour.
Your accuracy target goal range is 95% to 100%.

With each repetition of the drill, try to improve your speed without lowering your accuracy score. If your percent-of-accuracy score falls below 95%, review your finger position and technique. Then try again.

Instructions: *Start Touch Key. Complete Drill 6, 0 through 9, Parts A through E, One-Minute Timings. Write your scores for strokes per hour and percent of accuracy below.*

Touch Key Drill 6—The 0 through 9, Decimal, and Minus Keys, Five-Digit Numbers (Mixed), One-Minute Timings

Today's Date	Strokes per Hour	Percent of Accuracy
A.		
B.		
C.		
D.		
E.		

PART 2   *Business Math Skills*

FINANCIAL STATEMENTS

Financial statements are used to report a company's income and financial condition. Financial statements are audited and, for public corporations, are available to the general public. Analysis of the financial statements helps the owners and/or investors make business decisions. Companies may use financial statements of other companies for comparison.

Financial statements that will be discussed in this chapter are the balance sheet and the income statement. Also to be discussed are methods for analyzing financial statements, including horizontal and vertical analyses and ratios.

BALANCE SHEET

A **balance sheet** lists the assets, liabilities, and for a single proprietorship, the amount of owner's equity *on a specific date*. **Assets** are cash and other items of value owned by a business such as accounts receivable, merchandise inventory, furniture, and equipment. **Liabilities** are amounts owed by the business such as accounts payable and notes payable. A **single proprietorship** means the business has one owner. Other types of ownership include partnerships and stockholdings. The difference between the assets and the liabilities of a company is the owner's equity. **Owner's equity** or **stockholders' equity** is the amount of ownership or owner's rights to the business. Notice the relationships in the formulas in Figure 27.1.

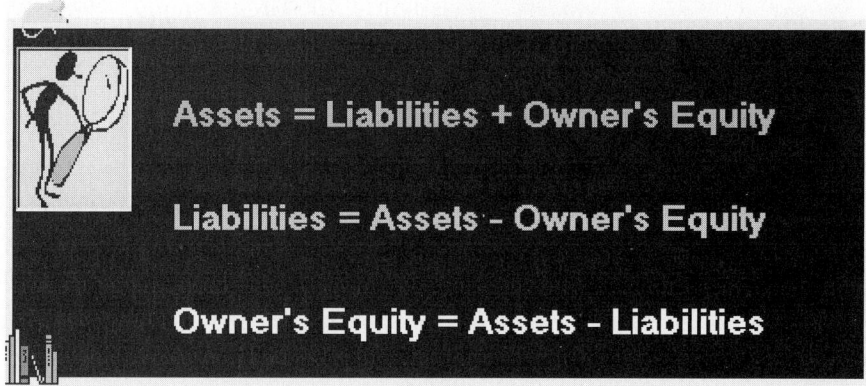

FIGURE 27.1

INCOME STATEMENT

An **income statement** shows the net income or loss of a business *over a period of time*, such as 1 month, one quarter, or 1 year. An income statement lists the **revenue**, which may consist of sales, other revenue such as service fees, or a combination of both. An income statement also lists cost of goods sold (if any), operating expenses, and net income or loss for the period. An example of an income statement for a business selling goods would include

$$\text{Gross Sales} - \text{Returns} = \text{Net Sales}$$
$$\text{Net Sales} - \text{Cost of Goods Sold*} = \text{Gross Profit}$$
$$\text{Gross Profit} - \text{Operating Expenses} = \text{Net Income or Loss}$$

Note:

$$\text{Beginning Inventory} + \text{Purchases} - \text{Ending Inventory} = \text{Cost of Goods Sold}$$

The term *gross,* when used before another term such as sales or profit, means "before adjustments are made." The amount of **gross sales** is the total sales amount before returns or other adjustments are subtracted. **Gross profit** is the total profit before expenses are subtracted.

VERTICAL ANALYSIS OF A BALANCE SHEET

To perform a **vertical analysis of a balance sheet**, find the percent of each item to the total assets (Figure 27.2). For example, an asset such as cash would be divided by the amount of total assets. In this way cash and all other line items are compared to total assets. You may want to use the formula $P \div B = R$, where total assets is the base, the amount being compared to the base is the percentage (cash), and the resulting percent is the rate. Or you may want to remember this procedure as writing a ratio for the item and its base and converting it to a percent.

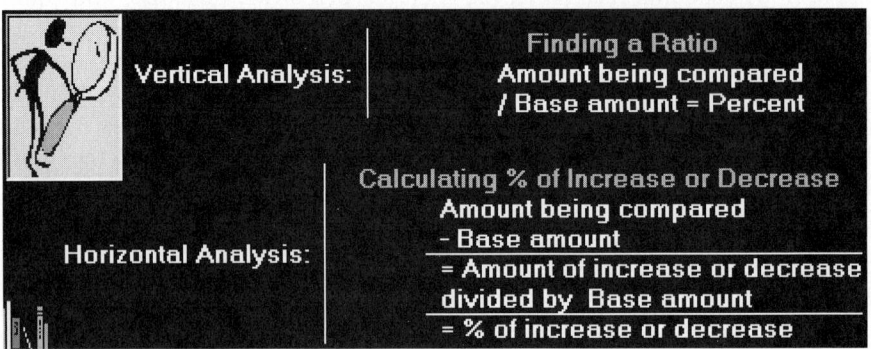

FIGURE 27.2

Refer to the balance sheet in Figure 27.3. The third column in the figure has been added to show the percents for each item after a vertical analysis has been performed. Each line item on the balance sheet has been divided by the amount of total assets.

Example: Cash ($2,000) ÷ Total Assets ($65,000) = 0.031 or 3.1%
Example: Accounts payable ($15,000) ÷ Total Assets ($65,000)
= 0.231 or 23.1%

Note: The percent for total assets as well as total liabilities and owner's equity is 100% ($65,000 ÷ $65,000 = 1 or 100%).

Check: When added, the total of the percents in the assets section should equal 100%. A slight difference may occur due to rounding. The total of percents for the liabilities and for the owner's equity should equal 100%. (Do not include percents calculated for subtotals such as total liabilities.)

Sea to Sea Cushions
Balance Sheet   December 31, 2000

Assets:	Cash	2,000	3.1%
	Accounts Receivable	8,000	12.3%
	Merchandise Inventory	20,000	30.8%
	Equipment	35,000	53.8%
Total Assets		65,000	100%
Liabilities:	Accounts Payable	15,000	23.1%
	Note Payable	20,000	30.8%
Total Liabilities		35,000	53.9%
Owner's Equity:	John Sea, Cap.	30,000	46.2%
Total Liabilities and Owner's Equity		65,000	100%

FIGURE 27.3

POCKET CALCULATOR AND DESKTOP CALCULATOR PROCEDURES

To perform a vertical analysis of the balance sheet shown in Figure 27.3:

Place the base in memory because it will be used many times. The memory recall key is used on the pocket calculator, and the memory subtotal key is used on the desktop calculator to display the total that has been stored in memory. On the desktop, set the decimal selector on F, and use the MT key to clear memory. Keys specific to the desktop calculator are shown in parentheses. For example, the pocket calculator key to clear memory and the desktop calculator key to clear memory are shown as MC(MT). On both machines, use the percent key so the answer will display as a percent rather than a decimal number.

Clear memory if necessary. Round answers to tenths.

$$\text{MC(MT) } 65{,}000 \text{ M+ } 2{,}000 \div \text{MR(MS) \% } \boxed{3.1}$$
$$8{,}000 \div \text{MR(MS) \% } \boxed{12.3}$$
$$20{,}000 \div \text{MR(MS) \% } \boxed{30.8}$$
$$35{,}000 \div \text{MR(MS) \% } \boxed{53.8}$$
$$65{,}000 \div \text{MR(MS) \% } \boxed{100}$$
$$15{,}000 \div \text{MR(MS) \% } \boxed{23.1}$$
$$20{,}000 \div \text{MR(MS) \% } \boxed{30.8}$$
$$35{,}000 \div \text{MR(MS) \% } \boxed{53.9}$$
$$30{,}000 \div \text{MR(MS) \% } \boxed{46.2}$$
$$65{,}000 \div \text{MR(MS) \% } \boxed{100}$$

Pocket Calculator Check

$$3.1 + 12.3 + 30.8 + 53.8 = \boxed{100}$$
$$23.1 + 30.8 + 46.2 = \boxed{100.1}$$

Desktop Calculator Check

$$3.1 + 12.3 + 30.8 + 53.8 + \text{T } \boxed{100}$$
$$23.1 + 30.8 + 46.2 + \text{T } \boxed{100.1}$$

VERTICAL ANALYSIS OF AN INCOME STATEMENT

Items on an income statement are compared to net sales when performing a **vertical analysis of an income statement**. The formula $P \div B = R$ can be used, where P is the amount of each item to be compared to the base and B is net sales. The resulting percent is R.

Note: Because the amount of net sales is the base, 100% is entered in the percent column.

Example: Purchases ($120,000) ÷ Net Sales ($245,000) = 49% (rounded)

The importance of analysis cannot be overstated. Note the percent of operating expenses to net sales. If it is determined that 28.2% is too high, efforts will be made in the near future to decrease expenses. Each decrease in expense is an increase in profit.

POCKET CALCULATOR AND DESKTOP CALCULATOR PROCEDURES

Perform a vertical analysis on the income statement shown in Figure 27.4 using memory and the percent key. On the desktop calculator, set the decimal selector on F, and use the MT key to clear memory and the MS key to display the total stored in memory. Keys specific to the desktop calculator are shown in parentheses. For example, the pocket calculator key to clear memory and the desktop calculator key to clear memory are shown as MC(MT).

$$\text{MC(MT) } 245{,}000 \text{ M+ } 250{,}000 \div \text{MR(MS) } \% \boxed{102}$$
$$5{,}000 \div \text{MR(MS) } \% \boxed{2}$$
$$245{,}000 \div \text{MR(MS) } \% \boxed{100}$$
$$18{,}000 \div \text{MR(MS) } \% \boxed{7.3}$$
$$120{,}000 \div \text{MR(MS) } \% \boxed{49}$$
$$20{,}000 \div \text{MR(MS) } \% \boxed{8.2}$$
$$110{,}000 \div \text{MR(MS) } \% \boxed{48.2}$$
$$127{,}000 \div \text{MR(MS) } \% \boxed{51.8}$$
$$69{,}000 \div \text{MR(MS) } \% \boxed{28.2}$$
$$58{,}000 \div \text{MR(MS) } \% \boxed{23.7}$$

Sea to Sea Cushions		
Income Statement For Year Ended December 31, 2000		
Gross Sales	250,000	102%
Less Sales Returns	5,000	2%
Net Sales	245,000	100%
Inventory, Jan. 1, 2000	18,000	7.3%
Purchases	120,000	49%
Less Inventory, Dec. 31, 2000	20,000	8.2%
Cost of goods sold	118,000	48.2%
Gross profit	127,000	51.8%
Operating expenses	69,000	28.2%
Net Income	58,000	23.7%

FIGURE 27.4

Pocket Calculator Check

The percents for cost of goods sold and gross profit should equal 100%:

$$48.2 + 51.8 = \boxed{100}$$

Desktop calculator check:

$$48.2 + 51.8 + \text{T} \boxed{100}$$

The percents for cost of goods sold, operating expenses, and net income should equal 100%:

$$48.2 + 28.2 + 23.7 = \boxed{100.1}$$
$$48.2 + 28.2 + 23.7 + \text{T} \boxed{100.1}$$

HORIZONTAL ANALYSIS

When performing a **horizontal analysis of a financial statement**, like items for two periods are compared by calculating the percent of increase or decrease. Percent of decrease (if any) should be shown in parentheses. A **comparative balance sheet** lists line items and amounts for two periods as shown in Figure 27.5. The balance sheet figures for years 2000 and

Sea to Sea Cushions Comparative Balance Sheet	Year 2000	Year 1999	Amt. of Inc./Dec.	% of Inc./Dec.
Assets: Cash	2,000	2,000	-0-	-0-
Accounts Receivable	8,000	5,000	3,000	60%
Merchandise Inventory	20,000	18,000	2,000	11.1%
Equipment	35,000	35,000	-0-	-0-
Total Assets	65,000	60,000	5,000	8.3%
Liabilities: Accounts Payable	15,000	12,000	3,000	25%
Note Payable	20,000	25,000	(5,000)	(20%)
Total Liabilities	35,000	37,000	(2,000)	(5.4%)
Owner's Equity: John Sea, Cap.	30,000	23,000	7,000	30.4%
Total Liabilities and Owner's Equity	65,000	60,000	5,000	8.3%

FIGURE 27.5

1999 are shown. Also included are columns for the amount of increase and/or decrease (increase/decrease) and for the percent of increase/decrease for each line item.

The method for calculating percent of increase/decrease (discussed in Chapter 13) is to:

1. Subtract the figure for the earlier year from the figure for the later year to find the amount of increase/decrease.
2. Divide the amount of increase/decrease by the earlier year (which is called the base year) to find the percent of increase/decrease. Using the figures for accounts receivable in Figure 27.5, the figures for 1999 are the bases. Subtract the base ($5,000) from $8,000. The amount of increase is $3,000. Divide $3,000 by the base ($5,000). The result (0.6) converted to a percent is a percent of increase of 60%.

POCKET CALCULATOR AND DESKTOP CALCULATOR PROCEDURES

To perform a horizontal analysis on the balance sheet shown in Figure 27.5 begin each item comparison by placing the base (the amount for the earlier year) in memory. Be sure to clear memory before comparing the next line item. Use the percent key to display the percent instead of a decimal number.

On the desktop calculator, set the decimal selector on F, and use the MT key to clear memory and the MS key to display the total stored in memory. Keys specific to the desktop calculator are shown in parentheses. For example, the pocket calculator key to clear memory and the desktop calculator key to clear memory are shown as MC(MT).

MC(MT) 2,000 − 2,000 = 0   There is no difference or percent of increase/decrease for this item

5,000 M+ 8,000 − MR(MS) =   Be sure to clear memory
3,000 ÷ MR(MS) % 60 MC(MT)

18,000 M+ 20,000 − MR(MS) = 2,000 ÷ MR(MS) % 11.1 MC(MT)

35,000 − 35,000 = 0   There is no difference or percent of increase/decrease

60,000 M+ 65,000 − MR(MS) = 5,000 ÷ MR(MS) % 8.3 MC(MT)

12,000 M+ 15,000 − MR(MS) = 3,000 ÷ MR(MS) % 25 MC(MT)

25,000 M+ 20,000 − MR(MS) =   The amount has decreased; thus
−5,000 ÷ MR(MS) % −20 MC(MT)   the resulting percent of decrease
                                            (−20%); the amount of decrease
                                            and the percent of decrease should
                                            both be written in parentheses.

37,000 M+ 35,000 − MR(MS) = −2,000 ÷ MR(MS) % −5.4 MC(MT)

23,000 M+ 30,000 − MR(MS) = 7,000 ÷ MR(MS) % 30.4 MC(MT)

60,000 M+ 65,000 − MR(MS) = 5,000 ÷ MR(MS) % 8.3 MC(MT)

HORIZONTAL ANALYSIS OF AN INCOME STATEMENT

The procedure for completing a **horizontal analysis of an income statement** is the same as for a balance sheet. Items on the income statement are compared for two different periods of time. The percent of increase/decrease is computed. Figure 27.6 shows an income statement on which the amount of increase/decrease and the percent of increase/decrease has been calculated.

Sea to Sea Cushions Comparative Income Statement	Year 2000	Year 1999	Amt. of Inc./Dec.	% of Inc./Dec.
Gross Sales	250,000	235,000	15,000	6.4%
Less Sales Returns	5,000	4,000	1,000	25%
Net Sales	245,000	231,000	14,000	6.1%
Beginning Inventory	18,000	22,000	(4,000)	18.2%
Purchases	120,000	115,000	5,000	4.3%
Less Ending Inventory	20,000	18,000	2,000	11.1%
Cost of goods sold	118,000	119,000	(1,000)	(0.8%)
Gross profit	127,000	111,000	16,000	14.4%
Operating expenses	69,000	65,800	3,200	4.9%
Net Income	58,000	45,200	12,800	28.3%

FIGURE 27.6

RATIOS

In addition to the vertical and horizontal analyses of financial statements, certain line items in the financial statements can be compared to each other to provide further information to decision makers in the form of **ratios**. How does a businessperson interpret a ratio? One of the ways is to compare the ratio with that of other businesses in a similar industry by looking at their financial statements. Publications such as *Standard and Poor's 500 Guide* (available at public libraries) list certain ratios for the top 500 companies. From these comparisons a manager can determine, for example, that inventory turnover for his or her business is higher than the "industry standard." He or she may then wish to take steps to lower the inventory turnover (more on inventory turnover later).

Recall from Chapter 24 that ratios are usually presented in the form 2:1, read two to one. The ratio may be converted to a percent such as 1:5 = 20%. These calculations have been traditionally referred to as ratios even though many are depicted as percents. Some of the ratios used for financial analysis purposes are shown below along with some of their uses.

TYPES OF RATIOS

The **working capital ratio** (Figure 27.7)—also known as the **current ratio**—is used to help determine the ability of a business to pay its creditors. Cash and assets that can be turned into cash within 1 year are **current assets**. Debts due within 1 year are **current liabilities**. Current assets minus current liabilities equals **working capital**. Current assets divided by current liabilities equals the working capital ratio.

The **acid-test ratio** (Figure 27.8), also known as the **quick ratio**, is similar to the current ratio, but, as its name implies, it is more stringent. It is used to help determine the ability of a business to pay its creditors quickly. In this ratio only cash and current assets that

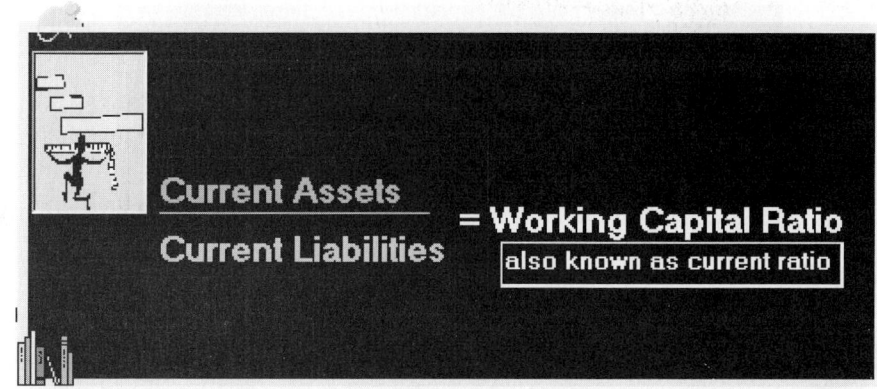

FIGURE 27.7

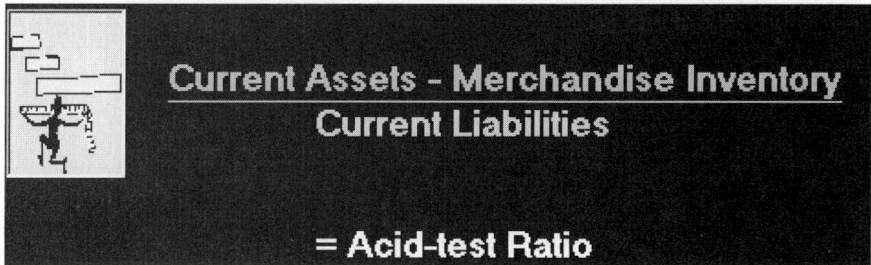

FIGURE 27.8

can be turned into cash quickly (such as accounts receivable, marketable securities, and notes receivable) are used. The asset merchandise inventory is not used. The difference of current assets minus merchandise inventory divided by current liabilities equals the acid-test ratio.

The **ratio of owner's or stockholders' equity to total liabilities** (Figure 27.9) is used to help determine the ability of the owner's or stockholders' equity to cover the debts of the business. Owner's or stockholders' equity is divided by total liabilities to find the ratio of owner's equity to total liabilities.

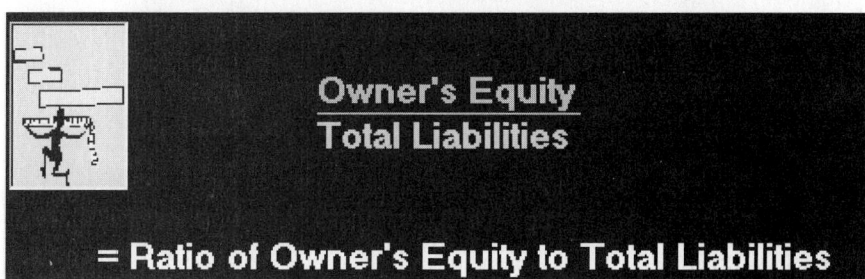

FIGURE 27.9

The **ratio of assets to owner's or stockholders' equity** (Figure 27.10) is used to help determine whether total assets can cover the owner's or stockholders' equity in a business. Divide total assets by owner's or stockholders' equity to find the ratio of assets to owner's or stockholders' equity.

The **ratio of accounts receivable to net sales** (Figure 27.11), when converted to a percent, indicates the percent of sales (or revenue) that have not yet been paid by customers. Divide accounts receivable by net sales to find the ratio of accounts receivable to net sales.

$$\frac{\text{Total Assets}}{\text{Owner's Equity}}$$

$$= \text{Ratio of Assets to Owner's Equity}$$

FIGURE 27.10

$$\frac{\text{Accounts Receivable}}{\text{Net Sales}}$$

$$= \text{Ratio of Accounts Receivable to Net Sales}$$

FIGURE 27.11

The **inventory turnover ratio** (Figure 27.12) indicates how many times merchandise inventory has been sold during a period of time. This valuable information is compared to that of other businesses in the same industry and can be used to make decisions concerning inventory. Turnover can also be calculated on specific items to find how fast those items are selling. To calculate inventory turnover:

1. Add the amounts of the beginning inventory and the ending inventory (from the income statement). Divide the total by two to find the average inventory.
2. Divide the amount of cost of goods sold (from the income statement) by the average inventory calculated in step 1 to find the inventory turnover.

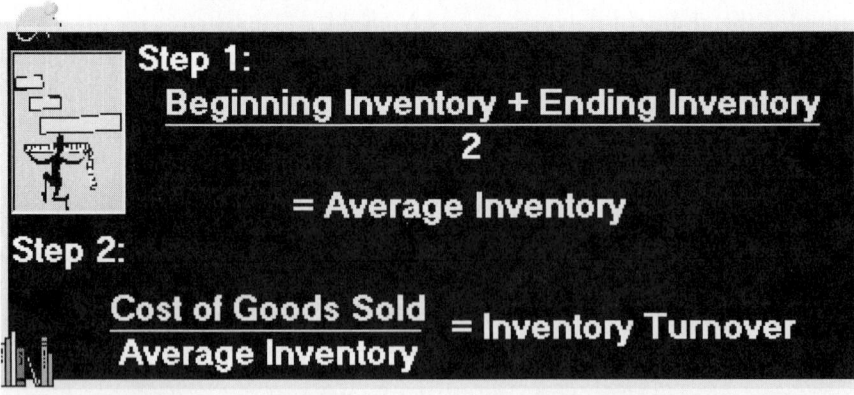

Step 1:
$$\frac{\text{Beginning Inventory + Ending Inventory}}{2}$$
$$= \text{Average Inventory}$$

Step 2:
$$\frac{\text{Cost of Goods Sold}}{\text{Average Inventory}} = \text{Inventory Turnover}$$

FIGURE 27.12

PROBLEM

An income statement for last month showed the beginning inventory to be $50,000, the ending inventory to be $40,000, and the cost of goods sold to be $90,000. Calculate the inventory turnover (Figure 27.13):

$$\$50,000 + \$40,000 = \$90,000$$

$$\$90,000 \div 2 = \$45,000 \quad \text{Average Inventory}$$

$$(\text{Cost of Goods Sold}) \ \$90,000 \div \$45,000 = 2:1 \quad \text{Rate of Inventory Turnover}$$

Step 1:

$$\frac{(50,000 + 40,000)}{2} = \$45,000$$

Step 2:

$$\frac{90,000}{45,000} = \text{2:1 Rate of Turnover}$$

FIGURE 27.13

The **operating ratio** (Figure 27.14) indicates whether a business has the ability to cover cost of goods sold and operating expenses with net sales (or net revenue). Total the cost of goods sold and operating expenses. Divide the total by the amount of net sales to find the operating ratio.

$$\frac{\text{COGS + Operating Expenses}}{\text{Net Sales}}$$

$$= \text{Operating Ratio}$$

FIGURE 27.14

The **gross profit margin ratio** (Figure 27.15) indicates the average difference between cost of goods sold and selling prices represented by the net sales amount. To calculate this ratio, subtract the cost of goods sold from the net sales to find the gross profit from sales, or take the gross profit from the income statement. Divide the gross profit from sales by the net sales (or net revenue) to find the gross profit margin ratio.

$$\frac{\text{Net Sales} - \text{COGS}}{\text{Net Sales}}$$

$$-\text{or-} \quad \frac{\text{Gross Profit from Sales}}{\text{Net Sales}}$$

$$= \text{Gross Profit Margin Ratio}$$

FIGURE 27.15

The **asset turnover ratio** (Figure 27.16) compares the net sales (or net revenue) to the average total assets. To find the average total assets, add the total assets for the base year and the total assets for the comparison year from a comparative balance sheet and then divide the total of the assets by two. Divide the net sales (net revenue) taken from the income statement for the comparative year by the average total assets to find the asset turnover ratio.

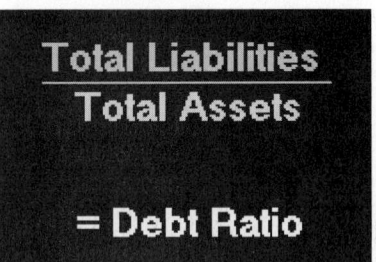

$$\frac{\text{Net Sales}}{\text{Average Total Assets}}$$

$$= \text{Asset Turnover Ratio}$$

FIGURE 27.16

PROBLEM

Calculate the asset turnover ratio using the balance sheet data shown in Figure 27.5 and the income statement data shown in Figure 27.6.

Add the total assets for 1999 ($60,000) and for 2000 ($65,000). Divide the total ($125,000) by two to find the average total assets ($62,500). Set up and calculate the ratio of the average total assets to the net sales for 2000 ($245,000):

$$\frac{62,500}{245,000}$$

The ratio is 1:4 (rounded). The percent of average total assets to net sales (62,500 ÷ 245,000) is 25.5% (rounded).

The **debt ratio** (Figure 27.17) indicates the indebtedness of a company for each 1 dollar of assets. Divide the total liabilities by the total assets to find the debt ratio.

$$\frac{\text{Total Liabilities}}{\text{Total Assets}}$$

$$= \text{Debt Ratio}$$

FIGURE 27.17

Name _____

Class/Section _____

Score (Correct Answers ÷ No. of Assigned Problems) _____

PART 2   *Business Math Skills*

Exercise 1

Complete a horizontal analysis on the following comparative balance sheet. Round percent answers to tenths.

Jostens Comparative Balance Sheet
December 31, 2002, and December 31, 2003

	Balance Sheet		Amount of Increase or Decrease	Percent of Increase or Decrease
	2002	2003		
Assets				
Current assets				
Cash	$50,000	$56,000		1. _____
Accounts receivable	25,000	30,000		2. _____
Merchandise inventory	30,000	35,000		3. _____
Total current assets	$105,000	$121,000		4. _____
Land, buildings, and equipment				
Land	80,000	80,000		5. _____
Buildings	250,000	250,000		6. _____
Equipment	60,000	50,000		7. _____
Total land, buildings, and equipment	390,000	380,000		8. _____
Total assets	$495,000	$501,000		9. _____
Liabilities and owner's equity				
Current liabilities				
Accounts payable	$28,000	$25,000		10. _____
Total current liabilities	28,000	25,000		11. _____
Long-term liabilities				
Note payable	10,000	9,000		12. _____
Mortgage payable	200,000	190,000		13. _____
Total long-term liabilities	210,000	199,000		14. _____
Total liabilities	$238,000	$224,000		15. _____
Owner's equity				
M. J. Josten, capital	257,000	277,000		16. _____
Total liabilities and owner's equity	$495,000	$501,000		17. _____

Exercise 2

Complete a vertical analysis on the following balance sheet. Round percent answers to tenths.

Jostens Balance Sheet
December 31, 2002

Cash	$50,000	18. _____
Accounts receivable	25,000	19. _____
Merchandise inventory	30,000	20. _____
Total current assets	$105,000	21. _____
Land	80,000	22. _____
Buildings	250,000	23. _____
Equipment	60,000	24. _____
Total land, buildings, and equipment	390,000	25. _____
Total assets	$495,000	26. _____
Accounts payable	$28,000	27. _____
Total current liabilities	28,000	28. _____
Note payable	10,000	29. _____
Mortgage payable	200,000	30. _____
Total long-term liabilities	210,000	31. _____
Total liabilities	$238,000	32. _____
M. J. Josten, capital	257,000	33. _____
Total liabilities and owner's equity	$495,000	34. _____

Exercise 3

Complete a vertical analysis of the following income statement. Round percent answers to tenths.

Jostens Income Statement
Month Ended April 30, 2003

Gross sales	$55,000	%	35.	_____
Less returns	1,250		36.	_____
Net sales	53,750		37.	_____
Inventory, April 1, 2003	25,000		38.	_____
Purchases	17,000		39.	_____
Less inventory, April 30, 2003	22,000		40.	_____
Cost of goods sold	20,000		41.	_____
Gross profit	33,750		42.	_____
Operating expenses	9,000		43.	_____
Net income	$24,750		44.	_____

Exercise 4

Complete a horizontal analysis on the following income statement. Round percent answers to tenths.

Jostens Comparative Income Statement
Months Ending March 31, 2003, and April 30, 2003

	March 31, 2003	April 30, 2003	Amount of Increase or Decrease	Percent of Increase or Decrease
Gross sales	$57,500	$55,000		45. _____
Less returns	2,200	1,250		46. _____
Net sales	55,300	53,750		47. _____
Beginning inventory	18,000	25,000		48. _____
Purchases	24,500	17,000		49. _____
Ending inventory	17,200	22,000		50. _____
Cost of goods sold	25,300	20,000		51. _____
Gross profit	30,000	33,750		52. _____
Operating expenses	12,000	9,000		53. _____
Net income	$18,000	$24,750		54. _____

PART 3   *Review and Practice Using Business Math FUNdamentals*

GOAL: Complete 9 of the 10 problems correctly.

Instructions: *Start Business Math FUNdamentals. Complete Tutorials 59 and 60 and Drills 47 and 48. If you are not satisfied with your score, repeat the drill. Write your scores below.*

Business Math FUNdamentals Drill 47

Today's Date	Score

Business Math FUNdamentals Drill 48

Today's Date	Score

Name _____

Class/Section _____

Strokes per Minute Score _____

Accuracy Score (Correct Strokes ÷ Total Strokes) _____

 PART 4   *Desktop Calculator*

Exercise 1

One-Minute Addition Timing (0 through 9 Keys, One- to Five-Digit Numbers, Mixed)

(Optional: Your instructor may wish you to use Touch Key on the computer for all your timings. Check with your instructor before completing this exercise.)

Complete as many of the problems as possible in 1 minute by adding. Work quickly and accurately. The number preceding each closing parenthesis indicates the cumulative number of strokes for problems attempted. For example, if you complete Problems 1 through 5 in 1 minute, your strokes-per-minute score is 250. If you complete all the problems, your strokes-per-minute score is 260.

1. 347.55	2. 910.24	3. 65.544	4. 2,900.6	5. 77.850	6. 69.200	7. 51.300	8. 31.001
758.5	576.9	51.35	790.2	45	28	60	61
237	462	800	701	650	123	100	318
57	39	15	64	995.6	−487.4	−930.7	−813.1
735.9	886.4	972.4	510.4	−5	8	5	4
8	7	−1	−3	229.9	223.6	451.9	671.2
−9.093	164.7	240.3	400.3	67	57	62	47
706	921	764	100	775	636	149	383
92	−96	30	88	900.3	514.3	230.7	238.5
63.870	11.009	35.300	79.100	4,556.8	3,250.6	9,142.9	2,468.3
50)	100)	150)	200)	250)	300)	350)	400)

9. 94.140	10. 7,690.1	11. 756.98	12. 477.9	13. 43.45	14. 49.661	15. −516.09	16. −9.9504
−86.64	44.26	22.22	153.1	29.99	78	13	26
585	361	455	120	995	885	738	400
76.61	−776.9	−170.4	135.3	27.22	9.655	9.014	4.870
6	5	9	−1	−3	−40	−43	−60
98	46	25	13	60	1	3	8
99.95	3.765	2.658	176.7	7.577	6.741	628.3	989.5
884	221	432	722	659	962	592	787
56	25	19	95	45	59.85	697.2	83.64
79.937	35.575	43.398	3,249.5	20.000	6.014	610.1	95.42
450)	500)	550)	600)	650)	700)	750)	800)

17. 911.55	18. 320.24	19. 41.544	20. 2,341.6	21. 29.850	22. 11.200	23. 42.300	24. 87.001
723.5	545.9	78.35	227.2	95	76	77	44
197	792	499	981	850	572	186	876
59	19	18	57	344.6	−981.4	−362.7	−459.1
125.9	236.4	312.4	597.4	−5	8	4	9
8	2	−6	−1	280.9	423.6	289.9	572.2
−9.643	927.7	255.3	226.3	87	17	50	27
772	331	831	579	775	236	150	588
33	−66	25	79	944.3	535.3	250.7	913.5
953.872	11.326	35.350	34.650	4,932.8	3,990.6	9,566.9	2,566.3
850)	900)	950)	1,000)	1,050)	1,200)	1,250)	1,300)

CHAPTER 27 *Terminology Review*

Acid-test ratio

Assets

Asset turnover ratio

Balance sheet

Comparative balance sheet

Current assets

Current liabilities

Current ratio

Debt ratio

Financial statements

Gross profit

Gross profit margin ratio

Gross sales

Horizontal analysis of a financial statement

Horizontal analysis of an income statement

Income statement

Inventory turnover ratio

Liabilities

Operating ratio

Owner's equity

Quick ratio

Ratio of assets to owner's or stockholders' equity

Ratio of owner's or stockholders' equity to total liabilities

Ratio of accounts receivable to net sales

Ratios

Revenue

Single proprietorship

Stockholders' equity

Vertical analysis of a balance sheet

Vertical analysis of an income statement

Working capital

Working capital ratio

Write the correct term next to the appropriate description.

1. _____ Total liabilities divided by total assets.

2. _____ Sales, service fees, or a combination of both.

3. _____ Total sales amount before returns or other adjustments are subtracted.

4. _____ Total profit before expenses are subtracted.

5. _____ Used to help determine the ability of a business to pay its creditors.

6. _____ When converted to a percent, indicates the percent of sales (or revenue) that has not yet been paid by customers.

7. _____ Lists the assets, liabilities, and for a single proprietorship, the amount of owner's equity *on a specific date*.

8. _____ Cash and other items of value owned by a business.

9. _____ Calculating the percent of increase or decrease for like items for two periods.

10. _____ Lists line items and amounts for two periods.

11. _____ Amounts owed by the business.

12. _____ A business with one owner.

13. _____ Shows the net income or loss of a business *over a period of time,* such as 1 month, 1 quarter, or 1 year.

14. _____ Compares net sales (or net revenue) to the average of total assets.

15. _____ Used to report a company's income and financial condition.

16. _____ Finding the percent of each item on the balance sheet to total assets.

17. _____ Comparing items on an income statement to net sales.

18. _____ Items for two periods of time on the income statement are compared.

19. _____ What persons in business compare with those of other businesses in the same industry to make better informed decisions.

20. _____ Cash and assets that can be turned into cash within 1 year.

21. _____ Debts due within 1 year are current liabilities.

22. _____ Current assets minus current liabilities.

23. _____ Current assets divided by current liabilities.

24. _____ Current assets minus merchandise inventory, divided by current liabilities.

25. _____ The amount of owner's rights to the business.

26. _____ Used to help determine the ability of the owner's or stockholders' equity to cover the debts of the business.

27. _____ Indicates how many times merchandise inventory has been sold during a period of time.

28. _____ Indicates whether a business has the ability to cover cost of goods sold and operating expenses with net sales (or net revenue). Given by (cost of goods sold plus operating expenses) divided by net sales.

29. _____ Indicates the average difference between cost of goods sold and net sales.

Chapter 27 Review Exercises

Exercise 1

Perform a horizontal analysis of the following comparative balance sheet.

ABC Company
Comparative Balance Sheet
December 31, 2002, and December 31, 2003

	Balance Sheet		Amount of Increase or Decrease	Percent of Increase or Decrease
	2002	2003		
Assets				
Current assets				
Cash	$150,000	$180,000	1. _____	
Accounts receivable	65,000	75,000	2. _____	
Merchandise inventory	80,000	103,000	3. _____	
Total current assets	$295,000	$358,000	4. _____	
Land, buildings, and equipment				
Land	180,000	185,000	5. _____	
Buildings	440,000	446,000	6. _____	
Equipment	960,000	1,050,000	7. _____	
Total land, buildings, and equipment	1,580,000	1,681,000	8. _____	
Total assets	$1,875,000	$2,039,000	9. _____	
Liabilities and owner's equity				
Current liabilities				
Accounts payable	$128,000	$175,000	10. _____	
Total current liabilities	128,000	175,000	11. _____	
Long-term liabilities				
Note payable	90,000	80,000	12. _____	
Mortgage payable	210,000	170,000	13. _____	
Total long-term liabilities	$300,000	$250,000	14. _____	
Total liabilities	$238,000	$425,000	15. _____	
Owner's equity				
Mark Miller, capital	1,637,000	1,614,000	16. _____	
Total liabilities and owner's equity	$1,875,000	$2,039,000	17. _____	

Exercise 2

Perform a horizontal analysis of the following comparative income statement.

ABC Company
Comparative Income Statement
Years Ending December 31, 2002, and December 31, 2003

	December 31, 2002	December 31, 2003	Amount of Increase or Decrease	Percent of Increase or Decrease
Gross sales	$1,187,500	$1,250,000		18. _____
Less returns	116,200	112,000		19. _____
Net sales	1,071,300	1,138,000		20. _____
Beginning inventory	138,000	155,200		21. _____
Purchases	642,100	670,000		22. _____
Ending inventory	155,200	190,000		23. _____
Cost of goods sold	624,900	635,200		24. _____
Gross profit	446,400	502,800		25. _____
Operating expenses	199,000	187,000		26. _____
Net income	$247,400	$315,800		27. _____

Exercise 3

Perform a vertical analysis of the following balance sheet.

ABC Company Balance Sheet
December 31, 2003

Cash	$180,000	28. _____
Accounts receivable	75,000	29. _____
Merchandise inventory	103,000	30. _____
Total current assets	$358,000	31. _____
Land	185,000	32. _____
Buildings	446,000	33. _____
Equipment	1,050,000	34. _____
Total land, buildings, and equipment	$1,681,000	35. _____
Total assets	$2,039,000	36. _____
Accounts payable	$175,000	37. _____
Total current liabilities	175,000	38. _____
Note payable	80,000	39. _____
Mortgage payable	170,000	40. _____
Total long-term liabilities	$250,000	41. _____
Total liabilities	$425,000	42. _____
Mark Miller, capital	1,614,000	43. _____
Total liabilities and owner's equity	$2,039,000	44. _____

Exercise 4

Perform a vertical analysis of the following income statement.

ABC Company
Income Statement
Year Ended December 31, 2003

		%	
Gross sales	$1,250,000		45. _____
Less returns	112,000		46. _____
Net sales	1,138,000		47. _____
Inventory, December 1, 2003	155,200		48. _____
Purchases	670,000		49. _____
Less inventory, December 31, 2003	190,000		50. _____
Cost of goods sold	635,200		51. _____
Gross profit	502,800		52. _____
Operating expenses	187,000		53. _____
Net income	$315,800		54. _____

Exercise 5

55. For the calendar year 2003, the ABC Company had beginning inventory of $225,000, an ending inventory of $195,000, and a cost of goods sold of $1,203,000. Calculate the company's inventory turnover for 2003. _____

56. Using the balance sheet shown in Exercise 3, calculate the following ratios:
    a. Ratio of owner's equity to total liabilities _____
    b. Ratio of assets to owner's equity _____
    c. Current ratio _____
    d. Acid-test ratio _____

57. Using the balance sheet shown in Exercise 3 and the income statement shown in Exercise 4, calculate the following ratios:
    a. Gross profit margin ratio _____
    b. Operating ratio _____
    c. Debt ratio _____
    d. Ratio of accounts receivable to net sales_____

58. Using the comparative balance sheet shown in Exercise 1 and the comparative income statement shown in Exercise 2, calculate:
    a. Asset turnover ratio _____
    b. Percent of average total assets to net sales _____

UNIT IV

Financial Mathematics for Business

CHAPTER 28

Compound Interest

 ## PART 1   *Speed and Accuracy Building Using Touch Key*

GOALS: Your speed goal is 12,000 strokes per hour.
Your accuracy target goal range is 95% to 100%.

With each repetition of the drill, try to improve your speed without lowering your accuracy score. If your percent-of-accuracy score falls below 95%, review your finger position and technique. Then try again.

Instructions: *Start Touch Key. Complete Drill 6, Parts A and B, Three-Minute Timings. (Parts C through E are optional.) Write your scores for strokes per hour and percent of accuracy below.*

Touch Key Drill 6—The 0 through 9, Decimal, and Minus Keys, Five-Digit Numbers (Mixed), Three-Minute Timings

Today's Date	Strokes per Hour	Percent of Accuracy
A.		
B.		
C.		
D.		
E.		

 ## PART 2   *Business Math Skills*

Special note: Two methods are given for calculating compound interest. Compound interest tables are usually used by businesses and are included at the end of this chapter. Formulas may also be used to solve compound interest problems. Formulas and procedures for working these problems on a calculator are also covered in this chapter. Note that the calculator used for these problems should have an exponent key $\boxed{x\text{\textasciicircum}y}$ similar to the Windows calculator in Scientific View. Please **check with your instructor** whether the table method or the formula method (or both) should be studied and used in this chapter.

COMPOUND INTEREST

In today's world, understanding compound interest is one of the most valuable skills in business and personal life. Understanding how time affects compound interest can help you to make decisions that can save thousands of dollars on a mortgage, reduce interest costs on major purchases, and increase your retirement income. The "magic of compound interest" can help to make your money work for you (Figure 28.1).

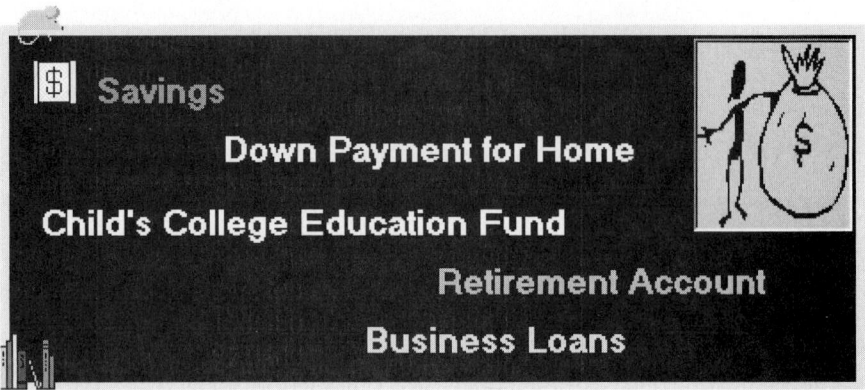

FIGURE 28.1

The difference between simple interest (discussed in Chapter 11) and compound interest is that when compound interest is used, the interest is paid on both the principal and any earned interest. Recall that interest is paid only on the principal when simple interest is used and that the formula for simple interest is I = PRT. When compound interest is used, a **compounding period** is stated that indicates the periods per year for which interest will be paid. Interest is paid at the end of each compounding period. This interest is added to the principal before interest is calculated for the next compounding period, and so on, until the end of the investment period.

Figure 28.2 shows a comparison of $100 invested at 12% simple interest for 1 year and $100 invested at 12% compounded quarterly for 1 year. Note that interest is added to principal each compounding period before interest for that period is calculated. Using the compound interest method results in a greater amount of interest than the simple interest method, which is good if you are the investor, not so good if you are paying back a loan.

Simple Interest:	Compound Interest:
$100 invested for 1 yr, at 12%	$100 invested for 1 yr, at 12%
100 + (100 × 1 × .12) = $112	compounded quarterly
maturity value	100 + (100 × .03) = $103
	103 + (103 × .03) = $106.09
	106.09 + (106.09 × .03) = $109.27
	109.27 + (109.27 × .03) = $112.55
	future value

FIGURE 28.2

There are several types of business situations that involve compound interest, including those relating to future value (also known as compound amount), present value, annuities, sinking funds, and amortizations. Tables, spreadsheets, and formulas for use on calculators can be used to help calculate interest. This chapter will explain the use of tables and calculator procedures for calculating compound interest.

Before calculating compound interest for any business situation, the compounding period must be known. This period may be monthly, quarterly, yearly, and so on. The **rate per period** is the stated (annual) interest rate divided by the number of compounding periods in a year. The **number of periods** in the investment period is the number of compounding periods in a year multiplied by the number of years of the investment.

FUTURE VALUE (COMPOUND AMOUNT)

The terms future value and compound amount may be used interchangeably. **Future value** or **compound amount** is the amount that an investment will be worth at some future date. Similar to maturity value, future value is the principal plus all the compound interest it will earn.

Table Method

The $1 Compounded table given at the end of this chapter is used to calculate future value. As the name implies, the part of the table labeled Compound Amount gives the compound amount for $1 invested for a certain number of periods at a certain rate per period.

PROBLEM 1

Calculate the future value of $100 invested at 8% compounded quarterly for 2 years (see Figure 28.3, where CA indicates the Compound Amount column and FV indicates Future Value).

First, calculate the rate per period. In this case quarterly periods are specified, so divide 8% by 4. The rate per period is 2%.

Second, calculate the total number of periods. Because quarterly periods are specified for 2 years, multiply 4×2 years. The number of periods in the investment period is 8.

Third, turn to the Rate 2% section of the $1 Compounded table. Look in the Periods column for 8 periods. Follow the 8 periods row across to the Compound Amount column. The future value of $1 is 1.171659381.

Fourth, multiply the factor from the table by the principal ($100). The future value is $117.17.

Problem: $100 invested at 8%, 2 years

Rate per period = 8%/4 = 2%

Number of periods = 2 yrs. x 4 qtrs. = 8 periods

Principal = $100

Factor from CA of $1 Table = 1.171659381

FV = 100 x 1.171659381 = $117.17

FIGURE 28.3

Formula Method

The **future value formula** is $P(1 + R)^n$, where P equals the original investment, R equals the rate per period, and the exponent n equals the number of periods in the investment.

PROBLEM 2

Calculate the future value of $100 invested at 8% for 2 years.

This calculation is shown in its entirety in Figures 28.4 and 28.5. The Windows calculator in Scientific View was used. The notation ^{n} means "raised to the power of n," that is, treat n as an exponent.

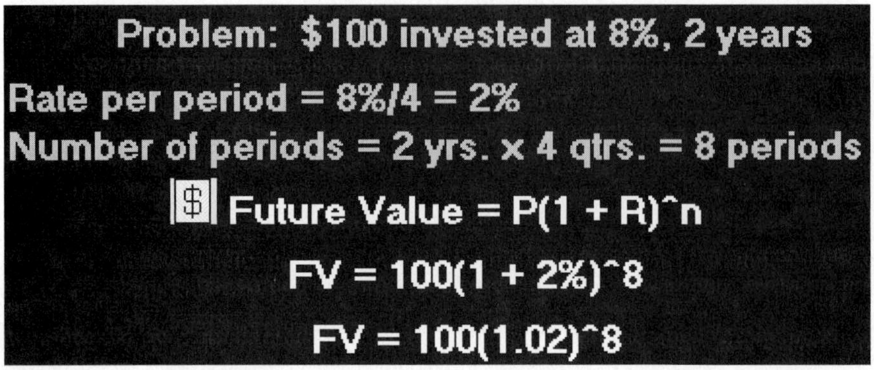

Problem: $100 invested at 8%, 2 years

Rate per period = 8%/4 = 2%
Number of periods = 2 yrs. x 4 qtrs. = 8 periods

$\boxed{\$}$ Future Value = P(1 + R)^n

FV = 100(1 + 2%)^8

FV = 100(1.02)^8

FIGURE 28.4

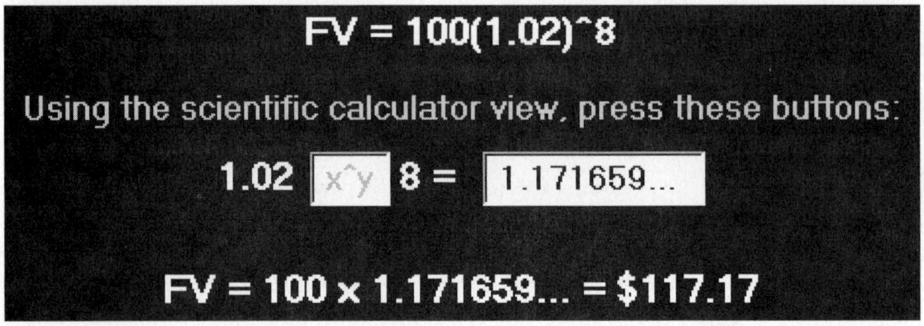

FV = 100(1.02)^8

Using the scientific calculator view, press these buttons:

1.02 $\boxed{x^y}$ 8 = $\boxed{1.171659...}$

FV = 100 x 1.171659... = $117.17

FIGURE 28.5

The rules of algebra tell us to perform the arithmetic operations in parentheses first, then apply the exponent, and finally multiply by P, or in this case, 100. Using a calculator, we have $1.02^8 = 1.02$ multiplied by itself 7 times:

$$1.02 \times 1.02 \times 1.02 \times 1.02 \times 1.02 \times 1.02 \times 1.02 \times 1.02$$

Windows Calculator Procedure

Alternatively, you may use the Windows calculator using Scientific View and use the exponent function, which appears on a key as $\boxed{x\char`^y}$.

Interest Compounded Daily

Interest may be compounded daily on savings accounts. Use the excerpt given in Figure 28.6 from a table listing the daily compounded interest on $100 to calculate interest on $1,200 invested at 12% annual interest compounded daily for 30 days. Because the interest amount given in the table is for $100, first divide savings by 100:

$$\$1,200 \div 100 = \$12$$

Multiply by the factor for 12% and 30 days from the table (0.991017):

$$\$12 \times 0.991017 = \$11.89 \text{ interest}$$

Daily Compounded Interest on $100

Days	Annual Rate				
	12%	12.5%	13%	13.5%	14%
1	0.032876	.0.34246	0.035616	0.036986	0.038356
10	0.329253	0.336123	0.356735	0.370473	0.384224
30	0.991017	1.032515	1.074029	1.115560	1.157107

Problem: $1200 invested at 12% annual interest, compounded daily for 30 days.

Step 1: $1200 / 100 = $12   Step 2: $12 x 0.991017 = $11.89

FIGURE 28.6

FUTURE VALUE OF AN ANNUITY

Table Method

An **annuity** is a series of regular savings, investments, or payments. When the same amount of money is saved on a periodic basis, such as monthly or yearly, it is called an annuity, and the future value (compound amount) of the annuity can be calculated. Retirement plans and saving for children's education are examples of annuities. Use the Amount of Annuity part of the $1 Compounded table to find how $1 per period will grow.

PROBLEM 3

Joan places $1,200 annually in an optional retirement plan that pays 12% interest compounded annually. What will the future value of the retirement plan be in 10 years? (See Figure 28.7. Where CA means future or compound amount of annuity.)

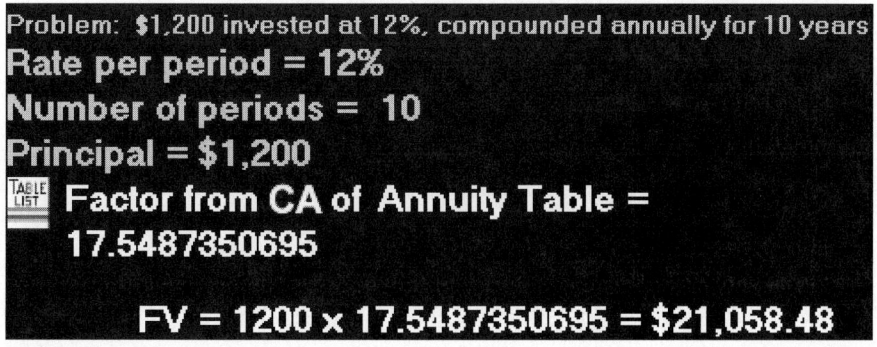

Problem: $1,200 invested at 12%, compounded annually for 10 years
Rate per period = 12%
Number of periods = 10
Principal = $1,200
Factor from CA of Annuity Table =
    17.5487350695

FV = 1200 x 17.5487350695 = $21,058.48

FIGURE 28.7

First, calculate interest rate per period. Because the compounding period is 1 year, the rate per period is 12%.

Second, because there is one (annual) compounding period, the number of periods is 10.

Third, consult the Amount of Annuity part of the $1 Compounded table for the factor for 10 periods at 12% (17.5487350695).

Fourth, multiply the factor by the yearly investment:

$$17.5487350695 \times \$1,200 = \$21,058.48$$

the amount that will be in the retirement account, which is 10 years if the payments in the account continue at $1,200 per year.

Formula Method

The formula for finding the future value of an annuity is shown in Figure 28.8. To solve Problem 2 using this formula, begin by replacing the variables in the formula with the known values wherever possible. Let P equal the payment ($1,200), R equal the periodic rate (12% or .12), and *n* equal the number of periods (10).

Rate per period = 12% annually
Number of periods = 10 periods
$ Future Value of an Annuity formula:

$$\text{Future Value} = P\left[\frac{(1 + R)^n - 1}{R}\right]$$

$$FV = 1200\left[\frac{(1 + .12)^{10} - 1}{.12}\right]$$

FIGURE 28.8

Using the rules of algebra, solve for the value in parentheses, then solve for the value in brackets.

1. Begin by finding the value in parentheses and then apply the exponent:

$$1 + .12 = 1.12$$
$$1.12 \text{ raised to the power of } 10 = 3.105848$$

Substituting these values, we see that the formula now looks like line 2 in Figure 28.9.

$$FV = 1200\left[\frac{(1 + .12)^{10} - 1}{.12}\right]$$

$$FV = 1200\left[\frac{3.105848 - 1}{.12}\right]$$

$$FV = 1200\left[17.54873...\right]$$

$$FV = \$21,058.48$$

FIGURE 28.9

2. Calculate the value of the numerator and divide by the denominator:

$$3.105848 - 1 = 2.105848$$
$$2.105848 \div .12 = 17.45873...$$

The dots indicate that more digits appear in the display and that this number has *not* been rounded.

Substituting this value, we now see that the formula looks like line 3 in Figure 28.9.

3. Multiply $1,200 by the number in brackets to find the future value of the annuity ($21,058.48).

Windows Calculator Procedure

Figure 28.10 illustrates how to solve the formula for the future value (compound amount) of an annuity using the Windows calculator, Scientific View. Do not round until the final answer.

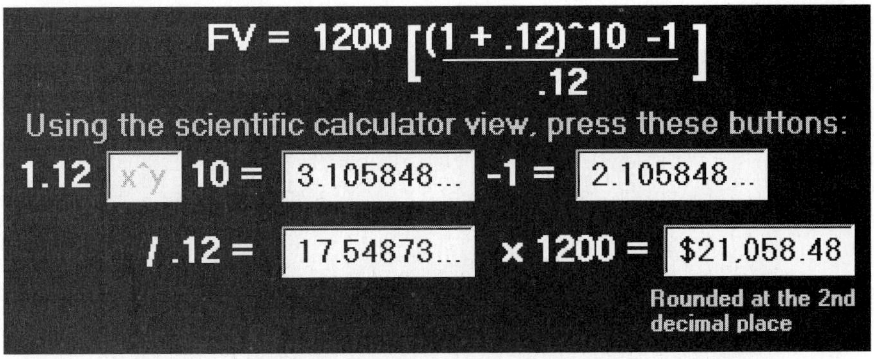

FV = 1200 [(1 + .12)^10 -1] / .12

Using the scientific calculator view, press these buttons:

1.12 [x^y] 10 = 3.105848... -1 = 2.105848...

/ .12 = 17.54873... × 1200 = $21,058.48

Rounded at the 2nd decimal place

FIGURE 28.10

SINKING FUND PAYMENT

Table Method

Sometimes businesses will make deposits into a special fund to ensure that a sufficient amount of cash will be on hand to make a large payment on a debt or to meet some other future obligation. An annuity referred to as a **sinking fund** may be used. The Sinking Fund part of the $1 Compounded table is used to help determine the amount of each payment to deposit in the sinking fund so that the money deposited plus the interest it earns will meet the requirement for cash when the obligation becomes due.

PROBLEM 4

A community water service needs $10,000 in 4 years to meet its debt obligation. An annual rate of 8% on an annuity investment is available. What is the amount of the payment the company needs to make into the sinking fund each of the 4 years?

Because the payment is an annual one, the rate per period is 8%. The number of periods is 4. Refer to the Sinking Fund part of the table to find the factor for 4 periods at 8% (.2219208045). Multiply the factor by the payment $10,000. The amount of the sinking fund payment is $2,219.21 (see Figure 28.11).

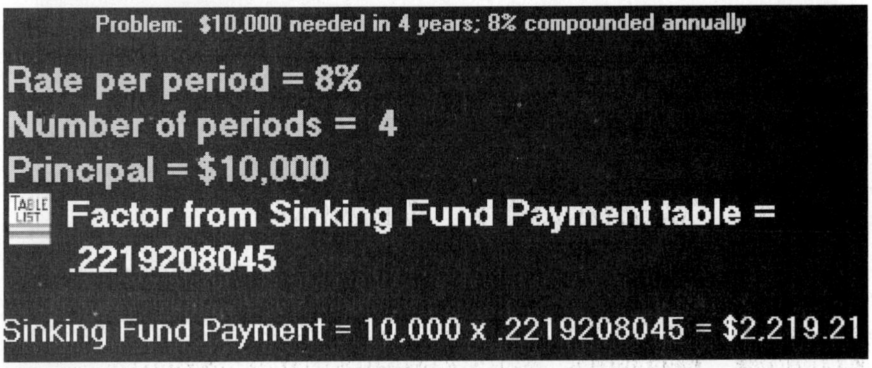

Problem: $10,000 needed in 4 years; 8% compounded annually

Rate per period = 8%
Number of periods = 4
Principal = $10,000
Factor from Sinking Fund Payment table = .2219208045

Sinking Fund Payment = 10,000 × .2219208045 = $2,219.21

FIGURE 28.11

Formula Method

The formula for calculating a sinking fund payment is shown in Figure 28.12. Let P equal the amount of the sinking fund payment that must be made in 4 years, R equal the rate per period (8%), and *n* equal the number of periods (4). Substitute these variables into the formula. The formula now looks like the last line in Figure 28.12.

$$\text{Rate per period} = 8\% \text{ annually}$$
$$\text{Number of periods} = 4 \text{ periods}$$
$$\$ \text{ Sinking Fund Payment formula:}$$
$$\text{Payment} = P\left[\frac{R}{(1+R)^\wedge n-1}\right]$$

$$\text{Payment} = 10{,}000\left[\frac{.08}{(1.08)^\wedge 4-1}\right]$$

FIGURE 28.12

Calculate the value in parentheses, apply the exponent, and subtract one to find the value of the denominator:

$$1 + .08 = 1.08$$
$$1.08 \text{ raised to the power of } 4 = 1.36048896$$
$$1.36048896 - 1 = 0.3604889 \quad \text{the value of the denominator}$$

The formula now looks like the one shown in line 2 of Figure 28.13.
Divide the numerator by the denominator:

$$0.08/0.3604889 = 0.22192084139 \quad \text{the value in brackets}$$

Multiply by $10,000 to find the amount of each payment into the sinking fund.

$$0.22192084139 \times \$10{,}000 = \$2{,}219.21$$

$$\text{Payment} = 10{,}000\left[\frac{.08}{(1.08)^\wedge 4-1}\right]$$

$$\text{Payment} = 10{,}000\left[\frac{.08}{.3604889}\right]$$

$$\text{Payment} = 10{,}000\left[.2219208\right] = \$2{,}219.21$$

FIGURE 28.13

Windows Calculator Procedure

The procedure for solving the sinking fund payment using the Windows calculator, Scientific View, is shown in Figure 28.14.

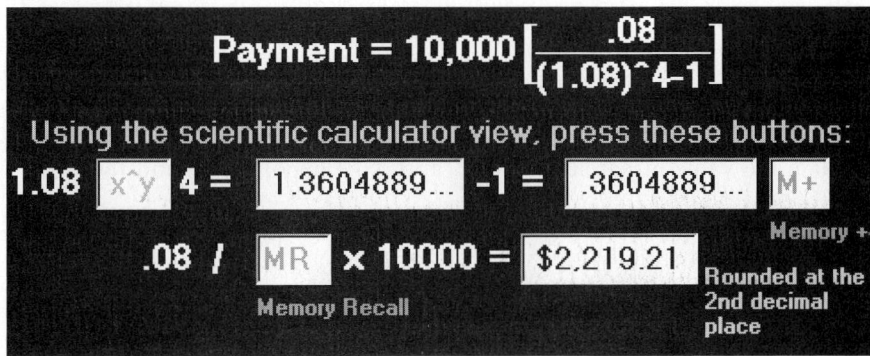

FIGURE 28.14

PRESENT VALUE

Table Method

Present value is today's worth of some future value. For example, if the specific amount needed at some future date is known, less than the full amount needed can be invested because money earns interest over time. How much? The amount needed can be found by calculating the present value of the amount needed. The Present Value part of the $1 Compounded table indicates what $1 due in the future is worth today.

PROBLEM 5

A young couple wants to buy a home in 2 years and will need $6,000 for the down payment. How much should they invest today at 12% compounded monthly?

Calculate the rate per period for monthly compounding:

$$12\% \div 12 = 1\% \text{ per period}$$

Calculate number of periods for monthly compounding for 2 years:

$$12 \text{ periods per year} \times 2 \text{ years} = 24 \text{ periods}$$

Consult the Present Value part of the table to find the present value for 24 periods at 1% (0.7875661274). Multiply by the total amount needed ($6,000) to find the present value of $6,000 ($4,725.40). See Figure 28.15.

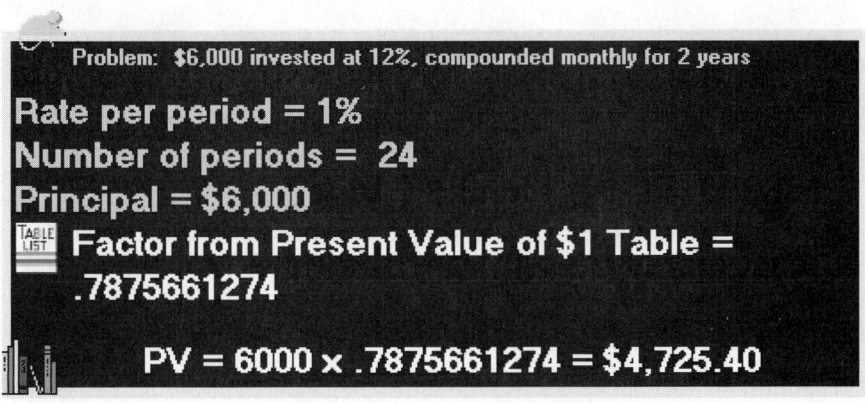

FIGURE 28.15

Formula Method

The present value formula is shown in Figure 28.16. Let P equal the amount needed in the future, R equal the rate per period, and *n* equal the number of periods. To solve Problem 4, substitute known values into the formula.

Calculate the value in parentheses and apply the exponent to find the value of the denominator:

$$1.01 \text{ raised to the power of } 24 \ = \ 1.26973464\ldots$$

Divide the numerator by the denominator:

$$1 \div 1.26973464\ldots \ = \ .787566\ldots$$

Multiply by $6,000:

$$.787566\ldots \times \$6{,}000 \ = \ \$4{,}725.40$$

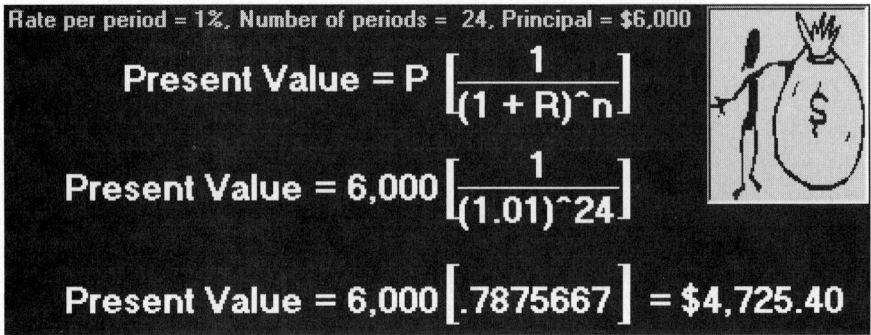

FIGURE 28.16

Windows Calculator Procedure

The procedure to find the present value (Problem 4) using the Windows calculator, Scientific View, is shown in Figure 28.17.

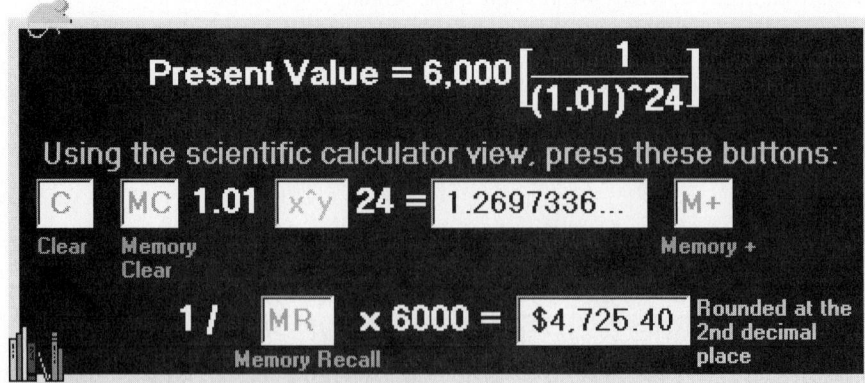

FIGURE 28.17

PRESENT VALUE OF AN ANNUITY

Table Method

There may be times when you need to decide whether to accept periodic payments (as in insurance settlements and lottery winnings) or to take the present value of those payments in one lump sum. Or you may need to invest an amount today to have a series of payments of a specific amount when you retire or for some other future need. The **present value of an annuity** can be found from the Present Value of Annuity part of the $1 Compounded table, which indicates the present worth of $1 per period. It indicates what $1 to be received periodically is worth today.

PROBLEM 6

Lottie estimates she will need $600 quarterly in extra retirement income for 6 years. How much should she invest when she retires if she can earn 12% compounded quarterly to meet these needs?
Calculate the rate per period and number of periods:

$$12\% \div 4 = 3\%$$
$$4 \times 6 \text{ years} = 24 \text{ periods}$$

Find the factor from the Present Value of Annuity part of the table for 24 periods at 3%. See Figure 28.18. Multiply the factor by the amount needed each quarter ($600).
Lottie will need to invest $10,161.33 today to receive the desired series of payments in the future.

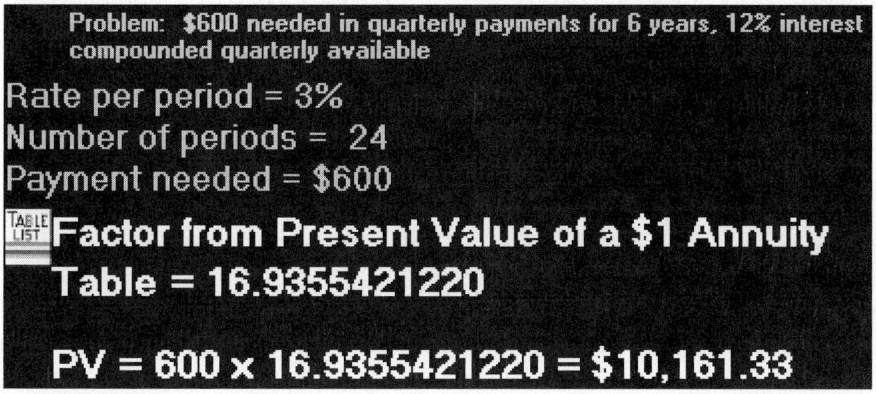

Problem: $600 needed in quarterly payments for 6 years, 12% interest compounded quarterly available

Rate per period = 3%
Number of periods = 24
Payment needed = $600

Factor from Present Value of a $1 Annuity Table = 16.9355421220

PV = 600 x 16.9355421220 = $10,161.33

FIGURE 28.18

Formula Method

The formula for the present value of an annuity is shown in Figure 28.19. Let P equal the amount of each of the payments needed in the series, R equal the rate per period, and *n* equal the number of periods.

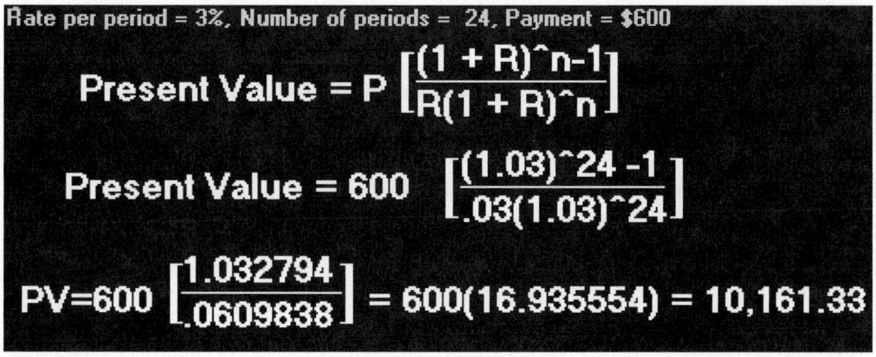

Rate per period = 3%, Number of periods = 24, Payment = $600

$$\text{Present Value} = P \left[\frac{(1 + R)^n - 1}{R(1 + R)^n} \right]$$

$$\text{Present Value} = 600 \left[\frac{(1.03)^{24} - 1}{.03(1.03)^{24}} \right]$$

$$PV = 600 \left[\frac{1.032794}{.0609838} \right] = 600(16.935554) = 10,161.33$$

FIGURE 28.19

Calculate the numerator. Calculate the value in parentheses, apply the exponent, and multiply by R to find the value of the denominator:

$$1.03 \text{ raised to the power of } 24 \; = \; 2.032794\ldots$$
$$2.032794 \times 0.03 \; = \; 0.0609838\ldots$$

Calculate the numerator in the same way:

$$2.032794\ldots \; - \; 1 \; = \; 1.032794\ldots$$

Divide the numerator by the denominator:

$$1.032794\ldots \; \div \; 0.0609838\ldots \; = \; 16.935554$$

Multiply the result by \$600 to find the present value of the desired annuity:

$$16.935554 \times \$600 \; = \; \$10{,}161.33 \text{ rounded}$$

Windows Calculator Procedure

The procedure for calculating the present value of an annuity (Problem 5) using the Windows Calculator is illustrated in Figure 28.20.

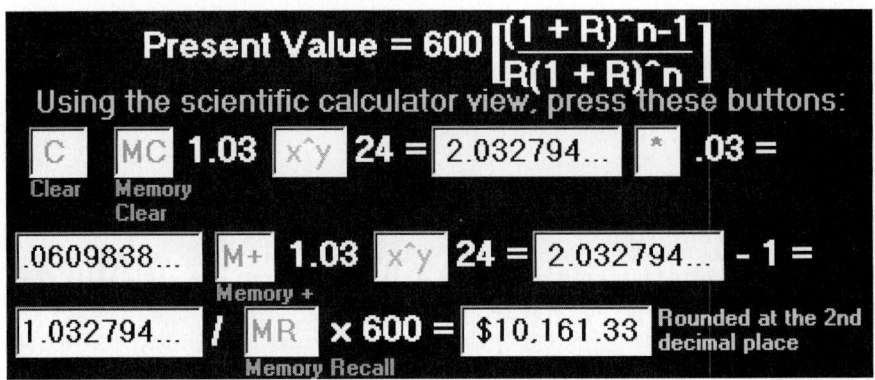

FIGURE 28.20

AMORTIZATION

When a loan is to be repaid in equal periodic payments and the interest is to be calculated on the unpaid balance each month, it is called an **amortization**. A typical example is the home mortgage. The principal of the loan is the amount of the loan. The Amortization part of the \$1 Compounded table indicates the periodic payment necessary to pay off a loan of \$1.

PROBLEM 7

Calculate the monthly payment for a \$2,000 loan amortized for 2 years at 18%.

Calculate rate per period:

$$18\% \; \div \; 12 \text{ months per year} \; = \; 1.5\%$$

Calculate number of periods:

$$12 \text{ months} \times 2 \text{ years} \; = \; 24 \text{ periods}$$

Consult the Amortization part of the table to find the factor for 24 periods at 1.5% (0.0499241020).

Multiply the factor by the amount of the loan ($2,000):

The monthly payment is $99.85 (Figure 28.21).

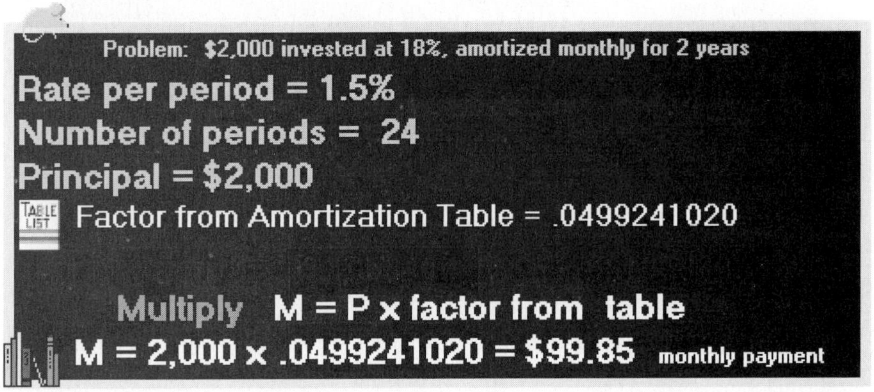

Problem: $2,000 invested at 18%, amortized monthly for 2 years

Rate per period = 1.5%

Number of periods = 24

Principal = $2,000

Factor from Amortization Table = .0499241020

Multiply   M = P x factor from table

M = 2,000 x .0499241020 = $99.85 monthly payment

FIGURE 28.21

Formula Method

The monthly payment formula is shown in Figure 28.22. Let P equal the amount of the loan, R equal the periodic rate, and *n* equal the number of periods.

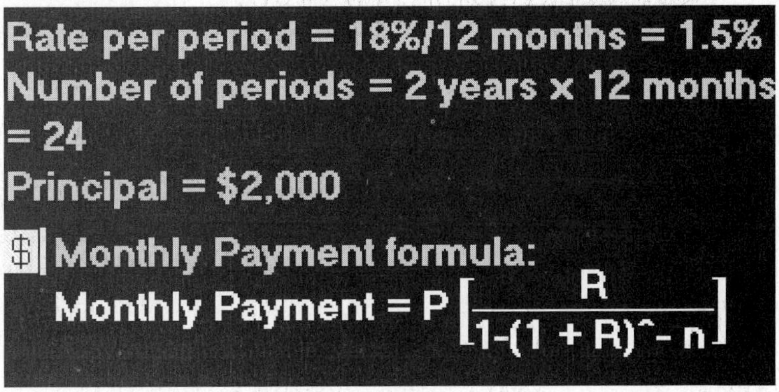

Rate per period = 18%/12 months = 1.5%

Number of periods = 2 years x 12 months = 24

Principal = $2,000

Monthly Payment formula:

$$\text{Monthly Payment} = P \left[\frac{R}{1-(1+R)^{-n}} \right]$$

FIGURE 28.22

Calculate the value of the denominator. Begin by calculating the value in parentheses and then apply the exponent. Subtract this amount from 1:

$$1 + .015 = 1.015$$
$$1.015 \text{ raised to the power of } -24 = 0.6995439\dots$$
$$1 - 0.6995439\dots = 0.300456\dots$$

Divide the numerator by the denominator:

$$0.015 \div 0.300456\dots = 0.049924\dots$$

Multiply this amount by P ($2,000) to find the amount of the monthly payment (Figure 28.23):

$$\$2,000 \times 0.049924\dots = \$99.85$$

$$\text{Rate per period} = 1.5\%, \text{Number of periods} = 24, \text{Principal} = \$2{,}000$$

$$M = 2{,}000 \left[\frac{.015}{1 - (1.015)^{-24}} \right]$$

$$M = 2{,}000 \left[\frac{.015}{.300456\ldots} \right]$$

$$M = 2{,}000 \left[\; .049924\ldots \; \right] = \$99.85 \;\; \text{rounded}$$

FIGURE 28.23

Windows Calculator Procedure

The procedure for calculating the monthly payment (Problem 6) using the Windows Calculator, Scientific View, is illustrated in Figure 28.24.

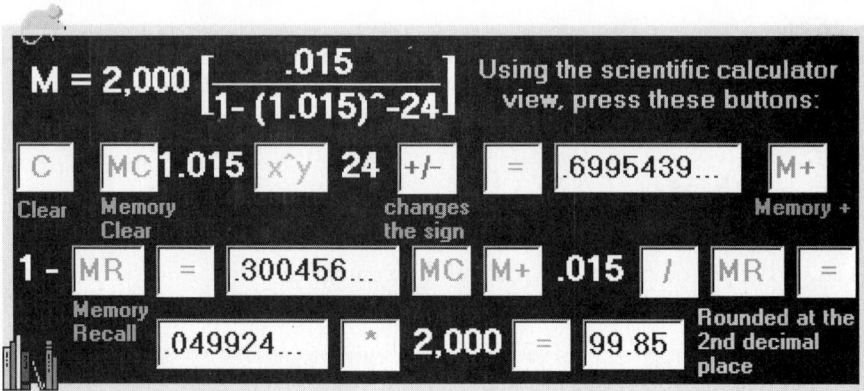

FIGURE 28.24

AMORTIZATION SCHEDULE

An **amortization schedule** lists each payment made on a loan, the part of the payment that is applied to interest, the part that is applied to principal, and the balance. Notice in the amortization schedule shown in Figure 28.25 that as the balance (amount owed) declines, the amount applied to interest decreases and the amount applied to principal increases.

Old balance × monthly interest rate (2,000 × .015) | Payment − amount applied to interest (99.85 − 30 = 69.85) | Old balance − amount applied to principal (2,000 − 69.85 = 1,930.15)

Amortization Schedule

Month	Payment	Applied to Interest	Applied to Principal	Balance
1	99.85	30.00	69.85	1,930.15
2	99.85	28.95	70.90	1,859.25
3	99.85	27.89	71.96	1,787.29
4	99.85	26.81	73.04	1,714.25

FIGURE 28.25

PROBLEM 8

Prepare an amortization schedule for the first 4 months of a $2,000 loan amortized monthly at 18% for a 2-year period.

The monthly payment ($99.85) was calculated in Problem 6.

Calculate the rate per period:

$$18\% \div 12 \text{ months} = 1.5\%$$

Calculate the amount of interest for month 1 (P × R):

$$\$2,000 \times 0.015 = \$30.00$$

Calculate the amount of the payment that will be applied to principal (payment minus interest):

$$\$99.85 - \$30 = \$69.85$$

Calculate the balance (principal minus amount applied to principal):

$$\$2,000 - \$69.85 = \$1,930.15$$

MORTGAGE TABLES

Mortgage tables are also available that list factors for monthly payments per $1,000 of mortgage. To use this table (also located at the end of this chapter), divide the mortgage by $1,000. Multiply by the factor for the rate and number of years (taken from the Monthly Payment per $1,000 of Mortgage table) to find the monthly payment.

PROBLEM 9

Calculate the monthly payment for $20,000 amortized monthly for 20 years at 8%:

$$\$20,000 \div \$1,000 = 20$$

$$20 \times \text{factor for 20 years at 8\%} = \text{monthly payment (Figure 28.26)}$$

$$20 \times \$8.37 = \$167.40$$

Problem: **$20,000 invested at 8%, amortized monthly for 20 years**

Step 1: Divide amount financed (20,000) by 1,000
Step 2: Multiply the amount from step 1 (20) by the factor from the table

 Factor from Monthly Payment per $1000 of Mortgage (8% for 20 years) = $8.37

M = (P/1,000) x factor from table
M = (20,000 / 1,000) x 8.37 = $167.40 monthly payment

FIGURE 28.26

TIPS THAT WORK

1. To determine whether simple or compound interest is involved, look for the words compound, compounded or amortized or a phrase such as "interest paid monthly," "quarterly," or so on, indicating that the interest is being compounded.

(continued)

2. Before using a table or a formula for a compound interest problem:
 a. Calculate the rate per period.
 b. Calculate the number of compounding periods of the loan or investment.
3. Key words for determining type of table to use:

Compound Amount. Look for a *single amount* that has been invested (or loaned) today and wording asking how much it will grow by some *future* date.

Amount of Annuity. Look for a *series of equal payments* that will be invested periodically and wording asking how much the investment will be worth at some date in the *future.*

Present Value. Use this table when:
 a. A *single amount* is expected to be received at a certain future date and you wish to know how much invested *today* would equal that amount by the specified future date.
 b. A *single amount* is needed at some future date and you wish to know how much must be invested *today* to equal the needed future amount.

Present Value of Annuity. Use this table when you wish to know *today's value* of a *series of payments* that you expect to receive over a period of time in the future.

Sinking Fund. Use this table when wording in a problem indicates that a certain amount is needed to meet a debt obligation at the end of a specified period of time and periodic payments are to be made into a fund. Use the sinking fund table to determine the *amount of the payments* necessary to accumulate the desired amount.

Amortization. Use this table to calculate the *periodic payment due* (such as monthly payment) when a series of equal payments is to be made on a loan, such as a mortgage.

Name _____

Class/Section _____

Score (Correct Answers ÷ No. of Assigned Problems) _____

PART 2 *Business Math Skills*

For these exercises, use six decimal places in the calculations. Round answers to hundredths.

Exercise 1

Calculate the rate per period and the number of periods.

Rate and Time	Rate per Period	Number of Periods
12% compounded monthly for 3 years		1. _____
6% compounded monthly for 2 years		2. _____
8% compounded quarterly for 2 years		3. _____
10% compounded semiannually for 5 years		4. _____
18% compounded monthly for 2 years		5. _____

Exercise 2

Find the factor from the appropriate table for each. Include six decimal places in the answers.

   6. Future value, 3% compounded annually for 8 years _____
   7. Present value, 5% compounded semiannually for 2 years _____

8. Sinking fund, 12% compounded quarterly for 4 years _____
9. Amortization, 6% compounded monthly for 5 years _____

Exercise 3

Complete the following calculations for future value (compound amount).

Rate (%)	Compounding Period	Time (Years)	Amount of Investment ($)	Future Value
7	Annually	10	7,500	10. _____
5	Semiannually	5	3,000	11. _____
12	Monthly	4	1,500	12. _____
15	Monthly	2	3,000	13. _____
8	Monthly	6	5,000	14. _____

Exercise 4

Complete the required calculations for the following investments.

Calculation Needed	Rate and Time	Rate	Number of Periods			
Compound amount	5% compounded annually for 5 years	_____	_____	Amount invested: $1,000	Future amount: _____	15.
Present value	6% compounded semiannually for 3 years	_____	_____	Amount needed in 3 years: $4,000	Today's value: _____	16.
Amount of an annuity	8% compounded quarterly for 5 years	_____	_____	Quarterly savings of $200 will be made	Future value: _____	17.
Present value of an annuity	7% compounded quarterly for 2 years	_____	_____	Quarterly payments of $120	Present value: _____	18.
Sinking fund	7% compounded semiannually for 4 years	_____	_____	$40,000 needed in 4 years	Amount to place in the sinking fund: _____	19.
Amortization	5% compounded monthly for 5 years	_____	_____	Amount of mortgage: $75,000	Monthly payment: _____	20.

PART 3 *Review and Practice Using Business Math FUNdamentals*

GOAL: Complete 9 of the 10 problems correctly.

Instructions: *Start Business Math FUNdamentals. Complete Tutorials 61 through 67 and Drill 49. If you are not satisfied with your score, repeat the drill. Write your scores below.*

Business Math FUNdamentals Drill 49

Today's Date	Score

 **PART 4** *Desktop Calculator*

TAPE 28.1:

```
        9·  ÷
       12·  =
      0·75  *

       12·  ×
        7·  =
      84·00 *

   15,000·  ×
   0·016089 =
    241·34  *

    241·34 M÷
   15,000·  ×
      0·75  %
    112·50  *

    112·50 -+
    241·34 M◇
    241·34  +
    128·84  *

    128·84 -+
  15,000·00 +
  14,871·16 *

  14,871·16 ×
      0·75  %
    111·53  ÷

    111·53 -+
    241·34 M◇
    241·34  +
    129·81  *

    129·81 -+
  14,871·16 +
  14,741·35 *
```

TAPE 28.2:

```
  14,741·35 ×
      0·75  %
    110·56  *

    110·56 -+
    241·34 M◇
    241·34  +
    130·78  *

    130·78 -+
  14,741·35 +
  14,610·57 *
```

AMORTIZATION SCHEDULE

Using the desktop calculator, calculate the monthly payment and prepare an amortization schedule for the first 6 months of a $15,000 loan at 9% for 7 years. Use the percent key % and the reverse sign key +/− for efficiency.

Procedure

Clear memory if necessary.

Calculate the rate per period and the number of periods:

$$9 \div 12 \text{ months} = .75\% \text{ or } 3/4\%$$
$$12 \text{ months} \times 7 \text{ years} = 84 \text{ periods}$$

Consult the Amortization part of the $1 Compound table for the factor for 84 periods at 3/4% (0.016089).

Multiply the principal ($15,000) by the factor to find the monthly payment. Place the amount of the monthly payment ($241.34) in memory:

$$15,000 \times 0.016089 = \boxed{241.34} \text{ M+}$$

Complete the amortization table.

Month 1

Principal (15,000) × rate per month (0.75%) = interest $\boxed{112.50}$ $\boxed{+/-}$
+ MS $\boxed{241.34}$ + T equals principal reduction $\boxed{128.84}$ $\boxed{+/-}$
+ principal (15,000) + T equals new balance (14,871.16)

Keystrokes for month 1:

15,000 × .75 $\boxed{\%}$ $\boxed{112.50}$ $\boxed{+/-}$ + MS $\boxed{241.34}$
+ T $\boxed{128.84}$ $\boxed{+/-}$ + 15,000 + T $\boxed{14,871.16}$

Month 2

Previous balance (14,871.16) × .75% = 111.53 interest $\boxed{+/-}$
+ MS $\boxed{241.34}$ + T $\boxed{129.81}$ (principal reduction) $\boxed{+/-}$
+ previous balance (14,871.16)
+ T equals new balance (14,741.35)

Keystrokes for month 2:

$\boxed{14,871.16}$ × .75 $\boxed{\%}$ $\boxed{111.53}$ $\boxed{+/-}$ + MS $\boxed{241.34}$
+ T $\boxed{129.81}$ $\boxed{+/-}$ + 14,871.16 + T $\boxed{14,741.35}$

Repeat for remaining months.

Keystrokes for month 3:

$$\boxed{14,741.35} \times .75 \boxed{\%} \boxed{110.56} \boxed{+/-} + \text{MS} \boxed{241.34}$$
$$+ \text{T} \quad 130.78 \boxed{+/-} + 14,741.35 + \text{T} \boxed{14,610.57}$$

Keystrokes for month 4:

$$\boxed{14,610.57} \times .75 \boxed{\%} \boxed{109.58} \boxed{+/-} + \text{MS} \boxed{241.34} + \text{T} \boxed{131.76} \boxed{+/-}$$
$$+ \boxed{14,610.57} + \text{T} \boxed{14,478.81}$$

Keystrokes for month 5:

$$\boxed{14,478.81} \times .75 \boxed{\%} \boxed{108.59} \boxed{+/-} + \text{MS} \boxed{241.34} + \text{T} \boxed{132.75} \boxed{+/-}$$
$$+ 14,478.81 + \text{T} \boxed{14,346.06}$$

Keystrokes for month 6:

$$\boxed{14,346.06} \times .75 \boxed{\%} 107.60 \boxed{+/-} + \text{MS} \boxed{241.34} + \text{T} \boxed{133.74} \boxed{+ /-}$$
$$+ 14,346.06 + \text{T} \boxed{14,212.32}$$

Your completed amortization should look like the one below.

Amortization Schedule

Month	Monthly Payment ($)	Interest ($)	Principal Reduction ($)	Balance ($)
1	241.34	112.50	128.84	14,871.16
2	241.34	111.53	129.81	14,741.35
3	241.34	110.56	130.78	14,610.57
4	241.34	109.58	131.76	14,478.81
5	241.34	108.59	132.75	14,346.06
6	241.34	107.60	133.74	14,212.32

TAPE 28.3:

```
14,610.57 x
     0.75 %
   109.58 ÷

   109.58-÷
   241.34M÷
   241.34 +
   131.76 ÷

   131.76-÷
14,610.57 ÷
14,478.81 ÷

14,478.81 x
     0.75 %
   108.59 ÷

   108.59-÷
   241.34M÷
   241.34 +
   132.75 ÷

   132.75-÷
14,478.81 ÷
14,346.06 ÷

14,346.06 x
     0.75 %
   107.60 ÷

   107.60-÷
   241.34M÷
   241.34 +
   133.74 ÷

   133.74-÷
14,346.06 +
14,212.32 ÷
```

Name _____

Class/Section _____

Score (Correct Answers ÷ No. of Assigned Problems) _____

 # PART 4 *Desktop Calculator*

Exercise 1

Complete the first 5 months of an amortization schedule for a loan that was made for $30,000 at 8% compounded monthly for 6 years.

Amortization Schedule

Month	Monthly Payment	Interest	Principal Reduction	Balance	
1	_____	_____	_____	_____	1.
2	_____	_____	_____	_____	2.
3	_____	_____	_____	_____	3.
4	_____	_____	_____	_____	4.
5	_____	_____	_____	_____	5.

Exercise 2

One-Minute Addition Timing (0 through 9, Decimal, and Minus Keys)

(Optional: Your instructor may wish you to use Touch Key on the computer for all your timings. Check with your instructor before completing this exercise.)

Complete as many of the problems as possible in 1 minute by adding. Work quickly and accurately. The number preceding each closing parenthesis indicates the cumulative number of strokes for problems attempted. For example, if you complete Problems 1 through 3 in 1 minute, your strokes-per-minute score is 252. Optional: 3- and 5-minute timings.

1.	2.	3.	4.	5.	6.
347.556	910.024	165.544	12,900.6	77,850.7	694,200
758.541	576.932	751.350	73,090.2	45,500.2	928.500
263.987	462.009	746.800	46,070.1	34,650.1	123,100
113.657	397.545	150.600	64,460.3	69,995.6	−487,400
735.987	886.041	972.400	53,010.4	57,359.1	821,006
883.524	719.000	199.500	−34,040.5	34,229.9	−223,005
−991.093	164.788	240.300	92,400.3	67,899.1	579,003
−706.835	654.921	−764.100	15,100.3	45,775.4	636,004
−920.569	−453.896	−403.300	−88,200.1	54,900.3	514,006
−563.870	−211.009	−535.300	79,100.2	34,556.8	−325,006
85)	168)	252)	335)	416)	491)

7.	8.	9.	10.	11.	12.
5,300.00	317,001	94.1400	7,690.01	756,987	14,477.9
6,609.00	619,003	−86.6420	44.2677	220,122	153.100
4,100.00	318,002	75.5850	36.3553	−160,455	120.666
9,300.00	813,001	76.6150	−776.998	−170,004	135.350
1,300.00	−919,004	−67.7700	−5,885.65	322,999	155.555
−1,200.00	671,002	98.8689	−1,743.22	−259,000	133.886
5,300.00	477,007	99.9599	−39,765.9	265,880	176.772
12,500.00	383,004	86.6884	−8,221.00	−110,432	1,722.50
5,600.00	238,005	−81.7256	−8,250.00	311,119	1,404.95
9,500.00	248,003	79.9374	−935.575	433,980	23,249.5
574)	646)	730)	818)	893)	974)

13.	14.	15.	16.
43.450	490,661	−516.000	−9.95004
29.995	789,000	−637.013	−88.2600
41.995	679,885	738.064	−76.4000
27.229	969,655	−539.014	−634.870
−30.759	−176,444	−430.045	−7,960.02
−60.999	−267,111	−727.023	−8,160.03
−37.577	−356,741	628.013	−989.514
−20.659	−452,962	592.053	−946.787
−45.695	−559,854	−697.024	−83.6412
−20.000	856,014	−610.011	−95.4600
1,051)	1,127)	1,215)	1,306)

CHAPTER 28 *Terminology Review*

Amortization
Amortization schedule
Amortization table
Amount of an annuity

Annuity
Compound amount
Compounding period
Future value
Future value formula
Mortgage tables
Number of periods
Present value
Present value of an annuity
Rate per period
Sinking fund

Write the correct term next to the appropriate description.

1. _____ The periods per year for which interest will be paid.
2. _____ The stated interest rate divided by the number of compounding periods in a year.
3. _____ The number of compounding periods in a year multiplied by the number of years of the investment.
4. _____ The amount that an investment will be worth at some future date.
5. _____ A series of regular savings, investments, or payments.
6. _____ Used by businesses to ensure that a sufficient amount of cash will be on hand to make a large payment on some future obligation.
7. _____ Today's worth of an amount that will be available in the future.
8. _____ Today's worth of a series of future payments.
9. _____ A loan that is to be repaid in equal periodic payments and the interest is to be calculated on the unpaid balance each month.
10. _____ List factors for monthly payments per $1,000 of mortgage.
11. _____ The amount that money invested on a periodic basis will be worth at some future date.

Name _____

Class/Section _____

Score (Correct Answers ÷ No. of Assigned Problems) _____

Chapter 28 Review Exercises
Exercise 1

1. Rocking Horse Hotel wished to expand. A loan was negotiated for $200,000 at 10% compounded annually for 8 years. Calculate the future value of the loan. _____
2. Jill Mercado purchased an annuity that will pay $450 per month for 5 years. What is the present value of the annuity if current rates are 6% compounded monthly? _____
3. Jonathan's grandmother left him $50,000, which he can claim on his 35th birthday. Jonathan is 25 years of age. What is the present value of the gift if investments are available at 4% compounded annually? _____
4. A school district floated a bond for $750,000. The bond matures in 8 years. If a rate of 6% compounded annually is available, how much should be deposited in the sinking fund annually for the school district to meet its obligations? _____

5. Kelly Richardson and his wife signed a mortgage agreement for $125,000 at 8% for 30 years. What is the amount of their monthly payment? Use the Monthly Payment for $1,000 of Mortgage table. _____

6. Marla's company offers an automatic savings plan that pays 6% compounded monthly. If she puts $125 into the plan monthly, how much will she have at the end of 5 years? _____

Exercise 2

Prepare an amortization schedule for the first 2 years of the mortgage described in Problem 5.

Amortization Schedule

Month	Monthly Payment	Interest	Principal Reduction	Balance
1				7. _____
2				8. _____

Exercise 3

9. Use the Monthly Payment per $1,000 of Mortgage Table to calculate the monthly payment for a $64,600 mortgage at 9% interest for 25 years. _____

10. Dan Johnson won a lottery for $55,000. The lottery is paid at $11,000 per year for 5 years. Dan is considering taking the cash option instead of the one-time payout. If a rate of 4% compounded annually is available for investments, what is the present value of the payments? _____

Exercise 4

The AJ Toy Co. invested part of its cash reserves ($60,000) in an investment that paid 5% annually in 1998, 1999, and 2000. The company invested the same amount ($60,000) during the years 2002, 2003, and 2004 at 2.5%. Calculate the values of the two investments at the end of the investment periods.

11. First investment value _____ Second investment value _____

Calculate the interest earned for each of the two investment periods.

12. First investment earnings _____ Second investment earnings _____
13. What was the difference in *earnings* for the two periods? _____

Exercise 5

14. Karen Yeh wishes to open her own business in 8 years. She will need $65,000 for the franchise. Right now, the cash value of her life insurance policy is $25,000. She also has savings of $10,000. If she invests both at 6% compounded monthly, will she have enough to pay for her franchise and start her business? _____ How much will she have? _____

15. Debbie and Kyle wish to save $32,000 for their 12-year-old child's college education. Kyle estimates that he can receive 12% compounded monthly on a monthly investment of $375. Will he have enough money when the child turns 18? _____ How much will he have saved? _____

16. Using the sinking fund part of the $1 Compounded table, calculate how much Debbie and Kyle from Problem 15 need to deposit each month at 12% compounded monthly to accumulate $32,000. _____

17. The Trifold Door Company can buy an additional building for $175,000 financed at 8½% for 30 years. Calculate the monthly payment. _____

18. The Trifold Door Company decided to save interest by financing the building for 20 years. What is the monthly payment? _____

19. Calculate total cost of the building (future value of the loan) for each of the following: 30-year loan _____ 20-year loan _____

20. How much would be saved by financing the building for 20 years instead of 30 years? _____

Rate/Period		Compound Amount	Amount of Annuity	Sinking Fund	Present Value	Present Value of Annuity	Amortization		Rate/Period
		Amount of $1	Amount of $1 per Period	Sinking Fund	Present Worth of $1	Present Worth of $1 per Period	Partial Payment		
		How $1 left at compound interest will grow.	How $1 deposited periodically will grow.	Periodic deposit that will grow to $1 at future date.	What $1 due in the future is worth today.	What $1 payable periodically is worth today.	Annuity worth $1 today. Periodic payment necessary to pay off a loan of $1.		
5/12%	56	1.2621903293	82.9256790222	0.0158917834	0.7922735397	49.8543504800	0.0200584300	56	5/12%
	57	1.2674494556	84.1878693514	0.0155792677	0.7889860977	50.6433365577	0.0197459344	57	
	58	1.2727304950	85.4553139071	0.0152775973	0.7857122964	51.4290488842	0.0194442639	58	
	59	1.2780335388	86.7280493021	0.0149862016	0.7824520794	52.2115009336	0.0191528683	59	
	60	1.2833586785	88.0060828408	0.0147045670	0.7792053903	52.9907063239	0.0188712336	60	
1/2%	21	1.1104200551	22.0840110145	0.0452816293	0.9005601037	19.8879792504	0.0502816293	21	1/2%
	22	1.1159721553	23.1944310696	0.0431137973	0.8960797052	20.7840589556	0.0481137973	22	
	23	1.1215520161	24.3104032250	0.0411346530	0.8916215972	21.6756805529	0.0461346530	23	
	24	1.1271597762	25.4319552411	0.0393206103	0.8871856689	22.5628662218	0.0443206103	24	
	25	1.1327955751	26.5591150173	0.0376518570	0.8827718098	23.4456380316	0.0426518570	25	
	36	1.1966805248	39.3361049647	0.0254219375	0.8356449188	32.8710162393	0.0304219375	36	
	37	1.2026639274	40.5327854895	0.0246713661	0.8314874814	33.7025037207	0.0296713861	37	
	38	1.2086772471	41.7354494170	0.0239604464	0.8273507278	34.5298544484	0.0289604464	38	
	39	1.2147206333	42.9441266640	0.0232860714	0.8232345550	35.3530890034	0.0282860714	39	
	40	1.2207942365	44.1588472974	0.0226455186	0.8191388607	36.1722278641	0.0276455186	40	
	56	1.3222070192	64.4414038366	0.0155179735	0.7563112171	48.7377565704	0.0205179735	56	
	57	1.3288180543	65.7636108558	0.0152059777	0.7525484748	49.4903050452	0.0202059777	57	
	58	1.3354621446	67.0924289100	0.0149048114	0.7488044525	50.2391094977	0.0199048114	58	
	59	1.3421394553	68.4278910546	0.0146139240	0.7450790572	50.9841885549	0.0196139240	59	
	60	1.3488501525	69.7700305099	0.0143328015	0.7413721962	51.7255607511	0.0193328015	60	
	96	1.6141427085	122.8285416922	0.0081414302	0.6195239087	78.0952182532	0.0131414302	96	
	97	1.6222134220	124.442844006	0.0080358279	0.6164417002	76.7116699535	0.0130358279	97	
	98	1.6303244891	126.0648978226	0.0079324222	0.6133748261	77.3250347796	0.0129324222	98	
	99	1.6384761116	127.6952223118	0.0078311466	0.6103232101	77.9335579896	0.0128311466	99	
	100	1.6466684921	129.336984233	0.0077319369	0.6072867762	79.5424447658	0.0127319369	100	
2/3%	71	1.6028167225	90.4225063740	0.0110591933	0.6239016514	56.4147522952	0.0177258600	71	2/3%
	72	1.6135021673	92.0253250965	0.0108665739	0.6197698523	57.0345221475	0.0175332406	72	
	73	1.6242566484	93.6388272638	0.0106793307	0.6156654162	57.6501875637	0.0173459973	73	
	74	1.6350672407	95.2630861122	0.0104972455	0.6115881618	58.2617757256	0.0171639121	74	
	75	1.6459878224	96.8981733530	0.0103201120	0.6075379091	58.8695136347	0.0169867787	75	
3/4%	56	1.5195782526	69.2771003476	0.0144347843	0.6580773305	45.5896892633	0.0219347843	56	3/4%
	57	1.5309750895	70.7966786002	0.0141249564	0.6531784918	46.2428677551	0.0216249564	57	
	58	1.5424574027	72.3276536897	0.0138259704	0.6483161209	46.8911838760	0.0213259704	58	
	59	1.5540258332	73.8701110923	0.0135372749	0.6434899463	47.5346738224	0.0210372749	59	
	60	1.5656810269	75.4241369255	0.0132583552	0.6386996986	48.1733735210	0.0207583552	60	

FIGURE 28.27 Table for calculating the value of $1 using compounded interest.

(continued)

Rate/Period	Compound Amount — Amount of $1. *How $1 left at compound interest will grow.*	Amount of Annuity — Amount of $1 per Period. *How $1 deposited periodically will grow.*	Sinking Fund — Sinking Fund. *Periodic deposit that will grow to $1 at future date.*	Present Value — Present Worth of $1. *What $1 due in the future is worth today.*	Present Value of Annuity — Present Worth of $1 per Period. *What $1 payable periodically is worth today.*	Amortization — Partial Payment. *Annuity worth $1 today. Periodic payment necessary to pay off a loan of $1.*	Rate/Period
81	1.8316793102	110.8905746990	0.0090178990	0.5459470959	60.5403872168	0.0165178990	81
82	1.8454169051	112.7222540092	0.0088713627	0.5418829736	61.0822701903	0.0163713627	82
83	1.8592575319	114.5676709143	0.0087284658	0.5378491053	61.6201192956	0.0162284658	83
84	1.8732019633	116.4269284462	0.0085890783	0.5338452658	62.1539645614	0.0160890783	84
85	1.8872509781	118.3001304095	0.0084530761	0.5298712316	62.6838357930	0.0159530761	85
1% 6	1.0615201506	6.1520150601	0.1625483667	0.9420452353	5.7954764746	0.1725483667	6
7	1.0721353521	7.2135352107	0.1386282829	0.9327180547	6.7281945293	0.1486282829	7
8	1.0828567056	8.2856705628	0.1206902920	0.9234832225	7.6516777518	0.1306902920	8
9	1.0936852727	9.3685272684	0.1067403628	0.9143398242	8.5660175160	0.1167403628	9
10	1.1046221254	10.4622125411	0.0955820766	0.9052869547	9.4713045307	0.1055820766	10
21	1.2323919403	23.2391940347	0.0430307522	0.8114301687	18.8569831349	0.0530307522	21
22	1.2447158598	24.4715859751	0.0408637185	0.8033962066	19.6603793415	0.0508637185	22
23	1.2571630183	25.7163018348	0.0388858401	0.7954417887	20.4558211302	0.0488858401	23
24	1.2697346485	26.9734648532	0.0370734722	0.7875661274	21.2433872576	0.0470734722	24
25	1.2824319950	28.2431995017	0.0354067534	0.7797684430	22.0231557006	0.0454067534	25
36	1.4307687836	43.0768783592	0.0232143098	0.6989249496	30.1075050373	0.0332143098	36
37	1.4450764714	44.5076471427	0.0224680491	0.6920049006	30.7995099379	0.0324680491	37
38	1.4595272361	45.9527236142	0.0217614958	0.6851533670	31.4846633048	0.0317614958	38
39	1.4741225085	47.4122508503	0.0210915951	0.6783696702	32.1630329751	0.0310915951	39
40	1.4888637336	48.8863733588	0.0204555980	0.6716531389	32.8346861140	0.0304555980	40
46	1.5804588547	58.0458854703	0.0172277499	0.6327276392	36.7272360793	0.0272277499	46
47	1.5962634432	59.6263443250	0.0167711103	0.6264630091	37.3536990884	0.0267711103	47
48	1.6122260777	61.2226077682	0.0163338354	0.6202604051	37.9739594935	0.0263338354	48
49	1.6283483385	62.8348338459	0.0159147393	0.6141192129	38.5880787064	0.0259147393	49
50	1.6446318218	64.4631821844	0.0155127309	0.6080388247	39.1961175311	0.0255127309	50
71	2.0268310021	102.6831002079	0.0097387009	0.4933810461	50.6618953936	0.0197387009	71
72	2.0470993121	104.7099312100	0.0095501925	0.4884960852	51.1503914789	0.0195501925	72
73	2.0675703052	106.7570305221	0.0093670646	0.4836509903	51.6340509692	0.0193670646	73
74	2.0882460083	108.8246008273	0.0091890987	0.4788707825	52.1129217516	0.0191890987	74
75	2.1091284684	110.9124468356	0.0090160881	0.4751294876	52.5870512393	0.0190160881	75
1.25% 21	1.2980626971	23.8450157684	0.0419374854	0.7703788132	18.3696949474	0.0544374854	21
22	1.3142884808	25.1430784655	0.0397723772	0.7608679636	19.1305629110	0.0522723772	22
23	1.3307170868	26.4573669463	0.0377966561	0.7514745320	19.8820374430	0.0502966561	23
24	1.3473510504	27.7880840331	0.0359866480	0.7421970686	20.6242345116	0.0484866480	24
25	1.3641929385	29.1354350836	0.0343224667	0.7330341418	21.3572686534	0.0468224667	25

(continued)

Rate/Period	Period	Compound Amount — Amount of $1. How $1 left at compound interest will grow.	Amount of Annuity — Amount of $1 per Period. How $1 deposited periodically will grow.	Sinking Fund. Periodic deposit that will grow to $1 at future date.	Present Value — Present Worth of $1. What $1 due in the future is worth today.	Present Value of Annuity — Present Worth of $1 per Period. What $1 payable periodically is worth today.	Amortization — Partial Payment. Annuity worth $1 today. Periodic payment necessary to pay off a loan of $1.	Rate/Period
1.5%	21	1.3670578316	24.4705221099	0.0408654950	0.7314979490	17.9001367341	0.0558654950	1.5%
	22	1.3875636991	25.8375799415	0.0387033152	0.7206876345	18.6208243685	0.0537033152	
	23	1.4083771546	27.2251436407	0.0367307520	0.7100370783	19.3308614468	0.0517307620	
	24	1.4295028119	28.6335207953	0.0349241020	0.6995439195	20.0304053663	0.0499241020	
	25	1.4509453541	30.0630236072	0.0332634539	0.6892058320	20.7196111984	0.0482634539	
1.75%	6	1.1097023542	6.2687059550	0.1595225565	0.9011425417	5.6489976174	0.1770225565	1.75%
	7	1.1291221454	7.3784083092	0.1355305857	0.8856437756	6.5346413930	0.1530305857	
	8	1.1488817830	8.5075304546	0.1175429233	0.8704115731	7.4050529661	0.1350429233	
	9	1.1689872142	9.6564122376	0.1035581306	0.8554413495	8.2604943156	0.1210581306	
	10	1.1894444904	10.8253994517	0.0923753442	0.8407285990	9.1012229146	0.1098753442	
	81	4.0765037829	175.8002161671	0.0056882751	0.2453082478	43.1252429848	0.0231882751	81
	82	4.1478425991	179.8767199500	0.0055593631	0.2410891870	43.3663321718	0.0230593631	82
	83	4.2204298446	184.0245625491	0.0054340572	0.2369426899	43.6032748617	0.0229340572	83
	84	4.2942873669	188.2449923937	0.0053122263	0.2328675085	43.8361423702	0.0228122263	84
	85	4.3694473958	192.5392797606	0.0051937454	0.2288624162	44.0650047865	0.0226937454	85
2%	6	1.1261624193	6.3081209632	0.1585258123	0.8879713822	5.6014308907	0.1785258123	2%
	7	1.1486856676	7.4342833825	0.1345119561	0.8705601786	6.4719910693	0.1545119561	
	8	1.1716593810	8.5829690501	0.1165097991	0.8534903712	7.3254814405	0.1365097991	
	9	1.1950925686	9.7546284311	0.1025154374	0.8367552659	8.1622367064	0.1225154374	
	10	1.2189944200	10.9497209997	0.0913265279	0.8203482999	8.9825850062	0.1113265279	
	16	1.3727857051	18.6392852545	0.0536501259	0.7284458137	13.5777093143	0.0736501259	16
	17	1.4002414192	20.0120709596	0.0499698408	0.7141625625	14.2918718768	0.0699698408	17
	18	1.4282462476	21.4123123788	0.0467021022	0.7001593750	14.9920312517	0.0667021022	18
	19	1.4568111725	22.8405586264	0.0437817663	0.6864307598	15.6784620115	0.0637817663	19
	20	1.4859473960	24.2973697989	0.0411567181	0.6729713331	16.3514333446	0.0611567181	20
2.5%	1	1.0250000000	1.0000000000	1.0000000000	0.9756097561	0.9756097561	1.0250000000	2.5%
	2	1.0506250000	2.0250000000	0.4938271605	0.9518143962	1.9274241523	0.5188271605	
	3	1.0768906250	3.0756250000	0.3251371672	0.9285994109	2.8560235632	0.3501371672	
	4	1.1038128906	4.1525156250	0.2408178777	0.9059506448	3.7619742080	0.2658178777	
	5	1.1314082129	5.2563285156	0.1902468609	0.8838542876	4.6452484956	0.2152488609	

(continued)

Rate/Period	Compound Amount — Amount of $1 — How $1 left at compound interest will grow.	Amount of Annuity — Amount of $1 per Period — How $1 deposited periodically will grow.	Sinking Fund — Periodic deposit that will grow to $1 at future date.	Present Value — Present Worth of $1 — What $1 due in the future is worth today.	Present Value of Annuity — Present Worth of $1 per Period — What $1 payable periodically is worth today.	Amortization — Partial Payment — Annuity worth $1 today. Periodic payment necessary to pay off a loan of $1.	Rate/Period
6	1.1596934182	6.3877367285	0.1565499711	0.8622968660	5.5081253616	0.1815499711	6
7	1.1886857537	7.5474301467	0.1324954296	0.8412652351	6.3493905967	0.1574954296	7
8	1.2184028975	8.7361159004	0.1144673458	0.8207465708	7.1701371675	0.1394673458	8
9	1.2488629699	9.9545187979	0.1004568900	0.8007283618	7.9708655292	0.1254568900	9
10	1.2800845442	11.2033817679	0.0892587632	0.7811984017	8.7520639310	0.1142587632	10
3%							3%
1	1.0300000000	1.0000000000	1.0000000000	0.9708737864	0.9708737864	1.0300000000	1
2	1.0609000000	2.0300000000	0.4926108374	0.9425959091	1.9134696955	0.5226108374	2
3	1.0927270000	3.0909000000	0.3235303633	0.9151416594	2.8286113549	0.3535303633	3
4	1.1255088100	4.1836270000	0.2390270452	0.8884870479	3.7170984028	0.2690270452	4
5	1.1592740743	5.3091358100	0.1883545714	0.8626087844	4.5797071872	0.2183545714	5
6	1.1940522965	6.4684098843	0.1545975005	0.8374842567	5.4171914439	0.1845975005	6
7	1.2298738654	7.6624621808	0.1305063538	0.8130915113	6.2302829552	0.1605063538	7
8	1.2667700814	8.8923360463	0.1124563888	0.7894092343	7.0196921895	0.1424563888	8
9	1.3047731838	10.1591061276	0.0984338570	0.7664167323	7.7861089219	0.1284338570	9
10	1.3439163793	11.4638793115	0.0872305066	0.7440939149	8.5302028368	0.1172305066	10
16	1.6047064391	20.1568813033	0.0496108493	0.6231669392	12.5611020260	0.0796108493	16
17	1.6528476323	21.7615877424	0.0459525294	0.6050164458	13.1661184718	0.0759525294	17
18	1.7024330612	23.4144353747	0.0427086959	0.5873946076	13.7535130795	0.0727086959	18
19	1.7535060531	25.1168684359	0.0398138806	0.5702860268	14.3237991063	0.0698138806	19
20	1.8061112347	26.8703744890	0.0372157076	0.5536757542	14.8774748605	0.0672157076	20
21	1.8602945717	28.6764857236	0.0348717765	0.5375492759	15.4150241364	0.0648717765	21
22	1.9161034089	30.5367802954	0.0327473948	0.5218925009	15.9369166372	0.0627473948	22
23	1.9735865111	32.4528837042	0.0308139027	0.5066917484	16.4436083857	0.0608139027	23
24	2.0327941065	34.4264702153	0.0290474159	0.4919337363	16.9355421220	0.0590474159	24
25	2.0937779297	36.4592643218	0.0274278710	0.4776055693	17.4131476913	0.0574278710	25
3.5%							3.5%
6	1.2292553263	6.5501521813	0.1526682087	0.8135006443	5.3285530198	0.1876682087	6
7	1.2722792628	7.7794075076	0.1285444938	0.7859909607	6.1145439805	0.1635444938	7
8	1.3168090370	9.0516867704	0.1104766465	0.7594115562	6.8739555367	0.1454766465	8
9	1.3628973533	10.3684958073	0.0964460051	0.7337309722	7.6076865089	0.1314460051	9
10	1.4105987606	11.7313931606	0.0852413679	0.7089188137	8.3166053226	0.1202413679	10
16	1.7339860398	20.9710297094	0.0476848306	0.5767059117	12.0941168081	0.0826848306	16
17	1.7946755512	22.7050157492	0.0440431317	0.5572037794	12.6513205876	0.0790431317	17
18	1.8574891955	24.4996913004	0.0408168408	0.5383611396	13.1896817271	0.0758168408	18
19	1.9225013174	26.3571804960	0.0379403252	0.5201556904	13.7098374175	0.0729403252	19
20	1.9897888635	28.2796818133	0.0353610768	0.5025658844	14.2124033020	0.0703810768	20

(continued)

Rate/Period	Compound Amount — Amount of $1 — How $1 left at compound interest will grow.	Amount of Annuity — Amount of $1 per Period — How $1 deposited periodically will grow.	Sinking Fund — Sinking Fund — Periodic deposit that will grow to $1 at future date.	Present Value — Present Worth of $1 — What $1 due in the future is worth today.	Present Value of Annuity — Present Worth of $1 per Period — What $1 payable periodically is worth today.	Amortization — Partial Payment — Annuity worth $1 today. Periodic payment necessary to pay off a loan of $1.	Rate/Period
4% 1	1.0400000000	1.0000000000	1.0000000000	0.9615384615	0.9615384615	1.0400000000	1 **4%**
2	1.0816000000	2.0400000000	0.4901960784	0.9245562130	1.8860946746	0.5301960784	2
3	1.1248640000	3.1216000000	0.3203485392	0.8889963587	2.7750910332	0.3603485392	3
4	1.1698585600	4.2464640000	0.2354900454	0.8548041910	3.6298952243	0.2754900454	4
5	1.2166529024	5.4163225600	0.1846271135	0.8219277068	4.4518223310	0.2246271135	5
6	1.2653190185	6.6329754624	0.1507619025	0.7903145257	5.2421368567	0.1907619025	6
7	1.3159317792	7.8982944809	0.1266096120	0.7599178132	6.0020546699	0.1666096120	7
8	1.3685690504	9.2142262601	0.1085278320	0.7306902050	6.7327448750	0.1485278320	8
9	1.4233118124	10.5827953105	0.0944929927	0.7025867356	7.4353316105	0.1344929927	9
10	1.4802442849	12.0061071230	0.0832909443	0.6755641688	8.1108957794	0.1232909443	10
5% 1	1.0500000000	1.0000000000	1.0000000000	0.9523809524	0.9523809524	1.0500000000	1 **5%**
2	1.1025000000	2.0500000000	0.4878048780	0.9070294785	1.8594104308	0.5378048780	2
3	1.1576250000	3.1525000000	0.3172085646	0.8638375985	2.7232480294	0.3672085646	3
4	1.2155062500	4.3101250000	0.2320118326	0.8227024748	3.5459505042	0.2820118326	4
5	1.2762815625	5.5256312500	0.1809747981	0.7835261665	4.3294766706	0.2309747981	5
6	1.3400956406	6.8019128125	0.1470174681	0.7462153966	5.0756920673	0.1970174681	6
7	1.4071004227	8.1420084531	0.1228198184	0.7106813301	5.7863733974	0.1728198184	7
8	1.4774554438	9.5491088758	0.1047218136	0.6768393620	6.4632127594	0.1547218136	8
9	1.5513282160	11.0265643196	0.0906900400	0.6446089162	7.1078216756	0.1406900800	9
10	1.6288946268	12.5778925356	0.0795045750	0.6139132535	7.7217349292	0.1295045750	10
6% 6	1.4185191123	6.9753185376	0.1433626285	0.7049605404	4.9173243260	0.2033626285	6 **6%**
7	1.5036302590	8.3938376499	0.1191350181	0.6650571136	5.5823814396	0.1791350181	7
8	1.5938480745	9.8974679088	0.1010359426	0.6274123713	6.2097938110	0.1610359426	8
9	1.6894789590	11.4913159834	0.0870222350	0.5918984635	6.8016922745	0.1470222350	9
10	1.7908476965	13.1807949424	0.0758679582	0.5583947769	7.3600870514	0.1358679582	10
7% 6	1.5007303518	7.1532907407	0.1397957998	0.6663422238	4.7665396598	0.2097957998	6 **7%**
7	1.6057814765	8.6540210925	0.1155532196	0.6227497419	5.3892894016	0.1855532196	7
8	1.7181861798	10.2598025690	0.0974677625	0.5820091046	5.9712985062	0.1674677625	8
9	1.8384592124	11.9779887489	0.0834864701	0.5439337426	6.5152322488	0.1534864701	9
10	1.9671513573	13.8164479613	0.0723775027	0.5083492921	7.0235815409	0.1423775027	10

(continued)

503

Rate/Period		Compound Amount	Amount of Annuity	Sinking Fund	Present Value	Present Value of Annuity	Amortization		Rate/Period
		Amount of $1	Amount of $1 per Period	Sinking Fund	Present Worth of $1	Present Worth of $1 per Period	Partial Payment		
		How $1 left at compound interest will grow.	*How $1 deposited periodically will grow.*	*Periodic deposit that will grow to $1 at future date.*	*What $1 due in the future is worth today.*	*What $1 payable periodically is worth today.*	*Annuity worth $1 today. Periodic payment necessary to pay off a loan of $1.*		
8%	1	1.0800000000	1.0000000000	1.0000000000	0.9259259259	0.9259259259	1.0800000000	1	8%
	2	1.1664000000	2.0800000000	0.4807692308	0.8573388203	1.7832647462	0.5607692308	2	
	3	1.2597120000	3.2464000000	0.3080335140	0.7938322410	2.5770969872	0.3880335140	3	
	4	1.3604889600	4.5061120000	0.2219208045	0.7350298528	3.3121268400	0.3019208045	4	
	5	1.4693280768	5.8666009600	0.1704564546	0.6805831970	3.9927100371	0.2504564546	5	
10%	6	1.7715610000	7.7156100000	0.1296073804	0.5644739301	4.3552606995	0.2296073804	6	10%
	7	1.9487171000	9.4871710000	0.1054054997	0.5131581182	4.8684188177	0.2054054997	7	
	8	2.1435888100	11.4358881000	0.0874440176	0.4665073802	5.3349261979	0.1874440176	8	
	9	2.3579476910	13.5794769100	0.0736405391	0.4240976184	5.7590238163	0.1736405391	9	
	10	2.5937424601	15.9374246010	0.0627453949	0.3855432894	6.1445671057	0.1627453949	10	
12%	6	1.9738226652	8.1151890432	0.1232257184	0.5066311212	4.1114073235	0.2432257184	6	12%
	7	2.2106814074	10.0890117284	0.0991177359	0.4523492153	4.5637565389	0.2191177359	7	
	8	2.4759631763	12.2996931358	0.0813028414	0.4038832280	4.9676397668	0.2013028414	8	
	9	2.7730787575	14.4756563121	0.0676788888	0.3606100250	5.3282497918	0.1876788888	9	
	10	3.1058482083	17.5487350695	0.0569841642	0.3219732366	5.6502230284	0.1769841642	10	

Monthly Payment per $1,000 of Mortgage

Rate	20 Years	25 Years	30 Years
8.00%	$8.37	$7.72	$7.34
8.25	8.53	7.89	7.52
8.50	8.68	8.06	7.69
8.75	8.84	8.23	7.87
9.00	9.00	8.40	8.05
9.25	9.16	8.57	8.23
9.50	9.33	8.74	8.41
9.75	9.49	8.92	8.60
10.00	9.66	9.09	8.78
11.00	10.33	9.81	9.53

Note: Monthly payments including principal and interest.

CHAPTER 29

Consumer Credit, Installment Purchases Rule of 78 and Interest Refunds

PART 1 *Speed and Accuracy Building Using Touch Key*

GOALS: Your speed goal is 12,000 strokes per hour.
Your accuracy target goal range is 95% to 100%.

With each repetition of the drill, try to improve your speed without lowering your accuracy score. If your percent-of-accuracy score falls below 95%, review your finger position and technique. Then try again.

Instructions: *Start Touch Key. Complete Drill 6, Part A, Five-Minute Timing. (Parts B through E are optional.) Write your scores for strokes per hour and percent of accuracy below.*

Touch Key Drill 6—The 0 through 9, Decimal, and Minus Keys, Five-Digit Numbers (Mixed), Five-Minute Timing

Today's Date	Strokes per Hour	Percent of Accuracy
A.		
B.		
C.		
D.		
E.		

PART 2 *Business Math Skills*

CONSUMER CREDIT

Merchants may extend credit to customers through a closed-end loan or an open-end loan. A **closed-end loan** is one in which the amount of the loan is fixed. An example is an installment plan.

INSTALLMENT LOANS

Consumers may often purchase items such as large appliances and televisions on an installment plan, which is a type of loan. An **installment loan** is a retail agreement in which the consumer promises to pay the retailer an installment price, usually with a down payment and monthly payments. The **installment price** for a product includes the down payment, the installment payments, the finance charges, and any or all fees included in the retail credit agreement (Figure 29.1).

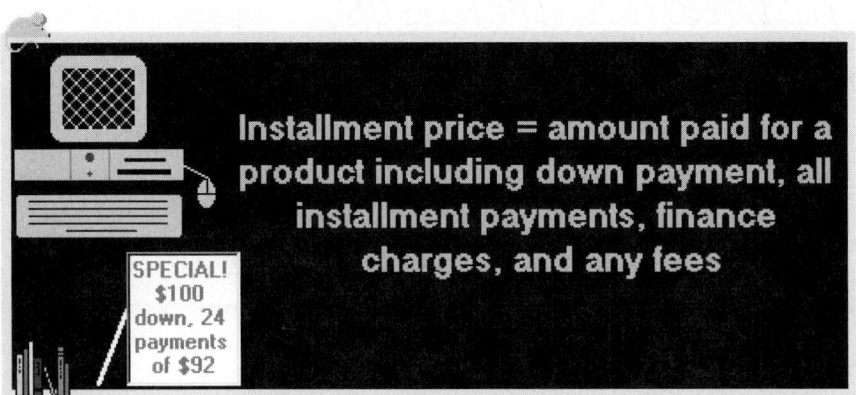

FIGURE 29.1

The **down payment** is the partial cash payment made at the time the product is purchased. The **amount financed** is the installment price minus the down payment. The **cash price** is the price of the product if cash is paid rather than using the installment plan. The cash price is usually lower because no fees, finance charges, and so on are involved.

Let us first look at two problems that do not involve finance charges to see how the installment price and payments are calculated.

PROBLEM 1

A computer system is advertised for $100 down and 24 payments of $92. No other fees apply.

Add the down payment to the total of the installment payments as shown in Figure 29.2. The installment price is $2,308.

Installment price = down payment + (no. of payments x payment amount)

1 0 0 + (2 4 X 9 2)

= $ 2 , 3 0 8

FIGURE 29.2

Pocket Calculator Procedure	Desktop Calculator Procedure
24 × 92 = 2,208 + 100 = 2,308	24 × 92 = 2,208 + 100 + T 2,308

PROBLEM 2

Find the amount of the installment payment for a sewing machine that costs $2,500 on the installment plan with terms of $200 down and the rest to be paid over 24 months.

First, subtract the down payment from the price. Divide the result by the number of payments to be made (in this case, 24) as shown in Figure 29.3. The amount of each installment payment is $95.83.

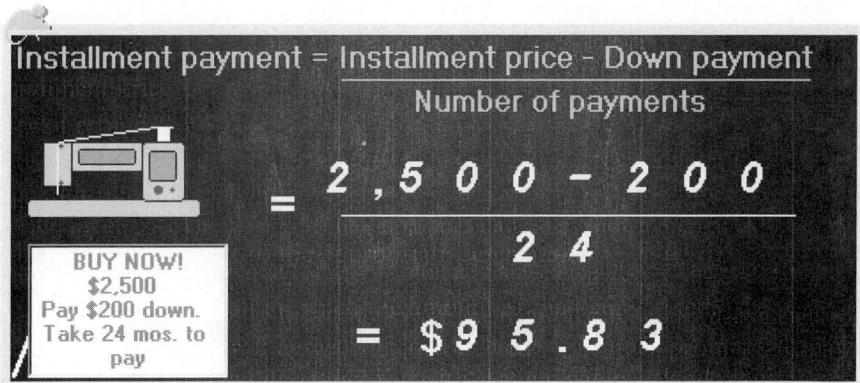

FIGURE 29.3

Pocket Calculator Procedure	Desktop Calculator Procedure
2,500 − 200 = 2,300 ÷ 24 = 95.83	2,500 + 200 − T 2,300 ÷ 24 = 95.83

The next problem involves an installment plan purchase with finance charges. The simple interest formula, Interest = Principal × Rate × Time, is used to calculate the finance charge, where interest equals the finance charge.

PROBLEM 3A

New office furniture was purchased for $8,000. The total amount was financed for 48 months at 18%. Use the simple interest formula to find the finance charge as shown in Figure 29.4. Because there was no down payment to subtract from the price, the entire amount of $8,000 will be financed:

Principal: $8,000

Rate: 18% annual interest

Time: 48 ÷ 12 months = 4 years

$$8,000 \times 0.18 \times 4 = \$5,760$$

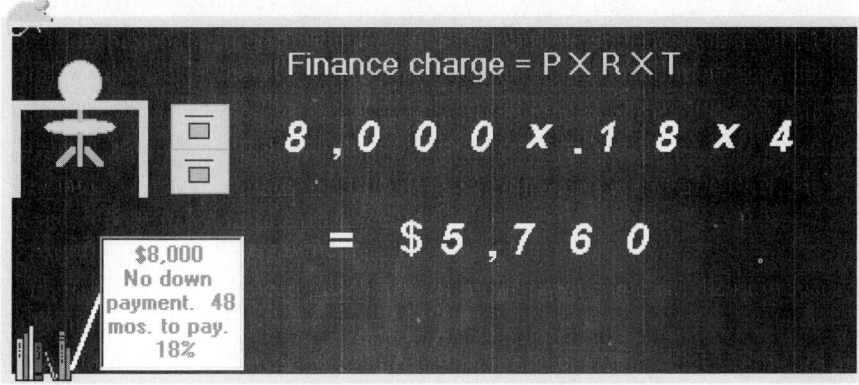

FIGURE 29.4

An alternative to converting months to years is to convert the annual finance charge to a monthly finance charge. Use the method with which you are most comfortable:

Principal: $8,000

Rate: 18% ÷ 12 months = 1.5% per month

Time: 48 months

The resulting formula returns the same result:

$$\$8,000 \times 0.015 \times 48 = \$5,760$$

PROBLEM 3B

Find the installment price.
Add the cash price and the total finance charge as shown in Figure 29.5.

Installment price = Cash price +
Finance charge

8,000 + 5,760

= $13,760

FIGURE 29.5

PROBLEM 3C

Find the amount of the monthly payment.
Subtract the down payment ($0) from the installment price. Divide the difference by the number of payments as shown in Figure 29.6.

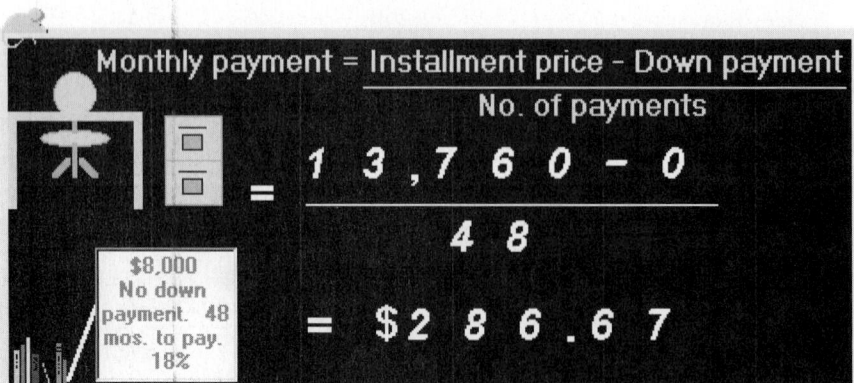

Monthly payment = Installment price - Down payment / No. of payments

$8,000 No down payment. 48 mos. to pay. 18%

= 13,760 - 0 / 48

= $286.67

FIGURE 29.6

Because the finance charge rate is usually stated as an annual rate and the payments are usually monthly, be sure to convert the annual rate to a monthly rate when working with installment plans.

INTEREST REFUNDS

An installment loan that is paid off early will result in an **interest refund** or **rebate**. Because more interest is paid during the early months of an installment loan than during the later months, a special method based on the **Rule of 78** is required to calculate the amount of interest to be refunded. With this method, the sum of the months' digits must be calculated for both the months the loan was paid off early and for the total months of the original loan. The name Rule of 78 comes from the fact that the sum of the digits for 12 months equals 78. The sum of the months paid off early is divided by the sum of the months' digits for the original loan. The result is the rate to be multiplied by the original finance charge to find the amount of interest to refund to the customer.

PROBLEM 4

A 12-month loan with an $84 finance charge was paid off 2 months early. Find the amount of interest to be refunded.

1. Calculate the sum of the months' digits for the 2 months the loan was paid off early.
2. Calculate the sum of the months' digits for the total months of the loan.
3. Divide as shown in Figure 29.7.

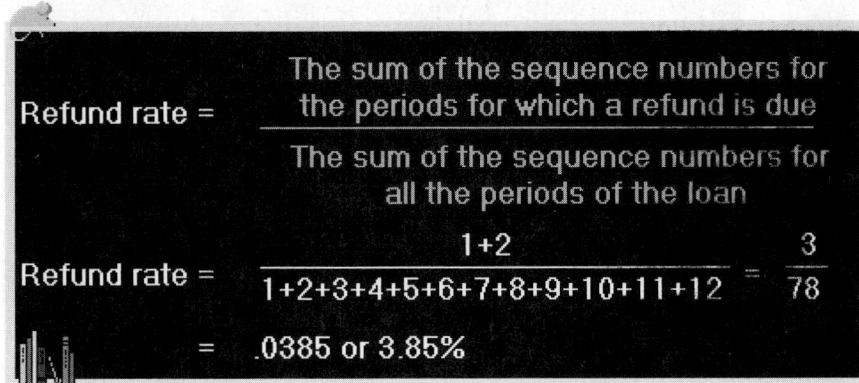

$$\text{Refund rate} = \frac{\text{The sum of the sequence numbers for the periods for which a refund is due}}{\text{The sum of the sequence numbers for all the periods of the loan}}$$

$$\text{Refund rate} = \frac{1+2}{1+2+3+4+5+6+7+8+9+10+11+12} = \frac{3}{78}$$

$$= .0385 \text{ or } 3.85\%$$

FIGURE 29.7

4. Multiply the rate calculated in step 3 by the interest (finance charge) for the loan as shown in Figure 29.8.

$$\text{Interest refund} = \text{Refund rate} \times \text{Amount of finance charge}$$

$$\text{Interest refund} = .0385 \times 84 = \$3.23$$

FIGURE 29.8

TABLE METHOD

You can use the table for the Sum of the Months' Digits to find the appropriate rate for large numbers of months. The sum-of-the-month's digits for a 12-month loan, for example, is 78.

Sum of the Months' Digits

Number of Months	Sum: 1 through Largest Month
6	21
9	45
10	55
12	**78**
15	120
18	171
24	300
36	666

SHORTCUT FORMULA METHOD

A shortcut for finding the sum of the months' digits, also called the sum of sequence numbers, is shown in Figure 29.9: [(largest number in sequence) times (largest number in sequence plus 1)] divided by 2. This formula may be handy when no table is available.

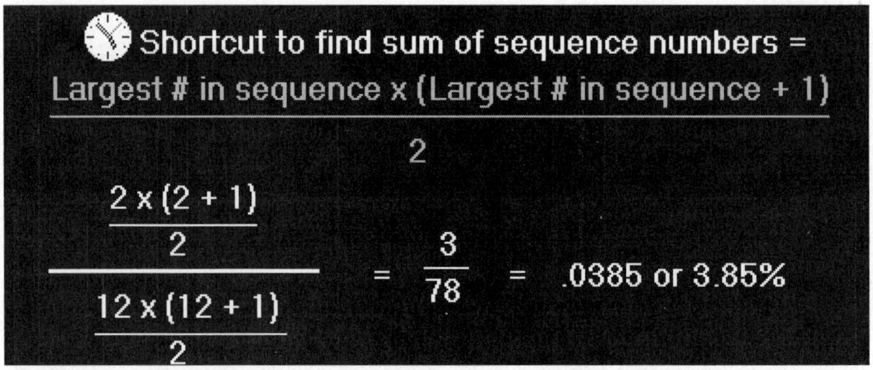

FIGURE 29.9

To use the shortcut formula to find the interest refund rate for a 12-month loan paid off 2 months early, use the second formula shown in Figure 29.9. To solve:

1. Calculate the sum of the months' digits for the 2 months the loan was paid off early (the numerator portion of the formula). Multiply the *largest number in the sequence* (2) times the *largest number in the sequence plus one* (2 + 1). Divide the result by 2.

2. Calculate the sum of the months' digits for the 12 months of the original loan (the denominator portion of the formula). Multiply the *largest number in the sequence* (12) times the *largest number in the sequence plus 1* (12 + 1). Divide the result by 2.

3. To find the interest refund rate, divide value of the numerator found in step 1 by the value of the denominator found in step 2.

PART 2 *Business Math Skills*

Exercise 1

1. A television is advertised for $3,559 with $200 down, 18 months to pay, and 0% interest. Calculate the amount of the monthly payment. _____

2. A sofa and chair combo is advertised at $2,000. It can be purchased on the installment plan for $75 down, 3% interest, and 36 months to pay. If it is purchased on the installment plan, calculate the following:
   a. Finance charge _____
   b. Installment price _____
   c. Monthly payment _____

3. A laser printer can be purchased for $50 down and $50 per month for 36 months. Calculate the installment price. _____

4. A jeweler offers a diamond bracelet for $2,500. It can be purchased for $300 down, with payments spread over 2 years at 18% interest. The jeweler also requires insurance and charges a finance fee. The insurance for the bracelet is $175. The finance fee is $25. If the bracelet is purchased on the installment plan, calculate the following:
   a. Finance charge _____
   b. Installment price _____
   c. Monthly payment _____

5. Use the shortcut formula to find the sum of the sequence of numbers and the interest refund rate for an 18-month loan paid off 3 months early. Show your work below.

6. Calculate the interest refund for a loan that was paid off 3 months early. The original loan was for 18 months with a finance charge of $60. _____

7. Calculate the interest refund for a $5,000 loan financed at 6% for 2 years. The loan was paid off 4 months early. _____

8. Use the Sum-of-the-Month's-Digits table to find the sum of the sequence for a 6-month loan. _____

9. A used Cessna was purchased for $12,000. It was financed for 3 years at 12%. The loan was paid off 9 months early. What was the amount of the interest refund? _____

PART 3 *Review and Practice Using Business Math FUNdamentals*

GOAL: Complete 9 of the 10 problems correctly.

Instructions: *Start Business Math FUNdamentals. Complete Tutorial 68 and Drill 50. If you are not satisfied with your score, repeat the drill. Write your scores below.*

Business Math FUNdamentals Drill 50

Today's Date	Score

 PART 4 *Desktop Calculator*

Exercise 1

One-Minute Addition Timing (0 through 9 Keys, One- to Five-Digit Numbers)

(Optional: Your instructor may wish you to use Touch Key on the computer for all your timings. Check with your instructor before completing this exercise.)

Complete as many of the problems as possible in 1 minute by adding. Work quickly and accurately. The number preceding each closing parenthesis indicates the cumulative number of strokes for problems attempted. For example, if you complete Problems 1 through 5 in 1 minute, your strokes-per-minute score is 250. Optional: 3- and 5-minute timings. If you complete all the problems in 5 minutes, your strokes-per-minute score is 260.

1. 911.55	2. 810.24	3. 35.544	4. 9,900.6	5. 27.850	6. 49.200	7. 91.300	8. 32.541
258.5	276.9	81.35	890.2	35	58	80	11
437	762	600	601	654	126	147	312
67	29	55	54	595.6	−187.4	−900.7	−313.1
735.2	886.5	972.3	510.1	−1	2	9	9
3	3	−2	−2	629.9	323.6	400.9	981.2
−5.093	100.7	940.3	900.3	57	47	82	87
906	900	864	300	774	635	147	673
32	−16	70	58	112.3	614.3	630.7	548.5
63.871	11.002	35.306	39.175	4,432.8	3,278.6	9,152.9	2,000.3
50)	100)	150)	200)	250)	300)	350)	400)

9. 12.140	10. 4,690.1	11. 126.98	12. 400.9	13. 93.45	14. 69.661	15. −916.09	16. −1.9004
−23.64	54.26	20.02	103.1	20.99	58	83	86
345	661	895	620	900	884	736	407
76.56	−777.9	−670.4	134.3	27.82	5.655	6.014	8.870
7	8	5	−2	−6	−41	−73	−92
13	99	35	63	67	5	8	5
19.95	9.765	2.653	176.3	1.577	5.741	928.3	189.5
284	800	832	952	259	662	892	237
36	95	79	91	35	59.45	696.2	83.32
79.934	35.578	43.396	3,009.5	24.009	6.013	610.8	25.42
450)	500)	550)	600)	650)	700)	750)	800)

17. 421.55	18. 120.24	19. 91.004	20. 9,341.6	21. 19.850	22. 34.200	23. 12.322	24. 54.901
756.5	245.9	88.35	827.2	25	85	37	75
817	392	799	781	853	972	145	876
52	49	68	67	444.6	−881.4	−212.7	−109.1
345.9	236.5	542.4	597.5	−1	7	3	1
5	5	−3	−4	580.9	623.6	233.9	142.2
−9.007	627.7	955.3	326.3	66	57	65	63
123	731	731	219	875	436	175	798
33	−86	65	90	774.3	533.3	259.9	962.5
123.872	10.320	15.355	74.050	9,232.1	8,992.6	1,500.8	2,731.3
850)	900)	950)	1,000)	1,050)	1,200)	1,250)	1,300)

CHAPTER 29 *Terminology Review*

Amount financed
Cash price
Closed-end loan
Down payment
Installment loan
Installment price
Interest refund
Rebate
Rule of 78

Write the correct term next to the appropriate description.

1. _____ A loan in which the amount of the loan is fixed.
2. _____ A retail agreement in which the consumer promises to pay the retailer an installment price, usually with a down payment and monthly payments.
3. _____ The amount paid for a product that includes the down payment, the installment payments, the finance charges, and any or all fees included in the retail credit agreement.
4. _____ The partial cash payment made at the time a product is purchased.
5. _____ The installment price of a product minus the down payment.
6. _____ The price of a product if cash is paid rather than using the installment plan.
7. _____ The result of an installment loan that is paid off early.
8. _____ The basis for a special method required to calculate the amount of interest to be refunded.

Name _____

Class/Section _____

Score (Correct Answers ÷ No. of Assigned Problems) _____

Chapter 29 Review Exercises
Exercise 1

1. A 2-horsepower outboard motor can be purchased for $99 down and nine payments of $99. Calculate the installment price. _____
2. An inflatable boat can be purchased for $850 on the installment plan with 10% down and the rest paid in monthly installments over 1 year. Calculate the amount of each installment payment. _____
3. A moped was advertised for $3,000. It can be financed with $500 down at 3% with 60 months to pay. The seller charges a $15 credit application fee. Calculate the following:
   a. Finance charge _____
   b. Installment price _____
   c. Monthly installment payment _____
4. A $4,500 used car financed at 8% for 24 months was paid off 12 months early. Use the formula to calculate the following:
   a. Original finance charge _____
   b. Interest refund rate _____
   c. Amount of interest to be refunded _____

5. A-Z Appliances offered local victims of a severe flood no down payment and 35 months to pay at 0% interest on any item in the store. The store sold a washer for $400, a dryer for $350, and a refrigerator for $900 to one customer. What was the monthly payment? _____

END-OF-CHAPTER TABLE

Sum of the Months' Digits

Number of Months	Sum: 1 through Largest Month
6	21
9	45
10	55
12	78
15	120
18	171
24	300
36	666

CHAPTER 30

Consumer Credit Continued, Revolving Charge Accounts, Annual Percentage Rate

 **PART 1** *Speed and Accuracy Building Using Touch Key*

GOALS: Your speed goal is 12,000 strokes per hour.
Your accuracy target goal range is 95% to 100%.

With each repetition of the test, try to improve your speed without lowering your accuracy score. If your percent-of-accuracy score falls below 95%, review your finger position and technique. Then try again.

Instructions: *Start Touch Key. Complete the Checks Test in Appendix A. Write your scores for strokes per hour and percent of accuracy below. If you are not satisfied with your scores, repeat the test until you are satisfied.*

Checks Test

Today's Date	Strokes per Hour	Percent of Accuracy
A.		
B.		
C.		
D.		
E.		

PART 2 *Business Math Skills*

ADDITIONAL TYPES OF CONSUMER CREDIT

An **open-end loan** is one in which additional purchases can be made without renegotiation of a loan or credit agreement. Examples are revolving charge accounts and bank credit cards.

REVOLVING CHARGE ACCOUNTS

A **revolving charge account** is a type of open-end loan. With this type of loan a business or person may be making payments to pay off a loan, but is also allowed to make additional purchases, thus increasing the amount of the loan (up to a specified limit) without further negotiations. Using a credit card is one such example. Credit cards are available for business or personal use. Some credit cards have an annual fee; some do not. A grace period may be allowed in which a customer has 25 or more days in which to pay off the entire balance without incurring finance charges. Credit cards used by businesses often have annual summaries of card use and other special features. Payments on the account are made monthly. Interest is quoted as an annual rate compounded monthly. There are two methods used for calculating interest: the unpaid balance method and the average daily balance method.

Unpaid Balance Method

Some credit card companies base their finance charges on the previous month's unpaid balance, as shown in Figure 30.1. In this **unpaid balance method,** the interest calculated and any purchases and cash advances made during the current month are added to the previous month's balance. Payments and credits to the account during the current month are subtracted.

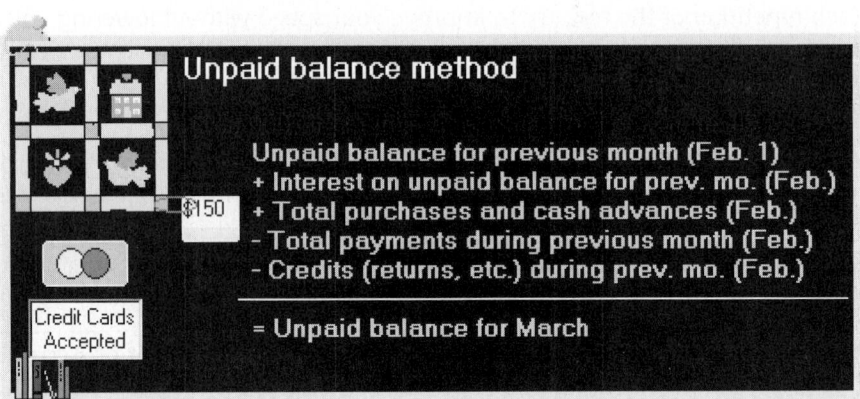

FIGURE 30.1

PROBLEM 1

A revolving charge account had an unpaid balance of $760 on February 1. During the month the customer made purchases of $150 and a payment of $200. This account carries an 18% finance rate and uses the unpaid balance method to calculate finance charges.

    a.   What is the interest on the unpaid balance?

    b.   What is the unpaid balance for March 1?

Answer a: To find the interest on the unpaid balance, multiply the unpaid balance by the monthly rate (18% ÷ 12 = 1.5%):

$$760 \times 1.5\% = \$11.40$$

Answer b: To find the unpaid balance for March, add the interest (finance charge) found in Problem 1a to the unpaid balance as of February 1. To the unpaid balance, add purchases and cash advances; subtract payments and any other credits made during February as shown in Figure 30.2.

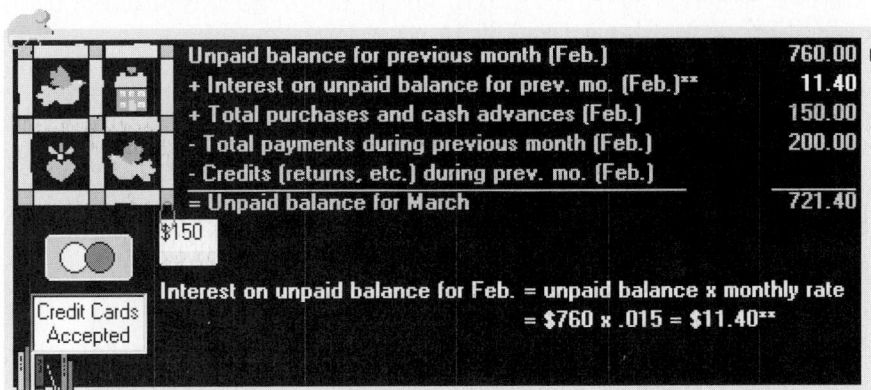

FIGURE 30.2

Average Daily Balance Method

To calculate finance charges when the **average daily balance method** is used, apply the monthly finance rate to the average daily balance during the billing cycle for that month. Finding the average daily balance is a two-step process:

1. First, find the daily unpaid balance. To the previous day's unpaid balance add any purchases and cash advances for the day and subtract any payments and credits for the day.
2. Second, find the average daily balance. Sum the total daily unpaid balances for the month's billing cycle. Divide this sum by the number of days in the billing cycle as shown in Figure 30.3.

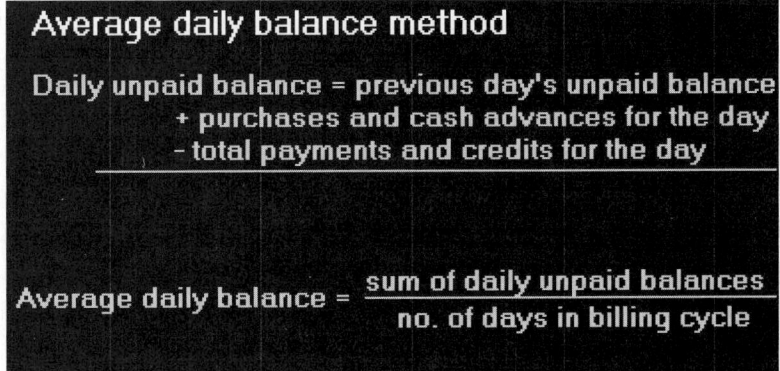

FIGURE 30.3

PROBLEM 2

A charge account had a daily balance of $390 for 10 days and $260 for 15 days during July. The company uses a 25-day billing cycle and charges a 10% finance rate. What is the finance charge for the current billing cycle if the average daily balance method is used?

1. Find the sum of the daily unpaid balances:

$$\$390 \times 10 = \$3,900$$
$$\$260 \times 15 = \$3,900$$
$$\$3,900 + \$3,900 = \$7,800$$

2. Find the average daily balance. Divide the sum by the number of days in the billing cycle:

$$\$7,800 \div 25 = \$312 \text{ average daily balance.}$$

3. Calculate the interest for the billing cycle. Multiply the average daily balance by the monthly finance rate (.10 ÷ 12) as shown in Figure 30.4.

Daily unpaid balance = previous day's unpaid balance
    + purchases and cash advances for the day
    - total payments and credits for the day

$$\text{Average daily balance} = \frac{\text{sum of daily unpaid balances}}{\text{no. of days in billing cycle}}$$

$$= \frac{(390 \times 10) + (260 \times 15)}{25} = \frac{7800}{25} = \$312$$

$$\text{Interest for billing cycle} = 312 \times \frac{.1}{12} = \frac{31.2}{12} = \$2.60$$

FIGURE 30.4

Pocket Calculator Method

390 × 10 = ⌐3900⌐ M+ 260 × 15 = ⌐3900⌐ M+ MT ⌐7800⌐ ÷ 25 = ⌐312⌐
× .1 = ⌐31.2⌐ ÷ 12 = $ ⌐2.60⌐   finance charge

ANNUAL PERCENTAGE RATE

Because purchase plans may specify finance charges compounded monthly, annually, quarterly, and so on, consumers find it difficult to compare finance charges. As discussed earlier, installment plans are interest payment plans. The finance charges include carrying charges, service charges, interest, insurance, and any other charges on credit sales. Merchants are required to disclose the **annual percentage rate** (APR), which includes all of these charges associated with a credit purchase in terms of an annual simple interest rate. The consumer can compare many different terms for paying interest or finance charges to terms of simple interest stated as the APR. A table for the annual percentage rate for monthly payment is used to help determine the APR. To use the table (included at the end of this chapter), find the number of installment payments. Read across this row to find the **finance charge per $100 of amount financed**. Use Finance Charge ÷ Amount Financed × 100 to find the finance charge per $100 of amount financed. At the top of the column containing the finance charge, read the annual percentage rate.

Note: The APR table may not include the exact amount of the finance charge per $100 of amount financed. In this case, use the closest number to the finance charge. If the finance charge is midway between two table values, use the larger value.

PROBLEM 3

A refrigerator was advertised for $1,000 cash. The customer elected to pay by the installment plan with terms of $100 down, a 10% finance charge, and 12 monthly payments. What is the APR if this appliance is purchased on the installment plan?

Step 1a: Calculate the finance charge as shown in Figure 30.5.
    Subtract the down payment from the cash price. Multiply the remainder by 10% and 1 year to find the finance charge ($90).
    Note that the annual rate of 10% (0.10) is used for rate and 1 year is used instead of 12 months.

Step 1b: Calculate the total cost of the refrigerator.

Installment Price ($900) + Down Payment ($100) + Finance Charge ($90) = $1,090

Step 1: Find the total cost of the refrigerator if purchased with the payment terms.
Cash price - Down payment = Balance
$1,000 - $100 = $900
Finance charge = $900 x .10 x 1 = $90
Total cost = Down payment + Balance + Finance Charge
Total cost = $100 + $900 + $90 = $1,090

FIGURE 30.5

Step 2: Find the finance charge per $100 of amount financed as shown in Figure 30.6:

Finance Charge ($90) ÷ Amount Financed ($900) × 100 = $10

Step 3: Find the APR. Follow the instructions for using the APR table contained in Figure 30.6. The APR is 18%.

Step 2: Find the finance charge per $100 of amount financed using the formula:
Finance charge / Balance x 100
$90 / $900 x 100 = $10
Step 3: Use the APR table.
Find 12 under the Number of Payments column. Read across to find the closest number to $10, which is 10.02. The percent at the top of this column is the APR (18%).

FIGURE 30.6

ESTIMATING APR

If an APR table is not available, it is possible to estimate the APR using the formula **APR = 2MI ÷ P($n + 1$)** as shown in Figure 30.8, where M equals the number of payments in a year (usually 12), I equals the finance charge, P equals the amount financed, and n equals the total number of payments. The formula for estimating the APR is explained more fully in Figure 30.7, where words are used instead of letters for variables. Both formulas will return the same result. This method should only be used for equal installment payments and for loans less than 10 years in length. Added fees increase the APR rate.

$$\text{estimated APR} = \frac{2 \times \text{no. of payments per yr.} \times \text{total interest}}{\text{amt. financed} \times (\text{total no. of payments})}$$

P = amt. financed = cash price - down payment
= 1,200 - 100 = $1,100
I = finance charge =
(no. of payments x monthly payment + fees) - cash price
= (15 x 90 + 10) - 1,200 = $160

FIGURE 30.7

PROBLEM 4

A refrigerator was advertised for $1,200 cash. The customer elected to pay by the installment plan with terms of $100 down and 15 monthly payments of $90. A credit application fee of $10 was required by the appliance store. Use the formula method to estimate the APR.

  a. To use the formula, we need to know the amount financed and the finance charge. Referring to Figure 30.7, we see that cash price ($1,200) minus down payment ($100) equals amount financed ($1,100).

  b. To find the finance charge, multiply the 15 months by the $90 payment and add the fee ($10) to the result. Subtract from the cash price to find the finance charge:

$$15 \times \$90 = \$1,350$$

$$\$1,350 + \$10 = \$1,360$$

$$\$1,360 - \$1,200 = \$160 \text{ finance charge}$$

Pocket Calculator Method

$$1200 - 100 = \boxed{1,100}$$

$$15 \times 90 = \boxed{1,350} + 10 = \boxed{1,360} - 1,200 = \boxed{160}$$

  c. Substitute the known values into the formula for estimating the APR as shown in Figure 30.8. If you are using a calculator, calculate the denominator first and add it to memory. Calculate the numerator and divide by memory recall. The percent key can be used to obtain the final result. Round the final answer to hundredths.

Refrigerator $1200, terms $100 down and 15 mo. payments of $90

$$\text{estimated APR} = \frac{2MI}{P(n+1)}$$

where
M = 12 (no. of payments in 1 yr.)
I = finance charge
P = amt. financed
n = total number of payments

$$\text{estimated APR} = \frac{2 \times 12 \times 160}{1,100\,(15 + 1)} = \frac{3,840}{17,600} = 21.82\%$$

FIGURE 30.8

Pocket Calculator Method

Clear memory if necessary.

MC 1,100 × 16 = $\boxed{17,600}$ M+

2 × 12 × 160 = $\boxed{3,840}$

÷ MR % $\boxed{21.82}$ estimated APR

DAILY PERIODIC RATE

The **daily periodic rate** that most credit card companies use is the APR the company charges divided by 365 days and rounded to the fourth or fifth decimal place. The average daily balance is multiplied by the daily periodic rate to find the daily finance charge. The daily finance charge is multiplied by the number of days in the billing cycle to find the periodic (monthly) finance charge.

If late fees are encountered, the fees are added to the unpaid balance in addition to the periodic finance charge.

PROBLEM 5

A credit card account has an average daily balance of $6,519.25 and an APR of 8.46%. Calculate the periodic finance charge for November if the billing cycle is 30 days.

1. Divide the APR by the number of days in a year to find the daily periodic rate. Round to four decimal places:

$$8.46 \div 365 = 0.0232\%(\text{rounded})$$

2. Multiply the average daily balance by the daily periodic rate. Multiply the result by 30 days to find the periodic finance charge.

Pen-and-Paper Method

Divide the average daily balance by 100 and multiply by the rate, 0.0232:

$$\$6,519.25 \div 100 \times 0.0232 = \$45.37$$

Or move the decimal two places to the left before multiplying by the rate:

$$\$6,519.25 \times 0.000232 \times 30 = \$45.37$$

Pocket Calculator Method

Be sure to use the percent key with the rate 0.0232:

$$6,519.25 \times 0.0232 \boxed{\%} \times 30 = \$45.37$$
$$\text{Or } 6,519.25 \times 0.0232 \times 30 \boxed{\%} \$45.37$$

Name _____

Class/Section _____

Score (Correct Answers ÷ No. of Assigned Problems) _____

PART 2   *Business Math Skills*

Exercises

1. A customer's revolving charge account showed a balance of $3,562 as of June 1 on the monthly statement. The customer charged $200 during June and made one payment of $500. The finance rate on the account is 9.25%. What is the unpaid balance as of June 30? _____

2. A business has a bankcard with an account balance of $1,945.16 and a finance rate of 9% on the average daily balance. The business made a purchase of $500 on July 10. A payment of $2,000 was made on July 20. Calculate the average daily balance if a 31-day billing cycle is used. _____

3. Calculate the July finance charge for Problem 2. _____

4. A store credit account with a balance of $5,290 on May 1 has a finance rate of 9.4% on the unpaid balance. A payment of $300 was made on May 15. No purchases were made during May. Calculate the finance charge for May. _____

5. Calculate the unpaid balance for Problem 4 as of the end of the finance period. _____

6. A credit card account has an APR of 9.2% and a 29-day billing cycle. The average daily balance this finance period is $2,995. Calculate the periodic finance charge. _____

PART 3 *Review and Practice Using Business Math FUNdamentals*

GOAL: Complete 9 of the 10 problems correctly.

Instructions: *Start Business Math FUNdamentals. Complete Tutorials 59 and 60 and Drills 47 and 48. If you are not satisfied with your score, repeat the drill. Write your scores below.*

Business Math FUNdamentals Drill 47

Today's Date	Score

Business Math FUNdamentals Drill 48

Today's Date	Score

Name _____

Class/Section _____

Strokes per Minute Score _____

Accuracy Score (Correct Strokes ÷ Total Strokes) _____

PART 4 *Desktop Calculator*

Exercise 1

One-Minute Addition Timing (0 through 9 and Decimal Keys, Six-Digit Numbers)

(Optional: Your instructor may wish you to use Touch Key on the computer for all your timings. Check with your instructor before completing this exercise.)

Complete as many of the problems as possible in 1 minute by adding. Work quickly and accurately. The number preceding each closing parenthesis indicates the cumulative number of strokes for problems attempted. For example, if you complete Problems 1 through 3 in 1 minute, your strokes-per-minute score is 243. Optional: 3- to 5-minute timings. If you complete all the problems in 5 minutes, your strokes-per-minute score is 259.

1. 1235.56	2. 5110.04	3. 1555.34	4. 5290.06	5. 2215.07	6. 1562.00	7. 2541.00	8. 6240.01
7582.33	5765.22	7513.34	3739.02	4554.22	9286.21	6256.00	6196.21
1339.87	3310.09	1218.00	5337.01	3005.01	1621.00	1220.00	6732.02
2254.57	3973.44	1502.33	6444.42	6992.24	4873.32	2123.00	1532.21
7354.43	4110.41	1424.00	1432.04	5115.91	5310.06	6522.00	1562.24
4115.24	7192.33	5325.00	3402.33	3426.22	2231.62	6532.00	3233.02
9913.24	4437.88	1223.00	4230.03	5119.91	1320.03	1532.00	4111.22
4438.35	6533.51	1231.00	1430.03	4574.22	6363.54	1535.00	1526.64
9202.24	4538.00	4034.56	4210.01	3560.03	4210.06	1520.00	6137.33
3344.11	2133.20	5355.33	3140.02	3456.01	3252.00	1330.00	5132.23
81)	162)	243)	324)	405)	486)	567)	648)

9. 9014.00	10. 7000.01	11. 7567.00	12. 9787.79	13. 9889.86	14. 9706.01	15. 5169.00	16. 8009.04
8678.90	4420.07	8761.22	1530.70	7768.75	7899.87	9960.13	8967.00
9981.50	3005.53	1609.76	8966.66	8869.50	9988.85	7389.97	9570.00
8532.50	7760.08	5970.04	1359.76	2728.76	9699.96	7690.14	6349.97
9987.00	5005.65	3227.07	8966.55	6885.90	7764.44	4309.76	9007.76
7796.89	1740.00	8770.00	9785.86	6099.60	2678.79	8860.23	9760.03
9015.99	3900.59	2656.97	1769.36	8977.70	9967.41	6287.69	9896.88
6978.84	8001.00	9764.32	1789.00	9900.90	4528.79	9980.53	7797.87
8178.56	8050.00	3117.98	7694.95	4568.87	9978.54	6979.07	8367.65
5113.74	9300.75	9789.80	2329.00	8890.00	9970.14	8760.11	8868.00
729)	810)	891)	972)	1,053)	1,134)	1,215)	1,296)

CHAPTER 30 *Terminology Review*

Annual percentage rate
APR $= 2MI \div P(n + 1)$
Average daily balance method
Daily periodic rate
Finance charge per $100 of amount financed
Open-end loan
Revolving charge account
Unpaid balance method

Write the correct term next to the appropriate description.

1. _____ A loan in which additional purchases may be made without renegotiation of the loan or credit agreement.

2. _____ A type of open-end loan.

3. _____ A method in which finance charges are based on the previous month's unpaid balance.

4. _____ A method in which the monthly finance rate is applied to the average daily balance of a finance period to calculate finance charges.

5. _____ Includes all of the charges associated with a credit purchase stated in terms of an annual simple interest rate.

6. _____ Equals Finance Charge ÷ Amount Financed × 100.

7. _____ The formula used to estimate APR.

8. _____ The APR the credit card companies charge divided by 365 days.

Chapter 30 Review Exercises
Exercise 1

Round credit card finance rates to four decimal places for these problems.

1. An $18,000 car can be financed at 7.5% for 60 months. Using the APR table, calculate the following:

    a. Original finance charge _____
    b. Finance charge per $100 of amount financed _____
    c. APR _____

2. A bankcard customer has an unpaid balance of $4,090 on her account and an 18% finance rate. How much will she save this month in finance charges if she changes to a bankcard with a 12% finance rate and both cards use the unpaid balance method? _____

3. A credit card company offered a special finance rate on balance transfers of 3.9% APR. The rate for purchases is 14.9% APR. Last month a customer transferred $10,000 to this company and made purchases of $565. The company has a 29-day billing cycle. Calculate the following:

    a. Finance charge daily rate for balance transfers _____
    b. Finance charge daily rate for purchases _____
    c. The periodic finance charge for the transfer _____
    d. The periodic finance charge for the purchases _____

4. The unpaid balance for April 30 on a credit card account is $2,995. The company uses the unpaid balance method, charges a 12% APR, and uses a 30-day billing cycle. In May the customer made a purchase of $75 and a payment of $200. Calculate the following:

    a. Daily finance rate _____
    b. Finance charge for May _____
    c. Unpaid balance for May _____

5. A customer's unpaid balance on a credit card is $995. The average daily balance for January is $1,010. The company charges 6.5% APR and uses a 31-day billing cycle for January. The customer made a $300 payment during the month and withdrew $100 in cash. The company charges a $2.00 cash advance fee. Calculate the following:

    a. Daily finance charge rate _____
    b. Periodic finance charge _____
    c. Unpaid balance for January _____

Annual Percentage Rate Table for Monthly Payment Plans

Annual Percentage Rate

No. of Payments	10	10.25	10.5	10.75	11	11.25	11.5	11.75	12	12.25	12.5	12.75	13	13.25	13.5	13.75
	Finance Charge per $100 of Amount Financed															
1	0.83	0.85	0.87	0.90	0.92	0.94	0.96	0.98	1.00	1.02	1.04	1.06	1.08	1.10	1.12	1.15
2	1.25	1.28	1.31	1.35	1.38	1.41	1.44	1.47	1.50	1.53	1.57	1.60	1.63	1.66	1.69	1.73
3	1.67	1.71	1.76	1.80	1.84	1.88	1.92	1.96	2.01	2.05	2.09	2.13	2.17	2.22	2.26	2.30
4	2.09	2.14	2.20	2.25	2.30	2.35	2.41	2.46	2.51	2.57	2.62	2.67	2.72	2.78	2.83	2.88
5	2.51	2.58	2.64	2.70	2.77	2.83	2.89	2.96	3.02	3.08	3.15	3.21	3.27	3.34	3.40	3.46
6	2.94	3.01	3.08	3.16	3.23	3.31	3.38	3.45	3.53	3.60	3.68	3.75	3.83	3.90	3.97	4.05
7	3.36	3.45	3.53	3.62	3.70	3.78	3.87	3.95	4.04	4.12	4.21	4.29	4.38	4.47	4.55	4.64
8	3.79	3.88	3.98	4.07	4.17	4.26	4.36	4.46	4.55	4.65	4.74	4.84	4.94	5.03	5.13	5.22
9	4.21	4.32	4.43	4.53	4.64	4.75	4.85	4.96	5.07	5.17	5.28	5.39	5.49	5.60	5.71	5.82
10	4.64	4.76	4.88	4.99	5.11	5.23	5.35	5.46	5.58	5.70	5.82	5.94	6.05	6.17	6.29	6.41
11	5.07	5.20	5.33	5.45	5.58	5.71	5.84	5.97	6.10	6.23	6.36	6.49	6.62	6.75	6.88	7.01
12	5.50	5.64	5.78	5.92	6.06	6.20	6.34	6.48	6.62	6.76	6.90	7.04	7.18	7.32	7.46	7.60
13	5.93	6.08	6.23	6.38	6.53	6.68	6.84	6.99	7.14	7.29	7.44	7.59	7.75	7.90	8.05	8.20
14	6.36	6.52	6.69	6.85	7.01	7.17	7.34	7.50	7.66	7.82	7.99	8.15	8.31	8.48	8.64	8.81
15	6.80	6.97	7.14	7.32	7.49	7.66	7.84	8.01	8.19	8.36	8.53	8.71	8.88	9.06	9.23	9.41
16	7.23	7.41	7.60	7.78	7.97	8.15	8.34	8.53	8.71	8.90	9.08	9.27	9.46	9.64	9.83	10.02
17	7.67	7.86	8.06	8.25	8.45	8.65	8.84	9.04	9.24	9.44	9.63	9.83	10.03	10.23	10.43	10.63
18	8.10	8.31	8.52	8.75	8.93	9.14	9.35	9.56	9.77	9.98	10.19	10.40	10.61	10.82	11.03	11.24
19	8.54	8.76	8.98	9.20	9.42	9.64	9.86	10.08	10.30	10.52	10.74	10.96	11.18	11.41	11.63	11.85
20	8.98	9.21	9.44	9.67	9.90	10.13	10.37	10.60	10.83	11.06	11.30	11.53	11.76	12.00	12.23	12.46
21	9.42	9.66	9.90	10.15	10.39	10.63	10.88	11.12	11.36	11.61	11.85	12.10	12.34	12.59	12.84	13.08
22	9.86	10.12	10.37	10.62	10.88	11.13	11.39	11.64	11.90	12.16	12.41	12.67	12.93	13.19	13.44	13.70
23	10.30	10.57	10.84	11.10	11.37	11.63	11.90	12.17	12.44	12.71	12.97	13.24	13.51	13.78	14.05	14.32
24	10.75	11.02	11.30	11.58	11.86	12.14	12.42	12.70	12.98	13.26	13.54	13.82	14.10	14.38	14.66	14.95
25	11.19	11.48	11.77	12.06	12.35	12.64	12.93	13.22	13.52	13.81	14.10	14.40	14.69	14.98	15.28	15.57
26	11.64	11.94	12.24	12.54	12.85	13.15	13.45	13.75	14.06	14.36	14.67	14.97	15.28	15.59	15.89	16.20
27	12.09	12.40	12.71	13.03	13.34	13.66	13.97	14.29	14.60	14.92	15.24	15.56	15.87	16.19	16.51	16.83
28	12.53	12.86	13.18	13.51	13.84	14.16	14.49	14.82	15.15	15.48	15.81	16.14	16.47	16.80	17.13	17.46
29	12.98	13.32	13.66	14.00	14.33	14.67	15.01	15.35	15.70	16.04	16.38	16.72	17.07	17.41	17.75	18.10
30	13.43	13.78	14.13	14.48	14.83	15.19	15.54	15.89	16.24	16.60	16.95	17.31	17.66	18.02	18.38	18.74
31	13.89	14.25	14.61	14.97	15.33	15.70	16.06	16.43	16.79	17.16	17.53	17.90	18.27	18.63	19.00	19.38
32	14.34	14.71	15.09	15.46	15.84	16.21	16.59	16.97	17.35	17.73	18.11	18.49	18.87	19.25	19.63	20.02
33	14.79	15.18	15.57	15.95	16.34	16.73	17.12	17.51	17.90	18.29	18.65	19.08	19.47	19.87	20.26	20.66
34	15.25	15.65	16.05	16.44	16.85	17.25	17.65	18.05	18.46	18.86	19.27	19.67	20.08	20.49	20.90	21.31
35	15.70	16.11	16.53	16.94	17.35	17.77	18.18	18.60	19.01	19.43	19.85	20.27	20.69	21.11	21.53	21.95

(continued)

FIGURE 30.9

Annual Percentage Rate

No. of Payments	10	10.25	10.5	10.75	11	11.25	11.5	11.75	12	12.25	12.5	12.75	13	13.25	13.5	13.75
	Finance Charge per $100 of Amount Financed															
36	16.16	16.58	17.01	17.43	17.86	18.29	18.71	19.14	19.57	20.00	20.43	20.87	21.30	21.73	22.17	22.60
37	16.62	17.06	17.49	17.93	18.37	18.81	19.25	19.69	20.13	20.58	21.02	21.46	21.91	22.36	22.81	23.25
38	17.08	17.53	17.98	18.43	18.88	19.33	19.78	20.24	20.69	21.15	21.61	22.07	22.52	22.99	23.45	23.91
39	17.54	18.00	18.46	18.93	19.39	19.86	20.32	20.79	21.26	21.73	22.20	22.67	23.14	23.61	24.09	24.56
40	18.00	18.48	18.95	19.43	19.90	20.38	20.86	21.34	21.82	22.30	22.79	23.27	23.76	24.25	24.73	25.22
41	18.47	18.95	19.44	19.93	20.42	20.91	21.40	21.89	22.39	22.88	23.38	23.88	24.38	24.88	25.38	25.88
42	18.93	19.43	19.93	20.43	20.93	21.44	21.94	22.45	22.96	23.47	23.98	24.49	25.00	25.51	26.03	26.55
43	19.40	19.91	20.42	20.94	21.45	21.97	22.49	23.01	23.53	24.05	24.57	25.10	25.62	26.15	26.68	27.21
44	19.86	20.39	20.91	21.44	21.97	22.50	23.03	23.57	24.10	24.64	25.17	25.71	26.25	26.79	27.33	27.88
45	20.33	20.87	21.41	21.95	22.49	23.03	23.58	24.12	24.67	25.22	25.77	26.32	26.88	27.43	27.99	28.55
46	20.80	21.35	21.90	22.46	23.01	23.57	24.13	24.69	25.25	25.81	26.37	26.94	27.51	28.08	28.65	29.22
47	21.27	21.83	22.40	22.97	23.53	24.10	24.68	25.25	25.82	26.40	26.98	27.56	28.14	28.72	29.31	29.89
48	21.74	22.32	22.90	23.48	24.06	24.64	25.23	25.81	26.40	26.99	27.58	28.18	28.77	29.37	29.97	30.57
49	22.21	22.80	23.39	23.99	24.58	25.18	25.78	26.38	26.98	27.59	28.19	28.80	29.41	30.02	30.63	31.34
50	22.69	23.29	23.89	24.50	25.11	25.72	26.33	26.95	27.56	28.18	28.80	29.42	30.04	30.67	31.29	31.92
51	23.16	23.78	24.40	25.02	25.64	26.26	26.89	27.52	28.15	28.78	29.41	30.05	30.68	31.32	31.96	32.60
52	23.64	24.27	24.90	25.53	26.17	26.81	27.45	28.09	28.73	29.38	30.02	30.67	31.32	31.98	32.63	33.29
53	24.11	24.76	25.40	26.05	26.70	27.35	28.00	28.66	29.32	29.98	30.64	31.30	31.97	32.63	33.30	33.97
54	24.59	25.25	25.91	26.57	27.23	27.90	28.56	29.23	29.91	30.58	31.25	31.93	32.61	33.29	33.98	34.66
55	25.07	25.74	26.41	27.09	27.77	28.44	29.13	29.81	30.50	31.18	31.87	32.56	33.26	33.95	34.65	35.35
56	25.55	26.23	26.92	27.61	28.30	28.99	29.69	30.39	31.09	31.79	32.49	33.20	33.91	34.62	35.33	36.04
57	26.03	26.73	27.43	28.13	28.84	29.54	30.25	30.97	31.68	32.39	33.11	33.83	34.56	35.28	36.01	36.74
58	26.51	27.23	27.94	28.66	29.37	30.10	30.82	31.55	32.27	33.00	33.74	34.47	35.21	35.95	36.69	37.43
59	27.00	27.72	28.45	29.18	29.91	30.65	31.39	32.13	32.87	33.61	34.36	35.11	35.86	36.62	37.37	38.13
60	27.48	28.22	28.96	29.71	30.45	31.20	31.96	32.71	33.47	34.23	34.99	35.75	36.52	37.29	38.06	38.83

Annual Percentage Rate

No. of Payments	14	14.25	14.5	14.75	15	15.25	15.5	15.75	16	16.25	16.5	16.75	17	17.25	17.5	17.75
	Finance Charge per $100 of Amount Financed															
1	1.17	1.19	1.21	1.23	1.25	1.27	1.29	1.31	1.33	1.35	1.37	1.40	1.42	1.44	1.46	1.48
2	1.75	1.78	1.82	1.85	1.88	1.91	1.94	1.97	2.00	2.04	2.07	2.10	2.13	2.16	2.19	2.22
3	2.34	2.38	2.43	2.47	2.51	2.55	2.59	2.64	2.68	2.72	2.76	2.80	2.85	2.89	2.93	2.97
4	2.93	2.99	3.04	3.09	3.14	3.20	3.25	3.30	3.36	3.41	3.46	3.51	3.57	3.62	3.67	3.73
5	3.53	3.59	3.65	3.72	3.78	3.84	3.91	3.97	4.04	4.10	4.16	4.23	4.29	4.35	4.42	4.48
6	4.12	4.20	4.27	4.35	4.42	4.49	4.57	4.64	4.72	4.79	4.87	4.94	5.02	5.09	5.17	5.24
7	4.72	4.81	4.89	4.98	5.06	5.15	5.23	5.32	5.40	5.49	5.58	5.66	5.75	5.83	5.92	6.00

(continued)

No. of Payments	14	14.25	14.5	14.75	15	15.25	15.5	15.75	16	16.25	16.5	16.75	17	17.25	17.5	17.75
					Finance Charge per $100 of Amount Financed											
8	5.32	5.42	5.51	5.61	5.71	5.80	5.90	6.00	6.09	6.19	6.29	6.38	6.48	6.58	6.67	6.77
9	5.92	6.03	6.14	6.25	6.35	6.46	6.57	6.68	6.78	6.89	7.00	7.11	7.22	7.32	7.43	7.54
10	6.53	6.65	6.77	6.88	7.00	7.12	7.24	7.36	7.48	7.60	7.72	7.84	7.96	8.08	8.19	8.31
11	7.14	7.27	7.40	7.53	7.66	7.79	7.92	8.05	8.18	8.31	8.44	8.57	8.70	8.83	8.96	9.09
12	7.74	7.89	8.03	8.17	8.31	8.45	8.59	8.74	8.88	9.02	9.16	9.30	9.45	9.59	9.73	9.87
13	8.36	8.51	8.66	8.81	8.97	9.12	9.27	9.43	9.58	9.73	9.89	10.04	10.20	10.35	10.50	10.66
14	8.97	9.13	9.30	9.46	9.63	9.79	9.96	10.12	10.29	10.45	10.62	10.78	10.95	11.11	11.28	11.45
15	9.59	9.76	9.94	10.11	10.29	10.47	10.64	10.82	11.00	11.17	11.35	11.51	11.71	11.88	12.06	12.24
16	10.20	10.39	10.58	10.77	10.95	11.14	11.33	11.52	11.71	11.90	12.09	12.28	12.46	12.65	12.84	13.03
17	10.82	11.02	11.22	11.42	11.62	11.82	12.02	12.22	12.42	12.62	12.83	13.03	13.23	13.43	13.63	13.83
18	11.45	11.66	11.87	12.08	12.29	12.50	12.72	12.93	13.14	13.35	13.57	13.78	13.99	14.21	14.42	14.64
19	12.07	12.30	12.52	12.74	12.97	13.19	13.41	13.64	13.86	14.09	14.31	14.54	14.76	14.99	15.22	15.44
20	12.70	12.93	13.17	13.41	13.64	13.88	14.11	14.35	14.59	14.82	15.06	15.30	15.54	15.77	16.01	16.25
21	13.33	13.58	13.82	14.07	14.32	14.57	14.82	15.06	15.31	15.56	15.81	16.05	16.31	16.56	16.81	17.07
22	13.96	14.22	14.48	14.74	15.00	15.26	15.52	15.78	16.04	16.30	16.57	16.83	17.09	17.36	17.62	17.88
23	14.59	14.87	15.14	15.41	15.68	15.96	16.23	16.50	16.78	17.05	17.32	17.60	17.88	18.15	18.43	18.70
24	15.23	15.51	15.80	16.08	16.37	16.65	16.94	17.22	17.51	17.80	18.09	18.37	18.65	18.95	19.24	19.53
25	15.87	16.17	16.46	16.76	17.06	17.35	17.65	17.95	18.25	18.55	18.85	19.15	19.45	19.75	20.05	20.36
26	16.51	16.82	17.13	17.44	17.75	18.06	18.37	18.68	18.99	19.30	19.62	19.93	20.24	20.56	20.87	21.19
27	17.15	17.47	17.80	18.12	18.44	18.76	19.09	19.41	19.74	20.06	20.39	20.71	21.04	21.37	21.69	22.02
28	17.80	18.13	18.47	18.80	19.14	19.47	19.81	20.15	20.48	20.82	21.16	21.50	21.84	22.18	22.52	22.86
29	18.45	18.79	19.14	19.49	19.83	20.18	20.53	20.88	21.23	21.58	21.94	22.29	22.64	22.99	23.35	23.70
30	19.10	19.45	19.81	20.17	20.54	20.90	21.26	21.62	21.99	22.35	22.72	23.08	23.45	23.81	24.18	24.55
31	19.75	20.12	20.49	20.87	21.24	21.61	21.99	22.37	22.74	23.12	23.50	23.88	24.26	24.64	25.02	25.40
32	20.40	20.79	21.17	21.56	21.95	22.33	22.72	23.11	23.50	23.89	24.28	24.68	25.07	25.46	25.86	26.25
33	21.06	21.46	21.85	22.25	22.65	23.06	23.46	23.86	24.26	24.67	25.07	25.48	25.88	26.29	26.70	27.11
34	21.72	22.13	22.54	22.95	23.37	23.78	24.19	24.61	25.03	25.44	25.86	26.28	26.70	27.12	27.54	27.97
35	22.38	22.80	23.23	23.65	24.08	24.51	24.94	25.36	25.79	26.23	26.66	27.09	27.52	27.96	28.39	28.83
36	23.04	23.48	23.92	24.35	24.80	25.24	25.68	26.12	26.57	27.01	27.46	27.90	28.35	28.80	29.25	29.70
37	23.70	24.16	24.61	25.06	25.51	25.97	26.42	26.88	27.34	27.80	28.26	28.72	29.18	29.64	30.10	30.57
38	24.37	24.84	25.30	25.77	26.24	26.70	27.17	27.64	28.11	28.59	29.06	29.53	30.01	30.49	30.96	31.44
39	25.04	25.52	26.00	26.48	26.96	27.44	27.92	28.41	28.89	29.38	29.87	30.36	30.85	31.34	31.83	32.32
40	25.71	26.20	26.70	27.19	27.69	28.18	28.68	29.18	29.68	30.18	30.68	31.18	31.68	32.19	32.69	33.20
41	26.39	26.89	27.40	27.91	28.41	28.92	29.44	29.95	30.46	30.97	31.49	32.01	32.52	33.04	33.56	34.08
42	27.06	27.58	28.10	28.62	29.15	29.67	30.19	30.72	31.25	31.78	32.31	32.84	33.37	33.90	34.44	34.97
43	27.74	28.27	28.81	29.34	29.88	30.42	30.96	31.50	32.04	32.58	33.13	33.67	34.22	34.76	35.31	35.86
44	28.42	28.97	29.52	30.07	30.62	31.17	31.72	32.28	32.83	33.39	33.95	34.51	35.07	35.63	36.19	36.76
45	29.11	29.67	30.23	30.79	31.36	31.92	32.49	33.06	33.63	34.20	34.77	35.35	35.92	36.50	37.08	37.66
46	29.79	30.36	30.94	31.52	32.10	32.68	33.26	33.84	34.43	35.01	35.60	36.19	36.78	37.37	37.96	38.56
47	30.48	31.07	31.66	32.25	32.84	33.44	34.03	34.63	35.23	35.83	36.43	37.04	37.64	38.25	38.86	39.46

(continued)

Annual Percentage Rate

Finance Charge per $100 of Amount Financed

No. of Payments	14	14.25	14.5	14.75	15	15.25	15.5	15.75	16	16.25	16.5	16.75	17	17.25	17.5	17.75
48	31.17	31.77	32.37	32.98	33.59	34.20	34.81	35.42	36.03	36.65	37.27	27.88	38.50	39.13	39.75	40.37
49	31.86	32.48	33.09	33.71	34.34	34.96	35.59	36.21	36.84	37.47	38.10	38.74	39.37	40.01	40.65	41.29
50	32.55	33.18	33.82	34.45	35.09	35.73	36.37	37.01	37.65	38.30	38.94	39.59	40.24	40.89	41.55	42.20
51	33.25	33.89	34.54	35.19	35.84	36.49	37.15	37.81	38.46	39.12	39.79	40.45	41.11	41.78	42.45	43.12
52	33.95	34.61	35.27	35.93	36.60	37.27	37.94	38.61	39.28	39.96	40.63	41.31	41.99	42.67	43.36	44.04
53	34.65	35.32	36.00	36.68	37.36	38.04	38.72	39.41	40.10	40.79	41.48	42.17	42.87	43.57	44.27	44.97
54	35.35	36.04	36.73	37.42	38.12	38.82	39.52	40.22	40.92	41.63	42.33	43.04	43.75	44.47	45.18	45.90
55	36.05	36.76	37.46	38.17	38.88	39.60	40.31	41.03	41.74	42.47	43.19	43.91	44.64	45.37	46.10	46.83
56	36.76	37.48	38.20	38.92	39.65	40.38	41.11	41.84	42.57	43.31	44.05	44.79	45.53	46.27	47.02	47.77
57	37.47	38.20	38.94	39.68	40.42	41.16	41.91	42.65	53.40	44.15	44.91	45.66	46.42	47.18	47.94	48.71
58	38.18	38.93	39.68	40.43	41.19	41.95	42.71	43.47	44.23	45.00	45.77	46.54	47.32	48.09	48.87	49.65
59	38.89	39.66	40.42	41.19	41.96	42.74	43.51	44.29	45.07	45.85	46.64	47.42	48.41	49.01	49.80	50.60
60	39.61	40.39	41.17	41.95	42.74	43.53	44.32	45.11	45.91	46.71	47.51	48.31	49.12	49.92	50.73	51.55

Annual Percentage Rate

Finance Charge per $100 of Amount Financed

No. of Payments	18	18.25	18.5	18.75	19	19.25	19.5	19.75	20	20.25	20.5	20.75	21	21.25	21.5	21.75
1	1.50	1.52	1.54	1.56	1.58	1.60	1.62	1.65	1.67	1.69	1.71	1.73	1.75	1.77	1.79	1.81
2	2.26	2.29	2.32	2.35	2.38	2.41	2.44	2.48	2.51	2.54	2.57	2.60	2.63	2.66	2.70	2.73
3	3.01	3.06	3.10	3.14	3.18	3.23	3.27	3.31	3.35	3.39	3.44	3.48	3.52	3.56	3.60	3.65
4	3.78	3.83	3.88	3.94	3.99	4.04	4.10	4.15	4.20	4.25	4.31	4.36	4.41	4.47	4.52	4.57
5	4.54	4.61	4.67	4.74	4.80	4.86	4.93	4.99	5.06	5.12	5.18	5.25	5.31	5.37	5.44	5.50
6	5.32	5.39	5.46	5.54	5.61	5.69	5.76	5.84	5.91	5.99	6.06	6.14	6.21	6.29	6.36	6.44
7	6.09	6.18	6.26	6.35	6.43	6.52	6.60	6.69	6.78	6.86	6.95	7.04	7.12	7.21	7.29	7.38
8	6.87	6.96	7.06	7.16	7.26	7.35	7.45	7.55	7.64	7.74	7.84	7.94	8.03	8.13	8.23	8.33
9	7.65	7.76	7.87	7.97	8.08	8.19	8.30	8.41	8.52	8.63	8.73	8.84	8.95	9.06	9.17	9.28
10	8.43	8.55	8.67	8.79	8.91	9.03	9.15	9.27	9.39	9.51	9.63	9.75	9.88	10.00	10.12	10.24
11	9.22	9.35	9.49	9.62	9.75	9.88	10.01	10.14	10.28	10.41	10.54	10.67	10.80	10.94	11.07	11.20
12	10.02	10.16	10.30	10.44	10.59	10.73	10.87	11.02	11.16	11.31	11.45	11.59	11.74	11.88	12.02	12.17
13	10.81	10.97	11.12	11.28	11.43	11.59	11.74	11.90	12.05	12.21	12.36	12.52	12.67	12.83	12.99	13.14
14	11.61	11.78	11.95	12.11	12.28	12.45	12.61	12.78	12.95	13.11	13.28	13.45	13.62	13.79	13.95	14.12
15	12.42	12.59	12.77	12.95	13.13	13.31	13.49	13.67	13.85	14.03	14.21	14.39	14.57	14.75	14.93	15.11
16	13.22	13.41	13.60	13.80	13.99	14.18	14.37	14.56	14.75	14.94	15.13	15.33	15.52	15.71	15.90	16.10
17	14.04	14.24	14.44	14.64	14.85	15.05	15.25	15.46	15.66	15.86	16.07	16.27	16.48	16.68	16.89	17.09
18	14.85	15.07	15.28	15.49	15.71	15.93	16.14	16.36	16.57	16.79	17.01	17.22	17.44	17.66	17.88	18.09
19	15.67	15.90	16.12	16.35	16.58	16.81	17.03	17.26	17.49	17.72	17.95	18.18	18.41	18.64	18.87	19.10
20	16.49	16.73	16.97	17.21	17.45	17.69	17.93	18.17	18.41	18.66	18.90	19.14	19.38	19.63	19.87	20.11

(continued)

Annual Percentage Rate

Finance Charge per $100 of Amount Financed

No. of Payments	18	18.25	18.5	18.75	19	19.25	19.5	19.75	20	20.25	20.5	20.75	21	21.25	21.5	21.75
21	17.32	17.57	17.82	18.07	18.33	18.58	18.83	19.09	19.34	19.60	19.85	20.11	20.36	20.62	20.87	21.13
22	18.15	18.41	18.68	18.94	19.21	19.47	19.74	20.01	20.27	20.54	20.81	21.08	21.34	21.61	21.88	22.15
23	18.98	19.26	19.54	19.81	20.09	20.37	20.65	20.93	21.21	21.49	21.77	22.05	22.33	22.61	22.90	23.18
24	19.82	20.11	20.40	20.69	20.98	21.27	21.56	21.86	22.15	22.44	22.74	23.03	23.33	23.62	23.92	24.21
25	20.66	20.96	21.27	21.57	21.87	22.18	22.48	22.79	23.10	23.40	23.71	24.02	24.32	24.63	24.94	25.25
26	21.50	21.82	22.14	22.45	22.77	23.09	23.41	23.73	24.04	24.36	24.68	25.01	25.33	25.65	25.97	26.29
27	22.35	22.68	23.01	23.34	23.67	24.00	24.33	24.67	25.00	25.33	25.67	26.00	26.34	26.67	27.01	27.34
28	23.20	23.55	23.89	24.23	24.58	24.92	25.27	25.61	25.96	26.30	26.65	27.00	27.35	27.70	28.05	28.40
29	24.06	24.41	24.77	25.13	25.49	25.84	26.20	26.56	26.92	27.28	27.64	28.00	28.37	28.73	29.09	29.46
30	24.92	25.29	25.66	26.03	26.40	26.77	27.14	27.52	27.89	28.26	28.64	29.01	29.39	29.77	30.14	30.52
31	25.78	26.16	26.55	26.93	27.32	27.70	28.09	28.47	28.86	29.25	29.64	30.03	30.42	30.81	31.20	31.59
32	26.65	27.04	27.44	27.84	28.24	28.64	29.04	29.44	29.84	30.24	30.64	31.05	31.45	31.85	32.26	32.67
33	27.52	27.93	28.34	28.75	29.16	29.57	29.99	30.40	30.82	31.23	31.65	32.07	32.49	32.91	33.33	33.75
34	28.39	28.81	29.24	29.66	30.09	30.52	30.95	31.37	31.80	32.23	32.67	33.10	33.53	33.96	34.40	34.83
35	29.27	29.71	30.14	30.58	31.02	31.47	31.91	32.35	32.79	33.24	33.68	34.13	34.58	35.03	35.47	35.92
36	30.15	30.60	31.05	31.51	31.96	32.42	32.87	33.33	33.79	34.25	34.71	35.17	35.63	36.09	36.56	37.02
37	31.03	31.50	31.97	32.43	32.90	33.37	33.84	34.32	34.79	35.26	35.74	36.21	36.69	37.16	37.64	38.12
38	31.92	32.40	32.88	33.37	33.85	34.33	34.82	35.30	35.79	36.28	36.77	37.26	37.75	38.24	38.73	39.23
39	32.81	33.31	33.80	34.30	34.80	35.30	35.80	36.30	36.80	37.30	37.81	38.31	38.82	39.32	39.83	40.34
40	33.71	34.22	34.73	35.24	35.75	36.26	36.78	37.29	37.81	38.33	38.85	39.37	39.89	40.41	40.93	41.46
41	34.61	35.13	35.66	36.18	36.71	37.24	37.77	38.30	38.83	39.36	39.89	40.43	40.96	41.50	42.04	42.58
42	35.51	36.05	36.59	37.13	37.67	38.21	38.76	39.30	39.85	40.40	40.95	41.50	42.05	42.60	43.15	43.71
43	36.42	36.97	37.52	38.08	38.63	39.19	39.75	40.31	40.87	41.44	42.00	42.57	43.13	43.70	44.27	44.84
44	37.33	37.89	38.46	39.03	39.60	40.18	40.75	41.33	41.90	42.48	43.06	43.64	44.22	44.81	45.39	45.98
45	38.24	38.82	39.41	39.99	40.58	41.17	41.75	42.35	42.94	43.53	44.13	44.72	45.32	45.92	46.52	47.12
46	39.16	39.75	40.35	40.95	41.55	42.16	42.76	43.37	43.98	44.58	45.20	45.81	46.42	47.03	47.65	48.27
47	40.08	40.69	41.30	41.92	42.54	43.15	43.77	44.40	45.02	45.64	46.27	46.90	47.53	48.16	48.79	49.42
48	41.00	41.63	42.26	42.89	43.52	44.15	44.79	45.43	46.07	46.71	47.35	47.99	48.64	49.28	49.93	50.58
49	41.93	42.57	43.22	43.86	44.51	45.16	45.81	46.46	47.12	47.77	48.43	49.09	49.75	50.41	51.08	51.74
50	42.86	43.52	44.18	44.84	45.50	46.17	46.83	47.50	48.17	48.84	49.52	50.19	50.87	51.55	52.23	52.91
51	43.79	44.47	45.14	45.82	46.50	47.18	47.86	48.55	49.23	49.92	50.61	51.30	51.99	52.69	53.38	54.08
52	44.73	45.42	46.11	46.80	47.50	48.20	48.89	49.59	50.30	51.00	51.71	52.41	53.12	53.83	54.55	54.26
53	45.67	46.38	47.08	47.79	48.50	49.22	49.93	50.65	51.37	52.09	52.81	53.53	54.26	54.98	55.71	56.44
54	46.62	47.34	48.06	48.79	49.51	50.24	50.97	51.70	52.44	53.17	53.91	54.65	55.39	56.14	56.88	57.63
55	47.57	48.30	49.04	49.78	50.52	51.27	52.02	52.76	53.52	54.27	55.02	55.78	56.54	57.30	58.06	58.82
56	48.52	49.27	50.03	50.78	51.54	52.30	53.06	53.83	54.60	55.37	56.14	56.91	57.68	58.46	59.24	60.02
57	49.47	50.24	51.01	51.79	52.56	53.34	54.12	54.90	55.68	56.47	57.25	58.04	58.84	59.63	60.43	61.22
58	50.43	51.22	52.00	52.79	53.58	54.38	55.17	55.97	56.77	57.57	58.38	59.18	59.99	60.80	61.62	62.43
59	51.39	52.20	53.00	53.80	54.61	55.42	56.23	57.05	57.87	58.68	59.51	60.33	61.15	61.98	62.81	63.64
60	52.36	53.18	54.00	54.82	55.64	56.47	57.30	58.13	58.96	59.80	60.64	61.48	62.32	63.17	64.01	64.86

CHAPTER 31

Life Insurance, Fire and Property Insurance, Auto Insurance

PART 1 *Speed and Accuracy Building Using Touch Key*

GOALS: Your speed goal is 12,000 strokes per hour.
Your accuracy target goal range is 95% to 100%.

With each repetition of the test, try to improve your speed without lowering your accuracy score. If your percent-of-accuracy score falls below 95%, review your finger position and technique. Then try again.

Instructions: *Start Touch Key. Complete the Order Test in Appendix A. Write your scores for strokes per hour and percent of accuracy below. If you are not satisfied with your scores, repeat the test until you are satisfied.*

Order Test

Today's Date	Strokes per Hour	Percent of Accuracy
A.		
B.		
C.		
D.		
E.		

PART 2 *Business Math Skills*

LIFE INSURANCE

Life insurance was developed as a means of protecting a breadwinner's family if he or she should die. Periodic payments called **premiums** were made during the insured's lifetime so that money would be available for burial expenses and, if the amount of the insurance policy was sufficient, for sustaining the family for a period of time. The money paid to the family might be in the form of a lump sum or an annuity. The same is true today, but more options are available. An **insurance policy** is the contract between a person and the company providing the insurance. The owner of the life insurance policy is referred to as the **insured**. The money paid on the insured's death is the **benefit**. The person designated by the insured to receive the benefits of the policy is the **beneficiary**. Usually, at least one additional beneficiary (the secondary beneficiary) is designated by the insured should the first beneficiary die before the insured person. A person who sells life insurance and meets certain requirements can earn the Certified Life Underwriter designation.

Premiums for life insurance policies are based on the life expectancies for men and women. **Actuarial tables** list the number of deaths per year by age for men and women and are used by insurance companies to establish the premiums. Other factors used to set premiums may include whether a person is a smoker or a nonsmoker and his or her weight, height, and medical history. Although types of life insurance policies vary by companies, basic types include whole life, paid-up life, term life, and variable universal life (Figure 31.1).

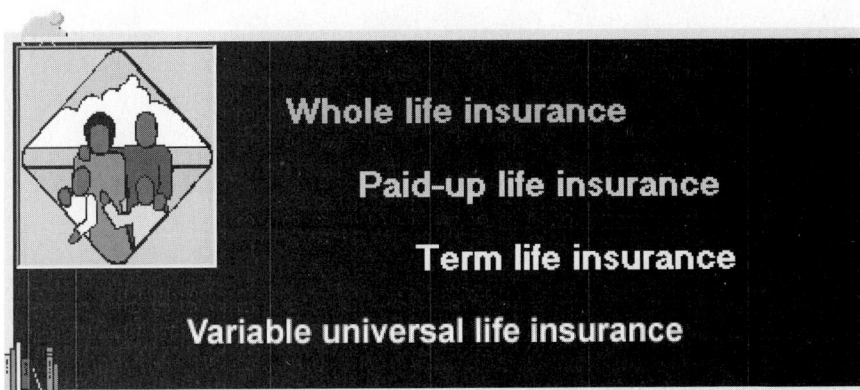

FIGURE 31.1

WHOLE LIFE

Premiums for **whole life** policies are paid during the insured's entire life, and a cash value accrues. **Cash value** is the amount returned to the insured person if the policy should be terminated or canceled before the insured person's death. The insurance company usually allows the insured to borrow against the cash value.

Calculating Whole Life Insurance Premiums

Tables listing life insurance premiums per $1,000 of insurance by age for male smoker, male nonsmoker, female smoker, female nonsmoker, and health condition are used to calculate monthly, quarterly, semiannual, or annual premiums.

PROBLEM 1

Calculate monthly premiums for $35,000 in whole life insurance for a nonsmoking man, age 47 years, in excellent health. Consult the Monthly Whole Life Insurance Premiums per $1,000 of Insurance table shown in Figure 31.2.

1. Find the number of $1,000 units of insurance:

$$\$35,000 \div \$1,000 = 35 \text{ units}$$

2. Use the table to find the monthly premium for $1,000 of insurance for a 47-year old nonsmoker (1.53). Multiply the premium by the desired number of $1,000 units of insurance found in step 1 (35):

$$\$1.53 \times 35 = \$53.55 \text{ monthly premium}$$

To find the annual premium, multiply monthly premium by 12:

$$\$53.55 \times 12 = \$642.60$$

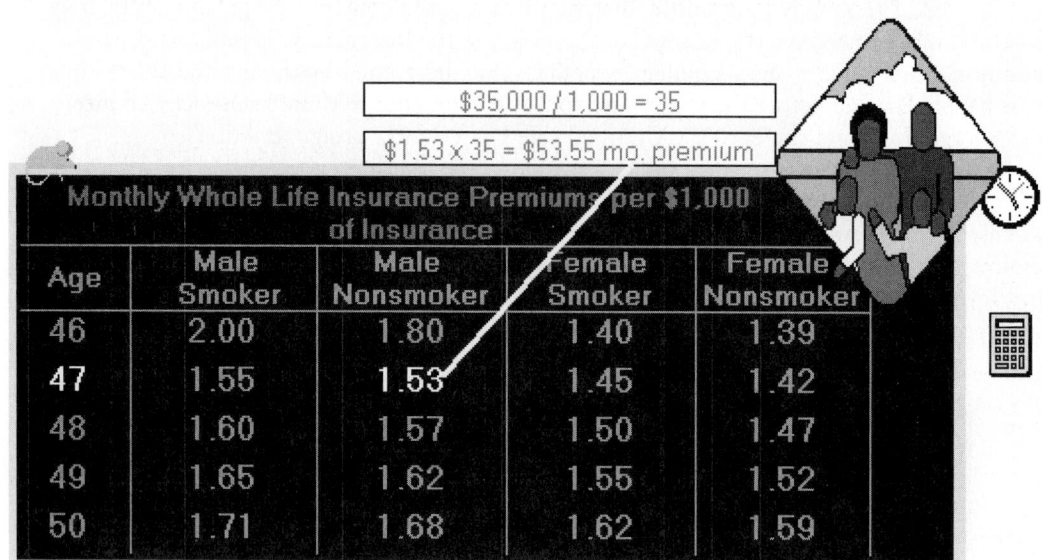

FIGURE 31.2

PAID-UP LIFE

Paid-up life insurance premiums are paid for a certain number of years. At the end of this time, the purchase price will have been paid and no further premiums are necessary. Cash value accrues. Loans may be taken against the cash value.

TERM LIFE

Term life insurance provides insurance in the case of death during a specific period of time. Benefits are paid only if the insured dies within that period. It is often considered to be the best choice for younger workers with family obligations because premiums are much less expensive than whole or paid-up life insurance. Workers can, therefore, afford more insurance for less cost. The policy is never considered to be paid up and no cash value accrues. For this reason, insurance agents sometimes refer to term life insurance as "pay-as-you-go" insurance.

The following table indicates representative monthly premiums for 10- and 20-year term life insurance for $250,000 and $500,000 policies for men and women by age. The premiums will not change during the 10- or 20-year terms or level periods.

Term Life Insurance Monthly Premiums for Level Periods

Amount of Coverage	10 Year $250,000	20 Year $250,000	10 Year $500,000	20 Year $500,000
Age 35 Man	14.85	19.80	23.40	33.30
Age 35 Woman	12.83	17.78	19.35	29.25
Age 45 Man	21.60	36.00	36.90	65.70
Age 45 Woman	19.80	28.13	33.30	49.95
Age 55 Man	47.25	82.13	88.20	157.95
Age 55 Woman	36.68	58.73	67.05	111.15

PROBLEM 2

Michael Connors, age 45, wishes to purchase $500,000 of 20-year term insurance. What is his monthly premium?

    Refer to the term life table to find the 20-year, $500,000 premium for a 45-year-old man: $65.70.

VARIABLE UNIVERSAL LIFE

A relative newcomer to the insurance world is the **variable universal life insurance** policy, a very flexible instrument that allows for increasing assets for the insured's retirement as well as insurance in the case of the insured's death. The insured's insurance premiums are invested in portfolios. Management fees are charged to the account. Cash accrues. The insured may make withdrawals or take tax-free loans for retirement or education funding. If the market is poor at the time of the insured's death, beneficiaries may elect to defer liquidating the portfolio until the market is more favorable. Premiums and the type of benefits desired may be changed at any time.

COMBINATION TABLE OF INSURANCE PREMIUMS

The following table shows annual premiums for $1,000 of various types of insurance policies—10-year term life, whole life, variable universal, and 20-year paid-up life—for nonsmoking men by age group.

Annual Life Insurance Premiums—Nonsmoker per $1,000 of Face Value for Male Applicants*

Age Issued (Years)	Term 10-Year	Whole Life	Variable Universal	20-Year Paid-Up Life
18	$6.81	$14.77	$18.36	$24.69
20	6.88	15.46	19.81	25.59
22	6.95	16.12	20.28	26.53
24	7.05	16.82	21.33	27.53
25	7.10	17.22	22.17	28.06
26	7.18	17.67	23.43	28.63
28	7.35	18.64	24.79	29.84
30	7.59	19.73	26.05	31.12
35	8.68	23.99	30.87	35.80
40	10.64	28.26	35.55	40.34
45	14.52	33.79	41.24	46.01
50	22.18	40.77	48.11	53.24
55	32.93	51.38	57.62	64.77
60	None	59.32	None	70.86

Note: Because of women's longer life expectancy, premiums for women (nonsmoking) are approximately equal to those of men who are 5 years younger.

PROBLEM 3

Using the above table, calculate the annual premium for a man, age 30, who wishes to purchase $50,000 in 20-year paid-up life insurance.

    First, divide $50,000 by $1,000 to find the number of $1,000 units of insurance desired:

$$\$50,000 \div \$1,000 = 50 \text{ units}$$

Second, multiply the units by the cost of one unit of insurance for a 30-year-old man, $31.12:

$$50 \times \$31.12 = \$1,556 \text{ annual premium}$$

FIRE AND PROPERTY INSURANCE

A business purchases **fire and property insurance** to insure buildings and building contents owned by the business from fire and other types of losses. Several factors affect the amount of fire and property insurance premiums including the following:

1. The amount of insurance desired—face value of the insurance policy
2. Type of area—location of the building
3. Class of building—type of materials from which the building is constructed
4. Class of contents—type of goods stored in the building

Should a fire occur, a business would receive money, called **compensation**, for the amount of loss up to the face value of the insurance policy.

Calculating Fire and Property Insurance Premiums

Tables containing annual rates per $100 of insurance are used to calculate annual fire and property insurance premiums.

PROBLEM 4

A small store valued at $60,000 with contents valued at $20,000 has an area rating of 1. The building and contents are rated as Class A. What is the annual premium?

Refer to the table in Figure 31.3. Because the table lists rates for each $100 of fire insurance, divide the building value and the contents value by $100. Multiply the result by the appropriate rate from the table:

1. Building: $60,000 ÷ 100 = $6,000
   The building is Class A, so multiply the result by .55 (from the table):

$$\$6,000 \times .55 = \$3,300$$

2. Contents: $20,000 ÷ 100 = $2,000
   The contents of the building are also Class A, so multiply the result by .60 (from the table):

$$\$2,000 \times .60 = \$1,200$$

3. Add the premiums for buildings and contents to find the total annual fire insurance premium:

$$\$3,300 + \$1,200 = \$4,500$$

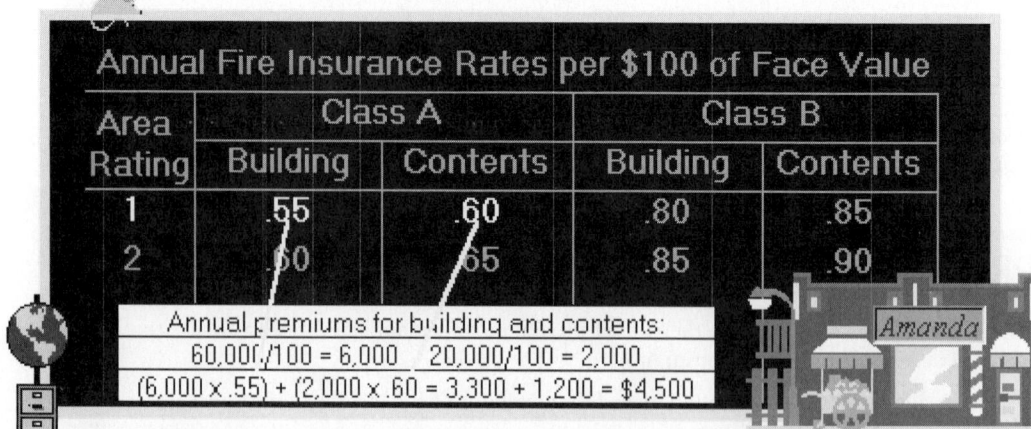

Annual Fire Insurance Rates per $100 of Face Value				
Area Rating	Class A		Class B	
	Building	Contents	Building	Contents
1	.55	.60	.80	.85
2	.60	.65	.85	.90

Annual premiums for building and contents:
60,000/100 = 6,000   20,000/100 = 2,000
(6,000 × .55) + (2,000 × .60 = 3,300 + 1,200 = $4,500

FIGURE 31.3

Coinsurance Clause

If the fire and property insurance plan includes a **coinsurance clause,** the insurance company will cover losses up to the face value of the insurance policy only if the property is insured for at least 80% of its value.

PROBLEM 5

A $120,000 building with $15,000 in contents is insured for $108,000. The insurance policy includes a coinsurance clause. If a fire causes $60,000 in damages, will the insurance company cover the entire loss?

To determine if 80% of the property is insured, multiply the total property value by 0.8. If the result equals or exceeds $108,000 (the amount for which the property has been insured), the total loss of $60,000 will be covered and the business will receive compensation from the insurance company for the full amount of loss ($60,000):

$$\$120,000 + \$15,000 = \$135,000$$
$$\$135,000 \times 0.8 = \$108,000$$

The business will receive full compensation.

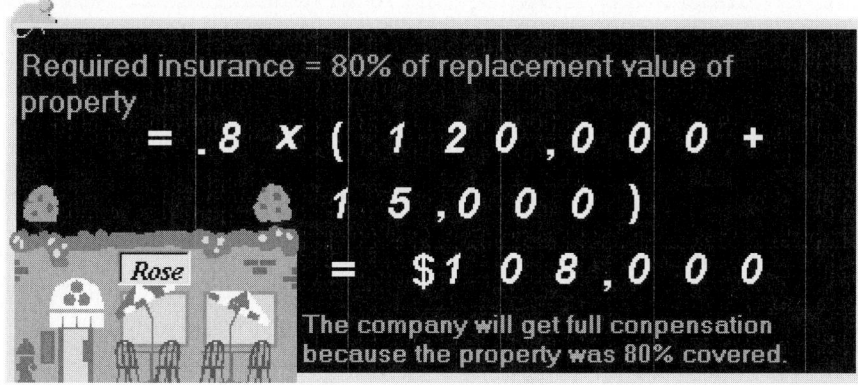

FIGURE 31.4

If an insurance plan contains a coinsurance clause and the property is insured for less than 80% of its value, the insurance company will pay part of the loss, not the full amount. In this case the amount of damage multiplied by the face value of the insurance policy would be divided by 80% of the building and contents worth to find the amount of compensation the insurance company will pay.

PROBLEM 6

A building and its contents valued at $135,000 are insured for $80,000. How much compensation would be received for $60,000 in fire damage?

Use the formula shown in Figure 31.5,

Compensation = Damage × Insurance Face Value ÷ 80% of Replacement Value

1. Multiply damage or loss by the face value of the insurance policy. You will need a calculator capable of displaying 10 digits, such as the Windows Calculator in Scientific View. (To open the Windows Calculator, select Start, Programs, Accessories, Calculator):

$$60,000 \times 80,000 = 4,800,000,000$$

2. Calculate the total worth of building and contents:

$$120,000 + 15,000 = 135,000$$

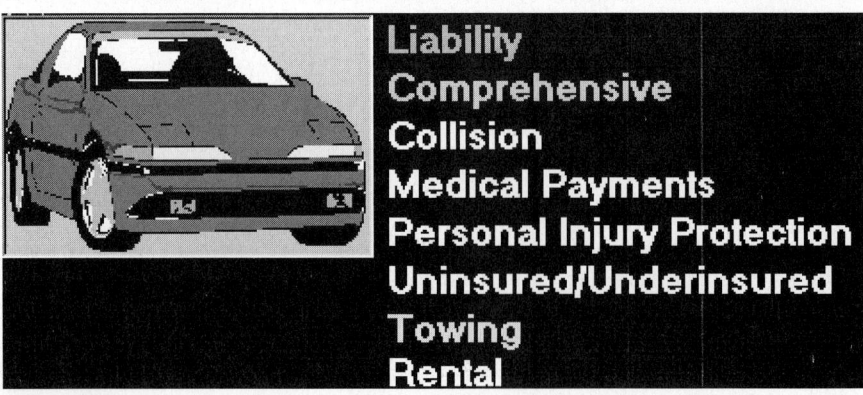

Compensation = damage x insurance face value
_____
              80% of replacement value

$$c = \frac{6\,0\,,\,0\,0\,0\ \times\ 8\,0\,,\,0\,0\,0}{.8\ \times\ (\ 1\,2\,0\,,\,0\,0\,0\ +\ 1\,5\,,\,0\,0\,0\ )}$$

$$= \$4\,4\,,\,4\,4\,4\,.\,4\,4$$

FIGURE 31.5

3. Multiply total worth by 80%:

$$135{,}000 \times 0.8 \ = \ 108{,}000$$

4. Divide the result from step 1 by the result in step 3. The amount the insurance company will pay in compensation for losses is $44,444.44:

$$4{,}800{,}000{,}000 \div 108{,}000 \ = \ \$44{,}444.44$$

AUTO INSURANCE

An auto insurance policy is a contract with an insurance company. The insured pays a premium and the insurance company promises to pay for certain automobile financial losses during the term of the policy. The policy usually covers you, relatives living in your household, and those who have permission to drive the vehicle covered by the policy.

Terms and Types

Covered loss: An amount for a specific incident agreed on by the insurance company.

Deductible: The portion of a covered loss that is the insured's responsibility, usually stated in the amounts of $100, $250, and so on. The deductible is applied to each covered loss.

Personal and business auto policies offer a range of choices of auto coverage including the following (Figure 31.6):

1. **Liability:** Pays for accidental bodily injury and property damages *to others* caused by an auto accident for which *the insured is responsible.* Bodily injury damages include

Liability
Comprehensive
Collision
Medical Payments
Personal Injury Protection
Uninsured/Underinsured
Towing
Rental

FIGURE 31.6

medical expenses, pain and suffering, lost wages, and other special damages. Property damage includes damaged property and may include loss of use. Liability coverage also pays legal defense and court costs. State laws usually determine the minimum amounts, but higher amounts are available.

2. **Comprehensive:** Pays for loss of or damage *to a covered vehicle* other than loss caused by collision or upset. Examples of covered losses include loss caused by fire, wind, hail, flood, vandalism, theft, or impact with an animal. A deductible may apply.

3. **Collision:** Pays for damage *to a covered vehicle* caused by collision with another object or by upset of the car. A deductible is required.

4. **Medical Payments:** Pays medical and funeral expenses *for covered persons*, regardless of fault, when those expenses are related to an auto accident. (Available in most states.)

5. **Personal Injury Protection:** Pays medical expenses *for covered persons*, regardless of fault, for treatment due to an auto accident. It may also pay for rehabilitation, lost earnings, replacement of services (child care if a parent is disabled, for example), and funeral expenses.

6. **Uninsured/Underinsured Motorist:** Pays damages when a *covered person* is injured in an auto accident caused *by a driver who has no liability insurance or insufficient insurance*. In some states this coverage may also pay for property damage. Policy provisions vary by state.

7. **Towing (Emergency Road Service):** Pays automobile towing expenses incurred as a result of a breakdown.

8. **Rental Reimbursement:** Pays expenses incurred for renting a car when your auto is disabled due to an auto accident. Daily allowances or limits vary by state or policy provisions.

Required Coverage

Some states require liability coverage and/or no-fault coverage to pay medical expenses for injuries to you and any passengers caused by a car accident regardless of fault. In other states, laws require drivers to be able to pay for any losses they cause to others in car accidents. Individuals usually elect to purchase insurance for any harm caused to others in a car accident and for repairing or replacing the insured's car if it is damaged or stolen. Companies that finance cars usually require coverage for vehicle damage.

Car insurance premiums are affected by the age and driving record of the driver, the use of the car, and the county or region in which the driver resides.

Examples of 6-month premiums for a household with a clear driving record and no underage drivers in a preferred county are shown in Figure 31.7. The insured car is a Ford Mustang GT two-door that is driven to and from work or school.

*$25,000 per person, $50,000 maximum

Liability		Collision		Uninsured/Underinsured	
$25,000	$90	$500 deduct. $186		25/50/25	$29
50,000	$95	$1000 deduct. $121		50/100/50	$41
100,000	$98	**Medical Payments**		100/300/100	$50
200,000	$104	25/50*	$80	**Towing**	
Comprehensive		50/100	$99	$40 limit	$1.00
		100/300	$125	$80 limit	$2.50
$100 deduct.	$186	250/500	$133	$120 limit	$3.00
$250 deduct.	$133	**Personal Injury Protection**		**Rental**	
$500 deduct.	$94				
$1000 deduct.	$73	$5,000	$28	$25/day, max $750	$15
		$10,000	$35	$30/day, max $900	$18

FIGURE 31.7

Looking at Figure 31.7 closely, we see that the premium for $25,000 of *liability* coverage is $90; for $50,000, $95; for $100,000, $98; and for $200,000, $104.

The premium for *comprehensive* coverage with a $100 deductible is $186; for a $250 deductible, $133; for a $500 deductible, $94; and for a $1,000 deductible, $73.

The premium for *collision* coverage with a $500 deductible is $186; for a $1,000 deductible, $121.

The premium for *medical payment* coverage of $25,000 per person ($50,000 maximum) is $80; for $50,000 per person ($100,000 maximum), $99; for $100,000 per person ($300,000 maximum), $125, and for $250,000 per person ($500,000 maximum), $133.

The premium for *personal injury protection* in the amount of $5,000 is $28; for $10,000, $35.

The premium for *uninsured and/or underinsured* motorists for $25,000 per person ($50,000 per accident) for bodily injury and $25,000 for property damage is $29; for $50,000 per person ($100,000 per accident) bodily injury and $50,000 for property damage, $41; for $100,000 per person ($300,000 per accident) bodily injury and $100,000 for property damage, $50.

The premium for $40 towing insurance is $1.00; for $80 towing, $2.50; and for $120 towing, $3.00.

The premium for rental car fees of $25 per day ($750 maximum) is $15; for $30 per day ($900 maximum), $18.

Compare the 6-month premiums shown in Figure 31.7 with those in Figure 31.8, which are representative for a single male driver under age 21, with one at-fault accident in the past three years, who drives a Ford Mustang GT two-door and lives in a county with a high accident rate. You will notice that rates in all categories are significantly higher.

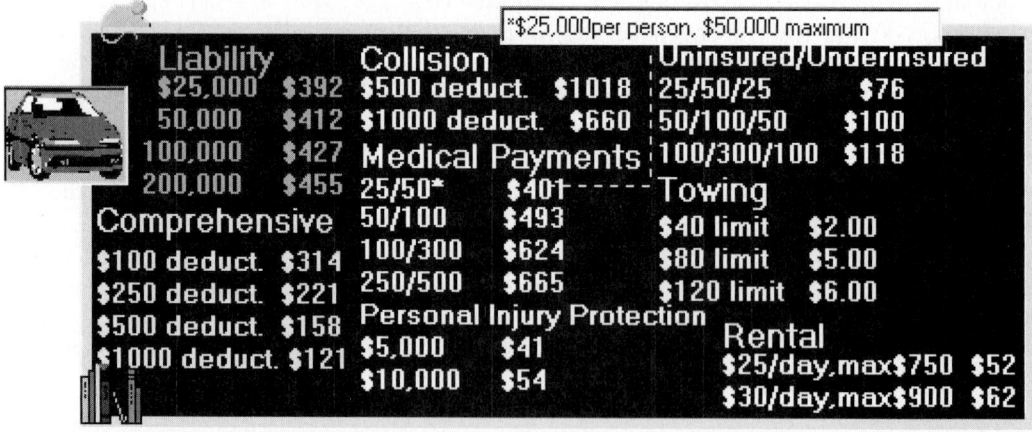

FIGURE 31.8

PROBLEM 7

Calculate the 6-month premium for the single male driver mentioned previously using the premiums shown in Figure 31.8 if he desires the following coverage:

Liability: $100,000

Comprehensive: $1,000 deductible

Collision: $500 deductible

Medical payment: $25/$50

Personal injury protection: $10,000

Uninsured/underinsured motorist: $50/$100/$50

Towing: $40 per day limit

Rental: $25 per day (maximum $750)

Add the premiums for the desired types of coverage as shown in Figure 31.9. The total 6-month premium is $2,175.

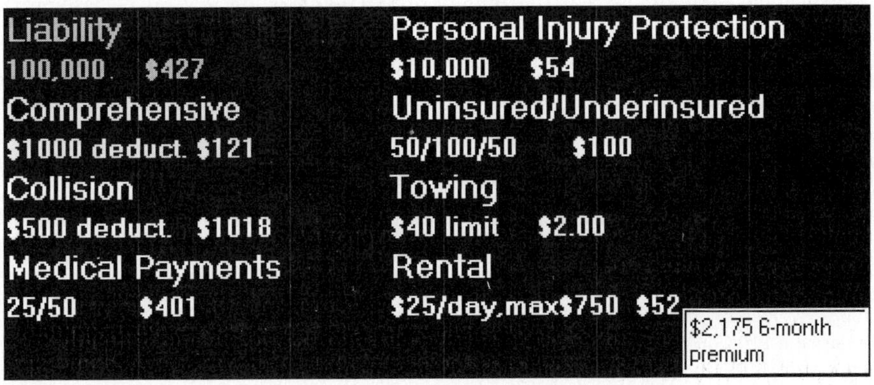

FIGURE 31.9

CALCULATING AUTOMOBILE INSURANCE USING TABLES

The Driver Classifications table at the end of the chapter indicates the annual multiple or rate to use for various types of drivers and intended car use. This rate is then multiplied by the annual premium listed for the desired coverage as shown in the Automobile Liability and Medical Payment Insurance table and the Comprehensive and Collision Insurance table, also included at the end of the chapter.

PROBLEM 8A

Jenny Bryant is a 20-year-old unmarried woman and has completed a certified driver-training course. She drives her car to work approximately 5 miles each way. What is the multiple or rate to use?

Refer to the Driver Classifications table, the row for young women age 20, DT (driver training), and under the column Drives to Work 3 to 9 miles each way.

The multiple is 1.15.

PROBLEM 8B

Consult the Comprehensive and Collision Insurance table at the end of the chapter. Jenny's car model is classified as (1) B. Her car's age group is classified as 2. She drives in a territory classified as 1. The coverages desired by Jenny are listed in the following worksheet. Use the worksheet to calculate the base premium and the actual premium for each of the coverages.

Desired Coverage	Deductible If Applicable	Base Premium	Multiple	Premium
Comprehensive	_____	_____	_____	_____
Collision	_____	_____	_____	_____
Bodily injury 15/30	_____	_____	_____	_____
Property damage $10,000	_____	_____	_____	_____
Medical payment $10,000	_____	_____	_____	_____

The base premium for comprehensive is $52. The base premium for collision with a $250 deductible is $77.

Refer to the Automobile Liability and Medical Payment Insurance table for:

1. Bodily injury coverage in the amount of 15,000/30,000 for Territory 1. The base premium is $81.
2. Property damage insurance in the amount of $10,000 for Territory 1. The base premium is $85.
3. Medical payment insurance in the amount of $10,000 for Territory 1. The base premium is $70.

Finally, multiply each of the base premiums just found by the multiple or rate found in Problem 8A. Add the results to find Jenny's total annual premium. Does your worksheet resemble the following worksheet?

Desired Coverage	Deductible If Applicable ($)	Base Premium ($)	Multiple	Premium ($)
Comprehensive		52	1.15	59.80
Collision	250	77	1.15	88.55
Bodily injury 15/30		81	1.15	93.15
Property damage $10,000		85	1.15	97.75
Medical payment $10,000		70	1.15	80.50
			Total annual premium	$419.75

Insurance companies rely on computer programs that take into account these and other variables affecting drivers and automobiles—such as safe driving records and car models with better crash ratings, restraints, and alarms—to calculate insurance premiums. It is possible to experience how these programs work by requesting instant rate quotes. This feature is available on many insurance company web sites, including http://www.statefarm.com, http://www.allstate.com, http://www.geico.com, and others.

COMMERCIAL VEHICLES

Commercial vehicles are rated based on factors such as cost or price new, age of the vehicle, weight, body style, number of axles, type of business use, and normal radius mileage of trips. Consult an insurance agent for insurance for commercial vehicles.

Name _____

Class/Section _____

Score (Correct Answers ÷ No. of Assigned Problems) _____

PART 2 *Business Math Skills*

Exercise 1

Use the combined Annual Life Insurance Premiums—Nonsmoker table to answer the following questions.

The following nonsmoking employees have listed their choices for supplemental life insurance. Calculate monthly premiums to be deducted from each employee's paycheck.

Employee	Type of Insurance	Age	Sex	Amount of Insurance ($)	Annual Premium ($)	Monthly Premium ($)
J. Jones	Whole	55	M	60,000		1. _____
A. Lawson	20-year paid-up life	60	F*	35,000		2. _____
G. Hajek	Term	29	F	75,000		3. _____
B. Hoelscher	Variable universal life	45	M	100,000		4. _____
A. Black	Term	33	F	120,000		5. _____

*Note: Use premiums for a man 5 years younger.

Exercise 2

6. Barry Klepper and his son are equal partners in a business worth $455,000. Barry would like to purchase enough whole life insurance so that at his death the insurance benefit could be used to pay his heirs (his son, who is also his partner, and three daughters) the value of his half of the business. Barry is 55 years old and does not smoke.
   a. How much insurance does he need? _____
   b. Calculate the monthly premium. _____
7. Amanda Barlow will be retiring in 20 years. She is 55 and does not smoke. She has decided to purchase $50,000 over the next 20 years in paid-up life insurance. Calculate the monthly premium. _____

Exercise 3

Use the Annual Fire Insurance Premiums for Buildings and Contents table to answer the following questions.

The department stores, warehouses, and contents owned by J. Berken and the amount of insurance for each are listed below along with the area rating and class for each. Calculate the annual premium for each building and contents and the total in annual premiums.

	Property	Amount of Insurance ($)	Area Rating	Class	Annual Premium ($)
8.	Building 101	315,000	1	A	_____
9.	Contents of Building 101	175,000	1	A	_____
10.	Building 102	225,000	2	A	_____
11.	Contents of Building 102	320,000	2	A	_____
12.	Building 103	250,000	2	B	_____
13.	Contents of Building 103	200,000	2	B	_____
14.	Building 104	375,000	1	A	_____
15.	Contents of Building 104	400,000	1	A	_____
16.			Total fire and property insurance premium		$ _____

17. A fire in Building 102 described above resulted in losses of $160,000 to the building and $320,000 to its contents. The fire insurance policy contained a coinsurance clause. The actual value of the building was $275,000. The actual value of the contents was $415,000. How much will the insurance company pay in compensation to the owner of the building? _____ Show your work.

Exercise 4

Use the Auto Insurance Driver Classification, Liability and Medical Payment, and Compensation and Collision tables at the end of the chapter to calculate insurance for the following drivers. The desired types and amounts of insurance are listed in worksheets for each driver. Use the worksheets to calculate the base premium, the actual premium, and the total annual premium for each driver.

18. Robert Black, age 35, uses his car in his business. His car model is classified as (4) L. His car's age group is classified as 1. He drives in a territory classified as 3.

Desired Coverage	Deductible If Applicable ($)	Base Premium ($)	Multiple	Premium ($)
Comprehensive				
Collision	250			
Bodily injury 50/100				
Property damage $50,000				
Medical payment $5,000				
		Total annual premium_____		

19. Justine Rankin, age 55, uses her car in her business. She is the only operator of her car. Her car model is classified as (3) K. Her car's age group is classified as 4. She drives in a territory classified as 2.

Desired Coverage	Deductible If Applicable ($)	Base Premium ($)	Multiple	Premium ($)
Comprehensive				
Collision	500			
Bodily injury 200/300				
Property damage $100,000				
Medical payment $10,000				
		Total annual premium_____		

20. Jack Kelly, age 24, is married and drives his car to work 12 miles each way. His car model is classified as (1) G. His car's age group is classified as 1. He drives in a territory classified as 2.

Desired Coverage	Deductible If Applicable ($)	Base Premium ($)	Multiple	Premium ($)
Comprehensive				
Collision	250			
Bodily injury 50/50				
Property damage $25,000				
Medical payment $5,000				
		Total annual premium_____		

PART 3   *Review and Practice Using Business Math FUNdamentals*

GOAL: Complete 9 of the 10 problems correctly.

Instructions: *Start Business Math FUNdamentals. Complete Tutorials 72 through 74 and Drill 52. If you are not satisfied with your score, repeat the drill. Write your scores below.*

Business Math FUNdamentals Drill 52

Today's Date	Score

Name _____

Class/Section _____

Strokes per Minute Score _____

Accuracy Score (Correct Strokes ÷ Total Strokes) _____

 **PART 4** *Desktop Calculator*

Exercise 1

One-Minute Addition Timing (0 through 9 Keys, Six-Digit Numbers)

(Optional: Your instructor may wish you to use Touch Key on the computer for all your timings. Check with your instructor before completing this exercise.)

Complete as many of the problems as possible in 1 minute by adding. Work quickly and accurately. The number preceding each closing parenthesis indicates the cumulative number of strokes for problems attempted. For example, if you complete Problems 1 through 3 in 1 minute, your strokes-per-minute score is 243. Optional: 3- and 5-minute timings. If you finish all the problems in 5 minutes, your strokes-per-minute score is 261.

1.	2.	3.	4.	5.	6.	7.	8.
9805.60	2202.40	9774.40	8899.60	9585.00	2120.00	4300.00	5775.10
7834.10	1233.20	6775.00	8770.20	6950.00	2895.00	5600.00	2700.30
2389.00	6200.90	5220.00	6970.10	3459.00	9910.00	6100.00	2700.20
1365.70	9754.50	1560.00	8460.30	3899.50	8798.00	3300.00	3900.10
7598.70	8604.10	9740.00	8750.40	1935.90	6700.60	4300.00	4800.40
8352.40	1900.00	1950.00	9940.50	3462.90	2387.50	6200.00	4600.20
9109.00	6478.80	2430.00	8600.30	9989.90	9200.30	5300.00	5560.70
7683.50	5492.10	9610.00	7400.30	4567.50	3695.40	7500.00	8990.40
9056.90	5389.60	8030.00	1200.10	9190.00	9600.60	1600.00	3877.50
5387.00	1100.90	5330.00	9345.20	3482.60	2589.60	9500.00	9900.30
81)	162)	243)	324)	405)	486)	567)	648)

9.	10.	11.	12.	13.	14.	15.	16.
8414.00	9869.00	9198.70	9677.00	9845.00	9661.90	1860.15	2,500.40
9664.20	8426.77	2093.20	5379.00	2976.50	8000.45	3013.72	8,260.00
9558.50	7635.53	6045.94	7666.60	8799.50	7885.13	3064.56	6,400.00
8661.50	9769.98	9100.40	3578.00	2796.90	6655.12	3014.75	3,487.00
7777.00	5885.65	2283.90	5555.86	3075.78	7444.87	3045.25	9,600.20
6886.89	6743.22	6500.00	9968.60	9683.90	6111.98	2023.46	1,600.30
7995.99	4976.59	6548.00	7658.20	9557.70	5741.63	2013.75	8,951.40
8668.84	5221.00	1043.95	7225.89	2082.90	5962.65	9053.68	4,678.70
9172.56	8250.00	9511.90	7959.50	4569.91	5854.61	9024.54	3,641.20
8993.74	7355.75	3367.00	3221.50	8500.00	5014.24	1011.18	5,460.00
729)	810)	891)	972)	1,053)	1,134)	1,215)	1,306)

CHAPTER 31 *Terminology Review*

Actuarial tables

Beneficiary

Benefit

Cash value

Coinsurance clause

Compensation
Covered loss
Deductible
Fire and property insurance
Insurance policy
Insured
Life insurance
Paid-up life insurance
Premiums
Term life insurance
Variable universal life insurance
Whole life

Write the correct term next to the appropriate description.

1. _____ A means of protecting a breadwinner's family if he or she should die.

2. _____ Periodic payments for life insurance.

3. _____ A contract between a person and a company providing insurance.

4. _____ The owner of an insurance policy.

5. _____ The money paid on the insured's death.

6. _____ The person designated by the insured to receive the benefits of the policy.

7. _____ Lists the number of deaths per year by age for men and women, and are used by life insurance companies to help establish premiums.

8. _____ Premiums are paid during the insured's entire life, and a cash value accrues.

9. _____ The amount returned to the insured person if the policy should be terminated or canceled before the insured person's death.

10. _____ Premiums are paid for a certain number of years, at which time the policy has been purchased and no further premiums are necessary.

11. _____ Provides insurance in the case of death during a specific period.

12. _____ A very flexible insurance that allows for increasing assets for the insured's retirement as well as insurance in the case of the insured's death.

13. _____ Insures buildings and building contents from fire and other types of losses.

14. _____ A provision that requires the insurance company to cover losses up to the face value of the insurance policy only if the property is insured for at least 80% of its value.

15. _____ Money received to cover losses due to fire and damages to property.

16. _____ An amount to be paid in compensation for a specific incident by the insurance company.

17. _____ The portion of a covered loss that is the insured's responsibility.

18. List the eight types of automobile coverage a consumer may purchase. _____

_____

Chapter 31 Review Exercises

Exercise 1

Use the Internet to obtain an instant quote for whole, term, paid-up, or variable universal life for yourself.

Exercise 2

Obtain an instant quote for car insurance on a make and model of your choice. Use the instant quote feature on the Internet site of your choice.

End-of-Chapter TABLES

Annual Life Insurance Premiums—Nonsmoker per $1,000 of Face Value for Male Applicants*

Age Issued (Years)	Term 10-Year	Whole Life	Variable Universal	20-Year Paid-Up Life
18	$6.81	$14.77	$18.36	$24.69
20	6.88	15.46	19.81	25.59
22	6.95	16.12	20.28	26.53
24	7.05	16.82	21.33	27.53
25	7.10	17.22	22.17	28.06
26	7.18	17.67	23.43	28.63
28	7.35	18.64	24.79	29.84
30	7.59	19.73	26.05	31.12
35	8.68	23.99	30.87	35.80
40	10.64	28.26	35.55	40.34
45	14.52	33.79	41.24	46.01
50	22.18	40.77	48.11	53.24
55	32.93	51.38	57.62	64.77
60	None	59.32	None	70.86

*Note: Because of women's longer life expectancy, premiums for women are approximately equal to those of men who are 5 years younger.

Annual Fire Insurance Premiums for Buildings and Contents per $100 of Face Value

Territory	Structure Class				Contents Class			
	A	B	C	D	A	B	C	D
1	$0.45	$0.56	$0.66	$0.75	$0.51	$0.79	$0.79	$0.98
2	0.58	0.64	0.78	0.80	0.68	0.86	0.91	1.03
3	0.63	0.72	0.85	0.93	0.71	0.89	0.95	1.12

Driver Classifications
Multiples of Base Annual
Automobile Insurance Premiums

			Pleasure; Less Than 3 Miles to Work Each Way	Drives to Work, 3 to 9 Miles Each Way	Drives to Work, 10 Miles or More Each Way	Used in Business
No young operators	Only operator is a woman, age 30 to 64		0.90	1.00	1.30	1.40
	One or more operators age 65 or over		1.00	1.10	1.40	1.50
	All others		1.00	1.10	1.40	1.50
Young women	Age 16	DT	1.40	1.50	1.80	1.90
		No DT	1.55	1.65	1.95	2.05
	Age 20	DT	1.05	1.15	1.45	1.55
		No DT	1.10	1.20	1.50	1.60
Young men (married)	Age 16	DT	1.60	1.70	2.00	2.10
		No DT	1.80	1.90	2.20	2.30
	Age 20	DT	1.45	1.55	1.85	1.95
		No DT	1.50	1.60	1.90	2.00
	Age 21		1.40	1.50	1.80	1.90
	Age 24		1.10	1.20	1.50	1.60
Young unmarried men (not principal operator)	Age 16	DT	2.05	2.15	2.45	2.55
		No DT	2.30	2.40	2.70	2.80
	Age 20	DT	1.60	1.70	2.00	2.10
		No DT	1.70	1.80	2.10	2.20
	Age 21		1.55	1.65	1.95	2.05
	Age 24		1.10	1.20	1.50	1.60
Young unmarried men (owner or principal operator)	Age 16	DT	2.70	2.80	3.10	3.20
		No DT	3.30	3.40	3.70	3.80
	Age 20	DT	2.55	2.65	2.95	3.05
		No DT	2.70	2.80	3.10	3.20
	Age 21		2.50	2.60	2.90	3.00
	Age 24		1.90	2.00	2.30	2.40
	Age 26		1.50	1.60	1.90	2.00
	Age 29		1.10	1.20	1.50	1.60

Note: DT indicates completion of a certified driver-training course.

Automobile Liability and Medical Payment Insurance
Base Annual Premiums

Coverage	Bodily Injury Territory 1	Territory 2	Territory 3	Coverage	Property Damage Territory 1	Territory 2	Territory 3
15/30	$81	$91	$112	$5,000	$83	$95	$100
25/25	83	94	115	10,000	85	97	103
25/50	86	97	120	25,000	86	99	104
50/50	88	101	125	50,000	87	101	107
50/100	90	103	129	100,000	90	103	108
100/100	91	104	131				
100/200	94	108	136	Medical Payment			
100/300	95	110	139	$1,000	$62	$63	$64
200/300	98	112	141	2,500	65	66	67
300/300	100	115	144	5,000	67	68	69
				10,000	70	72	74

Comprehensive and Collision Insurance
Base Annual Premiums

Model Class	Age Group	Territory 1 Comprehensive	$250 Deductible Collision	$500 Deductible Collision	Territory 2 Comprehensive	$250 Deductible Collision	$500 Deductible Collision	Territory 3 Comprehensive	$250 Deductible Collision	$500 Deductible Collision
(1)	1	$55	$82	$76	$59	$92	$80	$73	$100	$91
A-G	2,3	52	77	73	56	86	76	58	94	85
	4	49	71	67	51	79	70	54	85	78
(3)	1	63	111	101	69	128	108	75	141	127
J-K	2,3	59	103	95	64	118	101	68	131	118
	4	54	93	86	57	106	91	61	116	105
(4)	1	68	123	112	76	143	120	83	169	142
L-M	2,3	64	125	104	70	133	112	75	138	132
	4	57	102	94	62	117	100	66	129	117
(5)	1	77	140	126	86	164	136	95	183	162
N-O	2,3	70	130	117	77	151	126	85	168	150
	4	62	115	105	68	133	112	73	147	132

CHAPTER 32

Sales Tax, Property Tax, Corporate Income Tax

PART 1   Speed and Accuracy Building Using Touch Key

GOALS: Your speed goal is 12,000 strokes per hour.
Your accuracy target goal range is 95% to 100%.

With each repetition of the test, try to improve your speed without lowering your accuracy score. If your percent-of-accuracy score falls below 95%, review your finger position and technique. Then try again.

Instructions: *Start Touch Key. Complete the Payroll Test in Appendix A. Write your scores for strokes per hour and percent of accuracy scores. If you are not satisfied with your scores, repeat the test until you are satisfied.*

Payroll Test

	Today's Date	Strokes per Hour	Percent of Accuracy
A.			
B.			
C.			
D.			
E.			

PART 2   Business Math Skills

You have already learned that **sales tax** is a percentage problem in which the sales amount is multiplied by the rate of sales tax as shown in Figure 32.1. Sales tax is charged by most states. States decide which goods and services will be taxed. In addition, some cities charge sales tax. Some cities require a hotel tax as well. In such cases the rates are added together and then multiplied by the sales amount.

Use the percentage formula to find the amount of sales tax to be paid on taxable goods. Use the applicable state and city sales tax rates, if any.

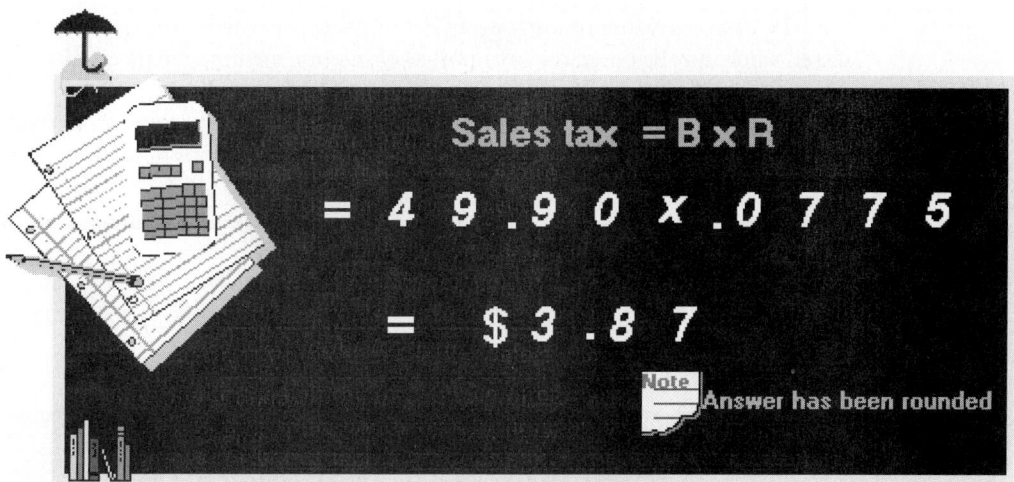

FIGURE 32.1

PROBLEM 1

Calculate the amount of sales tax for shoes that cost $49.90. The state sales tax is 7%. The city sales tax is 0.75%.

Convert the percents to decimal numbers and add. Multiply the rate by the sales amount:
$$\$49.90 \times 0.0775 = \$3.87$$

Pocket Calculator Method	**Desktop Calculator Method**
7 + .75 = $\boxed{7.75}$ × 49.90 $\boxed{\%}$ $\boxed{3.87}$	7 + .75 + T$\boxed{7.75}$ × $\boxed{49.90}$ $\boxed{\%}$ $\boxed{3.87}$

PROPERTY TAX

Property tax is levied by some states on real estate as a way to raise money. In addition, the city, county, and school district in which the property is located may levy a property tax. Some cities and states may also levy taxes for special purposes, such as a road and bridge tax to rebuild aging bridges and the roads connecting them (Figure 32.2). The tax rate for each entity is set by the local entities and is levied on property owned by individuals and businesses based on the assessed value and the tax rates currently in effect.

FIGURE 32.2

The **assessed value** of a property is the value on which property tax is levied. The assessed value may be based on any number of factors, including market value or intended use. Officials usually send an assessment report to property owners in advance of the tax bill to give property owners time to appeal the assessed valuation of their property. Using the percentage formula, multiply the assessed value by the tax rate to find the property tax due.

PROBLEM 2

A home was assessed at $120,000. The property tax rate is 3.8%. Calculate property tax due.
    As shown in Figure 32.3, $120,000 \times 0.038 = \$4,560$.

Property tax = B x R

1 2 0 , 0 0 0   X .0 3 8

= $ 4 , 5 6 0

FIGURE 32.3

Note: Tax rates may be stated as a dollar amount per $100 of property value. For example, the property tax rate in Problem 2 would be stated as $3.8 per $100 of property value. Notice that this calculation results in the same amount of tax as using the percentage method, $4,560:

$$\$120,000 \div 100 = \$1,200$$
$$\$1,200 \times 3.8 = \$4,560$$

How do the **taxing entities,** such as cities, school districts, and counties, determine the property tax rate? After setting a budget, the taxing entity divides it by the value of the taxable property in the district.

PROBLEM 3

The total assessed value of all taxable property in a school district was $45,000,000. The school needs $4,000,000 for its budget next year. What tax rate should the school set for school property tax?
    Using the percent formula, let percentage equal 4 million, let base equal 45 million, and let percent equal the school tax rate. Divide as shown in Figure 32.4. The new school tax rate should be set at 8.89%, or $8.89 per $100 of property value. (Note that the answer has been rounded to hundredths.)

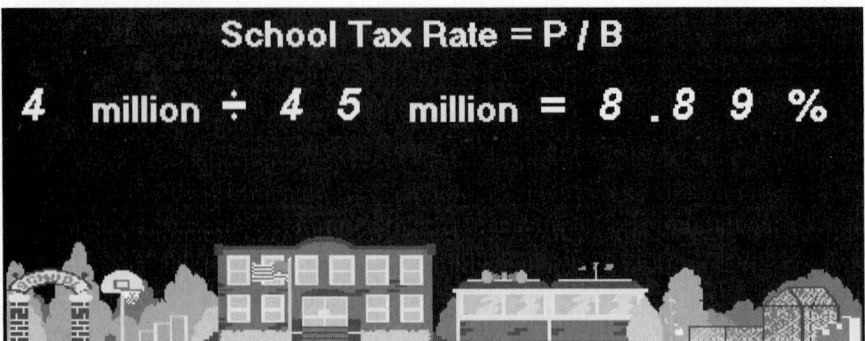

FIGURE 32.4

CORPORATE INCOME TAX

Corporations pay **corporate income tax** on taxable income. **Tables of corporate tax rates** are consulted to determine the amount of corporate income tax. A partial Corporate Income Tax Rate table is shown in Figure 32.5. To use the table, find the appropriate row for taxable income. Use the row for which the taxable income is more than the amount shown in column 1, but not more than the amount shown in column 2. Reading across the row, find the income tax rate as the amount shown in column 3.

PROBLEM 4

A consulting firm had taxable income of $225,000 in 2003. Using the table of Corporate Income Tax Rates in Figure 32.5, calculate the amount of corporate income tax the company must pay.

Consulting row 4, we see that $225,000 is over $100,000, but not over $335,000. The tax rate is 39% of taxable income:

$$\$225{,}000 \times 0.39 = \$87{,}750$$

Corporate Income Tax Rates—2004, 2003, 2002, 2001, 2000		
Taxable Income Over	**Not Over**	**Tax Rate**
$0	$50,000	15%
50,000	75,000	25%
75,000	100,000	34%
100,000	335,000	39%
335,000	10,000,000	34%
10,000,000	15,000,000	35%
15,000,000	18,333,333	38%
18,333,333	. . .	35%

FIGURE 32.5

Name _____

Class/Section _____

Score (Correct Answers ÷ No. of Assigned Problems) _____

PART 2 *Business Math Skills*

Exercise 1

1. Ken Watson sold a used car to a friend for $3,000. The city and state sales tax in his area is 8.5%. What is the total amount he should collect from his friend for the car? _____
2. Nadine Fisher Collectibles had sales of $5,165.92 on Monday. Calculate the total sales tax collected for the day if the city and state tax rate is 6.125%. _____

3. Joe wants to keep the price of his best-selling bar-b-que plate as close as possible to $8.00 but below that amount including tax. If the city and state sales tax is 7%, how much should he charge for the plate (before tax)? _____

4. Augustus Blake owns a business in Taxville. The land and building value of his property was assessed at $212,000. Calculate his property tax for the entities as listed.

Entity	Tax Rate/$100	Tax Amount
City	2.125	
County	0.5	
School	8.7	
College	2.1	
Road and bridge	1.2	
	Total	

5. The tax assessor/collector in Taxville has authority to grant discounts for early payment of taxes as follows. How much would Augustus pay if he paid his taxes in November? _____
Payment schedule:

If paid by . . .	Deduct . . .
October 31	3%
November 30	2%
December 31	1%

6. The county of Owen determined that a budget of $3.2 million would be needed for the next fiscal year. Total assessed property value in the county is $697 million. What tax rate should the county set for next year? Round the answer to hundredths. _____

7. A corporation specializing in automated car wash facilities had a taxable income of $60,000 the first year and $85,000 the second year. Calculate corporate income tax for the first year _____ For the second year _____

PART 3 *Review and Practice Using Business Math FUNdamentals*

GOAL: Complete 9 of the 10 problems correctly.

Instructions: *Start Business Math FUNdamentals. Complete Tutorials 75 through 77 and Drill 53. If you are not satisfied with your score, repeat the drill. Write your scores below.*

Business Math FUNdamentals Drill 53

Today's Date	Score

 # Part 4   Desktop Calculator

Exercise 1

One-Minute Addition Timing (0 through 9 Keys, Six-Digit Numbers)

(Optional: Your instructor may wish you to use Touch Key on the computer for all your timings. Check with your instructor before completing this exercise.)

Complete as many of the problems as possible in 1 minute by adding. Work quickly and accurately. The number preceding each closing parenthesis indicates the cumulative number of strokes for problems attempted. For example, if you complete Problems 1 through 5 in 1 minute, your strokes-per-minute score is 405. Optional: 3- and 5-minute timings. If you complete all problems in 5 minutes, your strokes-per-minute score is 261.

1. 1305.60	2. 9702.40	3. 1174.40	4. 2699.60	5. 3685.00	6. 9720.00	7. 1900.00	8. 9975.10
7856.10	1289.20	6726.00	8725.20	6937.00	2816.00	5618.00	2788.30
2389.16	6285.90	5220.45	6970.27	3459.38	9910.37	6100.17	2700.77
1265.70	9754.97	8660.00	2860.30	1299.50	1198.00	1600.00	1100.10
7597.80	4104.10	9795.00	8729.40	1945.90	6728.60	4315.00	4833.40
3252.40	1934.00	1950.98	9940.21	3462.67	2387.37	6200.14	4600.22
9134.00	6478.23	9730.00	2900.30	3189.90	3300.30	1200.00	5541.70
7683.50	7892.10	9674.00	7425.30	4551.50	3631.40	7513.00	8990.52
9056.35	5367.60	8030.72	1200.24	9190.62	9600.45	1600.15	6277.50
1617.00	1100.65	7430.00	2745.20	6721.34	4689.60	9560.00	9964.30
81)	162)	243)	324)	405)	486)	567)	648)

9. 3414.00	10. 2269.00	11. 2598.70	12. 1377.00	13. 3145.00	14. 7661.00	15. 1700.00	16. 2,500.40
9635.20	8421.77	2027.20	5332.00	2932.50	8320.00	3013.00	8,260.00
9558.36	7635.24	6045.17	7666.35	8799.41	7655.00	3064.00	6,400.00
3671.50	2669.98	9122.40	1378.00	4296.90	6648.00	3014.00	3,487.00
7739.00	5827.65	2283.25	5514.86	3043.78	5844.00	3045.00	9,600.20
6886.31	6743.31	6585.00	9968.15	9683.45	5111.00	2023.00	1,600.30
4295.99	5676.59	6548.12	1618.20	4657.70	9221.00	2013.00	8,951.40
8442.84	5267.00	2343.95	9925.89	2047.90	5202.00	9053.00	4,178.70
5672.56	5550.58	9525.90	9859.50	4569.50	5811.00	9024.00	3,641.20
8957.74	5355.75	3367.95	9321.50	8551.00	9014.00	1011.00	5,460.00
729)	810)	891)	972)	1,053)	1,134)	1,215)	1,306)

CHAPTER 32 *Terminology Review* _____

Assessed value

Corporate income tax

Property tax

Sales tax

Tables of corporate tax rates

Taxing entities

Write the correct term next to the appropriate description.

1. _____ A tax charged by most states on certain taxable items and services at the time a sale is made or a service is provided.
2. _____ Levied by some school districts, cities, counties, and college districts on real estate.
3. _____ The stated value on which property tax is levied.
4. _____ Cities, school districts, and counties that levy a property tax.
5. _____ Tax paid by corporations on taxable income.
6. _____ Used to determine the amount of corporate income tax owed.

Name _____

Class/Section _____

Score (Correct Answers ÷ No. of Assigned Problems) _____

Chapter 32 Review Exercises

Exercise 1

Renee Winegard purchased the following items. Taxable items are noted as txb. Sales tax in her area is 7.25%. Calculate the amount of tax and the total amount owed.

$15.90	txb
$5.47	
$3.90	
$1.90	
$7.03	txb
$.57	txb
$1.25	
$2.90	
$4.50	txb
$8.79	txb
$4.39	
$2.70	
$10.90	txb
	Tax 1.
	Total 2.

Exercise 2

Janet stayed at a hotel in a city that has a special hotel tax of 6%. Sales tax in the area is 9%. Hotel charges were $312.
3. What did she pay in taxes? _____
4. In total? _____
5. Bear County set a budget of $1,650,000 for next year. The county has $459,000,000 in taxable property. What property tax rate should the county set for next year? Round the answer to tenths. _____

Brad Smith's total property value is $109,000 including his homestead exemption. Property tax rates in his area are listed. Calculate his property tax for each entity, his tax discount if he paid his taxes in October, and the total amount he paid.

Early payment discount:

If paid by October   31   3%

If paid by November 30   2%

If paid by December 31   1%

Entity	Rate/$100	Tax ($)
County	1.90	6. _____
City	2.75	7. _____
School	5	8. _____
Road and bridge	.25	9. _____
College	.9	10. _____
	Total	11. _____
	Tax discount	12. _____
	Amount of taxes paid	13. _____

Exercise 3

Calculate the corporate income tax for each corporation listed using the table of Corporate Tax Rates (see Figure 32.5).

Name	Taxable Income ($)	Tax ($)
Company A	89,000	14. _____
Company B	59,800	15. _____
Company C	419,000	16. _____

END-OF-CHAPTER TABLE

Corporate Income Tax Rates—2004, 2003, 2002, 2001, 2000

Taxable Income Over	Not Over	Tax Rate
$0	$50,000	15%
50,000	75,000	25%
75,000	100,000	34%
100,000	335,000	39%
335,000	10,000,000	34%
10,000,000	15,000,000	35%
15,000,000	18,333,333	38%
18,333,333	. . .	35%

CHAPTER 33

Stocks and Bonds, Personal Investing

PART 1 *Speed and Accuracy Building Using Touch Key*

GOALS: Your speed goal is 12,000 strokes per hour.
Your accuracy target goal range is 95% to 100%.

With each repetition of the test, try to improve your speed without lowering your accuracy score. If your percent-of-accuracy score falls below 95%, review your finger position and technique. Then try again.

Instructions: *Start Touch Key. Complete the Invoice Test in Appendix B. Write your scores for strokes per hour and percent of accuracy below. If you are not satisfied with your scores, repeat the test until you are satisfied.*

Invoice Test

	Today's Date	Strokes per Hour	Percent of Accuracy
A.			
B.			
C.			
D.			
E.			

PART 2 *Business Math Skills*

STOCKS

To raise capital, a company may sell shares of the company, called **stocks**. **Dividends** are a portion of the company profits paid to stockholders. The two predominant types of stock are common and preferred. A **common stock** is one share of the company and carries the right to one vote. **Preferred stock** carries the right to a share of the earnings before dividends are paid to common stockholders. The amount of preferred dividend is usually stated as a dollars and cents value such as $.50 per share. **Dividends in arrears** consist of cumulative dividends owed to preferred stockholders that were not paid during the fiscal year, have been carried over to the next fiscal year, and will be paid when earnings are sufficient to do so. Stocks are bought and sold through exchanges such as the New York Stock

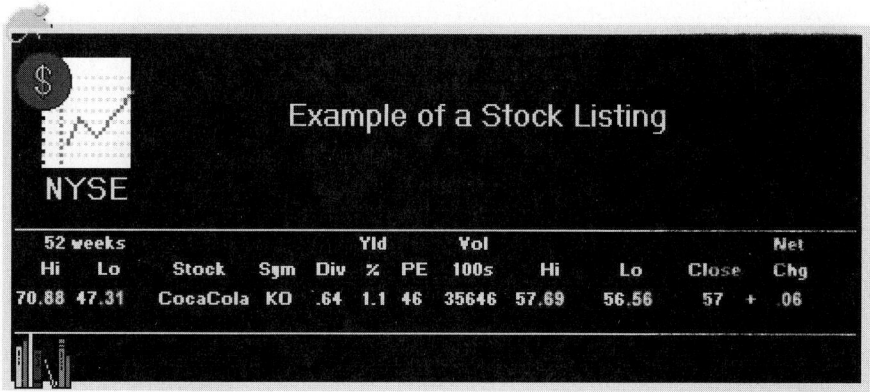

FIGURE 33.1

Exchange. Information about stocks is listed in major newspapers in sections for each exchange. An example of a listing for Coca Cola stock is shown in Figure 33.1.

HOW TO READ A STOCK LISTING

The example New York Stock Exchange (NYSE) listing for Coca Cola shows that:

1. The stock's highest price over the last 52 weeks was $70.88.
2. The lowest price over the last 52 weeks was $47.31.
3. The shortened name of the company is CocaCola.
4. The NYSE symbol for the company is KO.
5. The dividend last year was $.64.
6. The percent of yield (dividend divided by current price per share) is 1.1%.
7. The price–earnings ratio (price per share divided by annual earnings per share) is 46.
8. The number of shares sold on the date of the listing was 3,564,600.
9. The highest selling price on the date of the listing was $57.69.
10. The lowest price on the date of the listing was $56.56.
11. The price at the time the stock market closed on the date of the listing was $57.
12. Finally, the closing price on the date of the listing was up $.06 over the previous market day's closing price.

YTD % CHG
3.5
−6.1

Listings may also include a column showing year-to-date percent change (YTD % CHG). Minus signs are used to indicate a negative percent change.

DISTRIBUTING STOCK DIVIDENDS

Once a company has determined how much of its earnings will be paid in dividends, the company must determine how to distribute or pay out those dividends. Preferred stockholders must receive their promised dividends before any common stock shareholders are paid dividends.

PROBLEM 1

A company issued 50,000 shares of preferred stock with dividends of $.50 per share and 50,000 shares of common stock. This year, the company declared $75,000 available for paying dividends. Calculate the distribution of dividends.

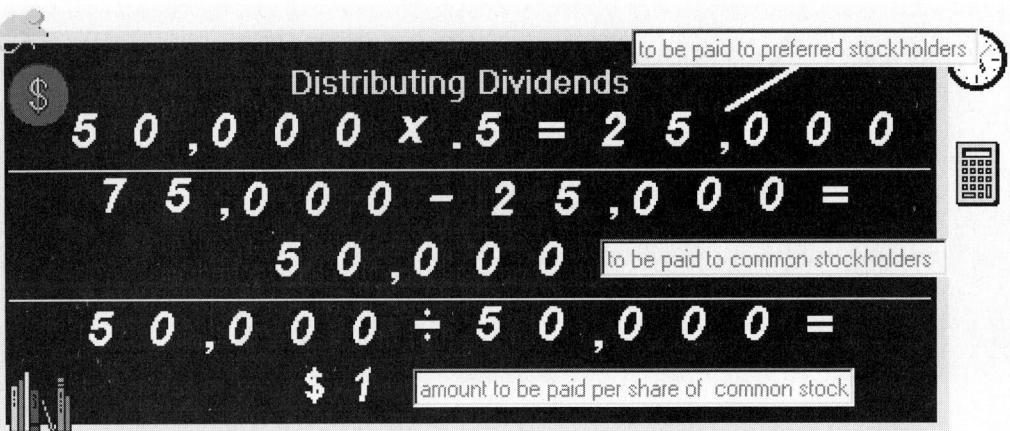

FIGURE 33.2

1. As shown in Figure 33.2, find the amount to be paid to preferred stockholders. Multiply the number of preferred stock shares by the preferred stock dividend:

$$\$50,000 \times .50 = \$25,000$$

2. Subtract the amount required for preferred stock dividend payouts from the amount available for paying dividends:

$$\$75,000 - \$25,000 = \$50,000$$

3. Divide the amount remaining by the number of common stock shares to find the dividend to pay for each share of common stock:

$$\$50,000 \div 50,000 = \$1 \text{ per share}$$

CALCULATING THE CURRENT STOCK YIELD

Investors use the current stock yield and compare it to other investment options to help them determine which is the best investment. **Current stock yield** is the annual dividend divided by the current market value. The current stock yield (1.1%) has been calculated for the CocaCola listing in Figure 33.3 by dividing $0.64 (annual dividend) by $57 (the current market value).

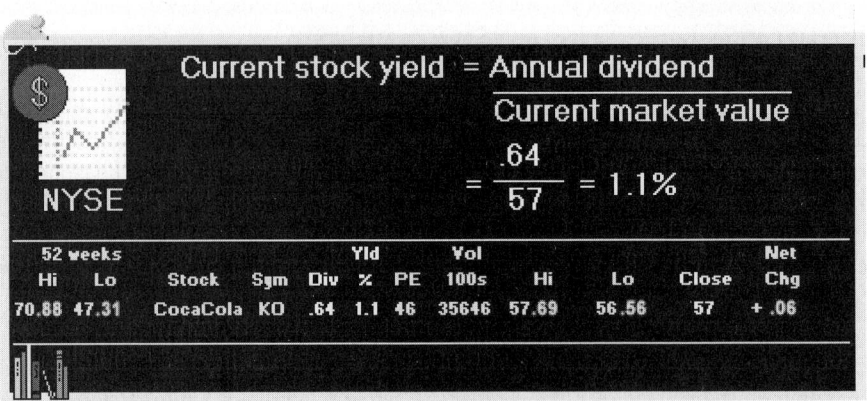

FIGURE 33.3

CALCULATING THE PRICE–EARNINGS RATIO AND ESTIMATED EARNINGS

A lower price–earnings ratio is desirable because it indicates higher earnings in relation to the stock's current market value. The **price–earnings ratio** (PE ratio) shown in the listing was calculated by dividing the current market value by the dividends declared by the company for the last four quarters. To estimate the company's annual dividends, divide the current market value by the price–earnings ratio (both are shown in the listing) or consult the company's annual financial statement for exact figures. The estimated annual dividend calculation is shown in Figure 33.4:

$$\$57 \div 46 = \$1.24 \text{ annual dividends}$$
$$\$57 \div \$1.24 = \text{price–earnings ratio}$$

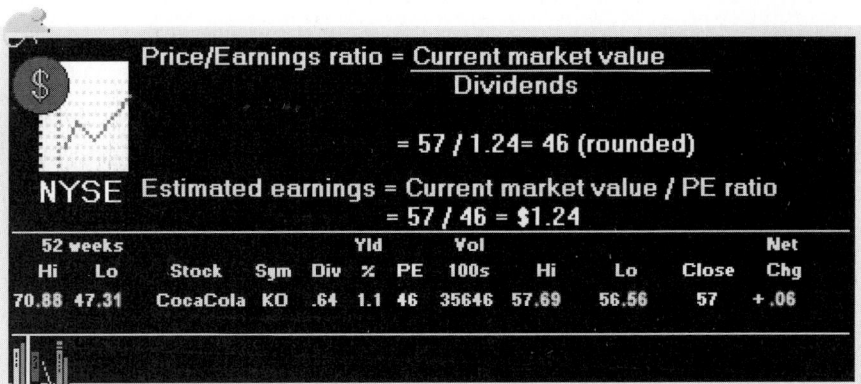

FIGURE 33.4

RETURN ON INVESTMENT

Return on investment is the percent of gain or loss that an investor experiences on an investment. It is calculated by dividing the total gain (loss) by the cost of the investment.

Cost equals the number of shares purchased times the cost per share plus commission.

Proceeds to the investor equal the selling price per share times the number of shares sold minus commission.

Total gain (loss) equals the proceeds minus cost plus dividends.

PROBLEM 2

Charles Brown bought 100 shares of Seaworthy Company last year at $50 a share on Ameritrade. A commission of $8.00 was paid. After 1 year, Charles sold the stock for $57 each, again using Ameritrade, and paid an $8.00 commission. During the year, a $1.24 dividend per share was paid. Calculate his return on investment (Figure 33.5).

1. Calculate cost:

$$(\text{Number of Shares Purchased} \times \text{Cost per Share}) \text{ plus Commission} = \text{Cost}$$
$$100 \text{ shares times } \$50 = \$5,000$$
$$\$5,000 + \$8 = \$5,008$$

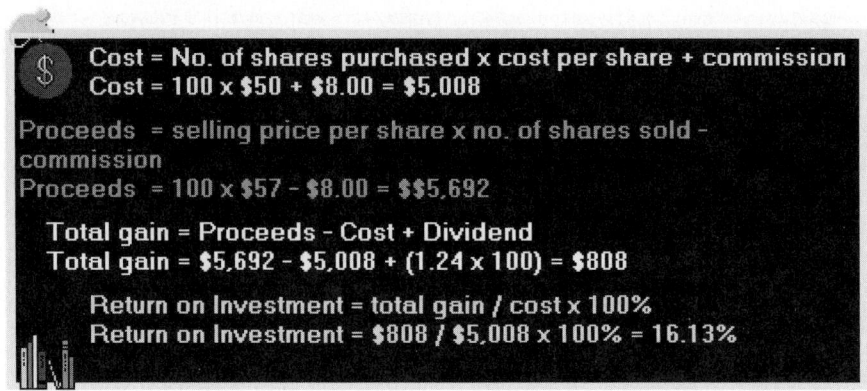

FIGURE 33.5

2. Calculate proceeds to investor:

(Selling Price per Share × number of Shares Sold) minus Commission = Proceeds

100 shares times $57 = $5,700

$5,700 − $8 = $5,692

3. Calculate total gain:

Proceeds − Cost + Dividends = Total Gain

a. Calculate gain on stock sale:

Proceeds − Cost = Gain on Stock Sale

$5,692 − $5,008 = $684

b. Calculate total dividends:

100 × $1.24 = $124

c. Add gain on stock sale to total dividends:

$684 + $124 = $808

4. Calculate return on investment:

Total Gain ÷ Cost = Return on Investment

$808 ÷ $5,008 = 0.1613, or 16.13% rate of return on investment

CORPORATE BONDS

Companies may elect to raise capital by selling corporate bonds, which are usually sold in multiples of $1,000. **Corporate bonds** are a debt obligation, a type of loan, issued by public and private corporations. The corporation promises to repay the face value on a specified date, referred to as the maturity of the bond, and to pay a stated rate of interest, usually semiannually. Unlike common stock, corporate bonds do not give the investor an owner-ship interest in the corporation.

Corporate bonds are classified by the types of **coupons** they carry:

1. **Fixed-rate coupon bonds** pay fixed payments of interest on a regular schedule for the life of the bond. The rate of interest of the bond may also be referred to as its fixed coupon.
2. **Floating-rate bonds** have variable interest rates that are adjusted periodically to an interest rate index such as the rate on short-term Treasury bills.
3. **Zero-coupon bonds** have no periodic interest payments, but are sold at a deep discount to face value.

In addition, bonds can be referred to as short-term, intermediate-term, and long-term bonds depending on the length of time to maturity:

1. Short-term bonds may have a maturity date of a few months to 5 years.
2. Intermediate-term bonds have a maturity date of 5 to 12 years.
3. Long-term bonds have a maturity date of 12 or more years.

Note: Although bonds have a maturity date, if the bond contains a "call" provision, the issuer may be allowed or required to repay the principal at a specified date before maturity. If the bond contains a "put" provision, the investor may require the issuer to repurchase the bonds at specified times prior to maturity.

Most bond transactions take place in the **over-the-counter market**. The OTC is made up of bond dealers and brokers who trade bonds by telephone or electronically.

Agencies providing ratings for bonds include Moody's Investor Service and Standard and Poor's Corp. Their highest ratings are AAA and Aaa, respectively. Bonds rated BBB and higher are considered to be investment grade. Bonds rated BB and lower are considered to be below investment grade.

Investors pay a **premium** when they buy a bond for more than its face value ($1,000). An investor buys at a **discount** when the bond is bought for less than the face value of $1,000. The price of a bond in the marketplace will fluctuate as a result of inflation and other factors, including interest rates. When interest rates rise, prices of outstanding bonds fall. When prevailing interest rates fall, prices of outstanding bonds rise. Therefore, if an investor sells a bond before it matures, the bond price may be more or less than the original purchase price.

The price of a bond is listed as a percent, with $1,000 representing 100%. A bond selling for $1,020 would be listed at 102% because $1,020 ÷ $1,000 = 1.02, or 102%. A bond selling for $995 would be listed at 99.5% because $995 ÷ $1,000 = 99.5%. See Figure 33.6.

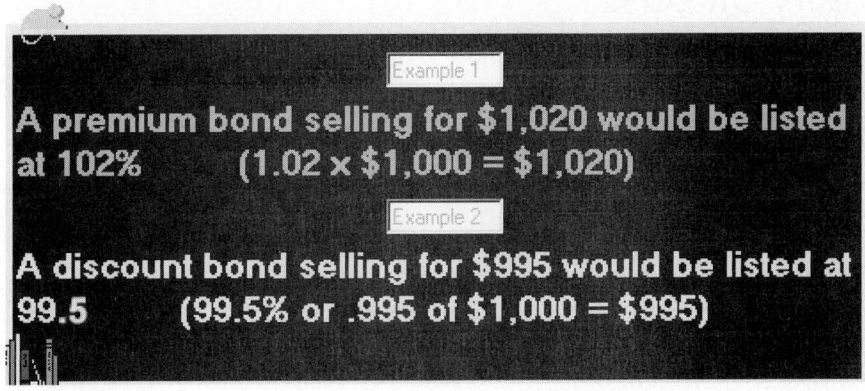

Example 1

A premium bond selling for $1,020 would be listed at 102%   (1.02 × $1,000 = $1,020)

Example 2

A discount bond selling for $995 would be listed at 99.5   (99.5% or .995 of $1,000 = $995)

FIGURE 33.6

An example of a bond listing for General Motors corporate bonds is shown in Figure 33.7. Notice the designation 8.375 and 2033 beside the name (GM). The number 8.375 in the designation indicates that the interest rate (the coupon) on the bond is 8.375%. The number 2033 in the designation indicates that the year of maturity of the bond is 2033. The coupon and maturity information may also be listed in separate columns. The following are also listed:

1. Last yield, which is 7.255%.
2. The last price is listed as a percent of the $1,000 face value. In this case, the closing price is 113.523%, or $1,135.23.
3. The estimated volume, 186,643, is the estimated dollar value of bonds traded in thousands ($186,643,000).

Bond yield is the return actually earned on a bond based on price paid and interest received.

Current bond yield is the annual return on the amount paid for the bond. The interest payment divided by the purchase price equals the current yield.

Example of a Bond Listing

Bonds	Last Yld	Last Price	Est. Vol
GMs8.375s2033	7.255	113.523	186,643

FIGURE 33.7

PROBLEM 3

Calculate the current yield this year for an 8% bond (face value $1,000) that cost $950.

Calculate interest paid:

$$\$1,000 \times 8\% = \$80 \text{ annual interest paid}$$

Calculate current yield:

$$\$80 \div \$950 = 8.42\%$$

Yield to maturity or **yield to call** is the total return if a bond is held until it matures or is called. All interest earned from the time of purchase until maturity or call is divided by the purchase price of the bond. This information can be received from a bond dealer or a broker.

CALCULATING NET GAIN OR LOSS

To calculate the net gain or loss on a bond investment, you must first calculate the cost of the bonds plus the commission for purchasing the bonds and the proceeds of the bonds minus the commission for selling the bonds.

PROBLEM 4A

What is the cost of 20 bonds bought at 999% if a $6 commission was charged for each bond?

Referring to Figure 33.8, calculate the cost of one bond, the cost of 20 bonds, and the amount of commission:

$$999\% \text{ of } \$1,000 = \$999 \text{ cost of one bond}$$
$$\$999 \times 20 = \$19,980 \text{ cost of 20 bonds}$$
$$20 \times \$6 = \$120 \text{ commission}$$
$$\$19,980 + \$120 = \$20,100 \text{ total cost of the 20 bonds}$$

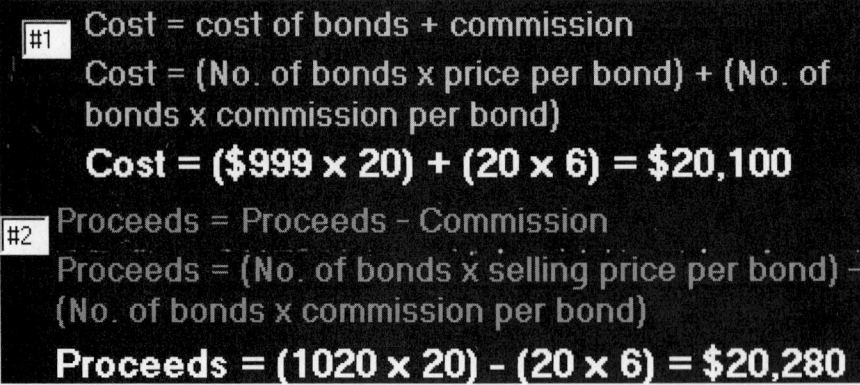

#1 Cost = cost of bonds + commission

Cost = (No. of bonds x price per bond) + (No. of bonds x commission per bond)

Cost = ($999 x 20) + (20 x 6) = $20,100

#2 Proceeds = Proceeds − Commission

Proceeds = (No. of bonds x selling price per bond) − (No. of bonds x commission per bond)

Proceeds = (1020 x 20) − (20 x 6) = $20,280

FIGURE 33.8

STOCKS AND BONDS, PERSONAL INVESTING

PROBLEM 4B

What are the net proceeds if the 20 bonds sold for 102% and a $6 commission was charged for the sale of each bond?

Calculate the selling price of one bond, the selling price of all 20 bonds, and the commission for selling the 20 bonds. Net proceeds equals selling price of all bonds minus commission for selling the bonds:

$$\$1,000 \times 102\% = \$1,020 \text{ selling price of one bond}$$
$$\$1,020 \times 20 = \$20,400 \text{ selling price for 20 bonds}$$
$$20 \times \$6 = \$120 \text{ commission}$$
$$\$20,400 - \$120 = \$20,280 \text{ net proceeds}$$

PROBLEM 4C

What was the gain or loss on the sale of the bonds?

Subtract the total cost of the bonds from the net proceeds:

$$\$20,280 - \$20,100 = \$180 \text{ net gain}$$

Any interest earned before the sale of the bonds is listed separately as interest earned, not as part of the gain or loss.

A WORD ABOUT PERSONAL INVESTING

Whenever investing in instruments with a fixed maturity date such as Certificates of Deposit (CDs) or bonds, consider laddering. **Laddering** involves buying CDs or bonds so that the maturity dates are spread over several years. As an example, consider $4,000 invested as follows:

$1,000 in a 2% CD that matures in 1 year

$1,000 in a 2.5% CD that matures in 2 years

$1,000 in a 3% CD that matures in 3 years

$1,000 in a 3.5% CD that matures in 4 years

At the end of each year the money from the CD is reinvested in a 4-year CD at the then–current rate of interest.

Advantages of investing in this way instead of placing all $1,000 in the same type of CD include the following:

1. At the end of each year, money is available ($1,000 plus interest) without penalty if the investor needs cash.
2. If interest rates go up, the investor can invest $1,000 plus interest at the higher interest rate.
3. If the interest rates go down, the investor will be investing only part of his or her money, $1,000 plus interest, at the lower rate.
4. The overall return is higher than if the entire $4,000 was invested in a 1-year CD at 2%.

AUTOMATIC SAVINGS ACCOUNTS

Many young people do not have a lump sum with which to begin investing. What is the best way to accumulate such a sum? Historically, the most successful method has been automatic deductions from one's paycheck deposited to a savings account. It works because the amount is deducted and placed in savings before the employee receives his or her paycheck, thus making it less likely that the employee will think it as part of his or her spendable money that pay period. This method, "paying yourself first," may be easily begun when a raise is received. Use the raise as the amount to be placed in an automatic savings plan. Another method involves deciding on a percentage of take-home pay to save each month and placing this amount in an automatic savings plan.

For more information about saving and investing, www.tomorrowsmoney.org is an interactive Web site especially designed for people new to investing.

Name _____

Class/Section _____

Score (Correct Answers ÷ No. of Assigned Problems) _____

PART 2 *Business Math Skills*

Exercise 1

Use the following listing of NYSE composite transactions to answer the following questions, (PE is the price–earnings ratio).

52-Week								
High	Low	Stock (Symbol)	Dividend	Yield %	PE	Volume 100s	Close	Net Change
25.60	13.05	LongsDrg LDG	.56	2.6	35	2,253	21.39	−0.43
60.42	34.83	Lowes Cos LOW	.12	.2	25	73,558	56.67	−1.71
33.97	18.55	MONY Gp MNY	.45	1.4	40	17,623	31.35	0.14
51.83	36.24	PepsiCo PEP	.64	1.2	24	60,018	52.09	0.34

1. What is the NYSE symbol for Longs Drug? _____
2. Did PepsiCo pay a dividend? _____
3. What was the percent of yield for Lowes Companies? _____
4. What was the volume for MONY Grp? _____
5. What was the price at close for PepsiCo? _____
6. What were the 52-week high and low for PepsiCo? High _____ Low _____

Exercise 2

7. A company issued 175,000 shares of common stock. The company declared $90,000 available for paying dividends. Calculate the distribution of dividends. _____
8. A company issued 100,000 in preferred stock paying a $.25 dividend and 200,000 in common stock. The company declared $175,000 available for paying dividends. Calculate the distribution of dividends. _____
9. A company issued 300,000 shares of $.40 preferred stock and 600,000 shares of common stock. The company has dividends in arrears of $120,000. The company declared $500,000 available for paying dividends. How much will each common share earn in dividends? _____
10. A 5-year, 3% bond price was listed at 112%.
    a. Did the bond sell for a discount or a premium? _____
    b. What was the total purchase price if five bonds were puchased? _____
    c. Calculate annual interest _____ and semiannual interest _____

PART 3 *Review and Practice Using Business Math FUNdamentals*

GOAL: Complete 9 of the 10 problems correctly.

Instructions: Start Business Math FUNdamentals. Complete Tutorials 75 through 77 and Drill 53. If you are not satisfied with your score, repeat the drill. Write your scores below.

Business Math FUNdamentals Drill 53

Today's Date	Score

Name _____

Class/Section _____

Strokes per Minute Score _____

Accuracy Score (Correct Strokes ÷ Total Strokes) _____

PART 4 *Desktop Calculator*

Exercise 1

One-Minute Addition Timing (0 through 9 Keys, Six-Digit Numbers)

(Optional: Your instructor may wish you to use Touch Key on the computer for all your timings. Check with your instructor before completing this exercise.)

Complete as many of the problems as possible in 1 minute by adding. Work quickly and accurately. The number preceding each closing parenthesis indicates the cumulative number of strokes for problems attempted. For example, if you complete Problems 1 through 3 in 1 minute, your strokes-per-minute score is 243. If you complete all problems in 5 minutes, your strokes-per-minute score is 216.

1. 9005.60	2. 5702.00	3. 2574.45	4. 2699.95	5. 3085.00	6. 9000.00	7. 8700.00	8. 1195.10
7800.10	1589.00	6156.00	8725.95	6907.00	2800.00	5686.00	2795.30
2009.16	6256.00	7520.45	6970.99	3450.59	9900.79	8900.79	2798.79
1200.70	9400.90	3295.00	2860.98	1099.59	1008.00	1698.00	1199.19
7005.80	4004.00	9756.00	8729.99	1905.59	6700.69	4399.00	4899.49
3252.00	1900.00	5750.95	9940.95	3460.49	2300.39	6298.49	4679.29
9004.00	6418.00	5630.00	2900.99	3089.99	3300.39	1295.00	5545.70
7600.50	7832.00	5774.00	7425.98	4501.59	3001.49	7599.00	8995.59
9056.00	5960.00	7520.75	1200.95	2190.69	9600.45	1696.59	6279.55
1967.00	1100.00	5990.00	2745.95	6901.39	4600.69	9595.00	9965.35
81)	162)	243)	324)	405)	486)	567)	648)

9. 1214.00	10. 9798.00	11. 9098.70	12. 6977.00	13. 4745.00	14. 3961.00	15. 3600.00	16. 9550.40
9642.20	8421.99	2094.20	5350.00	2957.50	8338.00	3500.00	3884.00
9558.15	9035.24	6045.85	5866.35	8799.56	7655.39	3700.00	4648.00
5171.50	2648.98	1422.40	1349.00	6596.90	1948.00	3900.00	9248.00
7723.00	5827.37	2251.25	5514.59	3075.78	5818.00	3500.00	1989.20
6886.45	9943.31	6585.99	5168.15	9683.95	5111.29	2500.00	2169.30
2595.99	5689.59	9848.12	1652.20	3057.70	3921.00	2550.00	7895.40
8435.84	5267.79	2378.95	9925.34	2040.90	5238.00	9500.00	4489.70
5672.12	9150.58	9525.79	1259.50	4569.95	5811.49	9550.00	5369.00
1568.74	5383.75	6967.95	9310.50	1419.00	1139.99	1500.00	9545.00
729)	810)	891)	972)	1,053)	1,134)	1,215)	1,306)

CHAPTER 33 *Terminology Review*

Bond yield
Common stock
Corporate bonds
Coupons
Current bond yield
Current stock yield
Discount
Dividends
Dividends in arrears
Laddering
Over-the-counter market
Preferred stock
Premium
Price–earnings ratio
Return on investment
Stocks
Year to call
Year to maturity

Write the correct term next to the appropriate description.

1. _____ Shares of a company.

2. _____ A portion of the company profits paid to stockholders.

3. _____ One share of a company that carries the right to one vote.

4. _____ A share of the company that carries the right to a share of the earnings before dividends are paid to common stockholders.

5. _____ Cumulative dividends owed to preferred stockholders.

6. _____ The annual dividend divided by the current market value.

7. _____ Is calculated by dividing the current market value by the dividends declared by a company for the last four quarters.

8. _____ Is calculated by dividing total gain or loss by the cost of the investment.

9. _____ A type of loan in which the company must repay the face value and pay the stated rate of interest or coupon each year.

10. _____ May be detached from a bond at the end of each interest-paying period and redeemed for the interest.

11. _____ Paid by an investor when a bond is purchased for more than the face value.

12. _____ What a bond is purchased at when the investor pays less than the face value.

Name _____

Class/Section _____

Score (Correct Answers ÷ No. of Assigned Problems) _____

Chapter 33 Review Exercises

Exercise 1

Calculate estimated annual earnings for each of the following stocks.

52-Week								
High	Low	Stock (Symbol)	Dividend	Yield %	PE	Volume 100s	Close	Net Change
25.60	13.05	LongsDrg LDG	.56	2.6	35	2,253	21.39	−0.43
60.42	34.83	Lowes Cos LOW	.12	.2	25	73,558	56.67	−1.71
33.97	18.55	MONY Gp MNY	.45	1.4	40	17,623	31.35	0.14
51.83	36.24	PepsiCo PEP	.64	1.2	24	60,018	52.09	0.34

Stock	Estimated Annual Earnings ($)
LDG	1. _____
LOW	2. _____
MNY	3. _____
PEP	4. _____

Exercise 2

5. James Mauldin bought 200 shares of PEP last year for $40 each. A commission of 1% was paid. After 1 year, James sold the stock for $51 and paid a 1% commission. During the year, James received $2.10 per share in dividends. Calculate:
   a. Cost _____
   b. Proceeds _____
   c. Gain (loss) _____
   d. Return on investment. Round the answer to hundredths. _____
6. What is the purchase price of a 5% bond listed at 99.54%? _____
7. Calculate the cost to an investor of ten 4% bonds purchased at 103%. A $2 commission was charged for each bond. _____
8. Calculate total semiannual interest for the bonds described in Problem 7. _____
9. Calculate proceeds _____ and net gain or loss _____ for the bonds described in Problems 7 and 8 if the bonds were sold after 1 year at 104.5% and a 3% commission for each bond was paid.
10. Calculate the current yield (annual) for the bonds described in Problems 7 and 8. Round to hundredths. _____

- Touch Key is a Windows program. It is compatible with Windows 95/98/2000/ME/XP/NT. It features attractive, colorful screens. Students and instructors will find the program easy to use.
- Touch Key is designed to teach 10-key by touch using the computer numberpad. Computer-assisted instruction allows for unlimited repetitions of exercises and for instant feedback.
- The software provides lessons, drills, and tests. Speed and accuracy are calculated and provided for each.
- Timing bars appear on screens to give students an idea of their progress during timed lessons, drills, and tests.
- Check marks in the pulldown menus indicate which activities have been completed.
- Logs containing scores for lessons, drills, and tests may be printed at any time. In addition, individual logs containing scores for Drills 1 through 6 may be printed. It is recommended that scores be printed on a regular basis in case of disk failure.
- Several partially completed spreadsheet files are included to allow the student to obtain experience in entering numeric data in spreadsheets.

SYSTEM REQUIREMENTS

- Intel 486 processor or equivalent
- 16 MB RAM (32 MB recommended)
- VGA (640 × 480) or SVGA (800 × 600) monitor, 256 color or higher
- CD-ROM drive (installation only)
- 3 MB available (Hard Disk Space)
- Windows 95, 98, 2000, ME, XP, or NT
- Windows Excel is required for completion of spreadsheet exercises
- 3.5″ Floppy drive
- 3.5″ Blank, formatted diskette

INSTALLATION INSTRUCTIONS

Note: It is recommended that all other Windows applications be closed before installing Touch Key.

1. Press Start on the Windows Taskbar.
2. Choose Run.
3. Type D:\Setup.exe (where D represents your CD-ROM drive).
4. Touch Key installation will begin. Follow instructions on screen.
5. Restart your computer if prompted to do so.
6. Touch Key setup is now complete.

GETTING STARTED

Before starting Touch Key, make sure your computer display is set properly. Select **Start, Settings, Control Panel, Display, Settings.** Change color palette to 256 color or higher. Change desktop to (640 × 480) or (800 × 600) pixels. Click OK and Yes to accept changes.

Also check that the correct default printer is selected. Select **Start, Settings, Printers.** Right click the appropriate printer icon, select **Set as Default,** if necessary.

ORGANIZATION OF TOUCH KEY LESSONS, DRILLS, AND TESTS

Table 1 outlines the content of each lesson and drill and the order in which the drills, lessons, and tests should be attempted. If this outline is followed, you will practice each key before you encounter that key in a drill or test. Thus, you are assured of "no surprises."

TABLE 1 Content of Touch Key Lessons, Drills, and Tests in Suggested Completion Order

Lesson 1. Home row keys and Enter key, three-digit numbers
Lesson 2. Top row keys, three-digit numbers
Lesson 3. Bottom row keys, three-digit numbers
Lesson 4. 4 through 9 keys, three-digit numbers
Lesson 5. 1 through 6 keys, three-digit numbers
Lesson 6. 1 through 9 keys, three-digit numbers
Lesson 7. 1 through 9 keys and 0 key, three-digit numbers
Drill 1. 0 through 9 keys, three-digit numbers
Lesson 8. 0 through 9 keys, four-digit numbers
Drill 2. 0 through 9 keys, four-digit numbers
Lesson 9. 0 through 9 keys, five-digit numbers
Drill 3. 0 through 9 keys, five-digit numbers
Lesson 10. 0 through 9 keys and decimal key, six-digit numbers
Drill 4. 0 through 9 keys and decimal key, six-digit numbers
Lesson 11. 0 through 9 keys, decimal key, and minus key, six-digit numbers
Drill 5. 0 through 9 keys, decimal key, and minus key, six-digit numbers
Drill 6. 0 through 9 keys, one- through five-digit numbers (mixed)
Check Test
Order Test
Payroll Test
Invoice Test

In Table 2, as you attain the following speed for each lesson, enter the date and the percent of accuracy.

Example: On the day you reach 6,000 strokes per hour for Lesson 1, enter the date and the percent of accuracy in the cell located beside Lesson 1 under 6,000.

STARTING TOUCH KEY

1. From the Windows Program manager, select the Touch Key icon. The Touch Key start-up screen will appear. The first time you use Touch Key follow the on-screen instructions to prepare a Touch Key student data disk.
2. Insert the Touch Key student data disk in drive A. The program will not proceed unless the Touch Key student data disk is in drive A.
3. Select Start.
4. On the Name, Course, and Password window type the requested information in the boxes provided.
   a. Type your name in the box, check it for accuracy, use the Backspace key to make necessary corrections, then press Enter.
      Note: You will want to be sure your name is correct because it will display at the top of the screen the entire time the program is in use. Information on this Window may not be changed after the Enter key has been pressed in the Password box.
   b. Type your course name and number as directed by your instructor. Check that you have typed it correctly before pressing Enter. This information will be displayed on all of your print jobs.

TABLE 2   Speed Progress Chart for Touch Key

	6,000	6,500	7,000	7,500	8,000	8,500	9,000	9,500	10,000	10,500	11,000	11,500	12,000
Lesson 1													
Lesson 2													
Lesson 3													
Lesson 4													
Lesson 5													
Lesson 6													
Lesson 7													
Drill 1													
Lesson 8													
Drill 2													
Lesson 9													
Drill 3													
Lesson 10													
Drill 4													
Lesson 11													
Drill 5													
Drill 6													
Checks													
Order													
Payroll													
Invoice													

    c.   Type a password. The password may be nine letters or numbers in length. Do not use special characters or symbols. (If you use your Social Security number as your password, do not type hyphens.)
- *Note: Remember your password. You will need it each time you start the program.*
- *Note: Keep your password **secret**.*

5. The Startup window will reappear. Select Start. Next, the Login window will appear, which contains the name and course information as you entered it on the Student Name, Course, and Password window.
6. You will need to type your password again, EXACTLY as you entered it on the Name, Course, and Password window.
7. In the future, each time you start the Touch Key program you will need to supply only your password.

Exiting the Program

You should always exit computer programs properly. Select Main Menu (if necessary), Exit. You should shut down the Windows software before turning the computer off. Check with your instructor for the specific lab procedure you should use.

MAIN MENU

The main menu contains the selections Lessons, Drills, Tests, Print, and Exit. Select the appropriate category to access a pulldown menu of options. A submenu lists the components of each lesson. A check mark appears beside an activity on the menu when the activity has been completed.

LESSONS

Each of the 11 lessons has five components labeled A through E. Each component of the lesson consists of fifty 3- to 6-digit numbers (problems) to be keyed. In each lesson, the number to be keyed appears in a white box. As you key, the numbers keyed will appear in a yellow box. Press the Enter key after each number. A progress bar is displayed so that you will have an indication of the number of problems remaining in the activity. Another aid will alert you when the last problem to be keyed has been reached. The numbers to be keyed will turn red.

Randomized numbers (problems) to be keyed ensure that no two lesson components are alike. Therefore, with your instructor's approval, activities may be repeated as many times as desired in an attempt to improve your keystrokes.

You may correct errors in a number with the Backspace key BEFORE the Enter key is pressed. However, the time clock will be running, so each correction will cost you time. It is recommended that you NOT correct while keying Touch Key lessons because correcting is detrimental to creating an even keystroking technique and to building speed.

After the last problem has been entered, Lesson Results are displayed. At this point, you may either Print or return to the Main Menu.

If Print is selected, the *problems and your actual keystrokes* will be printed on a report called Lesson Results. An asterisk beside the column of your keystrokes indicates errors. This is an important diagnostic tool. By comparing the two columns containing the problems and your keystrokes, you can identify troublesome keys.

Strokes per Hour, Total Errors, and Percent Accuracy are also printed on the Lesson Results report.

Note: It is important that you wait until the print job has finished and that you check for a successful print job before returning to the Main Menu. Once Main Menu has been selected, the actual keystrokes can no longer be printed.

However, Strokes per Hour, Errors, and Percent Accuracy are stored permanently in the Lesson Log on the student data disk and may be printed at any time. (This feature conserves disk space.) To print a Lesson Log, return to the Main Menu, select the Print menu, then Lesson Log.

Note: It is strongly recommended that you print logs on a regular basis and either submit the printed logs to the instructor or retain them in a folder in case of computer or disk failure. All logs will be personalized with your name, course, current date, and current time for each lesson, drill, or test taken.

DRILLS

Six drills are included, which consist of timings in which you will use specified keys covered in the lessons (see Table 1). Each drill has five components labeled A through E. You may choose 1-, 3-, or 5-minute timings at the Touch Key Timing Control window. You should complete five 1-minute, one 3-minute, and one 5-minute timing for each drill. (See Student Lesson Log.) A picture of the numberpad keys will display on the screen. The keys to be practiced in the selected drill are marked with a red asterisk.

Features contained in the lessons are also contained in the drills. You will key the number that appears in the white box and press Enter. A progress bar is displayed to give you an indication of the time remaining. When 5 seconds remain in the timing, the numbers to be keyed turn *red to alert you that time is almost up.*

After the drill, Strokes per Hour, Total Errors, and Percent Accuracy are displayed. At this point, you may print the drill including your actual keystrokes and error indicators.

You should wait until the print job has finished and check for a successful print job before returning to the Main Menu. Once Main Menu has been selected, the actual keystrokes can no longer be printed. However, Strokes per Hour, Total Errors, and Percent Accuracy are stored in the Drill Log on the student data disk and may be printed at any time.

Drills may be used as speed tests as well as speed-building exercises. Remember, no two drills are alike.

TESTS

Several exercises are included to give you practice with production jobs. There are maximum time limits given for the applications. Strokes per Hour, Errors, and Percent Accuracy are calculated and stored in the Test Log and may be printed at any time. These tests may be used for practice or grading purposes. Check with your instructor.

Check Verification Test

Similar to work done in the proofing departments of banks, in this test data must be entered from checks. You will be using simulated checks containing the data for this test.

Check Verification Instructions Read the following set of instructions before beginning the test. *The test may be canceled before the timing begins, but not after.*

- In proofing checks, the operator must always read and key the spelled-out amount, not the amount written in figures. You will follow this procedure also.
- Decimals must be keyed in the amount.
- Be careful not to lose your place. Information must be keyed in correct order.
- It is possible to correct information in a box by using the Backspace key. To move to a previous box, press Shift + Tab. To move to the next box, press Tab. It is not possible to move to a previous screen, however.
- The maximum time limit for this test is 8 minutes. The timing will stop when all data have been entered or when the time limit has been reached, whichever comes first.

Strokes per Hour, Errors, and Percent Accuracy are given. The test and your actual keystrokes may be printed at this point. Scores may be printed at any time from the Test Log under Print on the Main menu.

Begin the test with check number 7766.

Susan B. Anthony 7766
2200 Dollar Drive
Four Bits, Texas 77666   DATE *Feb. 5, 2001* 88-566/223

PAY TO THE ORDER OF *Jessica Long* $ 934.48

Nine hundred thirty-four dollars & 48/100 DOLLARS

Lotsa Money Federal Bank

MEMO *Susan B. Anthony*

⑆122345667⑆ ⑈77 51234⑈

Susan B. Anthony   **7767**
2200 Dollar Drive
Four Bits, Texas 77666   DATE *Feb. 5, 2001*   88-566/223

PAT TO THE ORDER OF *Natalie Waits* $ **152.48**

One hundred fifty-two dollars & 48/100   DOLLARS

Lotsa Money Federal Bank

MEMO   *Susan B. Anthony*

⑆123456 67⑆ ⑈77 51234⑈

Susan B. Anthony   **7768**
2200 Dollar Drive
Four Bits, Texas 77666   DATE *Feb. 5, 2001*   88-566/223

PAT TO THE ORDER OF *Mrs. Juan Velasquez* $ **364.92**

Three hundred sixty-four dollars & 92/100   DOLLARS

Lotsa Money Federal Bank

MEMO   *Susan B. Anthony*

⑆123456 67⑆ ⑈77 51234⑈

Susan B. Anthony   **7769**
2200 Dollar Drive
Four Bits, Texas 77666   DATE *Feb. 5, 2001*   88-566/223

PAT TO THE ORDER OF *Jennifer Dupree* $ **19.15**

Nineteen dollars & 15/100   DOLLARS

Lotsa Money Federal Bank

MEMO   *Susan B. Anthony*

⑆123456 67⑆ ⑈77 51234⑈

Susan B. Anthony   **7770**
2200 Dollar Drive
Four Bits, Texas 77666   DATE *Feb. 5, 2001* 88-566/223

PAT TO THE
ORDER OF *Robert Ainsley* $ *686.82*

Six hundred eighty-six dollars & 82/100   **DOLLARS**

Lotsa Money Federal Bank

MEMO _____   *Susan B. Anthony*

⑆1234566 7⑈ ⑇77 51234⑈

Susan B. Anthony   **7771**
2200 Dollar Drive
Four Bits, Texas 77666   DATE *Feb. 5, 2001* 88-566/223

PAT TO THE
ORDER OF *Lacey Anderson* $ *549.68*

Five hundred forty-nine dollars & 68/100   **DOLLARS**

Lotsa Money Federal Bank

MEMO _____   *Susan B. Anthony*

⑆1234566 7⑈ ⑇77 51234⑈

Susan B. Anthony   **7772**
2200 Dollar Drive
Four Bits, Texas 77666   DATE *Feb. 5, 2001* 88-566/223

PAT TO THE
ORDER OF *Julie Newman* $ *448.12*

Four hundred forty-eight dollars & 12/100   **DOLLARS**

Lotsa Money Federal Bank

MEMO _____   *Susan B. Anthony*

⑆1234566 7⑈ ⑇77 51234⑈

Susan B. Anthony
2200 Dollar Drive
Four Bits, Texas 77666

7773

DATE *Feb. 5, 2001* ⁸⁸⁻⁵⁶⁶/²²³

PAT TO THE
ORDER OF *Richard Nicks* $ 82.72

Eighty-two dollars & 72/100   DOLLARS

Lotsa Money Federal Bank

MEMO   *Susan B. Anthony*

⑈122345667⑈ ⑈77 51234⑈

Susan B. Anthony
2200 Dollar Drive
Four Bits, Texas 77666

7774

DATE *Feb. 5, 2001* ⁸⁸⁻⁵⁶⁶/²²³

PAT TO THE
ORDER OF *Donna Albright* $ 102.24

One hundred two dollars & 24/100   DOLLARS

Lotsa Money Federal Bank

MEMO   *Susan B. Anthony*

⑈122345667⑈ ⑈77 51234⑈

Susan B. Anthony
2200 Dollar Drive
Four Bits, Texas 77666

7775

DATE *Feb. 5, 2001* ⁸⁸⁻⁵⁶⁶/²²³

PAT TO THE
ORDER OF *Allen Wade* $ 539.15

Five hundred thirty-nine dollars & 15/100   DOLLARS

Lotsa Money Federal Bank

MEMO   *Susan B. Anthony*

⑈122345667⑈ ⑈77 51234⑈

Susan B. Anthony
2200 Dollar Drive
Four Bits, Texas 77666

7776

88-566/223

DATE *Feb. 5, 2001*

PAT TO THE
ORDER OF *Walter Smith* $ 982.10

Nine hundred eighty-two dollars & 10/100 DOLLARS

Lotsa Money Federal Bank

MEMO *Susan B. Anthony*

⑆1234566 7⑆ ⑈77 51234⑉

Susan B. Anthony
2200 Dollar Drive
Four Bits, Texas 77666

7777

88-566/223

DATE *Feb. 5, 2001*

PAT TO THE
ORDER OF *Wendel Holmes* $ 871.08

Eight hundred seventy-one dollars & 08/100 DOLLARS

Lotsa Money Federal Bank

MEMO *Susan B. Anthony*

⑆1234566 7⑆ ⑈77 51234⑉

Susan B. Anthony
2200 Dollar Drive
Four Bits, Texas 77666

7778

88-566/223

DATE *Feb. 5, 2001*

PAT TO THE
ORDER OF *Oliver Tobar* $ 631.13

Six hundred thirty-one dollars & 13/100 DOLLARS

Lotsa Money Federal Bank

MEMO *Susan B. Anthony*

⑆1234566 7⑆ ⑈77 51234⑉

Susan B. Anthony　　　　　　　　　　　　7779
2200 Dollar Drive
Four Bits, Texas 77666　　　DATE *Feb. 5, 2001* 88-566/223

PAT TO THE
ORDER OF *Andrew Johnson*　　　　　$ 555.72

Five hundred fifty-five dollars & 72/100　　DOLLARS

Lotsa Money Federal Bank

MEMO　　　　　　　　　　*Susan B. Anthony*

⑈123456673⑈ ⑈77 51234⑈

Susan B. Anthony　　　　　　　　　　　　7780
2200 Dollar Drive
Four Bits, Texas 77666　　　DATE *Feb. 5, 2001* 88-566/223

PAT TO THE
ORDER OF *Annie Taylor*　　　　　$ 398.44

Three hundred ninety-eight dollars & 44/100 DOLLARS

Lotsa Money Federal Bank

MEMO　　　　　　　　　　*Susan B. Anthony*

⑈123456673⑈ ⑈77 51234⑈

Susan B. Anthony　　　　　　　　　　　　7781
2200 Dollar Drive
Four Bits, Texas 77666　　　DATE *Feb. 5, 2001* 88-566/223

PAT TO THE
ORDER OF *Mrs. Elmer Jamison*　　$ 59.85

Fifty-nine dollars & 85/100　　　DOLLARS

Lotsa Money Federal Bank

MEMO　　　　　　　　　　*Susan B. Anthony*

⑈123456673⑈ ⑈77 51234⑈

Susan B. Anthony 7782
2200 Dollar Drive
Four Bits, Texas 77666 DATE *Feb. 5, 2001* 88-566/223

PAT TO THE
ORDER OF *Drew Leighton* $ 572.35

Five hundred seventy-two dollars & 35/100 DOLLARS

Lotsa Money Federal Bank

MEMO *Susan B. Anthony*

⑆122345667⑈ ⑈77 51234⑈

Susan B. Anthony 7783
2200 Dollar Drive
Four Bits, Texas 77666 DATE *Feb. 5, 2001* 88-566/223

PAT TO THE
ORDER OF *Lance Ferrell* $ 757.48

Seven hundred fifty-seven dollars & 48/100 DOLLARS

Lotsa Money Federal Bank

MEMO *Susan B. Anthony*

⑆122345667⑈ ⑈77 51234⑈

Susan B. Anthony 7784
2200 Dollar Drive
Four Bits, Texas 77666 DATE *Feb. 5, 2001* 88-566/223

PAT TO THE
ORDER OF *Linda Tennyson* $ 636.92

Six hundred thirty-six dollars & 92/100 DOLLARS

Lotsa Money Federal Bank

MEMO *Susan B. Anthony*

⑆122345667⑈ ⑈77 51234⑈

Susan B. Anthony
2200 Dollar Drive
Four Bits, Texas 77666

7785

88-566/223

DATE *Feb. 5, 2001*

PAT TO THE
ORDER OF *Jane Dawson* $ 982.42

Nine hundred eighty-two dollars & 42/100   DOLLARS

Lotsa Money Federal Bank

MEMO _____   *Susan B. Anthony*

⑆1234566 7⑈ ⑈77 51234⑈

Susan B. Anthony
2200 Dollar Drive
Four Bits, Texas 77666

7786

88-566/223

DATE *Feb. 5, 2001*

PAT TO THE
ORDER OF *Darrell Welden* $ 564.97

Five hundred sixty-four dollars & 97/100   DOLLARS

Lotsa Money Federal Bank

MEMO _____   *Susan B. Anthony*

⑆1234566 7⑈ ⑈77 51234⑈

Susan B. Anthony
2200 Dollar Drive
Four Bits, Texas 77666

7787

88-566/223

DATE *Feb. 5, 2001*

PAT TO THE
ORDER OF *Danny Johnson* $ 437.14

Four hundred thirty-seven dollars & 14/100   DOLLARS

Lotsa Money Federal Bank

MEMO _____   *Susan B. Anthony*

⑆1234566 7⑈ ⑈77 51234⑈

Susan B. Anthony
2200 Dollar Drive
Four Bits, Texas 77666

7788

88-566/223

DATE *Feb. 5, 2001*

PAT TO THE
ORDER OF *Dana Smith* $ *516.25*

Five hundred sixteen dollars & 25/100 DOLLARS

Lotsa Money Federal Bank

MEMO *Susan B. Anthony*

⑆1 2 2 3 4 5 6 6 7⑆ ⑈77 5 1 2 3 4⑈

Susan B. Anthony
2200 Dollar Drive
Four Bits, Texas 77666

7789

88-566/223

DATE *Feb. 5, 2001*

PAT TO THE
ORDER OF *John Johnson* $ *669.71*

Six hundred sixty-nine dollars & 71/100 DOLLARS

Lotsa Money Federal Bank

MEMO *Susan B. Anthony*

⑆1 2 2 3 4 5 6 6 7⑆ ⑈77 5 1 2 3 4⑈

Susan B. Anthony
2200 Dollar Drive
Four Bits, Texas 77666

7790

88-566/223

DATE *Feb. 5, 2001*

PAT TO THE
ORDER OF *William Jones* $ *444.41*

Four hundred forty-four dollars & 41/100 DOLLARS

Lotsa Money Federal Bank

MEMO *Susan B. Anthony*

⑆1 2 2 3 4 5 6 6 7⑆ ⑈77 5 1 2 3 4⑈

Susan B. Anthony   7791
2200 Dollar Drive
Four Bits, Texas 77666   DATE *Feb. 5, 2001* ⁸⁸⁻⁵⁶⁶/²²³

PAT TO THE
ORDER OF   *Janie Ireland* $ | 152.16 |

One hundred fifty-two dollars & 16/100   DOLLARS

Lotsa Money Federal Bank

MEMO _____   *Susan B. Anthony*

⑆1 2 2 3 4 5 6 6 7⑆ ⑈77 5 1 2 3 4⑈

Susan B. Anthony   7792
2200 Dollar Drive
Four Bits, Texas 77666   DATE *Feb. 5, 2001* ⁸⁸⁻⁵⁶⁶/²²³

PAT TO THE
ORDER OF   *Marilyn Rains* $ | 120.28 |

One hundred twenty dollars & 28/100   DOLLARS

Lotsa Money Federal Bank

MEMO _____   *Susan B. Anthony*

⑆1 2 2 3 4 5 6 6 7⑆ ⑈77 5 1 2 3 4⑈

Susan B. Anthony   7793
2200 Dollar Drive
Four Bits, Texas 77666   DATE *Feb. 5, 2001* ⁸⁸⁻⁵⁶⁶/²²³

PAT TO THE
ORDER OF   *Clara Schiller* $ | 191.11 |

One hundred ninety-one dollars & 11/100   DOLLARS

Lotsa Money Federal Bank

MEMO _____   *Susan B. Anthony*

⑆1 2 2 3 4 5 6 6 7⑆ ⑈77 5 1 2 3 4⑈

Susan B. Anthony   7794
2200 Dollar Drive
Four Bits, Texas 77666   DATE *Feb. 5, 2001* 88-566/223

PAY TO THE
ORDER OF *Ed Blakeney* $ 587.06

Five hundred eighty-seven dollars & 06/100   DOLLARS

Lotsa Money Federal Bank

MEMO _____   *Susan B. Anthony*

⑆122345667⑉ ⑈77 51234⑈

Susan B. Anthony   7795
2200 Dollar Drive
Four Bits, Texas 77666   DATE *Feb. 5, 2001* 88-566/223

PAY TO THE
ORDER OF *Patsy Dillon* $ 353.69

Three hundred fifty-three dollars & 69/100   DOLLARS

Lotsa Money Federal Bank

MEMO _____   *Susan B. Anthony*

⑆122345667⑉ ⑈77 51234⑈

Susan B. Anthony   7796
2200 Dollar Drive
Four Bits, Texas 77666   DATE *Feb. 5, 2001* 88-566/223

PAY TO THE
ORDER OF *Terry Miller* $ 668.11

Six hundred sixty-eight dollars & 11/100   DOLLARS

Lotsa Money Federal Bank

MEMO _____   *Susan B. Anthony*

⑆122345667⑉ ⑈77 51234⑈

Susan B. Anthony   **7797**
2200 Dollar Drive
Four Bits, Texas 77666   DATE *Feb. 5, 2001* 88-566/223

PAY TO THE
ORDER OF *Brenda J. Lee* $ 752.27

Seven hundred fifty-two dollars & 27/100   DOLLARS

Lotsa Money Federal Bank

MEMO _____   *Susan B. Anthony*

⑆122345667⑈ ⑈77 51234⑈

Susan B. Anthony   **7798**
2200 Dollar Drive
Four Bits, Texas 77666   DATE *Feb. 5, 2001* 88-566/223

PAY TO THE
ORDER OF *Robert Brewster* $ 121.57

One hundred twenty-one dollars & 57/100   DOLLARS

Lotsa Money Federal Bank

MEMO _____   *Susan B. Anthony*

⑆122345667⑈ ⑈77 51234⑈

Susan B. Anthony   **7799**
2200 Dollar Drive
Four Bits, Texas 77666   DATE *Feb. 5, 2001* 88-566/223

PAY TO THE
ORDER OF *Terry M. Albright* $ 119.19

One hundred nineteen dollars & 19/100 DOLLARS

Lotsa Money Federal Bank

MEMO _____   *Susan B. Anthony*

⑆122345667⑈ ⑈77 51234⑈

Susan B. Anthony
2200 Dollar Drive
Four Bits, Texas 77666
7800

DATE *Feb. 5, 2001* 88-566/223

PAT TO THE
ORDER OF *David Lassiter*
$ 828.81

Eight hundred twenty-eight dollars & 81/100 DOLLARS

Lotsa Money Federal Bank

MEMO
Susan B. Anthony

⑆1223456 67⑈ ⑉77 51234⑈

Susan B. Anthony
2200 Dollar Drive
Four Bits, Texas 77666
7801

DATE *Feb. 5, 2001* 88-566/223

PAT TO THE
ORDER OF *Ben Brown*
$ 911.19

Nine hundred eleven dollars & 19/100 DOLLARS

Lotsa Money Federal Bank

MEMO
Susan B. Anthony

⑆1223456 67⑈ ⑉77 51234⑈

Susan B. Anthony
2200 Dollar Drive
Four Bits, Texas 77666
7802

DATE *Feb. 5, 2001* 88-566/223

PAT TO THE
ORDER OF *Betty Patton*
$ 343.19

Three hundred forty-three dollars & 19/100 DOLLARS

Lotsa Money Federal Bank

MEMO
Susan B. Anthony

⑆1223456 67⑈ ⑉77 51234⑈

Susan B. Anthony   7803
2200 Dollar Drive
Four Bits, Texas 77666   DATE _Feb. 5, 2001_ 88-566/223

PAT TO THE
ORDER OF _Veronica Quinonez_ $ 952.93

Nine hundred fifty-two dollars & 93/100   DOLLARS

Lotsa Money Federal Bank

MEMO _____   _Susan B. Anthony_

⑆1234566⑆ ⑈77 51234⑈

Susan B. Anthony   7804
2200 Dollar Drive
Four Bits, Texas 77666   DATE _Feb. 5, 2001_ 88-566/223

PAT TO THE
ORDER OF _Larry Roberts_ $ 59.46

Fifty-nine dollars & 46/100   DOLLARS

Lotsa Money Federal Bank

MEMO _____   _Susan B. Anthony_

⑆1234566⑆ ⑈77 51234⑈

Susan B. Anthony   7805
2200 Dollar Drive
Four Bits, Texas 77666   DATE _Feb. 5, 2001_ 88-566/223

PAT TO THE
ORDER OF _Jim Ramirez_ $ 559.66

Five hundred fifty-nine dollars & 66/100   DOLLARS

Lotsa Money Federal Bank

MEMO _____   _Susan B. Anthony_

⑆1234566⑆ ⑈77 51234⑈

Susan B. Anthony   7806
2200 Dollar Drive
Four Bits, Texas 77666   DATE *Feb. 5, 2001* 88-566/223

PAT TO THE
ORDER OF *Donald Beck* $ 172.36

One hundred seventy-two dollars & 36/100   DOLLARS

Lotsa Money Federal Bank

MEMO   *Susan B. Anthony*

⑆1 2 2 3 4 5 6 6 7⑆ ⑈77 5 1 2 3 4⑈

Susan B. Anthony   7807
2200 Dollar Drive
Four Bits, Texas 77666   DATE *Feb. 5, 2001* 88-566/223

PAT TO THE
ORDER OF *Mark Blocker* $ 457.96

Four hundred fifty-seven dollars & 96/100 DOLLARS

Lotsa Money Federal Bank

MEMO   *Susan B. Anthony*

⑆1 2 2 3 4 5 6 6 7⑆ ⑈77 5 1 2 3 4⑈

Susan B. Anthony   7808
2200 Dollar Drive
Four Bits, Texas 77666   DATE *Feb. 5, 2001* 88-566/223

PAT TO THE
ORDER OF *Peter Haus* $ 14.49

Fourteen dollars & 49/100   DOLLARS

Lotsa Money Federal Bank

MEMO   *Susan B. Anthony*

⑆1 2 2 3 4 5 6 6 7⑆ ⑈77 5 1 2 3 4⑈

Susan B. Anthony   7809
2200 Dollar Drive
Four Bits, Texas 77666   DATE *Feb. 5, 2001* ^88-566/223

PAT TO THE
ORDER OF *Julie Tineman* $ 882.29

Eight hundred eighty-two dollars & 29/100   DOLLARS

Lotsa Money Federal Bank

MEMO _____   *Susan B. Anthony*

⑈1⑆2 2 3 4 5 6 6 7⑆ ⑈7 7 5 1 2 3 4⑈

Susan B. Anthony   7810
2200 Dollar Drive
Four Bits, Texas 77666   DATE *Feb. 5, 2001* ^88-566/223

PAT TO THE
ORDER OF *Kathy Leiberman* $ 164.19

One hundred sixty-four dollars & 19/100   DOLLARS

Lotsa Money Federal Bank

MEMO _____   *Susan B. Anthony*

⑈1⑆2 2 3 4 5 6 6 7⑆ ⑈7 7 5 1 2 3 4⑈

Susan B. Anthony   7811
2200 Dollar Drive
Four Bits, Texas 77666   DATE *Feb. 5, 2001* ^88-566/223

PAT TO THE
ORDER OF *Veronica Landen* $ 535.16

Five hundred thirty-five dollars & 16/100   DOLLARS

Lotsa Money Federal Bank

MEMO _____   *Susan B. Anthony*

⑈1⑆2 2 3 4 5 6 6 7⑆ ⑈7 7 5 1 2 3 4⑈

Susan B. Anthony 7812
2200 Dollar Drive
Four Bits, Texas 77666   DATE *Feb. 5, 2001*   88-566/223

PAT TO THE
ORDER OF *Amanda Jones* $ 546.16

Five hundred forty-six dollars & 16/100   DOLLARS

Lotsa Money Federal Bank

MEMO   *Susan B. Anthony*

⑆122345667⑆ ⑈77 51234⑈

Susan B. Anthony 7813
2200 Dollar Drive
Four Bits, Texas 77666   DATE *Feb. 5, 2001*   88-566/223

PAT TO THE
ORDER OF *Leon Letty* $ 576.49

Five hundred seventy-six dollars & 49/100   DOLLARS

Lotsa Money Federal Bank

MEMO   *Susan B. Anthony*

⑆122345667⑆ ⑈77 51234⑈

Susan B. Anthony 7814
2200 Dollar Drive
Four Bits, Texas 77666   DATE *Feb. 5, 2001*   88-566/223

PAT TO THE
ORDER OF *Paula Peyton* $ 543.49

Five hundred forty-three dollars & 49/100   DOLLARS

Lotsa Money Federal Bank

MEMO   *Susan B. Anthony*

⑆122345667⑆ ⑈77 51234⑈

Susan B. Anthony
2200 Dollar Drive
Four Bits, Texas 77666

7815

DATE *Feb. 5, 2001* 88-566/223

PAT TO THE
ORDER OF *Nancy Dawson* $ 912.43

Nine hundred twelve dollars & 43/100 DOLLARS

Lotsa Money Federal Bank

MEMO *Susan B. Anthony*

⑈12234566 7⑆ ⑈77 51234⑈

Susan B. Anthony
2200 Dollar Drive
Four Bits, Texas 77666

7816

DATE *Feb. 5, 2001* 88-566/223

PAT TO THE
ORDER OF *Pauline Lott* $ 994.93

Nine hundred ninety-four dollars & 93/100 DOLLARS

Lotsa Money Federal Bank

MEMO *Susan B. Anthony*

⑈12234566 7⑆ ⑈77 51234⑈

Susan B. Anthony
2200 Dollar Drive
Four Bits, Texas 77666

7817

DATE *Feb. 5, 2001* 88-566/223

PAT TO THE
ORDER OF *Rose Deighton* $ 117.16

One hundred seventeen dollars & 16/100 DOLLARS

Lotsa Money Federal Bank

MEMO *Susan B. Anthony*

⑈12234566 7⑆ ⑈77 51234⑈

Susan B. Anthony 7818
2200 Dollar Drive
Four Bits, Texas 77666   DATE *Feb. 5, 2001* 88-566/223

PAT TO THE
ORDER OF *Candace Smith* $ 525.63

Five hundred twenty-five dollars & 63/100 DOLLARS

Lotsa Money Federal Bank

MEMO _____   *Susan B. Anthony*

⑆1 2 2 3 4 5 6 6 7⑆ ⑈7 7 5 1 2 3 4⑈

Susan B. Anthony 7819
2200 Dollar Drive
Four Bits, Texas 77666   DATE *Feb. 5, 2001* 88-566/223

PAT TO THE
ORDER OF *Laura Jameson* $ 449.49

Four hundred forty-nine dollars & 49/100 DOLLARS

Lotsa Money Federal Bank

MEMO _____   *Susan B. Anthony*

⑆1 2 2 3 4 5 6 6 7⑆ ⑈7 7 5 1 2 3 4⑈

Susan B. Anthony 7820
2200 Dollar Drive
Four Bits, Texas 77666   DATE *Feb. 5, 2001* 88-566/223

PAT TO THE
ORDER OF *Kenneth Drew* $ 546.49

Five hundred forty-six dollars & 49/100 DOLLARS

Lotsa Money Federal Bank

MEMO _____   *Susan B. Anthony*

⑆1 2 2 3 4 5 6 6 7⑆ ⑈7 7 5 1 2 3 4⑈

Susan B. Anthony   7821
2200 Dollar Drive
Four Bits, Texas 77666   DATE *Feb. 5, 2001* 88-566/223

PAT TO THE
ORDER OF *Leslie Harper* $ *182.19*

One hundred eighty-two dollars & 19/100   DOLLARS

Lotsa Money Federal Bank

MEMO _____   *Susan B. Anthony*

⑆1 2 2 3 4 5 6 6 7⑆ ⑈77 5 1 2 3 4⑈

Susan B. Anthony   7822
2200 Dollar Drive
Four Bits, Texas 77666   DATE *Feb. 5, 2001* 88-566/223

PAT TO THE
ORDER OF *Janice Elliott* $ *511.59*

Five hundred eleven dollars & 59/100   DOLLARS

Lotsa Money Federal Bank

MEMO _____   *Susan B. Anthony*

⑆1 2 2 3 4 5 6 6 7⑆ ⑈77 5 1 2 3 4⑈

Susan B. Anthony   7823
2200 Dollar Drive
Four Bits, Texas 77666   DATE *Feb. 5, 2001* 88-566/223

PAT TO THE
ORDER OF *Andrew Mills* $ *726.16*

Seven hundred twenty-six dollars & 16/100   DOLLARS

Lotsa Money Federal Bank

MEMO _____   *Susan B. Anthony*

⑆1 2 2 3 4 5 6 6 7⑆ ⑈77 5 1 2 3 4⑈

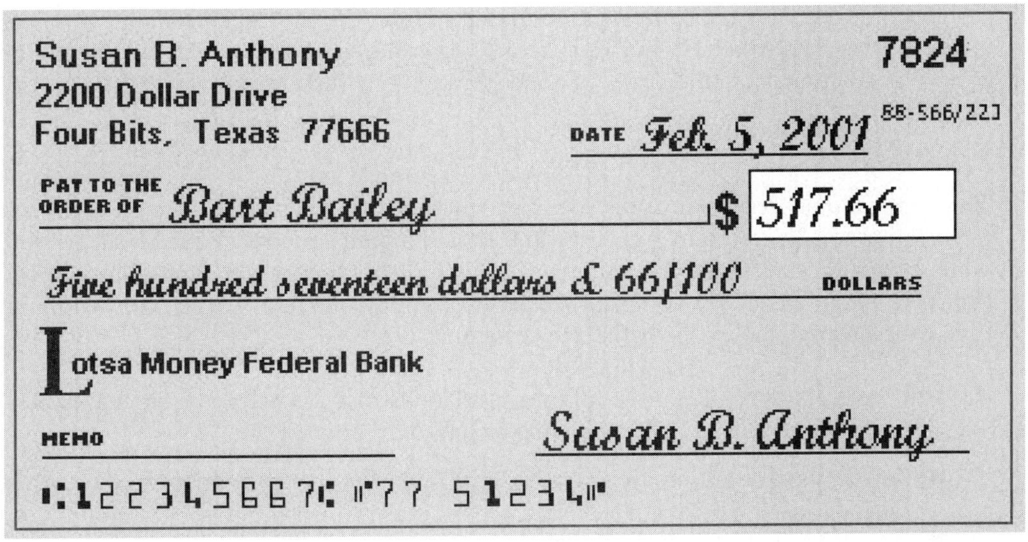
Susan B. Anthony
7824
2200 Dollar Drive
Four Bits, Texas 77666
DATE Feb. 5, 2001
88-566/223
PAY TO THE ORDER OF Bart Bailey
$ 517.66
Five hundred seventeen dollars & 66/100
DOLLARS
Lotsa Money Federal Bank
MEMO
Susan B. Anthony
⑆1223456670⑆ ⑈77 51234⑈

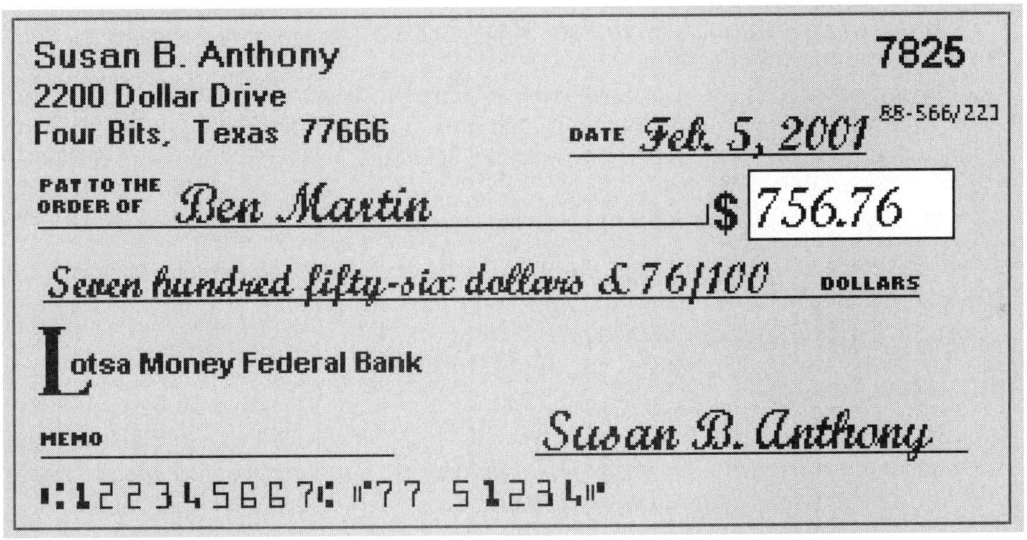
Susan B. Anthony
7825
2200 Dollar Drive
Four Bits, Texas 77666
DATE Feb. 5, 2001
88-566/223
PAY TO THE ORDER OF Ben Martin
$ 756.76
Seven hundred fifty-six dollars & 76/100
DOLLARS
Lotsa Money Federal Bank
MEMO
Susan B. Anthony
⑆1223456670⑆ ⑈77 51234⑈

Order Test

In this test, you will simulate data entry for a retail ordering system. The computer will generate all data needed for this test.

Order Instructions Read the following set of instructions before beginning the test. *The test may be canceled before the timing begins, but not after.*

- Similar to Touch Key lessons and drills, data to be keyed will appear in two white boxes. You will enter data in the two corresponding yellow boxes.
- Backspace, Shift + Tab, and Tab are functional during this test. It is not possible to move to a previous screen.
- This is a 5-minute test. A scroll bar appears on the screen to give you an indication of the time remaining. Also, during the last 10 seconds of the test, the numbers to be keyed will turn red.

After the test has been completed, Strokes per Hour, Errors, and Percent Accuracy are given. At this point, the test and your actual keystrokes may be printed. Scores may be printed at any time from the Test Log under Print on the Main menu.

Payroll Test

This application is designed to give you experience in keying numerical data using payroll information for Blue Water Chandlery. You should attempt to key as quickly as possible while maintaining accuracy. A maximum time limit of 10 minutes is given for this job. The timing will stop when you have finished keying the payroll data or when the maximum time limit has been reached, whichever comes first.

Payroll Instructions   Read the following set of instructions before beginning the test. *The test may be canceled before the timing begins, but not after.*

- Key the payroll information contained in Table 3 in the appropriate box and press Enter.
- Do not key hyphens in the Social Security numbers.
- Decimals must be keyed when entering amounts for Rates, Regular Hours, and Overtime Hours.
- If there are no overtime hours, press Enter to continue.
- Take care not to lose your place. Records MUST be keyed in the order in which they appear on the form.
- It is possible to correct information on a current screen using Backspace in the current box. To move to a previous box, press Shift + Tab (hold down the Shift key and press the Tab key). To move to the next box, press Tab. However, remember that the time clock is running.
- It is not possible to move to a previous screen.

After the test has been completed, Strokes per Hour, Errors, and Percent Accuracy will appear. At this point the application may be printed. Scores may be printed at any time from the Test Log on the Print menu.

Invoice Test

In this job, you are to enter data by customer number for invoicing by Crafter's Dreamland. *You must use care in entering the required data on the computer because the screen format is slightly different from that of the paper copy.*

Invoice Instructions   Read the following set of instructions before beginning the test. *The test may be canceled before the timing begins, but not after.*

- The Invoice Number and Customer Number MUST BE keyed along with each line item.
- Some information will appear automatically. When the customer number is entered, the customer name appears. When the item number is keyed, the nomenclature appears.
- Decimals MUST be keyed.
- Take care not to lose your place.

Hint: Keep your place with your left index finger on the line item while keying with the right hand. Then, when your eyes look elsewhere on the page to see the Invoice Number and Customer Number, you will be able to shift your eyes back to the next line item. This is essential because the items are not numbered.

- Backspace, Shift + Tab, and Tab are functional in this test. It is not possible to return to a previous screen, however.
- The maximum time limit for this application is 12 minutes. The timing will end when all data have been keyed or when the time limit has been reached, whichever comes first.

TABLE 3   Blue Water Chandlery, Victoria, TX Payroll Register
For Pay Period December 18, 1999, to December 25, 1999

Employee Number	Social Security Number	Regular Rate	Regular Hours	Overtime Hours
001	977766775	12.50	40.00	
002	828144362	12.75	40.00	5.50
003	819634856	7.50	32.00	
004	660459234	7.50	40.00	
005	578215591	15.25	40.00	
006	329371954	12.50	40.00	
007	958552951	12.50	40.00	8.00
008	596594592	12.50	32.00	
009	852923343	12.50	40.00	
010	439255221	12.75	38.00	
011	449771214	12.75	40.00	6.50
012	563794514	15.00	40.00	
013	485274747	15.05	40.00	
014	292543323	7.50	40.00	4.00
015	721536363	7.50	24.00	
016	855923443	12.50	40.00	8.50
017	696548211	12.50	40.00	8.00
018	392919155	7.50	40.00	4.00
019	879476654	11.00	40.00	8.00
020	439753226	8.50	40.00	
021	229664391	25.00	40.00	
022	957196825	7.50	40.00	9.50
023	234274791	8.75	40.00	8.00
024	559642287	9.05	40.00	
025	862575123	12.25	40.00	
026	621923161	9.75	40.00	5.75
027	551852891	10.25	40.00	4.50
028	459771888	12.50	32.00	
029	468212752	12.50	36.00	
030	793928585	8.00	40.00	
031	820583663	9.35	36.00	
032	309594774	12.50	40.00	
033	399600201	11.50	38.00	
034	484180491	7.50	40.00	4.00
035	885272333	7.50	40.00	
036	785533938	8.50	40.00	
037	435388822	7.75	40.00	4.50
038	413535577	9.25	32.00	
039	536114714	10.50	40.00	
040	262723669	7.55	40.00	8.50

When the test has been completed, Strokes per Hour, Errors, and Percent Accuracy will appear. At this point the test and actual student keystrokes may be printed. The scores may be printed at any time from the Test Log under Print on the Main menu.

Counting Errors

Each of the following is counted as one error.

- Incorrect keystroke
- Missing keystroke
- Incorrect place value

Crafter's Dreamland

1500 Bayou Way, Victoria, TX 77901

1-800-CRAFTER   Fax: 1-361-771-6464

Sold to: Jessica Long
              213 Waco St.
              Nashville, TN 53333

INVOICE **92001**

CUSTOMER No.   **860**

November 1, 2000

PAGE NO.	ITEM NO.	QUANTITY	DESCRIPTION	PRICE
209	100639	5	Peter Rabbit Quilt Panel Kit	19.99
420	900767	3	Willows Fabric Yardage	7.50
420	100508	10	Willows Fat Quarter Packet	10.99
209	100640	5	Peter Rabbit Fat Quarter Packet	11.99
20	100463	1	Flowers, Flowers Pattern	8.00
21	100513	5	Birdhouse Pattern	8.00

Crafter's Dreamland

1500 Bayou Way, Victoria, TX 77901

1-800-CRAFTER   Fax: 1-361-771-6464

Sold to: Natalie Waits
              634 N. Lakeview
              Coronado, CA 88888

INVOICE **92002**

CUSTOMER No.   **310**

November 1, 2000

PAGE NO..	ITEM NO.	QUANTITY	DESCRIPTION	PRICE
22	100747	1	Tulip Pattern	4.95
420	900767	6	Willows Fabric Yardage	7.50
420	100508	1	Willows Fat Quarter Packet	10.99
33	100559	3	Quilter's Vest	31.99
430	621251	2	1 3/4" Quilt Pins	2.95
430	621256	3	1 3/8" Red Glass-Head Silk Pins	4.98

Crafter's Dreamland

1500 Bayou Way, Victoria, TX 77901
1-800-CRAFTER   Fax: 1-361-771-6464

Sold to: Mrs. Juan Velasquez
            2000 Alamo Dr.
            San Antonio, TX 75000

INVOICE **92003**

CUSTOMER No.   **949**

November 1, 2000

PAGE NO.	ITEM NO.	QUANTITY	DESCRIPTION	PRICE
33	100559	1	Quilter's Vest	31.99
13	631334	2	Transparent Thread	4.25
13	631577	1	Metalic Thread Assortment	34.90
209	100640	1	Peter Rabbit Fat Quarter Packet	11.99
20	100463	3	Flowers, Flowers Pattern	8.00
26	122651	1	Polyester Thread	9.57

Crafter's Dreamland

1500 Bayou Way, Victoria, TX 77901
1-800-CRAFTER   Fax: 1-361-771-6464

Sold to: Jennifer Dupree
            1000 Circle Blvd.
            Atlanta, GA 80000

INVOICE **92004**

CUSTOMER No.   **329**

November 1, 2000

PAGE NO.	ITEM NO.	QUANTITY	DESCRIPTION	PRICE
420	100508	1	Willows Fat Quarter Packet	10.99
22	100747	6	Tulip Pattern	4.95
209	100640	14	Peter Rabbit Fat Quarter Packet	11.99
33	100559	3	Quilter's Vest	31.99
52	100188	2	Machine Quilting w/Decorative Threads	21.95
430	621256	3	1 3/8" Red Glass-Head Silk Pins	4.98

Crafter's Dreamland

1500 Bayou Way, Victoria, TX 77901
1-800-CRAFTER   Fax: 1-361-771-6464

INVOICE **92005**

CUSTOMER No.   **200**

November 1, 2000

Sold to: Robert Ainsley
P. O. Box 91202
Vicksburg, TN 52333

PAGE NO.	ITEM NO.	QUANTITY	DESCRIPTION	PRICE
53	223785	5	Holidays on Parade	15.95
22	100747	6	Tulip Pattern	4.95
209	100640	5	Peter Rabbit Fat Quarter Packet	11.99
54	100162	5	Creative Cotton Chenille	16.99
52	100188	2	Machine Quilting w/Decorative Threads	21.95
43	621672	36	Thread Heaven	2.80

Crafter's Dreamland

1500 Bayou Way, Victoria, TX 77901
1-800-CRAFTER   Fax: 1-361-771-6464

INVOICE **92006**

CUSTOMER No.   **551**

November 1, 2000

Sold to: Lacey Anderson Design Sop
8300 Santa Fe Dr., #222
Albuquerque, NM 55544

PAGE NO.	ITEM NO.	QUANTITY	DESCRIPTION	PRICE
424	100503	10	I0" Squares Packet	41.99
13	631577	12	Metalic Thread Assortment	34.90
209	100640	12	Peter Rabbit Fat Quarter Packet	11.99
33	100559	6	Quilter's Vest	31.99
21	100513	15	Birdhouse Pattern	8.00
209	100639	12	Peter Rabbit Quilt Panel Kit	19.99

Crafter's Dreamland

INVOICE **92007**

1500 Bayou Way, Victoria, TX 77901

CUSTOMER No.   **121**

1-800-CRAFTER   Fax: 1-361-771-6464

November 1, 2000

Sold to: Ms. Julie Newman
232 W. Grove St.
New York, NY 10000

PAGE NO.	ITEM NO.	QUANTITY	DESCRIPTION	PRICE
33	100559	1	Quilter's Vest	31.99
213	100534	1	House to House Pattern	8.25
224	900905	1	Natures Textures Fat I/4 Packet	14.90
209	100640	1	Peter Rabbit Fat Quarter Packet	11.99
20	100463	1	Flowers, Flowers Pattern	8.00
22	100747	1	Tulip Pattern	4.95

DATA ENTRY IN SPREADSHEETS

Six partially completed spreadsheet files are included on the Touch Key CD. To practice entering data in these spreadsheets, you will need to start Microsoft Excel software, open one of the spreadsheets, and, referring to the following pages, key numeric data to complete the spreadsheet.

Spreadsheet Instructions

1. Start Microsoft Excel.
2. Select File, Open, change to the CD drive on your computer (usually D:), select the folder named Spreadsheet.

If your instructor wishes you to save a completed spreadsheet, select File, Save As, change the drive to your floppy containing a data disk (usually A:), and type a new filename. Example: mileage2.xls

Select one of the following spreadsheets, turn to the corresponding page in this section, and key the data into the appropriate cells of the spreadsheet.

a. Mileage.xls   Mileage Between Toronto and Selected U.S. Cities

After keying the required data in the spreadsheet, select the Bar Chart tab at the bottom of the screen to view a bar chart reflecting the data you have just entered.

b. Budget.xls   Susan B. Anthony Basic Living Expenses, January 2006

After keying the required data, select the Pie Chart tab at the bottom of the screen to view a graphical representation of Susan's budget.

c. Sales.xls   2005 Sales by City & State

After keying the required data, select the Map USA tab to view a graphical representation of sales.

d. Expense.xls   Computers, Etc. Travel Expense Request for Reimbursement

e. USCanada.xls   United States/Canadian Mileage

f. Inventory.xls   Essentially Yours—Appliances & Furniture for the Home, Store #16—Inventory, January 31, 20xx

SUSAN B. ANTHONY
BASIC LIVING EXPENSES
JANUARY 1997

EXPENSE CATEGORY	EXPENSE AMOUNT	% OF TOTAL EXPENSES
Rent	$300.40	31.92%
Utilities	75.10	7.98%
Food	150.00	15.94%
Oil, Gas	69.15	7.35%
Car Insurance	100.00	10.63%
Cable	18.25	1.94%
Car Payment	200.00	21.25%
Phone	28.10	2.99%
TOTAL EXPENSES	$941.00	100.00%

MILEAGE BETWEEN TORONTO AND SELECTED U.S. CITIES

	TORONTO
LOS ANGELES	2,744
DALLAS	1,457
ATLANTA	959
NEW YORK	553

Mileage

Budget

COMPUTERS, ETC.
1996 SALES BY CITY AND STATE

CITY	STATE	SALES
LOS ANGELES	CALIFORNIA	12,655,456
SAN DIEGO	CALIFORNIA	5,800,500
FRESNO	CALIFORNIA	3,965,710
LAS VEGAS	NEVADA	7,645,958
PHOENIX	ARIZONA	9,850,550
SALT LAKE CITY	UTAH	3,678,832
SANTA FE	NEW MEXICO	2,145,760
DALLAS	TEXAS	7,890,450
HOUSTON	TEXAS	9,345,660
SAN ANTONIO	TEXAS	4,676,500
DENVER	COLORADO	6,098,555
TULSA	OKLAHOMA	2,245,897

Sales

EXPENSE	SUN	MON	TUE	WED	THU	FRI	SAT	TOTAL
Trans. (air)	427.00							427.00
Trans. (rental)								0.00
Trans. (.30/m.)								0.00
Lodging	96.59	96.59	96.59	96.59	96.59	96.59		579.54
Meals	15.30	39.00	28.50	37.91	41.09	22.96	4.55	189.31
Taxi/Limo	10.00						10.00	20.00
Telephone	6.79	4.50	2.20	8.90	7.57	2.39	0.57	32.92
Parking								0.00
Postage		3.00	1.28	10.00	1.60	3.00		18.88
Secretary Serv.		15.00	12.95	22.00	14.75	6.96		71.66
Entertainment		68.99	75.10	123.98	52.13	29.66		349.86
Miscellaneous			4.90	4.90	4.90	4.90		19.60

TOTAL REIMBURSEMENT ⟶ $1,708.77

Expense

UNITED STATES / CANADIAN MILEAGE

	VANCOUVER	CALGARY	REGINA	WINNIPEG	TORONTO	MONTREAL	MONCTON	HALIFAX	CHARLTTOWN	ST. JOHN'S
LOS ANGELES	1,382	1,692	1,968	2,126	2,744	3,080	3,726	3,861	3,835	4,713
SEATTLE	160	756	1,234	1,591	2,546	2,883	3,522	3,663	3,180	4,509
PHOENIX	1,654	1,543	1,650	1,943	2,069	2,638	3,172	3,345	3,285	4,154
DALLAS	2,255	1,885	1,644	1,335	1,457	1,763	2,256	2,429	23,669	3,238
MINNEAPOLIS	1,694	1,288	811	454	933	1,162	1,801	1,942	1,911	2,788
CHICAGO	2,461	1,735	1,258	900	519	856	1,501	1,636	1,611	2,488
CINCINNATI	2,772	2,046	1,568	1,211	506	824	1,396	1,482	1,506	2,383
DETROIT	2,750	2,023	1,546	1,189	231	568	1,212	1,348	1,322	2,198
ATLANTA	2,825	2,191	1,836	1,554	959	1,240	1,563	1,736	1,676	2,545
TAMPA	3,314	2,823	2,302	2,033	1,396	1,548	1,858	2,031	1,971	2,840
PHILADELPHIA	3,009	2,592	1,885	1,603	503	465	807	980	920	1,789
NEW YORK	3,449	2,699	2,222	1,865	553	383	738	799	846	1,730
BOSTON	3,440	2,714	2,236	1,846	568	341	515	576	624	1,502

USCanada

	A	B	C	D	E	F
1	ESSENTIALLY	YOURS - APPLIANCES AND FURNITURE FOR THE HOME				
2		STORE # 16 - INVENTORY				
3		JANUARY 31, 19xx				
4						
5	ITEM	PRODUCT	VENDOR	UNIT	ITEM	TOTAL
6	DESCRIPTION	NUMBER	NUMBER	COST	QUANTITY	COST
7						
8	Lamps, 12"	17504	10154	9.25	300	2,775.00
9	Lamps, 13"	17514	10154	12.50	26	325.00
10	Track Lighting, 4'	17499	10154	15.50	66	1,023.00
11	Track Lighting, 2'	17498	10154	7.25	145	1,051.25
12	Grow Lamp	17527	10154	19.90	1	19.90
13	Carriage Lamp	17521	10154	13.65	110	1,501.50
14	Door Mats	57789	25122	10.90	1275	13,897.50
15	Oval Rugs 3x5	49791	25122	16.95	121	2,050.95
16	Oval Rugs 2x3	49789	25122	12.30	560	6,888.00
17	Oval Rugs 4x6	49793	25122	20.50	31	635.50
18	Oval Rugs 8x12	49795	25122	30.00	10	300.00
19	Single Box Springs	21232	27156	126.40	30	3,792.00
20	Double Box Springs	21235	27156	134.80	44	5,931.20
21	King Box Springs	21238	27156	151.55	10	1,515.50
22	Single Mattress	31232	27156	139.20	48	6,681.60
23	Twin Mattress	31234	27156	135.50	23	3,116.50
24	Double Mattress	31235	27156	143.21	70	10,024.70
25	King Mattress	31433	27156	148.00	10	1,480.00
26	Arndeck Chairs	79981	22231	29.40	24	705.60
27	Laney Chairs	78882	22231	31.40	21	659.40
28	Single Bed Frame	20015	41713	19.00	5	95.00
29	Twin Bed Frame	20020	41713	19.00	3	57.00
30	Double Bed Frame	20025	41713	22.25	9	200.25
31	King Bed Frame	20030	41713	29.95	6	179.70
32	LXI Stereo	65721	00240	57.00	12	684.00
33	Portable CD	65723	00240	119.00	8	952.00
34	CD Player	65725	00240	214.50	3	643.50
35	Zenith TV 19" color	67556	87442	292.25	5	1,461.25
36	Zenith Console	67575	87442	625.00	3	1,875.00
37	VCR, 2 head	42177	87442	225.00	2	450.00
38	Zenith Large Screen	49002	87442	2,125.75	2	4,251.50
39	VCR, 4 hd. , stereo	42172	99250	268.50	2	537.00
40	Zenith 5", b/w	67545	99250	40.50	2	81.00
41	Zenith 9", b/w	61547	99250	49.00	24	1,176.00
42	Zenith 16" color	67552	99250	105.00	10	1,050.00
43	Zenith 19" color	67555	99250	286.00	9	2,574.00
44	Zenith am/fm Radio	60017	99250	33.30	42	1,398.60
45	GE Refrig.-Freezer	57129	31551	420.00	2	840.00
46	GE Refrig. 16 cu.ft.	57122	61551	440.00	3	1,320.00
47	GE Refrig. 20 cu.ft.	57123	31551	870.00	2	1,740.00
48	GE Refrig. 14 cu.ft.	57121	31551	300.00	4	1,200.00
49	Sony am/fm Radio	60006	25127	39.50	11	434.50
50	Sony am Radio	60002	25127	14.45	8	115.60
51	Sony Portable CD	60007	25127	63.00	10	630.00
52	Walkman	60001	25127	6.00	24	144.00
53	Entertainment Ctr.	65701	25127	240.00	2	480.00
54	RCA 19" TV color	67554	25237	280.00	4	1,120.00
55	RCA 21" TV color	67559	25237	340.00	4	1,360.00
56	RCA 25" TV color	67568	25237	490.00	2	980.00
57	RCA VCR, 2 head	42166	25237	1,340.00	3	4,020.00
58	RCA VCR, 4 head	42163	25237	150.00	1	150.00
59						
60			TOTAL INVENTORY COST ⟶			96,574.00
61						

Inventory

APPENDIX B *Answers to Selected Problems*

Chapter 1, Part 1

1. thirty-five
3. six hundred twenty-two
5. one hundred forty-four
7. one hundred fifteen
9. ten thousand four
11. 123
13. 56
15. 123,100
17. 365,000
19. 1,035,000

Chapter 1, Terminology Review

1. Arabic numerals
3. Order of entry
5. answer varies

Chapter 1, Review Exercises

1. thousand
3. ten thousand
5. one
7. hundred thousand
9. trillion
11. sixteen
13. forty-four
15. one hundred eighty-two
17. one million
19. four trillion, one hundred fifty-nine million
21. 169
23. 2,000,000
25. 12,102
27. 132,014
29. 23,191,000
31. 93 million

Chapter 2, Part 2, Exercise 1

1. 22	7. 28	13. 405	19. 700
3. 14	9. 990	15. 232	21. 45
5. 24	11. 160	17. 225	23. 68

Chapter 2, Part 2, Exercise 2

25. 30	31. 8
27. 37	33. 24
29. 31	35. 8

Chapter 2, Part 3, Exercise 1

1. 80	9. 120	17. 781
3. 102	11. 238	19. 312
5. 93	13. 814	
7. 40	15. 841	

Chapter 2, Part 3, Exercise 2

21. $104,719	25. $530,485	29. $111,023
23. $159,687	27. $102,551	31. $530,485

Chapter 2, Part 4, Exercise 1

1. 70	9. 1,030	17. 831
3. 22	11. 242	19. 711
5. 103	13. 870	
7. 97	15. 850	

Chapter 2, Part 4, Exercise 2

21. $254,719	25. $1,070,485	29. $221,023
23. $229,687	27. $192,551	31. $1,070,485

Chapter 2, Part 4, Exercise 3

1. 575	9. 616	17. 778	25. 726
3. 766	11. 719	19. 658	27. 726
5. 611	13. 696	21. 834	29. 814
7. 676	15. 739	23. 753	31. 804

Chapter 2, Terminology Review

1. grand total
3. addends
5. sum

Chapter 2, Review Exercises, Exercise 1

1. 210	7. 267	13. 24,670	19. 788
3. 322	9. 32,530	15. 690	
5. 303	11. 30,642	17. 1,049	

Chapter 2, Review Exercises, Exercise 2

21. Yes

Chapter 2, Review Exercises, Exercise 3

23. 25,719	27. 94,515	31. 21,022
25. 3,621	29. 18,547	33. 94,515

Chapter 3, Part 2, Exercise 1

1. 86	9. 6,097	17. 822	25. $114
3. 13	11. 46	19. 180	27. $26
5. 8	13. 383	21. 423	
7. 234	15. 76	23. 66,491	

Chapter 3, Part 2, Exercise 2

29. $11	35. $336
31. $4	37. $78
33. $116	

Chapter 3, Part 3, Exercise 1

1. 791
3. 113
5. 208
7. 501
9. 4,105
11. 146
13. 417
15. 13,576
17. 8,022
19. 299
21. 123

Chapter 3, Part 3, Exercise 2

23. $14,997
25. $35,868
27. $99,163
29. $2,551

Chapter 3, Part 4, Exercise 1

1. 79
3. 12
5. 8
7. 17
9. 22
11. 5,072
13. 1,147
15. 176
17. 824
19. −63
21. 1,291

Chapter 3, Part 4, Exercise 2

23. $135,997
25. $140,868
27. $589,163
29. $32,551
31. $160,364
33. $145,359
35. $647,714
37. $1,825

Chapter 3, Part 4, Exercise 4

1. 374
3. 631
5. 221
7. 331
9. 616
11. 719
13. 696
15. 739
17. 538
19. 655
21. 280
23. 718
25. 558
27. 521
29. 538
31. 264

Chapter 3, Terminology Review

1. credit balance
3. subtotal
5. difference
7. subtraction

Chapter 3, Review Exercises, Exercise 1

1. 19
3. 81
5. 34
7. −8
9. 2,211
11. 1,120
13. 938
15. 551
17. 21
19. 21
21. 1,092
23. 2,022
25. 3,100
27. 3,202

Chapter 3, Review Exercises, Exercise 2

29. $1,997
31. $11,870
33. $25,163
35. $109,547

Chapter 3, Review Exercises, Exercise 3

37. 33 gallons

Chapter 4, Part 2, Exercise 1

1. 40
3. 60
5. 30
7. 50
9. 900
11. 700
13. 400
15. 1,000
17. 1,200
19. 3,000
21. 4,000
23. 62,000
25. $42,800

Chapter 4, Part 2, Exercise 2

27. $800
29. $100
31. $1,500

Chapter 4, Part 2, Exercise 3

33. $1,600
35. $2,200
37. $800
39. $100
41. $4,900

Chapter 4, Part 3, Exercise 1

1. 1,115; 1,100
3. 1,407; 1,400
5. 446; 400
7. 957; 1,000
9. 7,973; 8,000
11. 5,394; 5,000
13. 15,993; 16,000
15. 3,576; 3,600
17. 17,022; 17,000
19. 999; 1,000
21. 3,123; 3,100

Chapter 4, Part 3, Exercise 2

23. $15,000
25. $37,000
27. $101,000

Chapter 4, Part 4, Exercise 1

1. 311; 310
3. 840; 840
5. 1,446; 1,450
7. 1,180; 1,180
9. 4,965; 5,000
11. 11,751; 11,800
13. 12,288; 12,300
15. 62,581; 63,000
17. 55,862; 56,000
19. 22,899; 23,000
21. 33,323; 33,000

Chapter 4, Part 4, Exercise 2

23. $621,714

Chapter 4, Part 4, Exercise 3

25. $2,000

Chapter 4, Part 4, Exercise 4

1. 664
3. 765
5. 721
7. 779
9. 616
11. 719
13. 696
15. 739
17. 738
19. 663
21. 727
23. 734
25. 697
27. 711
29. 755
31. 854

Chapter 4, Terminology Review

1. thousands place
3. estimate
5. five or greater

Chapter 4, Review Exercises, Exercise 1

1. 73
3. 111
5. 182
7. 96
9. −8
11. 5
13. 67
15. 6,151
17. 992
19. 1,720
21. 1,069
23. −547
25. 1,708
27. 2,225
29. 2,000
31. 388
33. 1,199
35. 900
37. 1,208

Chapter 4, Review Exercises, Exercise 2

39. $15,000
41. $34,000
43. $135,000

Chapter 4, Review Exercises, Exercise 3

45. $950
47. $1,010
49. $420

Chapter 5, Part 2, Exercise 1

1. 296	9. 321,280	17. 28,000	25. 720
3. 240	11. 16,800	19. 12,960	27. $75
5. 8,310	13. 8,125	21. 2,514,600	
7. 14,616	15. 385	23. 5,118,438	

Chapter 5, Part 2, Exercise 2

29. $30
31. $50
33. $135

Chapter 5, Part 2, Exercise 3

35. 3,000
37. 550

Chapter 5, Part 3, Exercise 1

1. 15,248	9. 5,640,426	17. 21,134,080
3. 35,720	11. 33,480	19. 417,882
5. 19,113	13. 66,321,990	21. 156,618
7. 14,812	15. 7,901,465	

Chapter 5, Part 3, Exercise 2

23. $1,553,904
25. $2,895,113
27. $8,804,583

Chapter 5, Part 3, Exercise 3

29. 5,280
31. 17,000

Chapter 5, Part 4, Exercise 1

1. 1,520	9. 11,254	17. 1,533,675
3. 4,864	11. 77,748	19. 212,282
5. 513	13. 7,817,472	21. 7,431,218
7. 1,456	15. 2,276,732	

Chapter 5, Part 4, Exercise 2

23. $1,311,264	27. $2,436,027
25. $146,647	29. $1,792

Chapter 5, Part 4, Exercise 3

31. $1,659
33. 265,140
35. 2,025,144

Chapter 5, Part 4, Exercise 4

1. 395	9. 304	17. 391	25. 541
3. 294	11. 381	19. 467	27. 469
5. 202	13. 369	21. 378	29. 335
7. 403	15. 276	23. 352	31. 243

Chapter 5, Terminology Review

1. constant
3. commutative property of multiplication
5. multiplier
7. multifactor multiplication
9. partial product

Chapter 5, Review Exercises, Exercise 1

1. 2,880	9. 6,378,126	17. 1,283,772
3. 1,552	11. 473,796	19. 47,000,072
5. 4,752	13. 272,368	
7. 5,313	15. 161,820	

Chapter 5, Review Exercises, Exercise 2

21. $1,960
23. $198
25. $3,918

Chapter 5, Review Exercises, Exercise 3

27. 520 miles
29. 9,000

Chapter 6, Part 2, Exercise 1

1. 81	9. 36	17. 136
3. 95	11. 1,263	19. 189
5. 37	13. 11	
7. 143	15. 43	

Chapter 6, Part 2, Exercise 2

21. Six sets
23. 12 minutes
25. 37 bags with 2 pounds left over

Chapter 6, Part 3, Exercise 1

1. 8	9. 19	17. 138	25. 3
3. 24	11. 26	19. 75	27. 502
5. 17	13. 256	21. 75	
7. 16	15. 244	23. 66	

Chapter 6, Part 3, Exercise 2

29. 25 boxes

Chapter 6, Part 4, Exercise 1

1. 7	9. 55	17. 38
3. 91	11. 88	19. 4
5. 29	13. 65	21. 8
7. 52	15. 59	

Chapter 6, Part 4, Exercise 2

Production Figures for September 2001, Oil Field #890

Oil Well	Total Income Produced ($)	Distribution of Income ($)			
		Adam Jackson	Bob Jackson	Patricia Maine	Harold Jackson
#14	8,000	23. 2,000	24.	25. 2,000	26.
#15	16,000	27. 4,000	28.	29. 4,000	30.
#16	24,000	31. 6,000	32.	33. 6,000	34.
#17	4,000	35. 1,000	36.	37. 1,000	38.
Totals	44.	39. 13,000	40.	41. 13,000	42.
				Total Distributions	43. $52,000

Chapter 6, Part 4, Exercise 3

45. 75 gallons

Chapter 6, Part 4, Exercise 4

1. 546	9. 564	17. 631	25. 559
3. 528	11. 561	19. 637	27. 496
5. 366	13. 575	21. 396	29. 359
7. 416	15. 516	23. 440	31. 266

Chapter 6, Terminology Review

1. Division
3. divisor, remainder
5. partial dividend
7. partial quotient
9. Accumulation of quotients

Chapter 6, Review Exercises, Exercise 1

1. 700	9. 27	17. 18
3. 250	11. 15	19. 62
5. 35	13. 7	
7. 330	15. 13	

Chapter 6, Review Exercises, Exercise 2

Biminis A'Loft Materials Check List
Current Orders: Order #86233, 85 Pacific Blue Biminis, Model S292

Inventory (Materials on Hand)	Materials Required for Order #86233	Sufficient Materials on Hand? Yes/No	Order Materials? Yes/No
3,500 square yards of Pacific blue Sunbrella fabric	16 square yards of Pacific blue Sunbrella each	21. Yes	25. No
350 six-foot YYK® zippers	4 six-foot zippers each	22.	26.
600 bobbins of white marine-grade thread	6 bobbins of white marine-grade thread each	23 Yes	27 No
1,200 yards of 1-inch Pacific blue webbing	12 yards of 1-inch Pacific blue webbing each	24.	28.
Begin manufacture? Yes/No			29. Yes
Warehouse supervisor		Date:	
Signature: *Your Name*		*Today's Date*	

Chapter 6, Review Exercises, Exercise 3

31. $2

Chapter 7, Part 2, Exercise 1

1. thirty-five and four tenths
3. twenty-two and three hundred fifty-five thousandths
5. fourteen and forty-five thousand five hundred ninety-eight hundred thousandths

Chapter 7, Part 2, Exercise 2

7. 14.3
9. 118.0005

Chapter 7, Part 2, Exercise 3

11. $39.69	19. 66	27. 168.8	35. 1/10
13. $63.00	21. 13.5967	29. $124.36	37. 98/100
15. $33.56	23. 92.5440	31. 76.284	39. 5/10
17. 0.286	25. 3.4597	33. $1.63	

Chapter 7, Part 3, Exercise 1

1. 341.855   7. 422.9
3. 169.640   9. $10.64
5. $10.02

Chapter 7, Part 3, Exercise 2

11. $344.35
13. $333.86
15. $178.66

Chapter 7, Part 3, Exercise 3

17. $110   23. $199
19. $25   25. $1,063
21. $21

Chapter 7, Part 4, Exercise 1

1. $197.94   13. 112   25. 41.856
3. $28.40   15. 162.581   27. 49.640
5. $124.46   17. 145.862   29. 1,121.025
7. $111.80   19. 912.899   31. −638,036.6967
9. 5   21. 553.323   33. 1.6322
11. 32   23. 32.0189   35. 644.3124

Chapter 7, Part 4, Exercise 2

1. 490.71   9. 37.44   17. 59.10   25. 438.37
3. 91.706   11. 473.5   19. 60.01   27. 646.81
5. 212.895   13. 408.5   21. 59.02   29. 515.53
7. 282.69   15. 301.7   23. 54.13   31. 675.88

Chapter 7, Terminology Review

1. decimal alignment
3. decimal point, decimal number
5. ten thousandths
7. floating decimal setting
9. b. 0.5
11. b. 6.11
13. c. $188

Chapter 7, Review Exercises, Exercise 1

1. ninety-six and nine tenths
3. eight thousand three hundred thirty-nine and three hundred thirty-six thousandths
5. one hundred sixteen thousand seven hundred eighty-two and ninety-nine thousand eight hundred fifty-two hundred thousandths

Chapter 7, Review Exercises, Exercise 2

7. 0.365
9. 10.42365

Chapter 7, Review Exercises, Exercise 3

11. $45.70   17. 1,290.5   23. 6.336   29. 6.81
13. $1.50   19. 87.456   25. 92   31. 5/10
15. 1,360.0   21. 26.267   27. 13   33. 75/100

Chapter 8, Part 2, Exercise 1

1. 52.5   11. 13   21. 288 oz   31. 6 hr
3. 14.25   13. 30   23. 1.4 gal   33. 8 qt
5. 552.42   15. 1.65   25. 3 pt
7. 0.67268   17. 7.8   27. 7.5 gal
9. 12.5   19. 880   29. 68 oz

Chapter 8, Part 2, Exercise 2

35. $33.00

Chapter 8, Part 3, Exercise 1

1. 73.8   9. 53.3077   17. 43.2 in   25. 16,896 ft
3. 32.76   11. 20.5558   19. 15 ft   27. 3.45 t
5. 243.04   13. 44.84   21. 23 yd
7. 29.06384   15. 444.4111   23. 2.75 mi

Chapter 8, Part 3, Exercise 2

29. $837,599.88
31. $2,717,819.80

Chapter 8, Part 3, Exercise 3

33. $111.10

Chapter 8, Part 4, Exercise 1

1. 3,404.39   9. 19.3771   17. 10.5 t
3. 1,125.36   11. 67.91   19. 15.188 qt
5. 301.41   13. 607.4167   21. 3.797 gal
7. 0.56   15. 2.5227   23. 211.2 lb

Chapter 8, Part 4, Exercise 2

25. $110.50
27. no

Chapter 8, Part 4, Exercise 3

1. 39,657   9. 40,322   17. 501.00   25. 542.34
3. 52,400   11. 50,186   19. 593.00   27. 462.69
5. 62,560   13. 35,730   21. 382.36   29. 335.45
7. 37,000   15. 41,660   23. 358.05   31. 802.43

Chapter 8, Terminology Review

1. intermediate answer
3. rounding up
5. repeating decimal number
7. A decimal point should be placed directly above the decimal point in the dividend.
9. false
11. true

Chapter 8, Review Exercises, Exercise 1

1. 47.64375   9. 45.8   17. 59.768 mi
3. 97.495   11. 76.92308   19. 6 c
5. 226.125   13. 34.53636   21. 23.1 yd
7. 70   15. 258.62069 23. 37.5 g

Chapter 8, Review Exercises, Exercise 2

25. 1.5 oz olive oil
27. 7.5 tsp sugar
29. 2.25 oz commercial yeast

Chapter 8, Review Exercises, Exercise 3

31. 126 mi
33. $58.50

Chapter 9, Part 2, Exercise 1

1. 2/5	9. 2	17. 1/12	25. 13 3/4
3. 3/10	11. 2/5	19. 2 1/3	27. 0.333
5. 6/7	13. 4 1/11	21. 1 1/3	29. 0.25
7. 3/4	15. 3/4	23. 3 3/5	31. 0.1

Chapter 9, Part 2, Exercise 2

33. 192 pieces	37. $7,200
35. 3 3/4″	39. 144 women

Chapter 9, Parts 3 & 4, Exercise 1

1. 0.625	9. 0.875	17. 0.41
3. 0.083	11. 0.1	19. 26.75
5. 0.667	13. 0.2	
7. 0.833	15. 7.875	

Chapter 9, Parts 3 & 4, Exercise 2

21. 0.106 increase
23. $21.55
25. 184″, 6 yd
27. 375 boxes
29. $292.50

Chapter 9, Parts 3 & 4, Exercise 3 for Desktop Calculators Only

1. 452,857	9. 304,322	17. 2,501.00	24. 3,546.10
3. 446,400	11. 788,186	19. 8,793.00	
5. 664,560	13. 423,730	21. 5,782.36	
7. 375,400	15. 418,860	23. 4,238.05	

Chapter 9, Terminology Review

1. mixed number
3. improper fraction
5. least common denominator
7. proper fraction
9. equivalent fraction

Chapter 9, Review Exercises, Exercise 1

1. 3 5/9	13. 10/11	25. 10 1/3	37. 0.273
3. 14 1/2	15. 7/27	27. 7/12	39. 0.27
5. 65/7	17. 1	29. 5/16	41. 0.063
7. 3	19. 4 17/21	31. 3 1/3	
9. 3	21. 2/15	33. 3/5	
11. 5/9	23. 2 9/10	35. 28 1/2	

Chapter 9, Review Exercises, Exercise 2

43. $3,155.33
45. 12 1/4 cakes

Chapter 9, Review Exercises, Exercise 3

47. 1/2 c lemon drink mix, presweetened with sugar
49. 1/4 c sugar

Chapter 10, Part 2, Exercise 1

1. 0.125	11. 60/100	21. 66.7%	31. 1,400
3. 1/8	13. 0.333	23. 0.8	33. 35%
5. 0.5/100	15. 1/3	25. 30/100	35. 41,666.67
7. 0.5	17. 0.1	27. 30%	
9. 1/2	19. 66.67/100	29. 0.375	

Chapter 10, Part 2, Exercise 2

37. $47.25
39. $4,778

Chapter 10, Part 3, Exercise 1

1. 0.53	9. 0.6225	17. 2,835
3. 0.5	11. 17,500	19. 101.82%
5. 1.02	13. 4%	21. 555,555.56
7. 0.755	15. 166,666.67	

Chapter 10, Part 3, Exercise 2

23. $237.93
25. $167.86
27. $37.43

Chapter 10, Part 4, Exercise 1

1. 0.12	5. 0.1675	9. 1.5512	13. 25.13%
3. 0.075	7. 0.062	11. 30	15. 1,271.43

Chapter 10, Part 4, Exercise 2

PURCHASE ORDER

Office Works, Inc.
PO Box 19
Victoria, TX 77900

TO:
[Computers and More Direct
2290 Palmer Drive
Long Beach, CA 90800]

SHIP TO:
Office Works, Inc.
200 S. Main St.
Victoria, TX 77901

P. O. NUMBER 56923
DATE June 7, 2002
REQUISITIONED BY AJ
SHIP BY June 10, 2002
SHIP VIA
F.O.B.
TERMS

Purchase order number must appear
on all forms relating to this order.

QTY	UNIT	DESCRIPTION	PRICE	AMOUNT
6	each	Model # S69501 6-outlet surge strip	4.99	17. 29.94
4	each	Model # H55302 4-port USB hub	9.99	
2	kits	Model # NK649 Gear to Go notebook kits	12.99	19. 25.98
10	each	Model # #509sc Sound cards	11.99	
1	each	Model # M300549 17" TFT LCD	499.99	21. 499.99

SUBTOTAL	
FREIGHT	0.00
TAX RATE	7.000%
TAX	23. 50.80
TOTAL DUE	

Jeremy Harrison   *June 7, 2002*
Authorized by   Date

Chapter 10, Part 4, Exercise 3

1. 481,857   7. 474,400   13. 446,730   19. 6,133.00
3. 661,400   9. 450,322   15. 661,860   21. 7,867.36
5. 612,560   11. 424,186   17. 6,191.00   23. 3,538.05

Chapter 10, Terminology Review

1. formula
3. base
5. proportion
7. purchase requisition
9. purchase order
11. true
13. false

Chapter 10, Review Exercises, Exercise 1

1. 0.8   13. 0.295   25. 20/100
3. 4/5   15. 5.9/20 or 59/200   27. 20%
5. 15/100   17. 0.2   29. 0.16
7. 0.05   19. 90/100   31. 144
9. 1/20   21. 90%   33. 2.67%
11. 94/100   23. 0.5   35. 857,142.85

Chapter 10, Review Exercises, Exercise 2

37. 3,534   43. 14.71%
39. $1,620   45. $26,547.50
41. 60%

Chapter 10, Review Exercises, Exercise 3

Advertising Budget

Month/Year: January 2003
Total Advertising Budget for Month: Percent of Sales: 5%
Dollar Amount: $424,500

Medium	Specific Outlet (Name of Specific Newspaper or Magazine, etc.)	Frequency of Ads	Total Cost ($)	Percent of Total Monthly Budget (%)	
Newspaper	Daily News	Daily	65,000	46.	
Magazine	Photo Monthly	Monthly	1,500	47.	.35
Television	KCEM	5 × daily	115,000	48.	
Radio	KLRR	20 × daily	120,000	49.	28.27
Internet	Isales.com	N/A	65,000	50.	
Outdoor	Boards, Inc.	N/A	58,000	51.	13.66
			Total %	52.	

Chapter 11, Part 2, Exercise 1

1. $180
3. $306.25
5. $11.60

Chapter 11, Part 2, Exercise 2

7. 85 days   13. $25.48   19. $187.74
9. 242 days   15. $243.93
11. $24.66   17. $6.02

Chapter 11, Part 2, Exercise 3

21. $600   27. 2.92%   33. 18 months
23. $12,888.89 29. 0.89%   35. 270 days
25. $4,500   31. 5 years

Chapter 11, Part 2, Exercise 4

37. a. $1,200 b. $78,800 c. $78,800 d. $10,000 e. $80,000

Chapter 11, Part 4, Exercise 1

1. $8,512.50, $93,637.50   5. 3.522%, $64,612.29
3. $32,000.00, $36,080.00   7. 90 days, $35,951.30

9. 170 days, $20,443.50   19. July 21
11. 40 months   21. $2,000, $8,000
13. 17 months   23. $345, $6,555
15. July 5   25. $24.06, $3,475.94
17. Oct. 9   27. $316.86, $3,983.14

Chapter 11, Part 4, Exercise 2

1. 2,396.57   7. 4,570.00   13. 3,573.20   19. 5,993.00
3. 8,524.00   9. 4,032.62   15. 4,166.60   21. 3,782.36
5. 5,925.60   11. 5,019.10   17. 4,901.00   23. 3,558.05

Chapter 11, Terminology Review

1. Interest   11. Exact interest
3. banker's interest 13. maker
5. Maturity value   15. false
7. Rate   17. true
9. promissory note

Chapter 11, Review Exercises, Exercise 1

1. $91, $5,691
3. $4,706.26, $4,768.75
5. 4.5%, $10,874.69
7. 52 months, $38,603.83

Chapter 11, Review Exercises, Exercise 2

9. 5-15-03
11. 9-6-03

Chapter 11, Review Exercises, Exercise 3

13. $300, $7,200
15. $108, $4,212
17. $6.27, $2,026.73

Chapter 11, Review Exercises, Exercise 4

19. 140 days, $63.29, $5,563.29
21. 96 days, $59.67, $8,309.67

Chapter 11, Review Exercises, Exercise 5

23. $5,563.29, 94 days, $94.42, $5,468.87
25. $8,309.67, 80 days, $166.19, $8,143.48

Chapter 12, Part 2, Exercise 1

1. 26	9. 75	17. 12	25. 10
3. 135	11. 100	19. 112	27. 5
5. 42	13. 10	21. 4	
7. 13	15. 3	23. 7	

Chapter 12, Part 2, Exercise 2

29. 1,750 sq in.; 190 in.
31. 385 cu in.
33. $2,250
35. $4,068.72 − $525.20 = n
    $3,543.52 = n$
37. $2n = 36, n = 72$ in.
39. $n + 3n = 138
    $n = 34.50 (Roger's portion)
    $3n = 103.50 (Don's portion)

Chapter 12, Part 4, Exercise 1

1. 46,149	7. 42,045	13. 36,615	19. 600.04
3. 52,950	9. 42,443	15. 50,870	21. 382.78
5. 60,740	11. 49,727	17. 580.02	23. 407.80

Chapter 12, Terminology Review

1. solution   5. mathematical expression
3. variables   7. equation

Chapter 12, Review Exercises, Exercise 1

1. 16	11. 5	19. 58	29. $n = 450$
3. 8	13. 10	21. $y = 10$	31. $y = 12$
5. $x = 18$	15. 9	23. $y = 14$	33. $n = 11$
7. $x = 30$	16. 2	25. $x = 3$	
9. 21	17. 16	27. $x = 3$	

Chapter 12, Review Exercises, Exercise 2

35. No, the outside dimensions are 138"
37. 24 cu ft

39. 12,457.95 cu in.
41. 1,384.74 sq in.

Chapter 12, Review Exercises, Exercise 3

Equations may vary.

43. $500 − $190 − $260 = n, or
    $190 + $260 + $n = $500, $50
45. 75(12) = n, $900
47. $j + j + 15 = 51$, 18 calls (John), 33 calls (Bob)
49. $r + (3/4)r = 1,500$, 857.14 red mugs, 642.86 blue mugs
    (857 red, 643 blue, rounded)

Chapter 12, Review Exercises, Exercise 4

1. 22,500   5. 30,000
3. 20,000   7. 15,000

Chapter 12, Review Exercises, Exercise 5

1. 450   5. 1,600   9. 1,800
3. 1,800   7. 3,200   11. 2,250

Chapter 13, Part 2, Exercise 1

1. 5.3%
3. 15.6%
5. (52.8%)

Chapter 13, Part 2, Exercise 2

7. 23.5%
9. (3.5%)
11. 9.5%

Chapter 13, Part 4, Exercise 1

1. (5.4%)
3. (9.3%)

Chapter 13, Part 4, Exercise 2

5. 8.4   9. 13.8   13. 4.2
7. 17.2   11. 34.8   15. 0.4

Chapter 13, Part 4, Exercise 3

1. 57,074	7. 56,829	13. 57,102	19. 613.83
3. 65,486	9. 36,165	15. 39,760	21. 431.57
5. 47,793	11. 51,946	17. 669.61	23. 587.31

Chapter 13, Terminology Review

1. The rate at which an amount increased over time.
3. (Amount − Base) ÷ Base = Percent of Increase or Decrease

Chapter 13, Review Exercises, Exercise 1

1. 14.3%
3. (12.3%)

Chapter 13, Review Exercises, Exercise 2

5. (11.6%)   9. 8.2%   13. 8.1%   17. (8.1%)
7. 10.5%   11. 8.2%   15. (0.4%)   19. (7.2%)

Chapter 14, Part 2, Exercise 1

1. 67.5
3. 15

Chapter 14, Part 2, Exercise 2

5. large
7. no
9. 28,000

Chapter 14, Part 4, Exercise 1

1. 50,914	7. 54,436	13. 49,478	19. 590.00
3. 32,846	9. 71,937	15. 42,897	21. 456.19
5. 50,255	11. 67,716	17. 435.86	23. 497.80

Chapter 14, Terminology Review

1. statistics   3. range   5. median

Chapter 14, Review Exercises, Exercise 1

1. 26,130   7. 85
3. 18,400   9. mean 970,000, median 800,000,
5. 79 (rounded)   mode 800,000, range 600,000

Chapter 15, Part 2, Exercise 1

1. 1985
3. 2,001
5. (2.85%) decrease

Chapter 15, Part 4, Exercise 1

1. 625,322	7. 370,000	13. 358,358	19. 609,390
3. 553,194	9. 679,322	15. 414,260	21. 447,703
5. 522,713	11. 410,978	17. 613,800	23. 416,829

Chapter 15, Terminology Review

1. pie chart   5. heading   9. bar chart   13. slope
3. labels   7. line chart   11. charts

Chapter 15, Review Exercises, Exercise 1

1. foreign stocks
3. increase

Chapter 15, Review Exercises, Exercise 2

Frontier Log Home Kits
2003 Yearly Sales Report

Model Number	Selling Price ($)	Units Sold	Totals ($)
198A	89,798.98	15	1,346,984.70
198B	69,799.99	12	
298A	75,898.88	26	1,973,370.80
298B	150,989.99	18	

Table for creating a bar chart:

Model Number	Totals ($)
198A	1,346,984.70
198B	
298A	1,973,370.80
298B	

Frontier Log Home Kits
2003 Yearly Sales

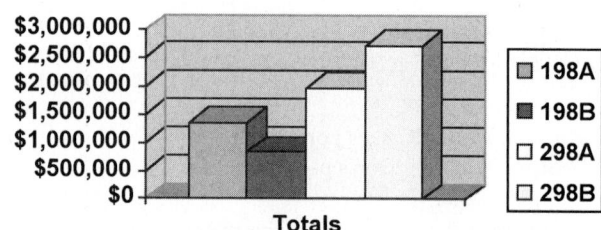

FIGURE 15.15

Chapter 16, Part 2, Exercise 1

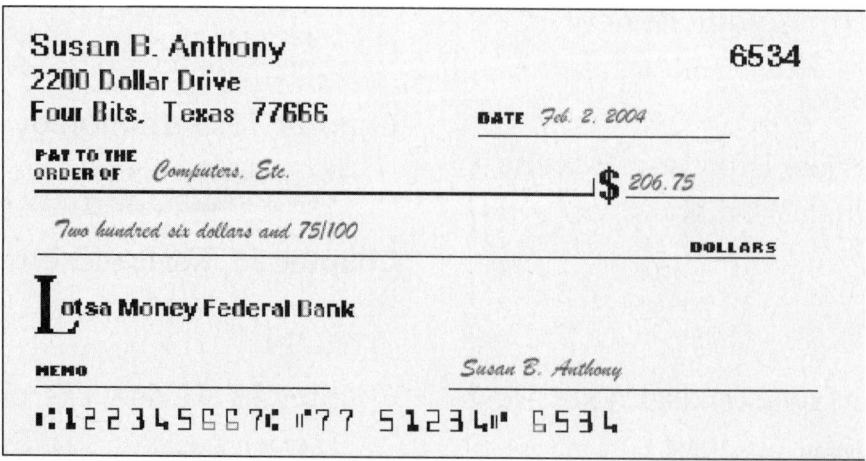

FIGURE 16.24

Chapter 16, Part 2, Exercise 3

7001		$ *609.00*	
Jan. 10		20 *04*	
To *Anderson Property Mgt.*			
For *rent*			
		Dollars	Cents
Balance Brought Forward		5,598	65
Deposits *1-10 ATM CD*		+ 200	00
Total		5,798	65
Amount of This Check		-609	00
Balance		5,189	65

FIGURE 16.25

Chapter 16, Part 2, Exercise 5

ENDORSE HERE

X *Student's Full Name*

DO NOT WRITE, STAMP, OR SIGN BELOW THIS LINE

Chapter 16, Part 2, Exercise 7

THIS IS PROVIDED TO HELP YOU BALANCE
YOUR BANK STATEMENT

BANK BALANCE
SHOWN ON THIS STATEMENT $ *4,559.42*

ADD + (IF ANY)
DEPOSITS NOT SHOWN
ON THIS STATEMENT   *943.76*

SUBTOTAL   *5,503.18*

SUBTRACT - (IF ANY)
CHECKS OUTSTANDING   *303.94*

BALANCE $ *5,199.24*
SHOULD AGREE WITH YOUR CHECKBOOK BALANCE

CHECKS OUTSTANDING	
NO.	AMOUNT
1790	55 69
1795	75 90
1796	104 35
1799	68 00
TOTAL	303 94

THIS IS PROVIDED TO HELP YOU BALANCE
YOUR BANK STATEMENT

CHECKBOOK BALANCE
AT STATEMENT DATE $ *5,699.01*

SUBTRACT - (IF ANY)
ACTIVITY CHARGES   *487.77*

SUBTOTAL   *5,211.24*

SUBTRACT - (IF ANY)
OTHER BANK CHARGES   *12.00*

BALANCE $ *5,199.24*
SHOULD AGREE WITH YOUR CHECKBOOK BALANCE

Chapter 16, Part 4, Exercise 1

37,229	91,544	27,850	50,000	81,400	66,987	40,450	96,000
78,877	75,920	48,500	67,000	65,420	22,122	29,005	36,013
23,651	74,807	34,950	10,800	55,750	60,455	41,990	38,564
13,324	83,600	69,915	30,010	66,110	70,014	20,229	39,064
75,256	97,930	57,355	30,003	77,706	22,992	30,059	30,044
83,117	19,788	94,229	10,000	28,689	19,000	60,909	47,023
91,339	67,300	68,899	32,000	93,599	63,880	37,570	25,013
76,541	76,460	45,975	50,800	66,784	10,132	50,659	92,653
90,471	40,303	54,980	60,090	17,216	11,139	40,695	97,054
77,870	18,300	34,557	50,004	99,372	33,982	20,990	10,016
1. 647,675	3. 645,952	5. 537,210	7. 390,707	9. 652,046	11. 380,703	13. 372,556	15. 511,444

18,900	45,100	87,349	76,213
62,100	76,120	66,855	28,500
55,340	93,713	54,198	20,938
72,546	78,100	46,647	75,163
28,500	95,890	21,875	71,452
18,500	49,145	32,423	88,632
76,370	23,100	31,000	61,285
27,219	88,210	70,005	25,729
17,900	89,500	40,045	97,115
35,270	28,490	80,100	26,873
17. 412,645	19. 667,368	21. 530,497	23. 571,900

Chapter 16, Terminology Review

1. debit card
3. debit memo
5. checking account
7. signature card
9. deposit
11. returned checks
13. adjusted bank statement balance
15. bank statement
17. bank statement reconciliation
19. POS

Chapter 16, Review Exercises, Exercise 1

1.

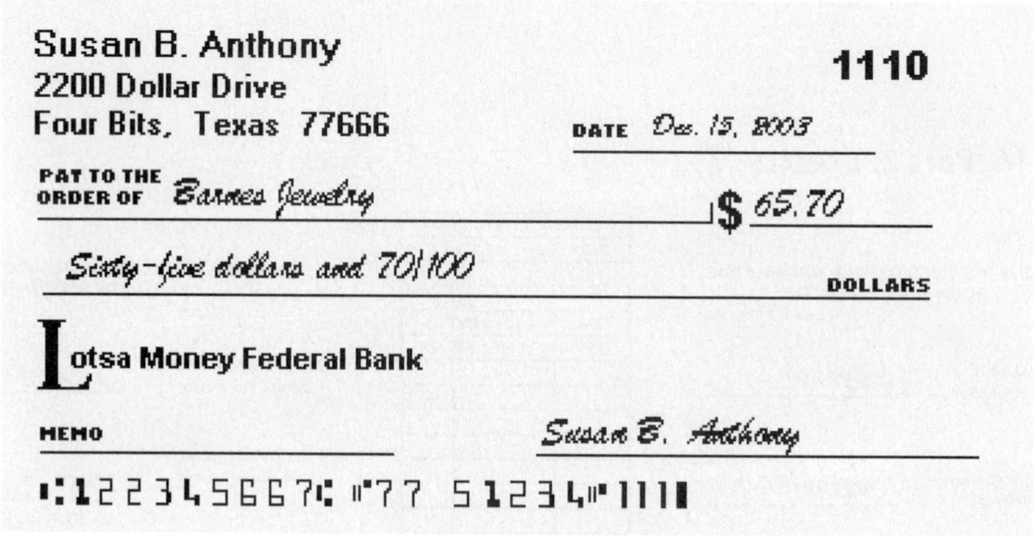
Susan B. Anthony
2200 Dollar Drive
Four Bits, Texas 77666
1110
DATE Dec. 15, 2003
PAY TO THE ORDER OF Barnes Jewelry $ 65.70
Sixty-five dollars and 70/100 DOLLARS
Lotsa Money Federal Bank
MEMO
Susan B. Anthony

FIGURE 16.26

Chapter 16, Review Exercises, Exercise 2

3.

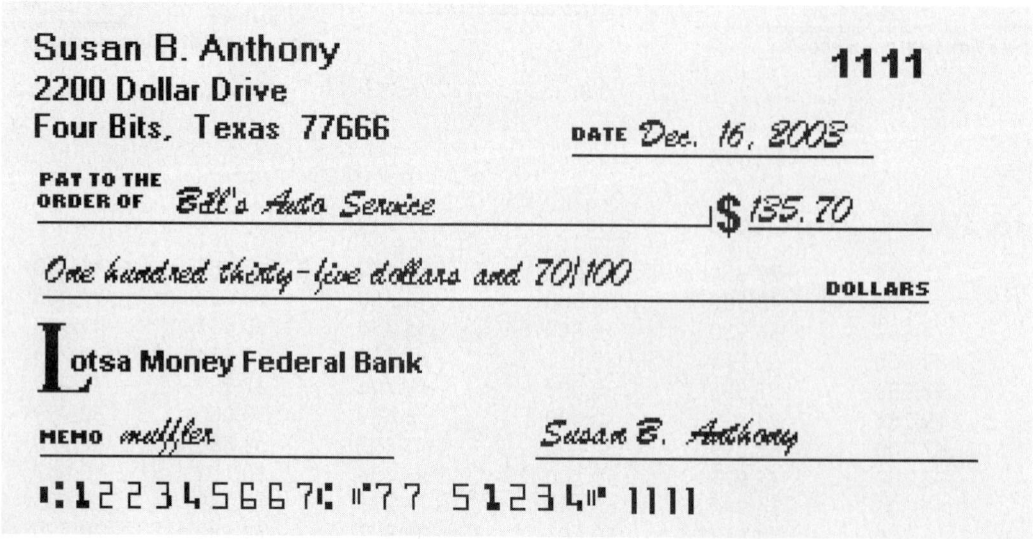
Susan B. Anthony
2200 Dollar Drive
Four Bits, Texas 77666
1111
DATE Dec. 16, 2003
PAY TO THE ORDER OF Bill's Auto Service $ 135.70
One hundred thirty-five dollars and 70/100 DOLLARS
Lotsa Money Federal Bank
MEMO muffler
Susan B. Anthony

FIGURE 16.27

Chapter 16, Review Exercises, Exercise 3

5.

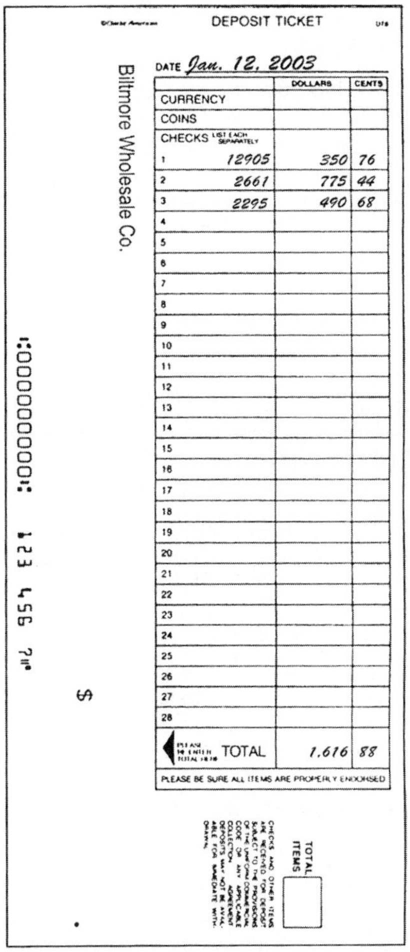
DEPOSIT TICKET

Biltmore Wholesale Co.

DATE *Jan. 12, 2003*

	DOLLARS	CENTS
CURRENCY		
COINS		
CHECKS LIST EACH SEPARATELY		
1 12905	350	76
2 2661	775	44
3 2295	490	68
TOTAL	1,616	88

PLEASE BE SURE ALL ITEMS ARE PROPERLY ENDORSED

TOTAL ITEMS

FIGURE 16.28

Chapter 16, Review Exercises, Exercise 4

7.

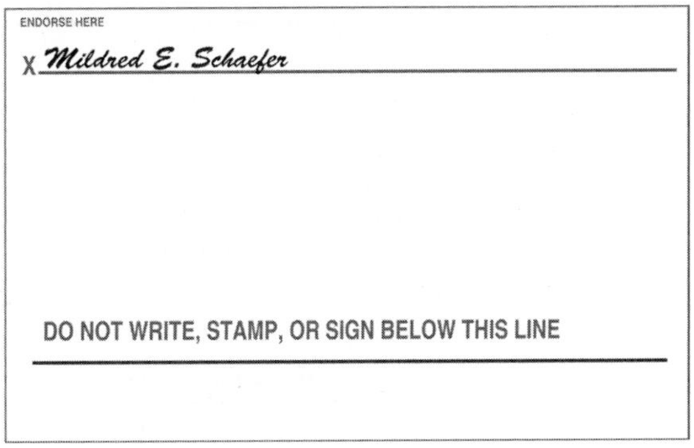
ENDORSE HERE

X *Mildred E. Schaefer*

DO NOT WRITE, STAMP, OR SIGN BELOW THIS LINE

Chapter 17, Part 2, Exercise 1

1. $3,354.17
3. $270
5. $3,200
7. $4,425

Chapter 17, Part 2, Exercise 2

9. $504.98
11. $718.61
13. $2,904.07

Chapter 17, Part 2, Exercise 3

15. $30
17. $154
19. $88

Chapter 17, Part 4, Exercise 1

ABC Co. Biweekly Time Card

Pay Period Ending 9/27/2003 *Employee Name Ed Jones* *Employee Number 350*

	Date	In	Out	In	Out	Regular Hours	Overtime Hours	
M	9/14	6:00	12:00	1:00	3:30	8	.5	1.
T	9/15	6:30	12:00	1:00	4:00			2.
W	9/16	7:00	12:00	1:30	5:00	8	.5	3.
T	9/17	8:00	12:30	1:30	5:00			4.
F	9/18	8:00	12:00	1:00	5:15	8		5.
S	9/19	7:00	11:00					6.
S	9/20			2:30	9:30		7	7.
M	9/21	8:00	12:00	1:00	6:00			8.
T	9/22	6:00	11:00	1:00	4:00	8		9.
W	9/23	7:00	12:00	1:00	4:00			10.
T	9/24	7:00	12:30	1:30	4:30	8	.5	11.
F	9/25	7:00	12:00	1:00	4:30			12.
S	9/26	7:00	10:00				3	13.
S	9/27							14.

For Office Use

	Hours Worked	Gross Pay ($)	*Employee Hourly Pay Rate* $13.60
Regular hours	80	1,088.00	15.
Overtime hours @ 1.5			16.
Overtime hours @ 2	7	190.40	17.
Totals			18.

Chapter 17, Part 4, Exercise 2

Payroll Register

For Week Ending August 16, 2003

	Employee Number	Employee Name	M/S	W.A.	Gross Pay ($)	YTD Earnings ($)	Deductions ($)				Total Deductions ($)	Net Pay ($)
							Federal	Social Security	Medicare	Other		
19.	1981	Brown, L.	S	0	950.98	28,529.40	165	58.96	13.79	55.50	293.25	657.73
20.	2222	Chaney, S.	M	2	1002.35	30,070.50						
21.	2527	Taylor, S.	M	4	750.56	22,516.80	41	46.53	10.88	28.12	126.53	624.03
22.	2679	Sung, L.	M	3	832.21	24,966.30						
23.	2780	Maybrey, I.	S	5	587.00	17,610.00	29	36.39	8.51	22.00	95.90	491.10
24.	2781	Canfield, J.	S	1	398.74	11,962.20						

Chapter 17, Part 4, Exercise 3

	Employee Name	Total Pieces	1 to 600 Pieces @ 0.55		601 to 800 Pieces @ 0.65		801 to 999 Pieces @ 0.75		Gross Pay ($)
25.	Lee, M.	810	600	330	200	130.00	10	7.50	467.50
26.	Johns, D.	790							
27.	Gaylor, K.	698	600	330	98	63.70			393.70
28.	Curry, T.	910							

Chapter 17, Part 4, Exercise 4

1. 590,590	9. 668,233	17. 447,835
3. 544,883	11. 358,954	19. 635,697
5. 461,961	13. 417,940	21. 548,211
7. 428,000	15. 527,181	23. 534,224

Chapter 17, Terminology Review

1. gross pay
3. withholding allowance
5. quota
7. sliding scale commission
9. salary plus commission
11. year-to-date earnings
13. social security
15. regular hours
17. overtime hours

Chapter 17, Review Exercises, Exercise 1

	Number	Name	Hours Worked	Regular Hours	Regular Hourly Rate ($)	Overtime Hours	Gross Pay ($)
1.	97	Balley, J.	45	40	12.80	5	608.00
2.	104	King, M.	48				
3.	125	Moore, S.	40	40	22.90		916.00
4.	152	Williams, B.	38				

Chapter 17, Review Exercises, Exercise 2

Payroll Register

For Week Ending August 16, 2003

	Employee Number	Employee Name	M/S	W.A.	Gross Pay ($)	YTD Earnings ($)	Deductions ($)				Total Deductions ($)	Net Pay ($)
							Federal	Social Security	Medicare	Other		
5.	101	Ross, J.	S	0	1,200	45,000	228	74.40	17.40	15.50	335.30	864.70
6.	222	Perez, T.	M	2	800	24,000						
7.	303	Douglas, S.	M	4	495	14,850	10	30.69	7.18	8.00	55.87	439.13
8.	309	Cain, E.	M	6	580	17,400						
9.	310	Smith, W.	S	5	540	16,200	23	33.48	7.83	12.00	76.31	463.69
10.	320	Jones, B.	S	1	657	19,710						

Chapter 17, Review Exercises, Exercise 3

11. $416.22
13. $1,523.20
15. $3,650; $2,593.77

Chapter 17, Review Exercises, Exercise 4

	Name	M/S	W.A.	Pieces	Gross Pay ($)	Federal ($)	Social Security ($)	Medicare ($)	Other ($)	Net Pay ($)
17.	Lee, J.	M	4	410	386.00	0	23.93	5.60	10.40	346.07
18.	Tucker, L.	S	2	380	349.00					
19.	Chu, K.	S	1	250	217.50	10	13.49	3.15	0	190.86
20.	Chen, L.	S	0	455	458.00					

Chapter 18, Part 2, Exercise 1

1. $2,930

Chapter 18, Part 2, Exercise 2

	Gross Earnings ($)	FUTA ($)	SUTA ($)
2.	6,070		
3.	14,090	56.00	378.00
4.	8,003		
5.	7,050	56.00	378.00
6.	4,339		

Chapter 18, Part 2, Exercise 3

Answers are in bold.

	Employee Number	Gross Earnings ($)	YTD Earnings ($)	Social Security ($)	Medicare ($)	FUTA ($)	SUTA ($)
7.	25	2,950.45	14,752.25	**182.93**	**42.78**	**0**	**0**
8.	46	3,040.91	6,081.82				
9.	30	5,092.84	25,464.20	**315.76**	**73.85**	**0**	**0**
10.	12	3,541.92	17,709.60				
11.	47	3,809.55	3,809.55	**236.19**	**55.24**	**30.48**	**205.72**
12.			Totals				

13. 2,286.04
15. 54.81

Chapter 18, Part 2, Exercise 4

17. 0
19. 0

Chapter 18, Part 4, Exercise 1

Answers are in bold.

Employee Name <u>Kenneth Lowden</u> Employee Number <u>#103</u> Year <u>2003</u>

Pay Period	Pay Period Ending	Gross Earnings ($)	Year-to-Date Earnings ($)	Deductions ($)				Total Deductions ($)	Net Pay ($)
				Federal Income	Social Security	Medicare	Insurance Premiums		
1	1/5	1,576.92	1,576.92	110.00	97.77	22.87	65.00	295.64	1,281.28
2	1/12								
3	1/19	**1,576.92**	**4,730.76**	**110.00**	**97.77**	**22.87**	**65.00**	**295.64**	**1,281.28**
4	1/26								
5	2/6	**1,576.92**	**7,884.60**	**110.00**	**97.77**	**22.87**	**65.00**	**295.64**	**1,281.28**
6	2/2								
7	2/9	**1,576.92**	**11,038.44**	**110.00**	**97.77**	**22.87**	**65.00**	**295.64**	**1,281.28**
8	2/16								
9	2/23	**1,576.92**	**14,192.28**	**110.00**	**97.77**	**22.87**	**65.00**	**295.64**	**1,281.28**
10	3/2								
11	3/9	**1,576.92**	**17,346.12**	**110.00**	**97.77**	**22.87**	**65.00**	**295.64**	**1,281.28**
12	3/16								
13	3/23	**1,576.92**	**20,499.96**	**110.00**	**97.77**	**22.87**	**65.00**	**295.64**	**1,281.28**
14	3/30								
15			First quarter totals	**$1,540.00**	**$1,368.78**	**$320.18**	**$910.00**	**$4,138.96**	**$17,937.92**

17. $2,737.56
19. $176.62

Chapter 18, Part 4, Exercise 2

17,556	71,544	97,850	30,393	41,987	46,987
72,341	75,250	48,500	60,363	66,979	25,122
23,390	74,830	34,750	10,585	55,979	60,655
13,647	15,604	69,965	30,252	66,878	70,074
75,985	57,400	57,355	30,282	77,797	22,998
13,524	16,500	94,229	20,939	88,789	99,000
92,093	24,700	69,899	30,696	99,898	60,880
76,335	76,180	45,075	50,828	66,884	10,932
90,549	40,309	54,990	60,528	17,877	11,189
53,875	53,311	34,558	50,639	99,987	33,987
1. 529,295	3. 505,628	5. 607,171	7. 375,505	9. 683,055	11. 441,824
73,450	82,000	28,900	31,100	82,349	96,213
24,995	85,013	29,100	72,700	86,215	28,500
41,995	28,064	52,800	93,700	58,156	28,435
27,229	39,614	22,300	32,100	18,647	36,163
30,471	30,735	28,500	93,100	81,535	39,452
76,999	37,023	12,500	39,100	82,451	28,432
37,777	38,013	26,600	38,100	51,460	61,615
67,659	93,053	22,200	28,500	57,545	28,781
78,695	96,023	28,900	23,500	56,245	30,485
73,000	13,011	25,000	16,492	86,100	26,983
13. 532,270	15. 542,549	17. 276,800	19. 468,392	21. 660,703	23. 405,059

Chapter 18, Terminology Review

Answers will vary.

Chapter 18, Review Exercises, Exercise 1

Answers are in bold.

	Employee	Status and W.A.	Earnings ($)	YTD Earnings ($)	Federal Income Tax ($)	Social Security ($)	Medicare ($)	FUTA ($)	SUTA ($)
1.	G. Mauldin	M-1	2,090.41	6,271.23	**118.00**	**129.61**	**30.31**	**16.72**	**112.88**
2.	J. Mauldin	M-1	5,060.10	15,180.30					
3.	J. Stanton	S-1	680.45	2,041.35	**22.00**	**42.19**	**9.87**	**5.44**	**36.74**
4.				Totals					

5. **$1,471.86**

Chapter 18, Review Exercises, Exercise 2

Answers are in bold.

	Amy Clarendon Month	Earnings ($)	YTD Earnings ($)	FUTA ($)	Rose Rodriguez Month	Earnings ($)	YTD Earnings ($)	FUTA ($)
1.	January	**1,500**	**1,500**	**12**	January	**1,990**	**1,990**	**15.92**
2.	February				February			
3.	March	**1,500**	**4,500**	**12**	March	**1,990**	**5,970**	**15.92**
4.	April				April			
5.	May	**1,500**	**7,500**	**8**	May	**1,990**	**9,950**	**0**
6.	June				June			
7.	July	**1,500**	**10,500**	**0**	July	**1,990**	**13,930**	**0**
8.	August				August			
9.	September	**1,500**	**13,500**	**0**	September	**1,990**	**17,910**	**0**
10.	October				October			
11.	November	**1,500**	**16,500**	**0**	November	**1,990**	**21,890**	**0**
12.	December				December			

Answers are in bold.

FUTA Worksheet

	First Quarter Month	FUTA ($)	Second Quarter Month (Amount Carried Over:)	FUTA ($)	Third Quarter Month (Amount Carried Over:)	FUTA ($)	Fourth Quarter Month (Amount Carried Over:)	FUTA ($)
13.	January	**27.92**	April	**20.24**	July	**0**	October	**0**
14.	February		May		August		November	
15.	March	**27.92**	June	**0**	September	**0**	December	**0**
16.	Total:		Total:		Total:		Total:	**0**

17. **Second quarter**

Chapter 18, Review Exercises, Exercise 3

19. **$121.50, $28.42**

Chapter 19, Part 2, Exercise 1

Answers are in bold.

	List Price ($)	Trade Discount (%)	Trade Discount Amount ($)	Net Price ($)
1.	10,700	2	**214.00**	**10,486.00**
2.	9,870	12		
3.	4,002	5.5	**220.11**	**3,781.89**
4.	65,000	3		
5.	125,000	6.25	**7,812.50**	**117,187.50**

Chapter 19, Part 2, Exercise 2

Answers are in bold.

	List Price ($)	Trade Discount (%)	Trade Discount Amount ($)	Net Price ($)
6.		3	97	
7.	55,000	**2.73**	1,500	**53,500.00**
8.	9,560	9.5		
9.	**3,333.33**	6	200	**3,133.33**
10.	12,000		450	

Chapter 19, Part 2, Exercise 3

Answers are in bold.

	List Price ($)	Trade Discount Series (%)	Net Decimal Equivalent	Net Price ($)
11.	200	7/5/2	.86583	173.17
12.	449	6/2/1		
13.	399	10/5	.855	341.15
14.	1,590	10/9/8		
15.	875	10/8/8	.76176	666.54

Chapter 19, Part 4, Exercise 1

Answers are in bold.

	Quantity	Description	Suggested List Price per Unit ($)	Net Price per Unit ($)	Total Amount ($)
1.	10 boxes	No. 2 yellow pencils	**25.00**	**12.60**	**126.00**
2.	5 boxes	Ruled notebook paper			
3.	2 boxes	College-ruled notebook paper	**36.00**	**18.14**	**36.28**
4.	5 boxes	Stick pens, black			
5.	10 boxes	Stick pens, blue	**5.90**	**2.97**	**29.70**
6.	6 boxes	One-inch plastic binders, assorted colors			
7.	12 boxes	Two-inch notebooks, assorted colors	**139.75**	**70.43**	**845.16**
8.	15 boxes	Computer/copy paper			
9.	4 boxes	Spiral-bound composition books	**259.00**	**130.54**	**522.16**
10.				**Total**	

Chapter 19, Part 4, Exercise 2

55,756	45,536	90,001	15,000	91,400	16,987
78,442	31,902	40,002	60,400	68,420	23,122
95,671	44,320	30,003	10,013	55,650	60,355
34,577	90,687	60,006	21,000	66,140	70,044
34,994	90,004	50,001	30,400	77,703	22,995
66,524	25,590	30,009	20,025	18,689	19,000
91,871	25,990	60,009	26,000	92,599	62,880
51,235	97,450	40,005	50,270	66,384	10,332
33,969	41,424	55,900	60,028	17,246	11,149
11,170	55,656	34,006	50,290	99,375	33,985
1. 554,209	3. 548,559	5. 489,942	7. 343,426	9. 653,606	11. 330,849
13,450	96,000	18,900	16,109	52,349	96,213
20,995	30,013	62,100	26,708	66,115	21,500
41,005	38,000	55,300	34,700	54,176	20,835
27,221	99,014	72,340	32,450	11,648	35,263
20,759	38,045	98,505	95,156	91,535	79,472
63,999	27,423	61,500	49,155	38,451	88,433
37,477	28,114	77,600	66,100	31,888	91,255
20,655	12,053	27,800	88,670	17,545	28,721
15,695	92,024	78,990	63,568	49,245	30,715
22,000	10,311	35,001	16,469	84,900	26,563
13. 283,256	15. 470,997	17. 588,036	19. 489,085	21. 497,852	23. 518,970

Chapter 19, Terminology Review

1. list price
3. net price
5. trade discount series
7. pattern of distribution of goods
9. trade discount amount

Chapter 19, Review Exercises, Exercise 1

Answers are in bold.

	List Price ($)	Trade Discount (%)	Trade Discount Amount ($)
1.	35.95	16	**5.75**
2.	79.59	22	
3.	3,457.49	35	**1,210.12**
4.	339.45	12	
5.	65.72	8	**5.26**

Chapter 19, Review Exercises, Exercise 2

Answers are in bold.

	List Price ($)	Trade Discount (%)	Net Price ($)
6.	698.00	26	
7.	4,529.90	25	**3,397.43**
8.	53.67	29	
9.	195.00	12	**171.60**
10.	0.25	15	

Chapter 19, Review Exercises, Exercise 3

Answers are in bold.

	List Price ($)	Trade Discount Series (%)	Net Price ($)
11.	54.00	15/10/10	**37.18**
12.	39.95	25/20/5	
13.	2.59	35/10/2	**1.48**
14.	10.59	24/10/10	
15.	33.99	10/9/8	**25.61**

Chapter 19, Review Exercises, Exercise 4

Answers are in bold.

	Trade Discount Series (%)	Net Decimal Equivalent
16.	5/4/4	
17.	10/7/5	**.79515**
18.	15/20/9	
19.	10/5/5	**.81225**
20.	5/2	

Chapter 19, Review Exercises, Exercise 5

Answers are in bold.

	List Price ($)	Trade Discount Series (%)	Net Decimal Equivalent	Net Price ($)
21.	5.95	5/3/2	**.90307**	**5.37**
22.	16.57	10/8/4		
23.	0.29	15/20/10	**.612**	**.18**
24.	312.11	25/10/5		
25.	15.43	20/10/3	**.6984**	**10.78**

Chapter 19, Review Exercises, Exercise 6

Answers are in bold.

	List Price ($)	Trade Discount Series (%)	Net Discount Equivalent	Complement of Net Discount Equivalent	Trade Discount Amount ($)
26.	1,300	12/5/3			
27.	6,950	10/8/5	**.7866**	**.2134**	**1,483.13**
28.	3,004	9/8/4			
29.	2,559	12/10/8	**.72864**	**.27136**	**694.41**
30.	10,000	10/9/5			

Chapter 19, Review Exercises, Exercise 7

1. $1,225
3. $3,963.47
5. $1,023.84, $556.16
7. $3,333.33
9. $49.34

Chapter 20, Part 2, Exercise 1

1. December 20; January 9
3. April 10; April 30
5. October 20, October 25, October 30; November 9

Chapter 20, Part 2, Exercise 2

7. August 11, August 21; .98; $736.23
9. April 20; .97; $75.17

Chapter 20, Part 2, Exercise 3

11. January 30; .98; $676.33
13. April 25, April 30; .99; $2,485.40
15. April 30; .97; $1,285.43

Chapter 20, Part 2, Exercise 4

17. 617.35
19. 887.76

Chapter 20, Part 4, Exercise 1

1. June 20, June 30; $7.00; $693.00
3. July 30;—;$1,112.00
5. October 10; $13.60; $666.40

Chapter 20, Part 4, Exercise 2

7. May 30, June 4; $353.54
9. April 10; $6,122.49

Chapter 20, Part 4, Exercise 3

1.

A-1 Automotive Suppliers,Inc.   # INVOICE

101 Main St.
Dallas, TX 75000
*   100-555-1234*
Fax: 100-555-1235

SOLD TO:

Gene's Auto Shop

PO Box 67001

San Antonio, TX 76000

INVOICE NUMBER	67008
INVOICE DATE	January 17, 2004
PURCHASE ORDER NO.	65332
TERMS	3/10,2/20,n30
SALES PERSON	S. Brown
SHIPPED VIA	UPS
F.O.B.	Shipping point

SHIPPED TO:

Gene's Auto Shop

1200 N. Rio Grande

San Antonio, TX 76000

QTY	DESCRIPTION	PRICE	AMOUNT
12	Part #36905	59.29	711.48
20	Part #20001	169.25	3385.00
10	Part #39607	65.05	650.50
5	Part # 37991	112.72	563.60
	Prices reflect terms of 20/10/10.		
	THANK YOU FOR YOUR BUSINESS!		

	SUBTOTAL	5310.58
	TAX	0.00
	FREIGHT	125.00
		5435.58
	TOTAL DUE	

FIGURE 20.13

3. $1,530.61, $2,035.53

Chapter 20, Part 4, Exercise 4

1. 4,713,322	9. 2,779,322	17. 2,713,800
3. 5,303,194	11. 5,410,978	19. 8,709,390
5. 5,062,713	13. 5,358,358	21. 6,747,703
7. 5,770,000	15. 8,314,260	23. 4,569,829

Chapter 20, Terminology Review

1. partial payment
3. cash flow
5. FOB shipping point
7. net amount
9. FOB destination
11. cash discount period

Chapter 20, Review Exercises, Exercise 1

Answers are in bold.

	Date of Invoice	Terms	Last Day of Discount Period(s)	Last Day to Pay Invoice
1.	March 22	3/15,n30	**April 6**	**April 21**
2.	June 26	2/10,1/15,n30		
3.	April 12	3/30,1/45,n90	**May 12, May 27**	**July 11**
4.	August 25	1/10,2/20EOM,n30EOM		
5.	February 20, 2004 (leap year)	2/10,n30	**March 1**	**March 21**

Chapter 20, Review Exercises, Exercise 2

Answers are in bold.

	Invoice Date	Invoice Amount ($)	Terms	Last Day of Discount Period(s)	Complement of Cash Discount Rate	Net Amount($)
6.	March 22	768.90	2/10,n30			
7.	July 20	1,102.91	2/10,1/20,n30	**July 30, August 9**	**.98**	**1,080.85**
8.	June 30	139.20	1/10EOM,n30EOM			
9.	March 30	82.56	2/10ROG,n30ROG (goods received March 15)	**April 25**	**.98**	**80.91**
10.	September 21	69.25	1/20ROG,n30ROG (goods received September 19)			

Chapter 20, Review Exercises, Exercise 3

Answers are in bold.

	Invoice Amount ($)	Invoice Date	Terms	Date Paid	Last Day of Discount Period(s)	Complement of Cash Discount Rate to Be Used	Net Amount ($)
11.	12,080.56	March 10	2/10,1/20,n30	March 25	**March 20, March 30**	**.99**	**11,959.75**
12.	16,895.90	March 20	2/10EOM,n30EOM	April 1			
13.	10,168.59	March 5	3/10,n30	March 9	**March 15**	**.97**	**9,863.53**
14.	15,670.98	April 2	3/10EOM,n30EOM	May 1			
15.	21,658.79	April 10	2/15EOM,n30EOM	May 14	**May 15**	**.98**	**21,225.61**

Chapter 20, Review Exercises, Exercise 4

Answers are in bold.

	Invoice Date	Terms	Partial Payment ($)	Amount to Credit Account ($)
16.	August 5	2/10,n30	55,000	
17.	August 30	2/10EOM	13,600	**13,877.55**
18.	June 22	3/10EOM	7,900	
19.	June 5	3/10ROG (goods received June 10)	21,000	**21,649.48**
20.	September 20	4/10,3/15,n30	5,000	

Chapter 20, Review Exercises, Exercise 5

21. $622.68
23. $842.42, February 7, March 4, $826.41
25. $773.20, $921.72

Chapter 21, Part 2, Exercise 1

Answers are in bold.

	Cost ($)	Markup Rate Based on Cost (%)	Selling Price ($)
1.	35	30	**84.50**
2.	79	25	
3.	220	40	**308.00**
4.	105	60	

Chapter 21, Part 2, Exercise 2

Answers are in bold.

	Cost ($)	Markup Rate Based on Cost (%)	Markup ($)	Selling Price ($)
5.	1.59	25	**.40**	**1.99**
6.	25.99	30		
7.	22.50	**44.44**	10.00	**32.50**
8.		15	22.00	
9.	30.00	**23.33**	7.00	**37.00**
10.		75	1,200.00	

Chapter 21, Part 2, Exercise 3

Answers are in bold.

	Cost ($)	Markup Rate Based on Selling Price (%)	Selling Price ($)
11.	399	15	**469.41**
12.	139	40	
13.	1,200	**25**	1,599
14.	769		1,200
15.	**71.25**	25	95
16.		35	1,096

Chapter 21, Part 2, Exercise 4

Answers are in bold.

	Markup Rate Based on Cost (%)	Markup Rate Based on Selling Price (%)
17.	35	**25.93**
18.	25	
19.	18	**15.25**
20.	30	
21.	75	**42.86**

Chapter 21, Part 2, Exercise 5

Answers are in bold.

	Markup Rate Based on Selling Price (%)	Markup Rate Based on Cost (%)
22.	29	
23.	25	**33.33**
24.	50	
25.	40	**66.67**

Chapter 21, Part 4, Exercise 1

537,556	476,544	677,850	130,765
258,341	575,350	545,500	260,564
226,890	267,800	534,650	210,276
513,657	457,600	469,995	230,755
265,987	657,400	757,359	430,586
583,524	569,500	634,229	420,003
491,093	464,300	567,899	330,005
576,835	456,100	745,775	150,006
490,569	540,300	454,900	160,005
245,870	453,300	434,556	450,004
1. 4,190,322	3. 4,918,194	5. 5,822,713	7. 2,772,969

121,400	956,987	943,450	916,000
564,420	700,122	869,995	737,013
455,320	350,455	741,995	838,064
166,150	477,004	527,229	539,014
427,700	500,999	630,759	630,045
383,689	759,000	860,999	337,023
499,599	965,880	937,577	618,013
356,884	610,432	820,659	562,053
517,656	511,119	945,695	197,024
599,374	833,980	720,000	522,011
9. 4,092,192	11. 6,665,978	13. 7,998,358	15. 5,896,260

418,900	432,100	398,331	300,213
642,100	142,700	920,215	200,500
130,800	433,700	320,156	120,435
800,300	120,100	901,647	715,163
121,500	142,100	312,535	971,452
421,500	142,100	632,451	288,432
200,600	153,100	531,460	821,255
421,200	123,500	477,545	822,721
214,900	321,500	846,245	330,115
142,000	301,490	504,100	736,543

17. 3,513,800 19. 2,312,390 21. 5,844,685 23. 5,306,829

Chapter 21, Terminology Review

1. markup
3. cost
5. selling price

Chapter 21, Review Exercises, Exercise 1

Answers are in bold.

	Cost ($)	Markup ($)	Selling Price ($)
1.	35.00	10.00	**45.00**
2.	165.00	38.00	
3.	129.00	**21.00**	150.00
4.	157.00		187.00
5.	**101.00**	59.00	160.00
6.		75.00	210.00

Chapter 21, Review Exercises, Exercise 2

Answers are in bold.

	Item	Cost per Pound ($)	Markup ($)	Selling Price ($)
7.	Fudge	3.00	**1.80**	**4.80**
8.	Pralines	3.25		
9.	Caramels	2.75	**1.65**	**4.40**
10.	Pecan clusters	3.50		
11.	Almond bark	3.10	**1.86**	**4.96**
12.	Jelly beans	2.19		

Chapter 21, Review Exercises, Exercise 3

Answers are in bold.

	Item	Cost ($)	Markup Rate Based on Selling Price (%)	Selling Price ($)
13.	Tie-dye T-shirt, adult size	1.50	**85**	9.95
14.	Tie-dye dresses, adult size	2.50		14.95
15.	Tie-dye T-shirt, child size	1.00	**83**	5.95

Chapter 21, Review Exercises, Exercise 4

Answers are in bold.

	Selling Price ($)	Markup Rate Based on Selling Price (%)	Cost ($)
16.	39.95	40	
17.	152.39	35	**99.05**
18.	19.95	50	

Chapter 21, Review Exercises, Exercise 5

Answers are in bold.

	Cost ($)	Markup Rate Based on Selling Price (%)	Selling Price ($)
19.	55.00	40	**91.67**
20.	5.95	60	

Chapter 21, Review Exercises, Exercise 6

Answers are in bold.

	Cost ($)	Markup Rate Based on Cost (%)	Selling Price ($)
21.	29.00	120	**63.80**
22.	35.00	65	

Chapter 21, Review Exercises, Exercise 7

23. $222.60
25. $1,250.98

Chapter 22, Part 2, Exercise 1

	Selling Price ($)	Markdown Rate (%)	Markdown ($)	Sale Price ($)
1.	45.59	15	6.84	38.75
2.	1,223.50	5		
3.	69.95	25	17.49	52.46
4.	129.67	20		
5.	101.50	10	10.15	91.35

Chapter 22, Part 2, Exercise 2

	Selling Price ($)	Markdown Rate (%)	Sale Price ($)
6.	5,923.60	12	
7.	7,500.25	15	6375.21
8.	16,780.22	20	
9.	1,567.90	5	1489.51
10.	235.12	18	

Chapter 22, Part 2, Exercise 3

	Selling Price ($)	Sale Price ($)	Markdown Rate (%)
11.	59.95	56.59	5.60
12.	3.19	2.69	
13.	39.95	35.00	12.39
14.	299.59	259.99	
15.	679.00	655.99	3.39

Chapter 22, Part 2, Exercise 4

	Cost ($)	First Markup (%)	Selling Price ($)	First Markdown (%)	Sale Price ($)	Second Markup (%)	New Selling Price ($)
16.	890	30		15		10	
17.	1,285	50	1,927.50	30	1,349.25	20	1,619.10
18.	500	150		25		15	
19.	0.39	200	1.17	50	0.59	15	0.67
20.	229.75	75		33		18	

Chapter 22, Part 2, Exercise 5

	Cost per Item	Quantity	Total Cost ($)	Markup (%)	Total Selling Price ($)	Spoilage Rate (%)	Quantity Expected to Sell	Selling Price per Item
21.	$1.19/lb	25 lb	29.75	60	47.60	20	20 lb	$2.38/lb
22.	$.45/lb	30 lb		25		10		
23.	$.15/lb	112 lb	16.80	15	19.32	5	106.4 lb	$.18/lb
24.	$2.99 each	50		35		12		
25.	$1.59 each	25	39.75	40	55.65	8	23	$2.42 each

Chapter 22, Part 4, Exercise 1

137,556	376,544	177,850	130,000	541,400	456,987
278,341	375,350	145,500	260,000	566,420	420,122
223,890	274,800	134,650	210,000	455,850	360,455
113,657	115,600	369,995	230,000	466,150	470,004
275,987	197,400	257,359	430,000	477,700	522,999
283,524	219,500	234,229	420,000	388,689	459,000
291,093	224,300	267,899	330,000	399,599	565,880
176,835	276,100	345,775	150,000	366,884	510,432
190,569	140,300	354,900	160,000	517,256	411,119
253,870	153,300	134,556	450,000	499,374	533,980
1. 2,225,322	3. 2,353,194	5. 2,422,713	7. 2,770,000	9. 4,679,322	11. 4,710,978
643,450	716,000	588,900	836,100	722,349	926,213
269,995	537,013	669,100	776,700	566,215	823,500
441,995	638,064	855,800	793,700	554,156	820,435
527,229	539,014	872,300	632,100	711,647	735,163
430,759	530,045	798,500	695,100	721,535	979,452
560,999	727,023	811,500	749,100	832,451	988,432
637,577	628,013	776,600	758,100	831,460	861,255
420,659	192,053	827,200	788,500	777,545	825,721
545,695	597,024	778,900	563,500	646,245	730,115
220,000	510,011	735,000	716,490	584,100	726,543
13. 4,698,358	15. 5,614,260	17. 17,072,444	19. 16,731,346	21. 16,344,419	23. 19,445,349

Chapter 22, Terminology Review

1. Series of markups/markdowns
3. Markdown rate
5. Sale price
7. Seasonal goods

Chapter 22, Review Exercises, Exercise 1

	Item	Selling Price ($)	Sale Price ($)
1.	Wash cloth	2.99	2.24
2.	Hand towel	6.99	
3.	Bath towel	9.99	7.49
4.	Bath sheet	15.99	
5.	Contour bath rug	13.99	10.49
6.	Lid cover	7.99	
7.	Rectangular bath rug	20.99	15.74
8.	Percale sheets, twin	29.99	
9.	Percale sheets, double	39.99	29.99
10.	Percale sheets, queen	49.99	
11.	Percale sheets, king	59.99	44.99
12.	Comforter, king	269.59	
13.	Bed ruffle, king	35.99	26.99
14.	Mattress pad, queen	35.98	
15.	Mattress pad, king	39.98	29.99

Chapter 22, Review Exercises, Exercise 2

	Selling Price ($)	Sale Price ($)	Markdown ($)	Markdown Rate (%)
16.	1,200	999	201.00	
17.	789	720	69.00	8.75
18.	159.98	99.98	60.00	
19.	2,999.95	2,759.95	240.00	8
20.	560.94	498.94	62.00	

Chapter 22, Review Exercises, Exercise 3

21. $45 - 20 \boxed{\%}$ discount $= \$36.00$; $\$36.00 - 10\%$ discount $= \boxed{\%} \$32.40$

23. $\$1,943 + 120 \boxed{\%}$ markup $= \$4,274.60$; 50 trees $- 5 \boxed{\%}$ unsold $= 47.50$ trees; Total Selling Price $\$4,274.60 \div$ Quantity Expected to Sell $= 47$ trees* $\$90.95$ per tree

   *If the quantity of trees expected to sell is rounded down to 47 (drop the half tree as unrealistic), the selling price for each tree is $90.95.

25. $\$0.75 \times 4 = \$3.00 + \$3.50 = \$6.50$; $\$6.50 + 20 \boxed{\%} \times \$6.50 = \$7.80$; $\$7.80 \div 4 = \$1.95$ each

Chapter 23, Part 2, Exercise 1

Answers are in bold.

	Asset	Cost ($)	Salvage Value ($)	Estimated Useful Life	Annual Depreciation ($)
1.	Building	375,000	25,000	30 years	**11,666.67**
2.	Furniture	80,000	15,000	15 years	
3.	Computer network	28,000	1,000	3 years	**9,000.00**
4.	SUV	51,000	5,500	5 years	
5.	Van	35,000	5,500	5 years	**5,900.00**

Chapter 23, Part 2, Exercise 2

Answers are in bold.

Asset Tractor Cost $85,000 Life 8 Years Salvage Value $20,000

	Year	Depreciation ($)	Accumulated Depreciation ($)	End-of-Year Book Value ($)
6.	1	8,125		
7.	2	8,125	16,250	68,750
8.	3	8,125		
9.	4	8,125	32,500	52,500
10.	5	8,125		
11.	6	8,125	48,750	36,250
12.	7	8,125		
13.	8	8,125	65,000	20,000

Chapter 23, Part 2, Exercise 3

15. $3,840

Answers are in bold. For all on this page.

Asset #322 Cost $32,000 Estimated Unit Production 600,000 Salvage Value $0 Depreciation per Unit _____

	Year	Units Produced	Depreciation ($)	Accumulated Depreciation ($)	End-of-Year Book Value ($)
16.	1	72,000			
17.	2	75,000	4,000	7,840	24,160
18.	3	67,500			
19.	4	75,250	4,013.33	15,453.33	16,546.67
20.	5	72,300			
21.	6	78,250	4,173.33	23,482.66	8,517.34
22.	7	82,300			
23.	8	77,400	4,128	31,999.99	0.01 changed to 0*

*Note: Slight difference due to rounding. Adjust one year of depreciation by $0.01 to make the end-of-year (EOY) book value equal to 0. For example, change the year 7 depreciation, $4,389.33, to $4,389.34. The EOY book value will then equal 0.

Chapter 23, Part 2, Exercise 4

Asset #500 Cost $15,590 Life 6 Years Salvage Value $300

	Year	Depreciation ($)	Accumulated Depreciation ($)	End-of-Year Book Value ($)
24.	1			
25.	2	3,640.48	8,009.05	7,280.95
26.	3			
27.	4	2,184.29	13,105.72	2,184.28
28.	5			
29.	6	728.10	15,290.01	0.01 changed to 0*

*Note: Slight difference due to rounding. Adjust depreciation for year 6 to $728.09 so that EOY book value will equal 0.

Chapter 23, Part 2, Exercise 5

Asset #230 Cost $2,000 Life 5 Years Salvage Value $100 Rate Straight Line

	Year	Depreciation ($)	Accumulated Depreciation ($)	End-of-Year Book Value ($)
30.	1			
31.	2	320	720	1,280
32.	3			
33.	4	204.80	1,180.80	819.20
34.	5			

Asset #560 Cost $5,150 Life 3 Years Salvage Value $500 Rate Double Declining

	Year	Depreciation ($)	Accumulated Depreciation ($)	End-of-Year Book Value ($)
35.	1	3,433.33	3,433.33	1,716.67
36.	2			
37.	3	72.22*	4,650.00	500.00

*Note: Depreciation is adjusted because EOY book value may not fall below the amount of the salvage value.

Asset #340 Cost $3,755 Life 3 Years Salvage Value $800 Rate 150%

	Year	Depreciation ($)	Accumulated Depreciation ($)	End-of-Year Book Value ($)
38.	1			
39.	2	938.75	2,816.25	938.75
40.	3			

Chapter 23, Part 2, Exercise 6

Answers are in bold. For all on this page.

Asset <u>Office Machines</u> Cost <u>$16,000</u> Class <u>5-Year</u>

	Year	Rate (%)	Depreciation ($)	Accumulated Depreciation ($)	End-of-Year Book Value ($)
41.	1	20	3,200	3,200	12,800
42.	2				
43.	3	19.2	3,072	11,392	4,608
44.	4				
45.	5	11.52	1,843.20	15,078.40	921.60
46.	6				

Chapter 23, Part 2, Exercise 7

47. $200
49. $750

Chapter 23, Part 4, Exercise 1

Asset <u>Bookshelves</u> Cost <u>$2,500</u> Life <u>7 Years</u> Salvage Value <u>$100</u>

	Year	Depreciation ($)	Accumulated Depreciation ($)	End-of-Year Book Value ($)
1.	1	342.86	342.86	2,157.14
2.	2			
3.	3	342.86	1,028.58	1,371.42
4.	4			
5.	5	342.86	1,714.30	785.70
6.	6			
7.	7	342.86	2,400.02	99.98 changed to 100*

*Note: Adjust year 7 depreciation to $342.88, so that EOY book value will equal $100.00.

Year	Annual Depreciation ($)	Accumulated Depreciation ($)	Book Value ($)	
1				8.
2	560	1,260	940	9.
3				10.
4	280	1,960	240	11.
5				12.

Asset <u>#200</u> Cost <u>$150,000</u> Estimated Hours of Production <u>15,000</u> Salvage Value <u>$500</u>

	Year	Hours of Use	Depreciation ($)	Accumulated Depreciation ($)	End-of-Year Book Value ($)
13.	1	3,000	29,900	29,900	120,100
14.	2	2,900			
15.	3	3,200	31,893.33	88,703.33	61,296.67
16.	4	5,500			

Answers are in bold.

Asset #119 Cost $7,000 Salvage Value $300 Declining-Balance Rate 0.25

	Year	Rate	Depreciation ($)	Accumulated Depreciation ($)	End-of-Year Book Value ($)
17.	1	.25	1,750	1,750	5,250
18.	2				
19.	3	.25	984.38	4,046.88	2,953.12
20.	4				

Chapter 23, Part 4, Exercise 2

452.556	4.76544	4.70050	−5132.12
−89.6321	7.75350	4.45500	76450.3
23.1321	−12.8100	7.92050	−100.341
13.0057	48.6300	8.69995	900.437
14.0987	390.400	3.50059	3500.79
5002.24	−20.5005	−9.34229	2071.00
9.81093	75.3006	5.00316	3001.00
185.835	6.06100	3.40075	50009.1
−84.3269	130.300	−1.54900	60.7939
43.1170	200.300	2.30056	500.671
1. 5,569.83643	3. 830.20004	5. 29.08972	7. 131,261.6309

4,158.61	−300.987	61.3451	176.905
66,429.1	720.002	20.2995	431.813
29,850.8	−800.455	40.1395	538.019
66,340.9	170.514	20.7249	−200.014
−77,708.1	922.990	30.0755	930.175
−88,689.6	459.968	80.0999	827.021
31,599.9	266.780	37.7577	398.013
66,614.5	910.495	−20.6659	−899.753
17,257.9	841.119	40.5595	697.062
31,374.1	238.480	−20.0946	3610.011
9. 147,228.11	11. 3,428.906	13. 290.2411	15. 6,509.252

Chapter 23, Terminology Review

1. Adjusted
3. Unadjusted basis
5. Section 179 deduction
7. Useful Life
9. Salvage value
11. Straight-line depreciation
13. Sum-of-the-years'-digits depreciatiation method
15. Declining-balance depreciation method
17. MACRS
19. Financial statements

Chapter 23, Review Exercises, Exercise 1

1. $8,700, $4,481.82, $49,036.36
3. year 1, $2,937.50; year 2, $2,517.86

5.

Answers are in bold.

Asset Furniture and Appliances Cost $37,000 Class 5-Year

Year	Rate (%)	Depreciation ($)	Accumulated Depreciation ($)	End-of-Year Book Value ($)
1	20	7,400	7,400	29,600
2	32	11,840	19,240	17,760
3	19.2	7,104	26,344	10,656

Chapter 23, Review Exercises, Exercise 2

7. a. $15,238.10
   b. $159,761.91
9. a. $9,600
   b. $165,400

Chapter 23, Review Exercises, Exercise 3

Answers are in bold.

Depreciation Worksheet for $2,000, 5-Year Property

Year	Method	Basis ($)	Rate (%)	Formula Used to Find Rate	Depreciation ($)	Half-Year Depreciation ($)	Check Method to Be Used	
Year 1	200% declining balance	2,000	40	2 + 5	800	**400**	✓	11.
	Straight line	2,000	20	1 + 5	400	200		
Year 2	200% declining balance							12.
	Straight line							
Year 3	200% declining balance	960	40		**384**		✓	13.
	Straight line	960	28.57	1 + 3.5	274.27			
Year 4	200% declining balance							14.
	Straight line							
Year 5	200% declining balance	345.6	40		138.24			15.
	Straight line	345.6	66.67	1 + 1.5	**230.41**	✓		
Year 6	200% declining balance	115.19						16.
	Straight line	115.19						

Chapter 24, Part 2, Exercise 1

1. 2.75/1
3. 1/1
5. 1/4

Chapter 24, Part 2, Exercise 2

7. $x = 312.50$
9. $x = 150$

Chapter 24, Part 2, Exercise 3

11. $x = \$9.92$
13. $x = 216.67$ miles
15. $x = \$816.67$

Chapter 24, Part 4, Exercise 1

347.556	765.544	77,850.7	−5,300.00
758.541	751.350	−45,500.2	6,609.00
263.987	746.800	−34,650.1	4,100.00
113.657	−150.600	−69,995.6	9,300.00
735.987	972.400	−57,359.1	−1,300.00
883.524	199.500	34,229.9	−1,200.00
−991.093	240.300	67,899.1	5,300.00
−706.835	−764.100	45,775.4	1,250.00
−920.569	−403.300	54,900.3	−5,600.00
−563.870	−535.300	34,556.8	9,500.00
1. −79.115	3. 1,822.594	5. 107,707.2	7. 22,659.00

94.1400	7.56987	143.450	16.0036
−86.6420	22.0122	29.9957	63.7013
−75.5850	−16.0455	41.9951	73.8064
76.6150	−1.70004	27.2293	83.9014
−67.7700	322.999	−30.7594	53.0045
98.8689	−2590.00	−60.9992	62.7023
99.9599	2658.80	−37.5771	82.8013
86.6884	−110.432	−20.6594	99.2053
−81.7256	31.1119	45.6951	59.7024
79.9374	4.33980	120.000	61.0011
9. 224.487	11. 328.65523	13. 258.3701	15. 655.8296

Chapter 24, Terminology Review

1. ratios
3. proportion method
5. proportions
7. Base/100 $= x$/Percent

Chapter 24, Review Exercises, Exercise 1

1. 2/1   7. $x = 12$
3. 1.5/2   9. $x = 25$
5. 1/8

Chapter 24, Review Exercises, Exercise 2

11. $750
13. $14.67
15. $18,750

Chapter 24, Review Exercises, Exercise 3

17. $1.53   23. 312.5 acres of corn
19. 1,280 sq ft   25. 172.22 miles
21. $3.34

Chapter 25, Part 2, Exercise 1

1. $15,100

Chapter 25, Part 2, Exercise 2

Answers are in bold.

Date	Item	Quantity	Cost/ Each ($)	Total Cost per Item ($)	
March 10	#210	5,000	1.29	**6,450.00**	3.
March 20	#210	5,250	1.31		4.
March 29	#210	4,500	1.32	**5,940.00**	5.
Totals					6.
		Weighted average		$1.31 (rounded)	7.

Chapter 25, Part 2, Exercise 3

Date of Purchase	Quantity	Cost ($)	Total Cost ($)	
May 15	16	2.25	36	9.
May 30	50	2.27		10.
June 15	50	2.29	114.50	11.
June 29	45	2.30		12.

13. $124.53 [(16 × 2.25) + (39 × 2.27)]
15. $172.20 [(30 × 2.29) + (45 × 2.30)]

Chapter 25, Part 2, Exercise 4

Date of Purchase	Quantity	Cost ($)	Total Cost ($)	
December 10	500	3.20	1,600.00	17.
December 20	520	3.25		18.
January 13	610	3.33	2,031.30	19.
January 22	650	3.30		20.
January 28	650	3.45	2,242.50	21.

23. $6,418.80 [(610 × 3.33) + (650 × 3.30) + (650 × 3.45)]
25. $7,692.80

Chapter 25, Part 2, Exercise 5

27. $2,554.00
29. $1,324

Chapter 25, Part 2, Exercise 6

31. $38,000 ($3,000 + $35,000)
33. $6,000 ($38,000 − $32,000)
35. $24,421.05

Chapter 25, Part 4, Exercise 1

Date	Inventory	Quantity	Unit Cost ($)	Total Cost ($)	
January 1	Beginning inventory	75	10.98	823.50	1.
March 8	Purchases	250	11.20		2.
May 13	Purchases	100	11.98	1,198.00	3.
August 24	Purchases	150	11.90		4.
November 29	Purchases	100	12.19	1,219.00	5.
Total merchandise available for sale					6.

7. Ending inventory $899.75, cost of goods sold $7,000.75
9. Ending inventory $914.25, cost of goods sold $6,911.25

Chapter 25, Part 4, Exercise 2

192.556	3.76544	2.77750	−3000.12
13.6321	2.75350	3.45500	60000.3
23.1001	−74.8100	5.34650	−100.561
−13.1657	15.6300	6.69995	300.437
75.4987	297.400	9.57359	3000.79
1322.24	−19.5005	−1.34229	2001.00
−1.81093	24.3006	5.67899	3008.00
736.835	7.06100	3.45775	50000.1
90.3269	430.300	−8.54900	60.7989
43.0070	536.300	1.34556	500.679
1. 2,508.55057	3. 1,223.20004	5. 28.44355	7. 115,771.4239
4,140.61	−356.987	60.3451	346.905
66,420.9	720.122	20.9995	437.013
55,850.8	−860.455	40.1995	538.064
66,150.9	170.004	20.7229	−939.014
−77,700.1	922.999	30.0759	930.045
−88,689.3	359.968	60.0999	227.023
99,599.9	265.880	30.7577	328.013
66,884.5	910.432	−20.0659	−892.053
17,256.2	511.119	40.5695	697.024
99,374.1	233.980	−20.0986	810.011
9. 309,288.51	11. 2,877.062	13. 263.6055	15. 2,483.031

Chapter 25, Terminology Review

1. merchandise
3. merchandise inventory
5. ending inventory
7. perpetual inventory method
9. weighted-average method
11. lower-of-cost-or-market (LCM) inventory method
13. Last in, first out

Chapter 25, Review Exercises, Exercise 1

Answers are in bold.

Date	Inventory	Quantity	Unit Cost ($)	Total Cost ($)	
May 1	Beginning inventory	35	2.98	**104.30**	1.
May 8	Purchases	100	3.20		2.
May 13	Purchases	74	1.98	**146.52**	3.
May 24	Purchases	15	3.90		4.
May 28	Purchases	25	2.69	**67.25**	5.

7. $102.35
9. $594.22

Chapter 25, Review Exercises, Exercise 3

Answers are in bold.

Inventory Number	Quantity on Hand	Unit Cost ($)	Retail Value ($)	Lower of Cost or Market Value ($)	
C56	56	.39	1.25	**21.84**	11.
D759	44	1.50	4.50		12.
C311	27	3.95	8.65	**106.65**	13.
D32	20	6.19	12.90		14.
D12	12	.59	.29	**3.48**	15.

Chapter 25, Review Exercises, Exercise 4

17. Ending inventory $98.12, cost of goods sold $348.88
19. FIFO

Chapter 26, Part 2, Exercise 1

Answers are in bold.

	Department	Sales ($)	Overhead Based on Sales ($)	Square Feet	Overhead Based on Square Feet ($)
1.	230	15,000	**2,727.27**	12,500	**2,840.91**
2.	231	22,000		16,200	
3.	233	7,000	**1,272.73**	6,500	**1,477.27**
4.	Totals				

Chapter 26, Part 2, Exercise 2

Answers are in bold.

	Department	Stated Rate (%)	Amount of Overhead ($)
5.	A	29	**20,880**
6.	B	37	
7.	C	18	**12,960**
8.	D	16	
9.	Totals	**100**	**72,000**

Chapter 26, Part 2, Exercise 3

Answers are in bold.

Department	Sales ($)	Departmental Overhead ($)	
212	35,000		10.
213	40,100	**4,365.47**	11.
214	12,500		12.
215	22,000	**2,395.02**	13.
216	19,000		14.
Totals	**128,600**	**13,999.99**	15.

Chapter 26, Part 4, Exercise 1

45.8236	4.76544	7.7775	−6000.12
−90.6321	2.5535	6.455	6900.03
93.1001	−7.461	9.3465	−1075.61
83.1657	1.567	1.69995	3009.37
33.4987	2.9748	4.57359	8000.79
83.9824	−1.95009	−8.34229	2401
48.7693	9.43006	4.67899	3068
1073.68	7.861	6.45775	5002.01
−90.3213	4.373	−8.549	6079.09
43.5629	5.366	3.34556	5006.72
1. 1,324.6293	3. 29.47971	5. 27.44355	7. 32,391.28
1140.61	−756.987	4004.51	200.905
6621.09	760.122	1300.95	100.013
5585.31	−865.455	4009.95	520.064
4115.09	170.403	2072.29	−900.014
−7742.01	922.939	3007.59	180.045
−8868.43	359.962	6009.99	227.128
5159.99	165.88	3005.77	328.997
6662.45	920.432	−2006.59	−100.053
1725.61	513.119	4006.95	623.024
4137.41	233.48	−2009.86	867.711
9. 18,537.12	11. 2,423.895	13. 23,401.55	15. 2,047.82

Chapter 26, Terminology Review

1. allocation of overhead expense
3. false
5. true

Chapter 26, Review Exercises, Exercise 1

Answers are in bold.

Department	Sales ($)	Departmental Overhead ($)	
A	15,000	**2,975.65**	1.
B	24,500		2.
C	18,200	**3,610.46**	3.
D	22,000		4.
E	31,200	**6,189.36**	5.
Totals			6.

Chapter 26, Review Exercises, Exercise 2

Answers are in bold.

Department	Square Feet	Departmental Overhead ($)	
A	39,250	**3,146.04**	7.
B	41,210		8.
C	37,500	**3,005.77**	9.
D	25,900		10.
E	43,280	**3,469.06**	11.
Totals			12.

Chapter 26, Review Exercises, Exercise 3

Answers are in bold.

Department	Rate (%)	Departmental Overhead ($)	
A	22	**2,750.00**	13.
B	24.5		14.
C	18	**2,250.00**	15.
D	12		16.
E	23.5	**2,937.50**	17.
Totals			18.

Chapter 26, Review Exercises, Exercise 4

19. Painting $10,625.91, welding $5,856.98, bending $19,742.61, finishing $8,774.50

ANSWERS TO SELECTED PROBLEMS

635

Chapter 27, Part 2, Exercise 1

Answers are in bold.

Jostens Comparative Balance Sheet December 31, 2002, and December 31, 2003

	Balance Sheet		Amount of Increase or Decrease	Percent of Increase or Decrease	
	2002	2003			
Assets					
Current assets					
Cash	$50,000	$56,000	**$6,000**	**12%**	1.
Accounts receivable	25,000	30,000			2.
Merchandise inventory	30,000	35,000	**5,000**	**16.7**	3.
Total current assets	$105,000	$121,000			4.
Land, buildings, and equipment					
Land	80,000	80,000	**0**	**0**	5.
Buildings	250,000	250,000			6.
Equipment	60,000	50,000	**(10,000)**	**(16.7)**	7.
Total land, buildings, and equipment	390,000	380,000			8.
Total assets	$495,000	$501,000	**$6,000**	**1.2**	9.
Liabilities and owner's equity					
Current liabilities					
Accounts payable	$28,000	$25,000			10.
Total current liabilities	28,000	25,000	**(3,000)**	**(10.7)**	11.
Long-term liabilities					
Note payable	10,000	9,000			12.
Mortgage payable	200,000	190,000	**(10,000)**	**(5)**	13.
Total long-term liabilities	210,000	199,000			14.
Total liabilities	$238,000	$224,000	**($14,000)**	**(5.9)**	15.
Owner's equity					
M. J. Josten, capital	257,000	277,000			16.
Total liabilities and owner's equity	$495,000	$501,000	**$6,000**	**1.2%**	17.

Chapter 27, Part 2, Exercise 2

Jostens Balance Sheet December 31, 2002

Cash	$50,000		18.
Accounts receivable	25,000	**5.1%**	19.
Merchandise inventory	30,000		20.
Total current assets	$105,000	**21.2**	21.
Land	80,000		22.
Buildings	250,000	**50.5**	23.
Equipment	60,000		24.
Total land, buildings, and equipment	390,000	**78.8**	25.
Total assets	$495,000		26.
Accounts payable	$28,000	**5.7%**	27.
Total current liabilities	28,000		28.
Note payable	10,000	**2.0**	29.
Mortgage payable	200,000		30.
Total long-term liabilities	210,000	**42.4**	31.
Total liabilities	$238,000		32.
M. J. Josten, capital	257,000	**51.9**	33.
Total liabilities and owner's equity	$495,000		34.

Chapter 27, Part 2, Exercise 3

Jostens Income Statement Month Ended April 30, 2003

Gross sales	$55,000	102.3%	35.
Less returns	1,250		36.
Net sales	53,750	100.0	37.
Inventory, April 1, 2003	25,000		38.
Purchases	17,000	31.6	39.
Less inventory, April 30, 2003	22,000		40.
Cost of goods sold	20,000	37.2	41.
Gross profit	33,750		42.
Operating expenses	9,000	16.7	43.
Net income	$24,750		44.

Chapter 27, Part 2, Exercise 4

Jostens Comparative Income Statement Months Ending March 31, 2003, and April 30, 2003

	March 31, 2003	April 30, 2003	Amount of Increase or Decrease	Percent of Increase or Decrease	
Gross sales	$57,500	$55,000	($2,500)	(4.3%)	45.
Less returns	2,200	1,250			46.
Net sales	55,300	53,750	(1,550)	(2.8)	47.
Beginning inventory	18,000	25,000			48.
Purchases	24,500	17,000	(7,500)	(30.6)	49.
Ending inventory	17,200	22,000			50.
Cost of goods sold	25,300	20,000	(5,300)	(20.9)	51.
Gross profit	30,000	33,750			52.
Operating expenses	12,000	9,000	(3,000)	(25.0)	53.
Net income	$18,000	$24,750			54.

Chapter 27, Part 4, Exercise 1

347.55	65.544	77.850	51.300	94.140	756.98
758.5	51.35	45	60	−86.64	22.22
237	800	650	100	585	455
57	15	995.6	−930.7	76.61	−170.4
735.9	972.4	−5	5	6	9
8	−1	229.9	451.9	98	25
−9.093	240.3	67	62	99.95	2.658
706	764	775	149	884	432
92	30	900.3	230.7	56	19
63.870	35.300	4,556.8	9,142.9	79.937	43.398
1. 2,996.727	3. 2,972.894	5. 8,292.45	7. 9,322.1	9. 1,892.997	11. 1,594.856
43.45	−516.09	911.55	555.19	29.850	42.300
29.99	13	723.5	78.35	95	77
995	738	197	499	850	186
27.22	9.014	59	18	344.6	−362.7
−3	−43	125.9	312.4	−5	4
60	3	8	−6	280.9	289.9
7.577	628.3	−9.643	255.3	87	50
659	592	772	831	775	150
45	697.2	33	25	944.3	250.7
20.000	610.1	953.872	35.350	4,932.8	9,566.9
13. 1,884.237	15. 2,731.524	17. 3,774.179	19. 2,603.59	21. 8,334.45	23. 10,254.1

Chapter 27, Terminology Review

1. debt ratio
3. gross sales
5. working capital ratio
7. balance sheet
9. horizontal analysis
11. liabilities
13. income statement
15. financial statements

17. vertical analysis of an income statement
19. ratios
21. current liabilities
23. working capital ratio
25. owner's equity
27. inventory turnover ratio
29. gross profit margin ratio

Chapter 27, Review Exercises, Exercise 1

Answers are in bold.

ABC Company Comparative Balance Sheet December 31, 2002, and December 31, 2003

| | Balance Sheet | | Amount of Increase | Percent of Increase | |
	2002	2003	or Decrease	or Decrease	
Assets					
Current assets					
Cash	$150,000	$180,000	**$30,000**	**20%**	1.
Accounts receivable	65,000	75,000			2.
Merchandise inventory	80,000	103,000	**23,000**	**28.8**	3.
Total current assets	$295,000	$358,000			4.
Land, buildings, and equipment					
Land	180,000	185,000	**5,000**	**2.8**	5.
Buildings	440,000	446,000			6.
Equipment	960,000	1,050,000	**90,000**	**9.4**	7.
Total land, buildings, and equipment	1,580,000	1,681,000			8.
Total assets	$1,875,000	$2,039,000	**$164,000**	**8.7%**	9.
Liabilities and owner's equity					
Current liabilities					
Accounts payable	$128,000	$175,000			10.
Total current liabilities	128,000	175,000	**47,000**	**36.7**	11.
Long-term liabilities					
Note payable	90,000	80,000			12.
Mortgage payable	210,000	170,000	**(40,000)**	**(19)**	13.
Total long-term liabilities	$300,000	$250,000			14.
Total liabilities	$428,000	$425,000	**($3,000)**	**(0.7%)**	15.
Owner's equity					
Mark Miller, capital	1,447,000	1,614,000			16.
Total liabilities and owner's equity	$1,875,000	$2,039,000	**$164,000**	**8.7%**	17.

Chapter 27, Review Exercises, Exercise 2

ABC Company Comparative Income Statement Years Ending December 31, 2002, and December 31, 2003

	December 31, 2003	December 31, 2003	Amount of Increase or Decrease	Percent of Increase or Decrease	
Gross sales	$1,187,500	$1,250,000			18.
Less returns	116,200	112,000	**($4,200)**	**(3.6%)**	19.
Net sales	1,071,300	1,138,000			20.
Beginning inventory	138,000	155,200	**17,200**	**12.5**	21.
Purchases	642,100	670,000			22.
Ending inventory	155,200	190,000	**34,800**	**22.4**	23.
Cost of goods sold	624,900	635,200			24.
Gross profit	446,400	502,800	**56,400**	**12.6**	25.
Operating expenses	199,000	187,000			26.
Net income	$247,400	$315,800	**$68,400**	**27.6**	27.

Chapter 27, Review Exercises, Exercise 3

Answers are in bold.

ABC Company Balance Sheet December 31, 2003

Cash	$180,000		28.
Accounts receivable	75,000	3.7%	29.
Merchandise inventory	103,000		30.
Total current assets	$358,000	**17.6**	31.
Land	185,000		32.
Buildings	446,000	**21.9**	33.
Equipment	1,050,000		34.
Total land, buildings, and equipment	$1,681,000	**82.4**	35.
Total assets	$2,039,000		36.
Accounts payable	$175,000	**8.6%**	37.
Total current liabilities	175,000		38.
Note payable	80,000	**3.9**	39.
Mortgage payable	170,000		40.
Total long-term liabilities	$250,000	**12.3**	41.
Total liabilities	$425,000		42.
Mark Miller, capital	1,614,000	**79.2**	43.
Total liabilities and owner's equity	$2,039,000		44.

Chapter 27, Review Exercises, Exercise 4

ABC Company Income Statement Year Ended December 31, 2003

Gross sales	$1,250,000	**109.8%**	45.
Less returns	112,000		46.
Net sales	1,138,000	**100%**	47.
Inventory, December 1, 2003	155,200		48.
Purchases	670,000	**58.9**	49.
Less inventory, December 31, 2003	190,000		50.
Cost of goods sold	635,200	**55.8**	51.
Gross profit	502,800		52.
Operating expenses	187,000	**16.4**	53.
Net income	$315,800		54.

Chapter 27, Review Exercises, Exercise 5

55. 5.7 to 1
57. a. 0.6 to 1, or 1.7 to 1
    b. 0.7 to 1, or 1 to 1.4
    c. 0.2 to 1, or 1 to 5
    d. 0.06 to 1, or 1 to 16.7

Chapter 28, Part 2, Exercise 1

Rate and Time	Rate per Period (%)	Number of Periods	
12% compounded monthly for 3 years	1	36	1.
6% compounded monthly for 2 years			2.
8% compounded quarterly for 2 years	2	8	3.
10% compounded semiannually for 5 years			4.
18% compounded monthly for 2 years	1.5	24	5.

Chapter 28, Part 2, Exercise 2

7. 0.905950
9. 0.065189

Chapter 28, Part 2, Exercise 3

Rate (%)	Compounding Period	Time (Years)	Amount of Investment ($)	Future Value ($)	
7	Annually	10	7,500		10.
5	Semiannually	5	3,000	**3,840.25**	11.
12	Monthly	4	1,500		12.
15	Monthly	2	3,000	**4,042.05**	13.
8	Monthly	6	5,000		14.

Chapter 28, Part 2, Exercise 4

Calculation Needed	Rate and Time	Rate (%)	Number of Periods			
Future value	5% compounded annually for 5 years	5	5	Amount invested: $1,000	Future amount: $1,276.28	15.
Present value	6% compounded semiannually for 3 years	3	6	Amount needed in 3 years: $4,000	Today's value:	16.
Future value of an annuity	8% compounded quarterly for 5 years	2	20	Quarterly savings of $200 will be made	Future value: $4,859.47	17.
Present vlaue of an annuity	7% compounded quarterly for 2 years	1.75	8	Quarterly payments of $120	Present value:	18.
Sinking fund	7% compounded semiannually for 4 years	3.5	8	$40,000 needed in 4 years	Amount to place in the sinking fund: $4,419.04	19.
Amortization	5% compounded monthly for 5 years	5/12	30	Amount of mortage: $75,000	Monthly payment:	20.

Chapter 28, Part 4, Exercise 1

Amortization Schedule

Month	Monthly Payment ($)	Interest ($)	Principal Reduction ($)	Balance ($)	
1	525.99	225.00	300.99	29,699.01	1.
2					2.
3	525.99	220.47	305.52	29,090.24	3.
4					4.
5	525.99	215.87	310.12	28,472.31	5.

Chapter 28, Part 4, Exercise 2

347.556	165.544	77,850.7	5,300.00
758.541	751.350	45,500.2	6,609.00
263.987	746.800	34,650.1	4,100.00
113.657	150.600	69,995.6	9,300.00
735.987	972.400	57,359.1	1,300.00
883.524	199.500	34,229.9	−1,200.00
−991.093	240.300	67,899.1	5,300.00
−706.835	−764.100	45,775.4	12,500.00
−920.569	−403.300	54,900.3	5,600.00
−563.870	−535.300	34,556.8	9,500.00
1. −79.115	3. 1,523.794	5. 522,717.2	7. 58,309
94.1400	756,987	43.450	−516.000
−86.6420	220,122	29.995	−637.013
75.5850	−160,455	41.995	738.064
76.6150	−170,004	27.229	−539.014
−67.7700	322,999	−30.759	−430.045
98.8689	−259,000	−60.999	−727.023
99.9599	265,880	−37.577	628.013
86.6884	−110,432	−20.659	592.053
−81.7256	311,119	−45.695	−697.024
79.9374	433,980	−20.000	−610.011
9. 375.657	11. 1,611,196	13. −73.02	15. −2,198

Chapter 28, Terminology Review

1. compounding period
3. number of periods
5. annuity
7. present value
9. amortization
11. amount of an annuity

Chapter 28, Review Exercises, Exercise 1

1. $518,748.40
3. $33,778.20
5. $917.50

Chapter 28, Review Exercises, Exercise 2

Amortization Schedule

Month	Monthly Payment ($)	Interest ($)	Principal Reduction ($)	Balance ($)	
1	917.50	625.00	292.50	124,707.50	7.
2					8.

Chapter 28, Review Exercises, Exercise 3

9. $542.64

Chapter 28, Review Exercises, Exercise 4

11. First investment value $69,457.50, second investment value $64,613.40
13. $4,844.10 less was earned by the second investment

Chapter 28, Review Exercises, Exercise 5

15. Yes, $39,266.22
17. $1,345.75
19. 30-year loan $484.470, 20-year loan $364,560

Chapter 29, Part 2, Exercises

1. $186.61
3. $1,850
5. $\dfrac{\dfrac{3 \times (3 + 1)}{2}}{\dfrac{18 \times (18 + 1)}{2}} = \dfrac{6}{171} = 0.0351$
7. $19.98
9. $811.20

Chapter 29, Part 4, Exercise 1

911.55	35.544	27.850	91.300	12.140	126.98
258.5	81.35	35	80	−23.64	20.02
437	600	654	147	345	895
67	55	595.6	−900.7	76.56	−670.4
735.2	972.3	−1	9	7	5
3	−2	629.9	400.9	13	35
−5.093	940.3	57	82	19.95	2.653
906	864	774	147	284	832
32	70	112.3	630.7	36	79
63.871	35.306	4,432.8	9,152.9	79.934	43.396
1. 3,409.028	3. 3,651.8	5. 7,317.45	7. 9,840.1	9. 849.944	11. 1,368.649
93.45	−916.09	421.55	91.004	19.850	12.322
20.99	83	756.5	88.35	25	37
900	736	817	799	853	145
27.82	6.014	52	68	444.6	−212.7
−6	−73	345.9	542.4	−1	3
67	8	5	−3	580.9	233.9
1.577	928.3	−9.007	955.3	66	65
259	892	123	731	875	175
35	696.2	33	65	774.3	259.9
24.009	610.8	123.872	15.355	9,232.1	1,500.8
13. 1,422.846	15. 2,971.224	17. 2,668.815	19. 3,352.409	21. 12,869.75	23. 2,219.222

Chapter 29, Terminology Review

1. closed-end loan
2. installment loan
3. installment price
5. amount financed
7. interest refund or rebate

Chapter 29, Review Exercises, Exercise 1

1. $990
3. a. $377.25
   b. $2,892.25
   c. $48.20
5. $45.83

Chapter 30, Part 2, Exercises

1. $3,289.46
3. $11.81
5. $5,031.44

Chapter 30, Part 4, Exercise 1

1235.56	1555.34	2215.07	2541.00
7582.33	7513.34	4554.22	6256.00
1339.87	1218.00	3005.01	1220.00
2254.57	1502.33	6992.24	2123.00
7354.43	1424.00	5115.91	6522.00
4115.24	5325.00	3426.22	6532.00
9913.24	1223.00	5119.91	1532.00
4438.35	1231.00	4574.22	1535.00
9202.24	4034.56	3560.03	1520.00
3344.11	5355.33	3456.01	1330.00
1. 50,779.94	3. 30,381.9	5. 42,018.84	7. 31,111.00
9014.00	7567.00	9889.86	5169.00
8678.90	8761.22	7768.75	9960.13
9981.50	1609.76	8869.50	7389.97
8532.50	5970.04	2728.76	7690.14
9987.00	3227.07	6885.90	4309.76
7796.89	8770.00	6099.60	8860.23
9015.99	2656.97	8977.70	6287.69
6978.84	9764.32	9900.90	9980.53
8178.56	3117.98	4568.87	6979.07
5113.74	9789.80	8890.00	8760.11
9. 83,277.92	11. 61,234.16	13. 74,579.84	15. 75,386.63

Chapter 30, Terminology Review

1. open-end loan
3. unpaid balance method
5. annual percentage rate
7. APR $= 2MI \div P(n + 1)$

Chapter 30, Review Exercises, Exercise 1

1. a. $6,750
   b. 37.50
   c. 13.25%
3. a. 0.0107%
   b. 0.0408%
   c. $31.03
   d. $6.69
5. a. 0.0178%
   b. $5.57
   c. $802.57

Chapter 31, Part 2, Exercise 1

Answers are in bold.

Employee	Type of Insurance	Age	Sex	Amount of Insurance ($)	Annual Premium ($)	Monthly Premium ($)	
J. Jones	Whole	55	M	60,000	**3,082.80**	**256.90**	1.
A. Lawson	20-year paid-up life	60	F	35,000			2.
G. Hajek	Term	28	F	75,000	**528.75**	**44.06**	3.
B. Hoelscher	Variable universal life	46	M	100,000			4.
A. Black	Term	34	F	120,000	**882.00**	**73.50**	5.

Chapter 31, Part 2, Exercise 2

7. $221.83

Chapter 31, Part 2, Exercise 3

Answers are in bold.

	Property	Amount of Insurance ($)	Area Rating	Class	Annual Premium ($)
8.	Building 101	315,000	1	A	
9.	Contents of Building 101	175,000	1	A	**892.50**
10.	Building 102	225,000	2	A	
11.	Contents of Building 102	320,000	2	A	**2,176.00**
12.	Building 103	250,000	2	B	
13.	Contents of Building 103	200,000	2	B	**1,720.00**
14.	Building 104	375,000	1	A	
15.	Contents of Building 104	400,000	1	A	**3,800.00**
16.	Total fire and property insurance premium				

17. $473,913.04
    Procedure:

    $225,000 + $320,000 = $545,000 (insured amount)

    ($415,000 + $275,000) × .8 = $552,000 (80% of actual value)

The insured amount is less than 80% of the actual value, so the insurance company will not pay the full amount of damages:

$$\frac{\$480,000 \times \$545,000}{0.80 \times (\$275,000 + \$415,000)} = \$473,913.04$$

amount of compensation insurance company will pay

Chapter 31, Part 2, Exercise 4

Answers are in bold.

Desired Coverage	Deductible if Applicable ($)	Base Premium ($)	Multiple	Premium ($)
Comprehensive		57	1.4	79.80
Collision	500	91	1.4	127.40
Bodily injury 200/300		112	1.4	156.80
Property damage $100,000		103	1.4	144.20
Medical payment $10,000		72	1.4	100.80
			Total annual premium	$609.00

Chapter 31, Part 4, Exercise 1

9805.60	9774.40	9585.00	4300.00
7834.10	6775.00	6950.00	5600.00
2389.00	5220.00	3459.00	6100.00
1365.70	1560.00	3899.50	3300.00
7598.70	9740.00	1935.90	4300.00
8352.40	1950.00	3462.90	6200.00
9109.00	2430.00	9989.90	5300.00
7683.50	9610.00	4567.50	7500.00
9056.90	8030.00	9190.00	1600.00
5387.00	5330.00	3482.60	9500.00
1. 68,581.90	3. 60,419.40	5. 56,522.30	7. 53,700.00

8414.00	9198.70	9845.00	1860.15
9664.20	2093.20	2976.50	3013.72
9558.50	6045.94	8799.50	3064.56
8661.50	9100.40	2796.90	3014.75
7777.00	2283.90	3075.78	3045.25
6886.89	6500.00	9683.90	2023.46
7995.99	6548.00	9557.70	2013.75
8668.84	1043.95	2082.90	9053.68
9172.56	9511.90	4569.91	9024.54
8993.74	3367.00	8500.00	1011.18
9. 85,793.22	11. 55,692.99	13. 61,888.09	15. 37,125.04

Chapter 31, Terminology Review

1. life insurance
3. insurance policy
5. benefit
7. actuarial tables
9. cash value
11. term life insurance
13. fire and property insurance
15. compensation
17. deductible

Chapter 31, Review Exercises, Exercise 1

Answers will vary.

Chapter 31, Review Exercises, Exercise 2

Answers will vary.

Chapter 32, Part 2, Exercise 1

1. $3,255
3. $7.47
5. $30,384.90
7. First year, $15,000; second year, $28,900

Chapter 32, Part 4, Exercise 1

1305.60	1174.40	3685.00	1900.00
7856.10	6726.00	6937.00	5618.00
2389.16	5220.45	3459.38	6100.17
1265.70	8660.00	1299.50	1600.00
7597.80	9795.00	1945.90	4315.00
3252.40	1950.98	3462.67	6200.14
9134.00	9730.00	3189.90	1200.00
7683.50	9674.00	4551.50	7513.00
9056.35	8030.72	9190.62	1600.15
1617.00	7430.00	6721.34	9560.00
1. 51,157.61	3. 68,391.55	5. 44,442.81	7. 45,606.46
3414.00	2598.70	3145.00	1700.00
9635.20	2027.20	2932.50	3013.00
9558.36	6045.17	8799.41	3064.00
3671.50	9122.40	4296.90	3014.00
7739.00	2283.25	3043.78	3045.00
6886.31	6585.00	9683.45	2023.00
4295.99	6548.12	4657.70	2013.00
8442.84	2343.95	2047.90	9053.00
5672.56	9525.90	4569.50	9024.00
8957.74	3367.95	8551.00	1011.00
9. 68,273.50	11. 50,447.64	13. 51,727.14	15. 36,960.00

Chapter 32, Terminology Review

1. sales tax
3. assessed value
5. corporate income tax

Chapter 32, Review Exercises, Exercise 1

$15.90	txb	
$5.47		
$3.90		
$1.90		
$7.03	txb	
$.57	txb	
$1.25		
$2.90		
$4.50	txb	
$8.79	txb	
$4.39		
$2.70		
$10.90	txb	
$3.46	Tax	1.
	Total	2.

Chapter 32, Review Exercises, Exercise 2

3. $46.80
5. 3.6%

Answers are in bold.

Entity	Rate/$100	Tax ($)	
County	1.90		6.
City	2.75	**2,997.50**	7.
School	5		8.
Road and bridge	.25	**272.50**	9.
College	.9		10.
Total		**$11,772.00**	11.
Tax discount			12.
Amount of taxes paid		**$11,418.84**	13.

Chapter 32, Review Exercises, Exercise 3

Answers are in bold.

Name	Taxable Income ($)	Tax ($)	
Company A	89,000		14.
Company B	59,800	**14,950**	15.
Company C	419,000		16.

Chapter 33, Part 2, Exercise 1

1. LDG
3. 0.2%
5. $52.09

Chapter 33, Part 2, Exercise 2

7. $.51 per common share
9. $.43 per common share

Chapter 33, Part 4, Exercise 1

9005.60	2574.45	3085.00	8700.00
7800.10	6156.00	6907.00	5686.00
2009.16	7520.45	3450.59	8900.79
1200.70	3295.00	1099.59	1698.00
7005.80	9756.00	1905.59	4399.00
3252.00	5750.95	3460.49	6298.49
9004.00	5630.00	3089.99	1295.00
7600.50	5774.00	4501.59	7599.00
9056.00	7520.75	2190.69	1696.59
1967.00	5990.00	6901.39	9595.00
1. 57,900.86	3. 59,967.60	5. 36,591.92	7. 55,867.87

1214.00	9098.70	4745.00	3600.00
9642.20	2094.20	2957.50	3500.00
9558.15	6045.85	8799.56	3700.00
5171.50	1422.40	6596.90	3900.00
7723.00	2251.25	3075.78	3500.00
6886.45	6585.99	9683.95	2500.00
2595.99	9848.12	3057.70	2550.00
8435.84	2378.95	2040.90	9500.00
5672.12	9525.79	4569.95	9550.00
1568.74	6967.95	1419.00	1500.00
9. 58,467.99	11. 56,219.20	13. 46,946.24	15. 43,800.00

Chapter 33, Terminology Review

1. stocks
3. common stock
5. dividends in arrears
7. price–earnings ratio
9. corporate bonds
11. premium

Chapter 33, Review Exercises, Exercise 1

1. $.61
3. $.78

Chapter 33, Review Exercises, Exercise 2

5. a. $8,080
   b. $10,098
   c. $2,018
   d. 24.98%
7. $10,320
9. $10,420 proceeds, $500 gain

index